Travels In India

By

Jean-Baptiste Tavernier

Baron of Aubonne

Translated from the Original French Edition of 1676 with a biographical sketch of the Author, Notes, Appendices etc.

By

V. Ball

Second Edition

Edited By

William Crooke

Jean-Baptiste Tavernier

Travels in India *by* Jean-Baptiste Tavernier

Baron of Aubonne

In 2 Vols.
(Bound in 1)

Translated from the Original French Edition of 1676 with a biographical sketch of the Author, Notes, Appendices etc.

by
V Ball

This edition, second, edited by
William Crooke

Vol. 1

Low Price Publications
2015

Valentine Ball (1843-1894)
William Crooke (1848-1923)

First Edition Published 1889
This Edition Reproduced from Second Edition Published 1925
Reprinted in **LPP** 2000, 2007, 2015

ISBN 10: 81-7536-206-5
ISBN 13: 978-81-7536-206-2

Published by
Low Price Publications
A-6, 2nd Floor, Nimri Commercial Centre,
Ashok Vihar Phase 4, Delhi 110052 (INDIA)
tel.: +91-11-27302453 fax.: +91-11-47061936
url: www.LPPindia.com e-mail: info@LPPindia.com

Printed at
D.K. Fine Art Press Pvt. Ltd.
Delhi

PRINTED IN INDIA

CONTENTS OF VOL. I

ILLUSTRATIONS

ILLUSTRATIONS contained in the portion of the original work included in this Volume i, but not reproduced here :—

Numerical figures—French and Indian.
Touchstones of the money-changers for testing silver.
Seals or monograms of the Kings who have reigned.

PREFACE OF DR. V. BALL

VOL. I

TAVERNIER'S name, owing to its frequent mention in histories and in works on precious stones, has long been known as that of one of the most renowned travellers of the seventeenth century. Possibly it would not be incorrect to speak of Tavernier as in some respects the most renowned traveller during that period when so much was done to bring home to the people of Europe information about countries which had previously been but little known.

Such being the case, it is not only somewhat surprising that there should be so much error in the published accounts of his life, but also that his *Travels*, although they have been frequently issued in various languages, have not, as a whole, been subjected to critical examination and elucidation with the aid of our modern knowledge of the countries which they describe.

Of Tavernier's life and work Prof. Charles Joret has given an exhaustive survey in a recently-published monograph. In the present volumes it is sought to present an approximately literal translation of the portion of the *Travels* which refer to India, accompanying it by such identifications of localities with modern sites, and such elucidation of obscure points, as have been possible.

As will be explained more particularly in the biographical sketch, the chief faults in Tavernier's encyclopaedic volumes consist in a want of systematic arrangement of the subjects, a fuller and more carefully correlated chronology, and a reconciliation of really or apparently contradictory statements; such work, in short, as should have been done by the editors whom he employed, but which they appear to have either wilfully shirked or omitted to recognize as a part of their duty.

Upwards of two hundred years have elapsed since an English translation, that by John Phillips, has appeared; but owing to that translator's misconception of the author's meaning, through want of local knowledge, and to serious abridgement, it gives a very inadequate idea of the true merits of the work, which, except to those who have read it in the original, have therefore been practically unknown to English readers.

A word of explanation is due to the readers of these volumes as to how it has happened that the present editor came to undertake the onerous task of translation and annotation.

For a long time I have been well acquainted with the portions of Tavernier's works which deal with the economic mineral resources of India, and although I have published some accounts of these, having succeeded in identifying the sites of the diamond mines described by him, which were for a long time supposed by authors to be beyond the reach of recognition, I have felt that in order to truly represent him a new English edition, at least of the Indian travels, was much wanted, which would give his facts in their own setting and substantiate, by means of modern illustration, the strong claim which he has to be regarded as a veracious and original author.

Being fully mindful of my deficiencies as a philological and historical critic, I had, when further acquainted with the work, determined not to undertake the task myself, as I felt that such qualifications as I possessed, which were mainly derived from a long experience of travelling in India in connexion with the Geological Survey of that country, would not make up for the lack of special knowledge in the subjects just alluded to.

Acting, however, under the advice of Colonel Sir H. Yule, I commenced the translation and annotation in the year 1886 and have devoted the greater portion of my spare time since then to this work.

In speaking of the aid which Colonel Yule has ever been most ready to afford, I must guard against implying that the work has been completed in any way under his supervision; that for various reasons has not been possible, and it would be an ill return for so much assistance as I have received to lay upon him any responsibility for opinions which he has not had an opportunity of considering. At the same time the direct acknowledgements of his advice which are made in the footnotes by no means cover the extent of my indebtedness, and

I regret the impossibility of doing more now than to give expression to my gratitude to him for his labour and advice in these somewhat general terms.

To Mr. V. A. Smith of the Bengal Civil Service I am indebted for much assistance and advice while passing this first volume through the press. His departure for India has deprived me of a continuation of his valuable aid in connexion with the second volume.

INTRODUCTION[1]

LIFE OF J.-B. TAVERNIER

JEAN-BAPTISTE TAVERNIER was born in Paris in the year 1605. This has been ascertained from a statement in the volume of his *Relations*, namely that in 1679 he was seventy-four years old. But there is no direct evidence as to the exact month or day of his birth, and they cannot now be ascertained owing to the disappearance of the registers of the church at Charenton, where he was baptized.

Not very much is known of the family of his father Gabriel, of whom, however, it is recorded that he fled from Antwerp to Paris in 1575, together with his brothers Melchior and Nicolas, in order to avoid religious persecution, they being Protestants. They readily accepted French nationality, and it is suggested by M. Joret that their ancestors may have originally migrated from France to Belgium. Melchior became famous as an engraver and printer to the King; he was born in 1544, and died in 1641, at the age of ninety-seven years. Of Nicolas the record is more scanty, it being only known that he was married to Claudine le Bert, by whom he had a son named Jacques. Of Gabriel it is known that like Melchior he was a geographer, but he appears to have been rather a merchant than an artist. He married Suzanne Tonnelier, by whom he had three sons—Melchior, baptized in 1594; Jean-Baptiste, who, as already stated, was born in 1605; and Gabriel, born in 1613. As will be seen hereafter, Tavernier mentions a brother Daniel[2] who died at Batavia in the year 1648, and there also appears to have been a brother named Maurice, whose son accompanied Tavernier on his sixth voyage. The possibility of Gabriel being identical with either Daniel or Maurice has been discussed, but there would be no advantage in retailing the various opinions

[1] Largely based on the excellent life of *J.-B. Tavernier* by Prof. Charles Joret, Paris, Plon, 1886.

[2] See Book III, chap. xxvi. The name Daniel is printed on the map of Tonquin in Tavernier's account of that Kingdom.

here, as none of them are conclusive. Melchior, like his uncle, became distinguished as a cartographer; he died in 1665, during the last of Jean-Baptiste's voyages to the East.

The geographical surroundings of Jean-Baptiste, and the discussions which learned men held with his father, and to which he listened with avidity, served to inflame in his mind from his earliest years a strong desire to see foreign countries; but minute as are his descriptions of his travels, he, so far as his own autobiographical account is concerned, ignores the events of his early youth; and indeed it may be said that throughout he sinks his personality to such an extent that the actual period at which some of his adventures took place can only be arrived at by the casual mention of incidents and dates which are scattered about through his works, while with regard to others there are no indications whatever, and in reference to some periods of his life we are left in complete darkness as to where and how they were spent.

By the age of twenty-two he had, he states in his 'Design', seen the best parts of France, England, Holland, Germany, Switzerland, Poland,[1] Hungary, and Italy, and had acquired a fair knowledge of the most useful European languages. It would appear from M. Joret's estimate that these rambles must have commenced when he was only fifteen years old. It is not necessary to follow the details of these European travels here, as they are fully set forth on following pages in 'The Design of the Author'.

First Voyage.—Contrary to those writers who have stated that Tavernier started on his first voyage to the East in 1636, M. Joret has, I think, very clearly proved, by reference to the easily ascertained dates of historical events which took place while he was in Constantinople, that his departure cannot have been later than January or February 1631; and that, in 1633, after visiting Persia, he returned to Europe by Aleppo and Alexandretta to Malta, from whence he made his way to Italy, bringing with him some Persian turquoises as articles of trade. During the next five years his occupation is unknown, the record being almost blank.

[1] Poland, as pointed out by M. Joret, does not appear to have been visited till he was twenty-five years old.

Second Voyage.—On the 13th of September 1638 we find him again starting from Paris for the East, taking ship at Marseilles for Alexandretta, with a following consisting of a young artist, a surgeon, and his brother Daniel. He was, moreover, on this occasion well equipped as a merchant. After spending six weeks at Aleppo he left it on the 27th December [1] with a caravan, and passing through Mashhad, Basra, and Shīrāz, reached Ispahān at the end of April or beginning of May 1639. Here he visited the King, Shāh Safavi, grandson of Shāh 'Abbās. Our next record of him shows him to have been in Hindustān early in 1641, but as to the route which he followed, whether by sea or by land, and at what date he traversed it, there is no direct evidence. M. Joret suggests that he left Ispahān at the end of 1639, that he paid his first visit to Dacca in 1640, and that he remained in Agra during the winter of 1640–1. In 1641 he tells us that he was at Burhānpur on the journey from Agra to Surat, and elsewhere that he was at Goa at the close of the same year. His journey up from Surat to Agra in 1640, unlike the journey back *via* Burhānpur, was probably made by the Ahmadābād route which is described on pp. 40–73. At Agra he found Shāhjahān enjoying a peaceable reign. From Goa he appears to have visited Golkonda and made full inquiries and perhaps visited the diamond mines—returning to Surat by the land journey throughout, in the spring of 1642. How he occupied himself during the remainder of this year is uncertain ; but he states that he paid a visit to Ahmadābād, probably while awaiting the season for sailing, towards the end of the year 1642 or the beginning of 1643, when he states he was in Bandar 'Abbās.

Third Voyage.—We do not know when he reached Paris nor what route he followed ; but we find him towards the close of 1643, namely on the 6th of December, starting thence on his third voyage to the East, arriving as before at Alexandretta. On the 6th of March 1644 he started from Aleppo in the company of two Capuchin monks, arriving at Ispahān on the 3rd of May, where M. Joret considers he must have remained

[1] I do not think it necessary to enter into any discussion here as to the enigmas presented by the incompatibility of some of his statements with these dates. (See Joret, p. 48.)

for some months, reaching Surat in January 1645, most probably by the Bandar 'Abbās route. On the 19th of January he started *via* Daulatābād and Nānder for Golkonda, whence he visited the diamond mines, regarding which he had ascertained particulars, if he had not actually seen them, on the occasion of his previous journey. After visiting the mine of Raolconda, *i. e.* the modern Ramalakota, eighteen miles south of Karnūl, he appears to have returned to Golkonda and afterwards proceeded to the mine which he called Gani or Coulour ; this, it will be seen, stands for Kān-i-Kollūr on the Kistnā, at seven days' journey eastwards, or more correctly south-eastwards, from Golkonda. (See vol. i, 139.) How the remainder of this year and the whole of 1646 were employed we cannot say. In connexion with the descriptions of the above-named mines he also describes one at Soumelpour (see vol. ii, 65 ff.), which was situated on the Koel river, an affluent of the Son, in the District of Lohārdagā in Western Bengal, but as to when he visited it, if ever, he gives no certain indication. There are some grounds for supposing that in 1647 he visited Persia, indeed he actually states (Book I, chap. viii) that he was in Ispahān towards the end of that year. Be this as it may, we find him on the 11th of January 1648 at Mingrela, that is to say Vengurla, on the west coast of India, where he had arrived from Surat in a Dutch vessel called the *Maestricht*. After nine days spent there, during which time he enjoyed the hospitality of the Dutch, who had a factory there, he embarked on an armed vessel for Goa, where he arrived on the following day, and was much struck with its decadence since his previous visit in 1641. During the two months which he spent in Goa he was on the most friendly terms with the Viceroy—the wealthy Dom Filippe de Mascarenhas,—the Archbishop, and the Inquisitor-General, by all of whom he was treated with much kindness, the latter having first satisfied himself that he had left his Bible behind him at Vengurla. On the 11th of March he returned to Vengurla, where he remained for more than a month, or till the 14th of April, when he embarked for Batavia, for the ostensible reasons of seeing so famous a place and of rendering a service to the Dutch by conveying to them information about a new port in Africa which had been discovered by the Portuguese. M. Joret probably rightly concludes that he was anxious to seek for and meet with his brother Daniel, whom he had not seen for ten years.

On this voyage Tavernier narrowly escaped shipwreck off the coast of Malabar, but at length succeeded in reaching the harbour of Pointe de Galle, in Ceylon, where, as usual, he was well received by the Dutch authorities. On the 25th of June, the merchandise having been transhipped to another vessel, the voyage was continued, and on the 17th of July the coast of Sumatra was sighted, and on the 22nd Tavernier reached Batavia. On the following day he went to pay his respects to the General, Vanderling, and the Director-General, Caron, by whom he was at first well treated. Subsequently, however, he was involved in tedious investigations in reference to his relations with M. Constant, the Commander at Bandar 'Abbās, for whom he had purchased diamonds at the mines. These inquiries suddenly collapsed when Tavernier disclosed the fact that he possessed a very considerable amount of compromising information concerning the illicit transactions of the members of the Council at Batavia who proposed to try him.

His stay at Batavia was interrupted by two short visits to Bantam, where he was well received by the King, of whom his brother was a boon companion ; and he also experienced much kindness from the English Resident, who offered him a free passage to England, which he at first accepted, but subsequently declined in favour of a similar offer made by the Dutch. Thereupon followed a serious contention about certain Dutch pay-bills which he had purchased at a considerable discount, intending to sell them at par in Holland, and so employ his capital during the voyage. This traffic having been prohibited, those who had bought bills were all, with the exception of Tavernier, both compelled to give up what they had purchased, and otherwise severely mulcted and punished. Tavernier held out to the last moment, but finally handed up the bills on promise of an order for payment of his outlay in Holland. Ultimately he sailed without this promise being fulfilled, and it was only after several years and the institution of an action against the Company in Holland that he, or rather his brother for him, received part of the sum due. From all these circumstances he, perhaps naturally enough, became a bitter enemy of the Dutch, and availed himself of every opportunity for manifesting his hostility.[1]

After his second return to Batavia from Bantam he was about to visit certain Kings in Sumatra, when his brother Daniel arrived in a dying state from Bantam; and shortly afterwards died, in spite of all that could be done to cure him.

Somewhere about the month of October, according to M. Joret's estimate, Tavernier sailed for Holland in a ship called the *Provinces*, which having passed the Sunda Straits, and failing to make the Cocos Islands, steered for the Cape of Good Hope, where it arrived in fifty-five days; and the fleet, after remaining there twenty-two days for the recovery of the sick, &c., proceeded to St. Helena, which was reached in eighteen days; and then halted for a further twenty-two days, when the crews and passengers of the several vessels in the port entertained one another. Ultimately, after some delays on account of contrary winds, the fleet reached Holland, where the Directors treated Tavernier with much politeness and hospitality; as regards his claim against them, they denied all knowledge of it at first, but finally offered to give him a free passage back to Batavia in order that he might get it paid there: this offer he declined to accept.

There is no precise intimation in the text as to when he arrived in Holland. M. Joret concludes that the voyage must have taken six months, and that, allowing for delays in Holland, he could not have reached Paris till the spring of 1649.

Fourth Voyage.—Two years having been spent in Europe which were occupied in the sale of the precious stones brought by Tavernier from India, and in repeated efforts to recover his debt from the Dutch Company, he again started for the East, leaving Paris on the 18th June 1651. It was not till the 25th of August, however, that he sailed in the *St. Crispine* from Marseilles; and after touching at Malta and Larnaca in Cyprus, reached Alexandretta on the 4th of October, and Aleppo on the 7th. Owing to disturbances in the country he was unable to resume his journey eastwards till the last day of the year. It is needless here to detail his adventures in Persia from this time

[1] See his *Histoire de la Conduite des Hollandois en Asie.*

forwards till the 11th of May, when he embarked at Bandar 'Abbās on a ship belonging to the King of Golkonda, which was bound for the port of Masulipatam, on the east coast of India. After narrowly escaping shipwreck he reached Masulipatam on the 2nd of July—or perhaps for 2nd we should read 12th, and on the 21st of July, together with M. du Jardin, he set out to march to Gandikot *via* Madras, which latter place he reached on the 13th of August. The description of this march will be found in Book I, chap. xviii. Here it need only be pointed out that, conformably to his custom, he made friends with the English who were residing in Fort St. George, and visited the Portuguese Governor and Catholic brotherhoods at St. Thomé. On the 22nd of the same month he started by the valley of the Penner River for Gandikot, which he might have reached from Masulipatam by a more direct and shorter route had he not desired to visit Madras. On the 1st of September he reached Gandikot, which Mīr Jumla, on behalf of the King of Golkonda, had just captured. As Mīr Jumla was not only the General of the troops but also Prime Minister, Tavernier had gone to him in order to show him—as he was bound to do, not merely as an act of courtesy but because it was the custom—the pearls and precious stones which he proposed to sell to the King. Several interviews which he had with Mīr Jumla served to impress him with a high opinion of that General's abilities. On the 15th Tavernier took leave after receiving his assurance that he had recommended him to his son at the Golkonda court. His march northwards lasted till the 2nd of October, when he reached Golkonda. After some delay negotiations were opened with reference to the sale of the precious stones, but in consequence of a remark by a eunuch that the prices asked by Tavernier were too high, he took offence, and, together with M. du Jardin, left at once for Surat, following the same route as he had come by to Golkonda in 1643.

In some of the editions the date of his showing the precious stones is given as the 25th (of October), but in the 1676 edition the 15th is mentioned ; and as he started on the following day, and the distance was twenty-one [1] days' journey, or five days

[1] In Book I, chap. ix, p. 120 of vol. i, he says, however, twenty-seven days.

less than by the Aurangābād route which was twenty-six days, he reached Surat either on the 5th or the 15th of November. Shortly afterwards his companion, M. du Jardin,[1] died, and Tavernier then set out for Ahmadābād, where he had been invited to bring his jewels by Shāista Khān, who was then Governor of Gujarāt. Thence he returned to Surat, and set out for Golkonda on the 6th of March 1653 by the Aurangābād route, arriving at Golkonda on the 1st of April. He then paid another visit to the mines, regarding which, as he gives no details, we must only conclude that any observations of importance made by him on this occasion are incorporated in the account of his previous visit in 1645, which has been above alluded to. He appears to have returned to Surat during the same year, as in Book III, chap. xiii, he refers to having, in the year 1653, when on the return journey from Golkonda to Surat, encountered a troop of pilgrims. He says M. d'Ardilière was with him, to which M. Joret objects that he had died in 1652. But had he? We know his father, M. du Jardin, had, but of himself there is, so far as I know, no such record. Tavernier next refers to being back at Surat, where he heard that war had been declared between the English and Dutch. On the 8th of January 1654 he sailed in one of a fleet of five Dutch vessels of war which were dispatched from Surat to intercept the English fleet, which was then expected to be on its way back from Hormuz. After a naval engagement, in which the English were beaten, and various delays, the Dutch fleet proceeded to Bandar 'Abbās, arriving there on the 7th of March. Tavernier then started for Ispahān, visiting Kermān *en route*, where he purchased a large quantity of the beautiful wool of that country for transport to France. After a protracted stay in Persia, where he visited many places which he had not previously seen, he returned to Paris apparently in the autumn of the year 1655, but the information he gives on this point is very vague.

FIFTH VOYAGE.—In February 1657 Tavernier started from Paris on his fifth voyage. Shortly after leaving Marseilles, the vessel in which he had embarked was chased by pirates, and was compelled to take refuge in a port near Toulon, from

[1] As will be seen there is some uncertainty about the identification of this M. du Jardin. (See Index for references.)

whence he returned by land, carrying on his person the jewels which he was taking with him to sell in the East, but allowing his heavier merchandise to proceed in the same vessel. At Marseilles he again took ship in an English vessel for Italy. In Italy he spent a short time, and visited Ferdinand II of Tuscany, who treated him with kindness and distinction. He then sailed for Smyrna in a Dutch ship, and, while awaiting the departure of the caravan, sent one of his servants to buy in Constantinople some pearls which he heard that a Jew residing there had for sale, because, he remarks, pearls were the best articles of trade which could be taken to India. At this time, according to him, Smyrna was the principal entrepôt for all kinds of goods which passed from Europe to Asia and from Asia to Europe. From the vague indications given by Tavernier Prof. Joret concludes that he started with the caravan from Smyrna in June 1657. The journey was made by Erivān and Tabrīz to Ispahān, without any event happening worthy of particular record. Owing to the accounts which reached him of the disturbed condition of India, in connexion with the usurpation by Aurangzeb of his father's throne, Tavernier appears to have prolonged his stay in Ispahān till the beginning of 1659 ; but before starting for Surat, which his letter addressed to Shāista Khān proves him to have reached in May of that year, he dispatched to Masulipatam, in charge of one of his servants for safety, and perhaps to evade dues, the bulk of the beautiful objects and rare curiosities which he had collected for Shāista Khān in Europe. Shāista Khān's reply to his letter was an invitation to visit him at Jahānābād, sending him a passport to enable him to do so with ease and safety. Delayed by the rains, Tavernier had not started before he received other letters, first asking him to come to Burhānpur and then to Aurangābād. When he went to take leave of the Governor of Surat, named Mīrzā Arab, he was informed by him that until instructions came from Aurangzeb, who had been informed of his arrival, he would not be allowed to depart. He then wrote to Shāista Khān, asking him to send an order to the Governor to let him go ; this was done, and at length, after six months' delay at Surat, he set out and found Shāista Khān laying siege to Chākan (Choupar) in the Deccan. As has

been seen on pp. 27 and 325, vol. i, there are some discrepancies in Tavernier's two accounts of the sale of and payment for his goods. It is inferred from a casual statement that, having concluded this transaction, he pursued his course farther southwards in order to visit the diamond mines at Golkonda again, from whence probably he returned to Surat about the end of 1660 or beginning of 1661.[1] In his *Persian Travels* he says (Book V, chap. ii) that he was in Persia in 1662, and during the same year he returned to Paris, his age being then fifty-six years. It was thought that, as he had by this time amassed a considerable fortune, and was married in the same year for the first time in his life, he would settle down and rest from his travels, which, as we have seen, commenced when he was only fifteen years of age. His wife was named Madeleine Goisse, a daughter of Jean Goisse, a jeweller, with whom he had had some business transactions, and who was a connexion by marriage of his brother Melchior.

Sixth Voyage.—Tavernier's original intention, expressed shortly after his marriage in 1662, was, however, to make a short journey to the East in order to close his affairs there. As months passed in preparation, this intention expanded, and on the 27th of November 1663 he started from Paris, and did not return again for five years. On this occasion he took with him a young nephew, son of Maurice Tavernier, and four attendants of different professions, including a surgeon. His stock of precious stones, goldsmith's work, &c., was valued at 400,000 livres, which at 1*s*. 6*d*. would be equal to £30,000. On the 10th of January 1664 he embarked at Marseilles for Leghorn, and after passing through many misadventures, including a narrow escape of being drowned, he ultimately reached Smyrna on the 25th of April, where he remained till the 9th of June, when he left with the caravan for Tabrīz. After three months' marching the caravan reached Erivān on the 14th of September, and Tabrīz on the 9th of November, where two of his followers, one a watchmaker and the other a goldsmith, died of sickness brought on by the fatigues of the journey. Here also Tavernier

[1] 'He then left Surat for Persia, in a Dutch vessel, which reached Gombroon on 5 July, N.S. (see *Dagh. Register*, Batavia, 1661, p. 442)': Foster, *Eng. Factories in India, 1655–60*, p. 235 *n*.

left his nephew Pierre in the charge of the Superior of the Capuchin Convent. On the 22nd of November, having beforehand dispatched his principal goods, he left with a small party for Ispahān, and arrived there on the 14th of December. Three days afterwards the King, Shāh 'Abbās II, who in 1657 had bought a quantity of jewels from him, summoned him to his palace, where he went in state accompanied by all the Franks, and bearing with him his most precious treasures, Father Raphael acting as interpreter. The Shāh first inquired to whom he had sold the jewels which he had with him on the occasion of his last voyage, and he informed him that it was to Shāista Khān, and that the price he received was 120,000 rupees, though he mentions no sum in the account of the transaction itself.

His present to the Shāh consisted of a large metallic mirror, which distorted the face of any one looking into it. All the jewels, with the exception of the pearls, were bought, after prolonged negotiation, at the high prices which Tavernier demanded. The Shāh being, however, well pleased, Tavernier besought his protection for his nephew, and requested that he himself should be allowed to sell his goods in Persia, free of duty, both of which requests were granted, and he was further complimented by the bestowal of a robe of honour, and by being appointed jeweller in ordinary. Further, out of regard for him a good reception was promised to all Franks arriving in Persia. A portrait of Tavernier prefixed to the *Recüeil*, published in 1679, and reproduced as a frontispiece to this volume, represents him clothed in this robe, with the addition of the mantle which was further conferred upon him by the express order of the Shāh. The total value of the sales made on this occasion was 3,900 tomāns, or £13,455, allowing £3 9*s*. for the tomān. The Shāh gave him several designs for ornaments, made by himself, which he desired to have executed in gold, enamel, and precious stones. Curiously enough, Chardin relates that a similar order was given to himself in 1666.

At length Tavernier left Ispahān for India on the 24th of February 1665, and reached Bandar 'Abbās about the end of the first week of April, having made several halts on the road. On the 5th of May we find him once more at Surat. On the occasion of this voyage an injury happened to him at the hands of the Dutch, which, added to what had previously been done to him in Batavia, served to perpetuate his enmity and contempt. Having been entrusted by the English Resident with an important packet of letters for Surat, which it was believed contained information of the outbreak of war in Europe, it was stolen by the Dutch, a parcel of blanks being put in its place. The English in Surat were naturally indignant when, instead of their letters, they received these blanks, and it is said that Tavernier was threatened with assassination, in consequence of which all the plans he had made for his Indian tour were thrown into confusion. He sent a strong protest against this scandalous treachery to the General at Batavia, and stated that if satisfaction were not rendered, he would, on his return to France, carry the matter further, and would also inform the Shāh of Persia. He does not appear to have received any direct satisfaction, and this probably led him to write his exposures contained in *The History of the Conduct of the Dutch in Asia.*[1]

On arrival at Surat the Governor told him that Aurangzeb wished to be the first to see his jewels; and he further learnt that Shāista Khān was in Bengal, so that although, in pursuance of his promise given on the last occasion, he desired to visit him first, he was compelled to go to Jahānābād, travelling probably by Burhānpur, Sironj, Gwalior, and Agra, and arriving at Jahānābād in September. On the 12th of the same month he went to salute the Great Mogul, to whom, as well as to the nobles of the Court and others, he made presents amounting in all to the value of 23,187 livres. He then sold to the Great Mogul, Aurangzeb, a number of his most precious stones; and Ja'far Khān, the Mogul's uncle, bought several, but disputed the price of a large pearl, which he sought to buy at 10,000 rupees less than Tavernier demanded. Subsequently, it was bought by Shāista Khān, who was then in Dacca, but with him too it became the subject of a serious dispute.

[1] Described by Chardin, Amsterdam ed., 1711, vol. iii, p. 154, as 'a collection of the adventures of insignificant people, mostly Dutch; published out of a spirit of flattery, or on account of French animosity at the time.'

Tavernier remained two months at Jahānābād, and on the 1st of November, when he went to take leave, Aurangzeb pressed him to remain in order to witness his annual festival which was then close at hand, promising him, if he would do so, that he would allow him to see all his jewels after it was over. So tempting an offer was at once accepted by Tavernier, and to this we owe some of the most interesting chapters in the whole of his travels.

The fête having concluded on the 9th of November, he was on the following day shown the jewels, including the great Mogul diamond. Shortly afterwards he left for Agra, and on the 25th (not the 15th, as an obvious though frequently repeated misprint has it in various editions) he started for Bengal, being accompanied by the celebrated French physician named Bernier and another friend named Rachepot. They reached Allāhābād on the 7th of December, where they found Claude Maillé of Bourges installed as physician and surgeon to the Governor, but no hint is given as to whether he was the same person or not whom Tavernier mentions under the same name in the capacity of gun-founder at Gandikot for Mīr Jumla. Having obtained permission to cross the Ganges, they followed its left bank and arrived at Benares on the 11th, where they remained for two days, and then proceeded along the right bank to Patna, which they reached on the 20th. It is clear that on this occasion Tavernier did not turn down the valley of the Son to Rohtās and the diamond mine at Soumelpur, and it is uncertain whether he ever went there; but he may have done so on his return and prolonged visit to Patna and its neighbourhood, which is mentioned below, or during his first journey to Dacca in 1640. After eight days spent at Patna he embarked on the 29th December (not January, as by an obvious misprint it is given in several of the editions), and passed down the Ganges, reaching Rājmahāl on the 4th of January 1666. On the 6th M. Bernier left him to go to Kāsimbāzār, while he proceeded to Dacca, which he reached on the 13th, and on the following day went to visit the Nawāb, Shāista Khān, to whom he made a valuable present. After selling him the goods which he had brought for him, and having received an order for payment on Kāsimbāzār, he started for that place on the 29th, and reached it on the 12th of February, being well received by Van Wachtendonk, the Director of all the Dutch factories in Bengal. On presenting his order for payment to the Mogul's Treasurer, he was informed by him that three days previously he had received an order not to pay it. Subsequently this Treasurer, acting under Shāista Khān's instructions, offered to pay him the debt, less by 20,000 rupees. Tavernier enlarges on the causes which led to this treatment, attributing it to the machinations of Aurangzeb's officers to spite him for not having sold the jewels to them, in order that they might resell them to their master at an enhanced rate. There is no direct record of his subsequent movements, but he appears to have spent June and July in Patna, where, on the second day of the last-named month, he witnessed an eclipse of the sun. In August he probably reached Agra, where he seems to have met the representatives of the French company 'for establishing commerce in Persia and India'. He ultimately reached Surat on the 1st of November, and met there M. Thévenot, who was returning from Madras and Golkonda, and of whose travels the published account serves to elucidate some points in Tavernier's narratives. Early in the year 1667 Tavernier left Surat—probably, as ingeniously calculated by M. Joret, in the month of February—for Bandar 'Abbās, where he met, among other Europeans, the famous traveller Chardin. At Ispahān he remained for some months, probably till the end of 1667. In the early part of the year 1668 he reached Constantinople, and made a prolonged stay there, finally reaching Paris on the 6th of December ; and being then sixty-three years old, he resolved to enjoy the riches he had acquired and rest from his labours. His first care, he tells us, was to render thanks to God, who had protected him through all perils by sea and land during the space of forty years. His life after this period for sixteen years cannot be followed out in detail here from want of space. Those who desire details are referred to M. Joret's excellent volume. It is only possible to mention here a few of the principal events.

Soon after his arrival in France he had an interview with Louis XIV, who was anxious to see so famous a traveller ; and the distinguished traveller did not forget his business as a merchant, for he sold the King a large number of diamonds and other precious stones, and in February 1669, in consideration of his eminent services to France, he was granted letters which conferred upon him a title of nobility; this was the full complement of his success. In April 1670 he purchased the barony of Aubonne, near Geneva, and in the following month he took the oaths, and was received by their Excellencies of Berne as 'Seigneur Baron d'Aubonne'. He restored the Castle and orientalized its decorations, and it was here he prepared his notes for publication. It is commonly said that the *Voyages* were written from Tavernier's dictation by a French Protestant named Samuel Chappuzeau; but it is evident from many remarks scattered through the volumes, and, indeed, is sufficiently proved from the nature of the facts recorded, that many pages must have been written at or shortly after the time when the events took place, and by Tavernier himself. Chappuzeau, who had obtained considerable reputation as an historian and writer of theatrical plays, was prevailed on to edit Tavernier's notes, or, as he afterwards described it, to give form to the chaos, as the confused memoirs of the six voyages might be called.[1] The statement made by Chappuzeau and quoted by Bayle, that the only written portions were by Father Gabriel de Chinon, Capuchin, seems to be somewhat inconsistent with this. Chappuzeau states that it was with the greatest repugnance he undertook the work, and then only in consequence of Tavernier's having used his interest to get the King to prevail upon him to do so. His friendship for Tavernier was completely broken under the 'mortification if not martyrdom' which he suffered, as he says, for the space of a year, while exposed to the rough humour of Tavernier and the ridicule of his wife. I agree completely with M. Joret in the opinion that the internal evidence is too strong to admit of the supposition that Tavernier was not personally the author of the larger part of the memoirs, and that from their very nature they could not

[1] According to a note in the MS. Catalogue of the Bibliothèque Impériale the *Voyages* of Tavernier were compiled from his own notes, in part by his friend Chappuzeau, and in part by Danlier des Landes, author of *Les Beautés de la Perse*, Paris, 1673, who accompanied him on one of his voyages.

have been written from mere verbal dictation. Chappuzeau doubtless edited them, and did his work very badly, as the numerous omissions and contradictions prove.

In the year 1675 Tavernier's first publication appeared under the title, *Nouvelle Relation du Serrail du Grand Signior*. His *magnum opus*, the *Six Voyages*, appeared in the following year;[1] and the 'Design of the Author' which is prefixed conveys the idea that the whole was his own handiwork. The interest aroused in these works was considerable, and the number of editions which appeared in rapid succession (see Bibliography) amply attest the popularity of the work. In 1679 he published another volume, the *Recueil de plusieurs Relations*. In the preparation of this work he received the assistance of M. de la Chapelle, Secretary to M. de Lamoignon, M. Chappuzeau having refused to aid him further; but to what extent this assistance went it is impossible to say. This latter volume contains two portraits of Tavernier, one a bust, which is a work of high art (frontispiece to vol. ii), as also are the dedicatory verses by Boileau printed underneath it. The other is a full figure representing Tavernier in the robe of honour given him by the Shāh of Persia, to which reference has already been made on a previous page. Translations of these works soon appeared in English, German, and Italian, as will be seen in the Bibliography.

Some who were jealous of Tavernier's success did not hesitate to contrast his works with those of Thévenot, Bernier, and Chardin—who were perhaps better educated men and of a more philosophical turn of mind than he was, but it cannot be maintained that their works met with equal success; and it is apparent that the reading public preferred his facts and personal observations to the philosophic speculations which were added to the facts recorded by his rivals. Voltaire and others, though they wrote somewhat contemptuously of the value of Tavernier's work, did not influence the tide of opinion which had set strongly in his favour.

It is noteworthy, however, that Tavernier, in his references to the above-named travellers, speaks of them all with the utmost courtesy, when referring to his having met them, while

[1] Paris, Gervais Clouzier, 1676, 2 vols. 4to.

they are either silent about him, or, like Chardin, mention him only to abuse him.[1]

In the footnotes to the present work it will be seen that while obscurity and contradiction are not absent from the text, and the effects of careless editing of the original are much to be deplored, the general accuracy of the recorded facts, when submitted to critical examination in the light of our modern knowledge of India, is much greater than it was ever believed to be, even by his greatest admirers, who supposed them to be beyond the reach of elucidation or confirmation. Gemelli Careri [2] speaks of Tavernier as a dupe rather than a liar; but as I have met with no indications of either of these characteristics, I have not troubled to follow up his charges of error, as they refer chiefly to Persia, and M. Joret affirms that they have for the most part no foundation.

In a certain sense, to a limited degree, Tavernier may have been a plagiarist, but he openly avowed his endeavours to obtain information wherever he could. His historical chapters for instance, may have been derived from Bernier's writings, or, what is more probable, from conversations with him when they travelled together down the Ganges; while the chapters on places he had not himself visited were, of course, founded on information collected from various sources, but principally from persons who gave him their own personal experiences. Thus, probably, is to be explained the resemblance noted by Dr. Hyde [3] between a passage by Tavernier and one by Louis Morera in a work published at Lyons in 1671, which was founded on papers by Father Gabriel de Chinon. We know that Tavernier saw much of Father Gabriel in Persia, and he may have learned the facts from him if he did not himself observe them.

M. Joret gives an interesting account of the controversies and polemical literature which were roused in the seventeenth century by the publication of Tavernier's volumes;

[1] Sir W. Ouseley, in his *Travels in various Countries of the East* (ii. 497), devotes some pages to a criticism of Tavernier's errors regarding Persia; for the opinion of Lord Curzon, see p. xxxii, below.

[2] *Voyage autour du Monde*, translated from the Italian. Paris, 1727. 12mo.

[3] See Rose's *Biographical Dictionary*, Art. 'Tavernier'.

and in discussing the published biographies of Tavernier he points out that they are all founded on the erroneous and amplified statements of Henrick van Quellenburgh,[1] Jurieu,[2] Chappuzeau,[3] Bayle, and others. M. Joret asserts that the article on Tavernier in the *English Cyclopaedia* alone, of all the biographies, does full justice to his character.

During the period which elapsed from the publication in 1679 of his last volume up to 1684 there is reason for believing that Tavernier lived an active, commercial, though somewhat retired life. In 1684 he started from Paris for Berlin, being called thither by Frederick William, Elector of Brandenburg, to advise with him on his projects of colonization and commercial enterprise in the East, and to undertake to open up negotiations on his behalf with the Great Mogul. M. Joret maintains that there is no foundation for the view that Tavernier had been ruined at this time by the misconduct of his nephew, to whom he entrusted a valuable cargo for the East. On the contrary, he went to Berlin, *en véritable grand seigneur*, at the age of seventy-nine years, attracted by the offer of becoming the Elector's ambassador to India, being still full of bodily energy and possessing an enterprising spirit. M. Joret, by means of an unpublished manuscript, has been enabled to trace his circuitous journey through the principal countries of Europe. Many interviews took place with the Elector, at which the arrangements for the Embassy and the formation of the trading company were discussed. Three armed vessels were to convey it, and Tavernier, besides being nominated Ambassador, was appointed to the honorary offices of Chamberlain to the Elector and Counsellor of Marine. Soon afterwards he resolved to sell his estate at Aubonne, probably to obtain capital for his own speculations.

After six weeks spent in Berlin, he left on the 15th of August for Hamburg, and then paid a number of visits to different

[1] *Vindicia Batavica ofte Refutatie van het Tractaat van J. B. Tavernier*, &c. Amsterdam, 1684. 4to.

[2] *L'Esprit de M. Arnaud tiré de sa conduite et des écrits de lui et de ses disciples*, &c. Deventer, 1684. 12mo.

[3] *Défense du Sr. Samuel Chappuzeau contre une satire intitulée l'Esprit de M. Arnaud.*

towns in Germany, Holland, &c., finally returning to Aubonne in November. In January 1685 he was again in Paris, when he sold the land and barony of Aubonne to the Marquis Henri du Quesne for 138,000 livres of French money, with 3,000 livres more for the horses and carriages, the actual transfer being made by his wife Madeline Goisse, as he himself was at the time still in Paris. This sale completed, he would have been free to go to Brandenburg, but was delayed, as M. Joret suggests, in order to realize the 46,000 écus provided for in the letters patent constituting the Company, and which were to cover the costs of equipment of the vessels required for the first voyage. The prejudice which existed against Protestants before the revocation of the Edict of Nantes accounts for some of the difficulties he experienced in settling his affairs. M. Joret is disposed to treat as unfounded the story that Tavernier was at this time imprisoned in the Bastille as one of those who suffered from the oppression practised on the Protestants. It is proved, however, by the manuscript archives of the Bastille, which M. Joret quotes, that some one of the name of Tavernier was incarcerated there on the 13th of January 1686. If he was not there he was probably somewhere in Paris, for by that time the projected company of the Elector had come to naught, and Tavernier's home at Aubonne in Switzerland had been sold. At upwards of eighty years of age his commercial instincts had led him to entrust a valuable cargo for India, worth 222,000 francs, to his nephew, Pierre Tavernier, son of the goldsmith of Uzès,[1] who, as we have seen, was left by him at Tabrīz in the year 1664 in charge of the Superior of the Capuchin Convent in order to learn the Persian language. It is commonly said that this nephew settled in Persia and defrauded him of his profits, which should have amounted to a million of livres. On the 9th of July 1687 we hear of Tavernier again as obtaining a passport to Switzerland for three or four months, subject to a bail of 30,000 livres. At this time he set out on his seventh journey

[1] The goldsmith of Uzès is supposed to have been Tavernier's fourth brother, but the archives of that town only mention a Maurice and a Jean Tavernier, whereas those at Charenton give only Melchior, Jean-Baptiste, and Gabriel. The younger brother who died in Batavia was almost certainly Daniel: Joret, *J.-B. Tavernier*, pp. 3–4 and 378–80.

to the East in order to recover his losses, as it is believed by some; but be this as it may, to M. Joret belongs the honour of having effectively followed up the question as to where the famous traveller ended his days. Traces of his having been in Copenhagen in 1689 (or more probably in 1688) were discovered by Prof. Steenstrup, to whom inquiries were addressed by M. Joret. In the Russian review, *La Bibliographie*, for the month of February 1885, M. T. Tokmakof has described how, in the year 1876, when visiting an old Protestant cemetery near Moscow, he discovered the tomb of Tavernier, as M. Guerrier described it in a letter to M. Joret, with the name still preserved in full, and a fragment of the obliterated date, 16—. Moreover, M. Tokmakof discovered documents proving that Tavernier, carrying with him the passport of the King of Sweden, arrived in Russia early in February 1689, and that instructions were sent to the frontier to facilitate the journey of the illustrious visitor to Moscow.

M. Joret concludes his sketch with a well merited panegyric on the subject of his biography—the merchant-traveller whose reputation no French writer has previously attempted to protect from hostile critics, although the anonymous writer of the article in the *English Cyclopaedia* has written in strong terms of his peculiar and unrivalled merits.

To the testimony thus given, and to that which is afforded by the popularity of Tavernier's works in the last century, the present writer confidently expects that readers of the following pages will accord a liberal and hearty confirmation.

INTRODUCTION TO THE SECOND EDITION

THIS edition of the *Travels in India* by Jean-Baptiste Tavernier, Baron of Aubonne, is republished from the English translation, with notes and appendixes, by the late Dr. Valentine Ball, issued in 1889. Messrs. Macmillan, and Mrs. Ball, widow of the editor, the owners of the copyright, have kindly consented to this reprint. After the publication of the first edition Dr. Ball revised the entire work, and added some notes and references, with the object of preparing a second edition, which he did not live to complete. These volumes, by the generosity of Mrs. Ball, have been placed at my disposal. The emendations in the original text largely consists of improvements in the style of the translation, and I have ventured to add some further corrections of the same kind, which will, I hope, make the book more readable. Dr. Ball's additional notes and references were not of great importance, but I have used many of them in this revision.

The chief value of Dr. Ball's work lies in his excellent version of the French original text ; in his careful investigation of the Indian diamond mines, and, in particular, his identification of the hitherto unknown site of the famous Soumelpour mine ; in his elaborate description of the Koh-i-Nūr[1] and other famous diamonds, their characteristics and history, which led to conclusions, based on patient scientific inquiries, now generally accepted by later writers who have discussed these difficult problems ; in his elaborate investigation of the currency,

[1] The latest contribution to the history of the Koh-i-Nūr is that by Mr. Henry Beveridge in the *Journal of the Royal Asiatic Society* (1921, p. 178 f.). He writes : 'The Koh-i-nūr is probably the diamond brought from the Deccan by that arch-robber Alāu-d-dīn Khiljī, and which afterwards passed into the hands of the Rajah of Gwalior, and was given by the family of the last Rajah to Humāyūn. Humāyūn dutifully surrendered the diamond to his father, who returned it to him. Humāyūn took it with him to Persia, and gave it, when hard pressed and a fugitive

3 Dr. Valentine Ball

weights and measures of India at the time of Tavernier's travels ; and, lastly in his complete bibliography of the various editions and translations of the *Travels*. On all these questions Dr. Ball's scientific knowledge, acumen, and patient inquiries provided a mass of novel information, the value of which it is difficult to overrate.

Dr. Ball's duties on the staff of the Geological Survey of India allowed him wider opportunities for leisurely travel through the country than generally fall to the lot of the military or civil official of the present day, who marches along well-metalled roads or uses the railway. He explored many wild districts seldom visited by Europeans, and he thus enjoyed ample opportunities for pursuing his favourite studies in the fields of geology, zoology, botany, and ethnology. The results of his wanderings are embodied in many of the notes added to this work.

Not only was the translator and editor of Tavernier's work an eminent worker in the Indian scientific field. His father, Robert Ball, LL.D., who held a post in the office of the Chief Secretary to the Lord Lieutenant of Ireland, was also a man of wide culture and one of the leaders of literary and scientific life in Dublin up to the time of his death in 1857. Three of his sons were distinguished in various branches of science : Sir C. B. Ball, Bart., a leading surgeon in Dublin ; Sir R. S. Ball, the distinguished astronomer and lecturer. The third brother, Valentine Ball, was born in 1843, graduated at Trinity College, Dublin, in 1864, and in the same year was appointed a member of the staff of the Geological Survey of India. He held this post till 1881, and during seventeen years' service visited many parts of the Indian Empire. He recorded some of these experiences in a charming book, *Jungle Life in India, or the Journeys and Journals of an Indian Geologist*, published in 1880. During his Indian service he contributed numerous

to Tahmāsp Shāh. The latter was too much of a bigot to care about a stone, and sent it as a present to a co-religionist in the Deccan. Possibly Mīr Jumla obtained it afterwards and presented it to Shāh Jahān. Professor Ball did not know, as pointed out by Mr. Stanley Lane Poole at p. 167 of his monograph on Bābar, that Bābar's diamond had been sent back to the Deccan.'

papers to scientific journals. In an appendix of his *Jungle Life* (pp. 702 ff.) he gives a list of 62 papers on various subjects contributed up to that time. After his work on the Geological Survey ended he continued his literary activity in the Proceedings of the Royal Irish Academy and other European learned societies. The results of his geological work in India were summed up in his *Economic Geology of India*, and in some annotations to the present work, which was undertaken at the suggestion of Sir Henry Yule.

On his retirement he was appointed to succeed Dr. S. Haughton as Professor of Geology and Mineralogy in the University of Dublin. He held this office for two years until his appointment as Director of the Science and Arts Museum in Dublin. The fine new buildings, opened in 1890, were completed under his supervision, and the rearrangement of the collections occupied the last years of his life, which ended in 1895. In 1889 the University of Dublin conferred on him the honorary degree of LL.D., and he was invested with the Companionship of the Order of the Bath in 1891. During his tenure of office as Director of the great Dublin Museum he did much to advance the interests of science, and by his kindliness and readiness to assist scientific workers he gained the affection of many friends. He married in 1897 Mary, daughter of John Stewart Moore, who, with two daughters, survives him. His only son, Robert Gordon, on the staff of the West African Medical Service, was invalided in the expedition to Togoland and the Cameroons, served in Europe in the later period of the War, and died in 1920. For these details of her father's life and services I am indebted to Miss Maude Ball.

The most important question connected with Tavernier's work is the credibility of the narrative. Lord Curzon,[1] dealing with his Persian travels, writes :—' I am aware that grave charges have been brought, with some truth, against Tavernier. Chardin said he never understood a word of Persian. One critic declares that he could neither read nor write. His descriptions of some places are manifestly incorrect. There is no doubt that his editors experienced some difficulty in arranging his papers, which were in a state of chaos. Never-

[1] *Persia and the Persian Question*, i. 24.

theless his work retains its value, both for its independence and general freedom from exaggeration.' Gibbon[1] describes him as 'that wandering jeweller, who had read nothing, but had seen so much and so well' Whatever may have been his knowledge of Persian, it is certain that he had little or no acquaintance with any of the languages of India, and he was always obliged to do his business through an interpreter. It is now impossible to say what record, in the shape of notes or diaries, he kept up during his wanderings; his book gives no information on this point. But it seems unlikely that he could have carried on his extensive business of the sale and purchase of precious stones, the weights and prices of which he carefully describes, or that he could have investigated the various products of the country, without systematic notes; still less that he could have trusted to his memory for the names of his many halting places. My personal impression coincides on the whole with that expressed by Dr. Ball, that his narrative, when tested by modern authorities, is much more accurate than it has often been supposed to be. The places which he visited, and the events which occurred under his own observation, appear to be described with honesty and candour, and occasionally with some caustic humour. For matters of which he was not an eye-witness he depended on the merchants' tales current in the ports and cities which he visited. A somewhat parallel case is that of Dr. John Fryer, who visited India about the same time. He includes hearsay information with the record of his personal experiences. Unfortunately neither of these writers thought it necessary to distinguish clearly between information based on his own experience and that acquired, in the case of Tavernier, from shipmasters or other travellers, particularly the priests and friars of the Roman Catholic Church, whose friendship he enjoyed.

By a study of the routes which he carefully records we are in a position to estimate the credibility of his narrative. On the whole they stand the test fairly well. The distances seem generally to be stated with substantial accuracy; but the places names are occasionally so distorted that it is now almost impossible to identify them on modern maps, or by the aid of

[1] *Decline and Fall of the Roman Empire*, ed. W. Smith, vi, 59 note.

gazetteers or other official publications. We can only speculate on the causes of inaccuracies such as these. They may be due to want of care in keeping up his notes or diaries ; to difficulties in understanding the statements of his interpreter or other persons from whom he derived his information ; to the carelessness or ignorance of those who edited his work from scattered or ill-written notes. At the same time, while we may admit the occasional inaccuracy of his geographical knowledge, it is certain that he did traverse the routes which he describes, and that he recorded them to the best of his ability. We must remember that many of his halts were made at Sarāīs or hostelries provided by the Mughal Government along the main roads, and these were often known by the names of their lessees or caretakers, of whom no recollection survives. Other journeys, again, were made through districts which were imperfectly opened up in the days of Tavernier, and now owing to the increase of cultivation and population, or from other causes, their condition has greatly changed. Dr. Ball, by his long experience of marches along frequented or unfrequented routes, was able to identify many of the places at which Tavernier halted. But there is no hope of finality in this kind of investigation. My personal knowledge of parts of northern India, and a comparison of the journeys of other travellers, such as Sir Thomas Roe and Peter Mundy, have enabled me to make some corrections. The routes through the territories of the Nizam of Hyderabad and the Madras Presidency are more perplexing. By the kind assistance of the British Resident at the Court of H.H. the Nizam, Mr. Yazdani, on the staff of the Archaeological Survey of the State, has been able to clear up several doubtful points. I am indebted to Mr. F. J. Richards, of the Madras Civil Service, for similar assistance, with the co-operation of several district officers ; Mr. P. L. Moore for the Kistna District ; Mr. F. W. Robertson for Guntūr ; Mr. H. J. Gharpuray for Cuddapah ; Mr. J. C. Molony for Karnūl ; Mr. F. W. Bateman, of the Revenue Survey, in other places. But even now the work of identification is not quite complete, and it must be left to other officers possessed of local information to settle some doubtful points. It may be objected that little is to be gained by an attempt to identify obscure villages and inns. But the work of Tavernier is a classic, and I venture to think that the task of tracing his routes is not altogether labour misspent.

In questions of science and topography Dr. Ball's annotations are excellent. But a careful examination of the book showed that in order to make the work more valuable to the reader, and to conform it with the system pursued in other volumes of this series of reprints of classical works on India, it was necessary to add further information on questions of archaeology, historical events and personages, the social and religious life of the people. This I have, to the best of my ability, endeavoured to supply.

Since the publication of the first edition in 1889 many important works have increased our knowledge. It is necessary only to mention the new edition of *The Imperial Gazetteer* ; Dr. Vincent Smith's *Early History of India*, *History of Fine Art in India and Ceylon*, and *The Oxford History of India* ; Professor Jadunath Sarkar's *History of Aurangzib* and other works on the later Mughal period ; Mr. W. Irvine's edition of Niccolao Manucci's *Storia do Mogor, or Mogul India*, and his *Army of the Indian Moguls* ; the editions of Bernier's *Travels in the Mogul Empire* ; Sleeman's *Rambles and Recollections of an Indian Official* ; Grant Duff's *History of the Mahrattas* ; and Tod's *Annals of Rajasthan*—all published in this series. To these may be added the editions published by the Hakluyt Society of *The Book of Duarte Barbosa*, the *Travels* of Sir Thomas Roe, Peter Mundy, and John Fryer. The use I was able to make of these and other authorities was limited by considerations of space, but it may be estimated by the references in the commentary.

With all its obvious limitations, the work of Tavernier is an important contribution to our knowledge of Mughal India. We must remember that he was not a scientifically trained observer who visited India with the intention of describing the country and its people. He observed it from the point of view of a merchant, and nothing engages his attention so much as a successful bargain. This devotion to trade interests enabled him to collect much valuable information on the conditions of commerce, the methods and tricks of the native banker, of the Shroff or money-changer. He gives precise accounts of the production and sale of the standard commodities—spices, snake-stones, bezoar, musk, indigo, ivory, and the like—which are an important contribution to the history of oriental commerce. Even more useful, because it was based on the knowledge of an expert, are his lucid descriptions of the varieties of precious stones and pearls.

He looks on Orientals as a foreign gentleman, new to the country, naturally would do. Many of his anecdotes illustrate his cleverness in bargaining and his acumen and presence of mind in dealing with Orientals. He shows no hesitation in describing his bravery during a naval action with a British fleet when he was a passenger on a Dutch vessel, and when he more than once endured grave perils of the sea. Some of his personal remarks are characteristic; as when the Dutch officials, by offering wine, tried to induce him to disclose trade secrets, he remarks that 'they need not have brought wine for that purpose to make me drink, because I differed from most men, who speak much and say more than they know when they have drunk, but, as for myself, it is then I talk least'. He thus sums up his philosophy of life: 'I praise God that notwithstanding the troubles I had experienced in Batavia, and of which I have as yet told only a part, and the small dissipations which one cannot altogether avoid in this country, I have taken such good care of myself that I have never been inconvenienced by the least headache, or by a bloody flux, which is the ailment that carries away many people. That which in my opinion has contributed most to my health is, that I do not think I have ever grieved on account of any misfortune which has happened to me. I have sometimes made great profits, and I have sometimes experienced severe losses; but when in unpleasant circumstances I have never been more than half an hour in deciding what course I should adopt, without thinking more of the past, having always in my mind the thought of Job, that God gives and takes away as it pleases Him, and that one should render thanks for all that happens, whether it be good or evil.'

He certainly showed great courage and self-reliance in his journeys by sea and land, along routes in the jungles and uninhabited tracts, where, unprotected by guards, he was constantly exposed to the attacks of wild beasts and snakes, or of the more dangerous robber bands, which the inefficient Mughal police were unable or unwilling to repress. His marches were not interrupted even in the hot and rainy seasons, when a traveller not provided with a full supply of tents, and forced to depend on the chance accommodation in Sarāīs along the main roads and peasants' huts in the less frequented districts, must suffer much hardship. An epicure like Tavernier, who loved good food and a good glass of wine, must have found it difficult to put up with the coarse, badly cooked food on which he was obliged to subsist. But he seldom complains of the many inconveniences to which he was exposed.

He always took care to pose, not as a common merchant, but as a gentleman trader, who brought novelties in art work from Parisian studios, and invested the proceeds in precious stones and pearls. He constantly boasted that he travelled under the patronage of the Kings of France and Persia, whose protection he was accustomed to claim when he was subjected to any special loss or indignity. By this means he gained the unique distinction of being admitted to familiar intercourse with the nobles of the Imperial Court, and was allowed to handle and weigh the jewels in the royal collection.

His account of the Koh-i-Nūr and other famous stones suggested the essays in which Dr. Ball discussed their characteristics and later history. To his intimacy with the Mughal nobility we owe his life-sketches of the leading personages of the time—of Shāista Khān and his dealings in precious stones; of Mīr Jumla at the siege of Gandikota and his remarkable method of administering justice and conducting business; of Ja'far Khān, the Wazīr, and his clever wife. From his pages we can draw a realistic picture of Mughal India: of the Court and army; of the splendid presents which the profits of his business allowed him to offer to the Emperor and his officials; of the Kāzī and the administration of justice; of the police and the custom-house officials. He displays no desire to make a case for or against the administration as he studied it, and in this respect his narrative is a document of great importance when contrasted with the more detailed statements of Bernier or Manucci.

He also gives us vivid sketches of the foreign powers and their servants who competed for the Eastern trade. He certainly brings some ugly charges against the Dutch. One of their officers, he says, stole his mail bag and some jewels; others cheated him over some pay warrants in which he speculated. In the former case he consoles himself by the fact that his enemies met with sudden death, in the second case we cannot say what the Dutch had to urge in their defence; but it would clearly seem that the Dutch were right in preventing these warrants from being sold at much below their value. At any rate, if the result was that Tavernier, a foreigner, lost his money, they punished their own officials more severely for similar offences.

To the archaeologist the evidence of Tavernier is of importance. He traversed northern India before Aurangzeb was led by his craze for iconoclasm to destroy Hindu temples, a policy which did much to alienate the loyalty of the Rājputs, the bulwark of the Mughal Empire. For those who know the ground covered in his wanderings it is interesting to visit Mathura in his company while the great temple of Kesava Deva was still standing, and before the shrine of Visvesvara had been demolished and replaced by the stately minarets which dominate the Benares of our time.

But his search for information was generally limited to objects like these. It is disappointing to find that he tells us little of the condition of the peasantry, of the revenue system, of the social economy of the jungle tribes which he encountered in his wanderings. He was lacking in the preliminary knowledge which would have helped him to understand the religions of the people—Islām, the dominant faith of the governing classes, and Hinduism, the faith of the masses tolerated, but kept in subjection, as yet not actively persecuted. What he noticed were only the externals of both religions: the temples and mosques, the wandering troops of Fakīrs and their austerities, parties of Hindus carrying their idols in procession to some place of pilgrimage. Sati, or the immolation of widows with their husbands, the various methods of which he carefully describes, naturally attracted his special attention. But his descriptions of religion and custom lack that clearness which can be gained only by minute observation, the study of the sacred books, and a knowledge of the vernacular dialects.

With the help of the *Travels* of Tavernier, the *Travels in the Mogul Empire* of Bernier, the *Storia do Mogor* of Manucci, John Fryer's *New Account of East India and Persia*, with the narratives which we owe to the Hakluyt Society, combined with the evidence from Indian sources which has been skilfully collected by Professor Jadunath Sarkar, and the *History of the Mahrattas* of Grant Duff, we can understand in some degree the early period of the decline and fall of the Mughal Empire.

Besides my obligations to the officers of the Madras service and that of Hyderabad, I am indebted to many other authorities for assistance in elucidating some of the difficulties in the narrative of Tavernier. Among these I may mention the following: Dr. L. D. Barnett, Keeper of the Oriental Printed Books and Manuscripts in the British Museum; his pupil, Mr. S. K. Chatterji; the late Mr. M. Longworth Dames, the learned editor of *The Book of Duarte Barbosa*; Sir G. Grierson; Mr. W. Foster, C.I.E.,[1] late Registrar and Superintendent of Records at the India Office; Dr. E. Sidney Hartland; Mr. E. Heawood, Librarian of the Royal Geographical Society; Rev. H. Hosten, S.J.; Mr. L. K. Anantha Krishna Iyer, Superintendent of the Ethnographical Survey, Cochin State; Sir H. H. Johnston; Sir A. Keith, Curator of the Museum, Royal College of Surgeons; Mr. J. P. Lewis, C.M.G., late of the Ceylon Civil Service; Sir G. Watt, K.C.I.E.; Mr. Ghulam Yazdāni, Archaeological Surveyor in the Dominions of H.H. the Nizam of Hyderabad.

W. CROOKE.

[1] Now Sir William Foster, K.C.I.E.

SOME ADDITIONAL NOTES ON TAVERNIER'S HISTORY AND GEOGRAPHY

As a historian Tavernier is not always to be trusted. Thus in his chapters xxi–xxvi of Bk. III (p. 286 ff. of vol. ii) he describes the King of Japāra as 'otherwise called the Emperor of Java', and formerly 'King of all the island, before the King of Bantam, who was only governor of a province, rebelled against him'. But according to Mandelslo Matāram was 'a great city and the residence of a powerful king who once pretended to the sovereignty over the rest of the island, and still styles himself Emperor of Java'.[1] Now Mandelslo had described the island in 1639 or 1640, not long before Tavernier, and the question is which was right in his relation. It seems certain that Mandelslo was the more accurate in his facts. Matāram had been an ancient empire of Hindu or Buddhist[2] origin, but it had decayed and ceased to exist about A. D. 1002. From its ruins rose in succession two empires, Pajajāran and Majapahit, but both had been destroyed by the Muhammadans before the end of the sixteenth century A. D. A period of disruption ensued, Java being split up into several states. By A. D. 1600, however, a Muhammadan family had raised itself from the position of *adipati* of a district to that of *senapati* of a province—the survival of these two Hindu titles is curious—and finally to that of Sultān of the resuscitated empire of Matāram, and it was the paramount power in Java when Tavernier visited it. Tavernier had, however, some excuse for his error. The kingdom of Majapahit was represented by Japāra; but the old regalia of the kings or emperors, both of Majapahit and Pajajāran, had come down to the Sultān of Pajang. From him the *senapati* wrested it, and its possession gave its holder a title to the suzerainty of the whole of Java.[3] Nevertheless Japāra had clearly not abandoned all its claims

[1] As quoted in *Java: Past and Present*, by Donald Maclaine Campbell, London, 1915, vol. ii, p. 814. But, as Sir William Foster justly points out, Mandelslo did not actually 'visit' Java.

[2] *Ibid.*, p. 718.

[3] *Ibid.*, i, pp. 97–108.

to be considered the imperial power *de jure*.[1] In the eyes of the ancient Javanese the king was often an incarnation of a god, and the emperors of Majapahit had assumed the style of Bitāra (Sanskr. *avatāra*, 'incarnation') which in itself gave them titular authority over all the subordinate kings of Java and the surrounding islands.[2] Moreover, Majapahit had taken over from Pajajāran the art of making damascened *krīses*, bringing it to its highest perfection, and the carrying of a *krīs* is said to characterize the people of all the countries which once acknowledged the sway of the first empire of Matāram.[3] Tavernier had probably been told stories of the ancient glories of Majapahit. He may possibly have been made use of for propaganda purposes. But Mandelslo was better informed as to the real power of Matāram.

Other travellers were similarly misled. Thus Captain Edmund Scott describes the Sultān of Bantam, where he resided from 1602 to 1605, as the most powerful ruler in the island; and no doubt it was a strong kingdom, as was Balambuan in Mandelslo's time. But others, e. g. Tugal, were independent if not equally powerful, and Matāram undoubtedly was the dominant state.

On p. 289 of vol. ii Tavernier alludes to a 'siege' of Batavia by the King of Bantam in 1659, but it is doubtful if such a siege actually occurred. In 1652 the Sultān of Bantam attacked the settlement with 60,000 men, but he seems to have achieved

[1] Tavernier's failure to get permission to visit Japāra is to me a complete puzzle. In 1646 the Dutch had made a treaty with Matāram, whereby they agreed to set all their Javanese prisoners, subjects of the Emperor, at liberty. The Dutch envoys went to Matāram *via* Japāra in April of that year. Now the Emperor Sūsūhūnan Ingalaga, who succeeded his father in 1645, had made himself master of Demak, Pajang, 'Japan', and other states, i. e. of virtually the whole of Java. Here 'Japan' appears to be an error for Japāra in Valentyn, *Oud en Nieuw Oostindien*, iv, p. 97: and the error is repeated in Du Bois, *Vies des Gouverneurs Généraux*, p. 135. Matāram may indeed have only reduced Japāra to a nominal dependence.

With Japāra no differences seem to have occurred, but in 1633 the Dutch had been invited by the King of Bali to join him in an attack against 'the Matāram'. These negotiations failed on that point: Du Bois, *op. cit.*, pp. 106, 112.

[2] Campbell, *op. cit.*, i, p. 63.

[3] *Ibid.*, i, pp. 51 and 64.

little beyond ravaging the country. In 1659 the Dutch effected a treaty with him whereby Bantam agreed to exchange all prisoners.[1]

Sir W. Foster justly takes exception to the statement on p. 268 *n.* of vol. ii that the Dutch took possession of Bantam as early as 1643. Crawford on this point is misleading, as Bantam did not even become a permanent Dutch station till much later. The allusions to its King in English writers are due to its cardinal value as a commercial and strategical port in the seventeenth century. Its story merits fuller mention, but a sketch of it may be useful.

The maritime kingdom of Bantam, as Mr. W. H. Moreland justly calls it, was the rival of its neighbour Jakatra, also a sea-power in the Spice Islands, and its importance to Western commerce lay in the fact that it could be reached by sea by way of the Strait of Sunda even when the Portuguese naval station at Malacca closed the Straits of Malacca to other powers. By 1602 the Dutch merchants were trading at Bantam, and had indeed been known there in 1596. In 1603 the Sultan allowed them to erect a stone building for the storing of merchandise, but after 1618 the Dutch Company complained of oppression by the rulers of Bantam and it was not until 1659 that a permanent peace was negotiated and a permanent factory established. The English had, especially in 1618–20, proved formidable rivals of the Dutch. The latter accused them of intrigues with the King of Bantam and other indigenous powers, but they seem to have contended solely for the policy of the open door against the Dutch claims to a monopoly of the trade in spices. By the peace of 1619 the Dutch and English Companies were to work in accord and conduct their business in the common interest. But the Dutch, who justly maintained that they had opened up their establishments in the Indies by their own sacrifices, complained that the English Company failed to contribute money, munitions or even instructions to advance the common cause. The Treaty had provided for the setting up of a joint Council of Defence at

[1] Campbell, *op. cit.* i, p. 234; cf. Du Bois, *Vies des Gouverneurs Généraux*, p. 182.

Batavia, and it is not clear that the English Company failed to provide the agreed naval support for its duties ; but its representatives on the Council refused to participate in the reduction of the Banda Islands, which was certainly not a defensive operation. Nevertheless the Companies continued outwardly at peace, despite the judicial aberration at Amboina in 1623, until the outbreak of war in 1652. Bantam, the eastern head-quarters of the English Company, was then abandoned by its factors, but after the war it was restored, and the factory was not closed until 1683, when the Dutch became masters of the town. And even then the English Company was able to establish a fortified post at Bencoolen in Sumatra. The events at Bantam in 1683 made a great impression in Europe and especially in England, according to Du Bois.

What, in view of these facts, did Tavernier mean when he wrote that, 'according to custom', permission to visit Bantam had to be obtained from the Dutch Governor-General at Batavia? All that he can have meant is that he asked for a safe-conduct or recommendation to the King of Bantam, and was refused it ; but was told by the Director-General, the Governor-General's subordinate, that he could go without any risk, as he could obviously do and actually did. In 1648 the Dutch seem to have had no open dispute with Bantam.

Still graver errors are to be found in Tavernier's account of 'the Raja of Narsingue' (in Bk. I, ch. x, pp. 128–9). As the late Dr. Vincent Smith pointed out, the great Hindu kingdom of Vijayanagar was often called by Europeans the 'kingdom of Narsingh', after its usurper Narasinga Sāluva, who was constantly at war with the Muhammadans.[1] Under Rāma Rāja this empire was overthrown by a combination of the Muhammadan Sultāns of Bījāpur, Ahmadnagar, Golkonda, and Bīdar at the great battle of Tālikota in 1565. These Sultanates had been founded earlier in the sixteenth century by provincial governors of the Bahmanī dynasty, the great Moslem power in

[1] *Oxford Hist. of India*, p. 303. The Bahmanī kingdom broke up into five Sultanates, of which Tavernier only mentions three, omitting Berār and Bīdar, but including Burhānpur, which did not form a province of Vijayanagar or of the Bahmanī kingdom. His Daulatābād represents the Sultanate of Ahmadnagar.

the Deccan. Burhānpur, capital of the small Muhammadan kingdom of Khāndesh, formed no part of the Bahmanī domains. Akbar's conquest of it had been preceded by the annexation of Berār, then a province of Ahmadnagar, but that Sultanate was not finally overthrown till the reign of Shāh-jahān in 1632. Bījāpur became virtually tributary in 1636[1] and surrendered much of its territory in 1657.[2] Golkonda had submitted to the Mughal claim to suzerainty in 1635–6. What event Tavernier alludes to when he speaks of the *fameuse victoire sur le Mogol* achieved by them (the four generals who set up the four Sultanates) a few days after the death of the Rāja of Narsingue, it is difficult to conjecture. The Sultāns never combined against the Mughals. Individually no doubt each Sultanate inflicted reverses on Mughal armies, but collectively they fought no famous fight. Tavernier clearly confused the disruption of the Muhammadan Bahmanī power with the later overthrow of the Hindu empire of Vijayanagar, a mistake the less excusable in that the former monarchy lay to the north of the Krishnā River, and the latter to its south.[3]

Tavernier was certainly not always an eye-witness to events which he claims to have seen. Thus he could not have been present, as he says he was (vol. i, p. 144), when the English captives returned to Surat after their ransom from the Malabar pirates. Sir W. Foster has demonstrated this on p. xv of his Introduction to *The English Factories in India 1637–41* (wherein Clark's own account of their capture is given).

Tavernier's account of Bījāpur has raised a surmise that he never visited that city, by his time adorned by some of the finest buildings in India and by no means merely *une grande villace qui n'a rien de remarquable . . . pour les édifices publiques.* Yet he states expressly that he was there in 1641. The kingdom was then flourishing under Muhammad Shāh 'Ādil-Shāhī (1526–56). On his death he was succeeded by his only son, 'Alī 'Ādil Shāh II, aged eighteen or nineteen, but his claim to the throne was disputed by the Mughals without any valid ground. Tavernier appears to give the Mughal side of the dispute, but he

[1] *Oxford Hist. of India*, p. 399.
[2] *Ibid.*, p. 407.
[3] *Ibid.*, p. 275.

may have misunderstood it. The Queen could hardly, under strict Muhammadan law, have adopted an heir to the Crown even after her husband's death, and certainly not in his lifetime. Did Tavernier mean that 'Alī 'Ādil Shāh was declared to be a supposititious son by Aurangzeb, not an adopted son? Such a charge would be quite in harmony with Indian methods. The problem has been discussed by Professor Jadunath Sarkar at p. 285 of his *History of Aurangzib*, i. He suggests that the boy was really the son of a slave-girl.[1] It may be further suggested that: (1) he was 'adopted' by the Queen, Indian usage apparently recognizing the adoption of a stepson born to a co-wife or concubine by a Queen (an instance of a similar adoption by a noble's wife is recorded in the same writer's *Studies in Mughal India*, p. 116); and (2) the precisian Aurangzeb took exception to the unorthodox usage and seized upon it as a pretext for intervention. However this may be, Bījāpur was not left without a sovereign on its throne, and the first attack on it came from Aurangzeb, with Mīr Jumla's aid, not from Sivajī.

But despite his propensity to omit important facts in his history, Tavernier in his record of contemporary events is valuable to the English reader. He was in India much during the early period of the golden age of Dutch enterprise in the East, 1640–1750. *The Oxford History of India* states that in Aurangzeb's day the Portuguese were of little account, that the struggle for the Eastern maritime trade then lay between the English and the Dutch, and that the latter devoted their attention chiefly to the commerce with the Indian Archipelago and Spice Islands. But the Dutch had already, by Tavernier's time, learnt the value of Asiatic troops under good leadership, as he points out (vol. i, p. 188). No doubt they directed their energies largely to the Far East. In or about 1634 they had sent from Batavia an embassy to China—the one mentioned by Tavernier (ii, p. 235) thus being by no means their earliest

[1] 'A slave girl's son comes to no good,
Even though he may have been begotten by a King'.

sang Aurangzeb in one of his despatches: Sarkar, *Ahkam-i-Alamgiri*, p. 78. Aurangzeb, in thus addressing his youngest son, Kām Bakhsh, was at least consistent if 'Alī 'Ādil Shāh was a slave-girl's son.

attempt to open up trade with that country. They ousted the Portuguese from Japan and wrested Malacca from them in 1641. In 1624 they had expelled the Spaniards from Formosa.[1] Tavernier fully realized the decay of Portugal's power in the Far East. At first his sympathies clearly lay with the Dutch, and though they incurred his resentment in the event, he does not minimize their successes in India. There they had governors with councils at Cochin, the siege of which Tavernier describes, as well as the surrender of Cannanore (i, pp. 187–93); at Pulicat, whence all the Dutch factories on the coast of Pegu—as well as Coromandel—were controlled; Hughli; and Surat. The Dutch as a military power were in brief well on the way to establishing a dominant position, not only in Ceylon, but also in southern India. On the sea they were superior to the English and the French, severally, and yet able to maintain blockades of Goa, supplying their squadron from their depot at Vengurla, as Tavernier relates (i, p. 148).

The Dutch blockaded Goa from 1639 to 1642, and in spite of a ten-year cessation of arms agreed upon in the latter year the war was resumed in 1649. Again in 1680 they blockaded the harbour of Goa but failed to take the city. They had built a fortified factory at Vengurla previous to 1641 (*Bombay Gazetteer*, I, Pt. ii, p. 63).

On p. 288 of vol. i we read: 'M. Chevres (Cheveres in the edition of 1678), a Councillor of India, and the Major.' Le sieur Cheveres is not traceable with certainty, but a Salomon Zweris, Councillor in 1644–5, appears to be meant. His name is also spelt Zweers. The Major was possibly the Sergeant-Major (an office of importance) Willem Verbeek or van der Beek, who held that post in 1620–, 1640–51, and 1661–3. From 1651–4 he was Councillor Extraordinary and from 1654–6 an Ordinary Councillor of India.

The 'Sieur' Cheteur of vol. i, pp. 231 and 241, can only be

[1] In vol. ii, p. 172, Tavernier has a circumstantial account of the loss of the English fort in Formosa to the Dutch, who treacherously massacred the principal officers in it. This charge is flatly denied by Du Bois, *Vies des Gouverneurs Généraux* (1763), p. 150. He asserts that the Dutch Council at Formosa purchased the site required for their post from the Islanders, a fact obviously not inconsistent with Tavernier's story. But I have failed to trace anything to support the accusation.

Dirk Steur, whose earlier career cannot be traced, but he was Accountant (Boekhouder) General at Batavia from 1645–51, Councillor Extraordinary 1642–5, and Ordinary 1655–63.

The General Vandime of vol. ii, pp. 68, 268, and 307, was Antoni van Diemen, Governor-General of Batavia from December 31st, 1635, to April 19th, 1645, when he died at Batavia. His widow is said to have married again, Constant becoming her second husband (as Tavernier relates on p. 254), though Valentyn describes him as Directeur in Persia, not as Commander at Gombroon : *op. cit.*, 4, p. 295.

The fourth volume of François Valentyn's exhaustive work, *Oud en Nieuw Oostindien*, contains biographies and portraits of the Dutch Governors-General of Batavia down to 1725. Referring to it, Dr. J. Ph. Vogel, Professor of Sanskrit at Amsterdam, points out that the General Vanderlin of vol. ii, p. 251, must have been Cornelius van der Lyn, who rose to be Governor-General from April 19th, 1645, to December 11th, 1650. On p. 262 Tavernier styles him Commander Vanderlin. If this is right, it shows that in Van der Lyn's earliest days the Dutch had a fortified 'Commandery' at Gombroon or near it—probably at Basra, though in 1650 Basra was only a Hoofd-Comptoir or 'chief-factory' and in 1725 a Directory : *v. The Dutch in Malabar*, pp. 3–4. Incidentally too Tavernier shows that a golden bridle was regarded as too ostentatious in a Commandeur. It was presumably part of a Governor's insignia.

The following data are also culled from Valentyn's tome 4. As a preliminary it may be noted that in the Dutch bureaucracy the Gouverneur-Generaal was also styled Opperlandvoogd. This office was apparently created in 1610. An official could attain to it and the process is illustrated by the career of Joan Maatsuiker (*sic*). After holding one or two minor posts, he was from 1637–8 'President of Voorzitter van Schepenen' : then Baillu (of Batavia) from 1638–40 : from 1641–4 he was a Councillor Extraordinary : from 1640–50 his name becomes Johan Maatsuiker and is in the list of Ordinaris Raaden or Councillors. As Joan again he figures in that of the Directeurs-Generaal from 1650–3 ; and from May 18th, 1653, to January 4th, 1678, he was Gouverneur-Generaal.

So he seems to have been Gouverneur, as Tavernier correctly renders Landvoogd, at Pointe de Galle while also holding his seat on the Council.

But Tavernier is not so accurate in his use of the term 'General'. He uses it loosely; sometimes in anticipation of its holder's future appointment as Governor-General. For example, at the siege of Cochin Rijklof van Goens was in supreme command as Admiral, and it was not till 1678 that he became Gouverneur-Generaal. Under the Dutch system an official might begin as a commercial employé, rise to be Directeur[1] of an unfortified factory, Commandeur of a fortified factory, Gouverneur of a more important settlement with a strong garrison, exercising some sort of sovereign powers, and eventually become Gouverneur-Generaal. And from such appointments he might be seconded for important military duties and equally responsible diplomatic missions. The career of van Goens is typical of this *cursus honorum*. It is outlined by Galletti, *The Dutch in Malabar*, p. 8.

Van Goens, that very able servant of the Dutch Company, cannot have been the 'General' of vol. i, p. 193, whom Tavernier pleasantly describes as once a ship's cook out of Holland.[2] That personality must have been Jacob Hustaart or Hustaert, whose early career I have failed to trace until he suddenly appears as a Councillor Extraordinary (1662–5), and then as a Councillor till 1665. But he never became Governor-General, and when he acted for van Goens in the operations against Cochin from March to November, 1662, and under him till the fall of that place, he was 'on deputation' from his seat on the Council, it would seem, but held no title of General.

In the edition of 1678 Tavernier does not say that the Gouverneur-Generaal of Ceylon sent out pilots, but that the Gouverneur did so, which is correct. On p. 246 of vol. ii Governor-General is an error. Later, on the same page, he is, however, himself misleading in speaking of the Gouverneur Maatsuiker (the name is correctly given in the edition of

[1] Or Opperbestierder, according to Valentyn.

[2] This incident was certainly true of Caron, who shipped as cook on a vessel bound for Japan, cut his ship on arrival, and remained in the Dutch factory.

1678) as 'at present General at Batavia', since he means Gouverneur-Generaal. As Mr. A. Galletti points out, Major seems to have been at this period the highest military title conferred in the Dutch colonial service: *The Dutch in Malabar*, p. 8. But the highest rank seems to have been that of Opperbevelhebber, or chief commander, and it carried with it authority over all the forces, naval and military, engaged.

Signor (i. q. Sieur) David Bazeu, the Dutchman styled Bazu in ii, 99, followed Tavernier to India in the next ship from Gombroon in 1665. He too had done good business with the King of Persia and proceeded to the Mughal Court: Thévenot, *Suite de Voyage*, v, 216, 389, 322: and Foster, *Report on the Finch MSS.*, i, 493.

Jacob Casembrood was Baillu from 1664 to 1686: ib., p. 379. Reinier Casembrood rose to be an Extraordinary Councillor of Dutch India in 1684–5, that is a good many years later.

The M. Cant, one of the Councillors of India, also mentioned in vol. ii p. 278, as having died at Batavia while Tavernier was there (in 1648), is not traceable in the lists of Councillors, Ordinary or Extraordinary, nor can the death of any Councillor be traced as having occurred in that year. But Tavernier is so positive in his statements about M. Cant that one is tempted to think that he meant by him Antoni Caan, who in Valentyn's tome appears as Councillor from 1639–43, and that the latter date is a mistake for 1648. The M. Cam of p. 266 may be the same. Antoni Caan or Kaan had taken Trincomalee in 1639 and merited the military funeral given to M. Cant, whose origin and horsemanship Tavernier so scathingly disparages.[1]

The Advocàat Fiscaal at Batavia in 1646–9 was Gerard Herberts.

M. ('le sieur') Faure cannot be traced. A Kornelis Faber was one of the Commissaries of Huwelykze en Kleine Zaken in 1648: Valentyn, 4, p. 404.

The M. Croc of vol. ii, pp. 249–50, and the Croke of p. 234 seem to be one and the same person, to wit Arnold Krook,

[1] Valentyn, *op. cit.*, iv, pp. 369, 370 and 294. The Admiral Caan, whose ruthless proceedings at Amboina in 1743 even Du Bois censures, may have been a descendant: *Vies des Gouverneurs Généraux*, p. 130.

possibly, who had been Chief Merchant of the Castle at Batavia till 1622. But Paulus Krook whose last appearance was as President of the Law Council (van Justitie) in 1644, is nearer Tavernier's time: Valentÿn, *op. cit.*, iv, pp. 375 and 384. But Tavernier's somewhat scandalous allusions to Krook convey quite an inadequate idea of the importance of his employment as envoy to Achīn. That kingdom does not seem to have embraced the whole of Sumatra, but it was certainly a naval power of respectable weight. In 1615 it could put 60,000 men on its fleet of 500 sail; and in 1641 it aided the Dutch to destroy the Portuguese position at Malacca. Tavernier does not controvert the arguments of the Jesuit diplomatists at the court of China (ii, 236) that the Dutch had not kept faith with the King of Kandy; but Du Bois asserts that the Dutch did in fact make over 'Baticalo, Trinquemale and Punto-Gale'[1] to the King, though their treaty with him did not oblige them to do so. If the Dutch had broken faith with Kandy it is not very probable that the Achinese would have lent them powerful aid against Malacca. When Tavernier says that the King of Achīn agreed to hold the coast [of Ceylon] with a sufficient number of small armed frigates, of which he always maintained several (ii, 247), he seems to have entirely underrated the Achinese naval resources. He does not say what the King of Achīn was to receive in return for his support against the Portuguese in Ceylon, but it is clear that he had no serious grievance against them; and the broken promise alluded to on p. 248 must have related to the price of his subsequent co-operation against Malacca (p. 236). Tavernier hints that the Achinese king could have had the aid of Kandy[2] against the Dutch, but preferred to decree an embargo on their export of pepper from his dominions and even declared war on them (ii, 248–9). Du Bois says no word about Achinese aid against Malacca or an Achinese declaration of war either after the operations in

[1] Yet, he says, Coster became the first Governor of Pointe de Galle, already ceded to Kandy: *Vies des Gouverneurs Généraux*, p. 126.

[2] Du Bois alleges that its perfidious prince, incensed by Coster's insults, caused him to be murdered and then secretly favoured his old enemies the Portuguese: *ibid.*

Ceylon or those against Malacca. It is clear that in 1641 Achīn was not in a position to wage such a war because in that very year Iskandar Muda died and was succeeded by his widow, and she by three more queens. Incidentally, Krook cannot have been envoy to Achīn after 1641. And in 1643 it was André Soury who was sent as the Company's ambassador to congratulate the widow on her accession to the throne.[1]

Daniel Tavernier doubtless supplied much of the information about Macassar, but the account of the operations there in 1660 (ii, 236–8) is rather loosely written. The Dutch attack on the forts of Panakoke and Samboupo (in this latter was the palace of the kings) was not begun until the Portuguese squadron from Macao had been defeated.[2] The Dutch did not take any booty from the five vessels burnt or sunk. But they captured a sixth, which Schouten says was called Notre-Dame des Remèdes, and found her richly laden. Schouten implies that the six Portuguese vessels were attacked by only two Dutch, the two Dutch Admirals, and his account as a whole suggests that there was an element of surprise in their action as they had originally been detached from the main fleet to make proposals of peace to the King.

Another instance of the looseness of Tavernier's style is in vol. i, p. 165, where his meaning is that de Mascarenhas had been Governor of Ceylon, that is of all the Portuguese settlements on that island, with Colombo as his residence. As he became Viceroy at Goa in 1646 (till 1651) the incident of his rescue by the French adventurers must have occurred in that year. Tavernier's estimate of these Frenchmen's aid in the siege of Negombo is indirectly supported by Manucci (III, 240) who says that the final expulsion of the Portuguese from Ceylon was due to the King of Kandy's calling in Dutch assistance. They came against Colombo with a fleet of twelve vessels, under a Dutch captain of sea and war called Riclof, manned by

[1] *Ibid*., p. 129.

[2] Du Bois. *op. cit.*, p. 166. The King bore the non-Moslem name of Sombanco, Tavernier's Sumbaco. But that may have been a title added to his Muhammadan name. He was followed by a Hasan-ud-Dīn, one of whose nobles, a Būgī, bore the Hindu title of 'Rājā' Palaka; p. 167.

6,000 Europeans, mostly of French nationality, commanded by a general named Tuf de Barbon (Geeraart Hulft, ? of Brabant) and other valiant leaders, such as Arriam Vandermuis Coquinto and others like him.' Adriaan vander Meiden, who had succeeded Kittenstein as Governor of Ceylon, took over command of the troops on the 10th of April, 1656, when Hulft was killed by a shot, and on May 12 Colombo fell, after 150 years of Portuguese dominion. It became the principal Dutch factory (*comptoir*) in Ceylon. In 1658 Major van der Laan took Tuticorin and Nagapatam, while the Admiral Ryklof van Goens seized Manar, Fort Caïs and Jaffanapatam ; Du Bois, *op. cit.*, p. 187.

I can trace no corroboration of the statement in the *Ency. Brit.* (xxiv, 8) that in 1651 the Dutch abandoned St. Helena. 'The Dutch', observes Sir W. Foster, 'had not settled at St. Helena (see *Court Minutes of the E. I. Co., 1655–9*, p. xxx *n.*) The English established themselves there in 1659' (not in 1658) ; and on p. 27 of vol. ii Tavernier makes no mention of any earlier Dutch settlement on the island, merely complaining that heretofore it had been free to all the world as a place for revictualling.

Tavernier's version of the abstraction of the postal packet entrusted to him (ii, 129) must be accepted as correct. It was made over to him by Mr. Flower. Hendrik van Wyk, Directeur in Persia [1], believing that its contents would yield later information than he had received concerning the critical situation in Europe, managed to get it into his possession. The English Council at Surat stigmatized Tavernier as a 'Dutchified Frenchman' and suspected him of complicity, but van Wyk's own letter to Batavia negatives that theory. The private letters in the packet were never recovered.

In vol. ii, p. 196, Tavernier has a circumstantial account of the Indian Governor's assassination at Surat in 1653, while he was in that city. Sir W. Foster finds no support for this story in the contemporary English records. The Governor from 1652 to 1656 was Hãfiz Nasr, and he was dismissed in the latter year. It might be added that it could hardly be one of the Governor's functions to collect the octroi on a few

[1] From 1663–65 : Valentyn, 5 i, p. 205.

rupees' worth of cloth. Tavernier's tale may be founded on fact, but he has substituted the Governor for some official underling or misplaced the incident at Surat.

One of the most interesting figures which flit across Tavernier's stage is that of François Caron, whom Valentyn first mentions as 'oud Japans Voorzitter' and as President of the Heeren Schepenen in 1641. In that year too he was a Councillor Extraordinary, and Ordinary from 1642–7, in which last year he became Directeur-Generaal,[1] holding that post till 1650. So Tavernier describes him correctly on p. 251 of vol. ii. In n. 5 on that page he is said to have founded the first French factory in India in 1668, fully twenty years after, apparently, he had left the Dutch service. But he was no 'renegade' as the *Imperial Gazetteer* calls him. At the gravest perils of his life he had served the Dutch in Japan and elsewhere. For some reason he was dismissed by their Company, but Kornelis van der Lyn stood by his friend, whose conspicuous services he rated far above his own, and insisted on resigning his office as Governor-General as a protest. Together he and Caron sailed for Holland, where van der Lyn became Burghermaster of Alkmaar.[2] If Caron entered the French service he was amply justified in so doing. The Dutch, to judge by their officers' names, employed many foreigners, and Caron was in fact born in Holland, of a refugee French Protestant family, and probably by nationality a Frenchman (cf. Joret, *op. cit.*, p. 95 n.). For some reason Tavernier does not mention that the capture of Negombo in 1644 was effected by Caron, then Commander-in-Chief of the Dutch Company's forces in those parts, though he mentions the French adventurers who were there engaged: i, p. 164. Now Negombo had been taken from the Portuguese in 1640, retaken by them as Tavernier relates (i, 155) and finally fell to the Dutch in 1644—all during van Diemen's rule as Governor-General. But his relative, the young man recently arrived from Holland, whose nomination as its governor caused St. Amant to desert, was not, I think, Caron.

[1] Or Algemeene Bestierder van den Handel, i. e. 'Controller-General of Commerce.'

[2] Valentyn, *op. cit.*, iv, p. 296.

Tavernier's accuracy in topography has also been impugned, but caution is required. In any attempt to trace the route of an early traveller in India it must be borne in mind that names of places are often changed, new towns built near older ones, ruined or decayed, and stages reorganized. Occasionally, too, a halting-place bore a name conferred on it by the builder of its inn, to commemorate his beneficence and puzzle latter-day topographers. As an instance we may take Sera-dakan. Tavernier mentions this as a stage on p. 77, vol. i. This must have been the Sarāī of that name at the well-known town of Jullundur. The building still exists, or did exist a few years ago. Many of these Sarāīs were strongly built enclosures, capable of holding a strong force and indeed hardly defensible without one, in spite of their lofty walls with loop-holed parapets. A few still survive, but many have disappeared, a fate little to be regretted as there was a monotonous sameness in their architectural design. Hence intimate local knowledge or close investigation on the route is essential in such attempts. Regarding the identification of Tavernier's *Bergam* or *Bergant* with Bāglānā, Sir W. Foster observes that Bāglānā is nowhere near the Āgra-Ahmadābād route, and points out that John Jourdain (*Journal*, Hakluyt Soc. ed., p. 168) gives 'Berghee' near Merta as one of the stages on this route. Berghee has not been traced, but it may have been one of those Mughal refuges for travellers, imposing in its day, but now a ruin or at best concealed in a hamlet which has been built into its frame-work. It is, however, equally probable that Tavernier mixed up the two routes and really had Bāglānā in mind.

Sir W. Foster more closely identifies the Belli-porto of vol. i, p. 187, with Palliport at the northern end of Vapīn Island, some fifteen miles north of Cochin (*v. Eng. Factories, 1661–4*, p. 247, where the Dutch version of the attack is given ; also Galletti's *Dutch in Malabar*, p. 9). Sir William further points out that the *Touan* of p. 191 in the same volume is not Tuban in Java at all, but that it can only be Taiwan, the castle on the Island of Formosa whence the Chinese expelled the Dutch in 1661, capturing £300,000 in treasure and sending the shares in the Dutch Company down 30 per cent. Taiwan is mentioned in vol. ii, p. 270 n. In August of that year the Dutch Council at Batavia decided that it was too late in the season to send a fleet against Macao, and that all their forces should be concentrated against the Malabar Coast. In 1662 they seemingly made an attempt to recover Formosa, but the expedition was a failure.[1] Owing perhaps to this diversion it was not till January 1663 that they took Cochin. In that city the English had no factors in residence, as stated in vol. i, p. 192, n. 1.[2] Cochin was, next to Goa, the greatest Portuguese colony in the East, and a centre of Portuguese civilization.[3] The Dutch were intent on making themselves masters on the Coast of Malabar before the peace with Portugal could be ratified. The English Factories on the Coast of Malabar at this time were Kāyal, near Tuticorin : Porakād, between Quilon and Cochin : and Kārwār, a little south of Goa. In 1663 the Dutch were boasting that they would expel the English from both Porakād and Kārwār, and they stopped all the East India Company's trade at the former Factory, though its factors, Harrington and Grigsby, stubbornly maintained their footing there and refused to leave without orders from their superiors at Surat.[4] Tavernier mentions Dutch deserters as aiding the Portuguese in the defence of Cochin, and this is confirmed by Du Bois, *Vies des Gouverneurs Généraux*, p. 197.

Ball, in vol. ii, p. 7, described Raout as unidentified, but Sir W. Foster cites Roe (*Embassy*, i, 89) who calls it Arawd, and *English Factories*, 1630–33, 138, where it is called Roude. Roe places it about 51 miles from Burhānpur. This would indicate that it was Arāvad, in Chopra subdivision, East Khāndesh District. Dr. Crooke restored the name as 'Rāwat', which is tempting. But that is, at least in northern India, a tribal

[1] Du Bois is very brief in his mention of this expedition. The Dutch fleet returned to Batavia in March, 1663, after losing one of its twelve ships : *Vies des Gouverneurs Généraux*, p. 214.

[2] Ponnānī is not mentioned in *Eng. Factories 1661–4*. Possibly the *Imperial Gazetteer*, x, p. 355, is based on a local record. But the place seems to have been held by the Dutch as an unfortified factory : Galletti, *op. cit.*, p. 4 n. 2.

[3] Galletti, *op. cit.*, p. 10 : cf. *Eng. Factories, 1661–4*, p. 125.

[4] *Eng. Factories 1661–4*, pp. 250, 251, and 341.

name or title. Whatever Arāvad may signify there can be no real doubt as to its identity with Raout, Roude, and Arawd.

On p. 14 of vol. ii, Tavernier was unquestionably in error in imagining that his Damne was Van Diemen's Land. Sir W. Foster suggests that it is Damm, an island or group of islands south of the Bandas and NE. of Timor.

By Bhutān, Sir W. Foster suspects, Tavernier means Tibet throughout ; and it is self-evident that he confused the King of Bhutān with the Grand Lāma on p. 211 of vol. ii, though camels would be as impossible in Tibet as in Bhutān. The only possible explanation is that Tavernier mixed up his information about Bhotant (Tibet) with what he learnt about Bhutān ; and that his informant had a lively imagination.

Tavernier's account of his voyage to Batavia (ii, p. 251) raises a slight difficulty. Having crossed the Line from the North on June 2nd, he reaches 'the island called Nazacos' on the 6th, but does not sight the coast of Sumatra till the 17th. Now the island of Nacous in the tale of Sindbad the Sailor seems to be identifiable with the Nicobar Islands.[1] Was Tavernier's ship driven back to the North and East by the monsoon ? He does not say so, but it is not unlikely. The alternative would be to identify Nazacos Island with Nias, off the west coast of Sumatra, but so close to it that the ship could hardly have taken eleven days more to sight that coast. Nias was a well-known island, famous for the loveliness of its women, who were kidnapped wholesale for slaves.[2] It too lies to the north of the Equator, but not far from it. The balance inclines to the Nicobars.

The Bishop of Heliopolis (ii, 225) is not named by Tavernier, but if he was François Fallu, the bishop sent from France in 1662 to supervise the missions in Siam, &c. (*Eng. Factories, 1661–64*, p. 270), the fact would lend some support to Tavernier's statement that in 1662 he was at the capital of Persia. The Bishop must, however, have been at Alexandretta late in that year as he only reached Masulipatam in April, 1663. And Tavernier appears to have sailed home from Smyrna, not Alexandretta, arriving in France some time in 1662 ; *v.* Joret, *J.-B. Tavernier*, pp. 159–62.

[1] Campbell, *op. cit.*, i, p. 90, and ii, p. 1094.
[2] Campbell, *op. cit.*, i, p. 221.

Tavernier is a little confused in his account of the Orders at Goa (vol. i, p. 159). He does not mention the Theatines (cf. Manucci, iii, pp. 117 and 135 *nn.*), and he writes as if the Cordeliers and Recollects were not both Franciscans, if not indeed absolutely identical (*ib.* p. 165 *n.*). The Augustinians' church and convent at Goa seem also to be misdescribed (cf. *ib.*, p. 165 *n.*)

When a writer is found to be incautious about facts, the reader's mind, though not by nature sceptical, tends to become suspicious not merely of the writer himself but of his informants' statements as well. On p. 169 of vol. i we have M. des Marests' story, as presumably he told it to Tavernier, of the Polish Princes in Constantinople. Seeking confirmation of this story one finds that a very similar event did in fact occur, but that, unless history repeated itself, M. des Marests' tale inspires little conviction. It is a historical fact that in 1617 a Polish nobleman effected his escape from the Seven Towers in disguise. He was aided by M. Achille de Harlay, First Secretary of the French Embassy. The result was that the whole Embassy was arrested, including the Ambassador, M. de Savary de Brèves: R. Davey, *The Sultan and his Subjects*, p. 145. This *affaire* occurred rather too early to fit in with that in which des Marests was concerned, and I have not been able to trace any corroboration of his alleged enterprise. *Prima facie* this raises a suspicion that des Marests annexed a real event to his own experiences, though he had taken no part in it; and only further research can settle the doubt.

Writing in the middle of the seventeenth century the Turkish traveller Evliya confirms Tavernier's account of the Kūmūks of Dāghistān, the 'mountain country' south-east of Darband. Evliya styles them worst of all enemies: *Travels.* Trans. into English from the German Trans. of von Hammer, pp. 157, 165, and 167, vol. i.

Tavernier allows that he was not skilled in oriental languages, though he had acquired several European tongues in his earlier travels. All that he seems to have learnt in the East was a stray word or two. Incidentally, he uses the Turki term *sū* for 'river' and applies it to purely Indian names. It is unknown to modern Urdu, but not impossible that it was used by the Mughals, Persianised though they were. Or Tavernier may have learnt it on his travels before he reached India. No one at all versed in the Hindi of northern India would have written of Rājā Naktī Rānī, ' King Noseless Queen.'

It may be suggested that the explanation given on p. 204 n. of vol. i of the term *shāhmīyāna*, which is taken from *Hobson-Jobson*, p. 821, is incorrect. The word appears to be derived from *shāh*, ' king ', and *mīyān*, ' prince ', and to signify a canopy or tent for the use of royal and princely personages. If this is right, the *shāhmīyāna* of a ship may well have been the mainsail: cf. our term ' royal '.sail. The tent was not always without walls or sides—such a tent would have been too exposed for use in bad weather in the cold season—but its distinctive feature seems to have been that it resembled a canopy and was in fact a huge square umbrella, one of the ensigns of royalty, with or without the addition of side-pieces: vide *Hobson-Jobson*, p. 952.

As regards the theory propounded by Dr. Ball and others that Mīr Jumla's diamond was the original of the Koh-i-Nūr, Sir W. Foster has pointed out the hopeless discrepancies in Manucci's weight, 411 *ratis* = 360 carats (if the Florentine carat be meant), and Tavernier's 319½ *ratis*, when cut down from the 900 *ratis* which it scaled when received from Mīr Jumla: *Eng. Factories, 1655–60*, p. 70. The problem cannot be taken as yet solved.

It would be a great ' find ' if Tavernier's original MS. were to be discovered. His handwriting must have puzzled his transcribers or compositors. Thus in vol. ii, p. 246, Masudere or Madsuere must be Joan Matsuyker,[1] Governor in Ceylon from 1646 to 1650. Then again his memory occasionally failed him, for, though the English President at Bantam gave him and his brother a *grand accüeil* (ii, p. 269), he failed to recall or record that worthy's name. It must have been Aaron Baker, President from 1639 to 1641 and from 1646 to 1649.[2] This last

[1] Indeed in the ed. of 1678 we have ' Maatsuiker ', showing that attempts were made to correct errors in earlier editions.

[2] Campbell, *op. cit.*, i, p. 595, where the name is spelt Backer: but, as Sir William Foster notes, that must be the Dutch version of the name.

year fits in with Tavernier's statement that his term of office at Bantam had expired when he offered his guest a passage to Europe. Baker was a friendly person who managed to keep on good terms with the difficult Dutch. In 1652 he transferred himself to Madras (under orders from home) and was there too President.

Sir William Foster in conclusion points out that Tavernier used New Style dates while Dr. Ball in his notes generally used Old Style. The reader is indebted to him and also to Miss Z. M. Anstey for an exhaustive scrutiny of the proofs and many valuable corrections and additions.

H. A. ROSE.

JERSEY, *August* 1924.

BIBLIOGRAPHY

BY DR. BALL

As I cannot find in any of the Bibliographical Dictionaries an exhaustive treatment of the numerous editions of Tavernier's works, I have felt it necessary to go into fuller detail here than would have otherwise been advisable, owing to the amount of space required for proving the distinction between various issues, which can only be done by quoting titles. Such an analysis as that given below should prove of use, as I have had occasion to observe that copies have sometimes been incorrectly bound up, Tavernier's works being in consequence not readily distinguishable from those of other authors with which they have been mingled.

Primarily this list is based upon one by Professor Joret,[1] but, as will be seen on comparison, his catalogue has been much modified and amplified, the number of editions and translations being raised from twenty-six to thirty-eight.

My work having been done in Dublin, I have been interested to find what a number of the editions of Tavernier's volumes there are in the libraries of that city. In one which is seldom resorted to, namely that of Archbishop Marsh, there are six, though the library has been generally supposed to contain only ecclesiastical literature.

My thanks are due to the Bishop of Down and Connor for information regarding the copies in Armagh Library, and to the Librarians of the Bodleian and University College libraries for information about editions mentioned in their catalogues regarding which there were some statements which did not agree with other information available to me.

I

THE FRENCH EDITIONS OF THE 'VOYAGES' AND 'RELATIONS' OF TAVERNIER

FRENCH

1. **1675**.—*Nouvelle | Relation | De l'intérieur | Du Serrail | du | Grand Seigneur | contenant plusieurs singularitez | qui jusqu'ici n'ont pas esté mises en lumière | Par J. B. Tavernier escuyer Baron | d'Aubonne. A Paris | chez Olivier de Varennes* | MDCLXXV | 4to.

   There is a copy of this in Marsh's Library, Dublin.

---

[1] *Jean-Baptiste Tavernier*, Paris, Plon, 1886.

1676.—*Les Six | Voyages | de Jean-Baptiste | Tavernier, | Escuyer Baron D'Aubonne, | Qu'il A Fait | en Turquie, en Perse, | Et Aux Indes, | Pendant l'espace de quarante ans, & par toutes les | routes que l'on peut tenir: accompagnez d'obser- | vations particulieres sur la qualité, la religion, | le gouvernment, les coûtumes & le commerce | de chaque pais; avec les figures, le poids, & la | valeur des monnoyes qui y ont cours | Premier Partie | Où il n'est parlé que de la Turquie, & de la Perse.* | Volume II has the same general title, save for the last two lines, which run *Seconde Partie | Où il est parlé des Indes, & des Isles voisines | —A Paris, | Chez Gervais Clouzier &c. | et | Claude Barbin, &c. | au Palais* MDCLXXVI. 2 vols. 4to.

It is from this, the best edition, that the present translation has been made. For the most part the misprints which it contains are repeated in the subsequent editions.

3. **1677.**—A reprint of the above, but the pages are, I think, smaller. I have seen two copies.

4. **1678.**—*Nouvelle relation de l'intérieur du serrail du Grand Seigneur,* etc. (as in No. 1, above). Amsterdam. J. Van Someren. 12mo. (Brunét and M. Joret.)

5. **1678.**—*Les Six | Voyages | de | Jean-Baptiste Tavernier | Écuyer Baron d'Aubonne | Qu'il a fait en Turquie, en Perse | et aux Indes,* etc. [*Suivant la copie | Imprimée | à Paris.* | *Amsterdam* [on the engraved title] *chez Johannes Van Someren l'an 1678.* 2 vols. 12mo.

I have seen two copies of Vol. I and one of Vol. II of this edition. The page and type are smaller than in No. 9 below. There are copies in Marsh's and University College (London) Libraries, and I am informed by the Librarian of the latter that it is incorrectly described in the catalogue as 18mo. Brunét says the edition is rare, but neither fine nor complete.

6. **1679.**—Reprint of No. 2 (according to Brunét).

7. **1679.**—*Recüeil | de Plusieurs | Relations | et | Traitez singuliers et curieux | De | J. B. Tavernier | Escuyer Baron d'Aubonne | Qui n'ont point esté mis dans ses six premiers Voyages | Divisé en cinq Parties,* etc. *A Paris chez Gervais Clouzier* MDCLXXIX, 4to.

Contains two fine portraits of Tavernier. It makes a uniform third volume to No. 2. Facsimiles of these portraits are given in the present edition.

8. **1681.**—A reprint of No. 7 (according to Brunét).

9. **1679** (I and II), **1681** (III).—*Les Six Voyages,* etc. (Same title as No. 5.) *Suivant la copie imprimée à Paris.* Engraved title in some copies as in No. 5, therefore probably by Van Someren of Amsterdam. 3 vols. in 12mo. Vols. I and II are in Trinity College Library, Dublin, and I have Vols. II and III, but they contain no indication of printer, publisher, nor place of publication.

Brunét says there were two issues of Vols. I and II, and I find that the two above-mentioned copies of Vol. II vary slightly in the ornament on the title. Vol. I contains the Persian Travels, Vol. II the Indian Travels, and Vol. III the Recüeil and Seraglio.

10. **1692.**—Reprint of No. 9. 3 vols. 12mo.

11. **1702 and 1703.**—This edition is mentioned in the references below. I know no more about it. Probably it was a small 8vo.

12.—*Les Six Voyages de J. B. Tavernier*, etc. Utrecht. 2 vols. 12mo.

Recueil de plusieurs relations et traitez, etc. Utrecht 1702 (should be 1712 ?). 1 vol. 12mo.

There is possibly a mistake in describing these two last as being 12mo, for I am informed that the Bodleian contains an edition as follows: *Les Six Voyages*, etc. Part I. Utrecht, 1712. Small 8vo.—leaves only 6⅛ in. high, with engraved title 1702. Do. do. Part II, *Suivant la copie imp. à Paris*, 1703. Small 8vo, as Part I. Part (Vol.) III, *Recueil de plusieurs . . . avec la relation de l'intérieur du serail suivant la copie imp. à Paris*, 1702. Small 8vo.

13. **1713.**—*Les Six Voyages de J. B. Tavernier*, etc. Nouvelle éd., Paris. Ribou. 5 vols. 12mo.

Brunét says it is badly printed.

14. **1713.**—*Les Six Voyages de J. B. Tavernier*, etc. Rouen, Machuel (according to Joret). 6 vols. 12mo.

15. **1713.**—An edition similar to the last, but differs in having the name Eustache Herault on the title-page. There is a copy in the India Office Library.

16. **1715.**—*Les Six Voyages*, etc. La Haye. 3 vols. 12mo.

This is on the authority of M. Joret. Perhaps identical with next.

17. **1718.**—*Les Six Voyages*, etc. La Haye, H. Schwendler. 3 vols. (in 6 parts). Small 8vo, pages barely exceeding 6 inches. Utrecht 1702 on engraved title. There is a copy in the Bodleian.

18. **1718.**—*Les Six Voyages*, etc. Amsterdam (Rouen). 3 vols. (in 6 parts). 12mo (according to M. Joret).

19. **1724.**—*Les Six Voyages*, etc. Rouen, Machuel le Père. 6 vols. 12mo (according to M. Joret).

20. **1724.**—*Les Six Voyages*, etc. Rouen, Machuel le Jeune. 6 vols. 12mo (according to M. Joret).

The Bodleian contains two vols. of one of the two last editions or separate issues. They are described as follows: *Les Six Voyages*, etc., Nouv. Ed. Tome I. Rouen, 1724. 12mo (leaves 6¼ in. long) . . . . . . *Suite des Voyages*, etc., Nouv. Ed. Tome II. Rouen, 1724. Tome I has the engraved title, dated 1712.

21. **1755.**—Considerable extracts from Tavernier's travels are given

in the *Histoire Générale des Voyages*, by M. l'Abbé Prévost, which was republished with additional notes in Holland (La Haye) in 1755. Most of these extracts are included in Vol. XIII of the latter edition.

22. **1810.**—*Les Six Voyages de J. B. Tavernier, &c. Edition entièrement refondue et corrigée, accompagnée d'éclaircissements historiques et critiques etc. par J. B. J. Breton. Paris, Veuve Lepetit.* 7 vols. 18mo.

I regret not having had an opportunity of seeing a copy of this edition, which may contain some useful critical information.

23. **1882.**—*Les Six Voyages de J. B. Tavernier en Perse et dans les Indes pendant quarante années. Et par toutes les routes que l'on peut tenir, Racontés par lui-meme, Réduits et annotés par Maxime Petit.* Dreyfus, Paris. 12mo.

This edition is in a popular and abridged form; it contains no critical information of importance.

II

Translations of Tavernier's Travels into Different Languages

A.—English [1]

1. **1677.**—*A New | Relation | of | the Inner Part | of the | Grand Seignors | Seraglio | containing | Several Remarkable Particulars never before ex | pos'd to publick View | by J. B. Tavernier Baron of Aubonne | London | Printed and Sold by R(obert) L(ittlebury) and Moses Pitt |* 1677 |

2. **1677.**—*The Six | Voyages | of | John Baptiste Tavernier Baron of Aubonne | through | Turky into Persia | and the | East Indies | for the Space of Forty Years | giving an | Account of the Present State of those countries, viz. of the Religion, Government | Customs and Commerce of every country; and | the figures weight and value of the money | currant all over Asia | To which is added | The Description of the Seraglio | made English by* [2] *J(ohn) P(hillips) | Added likewise | A voyage into the Indies &c. By an English Traveller never before printed | London | Published by Dr. Daniel Cox | London | Printed by William Goodbid for Robert Littlebury at the King's Arms in Little Britain & Moses Pitt at the Angel in St. Paul's Churchyard 1677.* 1 vol. fol.

There is a copy of this in Marsh's Library, Dublin.

---

[1] Abstract in *Philosophical Transactions*, No. 129, 30 November, 1676, p. 711; No. 30, 14 December, 1676, p. 751.

[2] The J is printed like an F, and is sometimes erroneously quoted as such (see Professor Joret's list). I can find no confirmation of the existence of an edition by Phillips dated 1676, which is given by Professor Joret.

3. **1678**.—This edition differs from the preceding in the title and date, having after the word London—*Printed and sold by Robert Littlebury at the King's Arms in Little Britain and Moses Pit*[1] *at the Angel in St. Paul's Church Yard 1678.* 1 vol. fol.

There is a copy of this edition in the India Office Library.

Both titles contain a blunder about the 'Voyage into the Indies by an English Traveller', as the paper referred to itself bears the title 'A Description of all the Kingdoms which encompass the Euxine and Caspian seas', and contains no mention of India; it is signed 'Astrachan', and the writer says he was an Irishman. It is dated 1677 on its own title.

4. **1678**.—*The Six | Voyages | of | John Baptista | Tavernier | A noble man of France now living | through | Turky into Persia | and the | East-Indies | Finished in the year 1670 | Giving* etc. etc. 1 vol. Fol.

The blunder just referred to is corrected in this title, and there is some variation in the names of the printers, etc.

Both the last editions contain a letter to Sir Thomas Davies, Lord Mayor of London, and in the last there is also a dedication by J. Phillips to Dr. Daniel Cox. There are two copies of this edition in Trinity College Library, Dublin.

5. **1680**.—*A | Collection | of Several | Relations and Treatises | singular and curious | of | John Baptista Tavernier | Baron of Aubonne | not printed among his first six voyages,* | etc. etc. *Published by Edmund Everard Esq.* | *Imp.* etc. | *London* | *Printed by A. Goodbid, and J. Playford for Moses Pitt at the* | *Angel in St. Paul's Churchyard.* 1680. Folio.

This contains a dedication to Sir Robert Clayton, Lord Mayor elect, and it consists of five parts.

There are copies in Trinity College, Dublin (2), the Bodleian, Marsh's, and the Armagh Libraries.

6. **1684**.—*Collections | of | Travels | Through | Turkey into Persia & the East Indies | Giving an account of the | Present State of these countries | as also | A full relation of the Five years wars between | Aurengzebe & his Brothers,* etc . . . | *Being | the Travels of Monsieur Tavernier, Berniez | and other great men, Adorned with many copper Plates | The First Volume | London | Printed for Moses Pitt at the Angel in St. Paul's Churchyard* | MDCLXXXIV. Folio. 2 vols. in 1.

This contains a preface by Edmund Everard, who says that '*In this work was employed the Help of another Worthy Gentleman,*[2] *who labour'd in the first Volum of Tavernier's Translation;*

---

[1] M. P., or Moses Pitt, was not particular as to the spelling of his name, as we have Pitt, Pit, and Pytt.

[2] The worthy gentleman was presumably John Phillips, the translator of the previous editions. Whether his character justified this description is doubtful. He was a nephew of John Milton, his mother having been Milton's sister.

but it was brought to an end & perfection by me, who had the occasion to be more particularly acquainted with Monsieur Tavernier himself, his Native Tongue, and other Particularities abroad.'

Vol. II contains the same general title; it includes, together with Tavernier's *Relation* etc., the paper on the Euxine etc., referred to above, which is prefixed by a special 'Publisher unto the Reader', pp. 95–100, but the writer's name is not given: perhaps he was John Phillips or Dr. Cox. The latter part of the Volume consists principally of translations of Bernier's books and letters.

There are copies of this edition in the India Office and Marsh's Libraries, and I possess one which was obtained a few years ago from Mr. Quaritch.

7. **1688.**—An issue of this year has the same general title-page as the preceding, and the pagination is identical throughout, but the following is different:—*The first Part | London Printed for M(oses) P(itt) and are to be sold by George Monke at the White Horse | without Temple Bar and William Elevey at the Golden Lyon and Lamb | over against the Middle Temple Gate* MDCLXXXVIII.

   There is a copy of this in the King's Inns Library, Dublin. It contains no dedication.

8. **1764.**—Harris, in his *Voyages and Travels*, gives large extracts from Tavernier.

9. **1811.**—Pinkerton (*Travels*, Vol. VIII, pp. 235–57) gives Tavernier's Book II, chaps. xv, xvi, xvii, xviii, xix, xx, xxi, and Baron's animadversion on Tavernier's account of Tonquin is in Vol. IX, pp. 656 and 692.

B.—German

1. *Tavernier, J.-B.: Beschreibung der sechs Reisen in Türkey, Persien und Indien nebenst der Beschreibung des Türkischen serails und der Krönung des Kœnigs Soliman in Persien, herausgegeben von J. H. Widerhold,* 3 Theile mit Portraits, Karten, und Abbildungen. Genf. 1681. Folio.

2. *Kurtzer Begriff,* etc. Genf, J. H. Widerhold. 1681. Folio.

3. The *Nouv. Biog. Générale* mentions a German edition of 1684, perhaps a mistake for the English ed. of that year.

4. *John-B. Tavernier weyl. Ritters und Freyherrn von Aubonne in der Schweiz, Beobachtungen über das Serrail des Grossherrn.* Auf seiner sechsmaligen Reise nach der Türkey gesammelt. Nebst vielen eingestreuten Bemerkungen über die Sitten und Gewohnheiten der Türken. Memmingen, 1789, bei Andreas Seiler In 12mo, 179 pages. (According to Joret.)

C.—Dutch

1. An edition in Dutch in 1682. 4to. According to *Nouv. Biog. Générale*. (But Joret cites the *Nouvelle Bibliographie universelle*, art. *Tavernier*; and doubts its existence.)

D.—Italian

1. *Tavernier J. B.: Viaggi nella Turchia, nella Persia e nell' India stampati in lingua francese ed ora tradotti da Giovanni Luetti, Roma* 1682. 2 vols. in 4to.
   Same title, Bologna, 1690. 3 vols. 12mo.

[*Original title page.*]

LES SIX VOYAGES DE JEAN BAPTISTE TAVERNIER,

ECUYER BARON D'AUBONNE,

QU'IL A FAIT

EN TURQUIE, EN PERSE, ET AUX INDES,

Pendant l'eſpace de quarante ans, & par toutes les routes que l'on peut tenir : accompagnez d'obſervations particulieres ſur la qualité, la religion, le gouvernement, les coûtumes & le commerce de chaque pais ; avec les figures, le poids, & la valeur des monnoyes qui y ont cours.

SECONDE PARTIE.

Où il eſt parlé des Indes, & des Iſles voiſines.

A PARIS,

Chez { GERVAIS CLOUZIER, ſur les degrez en montant pour aller à la Ste Chapelle, à l'Enſeigne du Voyageur. ET CLAUDE BARBIN, ſur le ſecond Perron de la ſainte Chapelle. } au Palais

M. D. C. LXXVI.

AVEC PRIVILEGE DU ROY.

DEDICATION

TO THE KING

SIRE—

The zeal which I have for the service of your Majesty, and for the honour of France, does not permit me to enjoy the repose which I believed had come to me after such prolonged labours. My age not permitting me to undertake new voyages, I have experienced a kind of shame at finding myself of no use to my country, and at not acquitting myself of all which it expects from me. I have thought it to be my duty to it to render an account of my observations upon that which I have seen, and have not been able to excuse myself from making public. I hope, Sire, that these exact and faithful accounts which I have written, since my return, from the notes which I have collected, will not be less useful to my country than the valuable articles of merchandise which I have brought back from my travels. For my object in this work is not merely to assuage public curiosity. I have proposed for myself a more noble and more elevated aim in all my deeds. As the hope of legitimate gain alone has not made me traverse these regions, so the sole desire of placing my name in this book has not caused me to-day to have it printed. In all the countries which I have traversed, my strongest desire has always been to make known the heroic qualities of Your Majesty, and the wonders of your reign, and to show how your subjects excel by their industry and by their courage all other nations of the earth. I venture to say to Your Majesty that I have done so with more boldness, and even more success, than those who had a title and an authority to speak. My method of action, hostile to deception, and possibly somewhat too free, has exposed me to many risks among the nations jealous of our prosperity, who defame us as far as they can in order to exclude us from trade. I have often risked both mv fortune and my life by exalting Your Majesty by my words above all the monarchs of Europe and these Kings of the East—even in their very presence. I have emerged with honour from all these dangers by impressing a respect for your name in the hearts of these barbarians. Under the shadow of this august name, respected throughout the world, I have travelled more than 60,000 leagues by land in perfect safety. I have six times traversed Turkey, Persia, and the better part of India, and was the first to attempt to go to the famous diamond mines. Too happy to have brought precious stones which Your Majesty has condescended to join to the jewels of your throne, but still more happy to have made observations in all these places, to which Your Majesty will possibly not deem it unworthy to devote some moments, as you will find there many details of three of the most powerful Empires of Asia. You will see the manners and customs of the people dwelling there at present. I have interposed in certain places stories, which may relieve the mind after a tedious march of caravans, imitating in that the Orientals, who establish caravansarāīs at intervals in their deserts for the relief of travellers. I am principally devoted to the description of the territories of Turkey, Persia, and the Mogul, in order to point out on the five different routes which one may take to go to them certain common errors with reference to the positions of the places. Although these accounts may be wanting in grace and in politeness of language, I hope that the diversity of the curious and important matters which they contain, and more particularly the veracity which I have scrupulously observed, will nevertheless cause them to be read, and possibly to be esteemed. I shall consider myself well repaid for my work if it has the good fortune to please Your Majesty, and if you accept this evidence of profound respect.

With which I am,

SIRE,

YOUR MAJESTY'S

Very humble, very obedient, and very faithful

Servant and Subject,

J. B. TAVERNIER.

DESIGN OF THE AUTHOR[1]

Wherein he gives a brief account of his first travels in the fairest parts of Europe up to Constantinople

IF the first education is, as it were, a second birth, I am able to say that I came into the world with a desire to travel. The interviews which many learned men had daily with my father upon geographical matters, which he had the reputation of understanding well, and to which, young as I was, I listened with pleasure, inspired me at an early age with the desire to go to see some of the countries shown to me in the maps, which I could not then tire of gazing at.

At the age of twenty-two years I had seen the best parts of Europe, France, England, Holland, Germany, Switzerland, Poland, Hungary, and Italy, and I spoke fairly the languages which are the most necessary, and which have the greatest currency.

My first sortie from the Kingdom was to go to England, where the reigning monarch was James I, Sixth King of Scotland, who caused himself to be called King of Great Britain, to satisfy both the English and Scotch by a name common to these two nations. From England I passed into Flanders, to see Antwerp, my father's native land. From Flanders I continued my journey to the United Provinces, where my inclination to travel increased on account of the concourse of so many strangers, who came to Amsterdam from all parts of the world.

After having seen all that was most important throughout the Seventeen Provinces, I entered Germany, and having arrived at Nuremburg, by Frankfort and Augsburg, the noise of the armies which were marching to Bohemia to retake Prague made me desire to go to the seat of war, and acquire something of the art, which would be of service to me in the course of my travels. I was but one day's distance from Nuremburg when I met a colonel

[1] From Vol. I, *Persian Travels.* Paris, 1676,

of cavalry, named Hans Brener, son of Philip Brener, Governor of Vienna, who engaged me to follow him into Bohemia, being glad to have a young Frenchman with him. My intention is not to speak here of what happened at the battle of Prague; the discourse would be long, and the history of this century speaks sufficiently of it. Some years afterwards I followed this colonel to Vienna. He presented me to the Governor of Raab, his uncle, to whom belonged the title of Viceroy of Hungary. This Governor received me into his house to be one of his pages. It is usual to serve in this position in Germany up to the age of twenty-five years, and one never quits the service without being prepared to carry arms, and without obtaining a Cornetcy or an Ensign's Commission. I had been four and a half years with the Viceroy when the Prince of Mantua arrived at Vienna to urge the Emperor to the designs which the Duke his father desired, but he was unable to accomplish anything; and even the negotiation of M. de Sabran, Ambassador of the King to his Imperial Majesty, for the arrangement of the investiture which was the subject of his mission, was also fruitless. During the years I spent in Hungary I had time to learn something of war, having been with the master whom I served on many noteworthy occasions. But I shall say nothing of the affairs which we had with the Turks, because so many have treated of the subject, and because they have nothing to do with the subject of my travels. The Viceroy had espoused, on his second marriage, a sister of Count d'Arc, Prime Minister of State of the Duke of Mantua, and Envoy at Vienna with the Prince his son, and this Count was a relative of the Empress, who was of the House of Gonzague. The Count having come to see the Viceroy, I was ordered to attend on him during his sojourn at Javarin, and when about to depart he told the Viceroy that the Prince of Mantua, having no one with him who knew the language, he would please him by permitting me to attend on him while he remained at the Emperor's court. The thing was readily granted to the Count d'Arc, who took me to Vienna, and as I had the good fortune to be not unpleasing to the Prince, he assured me on his departure that he would be much pleased to see me at Mantua, where, as he believed the war would end satisfactorily, he would remember the service which I had done him. This was sufficient to arouse in me straightway a desire to pass into Italy, and continue the travels which I meditated.

I sought to obtain the Viceroy's approval of my design, who at first consented with reluctance, but at length, pleased with my service, granted me permission with a good grace, and presented me, according to custom, with a sword, a horse, and a pair of pistols, adding to them a very handsome gift of a purse full of ducats. M. de Sabran then left for Venice, and as he wished to have in his company a Frenchman who knew how to speak German, I availed myself of the opportunity, and we reached Venice in eight days. M. le Comte d'Avaux was then Ambassador of France to the Most Serene Republic, and he gave a grand reception to M. de Sabran, who visited him by order of the King. As the Venetians had no less an interest in the war of Mantua than the House of Gonzague, the Republic received M. de Sabran very well, and presented him with eight great basins of confections, upon one of which there was a heavy golden chain, which he placed on his neck for a moment, and then in his pocket. M. le Duc de Rohan was then in Venice with his family, and two of these basins having been distributed to those present in the hall, M. de Sabran directed me to convey the six others, on his account, to Mademoiselle de Rohan, who received them with a very good grace. During some days which we remained at Venice I studied with pleasure this town, so celebrated and so unique among all others in the universe; and as it has many things in common with Amsterdam—the site, the size, the splendour, the commerce, and the concourse of strangers—it contributed no less to increase the desire which I had of becoming thoroughly acquainted with Europe and Asia.

From Venice I went to Mantua with M. de Sabran, and the Prince, who testified his joy at beholding me again, gave me at first the choice of an Ensigncy or a commission in the Artillery Regiment of the Duke his father. I accepted the latter offer, and was well pleased to be under the command of M. le Comte de Guiske, who was its Captain, and is at present Mareschal de Grammont. A long sojourn at Mantua did not agree with the desire which I had for travelling, but the Imperial army having laid siege to the town, before thinking of my departure I wished to see what would be the issue of the war. We at length compelled the Imperialists to raise the siege. This they did one Christmas Eve, and on the following day some troops were sent out to see if it was not a feint, and whether they had entirely withdrawn.

The siege did not last long, and no considerable action took place—nothing which could instruct young soldiers. I shall only say that one day eighteen men having been commanded to go to reconnoitre the width and depth of the ditch which the enemy had made by cutting a dyke for the defence of a small fort from whence he had driven us, and eight troopers of our company being of this number, I obtained from the Prince, with great trouble, permission to be one of these eight, he having had the goodness to say to me privately that a heavy fire would have to be faced. In short, of the eighteen of us who went out but four returned, and we having gone the length of the dyke among the reeds, as soon as we appeared on the border of the ditch the enemy fired so furious a discharge that they did not give us time to make observations. I selected in the magazine a very light cuirass, but of good material. This saved my life, having been struck by two bullets, one of which struck the left breast and the other below, the iron being indented in both places. I suffered some pain from the blow which had struck the breast, and when we went to make our report, M. le Comte de Guiske, who perceived the good quality of my cuirass, had it decorated, and retained it, so that I have not seen it since.

Some time after I obtained my discharge from the Prince, who had promised to give it to me whenever I desired, and he accompanied it with an honourable passport, by reason of which six troopers came with me to Venice, where I left them. From Venice I went to Loretto, from thence to Rome, and from Rome to Naples, from whence, retracing my steps, I spent ten or twelve days more at Rome. Afterwards I went to see Florence, Pisa, Leghorn, and Genoa, where I embarked for Marseilles. As for the remainder of Italy, I have had opportunities of seeing it on other journeys which I have made; and I say nothing of this beautiful country, nor of its fine towns, because there are plenty of people who have written about them.

From Marseilles I came to Paris, where I did not remain long, and wishing to see Poland, I entered Germany by Switzerland. After having traversed the principal cantons, I descended the Rhine in order to reach Brisac and Strassburg, then ascending by the Swabe I passed to Ulm and Augsburg to go to Munich. I saw the magnificent palace of the Dukes of Bavaria, which William V had commenced and Maximilian his son accomplished during the heat of the wars which troubled the Empire. From thence I went, for the second time, to Nuremburg and to Prague, and going from Bohemia I entered Silesia and crossed the Oder to Breslau. From Breslau I went to Cracow, one of the largest towns of Europe, or rather one composed of three towns, and the ancient abode of the Kings of Poland. I then went to Warsaw, on the left bank of the Vistula, and saw the tomb of King Sigismund, which was beautiful and magnificent.

From Warsaw I returned to Breslau, and took the route to Lower Silesia, to visit one of the principal officers of the Emperor's household whom I knew very well. But at two leagues from Glogau I was turned from my intention by meeting, and the pressing invitation of, Colonel Butler, a Scotchman, who commanded a regiment of cavalry for the Emperor, and who since killed Wallenstein on account of the order which he received. His wife, who was with him, was fond of the French, and both of them having treated me with much kindness, accompanied by some presents, to induce me to remain with them, I was unable to resist such evidences of kindness. The King of Sweden at that time was invading Pomerania, and the army of the Emperor marched towards Stettin to prevent his entry. We were not more than four leagues off when we heard that the Swedes were in it. This news caused great disorders in the Imperial army, of which Tureste-Conte was the General, and out of 40,000 men, of which it was composed, he disbanded 9,000 or 10,000, which compelled the remainder to withdraw themselves to Frankfort-on-the-Oder and its environs.

It was then that I heard that the Emperor was going to Ratisbon with his son, Ferdinand III, in order to have him crowned King of the Romans. I had witnessed the crowning of the Kings of Hungary and of Bohemia, and being desirous to witness this third ceremony, which should be finer than the others, I took leave of my Colonel and came quickly to Ratisbon. All took place with much magnificence, and many young gentlemen showed their skill in the tournaments. In front of the course where they tilted the ring there were two platforms. The grandest was for the Emperor and the Empress, and all the ladies of the Court; the other resembled a large shop, where were suspended many jewels of great price. They made parties of seven or eight cavaliers, who with a lance touched the object for which they wished to run; and there were some of the jewels worth 10,000 écus and more. He who had the good fortune to win had nothing to pay; it was the others who had competed with him who had to pay the merchant for it. The conqueror received it from the hands of the Prince of Ekemberg, First Minister of State of the Emperor, and having placed it at the end of his lance went to present it to the Empress, who would not receive it; this allowed him to offer it to that one of the ladies of the Court for whom he had the most esteem.

There came then to Ratisbon jewellers from different places, and one of them perished unfortunately on his arrival by an adventure so tragic that all the Court was moved to compassion. He was the only son of the richest merchant in Europe, who dwelt at Frankfort, and his father had sent him to the coronation to sell precious stones. Through fear of his being robbed on the way his father sent them by a safe means to a Jew at Ratisbon, who was his correspondent, with an order to place them in the hands of his son. This young man on his arrival at Ratisbon went to find the Jew, who told him that he had received a small box full of precious stones, and that he might take possession of them whenever he wished. At the same time he invited him to drink, and took him to the house of the Dauphin on the quay at Ratisbon, where they enjoyed themselves till one o'clock at night, when the Jew, taking the young man by a street where there were no shops, and where there were no passers, stabbed him in the stomach eight or ten times with a knife, and left him lying on the pavement. The miserable Jew thought that he would escape by writing to the jeweller in Frankfort that he had handed over the small box to his son, and that no one would suspect him of the murder. But by God's will, on the very same evening the crime was discovered and the guilty one was in the hands of justice.

The matter was discovered thus. Immediately after this cruel murder a herald of the Emperor, named Jean-Marie, passing through this obscure street, struck his feet against the body of this young man, who still breathed, and fell on top of him. Feeling some moisture on his hand, he at first thought that he was a drunken man who had been ill and was unable to stand. But on second thoughts it occurred to him that it might be a wounded man. He ran for a light to an office of the Marshal at the corner of the street. The Marshal and his companions took a lantern, and on arriving at the place with the herald saw the melancholy spectacle of a young man bathed in his own blood, who had but few moments to live. The Marshal would not allow them to carry him to his office, in order not to embarrass justice, and they found nowhere more suitable for prompt aid than the house of the Dauphin, which was not far off. He was at once taken there, and as soon as they had washed his face, which was covered with blood and dust, the mother and daughter of the house at once recognised him as the person who came to drink there with the Jew. He expired a moment afterwards, without having been able to speak or to give any sign of consciousness, and it was in this way that they discovered the murderer, who was taken in his own house the same evening, and straightway confessed his crime. The enormity of the deed justified that the guilty one should be condemned to a very severe sentence, and the judgement provided that he should be hung to a gallows, head downwards, between two large dogs, suspended close to him, so that in their rage they should eat out his vitals, and so make him suffer more than one death by the protraction of the torment. It is the sentence provided by the Imperial law for a Jew who has killed a

Christian, and the method of this assassination had about it something more horrible than ordinary murders. However, the Jews of Ratisbon made such large presents to the Empress and to the two Princesses that they obtained an alteration in the sentence. and the culprit was condemned to a shorter execution, but which was not less rigorous. He was torn with hot irons in various parts of the body and in different quarters of the town, and as the pincers tore out the flesh molten lead was poured into the openings, after which he was taken outside Ratisbon and broken on the wheel at the place destined for the execution.

The coronation ceremony having been accomplished, I heard that the Empress was sending the Sieur Smit as Resident to the Porte of the Grand Seigneur. From the information which my friends gave me I hoped that he would be gracious enough to allow me to accompany him. I was unwilling to be a cause of expense to him, and I had, in order to make the voyage, a sufficient number of ducats, which I had saved while I served under Colonel Butler, who showed me much affection. I was about to leave Ratisbon when Father Joseph, who was in the service of the King, and who had known me at Paris, proposed to me to accompany M. Bachelier, whom his Majesty was sending to the Duke of Mantua, or to accompany M. l'Abbé de Chapes, brother of the late M. le Mareschal d'Aumont, and M. de Saint Liebau in the voyage which they had designed to make to Constantinople and even to Palestine. I liked this latter proposition, having no intention to return to Italy, and wishing to see new countries. Without hesitating about the selection, I told Father Joseph how indebted I was to him for the offer which he made me, and I joined these two latter gentlemen, from whom I did not part till they were about to leave Constantinople for Syria. Before quitting Germany these gentlemen desired to see the court of Saxony, where we arrived in a short time. You pass through Freiburg on this route, a small town, but well worthy of being seen, because it contains the tombs of the Electors, which, whether as regards material or form, are the finest in Europe. From thence we went to see the splendid Castle of Augustburg, which is on a high mountain, wherein there are many remarkable things. There is a hall which, for sole decoration from top to bottom, has a multitude of horns of all kinds of animals hung on the walls, and you see the head of a hare with two small horns, which was sent to the Elector as a great curiosity by the King of Denmark. There is in one of the courts of this castle a tree of such enormous size, and the branches of which are so extended, that one can place underneath it a great number of tables. I did not count them, but the concierge told us that there were as many as there are days in the year. That which makes this tree more wonderful is that it is a birch, which it is rare to see attain to such a size. There is also in this castle a well so deep that one cannot draw water from it in less than half an hour, and considering the altitude of the place, one cannot sufficiently admire the boldness of the designer.

All Germany is so well known that I shall not delay to describe Dresden, which is the residence of the Elector. I shall merely say that the town is not large, but that it is very beautiful and well fortified, and that the Elbe, over which there is a fine stone bridge, separates the old and the new towns. The palace of the Elector is one of the largest and most beautiful in Germany, but it lacks an open space in front, and its principal gate is at the bottom of a cul de sac. The treasure-rooms,[1] to the number of sixteen, are open to all strangers of distinction; and there are catalogues, both in German and in other languages, of all that is beautiful and rare in each. MM. l'Abbé de Chapes and de Saint Liebau were very well received by the Elector—father of him who reigns to-day; he kept them to supper, and treated them with much kindness. A grand buffet had been arranged this evening, upon which all the pieces were of a perfectly beautiful and shining stone, which was obtained in the silver mines of Saxony, and on a lower shelf there were several goblets of silver gilt of different sizes. The Elector, wishing to give the health of the King to these gentlemen, allowed them to select of these goblets the one from which they wished to drink, on condition of drinking it full, according to the custom of the country. M. l'Abbé de Chapes caused one to be brought

[1] The famous green vaults.

which did not appear to be large, and M. de Saint Liebau asked for another which held a little more. But l'Abbé de Chapes was much surprised when, having taken the goblet which he had chosen, it expanded in his hands when he touched a spring, like a tulip which opens to the sun, and it became forthwith a large cup capable of containing nearly a pint. He was not forced to drink it full, and the Elector forgave him, contenting himself with a laugh at his surprise.

From Dresden we went to Prague, and it was for the third time that I saw this grand and beautiful town, or, if you wish it, these three towns, separated by the Molde, which falls into the Elbe 5 or 6 leagues below. Having traversed Bohemia through the middle, and touched an angle of Moravia, we entered Austria and came to Vienna, intending to embark at once, the cold beginning to make itself already felt. These gentlemen confiding on me the arrangements of the journey, I went to ask the Governor of Vienna to write in their favour to the Viceroy of Hungary, his brother, to give us necessary passports; this he granted with a good grace, and he also gave two boats to these gentlemen, one for themselves, which had a good room, and the other for the kitchen. We remained one day at Presburg, to see the great church and a quantity of relics which they had to show there, and from thence we descended to Altemburg.

Altemburg is a town and county which belong to Comte d'Arach. It was the property of a Queen of Hungary, who presented it when dying to a noble of her court, on condition that he and his successors should always keep in this castle a certain number of peacocks, which this Queen was very fond of; and that if any one omitted to do so the county should revert to the throne.

We arrived at Sighet after midday, and immediately I took a small boat and went quickly to Raab, formerly called Javarin, which is only two hours distant. I gave the Viceroy the letter which his brother had given me, and I informed him of the arrival of MM. de Chapes and de Saint Liebau. As I had had the honour of being some years in his service, he told me he was glad to see me again, and that he would do everything to satisfy those whom his brother recommended.

On the following day he ordered 300 cavalry and two carriages to go and bring them to Javarin. He received them very politely, and during the sojourn which they made the principal officers sought to make them pass the time agreeably. It was necessary to wait eight or ten days to receive the reply of the Bacha of Buda, a message having been sent to the Governor of Comorre to ascertain if he would grant a passage to two French gentlemen and their suite. In order to facilitate the matter they were represented to be relatives of M. de Cessy,[1] Ambassador of France at the Porte, and the reply of the Bacha having come in the affirmative, we descended to Comorre, where the Governor gave us other boats. They conveyed us half way to Buda, where we found others, which, on the receipt of the notice of our departure, came from Buda to meet us. These boats are a kind of brigantines well armed and very convenient, and they make, by force of oars, much way in little time, because they are very light. It is between Comorre and Buda on the frontiers of the two Empires, where the Ambassadors relieve one another, which happens on both sides every six years, and in the same time the alliance is renewed, and it is necessary that the number of persons on each side shall be equal.

From Vienna to Javarin we were three days on the water, because the Danube makes a great circuit, though one can make the land journey in two hours. From Javarin one goes to Comorre, and from Comorre we descended to Buda in less than two days. The journey from Raab to Buda is seldom taken by land, because the country being on the frontier there are brigands on both sides whom it is dangerous to meet. In the fine season one can go from Buda to Belgrade in less than eight days ; but we took eight, the cold and snow delaying our progress. We took an equal time up to Constantinople, where we did not arrive till the 29th day after our departure from Belgrade, because the days were short and the way bad.

It is the custom in Hungary, especially on routes little frequented by strangers, to take no money from travellers ; a householder lodges them and treats them well, and the

[1] Spelt 'de Cesi' in vol. i, p. 170, and below, p. lxxxvi.

mayor of the place repays him at the end of the year out of the public revenue for the expense which he has incurred. But it should be remembered that they are not charged with a great number of travellers, and that in Hungary, which is one of the best countries in Europe, food is so cheap that we did not expend at Belgrade for fourteen months as much as two crowns a day.

Buda is on the right of the Danube, distant from the river about half an hour. As soon as the Bacha had news of our arrival he sent his equerry with horses led by well-dressed slaves for our conduct to the town. Among these slaves were two Parisians, and our gentlemen, knowing their families, offered unavailingly up to 800 crowns for their ransom.

We remained twelve days at Buda before we could have audience of the Bacha, who was unwell. He sent us our food daily—a sheep, fowl, butter, rice, and bread, with two sequins for other fresh supplies; and on the day upon which he granted an audience to MM. de Chapes and de Saint Liebau, they presented him with a watch, the case of which was covered with diamonds. The Bacha is a man of good figure and pleasing countenance; he received them with much civility, and on their departure for Belgrade, which was on the fourteenth day of their arrival at Buda, he sent them six chariots with two soldiers to conduct them, and an order to defray their expenditure for food throughout, of which they did not wish to avail themselves.

On our arrival at Belgrade we entered an old caravansarāī, but four of the principal merchants of Ragusa, who do a large trade in this place, took us from this poor inn to convey us to the house of a good citizen. The Ragusans carry cloth to Belgrade, and take wax in exchange, and quicksilver, which they obtain from Upper Hungary and from Transylvania.

If we had reason to congratulate ourselves on the good reception of the Bacha of Buda, we had also reason to complain of the rude manner which the Sangiac [1] of Belgrade displayed towards us, as he compelled us to contest for fifteen or sixteen days the ridiculous demand that he at first made of 200 ducats

[1] Misused for Sanjakbeg, governor of a Sanjak or district of the Turkish Empire: Turkish *sanjāq*, 'banner'—*New English Dict.*, *s.v.*

per head. The merchants of Ragusa went to speak to him, and all they could obtain was that we should each give him fifty ducats. The Sangiac continuing to act badly, I went to see him with our interpreter, and at first spoke to him with civility. But seeing that he paid no attention to me, and that it was necessary to address him otherwise, I intimated so well by threats that I would send an express to the Porte to complain of his rude conduct towards two gentlemen, relatives of the French Ambassador, that notwithstanding the 200 ducats which he demanded per head, he contented himself with fifty for all, which were forthwith given to him. During this fifteen days' detention we had the small consolation of enjoying good fare. The bread, the wine, and the meat are all excellent and cheap in this place; and Belgrade being built on a point of land where two great rivers—the Danube and Save—join, so large a quantity of large pike and fine carp were caught that we only used the livers and milts, giving the fish to the poor. Two Jesuit Fathers, chaplains of the merchants of Ragusa, contributed much to dissipate the annoyance which these gentlemen experienced from the delay of their journey, caused by the injustice of the Sangiac. The merchants too, did not limit themselves to the good services which they rendered on several occasions; they added a magnificent banquet to which they invited them on Christmas Eve, after which they went to the midnight mass, accompanied by music and instruments, with which they were pleased.

We took saddle horses and chariots at Belgrade for Adrianople, each selecting the mode of conveyance he considered most comfortable. As for me, I preferred a chariot, wherein, covering myself with straw, my body being clad in a good sheep skin, I did not feel the cold. We came to Sophia, a large and populous town, the capital of the old Bulgarians, and the residence of the Bacha de Romeli.[1] You see there a beautiful mosque, which was once a Christian church, with a tower so artfully made that three persons can ascend it at the same time without seeing one another.

From Sophia we came to Philippopolis, and between this last

[1] Pāsha of Roumelia.

town and Adrianople we met two well-mounted companies of Tartars. They come to make raids on this side of the Danube, and indeed farther into the portion of Hungary which belongs to the house of Austria. As soon as they saw us they hastily ranged themselves in two lines on either side, to allow us to pass through them, designing, doubtless, to attack us, being without hope of vanquishing us except by numbers and surprise. They had for their only arms a poor sort of sabre, and we on our side had wherewithal to prevent their approach, each having a musket and a pair of pistols, and the majority good sporting guns also. For fear they should come to attack us if we neglected to defend ourselves, we stood our ground and made a barricade of our chariots. However, our two guards with our interpreter were sent to the chief of these Tartars to tell him that we should not move till they decamped, and that being soldiers like them they would obtain nothing from us. The chief replied that he had only drawn up his men in order to honour us, and that, as we wished it, they would pass on if we gave them something to buy tobacco. We speedily satisfied them ; and our interpreter having taken them four sequins, they drew off and left our passage open.

We reached Adrianople on the twenty-third day after our departure from Belgrade, and we hired other horses and chariots for Constantinople. Adrianople derives its name from the Emperor Adrian, who enlarged and embellished it ; it was previously called Oreste.[1] It is pleasantly situated at the mouths of three rivers, which debouch together in the Archipelago. The old town is not very large, but the Turks have added splendid suburbs, and it is one of the residences of the Ottoman Emperors, who often come there, whether called by business or for the pleasure of the chase, especially of ducks and herons. When these three rivers overflow the marshes and neighbouring fields they make, as it were, a sea, which is covered by a multitude of these birds, as also cranes and wild geese, and the Grand Seigneur takes them with the eagle and the falcon, which are very well trained to this kind of sport.

On the fifth day after our departure from Adrianople, and

[1] Orestis, land of the Orestae tribe.

the fifty-second after we left Vienna, we arrived happily at Constantinople, at eight o'clock in the morning. Having traversed the town and passed to Galata, they led us to the house of the French Ambassador, which we did not leave till after dinner, and in the evening we went to take possession of a house belonging to a Greek close to that of the Ambassador. MM. de Chapes and de Saint Liėbau remained two months at Constantinople, where they expended a large sum, always keeping open house. We made during the winter a small trip to the Dardanelles and the ruins of Troy, where we only saw stones, which were assuredly not worth the trouble of going there.

Curiosity to see a room furnished in the French fashion, of which they gave us a great account, led us to go to the serrail [1] at Scutari. Two eunuchs who guarded it made much fuss about permitting us to enter, for which we had to pay well, and we saw nothing but a bed after our pattern, of rich material, with the chairs and carpets, which constituted the whole lot. On another day we took boats with our friends to go to Chalcedonia, which is on the margin of the sea. There is a very ancient church there, in which one sees the council hall, with the original chairs still preserved. It is to-day a monastery, and two bishops who were there, after having conducted us all through, civilly presented us with a collation.

We then went to see Pompey's Pillar, at the mouth of the Black Sea, and going from serrail to serrail, which are the royal houses of the Grand Seigneur, we occupied eight days upon this pleasant outing. But one might do it in two, if content to see the pillar without stopping anywhere. We met in one of these serrails an old French eunuch, who was delighted to see us, and gave us all possible good cheer.

I shall make here a remark about the Black Sea canal. There is no strait of the sea without a current, and this has two opposite ones. That from the European side carries vessels towards the Black Sea, and that which is from the Asiatic side brings them back towards the Mediterranean. Thus in the trip which one often makes from Constantinople to the mouth of

[1] See Yule, *Hobson-Jobson*, s.v Serai.

the canal, both in going and returning you find the stream favourable, and you have but to cross from one bank to the other.

The rigour of winter being over, MM. de Chapes and de Saint Liebau continued their journey, and accompanied by two guards, engaged two brigantines for the journey to Alexandretta. I have since heard that they saw all that is most remarkable in the Archipelago and along the coasts of Natalie; that from Alexandretta they went to Aleppo, from thence to the Euphrates, and that, retracing their steps to Aleppo, they went to Damascus, and from thence to Jerusalem.

As for me, having another journey in view, and wishing to see Persia, I remained at Constantinople, awaiting a caravan which I was encouraged to hope for from one month to another. But without that it often happened that eight or ten merchants, joining together, made the journey in safety to Ispahān. My ignorance was the reason for my making a much longer stay at Constantinople than I had contemplated. I remained eleven months, during which time I saw M. de Marcheville arrive, who came to relieve M. de Cesi. He had an audience of the Grand Seigneur as Ambassador of France, but M. de Cesi, who did not wish to retire, intrigued so well with the Grand Vizir that he remained Ambassador at the Porte, while M. de Marcheville was compelled to return to France. I was in his cortège on the day when he had audience with his Highness, as I have stated in my account of the Serraglio.

At length, after eleven months' delay, a well-equipped and numerous caravan left Constantinople for Ispahān, and I joined it on the road, for my first journey to Asia.[1] It has been followed by five others, and I have thus had time to observe the nature of the country well, and the genius of the populations. I have pushed the three last beyond the Ganges and to the island of Java; and during the space of forty years I have traversed more than 60,000 leagues by land, only having once returned from Asia to Europe by sea. Thus I have seen at my leisure in my six journeys, and by different routes, the whole

[1] M. Joret, by means of the incident about the Ambassadors just referred to, has fixed this date as January or February 1631. Those who give it as 1636 are therefore clearly in the wrong.

of Turkey, all Persia, and all India, and especially the famous mines of diamonds, where no European had been before me.[1] It is of these three grand Empires that I propose to give a full and exact account, and I shall commence with the different routes which one may take to go from Paris to Persia.

[1] As elsewhere pointed out in the following pages, there were European visitors before Tavernier's time, as Caesar Frederick before 1570, Methold before 1622, and also some others.

TABLE OF THE BOOKS AND CHAPTERS

BOOK I

BOOK II

BOOK I

Concerning routes which one may take to go from Ispahān to Agra, and from Agra to Delhi and Jahānābād,[1] where the Court of the Great Mogul is at present ; as also to the Court of the King of Golkonda and to that of the King of Bījāpur,[2] and to several other places in India.

[1] Dehly and Gehanabat in the original. Shāhjahān rebuilt Delhi (A. D. 1638–48), and called the new city Shāhjahānābād, which retains its form and fortifications to the present time, and is the Delhi of to-day.

[2] Visapour, in the original, was an early corruption of the name Bījāpur (Vijayapura). It is the principal town of what is now the Bījāpur District of the Bombay Presidency. An account of its buildings is given in Fergusson's *History of Indian and Eastern Architecture* ; but this has recently been superseded by the monograph by H. Cousens, *Bījāpur and its Architectural Remains, with an Historical Outline of the ʻAdil Shāhī Dynasty*, Bombay, 1916.

TRAVELS IN INDIA

CHAPTER I

Route from Ispahān to Agra by way of Gombroon,[1] *where particular mention is made of the navigation from Hormuz*[2] *to Surat.*[3]

I SHALL follow in this account of my Indian travels the same order as I observed in that of my Persian travels, commencing with a description of the routes by which one can go from Ispahān, to Delhi and Jahānābād, where the Great Mogul at present resides.

Although India presents a frontier towards Persia of more than 400 leagues, extending from the ocean to that long chain of mountains which traverses the centre of Asia from west to east—and has been known to antiquity under the name of Mount Taurus or Mount Caucasus[4]—there are, notwithstanding, not so many ways for passing from Persia into India as there are from Turkey into Persia, because between Persia and India there are only sands and vast deserts where

[1] Gomron in the original, for Gombroon, the modern Bandar 'Abbās, in the Persian Gulf; see Barbosa, ed. M. L. Dames, Hakluyt Society, 1918, vol. i. 77; Curzon, *Persia*, ii. 418 f.

[2] Ormus in the original, the modern Hormuz, more properly Hurmūz, formerly a city and kingdom near the mouth of the Persian Gulf. See Barbosa, ed. Dames, i, p. 68 ff., 90 ff.

[3] Surate in the original, the modern Surat, spelt Suratte in the French edition of 1713.

[4] Mount Taurus or Mount Caucasus. The former name was used by some of the ancient geographers for a supposed continuous range from west to east, through the whole of Asia, and embracing the real Taurus of Asia Minor, the Persian Elburz, the Hindu Kush, and the Himalayas. 'India is bounded on the north from Ariana to the eastern sea by the extremities of the Tauros which the Macedonians call the Kaukasos, while the natives give distinctive names to the several parts, such as Paropamisos [Paropanisos], Emodus, and Imaos,' &c. (Strabo, bk. xv, c. i, § 11; McCrindle, *Ancient India as described in Classical Literature*, 15 f.).

there is no water to be found. Thus, in order to go from Ispahān to Agra there are but two routes to select from—one partly by land and partly by sea, by taking ship at Hormuz ; and the other altogether by land, passing through Kandahār. The first of these routes has been fully described up to Hormuz towards the end of the last book of my travels in Persia,[1] and I have now to speak of the navigation from Hormuz to Surat.

Navigation in the Indian seas is not carried on at all seasons, as it is in our European seas, it being necessary to take the proper season, outside which no one ventures to put to sea. The months of November, December, January, February, and March, are the only months in the year in which you embark at Hormuz for Surat, and at Surat for Hormuz : with this difference, however, that you can rarely leave Surat later than the end of February,[2] but for leaving Hormuz you may wait till the end of March, and even till the 15th of April, because the western wind, which brings the rains to India, begins to blow then. During the first four months a wind from the north-east prevails with which you may sail from Surat to Hormuz in fifteen or twenty days ; afterwards, veering by degrees to the north, it serves equally the vessels going to Surat and those coming from it ; during this period the merchants generally reckon on spending thirty or thirty-five days at sea ; but if you desire to make the passage from Hormuz to Surat in fourteen or fifteen days, you must embark in the month of March or at the beginning of April, because you then have the western wind astern all the way.[3]

Vessels leaving Hormuz steer for Muscat,[4] on the coast of Arabia, so as not to approach too near that of Persia, and to

[1] Bk. v, ch. xx, xxi, xxii, p. 653 et seq. The second route up to Kandahār is described in bk. v, ch. xxiv, p. 693, *Persian Travels*, Paris edition of 1676.

[2] This indication of the periods of the monsoons is of interest. It is utilized by M. C. Joret, in his *J.-B. Tavernier*, Paris 1886, p. 64, as a factor in determining the dates of Tavernier's journeys, regarding which his direct statements are so few, vague, or even contradictory.

[3] For the monsoons see *Imperial Gazetteer of India*, i. 109 ff.

[4] Mascaté in the original, the modern Muscat, or more properly Maskat, the capital of Oman, in North-East Arabia (Barbosa, i. 71 ; Curzon, *Persia*, ii. 439).

give it a wide berth. Those coming from Surat do the same, in order to find the entrance to the gulf, but in neither case do they ever touch at Muscat, because custom dues have to be paid to the Arabian Prince who captured it from the Portuguese.

Muscat is a town on the sea-coast, facing three rocks, which render the approach to it very difficult, and it lies at the foot of a mountain upon which the Portuguese had three or four forts. It may be remarked that Muscat, Hormuz, and Bassora [1] are the three places in the East where the heat is most unbearable. Formerly the English and Dutch monopolized this navigation; but for some years past the Armenians, Musalmāns of India and Banians [2] had their own vessels also, on which, however, you do not feel so safe as on those of the Franks,[3] because necessarily the Indians do not understand navigation so well, and do not employ such good Pilots.

Vessels sailing for Surat, which is the sole port in the whole empire of the Great Mogul, steer for Diu and Point St. Jean,[4] and then anchor in the roads at Suwālī,[5] which is only four leagues distant from Surat, and but two from the mouth of the river, bearing from it northwards. Merchandise is conveyed from one place to the other either by cart or by boat, as large vessels cannot enter the river at Surat until after they are unloaded, on account of the sandbanks at the mouth. The Dutch depart after having landed their goods at Suwālī, and the English need to do the same, neither being permitted

[1] Balsara in the original, Balsora of the *Arabian Nights*, the modern Bassora (Basra), in the Persian Gulf.

[2] Banianes in the original, the Vānia or Banya trading caste.

[3] Francs in the original, and Franguis on p. 49, names in the East for all Europeans except Greeks; Pers. *Farangī*.

[4] Diu and Point St. Jean. Diu is on an island (from which fact the name is derived—*dvīpa*, Sanskrit for 'an island') off the southern extremity of Gujarāt. It occupies an important position in the history of the Portuguese, and still belongs to them. St. Jean is the port in Gujarāt called Sajān or Sanjān, the Sindān of Arab writers, corrupted by the Portuguese into San Gens and the English into St. John's. (See Yule, *Hobson-Jobson*, 2nd ed., 782; H. Wilberforce Bell, *Hist. of Kathiawar*, 89 f.)

[5] Souali in original: Suwālī: a roadstead near the mouth of the Tāptī (Yule, op. cit., p. 883).

to enter into the Surat river ; but for some time back, the King has granted to the latter a place to winter [1] in during the rainy season.

Surat is a city of moderate size, with a poor fortress,[2] close to which you must pass, whether you approach it by water or by land. It has towers at each of its four angles ; and as the walls are not terraced, the guns are placed upon scaffoldings. The Governor of the fortress commands merely the soldiers of the garrison, and possesses no authority in the city, which has its own separate Governor to receive the customs and the other revenues of the King throughout the extent of his Province.[3] The walls of the city are built of earth,[4] and the houses of private persons are like barns, being constructed of nothing but reeds, covered with cow-dung mixed with clay, to fill the interstices, and to prevent those outside from seeing between the reeds what goes on inside. In the whole of Surat there are only nine or ten well-built houses, and the Shāh-bandar [5] or chief of the merchants, owns two or three of them. The others belong to the Musalmān merchants, and those of the English [6] and Dutch are not the least fine, every President and Commander taking care to keep them in repair, the cost of which is charged against the accounts of their Companies. These dwellings are, nevertheless, only hired houses, as the King does not permit any Frank to possess a house of his own,

[1] The term winter (*hiver*) is used by several early writers on India to indicate the rainy season, viz. June to October. (Yule, *Hobson-Jobson*, 970.)

[2] For illustrations of the fort see Rawlinson, *British Beginnings in Western India*, 48, 52.

[3] Ovington (*Voyage to Suratt*, 217) says that the Governor was appointed for three years, and never left the castle.

[4] Peter Mundy (Hakluyt Society, ii. 29) calls it ‘ a badde ditch ’; Mandelslo (p. 29), ‘ a good rampier of stone ’.

[5] Cha-bander in original, Shāh-bandar, i. e. harbour and customs master.

[6] The Surat House is ‘ of the best in Towne, very faire and stronglie built, the Rooffs in general flatt and tarassed aloft to walke on, very substantiallie done with lime. . . . Wee have also a garden which for its bignes is the neatest and costliest in all the Countrey hereabouts ’ (Mundy, ii. 25 f. ; and see Fryer, Hakluyt Society, i. 214.) W. Foster (Sir T. Roe, Hakluyt Society, ii. 510) gives a valuable note describing the various houses occupied by the English in Surat.

fearing that he would thereby possess what he might convert into a fortress. The Reverend Capuchin Fathers have built a very commodious one upon the model of the houses of Europe, with a beautiful church, and I myself furnished a large portion of the money which it cost;[1] but the purchase had to be made in the name of a Maronite merchant of Aleppo[2] named Chelebi, of whom I have spoken in my account of Persia.

CHAPTER II

Concerning the Customs, the Money, the Exchange, the Weights, and the Measures of India.

IN order to save repetition, which cannot be avoided in the course of a long journey, it is desirable to make the reader acquainted, from the first, with the practice in India in reference to customs, money, exchange, measures, and weights.

As soon as merchandise is landed at Surat it has to be taken to the custom-house, which adjoins the fort. The officers are very strict and search persons with great care.[3] Private individuals pay as much as 4 and 5 per cent. duty on all their goods; but as for the English and Dutch Companies, they pay less. But, on the other hand, I believe that, taking into account what it costs them in deputations and presents, which they are obliged to make every year at court, the goods cost them nearly the same as they do private persons.

Gold and silver are charged 2 per cent., and as soon as they have been counted at the custom-house the Mintmaster[4]

[1] For the French Capuchins in Surat see Manucci, *Storia do Mogor*, ed. Irvine, i. 62, iii. 309, iv. 266; *Diary of W. Hedges*, Hakluyt Society, ii. 305. Some remains of their chapel still exist, *Bombay Gazetteer*, ii. 304.

[2] Alep in original, for Aleppo, described bk. II, cap. ii, p. 134, of the *Persian Travels*, Paris, 1876. Chelebi in Turkish means 'a noble': 'Amongst them [the Persians] four degrees are most remarkable, Chawns, Coozel-bashes, Agaes, and Cheliby or Coridschey' (Sir T. Herbert, *Travels*, ed. 1677, p. 303). See also *Ency. of Islam*, i, pp. 831 ff.

[3] The officials of the Mughal custom-house at Surat had a bad reputation among the early European traders for severity and extortion. Ovington, *Voyage to Suratt*, 119 f.; P. della Valle, Hakluyt Society, i. 23, 126; Rawlinson, 145.

[4] The Mintmaster was called Dārogha (of the mint); the assays were made by the Sarrāf; other officials in the mints were the Amīn, who

removes them, and coins them into money of the country, which he hands over to the owner, in proportion to the amount and standard of the bullion. You settle with him, according to the nature of the amount, a day when he is to deliver the new coins, and for as many days as he delays to do so beyond the term agreed upon, he pays interest in proportion to the sum which he has received. The Indians are cunning and exacting in reference to coin and payments ; for when money has been coined for three or four years it has to lose ½ per cent., and it continues in the same proportion according to age, not being able, as they say, to pass through many hands without some diminution.

All sorts of silver may be imported into the Empire of the Great Mogul, because there is a mint in each of the frontier towns, where it has to be refined to the highest standard,[1] as is the case with all the gold and silver in India, by order of the King, and it then is coined into money of the country. Bar silver, or old silver plate which has been bought without payment for the workmanship, loses the least, for on coined silver the loss on coinage cannot be avoided. Sales are, in general, conditional on payment being made in money coined during the current year ; and if you are paid in old pieces you must submit to loss, according to the time they have been coined, as I have above said. In all places at a distance from towns, where the common people do not understand money well, and where there are no Changers, they will not accept a piece of silver until they have first put it in the fire to ascertain whether it is good or not ; and this is especially practised at the river crossings.[2] As the ferry boats are made of osiers,

was a kind of spy on the others ; the Mushrif, to keep the accounts, &c. (See *Āīn-i-Akbarī*, Blochmann's transl., i. 18.)

[1] The method of assaying which was practised in India is described in the *Āīn-i-Akbarī*, i. 19, and upon it there are some important remarks and explanatory notes to be found in Percy's *Metallurgy of Gold and Silver* ; Sir E. Maclagan, *Monograph on Silver and Gold Work in the Panjab*, 19 ff. For Musulmān coinage and mints, H. N. Wright, *Catalogue of Muhammadan Coins in the India Museum*, Oxford, 1907.

[2] Ball remarks that a few years ago he found the people in a remote part of the District of Raipur, in the Central Provinces, most unwilling to accept any payment in silver ; they would take copper, but preferred cowries.

covered only with oxhide, and are consequently very light,[1] the owners conceal them in the woods, and will not take them on their shoulders to carry them to the water before they have received payment.

As regards gold, the merchants who import it use so much cunning in order to conceal it, that but little of it comes to the knowledge of the customs' officers. The former do all they can to evade paying the customs, especially as they do not run so much risk as in the custom-houses of Europe. For in those of India, when any one is detected in fraud, he is let off by paying double, 10 per cent. instead of 5, the Emperor comparing the venture of the merchant to a game of hazard, where one plays double or quits. However, for some time back this has been somewhat changed, and it is to-day difficult to compound with the customs' officers upon that condition. The Emperor has conceded to the English Captains that they shall not be searched when they leave their vessels to go on shore ; but one day an English Captain, when going to Tatta,[2] one of the largest towns of India, a little above Sindi,[3] which is at the mouth of the river Indus,[4] as he was about to pass, was arrested by the customs' guards, from whom he could not defend himself, and they searched him in spite of anything he could say. They found gold upon him ; he had in fact already conveyed some in sundry journeys which he had made between his vessel and the town ; he was, however, let off on payment of the ordinary duty. The Englishman, vexed by this affront, resolved to have his revenge for it, and he took it in a funny manner. He ordered a sucking-pig to be roasted, and to be placed with the grease in a china plate, covered with a napkin, and gave it to a slave to carry with him to the town, anticipating exactly what would happen. As he passed in front of the custom-house, where the Governor of the town,

[1] Coracles. See Index for further references to them.

[2] Tata in the original, the modern Tatta, in Sind (see p. 14), a taluk in the Karāchī District.

[3] Scimdy in the original, sometimes written Simdi by Tavernier—e. g. p. 14—Diul Sind, Sind, or the harbour near Lārībandar or Karāchī, at the mouths of the Indus. (Yule, *Hobson-Jobson*, 320.)

[4] River of Indou in the original, i. e. Hindū or Sindhū—the Indus river.

the Shāh-bandar, and the Master of the Mint were seated in a divan, they did not fail to stop him, but the slave still advancing with his covered plate, they told his master that he must needs go to the custom-house, and that they must see what he carried. The more the Englishman protested that the slave carried nothing liable to duty, the less was he believed; and after a long discussion he himself took the plate from the hands of the slave, and proceeded to carry it to the custom-house. The Governor and the Shāh-bandar thereupon asked him, in a sharp tone, why he refused to obey orders, and the Englishman, on his part, replied in a rage that what he carried was not liable to duty, and rudely threw the plate in front of them, so that the sucking-pig and the grease soiled the whole place, and splashed up on their garments. As the pig is an abomination to the Musalmāns, and by their Law they regard as defiled whatever is touched by it, they were compelled to change their garments, to remove the carpet from the divan, and to have the structure rebuilt, without daring to say anything to the Englishman, because the Shāh-bandar and the Master of the Mint have to be careful with the Company, from which the country derives so much profit. As for the Chiefs of the Companies, both English and Dutch, and their deputies, they are treated with so much respect that they are never searched when they come from their vessels; but they, on their part, do not attempt to convey gold in secret as the private merchants do, considering it beneath their dignity to do so. The commerce of Tatta, which formerly was considerable, is decreasing rapidly, because the entrance to the river becomes worse from day to day, and the sands, which have accumulated, almost close the passage.[1]

The English, seeing that the custom of searching them had been adopted, had recourse to little stratagems in order to pass the gold, and the fashion of wearing wigs having reached them from Europe, they bethought themselves of concealing the

[1] In consequence of the silting of the channel, Aurangzeb was obliged to create a new port at a mouth of the Indus (Jadunath Sarkar, *History of Aurangzīb*, i. 123 f.). The trade and population of the town have much decreased since the seventeenth century (*Imperial Gazetteer*, xxiii. 255).

Jacobuses, rose-nobles, and ducats in the nets of their wigs every time they left their vessels to go on shore.[1] There was a merchant who desired to convey into Surat some boxes of coral without its coming to the knowledge of the customs' officers. When the vessel was about to enter the river, he had the boxes lashed to the stern, and as they were immersed two or three feet under the water, the officers who came to examine the merchandise on the vessel could not see them. Several days passed before the cargo was unladen, when at length it became possible to convey the boxes in safety into the town, without the customs' officers having wind of it. This was cleverly accomplished, but the merchant had cause to repent of it, and he found himself on the wrong side of his reckoning; for, as the river at Surat is always turbid and muddy, there attached itself to the coral, which had been a long time immersed in the water, a sort of slimy crust and a white skin, which gave them much trouble to remove, and after the coral was cleaned the loss to the merchant exceeded 12 per cent.

I now come to the coins current in India throughout the territories of the Great Mogul, and to all the kinds of gold and silver which, in order to secure most profit there, should be carried in ingots, rather than in coin.

In the first place it must be remarked that it is advantageous to purchase gold or silver which has been worked, in order to have it made into ingots, and to have it refined up to the highest standard; for, after being refined, you do not pay for the carriage of the alloy which was mixed with it before, and by not carrying the gold or silver in coin, you escape paying what the Prince and the mint have taken for their coinage dues.

If you import coined gold, the best pieces are rose-nobles,[2]

[1] Frauds were committed on the customs regarding exports, too, as will be seen in subsequent pages. M. Thévenot also mentions that he knew people who had conveyed away, with the aid of the Dutch commanders, numerous precious stones and other costly articles without paying any custom dues. (*Voyages des Indes*, Paris, 1684, p. 5.)

[2] Rose-nobles, also known as Angel, George, or Thistle nobles, first minted by Edward III (*New English Dict.*, s. v.). The noble was an English coin worth 6*s*. 8*d*. or 10*s*.

old Jacobuses,[1] Albertuses,[2] and other ancient pieces, both of Portugal and other countries, and all sorts of gold coins which have been coined in the last century: On these old pieces there is always some profit to be made by the merchant. Among the good gold coins which one may import into India, all the ducats of Germany, both those of Princes and of imperial towns, as also the ducats of Poland, Hungary, Sweden, and Denmark must be included; and all these kinds of ducats are accepted at the same standard. The golden ducats of Venice formerly passed as the best, and were each valued at four or five of our sols [3] more than the others; but, for the last twelve years or thereabouts, it seems that they have been altered, so that they are now valued only at the same price as the others. There are besides the ducats which the Grand Seigneur coins at Cairo,[4] and those of Salee [5] and Morocco,[6] but these three coins are the least valuable of all, and are generally worth four sols less than the others.

Throughout the Empire of the Great Mogul all the gold and silver is weighed by a weight called tolā, which amounts to 9 deniers 8 grains of our weight.[7] When a quantity of gold or silver is for sale, the Indians have brass weights, which bear the King's stamp, to prevent fraud; and with these weights they weigh all the gold or silver at a time, provided it does not exceed one hundred tolās. For the weights of the Changers range only from one tolā up to one hundred, and these hundred tolās are equivalent in our weight to 38 onces 21 deniers 8 grains. As for the uncoined gold or silver, if there is much of it, it is

[1] Jacobus, an English coin of James I, originally issued in 1603, under the name of the Sovereign, worth from 20*s.* to 24*s.* (*New English Dict.*, s. v.)

[2] Albertuses. The Alberts Dutch dollar, a silver coin, was worth in exchange something less than the rix-dollar, or 4*s.* 6*d.* (Kelly, *Universal Cambist*, i. 207, 288.)

[3] 5 sols = 4½*d.* (See Appendix.)

[4] Caire in the original.

[5] Salé in the original, the modern Salli, the ancient Sala, on the north-west coast of Africa. For the Sallee Rovers or Pirates see *Ency. Brit.*, xviii. 857.

[6] Maroc in the original.

[7] Tolla in the original: the tolā therefore = 224 French gr. = 187·5 grains Troy. The present British tola = 180 grains Troy, i. e. the weight of the rupee.

tested, and the test having been applied, the buyers bid for it as highly as they can, out of jealousy to one another.

As there are merchants who have sometimes as much as forty and fifty thousand ducats [1] and more, the Indians weigh the coins with a weight which is exactly equal to one hundred ducats, and it also bears the King's stamp. Should it happen that the hundred ducats weigh less than this weight, pebbles are added till the weights are equal and when the whole amount is weighed you must make good to the Changer the sum of the weights of these pebbles. But before weighing golden coins, be they ducats or other coins, the whole are placed in a large charcoal fire, where the pieces become red-hot, after which the fire is quenched by throwing water on it, and they are then withdrawn. This is done for the purpose of ascertaining if any of them are false, and in order to burn the wax or gum which is sometimes adroitly attached in order that they may weigh more. But since some of the pieces are so well forged that they cannot be detected even after they have been in the fire; in order to test them the Changers bend them one by one, and by bending they know whether the coin is good, and they cut all those which are not.[2] After having examined all, they cause those which they believe to be bad to be refined; and for the good gold obtained by this refining they pay as much as for good ducats. All this gold is made into coins, called golden rupees,[3] with the exception of the ducats which have a face on one side; these are seldom melted but they are sold to the merchants who come from Tartary and the other countries of the North, the kingdoms of Bhutān,[4] Assam,[5] and others more

[1] 50,000 ducats at 9*s*. 4*d*. = £23,500.

[2] But 'I have never seen any Clipt Money here [Surat], and 'tis rare if either the Gold or Silver Coin is falsified' (Ovington, 219.)

[3] Golden rupees (Roupies d'or) were of different values; but those with which Tavernier had to do averaged, as will be seen further on, from 14 to 14½ silver rupees in value, say 31*s*. 6*d*. to 32*s*. (See p. 16 *n*.) Gold rupees were the modern gold mohur (Bernier, 60.)

[4] Boutan in the original. But the limits of the region referred to by Tavernier extended far beyond those of the modern Bhutān: see ch. xv of bk. III in vol. ii (p. 211 f.).

[5] Assam. Asen in the original appears to be an unusual spelling of Assam. That Kingdom is described in bk. II, ch. xvii, pp. 216–24 of vol. ii.

distant. It is of this kind of ducat that the women in those countries make their principal ornament: they suspend them from their hair on their foreheads.[1] As for the other ducats which are without faces, they are not valued by the merchants from the North.

With reference to all the other gold coins, many are sold to the goldsmiths, to the gold-drawers, and in general to all those who employ gold in their work. For if they can be disposed of without being made into rupees, they are not coined; this indeed is seldom done, except when the Emperors are placed on the throne, when they are used as largess to the people, together with silver rupees; and also to be sold to the Governors of Provinces who require quantities, as likewise to other nobles of the kingdom, who present them to the Emperor on the day when he enters into possession of his dominions. For they cannot always obtain jewels or other things worthy to be presented to him, both on this day, and also at the grand ceremonial—of which I shall speak elsewhere—when the Emperor is weighed every year.[2] They are, I say, very glad to obtain golden rupees on these occasions, and they also require them in order to make presents to the courtiers, by whose interest they hope to obtain higher appointments and more important offices of government.

In one of my journeys I saw by an example, which happened before my own eyes, wherein the virtue of these golden rupees lay. Shāhjahān,[3] the father of Aurangzeb, who reigns at present, had given to one of the nobles of his court the government of the province of Tatta, of which Sindi is the capital town.[4] Although from the very first year of his government there were serious complaints against him of the tyranny with which he treated the people, and of his great extortions, the Emperor allowed him to govern the Province for close on four

[1] They are worn with many other amulets: see C. A. Sherring, *Western Tibet and the British Borderland*, 59; L. A. Waddell, *Buddhism of Tibet*, 572; *Lhasa*, 354.

[2] For the custom of weighing the Emperor see p. 301 below.

[3] Cha Gehan in the original.

[4] Tata and Simdi (see p. 9 *n.*). The chief town was known as Dewal or Diul Sindi, a name sometimes transferred in later days to Larry Bunder (Lārībandar), &c. (See *Hobson-Jobson*, 320.)

years, after which he recalled him. All the people of Tatta rejoiced, supposing that the Emperor had recalled him in order to put him to death. But it happened quite otherwise, for he was well received by the Emperor, who conferred upon him the government of Allahabad,[1] a much more considerable post than that of Tatta which he had just quitted. The cause of the good reception which he received from the Emperor was, that before he arrived at Agra he sent secretly to him as a present 50,000 golden rupees, which are equivalent to 105,000 [2] of our livres, and in addition about 20,000 golden rupees, both for the Begam Sāhib,[3] who then governed the whole kingdom, and for other ladies, and for some courtiers who could aid him with their support. All these courtiers are very glad to obtain plenty of gold in that way not only because it occupies small space, and it can be easily concealed, but also because they hold it honourable to leave large sums to their wives and children, at their deaths, of which the Emperor can have no knowledge: for, as I shall say further on, when a great noble dies the Emperor inherits his property, his wife remaining only mistress of her jewels.[4]

To return to the golden rupees. It should be stated that they are not current among the merchants; for although one is not worth more than 14 silver rupees, which are equivalent to 21 livres of our money, at 30 sols to the rupee,[5] and that these golden rupees are scarcely ever to be met with save in the houses of the nobles, still when it happens that the latter make any payment with them they always desire to estimate them at a silver rupee, or at least at a quarter more than they are worth, by which the merchant loses his profit. Shāista Khān,[6] uncle of the Emperor, to whom I sold commodities for

[1] Halabas in the original, elsewhere spelt Hallabas.

[2] This is wrong, as, at 21 livres to the golden rupee, the figure should be 1,050,000.

[3] Jahānārā Begam (1614–80), daughter of Shāhjahān and Mumtāz Mahall. (Bernier, 11; Jadunath Sarkar, *History of Aurangzīb*, iii. 66.)

[4] See p. 44 below.

[5] 30 sols = 2*s.* 3*d.* = one rupee, and the livre therefore = 1*s.* 6*d.* (See Appendix to this volume.)

[6] Cha Est Kan in the original: Shāista Khān died 1694, aged 93 lunar years. His original name was Abū Tālib or Mīrzā Murād, son of 'Āsaf

96,000 rupees,[1] when it came to the question of payment, asked me in what kind of money I wished him to pay me, whether in gold or silver coin. Before I replied, he added that if I would trust him I would take it in golden rupees, and that he did not give this advice under the belief that it would turn to his own advantage. I told him that I would follow his advice, and he immediately ordered golden rupees to be counted out to the amount due to me ; but he claimed to give the golden rupee for 14½ of silver,[2] although among the merchants they pass only for fourteen. I was not ignorant of that, but thought it would answer better to receive my payment as the Prince wished to make it to me, in the hope of recompensing myself otherwise to the extent of what he wished to make me lose, or at least a part of it. I allowed two days to pass, after which I went to visit him and I told him that I had endeavoured to dispose of the rupees for the price at which I had received them, but that I had failed ; and that accordingly, upon the payment which he had made me of 96,000 rupees, I should lose 3,428 $\frac{3}{16}$, the golden rupee which he wished me to take at 14½ rupees not being worth more than 14 ; whereupon he flew into a passion, and told me that he would give so many strokes of the slipper (for in India they never speak of blows with a stick),[3] to the Dutch Changer or Broker, which he would remember, believing that he was the cause of what I had come

Khān, Wazīr, and grandson of I'timādu-daula, father of Nūrjahān Begam, wife of the Emperor Jahāngīr. He was appointed Wazīr of Shāhjahān on his father's death in 1641 : Viceroy of the Deccan, 1659 : Governor of Bengal, 1666–89 : retired to Agra, where he died. He is several times mentioned by Tavernier and in other memoirs of his time. (Sir T. Roe, i. 115 ; Manucci, i. 194 ; Bernier, 13, 56 ; Diary of Hedges, i. 42, 133, 141.) [For further details *v.* Beale, *Or. Biog. Dy.*, p. 372.]

[1] This was at Ahmadābād, at the end of 1652. (See p. 245 ff. below.) A second sale to Shāista Khān took place in 1660, at Choupar (Chākan) in the Deccan (see p. 26) ; and a third at Dacca in 1666. (See p. 106 below.)

[2] If we take the gold mohur at 31*s.* 6*d.*, the value of the rupee at 14 would be 2*s.* 3*d.*, and at 14½ would be 2*s.* 2*d.* (See pp. 13 *n.* and 15 *n.*)

[3] Castigation with a slipper is a contemptuous form of punishment, as the slipper is defiled by touching the earth, and leather is used in magic (Russell, *Tribes and Castes, Central Provinces*, iii. 103), and a blow from anything made from the leather of the sacred cow causes pollution.

to tell him, of his not having been willing to take the golden rupees at the price he had given them to me, and that he would teach these people to understand money, and that they were all old rupees, and worth $\frac{1}{16}$th of a silver rupee more than those that were then being made. As I understood the humour of Asiatic princes, with whom it is useless to excite oneself, I allowed him to say all he wished, and observing that he became quieter and began to smile, I asked him to permit me to return to him on the following day the amount which he had caused to be counted out to me, or if not, that he would give me the balance of my payment which was still due, and that I would take the golden rupee at 14 $\frac{1}{16}$ rupees, as he had told me that it was value for so much.[1] The Prince then looked at me askance for some time without saying a word, and then he asked me whether I had with me that pearl which he had been unwilling to buy. I replied that I had, and thereupon drew it from my bosom and gave it to him. It was a large pearl of good water, but badly shaped, which had prevented him from taking it before.

After I had handed it to him, 'Say no more about it,' said he. 'In a word, how much do you want for this pearl?' I asked him 7,000 rupees for it, and it is true that rather than carry it back to France I would have taken 3,000. 'If I give you', he replied, '5,000[2] rupees for this pearl, you will be well repaid for the loss which you say you have sustained on the golden rupees. Come to-morrow and I shall pay you 5,000 rupees. I wish you to leave contented, and you shall have in addition a khil'at[3] and a horse.' I then made him a bow, and besought him to give me a young horse, fit for work, as I had a long journey to make. Accordingly, on the following day, I received as he had promised, the robe, mantle, two waistbands, and the turban, which constitute, as I have elsewhere described, the complete suit which these princes are

[1] On p. 245 f. below, alluding to the same transaction, he says he received them at 14$\frac{1}{8}$ rupees. M. Joret, p. 158 *n.*, has, Ball thought, mixed up this transaction with the one which took place at Chākan, as mentioned on p. 16 *n.*, in the year 1660. (See also p. 26.)

[2] In the earliest edition this figure is by an obvious misprint given as 7,000. In the 1679 edition it is 5,000, which is adopted here.

[3] Calaat in the original, khil'at, Hind., a robe of honour: see p. 18 *n.*

accustomed to bestow upon those whom they desire to honour.[1] The mantle and the robe were of gold brocade, the two waistbands striped with gold and silver ; the turban of cotton cloth was of fire colour striped with gold, and the horse, without a saddle, was covered by a housing of green velvet, with a small fringe of silver round it. The bridle was very narrow, and to it silver coins were attached in places. I believe the horse had never been mounted for as soon as it arrived at the Dutch house, where I lodged on this occasion, a young man mounted it, and it began to rear in so strange a manner and to shake him so that, having fallen when jumping over the roof of a hut which was in the court, the Dutchman narrowly escaped being killed. Having realized that this impetuous steed was not suitable for me, I returned it to Shāista Khān, and telling him what had happened, added that I believed he did not wish me to return to my country, as he had asked me to do in order to procure for him some rarity. During my discourse he only laughed, and then he called for the horse which his father used to ride. It was a large Persian horse, which had formerly cost 5,000 écus [2] when young, but it was then more than twenty-eight years old.[3] It was brought ready saddled and bridled, and the Prince desired me to mount it in his presence. It still had as good paces as any horse I had ever seen, and when I was mounted, he said 'Well, are you content ? He will not give you a fall.' I thanked him, and at the same time took my leave of him ; and the following day, before my departure, he sent me a large basketful of apples. It was one of six which Shāhjahān had sent to him ; they had come

[1] Khil'at, 'that of which a superior divests himself and presents to an inferior,' was the general term for the robe of honour. There were five degrees of the Khil'at—three, five, six, seven pieces, or clothes that the Emperor had actually worn himself. The full Khil'at of seven pieces is described by Tavernier (i. 132). See the description in Irvine, *Army of the Indian Moghuls*, 29, and references in Yule, *Hobson-Jobson*, 483 f.

[2] £1,125, at 4*s*. 6*d*. the écu.

[3] Here there are irreconcilable discrepancies between this account of the transaction and that on p. 247, as our author gives the original cost of the horse there at upwards of 3,000 écus, and states that he sold it for 400 rupees to a Frenchman whom he at the same time placed in Shāista Khān's service, as he did not require it for his journey.

from the kingdom of Kashmīr,[1] and there was also a large Persian melon in the basket. All taken together might be value for 100 rupees, and I presented them to the wife of the Dutch Commander. As for the horse, I took it to Golkonda, where I sold it, old as it was, for 500 rupees, because it was still able to render good service.

To return to the discourse on coins, I shall add to what I have already said of the gold pieces, that it does not do to carry Louis d'or, Spanish nor Italian pistoles to India, nor any other gold pieces coined of late years, because there is too much to be lost on them. The Indians, who have no experience of them as yet, refine all, and it is by this refining that they make their profit. For the rest, every one strives to land his gold without the master of the customs knowing it; and when the merchant has sufficient skill to conceal it, he makes a profit of five or six of our sols on every ducat.

I come now to the silver coins, which must be distinguished as coins of the country and foreign coins, and I shall speak first of the latter.

The foreign silver coins which are imported into India are German rix dalers [2] and Spanish reals.[3] The first are brought by the merchants who come from Poland, from Little Tartary, and from the direction of Moscovie; the others by those who come from Constantinople, Smyrna, and Aleppo, and the principal part by the Armenians who have sold their silks in

[1] Kachemir in the original. The Emperors procured large supplies of fruit from Kashmīr, Kābul, and Central Asia (Bernier, 118, 203, 249). The apples of Kashmīr were, and are, famous (Sir W. R. Lawrence, *The Valley of Kashmir*, 349 f.). Presents of fruit were then, as now, commonly made. 'Doubtlesse they suppose our felicitie lies in the palate, for all that I euer reciued was eatable and drinkable—yet no *aurum potabile*' (Sir T. Roe, i. 172).

[2] Richedales in the original, for rix daler, properly reichs thaler; according to Sir Isaac Newton's tables, most of the varieties were worth in sterling 4*s*. 7*d*. Tavernier's equivalent of 100 = 216 rupees gives, with the rupee at 2*s*. 3*d*., a value of 4*s*. 10¼*d*. As in other cases, the sterling value may have been somewhat less than the exchange value; hence the difference.

[3] Reale in the original, for real, or 'piece of 8 reals' of Seville varied from about 4*s*. to 4*s*. 10*d*., the rupee being taken at 2*s*. 3*d*., and the écu at 4*s*. 6*d*., to which latter it was on the average equal.

Europe. All the merchants strive to convey their silver through Persia without its being discovered, because, if the customs' officers have wind of it, it must be taken to the masters of the mint to be coined into 'abbāsīs [1], which is the coinage of the King, and these 'abbāsīs on arrival in India are again coined into rupees, by which there is a loss to the merchant of 10¼ per cent., both on account of the coinage and on account of the King's dues, which he has to pay in Persia.

In order to understand how this 10¼ per cent. is lost between Persia and India, and sometimes even more, according to the nature of the reals which are generally imported into Persia, it is necessary to remember what I have said of the coins and exchange in Persia in the preceding volume.[2] I have remarked that the real in Persia passes for 13 shāhīs,[3] which are equal to 3¼ 'abbāsīs, and that sometimes, when silver is scarce, half a shāhī more is given; that the 'abbāsī is worth 4 shāhīs, and the tomān [4] 50 'abbāsīs or 200 shāhīs. Thus the real passing for 13 shāhīs, you receive 6½ tomāns for 100 reals. If you take 6½ tomāns to India you receive for each tomān 29½ rupees, and, consequently, for 6½ tomāns 191¾ rupees. But if you take to India Sevillian reals, of which I shall speak further on, for 100 you receive from 213 to 215 rupees; and for Mexicans for 100 you receive only 212. When, then, for the 100 reals you receive only 212 rupees, you gain on these 100 reals 10¼ reals, and on the Sevillians you make a profit up to 11 per cent.

[1] Abassis in the original, for 'abbāsīs = from 1*s.* 5*d.* to 1*s.* 6*d.* (Yule, *Hobson-Jobson*, 389.) The 'abbāsī, or ⅕ of the kran, was recently worth less than 1½*d* (Curzon, *Persia*, i. 512.)

[2] *Persian Travels*, Paris edition, 1676, p. 120.

[3] Chaez in the original, for shāhī, Pers., = 4*d.* to 4½*d.* At present about 2⅛*d.* only. It is now worth ¼ 'abbāsī (Curzon, i. 514.)

[4] Tomān. In Fryer's time (1677) = £3 6*s.* 8*d.* (ii. 139). P. della Valle's estimate, sixty years earlier, was about £4 10*s.*; Sir T. Herbert's valuation, £3 8*s.* 4*d.*; at present only worth 7*s.* 6*d.* (Yule, *Hobson-Jobson*, 928.) Fifty 'abbāsīs, as above, equal £3 10*s.* to £3 15*s.* Forty-six livres (at 1*s.* 6*d.*, the equivalent given by Tavernier in vol. ii. 320) and 1⅕ denier = £3 9*s.*, while 29½ rupees at 2*s.* 3*d.* = £3 6*s.* 6½*d.* only, and 15 écus at 4*s.* 6*d.* = £3 7*s.* 6*d.* But Tavernier, in his account of Persian coins, expressly says that the value given in livres is the most exact. (See *Persian Travels*, p. 122, Paris edition of 1676.) In 1889–90 Lord Curzon found the tomān worth 5*s.* 6*d.*, but later, with the increased value of silver, it rose to 6*s.* (*Persia*, i. 471 f.)

It should also be remarked that there are three or four kinds of Spanish real, and that for 100, according to the standard, from 208 up to 214 and 215 rupees are given. The best of all are the Sevillians, and when they are of good weight you receive for 100, 213 rupees, and at some times up to 215, according to whether silver is scarce or plentiful.

The Spanish real should weigh 3 gros [1] and 7½ grains more than 2 rupees, but the silver of the rupees is much better, for the rupee is of the standard of 11 deniers and 14 grains, and the Sevillian real, like our white ecu, is of the standard of only 11 deniers. The Mexican real is of but 10 deniers and 21 grains. For the Spanish real which weighs 73 vāls you receive 4½ mahmūdīs, and a mahmūdī is worth 20 paisā, and thus for the Spanish real you receive 90 paisā, but they must be good,[2] and, as I have said, weighing 73 vāls; 81 vāls [3] making an ounce, the val being of 7 deniers (standard).

As for the German rix dalers, being heavier than the reals, you get for 100 up to 116 [4] rupees; upon which it should be remarked that, in getting for the 100 reals and the 100 rix

[1] The gros = 59 grains Troy, and the French grain = ·819 gr. Troy, ∴ 3 gros 7½ gr. = 187 grains Troy. The weight of the piastre, or Seville piece of eight, was 17 dwt. 12 gr., and that of two rupees = 14 dwt. 20 gr., both according to Sir Isaac Newton, the difference being, therefore, 2 dwt. 16 gr. or 64 gr.; Ball, therefore, concludes that the 3 gros above must either be a misprint for 1, or that the value given to the gros is three times too great; even so, the 62⅓ gr. so deduced as the difference is slightly less than the 64 gr. deduced from Sir Isaac Newton. The absolute weight of the real is given by Tavernier at 73 vāls, or say 438 gr. Troy; and the weight of two rupees, according to him also, was 18 deniers 2 gr. = 454 French gr. = 380 Troy gr., and the difference = 58 gr., also too little.

[2] Pecha in the original, for paisā. Taking the paisā at ·54 of a penny (see Appendix), 90 of them would be equal to 4*s.* 0½*d.*, i. e. the value of a Spanish real; but this is too low, and therefore these paisās must have been worth ·6 of a penny, or 'good!' as Tavernier remarks.

[3] Vāl. The French 'once', being equal to 472·18 gr. Troy, would give a value of nearly 5·84 gr. to the vāl. The tolā is said, on p. 29 to be = 32 vāls, and therefore the vāl = 7 French gr. = 5·73 gr. Troy. Thévenot gives the value at 3 gongy (ghūngchī), and this with the ghūngchī at 1·79 gr. = 5·37 gr. Troy. See Appendix to this volume. At present in Gujarāt 1 vāl = 3 ratī : 16 vāl = 1 gadīānā : 2 gadīānā = 1 tolā (*Bombay Gazetteer*, ii. 208).

[4] This must be a misprint for 216.

dalers up to 215 and 216 rupees, it appears as if every rupee should consequently be worth less than 30 sols. But, on the other hand, if the merchant adds up the cost of the carriage of the silver and the duties, he will find that each rupee costs him more. All these reals and rix dalers are weighed by the 100, and when the weight is short they add small pebbles as when they weigh gold, as I have related above. But, in order that the merchant shall obtain value he must take care that all the reals of Mexico and the Sevillians [1] weigh 21 deniers and 8 grains, i. e. 512 grains; and as for our white écu,[2] it ought to weigh 21 deniers and 3 grains, which are equal to 509 grains.[3]

I pass on to the coins of the country. The Indians have for their silver money the rupee, the half, the quarter, the eighth, and the sixteenth. The weight of the rupee is 9 deniers and 1 grain, and the standard of the silver 11 deniers and 14 grains. They have also a silver coin which they call mahmūdī,[4] but it is only current in Surat and in the province of Gujarāt.[5]

The small coinage of India is of copper, and is called paisā, worth about two of our liards. There are also some coins of half a paisā, of two paisā, and of four. According to the province you may be in, you receive for the silver rupee more or fewer of these paisā. On my last journey the rupee at Surat was quoted at 49 paisā, but there are times when it is

[1] The piastre, or Seville piece of eight, weighed, according to Sir Isaac Newton, 17 dwt. 12 gr. = 420 gr. Troy, and its sterling value in silver was 54*d.* = 4*s.* 6*d.*

[2] The old écu of France, of 60 sols Tournois, weighed also, according to Sir Isaac Newton, 17 dwt. 12 gr. = 420 gr. Troy, and its sterling value was also 4*s.* 6*d.*

[3] The 509 gr. of Tavernier is a misprint for 507; it is repeated in the edition of 1713. The equivalent of 507 French grains is 424·5 Troy grains, or 4·5 gr. more than Sir Isaac Newton's figure in preceding note.

[4] Mamoudi in the original, for mahmūdī, = 20 paisā, or two-fifths of a rupee ∴ = 10·8*d.*, the rupee being 2*s.* 3*d.* Other relations given by our author in his account of Persian money give a less value for the mahmūdī, namely, one-sixteenth of the Venetian sequin, and one-eighth of the Spanish dollar, or 7*d.* and 6½*d.* The value as deduced from the 'abbāsī would seem, however, to be the mean of these, or from 8½*d.* to 9*d.* nearly. Several writers give to the Surat mahmūdī a value of one shilling. It was subject to constant variation (Fryer, i. 139; Yule, *Hobson-Jobson*, 389, 707).

[5] Guzerate in the original.

worth 50, and others when it falls to 46.[1] At Agra and Jahānabād it is worth 55–56 paisā, the reason of that being, that the nearer you approach the copper mines [2] the more paisā you receive for the rupee. As for the maḥmūdī, it is always worth 20 paisā. There are still two other kinds of small money in use in the empire of the Great Mogul: these are small bitter almonds and shells. In the province of Gujarāt alone the inhabitants use as small change these bitter almonds, which are brought from Persia, as I have remarked in the first part of my history. They grow in dry and arid places among rocks, the tree which produces them closely resembling our broom. These almonds are called bādām,[3] and are so bitter that colocynth is not more so, so that there is no need to fear that children will amuse themselves by eating them. Sometimes 35, sometimes 40, of them are given for the paisā.[4]

The other small money consists of shells called cowries, which have the edges inverted; they are not found in any other part of the world save only in the Maldive Islands.[5] They are the principal source of revenue of the King of these Islands, for they are exported to all the States of the Great Mogul, to the kingdoms of Bījāpur and Golkonda, and even

[1] Fifty paisā at ·54*d.* (see p. 21) = 2*s.* 3*d.* Thévenot, although he says that the rupee = 29–30 sols, adds that it equalled 32½ to 33½ paisā only (*Voyages*, Paris, 1684, p. 52).

[2] There is no further indication as to the position of these copper mines; probably they were those now known at Singhānā and other localities in Rājputānā. Full accounts of the ancient mines there will be found in the *Economic Geology of India*, p. 259, and in Watt, *Economic Dictionary*, ii. 647 ff.

[3] Baden in the original, for bādām (Pers. and Hind.), fruit of *Amygdalus communis*, L., var. *amara*, D.C. The use of bitter almonds as small coinage is attested by many authorities (Barbosa, ed. Dames, i. 156; Linschoten, Hakluyt Society, i. 246; Ovington, 219; Mundy, ii. 311, iii. pt. i, 252). Compare the use of mats and seeds in Africa for the same purpose (Ovington, 71, 445).

[4] Thévenot says 68; perhaps he meant a double paisā (*Voyages*, p. 53).

[5] This is incorrect, as money cowries (*Cypraea moneta*) have a much wider distribution, though the Maldives have furnished a large proportion of the supply for currency. The name is cori in the original. See Pyrard de Laval, Hakluyt Society, i. 236 ff.; Yule, *Marco Polo*, 1st ed., ii. 222.

to the islands of America,[1] to serve as money. Close to the sea up to 80 are given for the paisā, but the number diminishes as you leave the sea, on account of the cost of carriage; so that at Agra you receive but 50 or 55 for the paisā. Finally, according to the manner of counting known to the Indians—100,000 rupees make a lekke,[2] 100,000 lekkes make a kraur,[3] 100,000 kraurs make a padan, 100,000 padans make a nīl.[4]

In India a village must be very small indeed if it has not a money-changer, called a Shroff,[5] who acts as banker to make remittances of money and issue letters of exchange. As, in general, these Changers have an understanding with the Governors of Provinces, they enhance the rupee as they please for paisā and the paisā for these shells. All the Jews who occupy themselves with money and exchange in the empire of the Grand Seigneur pass for being very sharp; but in India they would scarcely be apprentices to these Changers.[6]

[*Here follows, in the original, a table giving the letters used as numbers, which need not be reproduced.*]

They have a very inconvenient custom for payments, and I have already remarked upon it in reference to golden rupees when a payment is made in that coin. They say that the longer a rupee of silver has been coined the less is it worth in comparison with those newly coined, or which have been coined a short time, because the old ones having often passed by hand, become worn, and they are in consequence lighter. Thus, when you make a sale, it is necessary to say that you

[1] A trade in these cowries to the West Coast of Africa and the West Indies still exists (*Ency. Brit.*, xxiv. 833).

[2] Lākh, Hind.

[3] A crore, or more properly, karor (Hind.), is 100 lākhs, or 10,000,000 (ten millions). Tavernier is wrong in stating it to be one thousand times more. However, Thévenot makes a similar statement (*Voyages*, p. 52); and it may be remarked that there are to be found similar contradictory statements, by different authorities, as to the values of our billions, trillions, &c. Comp. *Āīn-i-Akbarī*, ed. Jarrett, ii. 111 f.

[4] The value of the padam is variously given as 10 to 1,000 billions. The nīl is 10 billions.

[5] For Cheraf in the original, from Ar. Sarrāf, a money-changer or banker.

[6] This remarkable testimony to the sharpness of the Indians is applicable also at the present day.

require to be paid in Shāhjahānī [1] rupees, i. e. in new silver, otherwise your payment will be made in rupees coined fifteen or twenty years or more, upon which there may be up to 4 per cent. of loss. For, in the case of those which have not been coined within two years, $\frac{1}{4}$ per cent. is demanded or at least $\frac{1}{8}$th; and the poor people who do not know how to read the year when these rupees or paisā were coined are liable to be cheated, because something is always deducted from them, one paisā or half paisā on a rupee, and on the paisā three or four cowries.

As for false silver, but little is met with. If by chance there should be a false rupee in a bag given by a private merchant, it pays better to cut it and to lose it than to say anything about it, because if it becomes known you run some risk, the order of the Emperor being that you must return the bag to him from whom you received it, and thence it passes from one to another until the false coiner is discovered, and when one is detected, for sole punishment a finger is merely lopped off.[2] If it happens that the false coiner is not found, and that he who has given the silver is pronounced to be not guilty, he is freed on payment of some fine. This it is which yields such large profits to the Changers, for whether one receives or makes any payment he must show them the silver, and they receive for their commission $\frac{1}{16}$th of a rupee per cent.

As for the silver issued from the sarquet [3] or Emperor's treasury it is never base, for all that goes into it is carefully examined by the Changers of the Emperor, and the great nobles also employ their own. Before the silver is lodged in the treasury it is thrown into a large charcoal fire, and when the rupees are red the fire is extinguished by means of water, after which they are withdrawn. If one be found which is not perfectly white, or has the slightest trace of alloy, it is immediately cut. Whenever rupees enter the treasury they are

[1] Cha Jenni in the original, i. e. coined in the reign of Shāhjahān.

[2] This punishment is recognized in Islām: 'If a man or woman steal, cut off their hands' (*Korān*, v. 42); but there are many exceptions to the rules (Hughes, *Dictionary of Islam*, 284 f.).

[3] Sarquet, possibly for zakhīra, Hind., i. e. treasure or treasury, but it more probably represents sarkār, an abbreviation for māl-i-sarkār, or khazāna-i-sarkār, i. e. the Government Treasury. For the Imperial treasuries see *Āīn-i-Akbarī*, i. 12 ff.

stamped with a punch, which makes a small indentation without piercing; some of them have seven or eight marks of this kind, i. e. they have entered the treasury seven or eight times.[1] They are all placed by the thousand in sacks with the seal of the grand treasurer, to which is added the number of years since they have been coined. It is by this that the treasurers make their profit, both those of the Emperor and those of the nobles of the kingdom. If you make a sale it is in new rupees, coined in the same year; but when you go to receive payment the treasurers try to pay you in old rupees, by which you stand to lose up to 6 per cent.; and if you wish to have new silver, you must make up your mind to compound with them. On my fifth journey I went to see Shāista Khān,[2] having promised him to do so on the preceding occasion, and having pledged myself that he would be the first who should see whatever I had brought. Immediately on my arrival at Surat I let him know, and I received a command to go to meet him at Choupart, a town of the Deccan [3] to which he had laid siege. Having reached him in a short time, I sold him at once the greater part of the goods I had brought from Europe, and he told me that he awaited from day to day the money which should be sent to him from Surat to pay the army and to pay me then for what he had bought from me. I could not believe, however, that this Prince was in command of so large an army

[1] On shroff-marked rupees see Russell, *Tribes and Castes, Central Provinces*, iv. 532 f.

[2] See p. 15 *n.*

[3] On p. 326 below, this place is spelt Choupar. Ball suggested that the 'Choupart' of the text was Sholapur; but Prof. Jadunath Sarkar points out that the place referred to is Chākan (J. N. Sarkar, *Shivaji and his Times*, 2nd ed., pp. 87, 90). After Sivajī's surprise of Shāista Khān at Poona in 1663, Prince Mu'azzam was appointed Viceroy of the Deccan, and the Mughal army retired, leaving strong detachments at Chākan, 18 miles north of Poona. See a full account of the fort and its history in *Bombay Gazetteer*, xviii. pt. 3, pp. 121–3; Grant Duff, *Hist. of the Mahrattas*, ed. 1921, i. 50 *n.* 5; Shāista Khān's capture of Chākan is described by Grant Duff, ed. 1921, i. 151. The sale was made in 1660, during Tavernier's fifth visit to India. In his *Persian Travels*, he states (bk. IV, p. 467) that on his sixth journey, when at Ispahān, in 1664, he told the King that he had sold the jewels, which he had shown to him on the previous occasion, to Shāista Khān for 120,000 rupees.

without having plenty of money with him, and I rather thought that he hoped to make me lose something on the gold or silver pieces which I should receive for my payment, as he had done on my previous journey. The result was as I had foreseen; but for my sustenance and that of my people and cattle, he ordered that food should be furnished in abundance, both evening and morning, and on most days he sent to invite me to dine with him. Ten or twelve days passed, during which I heard no mention made of the money for which he waited, and being resolved to take leave of him, I went to his tent. He appeared somewhat surprised, and, regarding me with a sullen countenance, 'Wherefore', said he to me, 'do you wish to leave without being paid? and who would pay you afterwards if you went away without receiving your money?' At these words, assuming a look as proud as his: 'My King', I replied, 'will cause me to be paid; for he is so generous that he will reimburse all his subjects who have not received satisfaction for what they have sold in foreign countries.' 'And in what manner would thy King recoup himself?' replied he, as in a rage. 'With two or three good vessels of war,' I replied, 'which he will send to the port of Surat or towards its coasts, to await ships returning from Mocha.' [1] He appeared stung by this reply, and, not daring to carry his ill-humour further, he at once commanded his treasurer to give me a letter of exchange on Aurangābād. At this I was very glad, as it was a place through which I had to pass in order to go to Golkonda,[2] and, moreover, because it spared me the carriage and risk to my money. The following day I received my letter of exchange and took my leave of the Prince, who was no longer angry, and he requested me if I returned to India not to omit to visit him; this I did on my sixth and last journey.[3] When I arrived at Surat he was in Bengal, where I joined him, and he bought

[1] This illustrates the nervousness of the Mughals about any interference with the mercantile and pilgrim traffic between Surat and the Red Sea.

[2] There appears to be no other indication of Tavernier's destination at this time; he probably spent, according to M. Joret, the latter part of this year (1660) in this journey to Golkonda and the return to Surat, embarking for Bandar 'Abbās at the end of the same year or the beginning of 1661.

[3] In 1666. (See p. 106 below.)

from me the residue of the goods which I had not been able to sell either to the King of Persia or to the Great Mogul.

To return to my payment, having arrived at Aurangābād, I called on the Grand Treasurer, who had never previously seen me, but he told me that he knew why I had come to see him; that three days previously he had received notice, and that he had already drawn from the treasury the money which he was to pay me.[1] When all the bags required for my payment had been produced, I had one of them opened by my Changer, who saw that it contained rupees on which 2 per cent. would be lost. Upon which I thanked the Treasurer, and told him that I did not understand that sort of thing, that I would send one of my people to complain to Shāista Khān and ask him to order me to be paid in new silver, or I would go to reclaim my goods: this I straightway did. But having sent a man to him, and getting no reply by the time that I might have received one, I went to the Treasurer to inform him that since I had no news from the Prince I was going myself to get back what I had sold. I believe he had already received instructions as to what he should do, for seeing I was resolved to start he said he would be grieved by the trouble I was taking and that it would be better we should agree with one another. In short, after several discussions concerning the 2 per cent. which he wished to subtract, I obtained 1 per cent. of it; and I would have lost the other except for a fortunate meeting with a Shroff who had to receive payment of a letter of exchange on Golkonda; for this Shroff, not having money at hand, was very glad to accommodate himself with mine, arranging for me to receive the same sum in new silver at Golkonda at fifteen days' sight.

Finally, these Changers, in order to test silver, make use of thirteen small pieces, one half of which is copper and the other of silver, which are the 'touches'.[2] These thirteen pieces,

[1] Elsewhere (p. 326 below) he says the payment was made at Dultabat (Daulatābād) by the Treasurer, who, four days previously, had received an advice of his coming. In that passage, so far from alluding to difficulties, he praises the exactitude of the Indians in reference to matters of trade.

[2] The French original contains a figure of the touchstones. A description of them, known as mihakk, will be also found in the *Āīn-i-*

being all of different standards, are not used by them except when a small quantity of silver or some worked silver is in question ; for in the case of a large amount it is taken to the refiner. Silver is bought by the weight called tolā, which weighs 9 deniers and 8 grains, or 32 vāls, and 81 vāls make, as I have said, one once ; [1] so that 100 tolās make 38 onces, 21 deniers and 8 grains.

The following are the different values of the 13 standards of silver. The first and lowest standard is taken at 15 paisā the tolā, which make of our money 9 sols 2 deniers ; [2] the 2nd at 18 paisā, which are equal to 10 sols 2 deniers ; 3rd at 20 paisā, which are equal to 12 sols 6 deniers ; 4th at 23 paisā, which are equal to 14 sols 6 deniers ; 5th at 26 paisā, which are equal to 15 sols 10 deniers ; 6th at 29 paisā, which are equal to 17 sols 6 deniers ; 7th at 33 paisā, which are equal to 19 sols 2 deniers ; 8th at 35 paisā, which are equal to 20 sols 10 deniers; 9th at 38 paisā, which are equal to 22 sols 6 deniers ; 10th at 40 paisā, which are equal to 24 sols 2 deniers ; 11th at 43 paisā, which are equal to 25 sols 10 deniers ; 12th at 46 paisā, which are equal to 27 sols 6 deniers ; 13th at 49 paisā, which are equal to 29 sols 2 deniers.

I must not forget to remark here on the extreme parsimony both of these Shroffs, or Changers, and of all Indians in general ; it will suffice to give an example of it which is very special, but of which Europeans are not as yet aware. It is, that of all the gold which remains on the touchstone after an assay has been made, and of which we here make no account, far from allowing so small a thing to be lost, they collect it with the aid of a ball, made half of black pitch, and half of wax, with which they

Akbarī, i. 19. 'They have a touchstone like us, and they test after our manner. When the touchstone is full of gold, they have a ball of a certain composition which resembles wax, and with this ball, when they wish to see if the gold be good or poor, they press on the touchstone and take away some gold from the said touchstone, and then they see in the ball the goodness of the gold. And when that ball is full of gold they melt it, and take out the gold which they have tested by the touchstone. The said money-changers are extremely acute in this business' (Varthema, Hakluyt Society, 165).

[1] See p. 21.

[2] As the sol was the sixtieth part of the écu of 4*s*. 6*d*., its value was ·9 of a penny, and the ordinary paisā of Tavernier was consequently worth ·54 of a penny. See p. 21 *n*. and Appendix.

rub the stone which carries the gold, and at the end of some years they burn the ball and so obtain the gold which it has accumulated. The ball is about the size of our tennis-court balls, and the stone is like those which our goldsmiths commonly use.[1]

This is all that I have been able to observe of special importance with regard to the customs and coins of India, and it only remains for me to speak of the exchange.

As all goods produced in the Empire of the Great Mogul, and a portion of those of the Kingdoms of Golkonda and Bījāpur, reach Surat to be exported by sea to different places of Asia and Europe, when you leave Surat to go for the purchase of these goods to the towns from whence they are obtained, as Lahor, Agra, Amadabat, Seronge, Brampour, Daca, Patna, Banarou, Golkonda, Decan, Visapour, and Dultabad,[2] you take silver from Surat and dispose of it at the various places, giving coin for coin at par. But when it happens that the merchant finds himself short of money in these places, and has need of some to enable him to pay for the goods which he has bought, he must meet it at Surat, when the bill is due, which is at two months, and by paying a high rate of exchange.[3]

At Lahore on Surat the exchange goes up to $6\frac{1}{4}$ per cent.; at Agra from $4\frac{1}{4}$ to 5; at Ahmadābād from 1 to $1\frac{1}{2}$; at Sironj to 3; at Burhānpur from $2\frac{1}{2}$ to 3; at Dacca to 10; at Patna from 7 to 8; at Benares to 6.

At these three last places letters of exchange are only given on Agra, and at Agra those on Surat, the whole amounting only to the sum just stated; at Golkonda from 4 to 5; and on Goa the same; at Deccan to 3; at Bījāpur to 3; at Daulatābād from 1 to $1\frac{1}{2}$.

[1] This trade of collecting the sweepings of goldsmiths' shops is carried out by workmen known as Niyāriyā, 'separators': see Crooke, *Tribes and Castes, North-West Provinces and Oudh*, iv. 91 f.

[2] Lahore, Agra, Ahmadābād, Sironj, Burhānpur, Dacca, Benares, Golkonda, Deccan, Bījāpur, and Daulatābād. These spellings will be used on subsequent pages.

[3] For an account of the business of an Indian banker and of the various forms of their bills of exchange, see *Bombay Gazetteer*, ix, pt. i, 82 ff. For banking in Bombay, see Edwardes, *Gazetteer Bombay City and Island*, i. 274 ff.

In some years the exchange rises from 1 to 2 per cent., when there are Rājās, or petty tributary Princes, who interfere with trade, each claiming that the goods ought to traverse his territory and pay him custom.[1] There are two in particular between Agra and Ahmadābād, one of whom is the Rājā of Antivar,[2] and the other the Rājā of Bergam,[3] who harry the merchants much in reference to this matter. One may, however, avoid passing the territories of these two Princes by taking another route from Agra to Surat by way of Sironj and Burhānpur ;[4] but these are fertile lands intersected by several rivers, the greater number of which are without bridges and without boats, and it is impossible to ford them until two months after the rainy season. For this reason the merchants who have to be at Surat by the season for going to sea, generally make their way through the country of these two Rājās, because it can be traversed at all seasons, even during the rains, which consolidate the sand of which nearly the whole country is composed. Besides, it is not to be wondered at that the exchange is so high, for those who lend the money must accept on their part the risk that if the goods are stolen the money is lost to them.

On arrival for embarkation at Surat, you find there plenty of money.[5] For it is the principal trade of the nobles of India to place their money on vessels in speculations for Hormuz, Bassora, and Mocha, and even for Bantam, Achīn, and the Philippines. For Mocha and Bassora the exchange ranges from 22 to 24 per cent., and for Hormuz from 16 to 20 ; and for the other places which I have named the exchange varies in proportion to the distance. But if the goods happen to be lost by tempest, or to fall into the hands of the Malabārīs,[6]

[1] For a good account of the status of these Rājās see Bernier, 207 f.

[2] A misprint, probably for Dantivar (see p. 58), i. e. Dāntā, or Dāntawārā, a State in Mahi Kāntha, Bombay Presidency.

[3] Probably the Bargant of p. 69 below. In the edition of 1713 it is given as Bergant. The proper name is probably Bāglānā.

[4] For description of Sironj and Burhānpur see pp. 42, 46 below (Jadunath Sarkar, *History of Aurangzīb*, i. 51 ; *Imperial Gazetteer*, vi. 190 ff. ; *Āīn-i-Akbarī*, ii. 251).

[5] On the prosperity of Surat during this period see Manucci, i. 61 ff. ; Rawlinson, *British Beginnings in Western India*, 35 ff.

[6] Malavares in the original. For their piracies see p. 143 below.

who are the pirates of the Indian seas, the money is lost to those who have risked lending it.

I have but one word to say, in addition, regarding the weights and measures. Here, in the margin, is the 10th part of the ell of Agra, and the 8th of the ell of Ahmadābād and Surat. As for the weights, the ordinary man is 69 livres, and the livre is of 16 onces ; but the man which is used to weigh indigo, is only 53 livres. At Surat you speak of a ser, which is $1\frac{3}{4}$ livres,[1] and the livre is 16 onces.

CHAPTER III

Concerning conveyances and the manner of travelling in India.

BEFORE setting out for Agra, it is appropriate to speak of the conveyances and of the manner of travelling in India, which, in my opinion, is not less convenient than all the arrangements for marching in comfort either in France or in Italy. Differing from the custom in Persia, you do not employ in India in caravans or journeys either asses, mules, or horses, everything being carried here on oxen or by waggon, as the country is sufficiently level.[2] If any merchant takes a horse from Persia he does it only for show, and to have him led by hand, or in order to sell him advantageously to some noble.

They give an ox a load weighing 300 or 350 livres,[3] and it is an astonishing sight to behold caravans numbering 10,000

[1] This must mean one $\frac{3}{4}$ths of a livre, as elsewhere in this volume ; that is about the relation, roughly speaking, namely, 12 French onces. The present authorized British weights are :

80 tolās (or rupee's weight) = 1 ser = $2\frac{1}{2}$ lb. Troy.
40 sers = 1 man or maund = 100 lb. Troy.

[2] The English translation of this passage by John Phillips, in 1677 and 1684 is, like many others, curiously inaccurate, and as a sample, it may be given here : 'Quite otherwise it is in Persia, where they neither make use of asses, mules, nor horses, but transport all their wares to the Indies upon oxen or in wains, their countries being so near to one another' !

[3] 'The normal load for continuous travel of a fair-sized elephant is 800 pounds, so the animal is equal to eight ponies, small mules, or asses : to five stout pack-mules or bullocks, and to three and one-third of a camel' (J. L. Kipling, *Beast and Man in India*, ed. 1892, p. 239).

or 12,000 oxen together, for the transport of rice, corn, and salt—in the places where they exchange these commodities—carrying rice to where only corn grows, and corn to where only rice grows, and salt to the places where there is none. They use camels also for caravans, but rarely, and they are specially reserved to carry the baggage of the nobles. When the season presses, and they wish to get the goods quickly to Surat, in order to ship them, they load them on oxen, and not on carts. As all the territories of the Great Mogul are well cultivated, the fields are enclosed by good ditches, and each has its tank or reservoir for irrigation. This makes it so inconvenient for travellers, because, when they meet caravans of this description in narrow roads, they are sometimes obliged to wait two or three days till all have passed. Those who drive these oxen follow no other trade all their lives ; they never dwell in houses, and they take with them their women and children.[1] Some of them possess 100 oxen, others have more or less, and they all have a Chief, who acts as a prince, and who always has a chain of pearls hanging from his neck. When the caravan which carries corn and that which carries rice meet, rather than give way one to the other, they often engage in very sanguinary encounters. The Great Mogul, considering that these quarrels were prejudicial to commerce and to the transport of food in his kingdom, arranged that the Chiefs of the two caravans should come to see him. When they arrived, the King, after he had advised them for their mutual benefit to live for the future in harmony with each other, and not to fight again when they met, presented each of them with a lākh, or 100,000 rupees,[2] and a chain of pearls.

In order to enable the reader to understand this manner of

[1] The well-known Banjārās used to perform most of this carrying trade in India. In the Central Provinces, South-Western Bengal, and the northern districts of Madras, Ball says he has met with large numbers of them ; and in Sambalpur he has seen their fixed dépôts, where the infirm are left while the others are on their journeys. Railways have driven them from many of the routes which they used to follow. The best accounts of the Banjārās will be found in the paper by N. R. Cumberlege, reprinted in *North Indian Notes and Queries*, iv. 163 ff., and R. V. Russell, *Tribes and Castes of the Central Provinces*, ii. 162 ff.

[2] See p. 24 *n*.

carrying in India, it should be remarked that among the idolaters of this country there are four tribes, whom they call Manaris,[1] of which each numbers about one hundred thousand souls. These people dwell in tents, as I have said, and have no other trade but to transport provisions from one country to another. The first of these tribes has to do with corn only, the second with rice, the third with pulse, and the fourth with salt, which it obtains from Surat, and even from as far as Cape Comorin. You can also distinguish these tribes in this manner —their priests, of whom I shall elsewhere speak, mark those of the first with a red gum, of the size of a crown, on the middle of the forehead, and make a streak along the nose, attaching to it above some grains of corn, sometimes nine, sometimes twelve, in the form of a rose. Those of the second are marked with a yellow gum, in the same places, but with grains of rice; those of the third with a grey gum, with grains of millet, and also on the shoulders, but without placing grains there.[2] As for those of the fourth, they carry a lump of salt, suspended from the neck in a bag, which weighs sometimes from 8 to 10 livres (for the heavier it is the more honour they have in carrying it), with which, by way of penance before praying, they beat their stomachs every morning. Generally all have a string, or tress, round the shoulders, from which hangs a small box of silver in the form of a reliquary, of the size of a good hazel nut, in which they keep a superstitious writing which their priests have enclosed in it.[3] They place them also on their oxen, and on the other animals born in their herds, for which they entertain a special affection, loving them as dearly as they would do their children, especially when they happen to be childless.

The dress of the women is but a simple cloth, white or coloured, which is bound five or six times like a petticoat from the waist downwards, as if they had three or four one above the

[1] Manaris, probably a corruption of the term Banjārā. See Yule, *Hobson-Jobson*, 114 f.

[2] Much of this is probably mere hearsay, and it is not corroborated by recent authorities.

[3] The ta'wīz, for which see Ja'far Sharīf, *Islām in India*, Oxford, 1921, 247 ff.

other. From the waist upwards they tattoo their skin with flowers, as when one applies cupping glasses, and they paint these flowers divers colours with the juice of roots,[1] in such a manner that it seems as though their skin was a flowered fabric.

While the men load their animals in the morning and the women fold up their tents, the priests who follow them set up in the most beautiful parts of the plain where they are encamped, an idol in the form of a serpent, entwined about a staff of six or seven feet in height,[2] and each one in order goes to make reverence to it, the girls turning round it three times. After all have passed, the priests take care to remove the idol and to load it on an ox assigned for that purpose.

The caravans of waggons do not ordinarily consist of more than one hundred or two hundred at the most. Each waggon is drawn by ten or twelve oxen, and accompanied by four soldiers, whom the owner of the merchandise is obliged to pay. Two of them walk on each side of the waggon, over which two ropes are passed, and the four ends are held by the soldiers, so that if the waggon threatens to upset in a bad place, the two soldiers who are on the opposite side hold the ropes tight, and prevent it turning over.

All the waggons which come to Surat from Agra or from other places in the Empire, and return by Agra and Jahānābād,[3] are compelled to carry lime, which comes from Broach, which, as soon as it is used, becomes as hard as marble.[4] It is a great source of profit to the Emperor, who sends this lime where he pleases; but, on the other hand, he takes no dues from the waggons.

I come to the manner of travelling in India, where oxen take

[1] The English translation of John Phillips has it juice of 'grapes'; but the original word is *racines*, not *raisins*. For an account of tattooing see Russell, *Tribes and Castes, Central Provinces*, iii. 124.

[2] Here the allusion is apparently to Nāga, or snake worship. But snake worship is not mentioned in recent accounts of Banjārās: see Russell, *Tribes and Castes, Central Provinces*, ii. 176 ff. For their distinctive dress, ibid. ii. 184 f.

[3] Janabat in the original.

[4] Coral or shell lime probably, which make the best chunam. For an account of cements see Watt, *Commercial Products of India*, 713 ff.

the place of horses, and there are some of them whose paces are as easy as those of our hacks. But you should take care when you buy or hire an ox for riding that he has not horns longer than a foot, because, if they are longer, when the flies sting him, he chafes and tosses back the head, and may plant a horn in your stomach, as has happened several times.[1] These oxen allow themselves to be driven like our horses, and have for a bridle only a cord, which passes through the tendon of the muzzle or the nostrils. In level tracts, where there are no stones, they do not shoe these oxen, but they always do so in rough places, both on account of the pebbles and because of the heat, which may injure the hoof. Whereas in Europe we attach our oxen by the horns, those of India have a large hump on the neck,[2] which keeps in position a leather collar about four fingers wide, which they have only to throw over the head when they harness them.

They have also, for travelling, small, very light carriages, which can carry two persons ;[3] but usually you travel alone, in order to be more comfortable, being then able to have your clothes with you ; the canteen of wine and some small requisites for the journey having their place under the carriage, to which they harness only a pair of oxen. These carriages, which are

[1] Oxen are now seldom ridden in northern India, but they were used for this purpose at Surat. 'The vulgar . . . are pleas'd with getting on a small Ox, as their Pad, to carry them in the Town, or round the Country' (Ovington, 253). P. della Valle (Hakluyt Society, i. 185) saw a Portuguese youth riding to school on 'a Carnero, or wether without horns'. 'The Pandārams and Jangamas, priests of Siva, go on horseback or in a palanquin, but their favourite mode of progression is riding on an ox' (Dubois, *Hindu Manners, Customs and Ceremonies*, 3rd ed., Oxford, 1906, p. 129).

[2] The hump on the shoulders was unknown to John Phillips, the author of the English translation of 1677 and 1684, so he renders this passage, 'the Indians only put a thick truss upon their necks, that keeps,' &c. This is a good example of the kind of mistake many translators have fallen into when, in ignorance of local facts, they have strained their author's words in order to make sense, as they conceive it.

[3] This is what is known as a bahal or bahlī. 'The Coaches in this Countrie are generally drawne with Oxen, never above 2 to a Coach, which haue but 2 wheeles, in all things resembling a little Carte, the Cover excepted, which is like that of a Coach in England' (Mundy, ii. 189) ; and see P. della Valle, i. 21.

provided, like ours, with curtains and cushions, are not slung; but, on the occasion of my last journey, I had one made after our manner, and the two oxen by which it was drawn cost me very nearly 600 rupees.[1] The reader need not be astonished at this price, for there are some of them which are strong, and make journeys lasting 60 days, at 12 or 15 leagues a day, and always at the trot. When they have accomplished half the journey, they give to each two or three balls of the size of our penny rolls, made of wheaten flour, kneaded with butter and black sugar, and in the evening they have a meal of chick-peas, crushed and steeped in water for half an hour. The hire of a carriage amounts to about a rupee a day. The journey from Surat to Agra occupies thirty-five or forty days' journey by road, and you pay for the whole journey from 40 to 45 rupees. From Surat to Golkonda it is nearly the same distance and the same price, and it is in the same proportion throughout the whole of India.

Those who can afford to take their ease make use of a palankeen,[2] in which they travel very comfortably. It is a kind of bed, 6 or 7 feet long and 3 feet wide, with a small rail all round. A sort of cane, called bamboo,[3] which they bend when young, in order to cause it to take the form of a bow in the middle, supports the cover of the palankeen, which is of satin or brocade; and when the sun shines on one side, an attendant, who walks near the palankeen, takes care to lower the covering. There is another, who carries at the end of a stick a kind of basket-work shield, covered with some kind of beautiful stuff, in order that he may be able promptly to

[1] Ball believes that as much as Rs. 500, and perhaps more, is sometimes given now in Bombay and the Central Provinces for a good pair of trotting bullocks. The pace they can keep up has to be experienced in order to be properly realized. For bullock-racing in India, see *Folk-lore*, xxviii. 157.

[2] Pallanquin in the original; pālkī in Hindi: see, for an illustration, Bowrey (Hakluyt Society), 86, with Temple's note; P. della Valle, i. 183; Ovington, 255 ff.

[3] Bambouc in the original. Bamboo (*Bambusa arundinacea*, &c.). It is not necessary to grow bamboos to a particular shape, as by means of fire they can be made to bend into the required forms. Still, they are so trained sometimes during growth: see Fryer, i. 97; Grose, 247.

shelter the occupant of the palankeen from the heat of the sun when it turns and strikes him on the face.[1] The ends of the bamboo are attached on both sides to the body of the palankeen between two poles, joined together in a saltier, or St. Andrew's Cross, and each of these poles is 5 or 6 feet long. Some of these bamboos cost as much as 200 écus, and I have paid 125 for one. Three men, at most, place themselves at each of these ends, and carry the palankeen on their shoulders, one on the right and the other on the left, and they travel in this way faster than our chairmen in Paris, and with an easier pace, being trained to the trade from an early age. When you wish to make haste, and travel as much as 13 or 14 leagues a day, you take 12 men to carry the palankeen, so that they may relieve one another from time to time. You pay each of them only 4 rupees a month inclusive, but you pay up to 5 rupees when the journey is long, and when they are required to travel for more than sixty days.

He who desires to travel with honour in India, whether by carriage or palankeen, ought to take with him 20 or 30 armed men, some with bows and arrows and others with muskets, and you pay them as much per month as those who carry the palankeen. Sometimes, for greater show, you carry a flag. This is always done by the English and Dutch, for the honour of their Companies. These attendants not only conduce to your honour, but they watch also for your protection, and act as sentinels at night, relieving one another, and striving to give you no cause of complaint against them. For it should be mentioned that in the towns where you hire them they have a head man who answers for their honesty, and when you employ them, each one gives him a rupee.[2]

In the large villages there is generally a Musalmān governor, and there you find sheep, fowl, and pigeons for sale ; but in the places where there are only Banians, you find only flour, rice, vegetables, and milk.

[1] The English translation of 1684 says, 'when he turns and lies on his face'. This sunshade is like the Āftābgīr, used by the Mughal Emperors (*Āīn-i-Akbarī*, i. 50).

[2] A custom still common in India, where the Kahār bearers are provided by a Chaudharī or head man of the caste ; but palankeen travelling is rapidly disappearing.

The great heat of India compels travellers who are not accustomed to it to travel by night, in order to rest by day. When they enter towns which are closed they must leave by sunset, if they wish to take the road. For when night comes, and the gates are closed, the Governor of the place, who has to answer for thefts which occur within his jurisdiction, does not allow any one to go out, and says that it is the Emperor's order, which he must obey. When I entered such places I took provisions, and left early, in order to camp outside under some tree in the shade, waiting till it was time to march.

They measure the distances of places in India by gos and by coss. A gos [1] is about four of our common leagues, and a coss [2] about one league.

It is time now to leave Surat for Agra and Jahānābād, in order to see what is remarkable on that route.

[1] The gos, or gau, is equal to 8 or 10 miles in Southern India, but in Ceylon, according to Sir Emerson Tennent (*Ceylon*, i. 567; ii. 582), it is only from 3½ to 4 miles (*Madras Manual of Administration*, iii. 229). The word is a vague measure of distance—as far as the lowing of a cow can be heard, or as far as a man can walk in an hour (P. della Valle, ii. 230). The gaukos in Northern India is as far as the lowing of a cow can be heard.

[2] In the original edition this word is spelt coste by mistake, as explained in the 'Avis'; in subsequent editions it is cosse. It has been thought better to substitute the ordinary Anglo-Indian term coss throughout in this translation. While here definitely, and elsewhere inferentially, Tavernier gives the coss an equal value with the league, Thévenot says the coss was only half a league. The old French 'lieue de poste' = 2 miles 743 yards, and Akbar's coss = 2 miles 1,038 yards. But the coss was and is a most variable unit, as, indeed, Tavernier himself remarks. In some parts of India it exceeds 3 miles, and the Bengal coss of 4,000 cubits or 2,000 yards = 1 m. 1 f. 3 p. 3½ yds. (See Appendix to this volume.) 'A Course, 12,000 of the said feete, is 2⅖ mile English' (Mundy, ii. 67). The Akbarī kos was 400 poles, each 12½ gaz or yards, or 5,000 gaz (*Āīn-i-Akbarī*, ii. 414). See Yule, *Hobson-Jobson*, 261.

CHAPTER IV

Route from Surat to Agra by Burhānpur and Sironj.[1]

The routes to all the principal towns of India are not less well known to me than are those of Turkey and of Persia, and, for six journeys which I have made from Paris to Ispahān, I have made double the number from Ispahān to Agra, and to several other places in the Empire of the Great Mogul. But it would weary the reader to cause him to pass more than once by the same roads while giving him an account of these different journeys, and of sundry small adventures with which they have been accompanied ; therefore it is that, without indicating the times at which I have made them, it will suffice to give an exact description of each route.

There are but two roads from Surat to Agra, one by Burhānpur and Sironj, and the other by Ahmadābād, and the first will form the subject of this chapter.

From Surat to Barnoly,[2] 14 coss. Barnoly is a large town where you cross a river by a ford, and traverse, in this first march, a country of mixed character, sometimes meeting woods, and sometimes fields of wheat and rice.

From Barnoly to Balor, 10 coss. Balor is also a large village, situated close to a tank which is about a league in circuit, and upon the margin of it there is a good fort, which, however, is not kept in repair. Three-quarters of a league on the near side of the village you pass a rivulet by a ford, but with much difficulty, because there are many rocks and stones under the water which may overturn a carriage. The route this second day lies nearly altogether through forests.

[1] The elucidation of these routes has been facilitated by the notes of Sir R. C. Temple on the Travels of Peter Mundy, and of Sir W. Foster on those of John Jourdain and Sir T. Roe, all published by the Hakluyt Society. The forms of the place-names used by Tavernier have been given in the text : those found in modern maps, in the notes.

[2] Bardoli, or Panoli of some maps. The distance from Surat as the crow flies is only about 18 miles. On p. 116 below it is said to be 12 coss only. The river crossed is the Pūrnā.

From Balor to Kerkoa,[1] or, as they now call it, the Begam's caravansarāī, 5 coss. This caravansarāī is large and spacious, and it was built by the order of Begam Sāhib, the daughter of Shāhjahān, as a work of charity. For formerly the stage from Balor to Navapoura was too long, and this place being on the frontier of the country of those Rājās who are generally unwilling to recognize the Great Mogul, whose vassals they are, scarcely a caravan passed which was not ill treated; moreover, it is a forest country. Between the caravansarāī and Navapoura you pass a river by a ford, and another close to Navapoura.[2]

From Kerkoa to Navapoura,[3] 15 coss. Navapoura is a large village full of weavers, but rice constitutes the principal article of commerce in the place. A river passes by it, which makes the soil excellent, and irrigates the rice, which requires water. All the rice which grows in this country possesses a particular quality, causing it to be much esteemed. Its grain is half as small again as that of common rice, and, when it is cooked, snow is not whiter than it is, besides which, it smells like musk, and all the nobles of India eat no other.[4] When you wish to make an acceptable present to any one in Persia, you take him a sack of this rice. The river which passes Kerkoa, and the others of which I have spoken, combine to form the Surat river.[5]

From Navapoura to Nasarbar, 9 coss; Nasarbar to Dol-Medan, 14 coss; Dol-Medan to Senquera, 7 coss; Senquera to Tallener,[6] 10 coss; at Tallener you cross the river which goes to Broach,[7] where it is very wide, and from thence it flows into the Gulf of Cambay. From Tallener to Choupre, 15 coss; Choupre to Senquelis, 13 coss; Senquelis to Nabir, 10 coss;

[1] Balor is the modern Ballōr; the site of Kerkoa, the modern Kirkā, or the Begam's caravansarāī, is near Behānā.

[2] These rivers are tributaries of the Tāptī.

[3] From Bardoli (Panoli) to Navapoura or Nārāyanpura the distance as the crow flies is about 42 miles; here it is given as 30 coss, and in ch. ix as 28 coss. This and the preceding stage indicate a value of something less than 1½ mile for the coss. (See p. 116 below.)

[4] This fine rice is known as 'perfumed' (bāsmatī, sukhdās): in Peshāwar, bārā.

[5] The Tāptī.

[6] The stages are: Nārāyanpura; Nandurbār; Sinkheda; Thālner.

[7] This is a mistake, as the river at Thālner is the Tāptī. It is the Narbadā which goes to Broach.

Nabir to Baldelpoura, 9 coss;[1] At Baldelpoura loaded carts have to pay the Brampour[2] customs dues, but the carts which carry only passengers pay nothing. Between Navapoura and Brampour it is all a good country for wheat, rice, and indigo. From Baldelpoura to Brampour, 5 coss.

Brampour[3] is a large, much-ruined town, the houses of which are for the most part thatched. It has a large castle still standing in the middle of the town, and there it is that the Governor resides.[4] The government of this province is so important that it is conferred only upon a son or an uncle of the Emperor, and Aurangzeb, who now reigns, was for a long time Governor of Brampour during the reign of his father. But since it has been realized how much can be yielded by the province of Bengal, which formerly bore the title of kingdom, as I shall elsewhere indicate, its government has become the most important in the Empire of the Great Mogul. There is a considerable trade in this town, and both at Brampour itself and in all the province an enormous quantity of very transparent muslins are made, which are exported to Persia, Turkey, Muscovie, Poland, Arabia, Grand Cairo, and other places. Some of these are dyed various colours and ornamented with flowers, and women make veils and scarfs of them; they also serve for the covers of beds, and for handkerchiefs, such as we see in Europe with those who take snuff. There are other fabrics, which are allowed to remain white, with a stripe or two of gold or silver running the whole length of the piece, and at each of the ends, from the breadth of one inch up to twelve or fifteen—in some more, and in others less—it is a tissue of gold, silver, and of silk with flowers, and there is no reverse, one side being as beautiful as the other. If those which they export to Poland, where they are in great demand, have not at both ends at least three or four inches of gold or silver, or if this gold and silver become black when crossing the ocean

[1] The stages are: Chopra; Sānklī; Raver; Balledā.

[2] Burhānpur, now a station on the Great Indian Peninsular Railway: in Nimār District, Central Provinces.

[3] For Burhānpur, see Sir T. Roe, i. 89 ff.; Bernier, 31, 36; *Imperial Gazetteer*, ix. 104 ff.; *Bombay Gazetteer*, xii. 589.

[4] The Lāl Qal'a, or Red Fort, built by Akbar.

between Surat and Hormuz, and from Trebizonde to Mangalia,[1] or other ports of the Black Sea, the merchant cannot dispose of them except at great loss. He ought to take great care that the goods are well packed, and that they are secured from damp: this, for so long a voyage, requires much care and trouble. Some of these fabrics are all banded, half cotton and half gold or silver, such pieces being called ornis.[2] They contain from fifteen to twenty ells, and cost from one hundred to one hundred and fifty rupees, the cheapest being not under ten or twelve rupees. Those which are only about two ells long serve ladies of rank for the purpose of making scarfs and veils which they wear on their heads, and they are also sold largely in Persia and Turkey. They make, also, other kinds of fabrics at Brampour, and there is hardly another province in the whole of India which has a greater abundance of cotton.

On leaving the town of Brampour there is another river to be crossed besides the large one [3] which I have mentioned above; as it has no bridge, you cross by a ford, when the water is low, and by boat in the rainy season. The distance from Surat to Brampour is 132 coss.[4] These coss are the smallest in India, a cart being able to traverse one in less than an hour.

I am reminded here of a strange commotion which arose at Brampour in the year 1641,[5] when I was returning from Agra to Surat. The origin of it was, in a few words, as follows.

[1] Mingrelia (?) in Transcaucasia, now Russian territory.

[2] Orhnī, Hind., Mahr. odanī, a woman's mantle. In vol. ii, pp. 4, 35, the word is spelt ornis, and in the 1679 edition ormus. 'Ornees, 16 coveds [cubits] longe, wrought with Silk and Gold', Mundy, ii. 155.

[3] The larger river is the Tāptī, and the other, one of its tributaries.

[4] As an illustration of the uncertainty of the calculation of distances, Mundy gives 170 kos; Fitch, 152; Jourdain, 166; Tieffenthaler, 150 (Mundy, ii. 50).

[5] In reference to this casual mention of a date, M. Joret remarks that Tavernier has been lost sight of from the spring of 1639, when he was at Ispahān, till he turns up thus in India in 1641. Towards the end of the same year he says he went to Goa (bk. I, ch. xii). It is probable, M. Joret adds, that he spent the winter of 1640–1 at Agra, and in the same journey paid his first visit to Dacca in Bengal, which he revisited in 1666–7. In bk. III, ch. xiv, he says, however, he was in Agra in 1642, which M. Joret thinks may be a misprint for 1641. (*Jean-Baptiste Tavernier*, par C. Joret, Paris 1886, pp. 54–60; see also the Introduction to this volume.)

The Governor of the Province, who was the Emperor's nephew on his mother's side, had employed as one of his pages a young man of handsome appearance and fairly good family, who had a brother who lived as a Dervish,[1] and for whom all the town entertained much veneration. One day . . . the page, observing that the Governor was about to commit an offence, stabbed him three times in the stomach, slaying him before he could open his lips to cry aloud. This done, the page left the palace without allowing any sign of emotion to appear on his face, the guards at the gate thinking that the Governor had sent him on some message. The Dervish having learnt from his brother what had happened, in order to preserve him from the fury of the people, and to disclose at the same time the infamy of the Governor, ordered all the other Dervishes, his comrades, to seize the banners of Muhammad [2] which were planted about the mosque, and at the same time they called upon all the Dervishes, Fakīrs and others, who were good Musalmāns, to follow them. In less than an hour a multitude of rabble assembled, and the Dervish, taking the lead with his brother, went straight to the palace, crying out with all their might, 'Let us die for Muhammad, or let them give up to us that infamous person in order that dogs may eat him after his death, as he is not worthy to be interred amongst Musalmāns.' The guard of the palace was not able to resist such a multitude, and would have yielded to them, if the Dārogha [3] of the town with five or six nobles had not found an opportunity of making themselves heard, and of appeasing the people, by warning them that they should have some respect for a nephew of the Emperor, and so induced them to withdraw. The same night the body of the Governor was carried to Agra, together with his harem, and Shāhjahān, who then reigned having heard the news, was not in the least distressed, because he inherited the property of all his subjects,[4] and he even bestowed on the page a small appointment in Bengal.

[1] Deruich in original, for Dervish, Pers. Darvesh.

[2] Probably the 'Alām, or standards, carried at the Muharram festival, which are described by Ja'far Sharīf in his account of the festival in the *Qānūn-i-Islām*. See Ja'far Sharīf, *Islām in India*, Oxford, 1921, p. 160.

[3] Deroga in original: head police official.

[4] 'It should also be borne in mind that the Great Mogol constitutes

From Brampour to Piombi-sera, 5 coss. Before proceeding further, it should be remarked that throughout this work wherever the word sera occurs, it signifies a great enclosure of walls or hedges, within which 50 or 60 thatched huts are arranged all round. Here there are some men and women who sell flour, rice, butter, and vegetables, and who make it their business to prepare bread and cook rice.[1] If by chance any Musalmān arrives, he goes into the village to seek for a piece of mutton or a fowl, when those who supply the food to the traveller clean out for him the room which he wishes to occupy, and they place in it a small bed of girths,[2] upon which he spreads the mattress which he carries with him on his journey. From Piombi-sera to Pander, 3 coss; Pander to Balki-sera, 6 coss; Balki-sera to Nevelki-sera, 5 coss; Nevelki-sera to Cousemba, 5 coss; Cousemba to Chenipour, 3 coss; Chenipour to Charoüa, 8 coss; Charoüa to Bich-ola, 8 coss; Bich-ola to Andy, 4 coss. At Andy Handiā (you cross a river which discharges itself into the Ganges between Benares and Patna).[3]

From Andy to Onquenas, 4 coss; Onquenas to Tiquery, 5 coss; Tiquery to Toolmeden, 4 coss; Toolmeden to Nova-sera, 4 coss; Nova-sera to Ichavour, 4 coss; Ichavour to Signor, 5 coss; Signor to Chekaipour, 3 coss; Chekaipour to Dour-ay, 3 coss; Dour-ay to Ater-kaira, 3 coss; Ater-kaira to

himself heir of all the Omrahs, or lords, and likewise of the Mansebdars, or inferior lords, who are in his pay' (Bernier, 204): cf. Ovington, 197. See p. 15 above.

[1] These people are known as Bhathiyārā, Crooke, *Tribes and Castes, North-West Provinces and Oudh*, ii. 34 ff.

[2] A charpoy (*chārpāī*, Hind.), with plaited tape (*newār*) stretched across the frame. Such beds are still to be found in the Government Rest Houses or Dawk Bungalows.

[3] Some of the intervening stages cannot be traced with certainty; the chief places on the route are: Borgām; Nau Sarāī, Seharā; Chainpur; Charwā; Handiā on the River Narbadā. Tavernier has raised a difficulty by confounding the River Narbadā with the Son. Handiā, mentioned by Manucci (i. 67) is an old Muhammadan town in the Hoshangābād District, Central Provinces, which fell into decay when the Mughal officials left the place about A. D. 1700, and a better road was made over the Vindhyan range, via Indore (*Central Provinces Gazetteer*, 1870, p. 201).

Telor, 4 coss; Telor to San-kaira, 3 coss; San-kaira to Seronge,[1] 12 coss.

Sironj is a large town, of which the majority of the inhabitants are Banian merchants and artisans, who have dwelt there from father to son, which is the reason why it contains some houses of stone and brick. There is a large trade there in all kinds of coloured calicoes, which they call chites,[2] with which all the common people of Persia and Turkey are clad, and which are used in several other countries for bedcovers and tablecloths. They make similar calicoes in other places besides Sironj, but the colours are not so lively, and they disappear when washed several times. It is different with those of Sironj; the more they are washed the more beautiful they become. A river passes here, of which the water possesses the property of giving this brightness to the colours; and during the rainy season, which lasts four months, the workers print their calicoes according to patterns which the foreign merchants have given them, because, as soon as the rains have ceased, the water of the river becomes more turbid, and the sooner the calicoes are washed the better the colours hold, and become brighter.

There is also made at Sironj a description of muslin which is so fine that when it is on the person you see all the skin as though it were uncovered. The merchants are not allowed to export it, and the Governor sends all of it for the Great Mogul's seraglio, and for the principal courtiers. This it is of which the sultanas and the wives of the great nobles make themselves shifts and garments for the hot weather, and the

[1] Here, again, some places on the route, small villages or temporary inns, cannot be identified with certainty. The main stages are: Handia; Tumrī; Nau Sarāī; Ichhāwar, in the Bhopāl State; Sīhor, a cantonment in Bhopāl; Shaikhpura; Duraibā; Hāthiyākherā; Dilod; Sironj. Sironj in the Mughal period was an important place in Tonk State, but the manufacture of chintzes and muslins, for which it was famous, has died out, and no recollection of its having once formed the staple trade of the place survives (*Imperial Gazetteer*, xxiii. 39). The river referred to in the text is a tributary of the Betwā. Bernier (p. 403) says that the inferiority of the water prevented the manufacture of Kashmīr shawls at Patna, Agra, and Lahore. See ii. 29 below on the effects of water on the dyeing of chintz. Jadunath Sarkar (*India of Aurangzīb*, Introd. cxiv f.) discusses this route.

[2] See p. 65.

King and the nobles enjoy seeing them wearing these fine shifts, and cause them to dance in them.[1]

From Brampour to Sironj there are 101 coss, which are greater than those between Surat and Brampour, for a cart takes an hour, and sometimes an hour and a quarter, to travel one of these coss. In these 100 leagues [2] of country you march for whole days among fertile fields of wheat and rice, which strongly resemble our fields at Beausse,[3] for one rarely meets with woods, and between Sironj and Agra the country is of much the same character. As the villages are very close to one another you travel in comfort, and make the day's journey as you please.

From Seronge to Magalki-sera, 6 coss; Magalki-sera to Paulki-sera, 2 coss; Paulki-sera to Kasariki-sera, 3 coss; Kasariki-sera to Chadolki-sera, 6 coss; Chadolki-sera to Callabas,[4] 6 coss.

Callabas [5] is a large town, where formerly a great Rājā

[1] This is the fabric, semi-transparent muslin, known as Āb-i-ravān, 'flowing water'. Aurangzeb is said to have remonstrated with his daughter for the scantiness of her dress, and the princess replied that she wore seven garments made of this material (Yule, *Hobson-Jobson*, 706).

[2] Here, as elsewhere, the league is used as the equivalent of the coss, and the fact pointed out on p. 43 and in the Appendix that the coss near Surat is a short one is referred to.

[3] La Beauce or Beausse, an ancient division of France in Orléanais. Its capital town was Chartres; it formed an extensive and very fertile plain; it is now comprised in the Department of Eure et Loire.

[4] The stages are: Sironj to Mughal Sarāī, in the Tonk State; Mughal Sarāī to Pālkī Sarāī; Pālkī Sarāī to Kachnor kī Sarāī; Kachnor kī Sarāī to Shāhdaurā; Shāhdaurā to Kālābāgh.

[5] Kālābāgh (?), the Collybaye of Jourdain (p. 151), a halting-place on the old Deccan road, about 100 miles south of Gwalior, not mentioned in the *Imperial Gazetteer*, or, much less probably, the Calabad or Calabay of Manucci (iii. 502, 509, iv. 429). [But Manucci describes it as a 'province' close to the Gwāliyār (Gwalior) fortress. Irvine suggests Kālpī; but 'the plains of Gohad', Tod's *Rajasthan*, i, 16, may be suggested. They lie north of Gwalior, whereas Tavernier's Callabas was 46 coss to the south of it.] Prof. Jadunath Sarkar suggests that the 'great Rājā' mentioned in the text was Champat Rāī Bundela, who rebelled against Aurangzeb. His territory was invaded by the Mughals, and he finally committed suicide in October 1661 (Jadunath Sarkar, *Hist. of Aurangzib*, iii. 30 ff.). Numerous instances of pillars of the skulls of enemies or criminals will be found in Fryer (ii. 245), and a sketch of such a Mīnār or pillar in Mundy (ii. 108).

resided who paid tribute to the Great Mogul. Generally, when caravans passed it, the merchants were robbed, and he exacted from them excessive dues. But since Aurangzeb came to the throne he cut off his head, and those of a large number of his subjects. They have set up towers near the town on the high-road, and these towers are pierced all round by several windows where they have placed in each one the head of a man at every two feet. On my last journey, in 1665, it was not long since this execution had taken place when I passed by Callabas; for all the heads were still entire, and gave out an unpleasant odour.

From Callabas to Akmate, 2 coss; Akmate to Collasar,[1] 9 coss. Collasar is a small town, of which all the inhabitants are idolaters. As I was entering it, on this final journey, there arrived there also eight large pieces of artillery, some forty-eight pounders, the others thirty-six pounders, each gun being drawn by twenty-four pairs of oxen. A strong and powerful elephant was following this artillery, and whenever there was a bad spot from which the oxen had difficulty in drawing it, they made the elephant advance, and push the gun with his trunk.

Outside the town, for the whole length of the high-road there are a number of large trees which they call *mengues*,[2] and in several places near these trees you see small pagodas, each of which has its idol at the entrance. This elephant, passing in front of one of these pagodas, near to which I was encamped, and where there were at the door three idols of about five feet in height, when he was close by, took one with his trunk and broke it in two; he then took the next, and threw it so high and so far that it was broken in four pieces; while as for the third, he knocked off the head with a blow of his trunk. Some thought that the driver of the elephant had ordered him to do so, and had given him the signal; this I did not observe. Nevertheless, the Banians regarded it with an evil eye, without daring to say aught, for there were more than 2,000 men in charge of the guns, all of them in the Emperor's

[1] Kolāras, a well-known town in Gwalior, though not mentioned in the *Imperial Gazetteer*. The total distance from Mughalsarāī to Kolāras, measured on the map, is about 62 miles.

[2] Mangoes, the fruit of *Mangifera Indica*.

service, and Musalmāns, with the exception of the chief gunners, who were Franks—French, English, and Dutch. The Emperor was sending this artillery to the province of Deccan, where his army was opposed to the Rājā Sivajī, who had pillaged Surat the previous year [1664], as I shall have occasion for describing elsewhere.[1]

From Collasar to Sansele, 6 coss; Sansele to Dongry,[2] 4 coss; Dongry to Gate; 3 coss. Gate [3] is a pass in the mountains, which is half a quarter of a league long, and which you descend when going from Surat to Agra. You still see at the entrance the ruins of two or three castles, and the road is so narrow that chariots can only pass one another with the greatest difficulty.

Those who come from the south, *en route* to Agra, as from Surat, Goa, Bījāpur, Golkonda, Masulipatam, and other places, cannot avoid traversing this pass, not having any other road except by taking that through Ahmadābād. There were formerly gates at each end of the pass, and at that which was on the Agra side there are five or six shops of Banians, who sell flour, butter, rice, herbs, and vegetables. On my last journey I halted at one of these shops while awaiting the coaches and carts, the passengers having descended from them for this transit. Close by them was a large store full of sacks of rice and corn, and behind these sacks a snake of thirteen or fourteen feet in length, and of proportionate girth, was concealed. A woman while taking some grain from the sacks was bitten on the arm by this snake, and, feeling herself wounded, left the shop, crying 'Rām, Rām!' that is to say, 'Oh God! Oh God!' Immediately several Banians, both men and women, ran to her aid, and they tied the arm above the wound, thinking they could prevent the poison from ascending higher. But it was unavailing, for immediately her face swelled, and then became blue, and she died in less than an hour.

[1] For the artillery sent to reinforce Jai Singh in his Deccan campaign see Jadunath Sarkar, *Hist. of Aurangzīb*, iv. 107 f.

[2] Sansele is Sīprī; Dongry, Dongri, 8 miles from Sīprī, which is 15 miles from Kolāras; Dungri-Ghāt is represented on some maps near Narwar.

[3] Gate stands perhaps for some separate ghāt or pass, probably near Gopālpur on the Sind river, about 6½ miles from Dongri.

The Rājputs,[1] who are considered to be the best soldiers in India, constitute the heathen soldiery, and make no scruple of killing when it is a question of attacking or defending. As this woman was on the point of death, four of these cavaliers arrived, and, having learnt what had happened, entered the store each with a sword and a short pike in his hand, and slew the serpent. The people of the place then took it and threw it outside the village, and immediately a great number of birds of prey perched on the carcase, which was devoured in less than an hour. The relatives of the woman took her body and carried it to the river to wash it, after which they burnt it. I was compelled to remain two days in this place, because there is a river [2] to cross, which, instead of becoming lower, increased from hour to hour on account of the rains which had fallen during three or four days, so that I had to cross it half a league lower down. You always strive to cross this river by ford, because in order to reach the boats it is necessary to unload the carts and coaches, and even to take them to pieces, so that they may be carried by hand for the whole of this half-league of road, which is the worst that it is possible to conceive. It is all covered with great rocks, and confined between the mountain and the river, so that when the waters are in flood they cover the whole road, none but the people of the country being able to traverse it. They obtain their livelihood from the passengers, from whom they take the most that they can; but for that it were easy to facilitate the passage by making a bridge, since there is no lack of either wood or stone.

From Gate to Nader,[3] 4 coss. Nader is a large town on the slope of a mountain,[4] above which there is a kind of fortress, and the whole mountain is surrounded by walls. Most of the

[1] Ragipous in the original, Rājputs, the warrior caste.

[2] The Sind river, a tributary of the Jumna.

[3] Narwar, in Gwalior, on right bank of Sind river, Lat. 25° 39′ 2″ N., Long. 77° 56′ 57″ E., 44 miles south of Gwalior; an ancient Hindu town, surrendered to Nāsiru-d-dīn, A. D. 1251. (*Imperial Gazetteer*, xvii. 396 ff.; Cunningham, *Arch. Survey*, ii. 307 ff.) The distance is given as 17 coss from Kolāras to Narwar, and the true distance is 35 miles, and the stages given between Mughalsarāī and Kolāras amount to 28 coss, while the true distance is about 63 miles. Taken together, 45 coss = 98 miles, would give nearly the usual average of 2 miles = 1 coss.

[4] A steep scarp of the Vindhyan range.

houses, as is the case in the other towns of India, are thatched, and have only one story; and those of the wealthy have but two, and are terraced. Several large tanks around the town were formerly lined with cut stone, but they are now neglected; about one league off there are still some beautiful tombs. The river we crossed the day before, and that must be crossed again four or five coss beyond Narwar, surrounds the three sides of the town and of the mountain, which form a sort of peninsula, and after a long and tortuous course it discharges itself into the Ganges.[1] They make at Nader a quantity of quilted coverlets, some white, others embroidered with flowers in gold, silver and silk.

From Nader to Barqui-sera, 9 coss; Barqui-sera to Trie, 3 coss; Trie to Goüaleor,[2] 6 coss. Gwalior, a large town, is like others ill-built, in the manner of India. A small river passes it. It is built along the side of a mountain which lies to the west, and towards the top it is surrounded by walls with towers. There are in this enclosure several ponds formed by the rains, and what they cultivate there is sufficient to support the garrison; this is why this place is esteemed one of the best in India. On the slope of the mountain which faces the north-west, Shāhjahān built a pleasure-house, from whence all the town is visible, and it is fit to serve as a fortress. Below this house there are to be seen several images in bas-relief, sculptured in the rock, all of which have the forms of demons, and there is one, among others, of an extraordinary height.[3]

[1] There are two fine Musalmān bridges over the Sind; the weaving industry has disappeared.

[2] The route is: Barkī Sarāī; Antrī; Gwalior, the last the chief town of the State of the same name, and the residence of Mahārājā Sindhia, situated in Lat. 26° 13′ N., and Long. 78° 12′ E., 65 miles south of Agra. The fort, which was surrendered to Sindhia in 1886 in exchange for Jhānsī, stands on an isolated hill of sandstone 342 feet high, 1½ mile long, and 300 yards wide. On its eastern side there are several colossal figures, sculptured in bold relief, our author mentions. The Jain and Hindu antiquities have been described by Mr. Fergusson, and by Cunningham, *Arch. Survey*, ii. 330 ff. (*Imperial Gazetteer*, xii. 438 ff.) The distance from Narwar to Gwalior is nearly 50 miles; here it is given as 18 coss, the coss thus exceeding 2½ miles. The river to which Tavernier refers is possibly the Vaisalī.

[3] This is the series of images of the Jain Tirthankaras, or twenty-four

Since the Muhammadan kings have taken possession of these countries, the fortress of Gwalior had become the place where they send princes and great nobles for safe custody.[1] Shāhjahān having ascended the throne by treachery, as I shall relate [2] in the course of my narrative, caused all the princes and nobles whom he believed to be able to injure him, to be arrested, one after the other, and sent them to Gwalior, but he allowed them all to live and to enjoy their revenues. Aurangzeb, his son, does just the contrary; for when he sends any great noble there, at the end of nine or ten days he causes him to be poisoned, and he does this so that the people may not say that he is a sanguinary monarch. As soon as he had in his power Prince Murād Bakhsh,[3] his younger brother, whom he encouraged to take arms against his father, Shāhjahān, and who, being Governor of the Province of Gujarāt, had proclaimed himself Emperor, he had him placed in this fortress, where he died.[4] They have erected in the town an appropriately magnificent tomb for him, in a mosque which they built for the purpose, with a great court in front, all surrounded by vaults under which there are several shops. It is the custom in India, when they build a public edifice, to surround it with a large market-place, with an endowment for the poor, to whom they give alms daily, and who pray to God for him who has caused the work to be done.

At 5 coss from Gwalior you cross, by ford, a river which is called Laniké.[5] From Goüalcor to Paterki-sera 3 coss; Paterki-sera to Quariqui-sera,[6] 10 coss.

great saints, constructed under the Tunwar dynasty (A. D. 1440–73, Sleeman, *Rambles*, 267).

[1] On Gwalior as the Mughal State prison, where the prisoners were dosed with pōst or infusion of opium, see Bernier, 106 ff.

[2] See pp. 260 ff. below.

[3] Morat Bakche in original. On his fate see Bernier, 107 f., and for his rebellion, Jadunath Sarkar, *Hist. of Aurangzīb*, i. 318 ff.

[4] Murād Bakhsh was murdered by two slaves on December 4, 1661, and buried in the 'Traitors' Cemetery' at Gwalior Fort; Sulaimān Shikoh was drugged to death in May 1662, and buried beside his uncle, Murād Bakhsh: Jadunath Sarkar, ii. 100, 236.

[5] This probably stands for Sanike, i. e. Sank river, a tributary of the Kunwārī river.

[6] Kunwārī-kī Sarāī.

There is a bridge at Paterki-sera,[1] with six large arches, and the river which flows under it is called Quarinadi.

From Quariqui-sera to Dolpoura,[2] 6 coss. At Dolpoura there is a great river called Chammel-nadi[3]—you cross it in a boat, and it discharges itself in the Jumna[4] between Agra and Allahābād. From Dolpoura to Minasqui-sera,[5] 6 coss. At (? Beyond) Mania (-ki-sarāī) there is a river called Iagou-nadi[6]—you cross it by a very long bridge built of cut stone, and called Iaoulcapoul.[7] From Minasqui-sera to this bridge, 8 coss.[8]

It is not far from this bridge that they examine goods, so that when you reach Agra[9] you are not able to evade the dues; but it is particularly to see if among the number of cases full of fruits preserved in vinegar, in glass pots, there are not any cases of wine. From the bridge of Iaoulcapoul to Agra, 4 coss.[10] Thus from Sironj to Agra is 106 coss, which are common coss, and from Surat to Agra 339.

[1] This is an obvious misprint for Quariqui-sera, where the bridge really was, namely, over the Quari (Kunwārī) nadī, 'Princess river', which joins the Sind river near its junction with the Jumna.

[2] Dholpur, the chief town of the State of the same name. It is 34 miles south of Agra, and 40 miles north-west of Gwalior (*Imperial Gazetteer*, xi. 331 f. The value of the coss as deduced from this would be very nearly two miles, 37 coss = 71 miles. The Chambal river lies three miles to the south of this town, which was built by Rājā Dholan Deo, in the eleventh century, and surrendered to the Emperor Bābur in 1526.

[3] Chambal river.

[4] Gemena in the original. The Chambal joins the Jumna 25 miles south-west of the town of Etāwah.

[5] Maniā.

[6] Jājau on the Utangan river, a tributary of the Jumna, where, on June 10, 1707, Mu'azzam defeated his brother 'Azam.

[7] Iaoulcapoul, for Jājau kā pul, or the bridge of the Jājau.

[8] Mundy's route (ii. 61 ff.) was: Monde Sara, Mundiākherā; Dhol-poore, Dholpur; Saya, Saiyan; Agra. Tavernier halted at Pater kī Sarāī, Kunwārī Sarāī, Dholpur, Maniā kī Sarāī, Jājau bridge.

[9] For description of Agra see p. 86.

[10] There is a good deal of error in the distances as above stated. From Dholpur to Maniā it is 9 miles, from Maniā to Jājau on the Utangan river 6 miles, from Jājau to Agra about 20 miles; total, say 35 miles, as against 16 coss wrongly divided.

CHAPTER V

Route from Surat to Agra by Ahmadābād

From Surat to Baroche,[1] 22 coss. The country between these two towns abounds with corn, rice, millet, and sugar-canes. Before entering Broach, a river which runs to Cambay is crossed by a ferry, and discharges itself afterwards into the gulf bearing the same name.

Baroche is a large town, containing an ancient fortress which has been neglected ; the town has been widely renowned from all time on account of its river, which possesses a peculiar property for bleaching calicoes, which for this reason are brought from all quarters of the empire of the Great Mogul where there is not so great an abundance of water. In this place baftas[2] or pieces of long and narrow calico are made in quantity ; they are very beautiful and closely woven cloths, the price of them ranging from 4 up to 100 rupees. Custom dues have to be paid at Broach on all goods, whether imported or exported. The English have a very fine dwelling there ;[3] and I remember that, on arrival one day when returning from Agra to Surat[4] with the English President, some jugglers immediately came to ask him whether he desired them to show him some examples of their art ; these he was curious to see. The first thing they did was to kindle a large fire, and heat iron chains to redness ; these they wound round their bodies, making believe that they experienced some pain, but not really receiving any

[1] Broach, chief town of district of same name in Gujarāt, situated on the right bank of the Narbadā, 30 miles from its mouth (*Imperial Gazetteer*, ix. 28 ff.). *Villace* in original, a big 'straggling town'.

[2] Bāftas, one of the numerous varieties of fine calico, which were formerly largely exported to Europe from India. (See Yule, *Hobson-Jobson*, p. 47.) The *New English Dict.* defines 'Baft, a kind of coarse and cheap (generally cotton) fabric, originally of oriental manufacture, but now made in Great Britain for export, especially to Africa : Pers. *bāfta*, wrought, woven.'

[3] The English factory was established in 1616. The building seems to have disappeared.

[4] In the English translation of 1684, by John Phillips, these names are transposed.

injury.[1] Next, having taken a small piece of stick, and planting it in the ground, they asked one of the company what fruit he wished to have. He replied that he desired mangoes,[2] and then one of the conjurers, covering himself with a sheet, stooped to the ground five or six times. I had the curiosity to ascend to a room in order to see from above, through an opening of the sheet, what this man did, and I saw that he cut himself under his arm-pits with a razor, and anointed the piece of wood with his blood. At each time that he raised himself, the stick increased under the eye, and at the third time it put forth branches and buds. At the fourth time the tree was covered with leaves, and at the fifth we saw the flowers themselves. The English President had his chaplain with him, whom he had brought to Ahmadābād to baptize a child of the Dutch Commander, and he had been asked to be the godfather, for it should be remarked that the Dutch have no clergymen save in those places where both merchants and soldiers are quartered together. The English Chaplain at first protested that he was unable to consent that Christians should be present at such spectacles, and when he saw that from a piece of dry wood these people in less than half an hour had caused a tree of four or five feet in height, with leaves and flowers, as in springtime, to appear, he insisted on breaking it, and proclaimed loudly that he would never administer the communion to any one who witnessed such things in future. This compelled the President to dismiss the jugglers, who travel from place to place with

[1] For tricks of this kind see Ja'far Sharīf, *Islām in India*, Oxford, 1921, p. 173.

[2] The mango trick. Also described by Bernier (p. 321), who, however, did not personally witness the performance, and by Ovington (258), who believed that it was due to Black Magic, because a gentleman became ill after eating one of the mangoes, and did not recover until, following a Brāhman's advice, he restored it to the magician. See Yule, *Hobson-Jobson*, 555 f., for other early accounts of this famous trick. On the only occasion when Ball witnessed it, he was not much impressed with it as an example of sleight of hand; but the juggler was not of the first class. And his experience is that of other observers. It seems probable that the above-mentioned juggler knew he was being watched by Tavernier, and therefore distracted his attention by means of the razor. Chardin speaks of the incident contemptuously, and also of Tavernier for being deceived by it. (*Voyages*, Amsterdam, ed. 1711, vol. iv, p. 133.)

their wives and children, like those whom we in Europe commonly call Egyptians or Bohemians [1]; and having given them the equivalent of ten or twelve écus,[2] they went away very well satisfied.

Those who wish to visit Cambay, need not go out of their way more than about five or six coss, or thereabouts ; and when at Broach, instead of going to Baroda, which is the ordinary route, they make directly for Cambay, from whence afterwards they reach Ahmadābād. Except for business, or out of curiosity, this route is not taken, not only because it is longer, as I have said, by five or six leagues,[3] but principally on account of the danger in passing the end of the gulf.

Cambay [4] is a large town at the end of the gulf which bears its name. Here those beautiful agates which come from India are cut into cups, handles of knives, beads, and other objects of workmanship.[5] Indigo [6] of the same kind as that of Sarkhej [7] is made, also, in the vicinity of the town, and it was celebrated for its traffic when the Portuguese flourished in India. In the quarter close to the sea, many fine houses, which they built and richly furnished after the manner of Portugal may still be seen ; but at present they are uninhabited, and decay from day to day. Such good order was maintained at that time in Cambay, that at two hours after dark every street was closed by two gates, which are still to be seen, and even now some of the principal of them are closed, especially those in the avenues

[1] In the Deccan and Bombay they probably belonged to castes like the Nat and Kolhāti (Russell, *Castes, Central Provinces*, i. 139 ; *Bombay Gazetteer*, vi. 240 f.).

[2] = £2 5*s*. to £2 14*s*., at 4*s*. 6*d*. per écu.

[3] Here again leagues and coss are treated as synonymous terms.

[4] Cambaya in the original. Cambay, chief town of the State of Cambay, Province of Gujarāt, Bombay Presidency, 52 miles south of Ahmadābād. (See the account by Pyrard de Laval, ii. 249.)

[5] A full account of this industry will be found in the *Economic Geology of India*, p. 506 ; Watt, *Commercial Products*, 561 f.

[6] The cultivation of indigo has much diminished of late in that part of India (*Bombay Gazetteer*, vi. 183).

[7] Sarquesse in the original, this is Sarkhej, the Surkeja of Major Scott's Madras route map, south-west of Ahmadābād (*Bombay Gazetteer*, iv. 89, 292). Tieffenthaler calls it Sarkés, *Géog. de l'Ind.*, par Bernoulli, Berlin, 1791, p. 377. See for further information Yule, *Hobson-Jobson*, p. 31. (Spelt Suarkej on p. 59 below.)

to the market-places. One of the principal reasons why this town has lost a part of her commerce is, that formerly the sea came close to Cambay, and small vessels were able to approach it easily; but for some years past the sea has been receding day by day, so that vessels are now unable to come nearer than four or five leagues to the town.[1]

Pea-fowl are abundant in India, and especially in the territories of Broach, Cambay, and Baroda. The flesh of the young bird is white and of good flavour, like that of our turkeys, and throughout the day they may be seen in flocks in the fields; for during the night they perch in the trees. It is difficult to approach them by day, because if they perceive the sportsman they fly away from him more rapidly than a partridge, and enter the jungle, where it is impossible to follow them, one's garment being torn at every step. Hence, they can only be captured easily at night; and this, in a few words, is the method employed. You approach the tree with a kind of banner, on which life-like peacocks are painted on each side.[2] On the top of the stick there are two lighted candles, the light of which attracting the peacock, causes him to stretch out his neck almost to the end of the stick, where there is a cord with a running noose, which the man who carries the banner draws when he sees that the peacock has placed his neck in it. However, you must be careful not to kill a bird, or any other animal, in the countries of Rājās, where the idolaters are the masters; it is not dangerous in the parts of India where the rulers of the country are Musalmāns, as they permit sport to be without restriction.[3] It happened one day that a rich merchant of Persia, when passing by the territory of the Rājā of

[1] The commercial decay of Cambay is due, partly, to competition with Bombay and Surat, partly to the silting up of the gulf and to the Bore or rushing tide (*Imperial Gazetteer*, ix. 297; *Bombay Gazetteer*, vi. 195).

[2] Peacocks are successfully approached by day by a native sportsman, who carries before him a cloth screen, on which a rude representation of a peacock is painted, some birds actually making a charge towards the screen.

[3] Kārttikeya, god of war, is represented as riding on a peacock, and many castes, particularly Jāts, venerate the bird in northern India. See Sleeman, *Rambles*, 259.

Dantivar,[1] either out of bravado or from not knowing the customs of the country shot a peacock on the road. The Banians, enraged by an act which is regarded among them as a horrible sacrilege, seized the merchant themselves, and also the money he had with him, which amounted to 300,000 rupees, and tying him to a tree, whipped him during three days so severely that the poor man died of it.

After Cambay you next reach a village which is only three coss distant, where there is a pagoda to which the majority of the courtesans of India come to make their offerings. This pagoda contains many nude figures, and among others a large figure like an Apollo, which has the private parts all uncovered. When the old courtesans have amassed a sum of money in their youth, they buy young female slaves, to whom they teach dances and lascivious songs, and all the tricks of their infamous trade. When these young girls have reached the age of eleven or twelve years their mistresses take them to this pagoda, as they believe that it will be good fortune to them to be offered and abandoned to this idol.[2]

From this pagoda to Chiidabad [3] it is 6 coss. Here is one of the most beautiful houses of the Great Mogul, and a vast enclosure, where there are extensive gardens and large tanks, with all the embellishments of which the genius of the Indians is capable. From Chiidabad to Ahmadābād it is but 5 coss. I return to Baroche and the ordinary route. From Baroche to Baroda,[4] 22 coss. Baroda is a large town built on a good soil, where there is a considerable trade in calicoes. From

[1] Dāntā, or Dāntawārā, a State under the Political Agency of Mahi Kāntha, Bombay. The Chief is a Hindu. It has been pointed out already that the Antivar of p. 31 is probably a misprint for Dantivar.

[2] This is a vague reference to the rite of initiation, by a form of marriage to the god, of the Devadāsī, 'handmaids of the god,' at Deccan temples: see Russell, *Tribes and Castes, Central Provinces*, iii. 374 ff., iv. 604 f. In western India they are called Bhāvin (*Bombay Gazetteer*, x. 126). For the custom see Barbosa, ed. Dames, i. 222 f.; Hastings, *Encyclopaedia of Religion and Ethics*, ix. 820, xi. 673. Local inquiries have failed to identify the temple described by Tavernier.

[3] Sayyidābād, which is not traceable on modern maps.

[4] Baroda, Broudra in original, the chief town of the territory of the Gāekwār. From Broach to Baroda, the distance measured on the map is about 48 miles.

Broudra to Neriade,[1] 18 coss; from Neriade to Amadabat,[2] 20 coss.

Ahmadābād is one of the largest towns in India, and there is a considerable trade in silken stuffs, gold and silver tapestries, and others mixed with silk; saltpetre, sugar, ginger, both candied and plain, tamarinds, mirabolans,[3] and indigo cakes, which are made at three leagues from Ahmadābād, at a large town called Suarkej.[4]

There was formerly a pagoda in this place, which the Musalmāns seized and converted into a mosque. Before entering it you traverse three great courts paved with marble, and surrounded by galleries, but you are not allowed to place foot in the third without removing your shoes. The exterior of the mosque is ornamented with mosaic, the greater part of which consists of agates of different colours, obtained from the mountains of Cambay, only two days' journey thence.[5] There are many tombs of ancient idolatrous kings, like so many small chapels of mosaic, with columns of marble sustaining small vaults by which the tombs are covered. A river [6] flows past Ahmadābād on the north-west, and during the rainy season, which lasts in India three or four months, it becomes very wide and rapid, and does great injury every year. It is the same with all the rivers of India, and when the rains have ceased, you must generally wait six weeks or two months before it is possible to ford the river at Ahmadābād, as there is no bridge.[7] There are two or three boats, but one cannot

[1] Nadiād in Kaira District (*Bombay Gazetteer*, iii. 173).

[2] Ahmadābād, the chief town in the District of the same name, in the Province of Gujarāt, Bombay Presidency. Tieffenthaler calls the town itself Guzarat.

[3] The dried unripe fruit of *Terminalia chebula*, Retz. (Watt, *Commercial Products*, 1073.)

[4] Sarkhej in the Ahmadābād District: see n. 7 on p. 56 above. The cultivation of indigo has greatly decreased, and Sarkhej is now known only for its fine tank (*Bombay Gazetteer*, iv. 18, 58).

[5] The reference is apparently to Sultān Ahmad's mosque, in the Bhadar or citadel, built A. D. 1414; first attempt by Hindus to build in the Musalmān style. There are tombs of Sultān Begada and of other kings of the dynasty at Sarkhej (ibid. iv. 276, 291 f.).

[6] The Sābarmatī.

[7] The Sābarmatī is now crossed by the Bombay-Baroda Railway bridge.

make use of them, save when the river falls, and it takes much time to cross. The peasants do not stand on ceremony, for in order to go from one bank to the other they make use of the skin of a goat,[1] which they fill with air and tie on between the chest and the abdomen. It is thus, by swimming this river, that the poor, both men and women, cross, and when they wish to take their children across with them they make use of round earthen pots, which have mouths four fingers in width, and placing a child in one of these pots they push it before them while swimming. This brings to my mind a circumstance which happened at Ahmadābād, while I was there in the year 1642,[2] which is too remarkable to pass by in silence.

A peasant and his wife were crossing the river one day in the manner I have just described, and having an infant with them of about two years of age they placed him in one of these pots, so that only his head could be seen from outside. In the middle of the river they landed on a small bank of sand where there was a large tree, which the water had carried down, and the father to rest himself pushed the pot containing the infant on the shoal. As he approached the foot of the tree, the trunk of which was somewhat raised above the water, a snake came out from between the roots, and jumped into the pot where the infant was. The father and mother, startled, and losing their wits, let the pot go, and when the river carried it away they remained some time half-dead at the foot of the tree. About two leagues lower down a Banian and his wife, with a little child, were bathing in the river before going to dinner. They beheld from afar the pot upon the water, and half the head of a child outside its mouth. The Banian immediately swam out, and pushed it ashore. The woman, followed by her child, came presently to lift out the other baby which was in the pot, And at that moment the snake, which had done no injury to

[1] This is the so-called mussuck (*mashak*, Hind.) deri, sarnā, sarnāī, zuk, consisting of the inflated skin of a goat; sometimes, as on the Sutlej, in the Himalayan regions, the skin of a buffalo is used for the same purpose. Gore, *Lights and Shadows of Hill Life*, 122; Conway, *Climbing and Exploration in the Karakorum Himalayas*, 172.

[2] This casual reference to a date is of use as confirmation of Tavernier having been in this part of India in that year. (See Joret, *J. B. Tavernier*, Paris, 1886, p. 64.)

the first child, left the pot, and entwined itself about the body of the Banians' child which was close to the mother, bit it, and injected its poison, which caused its immediate death.

This extraordinary adventure did not much distress these poor people, as they believed that it had happened by a secret dispensation of their god, who had taken from them one child in order to give them another, by which they were soon consoled. Some time after, the report of this adventure having reached the ears of the first peasant, he went to the Banian to tell him how it happened and to demand from him his child. This caused a fierce dispute between them, the second peasant maintaining that the child was his, and that his god had given it to him in the place of the one who was dead. In a word, the matter made a great noise, and was at length laid before the Emperor, who ordered that the infant should be returned to its father.

About the same time a somewhat amusing case occurred in the same town of Ahmadābād. The wife of a rich Banian merchant, named Saintīdās, had no children, and announced that she wished for some. A servant of her house one day took her apart, and said to her that if she was willing to eat what he would give her, she might feel certain that she would have a child. The woman desiring to know what she ought to eat, the attendant said that it was a little fish, and that she need only eat some three or four.[1] The religion of the Banians forbidding them, as I have elsewhere said, to eat anything which has had life, the woman was at first unable to bring herself to do what he suggested; but the servant having said that he knew how to disguise it so well that she would not know that what she was eating was fish, she resolved at length to try the remedy, and she lay the night following with her husband, according to the instruction she had received from the servant. Some time after, the woman perceiving that she was enceinte,

[1] In the East surprising effects are often attributed to a fish diet. See the *Kitāb 'Ajāib al-Hind* (*Les Merveilles de l'Inde*, Leyden, 1883), p. 131, for a remarkable instance. In many Hindu castes the bride and bridegroom are made to catch fish as a fertility charm. Manucci (ii. 37) speaks of a fish called *instinco* (saqanūr) used by men as a love stimulant. See Thurston, *Tribes and Castes of Southern India*, v. 203; E. S. Hartland, *Primitive Paternity*, i. 48 ff.

her husband died, and the relatives of the defunct wished to take possession of his effects. The widow objected, and told them they should have patience till they knew if the infant which she carried would arrive safely.

The relatives, surprised by this news, which they had not expected, treated it as a lie or a joke, the woman having been fifteen or sixteen years with her husband without bearing. When she found that these people tormented her, she threw herself at the feet of the Governor, to whom she related what had happened, and he ordered that the relatives should wait till the woman was delivered. Some days after her confinement the relatives of the deceased, who were persons of position, and desired to secure for themselves so considerable an inheritance, maintained that the infant was illegitimate, and that the woman's husband was not its father. The Governor, to ascertain the truth, assembled the doctors, who decided that the infant should be taken to the bath, and that if the remedy which the mother had adopted was genuine, the child would smell of fish; this was done and the thing happened accordingly. After this experiment the Governor ordered the effects of the deceased to be secured for the infant, as its parentage had been proved; but the relatives, annoyed that so good a morsel was escaping from them, appealed from this judgement, and went to Agra to inform the Emperor. In consequence of what they stated, His Majesty issued an order to the Governor to send the mother and the infant, that the same experiment might be made in his presence; this having turned out as on the first occasion, the relatives of the deceased withdrew their claim and the effects were secured for the mother and infant.

I remember also another amusing thing which was told me at Ahmadābād—where I have been ten or twelve times—during the stay I made there on one of my journeys, on my return from Delhi.[1] A merchant with whom I often dealt, and who was much loved by Shāista Khān, Governor of the Province and uncle of the Emperor, had the reputation of never having

[1] Joret (*J.-B. Tavernier*, Paris, 1886, p. 47) supposes that this was in the early part of 1667, but says the passage is too obscure to admit of any definite conclusion.

lied. Shāista Khān having completed the three years of his government, according to the custom in the Empire of the Great Mogul, and Aurangzeb, son of Shāhjahān, having succeeded, he withdrew to Agra, where the court then was. One day, as he was conversing with the Emperor he remarked that he had seen many uncommon things in all the governments with which His Majesty had honoured him, but one thing alone surprised him, which was that he discovered a rich merchant who had never told a lie, and who was upwards of seventy years old. The Emperor, surprised at such an extraordinary thing, told Shāista Khān that he desired to see the man of whom he had spoken, and ordered him to send him forthwith to Agra, which was done. This caused much distress to the old man, both on account of the length of the road, which is from twenty-five to thirty days' journey, and because it was necessary for him to make a present to the Emperor. In short, he offered a gift valued at 40,000 rupees; it was a gold box for keeping betel, ornamented with diamonds, rubies, and emeralds. After he had saluted the Emperor, and had made his present, the Emperor merely asked his name, to which he replied that he called himself the man who had never lied. The Emperor asking him further what his father's name was: 'Sire,' replied he, 'I know not.'[1] His Majesty, satisfied with this reply, stopped there, and, not desiring to know more, ordered them to give him an elephant, which is a great honour, and 10,000 rupees for his journey.

The Banians have a great veneration for monkeys, and they even feed them in some pagodas where they go to worship,[2] There are in Ahmadābād two or three houses which serve as

[1] The oriental version of the well-known saying: 'It is a wise father that knows his own child' (Shakespeare, *Merchant of Venice*, Act ii, Scene 2). Οὐ γάρ πώ τις ἑὸν γόνον αὐτὸς ἀνέγνω (Homer, *Odyssey*, i. 216). In India this belief prevails specially where the institution of Mother Right and of descent in the female line exists, as among the Khasi and Synteng of Assam, and the Nāyars and other castes in Malabar.

[2] Monkeys, representing the god Hanumān, are venerated and fed at many Hindu temples, perhaps the best-known example being the so-called Monkey Temple at the Durgā Kund, or pool of Durgā, at Benares (Sherring, *The Sacred City of the Hindus*, 158 f.; Greaves, *Kashi, the Illustrious*, 89). See Fryer, *New Account*, ii. 73.

hospitals,[1] especially for cows, oxen, monkeys, and other sick and disabled animals, and they convey there all that they are able to find, and feed them. It should be stated that on every Tuesday and Friday all the monkeys in the neighbourhood of Ahmadābād, of their own instinct, come in a body to the town, and ascend the houses, each of which has a small terrace where the occupants sleep during the great heat. On each of these days they do not fail to place upon these little terraces rice, millet, sugar-canes in their season, and other similar things; for if by chance the monkeys did not find their food on the terraces, they would break the tiles with which the rest of the house is covered, and cause great damage. It should be remarked that the monkey eats nothing which he has not first well smelt, and before swallowing anything he makes a store for future hunger, filling his two cheeks with provisions, which he keeps for the following day.[2]

I have said that the Banians have an especial veneration for the monkey, and this is an example in point among several others which I could quote. One day at Ahmadābād, at the Dutch House, a young man of that nation, who had arrived but a few days before to serve in the office, and was ignorant of the customs of the country, perceiving a large monkey on a tree in the court-yard, wished to give an example of his skill, or rather as it turned out, of his youth, by shooting it. At the time I was at table with the Dutch Commander, and we had scarcely heard the shot before there was a great uproar among the Banians in the service of the Dutch Company, who came to complain bitterly against him who had slain the monkey. They all wished to resign, and it was with much trouble and many apologies that they were appeased and induced to remain.

In the neighbourhood of Ahmadābād monkeys are numerous, and it may be said that in the places where there are many of these animals there are but few crows. For when the latter have built their nests and laid their eggs, the monkeys climb

[1] There are now six animal hospitals in the Ahmadābād District (*Bombay Gazetteer*, iv. 114). On these hospitals see Fryer, i. 138; Linschoten, Hakluyt Society, ed. i. 253; Ovington, 300 f.

[2] The retention of food in the pouch only lasts for a short time, the monkey masticating it at his leisure.

the trees and throw the eggs on the ground. One day, on my return from Agra, I left Ahmadābād with the English Chief or President who had come there for some business, and was returning to Surat. We passed, at four or five leagues from Ahmadābād, a small grove of the trees which are called mangoes. We saw overhead numbers of large monkeys, male and female, and several of the latter carried their young ones in their arms. We each had our carriage, and the English President stopped his to tell me that he had an excellent and curious gun which the Governor of Damān[1] had presented to him, and, knowing that I was a good shot, he asked me to prove it upon one of these monkeys. One of my attendants, who was of the country, signed to me not to risk it, and I sought to dissuade the President from his intention, but it was impossible; so taking his gun he shot a female monkey, which remained extended between two branches and let her young ones fall to the ground. What my attendant, who had signed to me, had foreseen followed at once. All the monkeys on the trees, to the number of more than sixty, descended immediately, in a rage, and jumped on the carriage of the President, and would have strangled him, but for the prompt assistance that some gave by closing the windows, while the crowd of attendants who were present drove them off. Although they did not come to my carriage, which followed at some paces distant from that of the President, I nevertheless feared for myself the fury of these monkeys, which were both large and powerful, and so much were they enraged that they pursued the carriage of the President for nearly a league.

Continuing our route from Surat to Agra. From Amadabat to Panser, 13 coss; from Panser to Masana, 14 coss; from Masana to Chitpour,[2] 14 coss.

Sidhpur is a fairly good town, so named on account of the great trade which it does in those coloured cottons which are called chites,[3] and at four or five hundred paces on the south

[1] The Portuguese settlement in Thāna District, Bombay (*Imperial Gazetteer*, xi. 128 ff.).

[2] The route is Pansār, Mehsānā, Sidhpur (Chitpur on the map in Bernier, p. 238).

[3] Chites (see p. 46), from Mahr. *chit* and Port. *chita* = chintz (Yule, *Hobson-Jobson*, 201 f.).

side there flows a small river. When I arrived at Sidhpur, on one of my journeys, I was encamped under two or three trees at one of the ends of a great open space near the town. A short time afterwards four or five lions [1] appeared which they brought to train, and they told me it generally took five or six months, and they do it in this way. They tie the lions, at twelve paces distance from each other, by their hind feet, to a cord attached to a large wooden post firmly planted in the ground, and they have another about the neck which the lion-master holds in his hand. These posts are planted in a straight line, and upon another parallel one, from fifteen to twenty paces distant, they stretch another cord of the length of the space which the lions occupy, when arranged as above. These two cords which hold the lion fastened by his two hind feet, permit him to rush up to this long cord, which serves as a limit to those outside it, beyond which they ought not to venture to pass when harassing and irritating the lions by throwing small stones or little bits of wood at them. A number of people come to this spectacle, and when the provoked lion jumps towards the cord, he has another round his neck which the master holds in his hand, and with which he pulls him back. It is by this means that they accustom the lion by degrees to become tame with people, and on my arrival at Sidhpur I witnessed this spectacle without leaving my carriage.

The following day I had another experience, which was a meeting I had with a party of Fakīrs, or Musalmān Dervishes.[2] I counted fifty-seven of them, of whom he who was their Chief or Superior had been master of the horse to Shāh Jahāngīr,[3] having left the court when Sultān Bulākī, his grandson, was strangled by order of Shāhjahān, his uncle, as

[1] These were true lions, and not chītās, or hunting leopards, as lions are known to have been so tamed, and the region is one in which they may very possibly have been obtained. Tame lions were kept by Jahāngīr and other Emperors (Terry, 184 f.; Sir T. Roe, i. 198 f.). Aelian (*On the Peculiarities of Animals*, iii. 26) says they were tamed and used in sport: but he confuses the lion with the *chītā*. The Malloi presented tame lions and tigers to Alexander the Great (Smith, *Early Hist. of India*, 3rd ed., p. 97).

[2] Dervichs in original, for Dervishes.

[3] Cha Gehan-guir in original, for Shāh Jahāngīr.

I shall relate elsewhere.[1] There were four others who, under the Superior, were Chiefs of the band, and had been the first nobles of the court of the same Shāhjahān. The only garment of these five Dervishes consisted of three or four ells of orange-coloured cotton cloth, of which they made waistbands, one of the ends passing between the thighs and being tucked between the top of the waistband and the body of the Dervish, in order to cover what modesty requires should be concealed, both in front and behind.[2] Each of them had also a skin of a tiger upon the shoulders, which was tied under the chin. They had eight fine horses, saddled and bridled, led by hand before them, three of which had bridles of gold and saddles covered with plates of gold; and the five others had bridles of silver, and the saddles also covered with plates of silver, and a leopard's skin on each. The other Dervishes had for their sole garment a cord, which served as a waistband, to which was attached a small scrap of calico to cover, as in the case of the others, the parts which should be concealed. Their hair was bound in a tress about their heads, and made a kind of turban. They were all well armed, the majority with bows and arrows, some with muskets, and the remainder with short pikes, and a kind of weapon which we have not got in Europe It is a sharp iron, made like the border of a plate which has no centre, and they pass eight or ten over the head, carrying them on the neck like a ruff.[3] They withdraw these circles as they require to use them, and when they throw them with

[1] Dāwar Bakhsh, son of Khusrū, and titular Emperor, is said by some to have been strangled, while others assert that he was allowed to escape to Persia (Smith, *Oxford Hist. of India*, 392). His nickname was Bulāqī, from *bulāq*, the ring worn by women in the septum of the nose. A boy is ornamented in this way in order that he may be supposed to be a girl, and thus escape from the effects of the Evil Eye. *V.* pp. 267 f.

[2] Cf. the account of naked Fakīrs by Bernier (p. 317).

[3] These are the chakar, thin sharp-edged metal quoits, which can be flung with marvellous accuracy and effect against an enemy. The Sikhs are especially proficient in their use. Bowrey (p. 22) describes a ring, seemingly of another kind, worn by Fakīrs: 'Some, nay Severall, that I have Seen doe weare a very broad plate of beaten iron about their necks. I judge it may be 4½ or 5 feet over, haveinge theire necks through a round hole in the midst thereof, and this fastened on by a smith very strongly rivotted on, so that the party cannot ly downe.'

force at a man, as we make a plate to fly, they almost cut him in two. Each of them had also a sort of hunting horn, which he sounds, and makes a great noise with when he arrives anywhere, and also when he departs, and also a rake, or instrument of iron, made something like a trowel. It is with this instrument, which the Indians generally carry in their journeys, that they level the places where they wish to halt, and some, collecting the dust in a heap, make use of it as a mattress and bolster in order to lie more comfortably. There were three of these Dervishes armed with long rapiers, which they had received, apparently, from some Englishman or Portuguese. Their baggage consisted of four boxes full of Arabic and Persian books and some cooking utensils, and they had ten or twelve oxen to carry those among the troop who were invalids. When these Dervishes arrived at the place where I was encamped with my carriage, having then with me fifty persons, both people of the country, whom one engages, as I have said, for travelling, as also my ordinary servants, the Chief or Superior of the troop, seeing me well accompanied, inquired who that Aga [1] was ; and then asked me to surrender to him the position I occupied, it being more commodious than any other about the place for camping with his Dervishes. As they informed me of the quality of this Chief and the four Dervishes who followed him, I was willing to do them a civility, and to yield that which they asked with a good grace ; and so I ceded the place to them, and took another which suited me as well. Immediately the place was watered with a quantity of water, and made smooth and level, and, as it was winter and was somewhat cold, they lighted two fires for the five principal Dervishes, who placed themselves between them in order to warm themselves both before and behind. During the same evening, after they had supped, the Governor of the town came to pay his respects to these principal Dervishes, and during their sojourn in the place sent them rice and other things which they were accustomed to eat. When they arrive in any place the Superior sends some of them to beg in the towns and villages, and whatever food they bring, which is given them out of charity, is immediately distributed to all

[1] Āghā, Pers., means lord or master.

in equal portions, each being particular to cook his own rice for himself. Whatever they have over is given every evening to the poor, and they reserve nothing for the following day.

From Chitpour to Balambour, 12 coss; from Balambour to Dantiuar,[1] 11 coss; Dantiuar to Bargant, 17 coss.

Bargant [2] is the territory of a Rājā, where one has to pay customs. On one of my journeys to Agra, when passing by Bargant, I did not see the Rājā, but only his lieutenant, who treated me with great civility, and presented me with rice, butter, and fruits of the season. In return I gave him three waistbands of calico, gold, and silk, four handkerchiefs of coloured cotton, and two bottles, one of brandy and the other of Spanish wine. On my departure he ordered me to be escorted for 4 or 5 coss by twenty horsemen.

When returning from the same journey I sent before me my heavier goods by wagon, and to shorten the road I purposed to return by the same route. I had with me sixty Peons or people of the country, and seven or eight attendants who ordinarily waited on me. One evening, being encamped on the frontiers of the territory of the Rājā of Bargant, all my Peons [3] assembled to tell me that by taking the route through Bargant we should run the risk of being all strangled, and that the Prince of that country spared no one, and lived by robbery alone. That at the least, if I did not engage one hundred other Peons, there was no possibility of escaping the hands of the runners, whom he would send from both sides, and that they were obliged, as much for my safety as their own, to give me this advice. I spent some time disputing with them, and reproaching them with their cowardice; but from fear lest they should not also reproach me for my temerity, I resolved to employ fifty more, and they went to search for them in the neighbouring villages. For traversing

[1] Balambour is Pālanpur, capital of the State of the same name (*Imperial Gazetteer*, xix. 354 f.). Dantiuar is Dāntā, or Dāntawārā, the chief town of the State of the same name (see p. 58 *n.*). It is 136 miles north of Baroda (ibid. xvii. 12 f.). The Antivar of p. 31 is apparently the same place.

[2] Called Bergam on p. 31.

[3] Pion in the original for Peon, Port., a foot soldier; whence the name 'pawn' in chess (Yule, *Hobson-Jobson*, 696 f.).

the territories of the Rājā during three days only, they asked four rupees each, which is as much as one gives them for a month. On the following day, when I wished to start, my Peons, showing themselves to be obstructive and irresolute, came to tell me that they would leave me, and that they did not wish to risk their lives, asking me not to write to their Chief at Agra, who was answerable for their not leaving me against my wish. There were three of my personal servants who also treated me as the others had done, and there remained with me only he who led my horse, my coachman, and three other attendants with whom I started under the protection of God, who has always aided me in my journeys. At about a coss from the place whence I started I perceived, on turning round, some of these Peons, who followed me at a distance. Having ordered my carriage to stop to await them, I told the first who advanced that if they wished to come with me they should march around my carriage and not follow at a distance; and seeing them to be still timid and irresolute, I said that I did not require cowards in my service, and dismissed them for the last time. When I had travelled another coss, I perceived on the side of a mountain about fifty horsemen, of whom four separated to advance towards me. When I saw them I got out of the carriage at once, and having thirteen fire-arms, I gave a gun to each of my people. The horsemen approaching, I placed the carriage between them and me, and got ready to fire, in case they prepared to attack me. But they at once made me a sign that I had nothing to fear, and one of them said that it was the Prince who was hunting, and who had sent them to ask what stranger passed through his territory; I replied I was the same Frank [1] who had passed five or six weeks previously. By good fortune, the lieutenant of the Rājā, to whom I had presented the brandy and Spanish wine, followed close behind these four horsemen, and having assured me how rejoiced he was to see me again, asked me forthwith if I had any wine. I told him that I never travelled without it; and in fact I was provided, the English and Dutch having presented me at Agra with several bottles. Immediately on the lieutenant returning to the Rājā, he him-

[1] Franguy in the original.

self came to meet me, and assuring me that I was welcome, told me that he wished me to halt at a place which he indicated under certain trees, a coss and a half from where we were, and that he would not fail to come to drink with me. He came towards evening, and we remained there two days together to amuse ourselves; and the Rājā summoned the Baladines,[1] without whom the Persians and Indians do not think they can enjoy themselves properly. On my departure, the Rājā gave me two hundred horsemen to accompany me for three whole days to the frontiers of his country, and I was let go for three or four pounds of tobacco, which was all the present I made them. When I arrived at Ahmadābād the people could hardly believe that I had received such good treatment from a Prince who had the reputation of ill-treating all strangers who passed through his country.

From Bargant to Bimal, 15 coss; from Bimal to Modra, 15 coss; from Modra to Chalaour, 10 coss. Chalaour[2] is an ancient town upon a mountain surrounded with walls, and difficult of access; formerly it was a strong place. There is a tank on the top of the mountain, and another below, between which and the foot of the mountain is the road to the town. From Chalaour to Cantap, 12 coss; from Cantap to Setlana, 15 coss; from Setlana to Palavaseny, 14 coss; from Palavaseny to Pipars, 11 coss; from Pipars to Mirda, 16 coss.

From Dāntawārā to Mirda it is three days' journey,[3] and

[1] Baladines, from the Portuguese Baladeira; the more usual form is Bayadère among authors; but it is never heard, and is practically unknown in India, as a name for Nāchnīs or dancing girls. (See Yule, *Hobson-Jobson*, 75.)

[2] Jālor, a town in the State of Jodhpur or Mārwār in Rājputānā. The fort, 800 yards long by 400 yards wide, is on an eminence 1,200 feet high, and commands the town. It is of considerable strength, and still contains two tanks. It was famous in Rājput history, being several times mentioned in Tod, *Annals of Rājasthān*; Erskine, *Gazetteer, Western States, Rājputānā*, 189 f. The stages are: Bhīnmāl, also a famous place (*Imperial Gazetteer*, viii. 111), and Modrā, to Jālor. There is apparently some confusion between Baglānā and Dāntawārā, as the distances cannot be reconciled with Bāglānā, mentioned on p. 69 above.

[3] This statement is somewhat inconsistent with the route given, which represents 9 stages and 125 coss. The stages are: Khandap;

it is a mountainous country belonging to semi-independent Rājās or Princes, who pay some tribute to the Great Mogul. But in return, the Great Mogul appoints them to important posts in his armies, from which they derive much more than the tribute which they are obliged to pay him.

Mirda is a large town, but badly built. When I arrived there, during one of my journeys in India, all the caravansarāīs were full of people, because the aunt of Shāhjahān, wife of Shāista Khān, was then on her way, taking her daughter to marry her to Sultān Shujā', second son of Shāhjahān. I was obliged to order my tent [1] to be pitched upon a bank where there were large trees on both sides, and two hours afterwards I was much surprised to see fifteen or twenty elephants which came to break off as much as they could of these great trees. It was a strange thing to see them break large branches with their trunks, as we break a piece of faggot.[2] This injury was done by order of the Begam to avenge herself of an affront by the inhabitants of Mirda, who had not received her, and had not made a present as they ought to have done.

From Mirda to Boronda, 12 coss; from Boronda to Coëtchiel, 18 coss; from Coëtchiel to Bandar-Sonnery, 14 coss; from Bandar-Sonnery to Ladona, 16 coss; from Ladona town to Chasou, 12 coss; from Chasou to Nuali, 17 coss; from Nuali to Hindoo, 19 coss; from Hindoo to Baniana, 10 coss.

These two last places are towns where, as in all the surrounding country, round indigo cake is made, and being the best of all the varieties of indigo it is consequently twice as dear.

From Baniana to Vettapour, 14 coss; Vettapour is a very old town where they make woollen carpets. From Vettapour to Agra, 12 coss; from Surat to Agra there are in all 415

Sītalwānā; Palāsnī; Pīpār; Mertā or Mairtā. Mertā is one of the most famous places in Rājput history, the scene of several bloody battles, described by Tod (Erskine, *Gazetteer, Western States, Rājputāna*, 203 ff.).

[1] This is the obvious meaning, tante being in the original a misprint for tente.

[2] The mahouts of the present day sometimes, for similar reasons, make their elephants do injury of this kind. (See p. 48.)

coss. If one could make equal stages of 13 coss each, he would accomplish the journey in thirty-three days; but, since one rests and halts in certain places, the journey lasts generally from thirty-five to forty days.[1]

CHAPTER VI

Route from Ispahān to Agra by Kandahār [2]

I HAVE already given an exact description of a part of this route, having conducted the reader as far as Kandahār.[3] It now remains for me to take him from Kandahār to Agra, to which there are only two routes via Kābul or Multān respectively. The latter is shorter than the other by ten days, but the caravan scarcely ever takes it, because from Kandahār to Multān it is a desert country almost all the way, and because one must march sometimes for three or four days without meeting water. Hence the most common and beaten track is by Kābul. From Kandahār to Kābul there are 24 stages; from Kābul to Lahore, 22; from Lahore to Delhi or Jahānābād, 18; and from Delhi to Agra, 6: these, with the 60 stages from Ispahān to Farah,[4] and the 20 from Farah to Kandahār, make in all, from Ispahān to Agra, 150 stages. But those merchants who have urgent business sometimes join in parties of three or four on horseback, and accomplish the journey in half the time, that is to say in 60 or 75 days.

Multān [5] is a town where quantities of calicoes are made, and they used to be all carried to Tatta before the sands had obstructed the mouth of the river; but since the passage has

[1] The stages from Mertā to Agra are: Bharūndā; Kuchhel; Bandar-Sindrī; Ludānā on the Bandī river in Jaipur; Chaksū; Lohwān; Hindaun, a partially ruined city in Jaipur (*Imperial Gazetteer*, xiii. 135); Bayānā, in Bharatpur State, an important town in Rājput history (*ibid.* vii. 137: Cunningham, *Archaeological Survey*, ii. 54, vi. 50, xx. 61): Fatehpur Sīkrī, the site of Akbar's famous palace, 23 miles west of Agra (*Imperial Gazetteer*, xii. 84; E. W. Smith, *The Mughal Architecture of Fatehpur Sīkrī*, Allahabad, 1894–5).

[2] Candahar in original. See p. 4.

[3] *Persian Travels*, bk. v, ch. xxiv, p. 693, Fr. ed., 4to. 1676.

[4] Farat in the original.

[5] Multān, on the Chenāb river.

been closed for large vessels they are taken to Agra, and from Agra to Surat, as are also some of the goods which are made at Lahore. As this carriage is very expensive, but few merchants go to make investments either at Multān or Lahore, and indeed many of the artisans have deserted; this has much diminished the revenues of the Emperor in these provinces. Multān is the place from whence all the Banians migrate who come to trade in Persia, where they follow the same occupation as the Jews, as I have elsewhere said, and they surpass them in their usury. They have a special law which permits them on certain days to eat fowls, and they have only one wife between two or three brothers, of whom the eldest is regarded as the father of the children.[1] Numerous Baladins and Baladines, who hail from this town, spread themselves in divers parts of Persia.

I come to the route from Kandahār to Agra by Kābul and Lahore. From Kandahar to Charisafar, 10 coss; Charisafar to Zelaté, 12 coss; Zelaté to Betazy, 8 coss; Betazy to Mezour, 6 coss; Mezour to Carabat, 17 coss; Carabat to Chakenicouzé, 17 coss.[2]

Between Kandahār and Chakenicouzé,[3] on the frontier of India, there is a country where many small Chiefs rule and render some allegiance to the King of Persia.

From Chakenicouzé to Caboul, 40 coss.[4] In these 40 coss

[1] Tavernier was misled in believing that the Bānias of the Panjāb and Sind ate meat of any kind or practised polyandry. (See Rose, *Glossary*, ii. 59 ff.) They are widely spread in Persia, Central Asia, and in ports along the Arabian Sea (Curzon, *Persia*, i. 384, 401, 407, 435; Badger, *Hist. of the Imams and Sayyids of 'Oman*, 81). On their reputation for astuteness in trade see Fryer, i. 211; Grose, *Voyage to the East Indies*, 169; Bowrey, 27; *Bombay Gazetteer*, ix. pt. i, 78.

[2] The route is Shahr-i-safā, 'city of purity' (Macgregor, *Central Asia* 672, Babur, *Memoirs*, trans. Erskine, 226); Kalāt-i-Ghilzāī; Āb-i-tāzī; Mansūr; Kārābāgh; Shigānū. See Jadunath Sarkar, *India of Aurangzīb*, introd. civ f.

[3] Colonel Yule suggests that Chakenicouzé may have been the Shigānu of Broadfoot and Sekaneh of Babur's *Memoirs*, trans. Erskine, 220. If not identical with Ghaznī, it was probably in or near its latitude. Ghaznī is 85 miles SW. of Kābul, and 145 miles NW. of Kalāt-i-Ghilzāī.

[4] The total distance here given from Kandahār to Kābul is 110 coss. The distance in miles is 318, which would indicate a coss of 3 miles nearly. Tieffenthaler gives the stages from Kābul to Ghaznī as follows:

of road there are only three poor villages, where bread and barley for the horses can seldom be obtained, and the safest plan therefore is to carry a supply with you. In the months of July and August a hot wind prevails in these quarters, which suffocates and kills suddenly, like the wind of which I have spoken in my accounts of Persia, which prevails also in certain seasons near Babylon and Mosul.[1]

Kābul is a large town, fairly well fortified, and it is there the people of Usbek [2] come every year to sell their horses; they estimate that the trade in them amounts annually to more than 60,000.[3] They take there from Persia also, many sheep and other cattle, and it is the great meeting-place for Tartary, India, and Persia. You can obtain wine there, and articles of food are very cheap.

Before passing further it is necessary to note here a curious fact concerning the people called Augans,[4] who inhabit (the country) from Kandahār to Kābul, towards the mountains of Balch,[5] and are powerful men, and great thieves at night. It is the custom of these Indians to clean and scrape the tongue every morning with a small curved piece of a particular root.[6]

Kābul to Argandī (Urghandī) 12 milles, thence to Jadussia 12 milles, thence to Scheschgaon (Shashgāo) 12 milles, thence to Gasni (Ghaznī) 10 milles, total 46 milles. (*Geog. de l'Ind.*, Bernoulli, Berlin, 1791, p. 69.)

[1] 'All over Kandahār province the summer heat is intense, and the sīmoon is not unknown. The hot season through this part of the country is rendered more trying by frequent dust storms and fiery winds' (*Ency. Brit.*, i. 310).

[2] A Turkish tribe of Central Asia (Yule, *Hobson-Jobson*, 960).

[3] Rupees.

[4] Afghāns. Mr. Longworth Dames has shown that Pathān is the true name of this people, and that the term Afghān, first applied by foreigners, appears to be of literary origin; it has now been adopted as a polite designation by the upper classes (Sir P. Sykes, *Hist. of Persia*, 2nd ed., ii. 217).

[5] Balkh, an ancient city of Turkestan, south of the Oxus.

[6] Accounts of this practice among the tribes on the North-west Frontier have not been traced. But in western India, Brāhmans, after cleaning their teeth, break the twig in half, and with one piece scrape their tongues (Mrs. S. Stevenson, *Rites of the Twice-born*, 212). In Siam, 'whatever confidence the Siamese may have in this mixture [betel] as to keeping their mouths clean, it is remarked that the tongue is in holes in several places, and they are obliged to scrape it every morning to

This causes them to throw up a quantity of foul matter, and excites them to vomit. And those who inhabit the country on these frontiers of Persia and India practise the same thing, nevertheless, they vomit but little in the morning; but instead, when they take their meals, as soon as they have eaten two or three mouthfuls, their heart is disturbed, and they are obliged to vomit, after which they return to eat with appetite. If they do not do so they live only to the age of thirty years, and they become dropsical.

From Caboul to Bariabé,[1] 19 coss; Bariabé to Niméla, 17 coss; Niméla to Alyboüa, 19 coss; Alyboüa to Taka, 17 coss; Taka to Kiemry, 6 coss; Kiemry to Chaour, 14 coss; Chaour to Novéchaar, 14 coss; Novéchaar to Atek,[2] 19 coss.

Attock is a town situated on a promontory where two great rivers meet. It is one of the best fortresses of the Great Mogul, and they do not permit any stranger to enter it if he does not hold a passport from the Emperor. The Reverend Jesuit Father Roux, and his companion, wishing to go by this route to Ispahān, and not having obtained a passport from the Emperor, were sent back from thence, and returned to Lahore, where they embarked upon the river to go to Sind, from whence they passed into Persia. From Atek to Calapané, 16 coss; Calapané to Roupaté, 16 coss; Roupaté to Toulapéca, 16 coss; Toulapéca to Keraly, 19 coss; Keraly to

cleanse the slime which these drugs cause (Turpin, *History of Siam*, in Pinkerton, *Voyages and Travels*, ix. 608).

[1] Col. Yule states that Barikāb is often mentioned by writers (Babur, *Memoirs*, ed. Erskine, pp. 275, 278, 290, and Moorcroft, ii, p. 373). There are caves hollowed in a bank there for the accommodation of travellers (Vigne, *Narrative of a Visit to Ghuzni, &c.*, 1840, pp. 239–40). Tieffenthaler mentions two three-day itineraries between Peshāwar and Attock as follows, the total distance being 30 so-called Indian milles —Peschaver to Schahabad 6 milles, to Akora 12 milles, to Attak 12 milles. The second is more detailed: Peschaver to Djouigousar 3 milles, Djouigousar to Schahabad 4 milles, Schahabad to Noschera (Naushahra) 8 milles, Noschera to Girdab 4 milles, Girdab to Akora 4 milles, Akora to Neri 4 milles, Neri to Khairābād 3 milles, thence across the Indus to Attak. (*Geog. de l'Indoustan*, par J. Bernoulli, Berlin, 1791.) Tavernier's route from Kābul to Attock was: Barikāb; Nimlabāgh; 'Alībāghān or Ilāhabāgha; Dakka; Khaibar; Peshāwar; Naushahra; Attock. See Jadunath Sarkar, *India of Aurangzīb*, Introd., cii ff.

[2] Attock is situated near the junction of the Indus and Kābul rivers.

Zerabad, 16 coss; Zerabad to Imiabad, 18 coss; Imiabad to Lahor, 18 coss.[1]

Lahore is the capital of a kingdom, and is built on one of the five rivers which descend from the mountains of the north to go to swell the Indus, and give the name of Penjab [2] to all the region which they water. This river at the present day flows at a quarter of a league distant from the town, being liable to change its bed, and the neighbouring fields often sustain much damage from its great overflowings.[3] The town is large, and extends more than a coss in length, but the greater part of the houses, which are higher than those of Agra and Delhi, are falling into ruins, the excessive rains having overthrown a large number. The palace of the Emperor is rather fine, and is no longer, as it was formerly, on the margin of the river, which has withdrawn, as I have said, about a quarter of a league. One can obtain wine at Lahore.[4]

I shall remark, *en passant*, that after leaving Lahore, and the kingdom of Kashmīr which adjoins it on the north, all the women are naturally unprovided with hair on any part of the body,[5] and the men have very little of it on the chin.

From Lahor to Menat-Kan, 12 coss; Menat-Kan to Faty-abad, 15 coss; Faty-abad to Sera-dakan, 15 coss; Sera-dakan to Sera-balour, 15 coss; Sera-balour to Sera-douraï, 12 coss; Sera-douraï to Serinde, 17 coss; Serinde town to Sera Mogoul, 15 coss; Sera Mogoul to Sera Chabas, 14 coss; Sera Chabas to Dirauril, 17 coss; Dirauril to Sera-Crindal,

[1] It has been suggested by Mr. A. B. Wynne, who knows this country well, that Roupaté should be identified with Rawāt, near the Manikyālā tope, 16 miles south of Rāwalpindi. The route is: Attock to Kālā kī Sarāī; Rawāt; Tulpurī; Kariālā, Sarāī Ālamgīr; Wazīrābād; Amīnābād; Lahore.

[2] Panj-āb, Pers., 'five waters or rivers'.

[3] The changes in the course of the river Rāvī are noticed in *Imperial Gazetteer*, xvi. 112.

[4] No inconsiderable recommendation in the eyes of Tavernier, who makes frequent references to the wine which he carried with him on his journeys, and with which he delighted to entertain his friends.

[5] In the case of women, the absence of hair was probably due to the use of depilatories, common among Musalmān women. See Ja'far Sharīf, *Islām in India*, Oxford, 1921, 68, 305.

14 coss; Sera-Crindal to Guienaour, 21 coss; Guienaour to Dehly, 24 coss.[1]

Before proceeding further it should be remarked that nearly all the way from Lahore to Delhi, and from Delhi to Agra, is like a continuous avenue planted throughout with beautiful trees on both sides, which is very pleasant to the view;[2] but in some places they have been allowed to perish and the people have not taken care to plant others.

Delhi is a large town, near the river Jumna,[3] which runs from north to south, then from west to east, and after having passed Agra and Kadioue,[4] loses itself in the Ganges. Since Shāhjahān has caused the new town of Jahānābād to be built, to which he has given his name, and where he preferred to reside rather than at Agra, because the climate is more temperate, Delhi has become much broken down and is nearly all in ruins, only sufficient of it remaining standing to afford a habitation to the poor. There are narrow streets and houses of bamboo as in all India, and only three or four nobles of the court reside at Delhī, in large enclosures, in which they have their tents pitched. Here also the Reverend Jesuit Father who was at the court had his dwelling.

Jahānābād, like Delhi, is a great straggling town, and a simple wall separates them. All the houses of private persons are large enclosures, in the middle of which is the dwelling, so that no one can approach the place where the

[1] The route is: Lahore to Amānat Khān; Fatehpur; Dehkhān; Phillaur; Daurāhī; Sirhind, Sahrind; Mughal Sarāī; Shāhābād; Tarāwarī; Karnāl; Gannaur; Delhi.

[2] On the map which accompanies the French edition of 1713 this avenue is represented; it is mentioned by Bernier (p. 284) and by Sir T. Roe (ii. 537, 544).

[3] Delhi, on the Jumna, here Gemna, and elsewhere spelt Gemené. The distance from Gannaur is only about 36 miles. Tavernier distinguishes between Old Delhi and Shāhjahānābād. Shāhjahān occupied Shāhjahānābād or New Delhi in 1648, ten years after the beginning of its building.

[4] Kadioue is not, as Ball suggested, Etāwah, but Khajwā or Khajuhā in the Fatehpur District, United Provinces, the place where Sultān Shujā' was defeated on January 5, 1659. See Jadunath Sarkar, *Hist. of Aurangzīb*, ii. 143 ff. The place is not on the bank of the Ganges, but 10 miles distant from that river. Bernier (p. 75) calls the place Kadjoüé, which confirms its identification with the Kadioue of Tavernier.

women are shut up. The greater part of the nobles do not live in the town, but have their houses outside, so as to be near the water. When entering Jahānābād from the Delhi side, a long and wide street is to be seen, where, on both sides, there are arches under which the merchants carry on their business, and overhead there is a kind of platform.[1] This street leads to the great square, where the Emperor's palace is; and there is another very straight and wide one, which leads to the same square near another gate of the palace, in which there are the houses of the principal merchants who keep no shops.

The Emperor's palace is a good half league in circuit.[2] The walls are of fine cut stone, with battlements, and at every tenth battlement there is a tower. The fosses are full of water and are lined with cut stone. The principal gate has nothing magnificent about it,[3] nor has the first court, where the nobles are permitted to enter on their elephants.

Leading from this court there is a long and wide passage which has on both sides handsome porticoes, under which there are many small chambers where some of the horse-guards lodge. These porticoes are elevated about two feet from the ground, and the horses, which are fastened to rings outside, take their feed on the edge. In certain places there are large doors which lead to different apartments, as to that of the women, and to the Judges' court. In the middle of this passage there is a channel full of water, which leaves a good roadway on either side, and forms little basins at equal distances. This long passage leads to a large court where the Omrahs,[4] i.e. the great nobles of the kingdom, who resemble the Bachas [5] in Turkey, and the Khāns in Persia, constitute

[1] Known at present as the Faiz Bāzār.

[2] The fort measures 1,600 feet east and west, by 3,200 feet north and south, exclusive of the gateways (Fanshawe, *Delhi Past and Present*, 22).

[3] Fergusson, on the contrary, describes the gate as 'the noblest entrance known to belong to any existing palace' (*Indian and Eastern Architecture*, 1910, ii. 309), and compare Fanshawe, p. 22.

[4] Omerahs and Omrahs in the original for *Umarā*, Arabic pl. of *Amīr*. (See Yule, *Hobson-Jobson*, 637.)

[5] Bachas for Pachas. Chardin quaintly says of the two modes of spelling that bacha means Head of the King; and pacha, Feet of the

the bodyguard. There are low chambers around this court for their use, and their horses are tethered outside their doors.

From this second court a third is entered by a large gate, by the side of which there is, as it were, a small room raised two or three feet from the ground. It is where the royal wardrobe is kept, and whence the khil'at [1] is obtained whenever the Emperor wishes to honour a stranger or one of his subjects. A little farther on, over the same gate, is the place where the drums, trumpets, and hautboys are kept,[2] which are heard some moments before the Emperor ascends his throne of justice, to give notice to the Omrahs, and again when the Emperor is about to rise. When entering this third court you face the Dīvān where the Emperor gives audience. It is a grand hall elevated some four feet above the ground floor, and open on three sides. Thirty-two marble columns sustain as many arches, and these columns are about four feet square with their pedestals and some mouldings.[3] When Shāhjahān commenced the building of this hall he intended that it should be enriched throughout by wonderful works in mosaic, like those in the chapel of the Grand Duke in Italy; but having made a trial upon two or three pillars to the height of two or three feet, he considered that it would be impossible to find enough stones for so considerable a design, and that moreover it would cost an enormous sum of money; this compelled him to stop the work, and content himself with a representation of different flowers.

In the middle of this hall, and near the side overlooking the court, as in a theatre, they place the throne when the Emperor comes to give audience and administer justice. It is a small bed of the size of our camp beds, with its four columns, the canopy, the back, a bolster, and counterpane; all of which are covered with diamonds.[4]

King (*Voyages*, Amsterdam, ed. 1711, vol. i, p. 35). The true explanation being, as Colonel Yule states (*Hobson-Jobson*, 70), that as Arabic has no p, they have substituted b, which the Turks have adopted.

[1] Khil'at (See p. 18.). This wardrobe was known as the Toshakhāna.

[2] The Naubat- or Naqqār-khāna (Bernier, 260; Fanshawe, 23, 26).

[3] It was sometimes called Chihal Sitūn, the hall of 'forty pillars'.

[4] Manucci (i. 88) says: 'It is like a table, adorned with all kinds of precious stones and flowers in enamel and gold. There are three

When the Emperor takes his seat, however, they spread on the bed a cover of gold brocade, or of some other rich quilted stuff, and he ascends it by three small steps of two feet in length. On one side of the bed there is a parasol elevated on a handle of the length of a short pike,[1] and to each column of the bed one of the Emperor's weapons is attached, to one his shield, to another his sword, next his bow, his quiver, and arrows, and other things of that kind.

In the court below the throne there is a space twenty feet square, surrounded by balustrades, which on some occasions are covered with plates of silver, and at others with plates of gold. At the four corners of this space the four Secretaries of State are seated, who both in civil as well as criminal matters fulfil the rôles of advocates. Several nobles place themselves around the balustrade, and here also is placed the music, which is heard while the Emperor is in the Dīvān This music is sweet and pleasant, and makes so little sound that it does not disturb those present from the serious occupations in which they are engaged. When the Emperor is seated on his throne, some great noble stands by him, most frequently his own children. Between eleven o'clock and noon the Nawāb,[2] who is the first Minister of State, like the Grand Vizir in Turkey, comes to make a report on what has passed in the chamber where he presides, which is at the entry of the first court, and when he has finished speaking, the Emperor rises. But it must be remarked that from the time the Emperor seats himself on his throne till he rises, no one, whosoever he may be, is allowed to leave the palace; though I am bound to say that the Emperor was pleased to exempt me from this rule, which is general for every one—and here, in a few words, is how it occurred.

cushions, a large one five spans in diameter, and circular, which serves as a support to the back, and two other square ones, one on each side, also a most lovely mattress. For in Turkey and throughout the whole of Hindustān, they do not sit upon chairs, but upon carpets or mattresses, with their legs crossed.' Cf. Bernier, 260 ff., for the etiquette at the Emperor's receptions.

[1] Demi-pique in the original. This is the Āftābgīr, 'sun-seizing' (*Āīn*, i. 50).

12 [2] Nabab in original, for Nawāb. The Wazīr was Ja'far Khān.

Wishing one day, while the Emperor was in the Dīvān, to leave the palace on urgent business which could not by any means be deferred, the Captain of the guards caught me by the arm, and told me roughly that I should not pass out. I argued with him some time, but at length, seeing that he would treat me with violence, I put my hand to my canjare,[1] and would have struck him in the rage I was in if three or four guards, who saw my action, had not restrained me. Happily for me the Nawāb, who was uncle of the Emperor, passed at the moment, and being informed of the subject of our quarrel, ordered the Captain of the guards to let me go out. He reported to the Emperor in due course what had occurred, and in the evening the Nawāb sent one of his people to tell me that His Majesty had notified that I might enter and leave the palace as I was pleased while he was in the Dīvān, for which I went on the following day to thank the Nawāb.

Towards the middle of the same court there is a small channel which is about six inches wide, where, while the Emperor is on his seat of justice, all strangers who attend the audience must stop. They are not allowed to pass it without being called, and even ambassadors themselves are not exempted from this rule. When an ambassador has arrived at the channel, the officer in charge of the introductions calls out towards the Dīvān, where the Emperor is seated, that such an ambassador wishes to speak to His Majesty. Then a Secretary of State repeats it to the Emperor, who very often does not appear to hear, but some time after lifts his eyes, and throwing them upon the ambassador, conveys a sign through the same Secretary that he may approach.[2]

From the hall of the Dīvān you pass on the left to a terrace from whence you see the river, and thence the Emperor enters

[1] Canjare for khanjar, Hind., a kind of dagger. Most of the khanjar in the Indian Museum have doubly-curved blades, and are about 12 inches long. In the *Āīn*, pl. xii, no. 5, it is shown as a bent dagger with a double curve in the blade and a hilt like a sword (Irvine, *Army of the Indian Moghuls*, 86 f.).

[2] An interesting account of the proceedings at the Grand Darbār of Shāhjahān will be found in Jadunath Sarkar, *Studies in Mughal India*, 6 ff. Compare the Court regulations of the Persian Sassanians and of the modern Shāh (Sir P. Sykes, *Hist. of Persia*, 2nd ed., i. 465, ii. 382 f.).

a small chamber from which he passes into his harem. It was in this little chamber I had my first audience with His Majesty, as I shall elsewhere relate.

To the left of this same court where the Dīvān is situated, there is a small well-built mosque, the dome of which is entirely covered by lead, and so thoroughly well gilt that some indeed believe that the whole is of massive gold.[1] This is where the Emperor goes daily to pray, save on Friday, when he visits the Grand Mosque, which is very magnificent, and is situate on a lofty platform higher than the houses of the town, and it is reached by many grand flights of stairs. On the day the Emperor goes to the mosque, a large net five or six feet in height is stretched round these stairs lest the elephants might approach them, and out of respect with which the mosque is regarded.

The right side of the court is occupied by porticoes which form a long gallery, elevated about six inches above the ground, and the whole extent of these porticoes constitutes the Emperor's stables, to which there are several doors. They are always full of very fine horses, the least valuable of which has cost 3,000 écus, and some are worth up to 10,000 écus. In front of each door of the stables hangs a kind of screen made of bamboos split like our osiers; but, unlike the way in which we weave our little twigs of osier with osier itself, the bamboo is woven with twisted silk representing flowers, and the work is very elaborate and requires much patience. These screens serve to prevent the flies from tormenting the horses, but that is not deemed sufficient, for two grooms are

[1] 'It is not a little singular, looking at the magnificent mosque which Akbar built in his palace at Fatehpur Sīkrī, and the Motī Masgid, with which Shāhjahān adorned the palace at Agra, that he should have provided no place of worship in his palace at Delhi. The little Motī Masgid which is now found there was added by Aurangzeb. . . . There is no place of prayer within the palace walls, of the time of Shāhjahān, nor, apparently, any intention of providing one. The Jāma Masgid was so near, and apparently part of the same design, that it seems to have been considered sufficient to supply this anomalous deficiency' (Fergusson, ed. 1891, iii. 600 f.; Fanshawe, 451). Possibly the mosque of which Tavernier speaks was only a temporary building, afterwards replaced by the Motī Masjid.

told off to each horse, one of whom is generally occupied in fanning it. There are also screens stretched before the porticoes, as before the doors of the stables, which are lowered and elevated according to necessity; and the floor of the gallery is covered with beautiful carpets, which are taken up in the evening in order to spread the bedding of the horses. This bedding is made of the horse's own droppings dried in the sun, and afterwards somewhat crushed.[1] The horses imported into India, whether from Persia or Arabia, or the country of the Usbeks, undergo a complete change of food, for in India they are given neither hay nor oats. Each horse receives for its portion in the morning two or three balls made of wheaten flour and butter, of the size of our penny rolls.[2] There is much difficulty in accustoming them to this kind of food, and often four or five months pass before it can be accomplished. The groom is obliged to hold the horse's tongue in one hand, and with the other he has to force the ball down its throat. In the sugar-cane or millet season they are given some at midday; and in the evening, an hour or two before sunset, they receive a measure of chick-peas which the groom has crushed between two stones and steeped in water. These take the place of hay and oats. As for the other stables of the Emperor, where he has also some fine horses, they are poor places, badly built, and do not deserve to be mentioned.

The Jumna is a fine river with large boats upon it, and, after passing Agra, it loses its name in the Ganges at Allāhābād. The Emperor keeps many small brigantines at Jahānābād for pleasure, and they are highly decorated after the manner of the country.

[1] This is also the custom in Persia (Wills, *Land of the Lion and Sun*, ed. 1891, p. 101).

[2] To old horses in Persia balls of dough made of barley, flour, and water, the usual camel food, are given (Wills, 103). See 'Horse-bread', with references in the *New English Dict.*, s. v. Tavernier does not mention the Dūb grass, dug up by grass-cutters, which was presumably supplied.

CHAPTER VII

Sequence of the same Route, from Delhi up to Agra

From Dehly to Badelpoura, 8 coss; From Badelpoura to Peluel-ki-sera, 18 coss; From Peluel-ki-sera to Cotki-sera, 15 coss; From Cotki-sera to Cheki-será [1], 16 coss.

At Cheki-sera there is one of the grandest pagodas in India with an asylum for apes, both for those commonly in the place and those from the neighbouring country, where the Banians provide them with food. This pagoda is called Mathura; [2] formerly it was held in much greater veneration by the idolaters than it is at present, the reason being that the Jumna then flowed at the foot of the pagoda,[3] and the Banians, both those of the place and those who came from afar in pilgrimage to perform their devotions there, were able to bathe in the river before entering the pagoda, and after coming out of it before preparing to eat, which they must not do without bathing; besides, they believe that by bathing in running water their sins are more effectually removed. But for some years back the river has taken a northerly course, and flows at a good coss distance from the pagoda; this is the reason why so many pilgrims do not visit it now.

From Cheki-sera to Goodki-sera, 5 coss; From Goodki-sera to Agra, 6 coss.[4]

[1] The stages are probably: Ballabhgarh; Palwal; Kosī; Shaikh kī Sarāī, for Shāh kī Sarāī, the Shāhganj Sarāī, then recently built (Growse, *Mathura*, 120, 127). It is to be noted that Tavernier calls Mathura the Shāh kī Sarāī, and gives the name Mathurā to the temple. A useful examination of this route will be found in Jadunath Sarkar, *India of Aurangzib*, Introd., xcvii f.

[2] Mathurā, or Muttra, on the right bank of the Jumna, about 30 miles above Agra. It was a centre of the Buddhist faith about the year A. D. 400, when visited by the Chinese pilgrim, Fa-Hian. Monkeys still swarm in the city, where they are fed by the inhabitants. In 1669–70 Aurangzeb visited the city, and destroyed many of its temples and shrines (Growse, 36; Smith, *Oxford Hist. of India*, 437).

[3] On the supposed change in the course of the Jumna see Growse, 119 f.

[4] On his second journey Tavernier made the distance from Mathurā to Agra 18 kos, which is about right. In this case he must have omitted one stage. If he made only two marches the natural halt would have 3
been Farah.

Agra is in 27° 31 latitude,[1] in a sandy soil; which is the cause of excessive heat in summer. It is the largest town in India, and was formerly the residence of the Emperors. The houses of the nobles are beautiful and well built, but those of private persons have nothing fine about them, as is the case in all the other towns of India. They are separated from one another, and are concealed by the height of the walls, from fear lest any one should see the women; so it is easy to understand that all these towns have nothing cheerful about them like our towns in Europe. It should be added to this that, Agra being surrounded by sands, the heat in summer is excessive, and it is, in part, this which induced Shāhjahān to abandon the place, and to remove his court to Jahānābād.

All then that is remarkable at Agra is the palace of the Emperor,[2] and some beautiful tombs both near the town and in the environs. The palace of the Emperor is a considerable enclosure with a double wall, which is terraced in some places, and above the wall small dwellings have been built for certain officers of the court. The Jumna flows in front of the palace; but between the wall and the river there is a large square where the Emperor makes his elephants fight.[3] They have purposely selected this spot near the water, because the elephant being excited by his victory, they would not be able to pacify him for a long time if they did not urge him into the river, to effect which it is necessary to use artifice, by attaching to the end of a handpike fuses and petards, which are set on fire to drive him into the water: and

[1] The true latitude of Agra is 27° 10′ 6″.

[2] The palace was commenced during the reign of Ibrāhīm Lodī; but the chief architectural monuments are due to Shāhjahān (*Arch. Survey*, iv. 12). New Delhi or Shāhjahanābād was occupied by the Court in 1648, some ten years after the beginning of the work. The Tāj at Agra was built between 1632 and 1653, but the central mausoleum was ready in 1643. The Pearl mosque was finished in 1653 (Smith, *Oxford Hist.*, 420 f.). The old fort at Agra was built by Salīm or Islām Shāh (A. D. 1545–53–4), and was called Bādalgarh, 'Cloud Fort'. It was blown up in 1556. For its rebuilding by Akbar see Smith, *Akbar the Great Mogul*, 76.

[3] On these animal fights see Fryer, i. 280; Bernier, 276 ff.; Mundy. ii. 127 f., iii, pt. i. 127 f.

when he is two or three feet deep in it he forthwith becomes appeased.

There is a large square on the side of the town in front of the palace, and the first gate, which has nothing magnificent about it, is guarded by some soldiers. Before the Emperor had given up his residence at Agra for that at Jahānābād whenever he went to the country on a visit he entrusted the custody of the palace, where his treasure was, to one of the principal and most trustworthy of his Omrahs, who, until the return of the Emperor, never moved, neither day nor night, from this gate where his lodging was. It was during such an absence that I was permitted to see the palace at Agra. The Emperor having left for Jahānābād, where all the court followed, and even the women too, the government of the palace was conferred on a noble who was a great friend of the Dutch, and, in general, of all the Franks.[1]

M. Velant, chief of the Dutch factory at Agra,[2] as soon as the Emperor had left, went to salute this noble and make him a present, according to the custom. It was worth about 6,000 [3] écus, and consisted of spices, Japanese cabinets, and beautiful Dutch cloths. He invited me to go with him when he went to pay his compliments to the Governor; but this noble was offended at being offered a present, and obliged him to take it back, telling him that, in consideration of the friendship he had for the Franks, he would take only one small cane out of six which formed a part of the gift. They were those Japanese canes which grow in short nodes; it was even necessary to remove the gold with which it had been embellished, as he would not receive it except in its unadorned condition. Compliments having passed on both sides, the Governor asked M. Velant what he desired him to do to serve him; and he having prayed him to have the goodness, as the court was absent, to permit him to see the interior of the palace, it was granted him, and six men were given to accompany us.[4]

[1] Franguis in the original, Franks, i. e. Europeans. (See pp. 5 and 49.)

[2] Bernier (p. 292) speaks of the Dutch factory at Agra.

[3] About £1,350.

[4] For buildings at Agra see Sleeman, *Rambles*, 312 ff., and Syad Muhammad Latif, *Agra*. Tavernier's visit was probably in 1648, as he

The first gate, where, as I have said, the dwelling of the Governor of the palace is situated, is a long and dark arch, after which you enter a large court surrounded with porticoes, like the Place Royale or Luxembourg at Paris. The gallery which is opposite is larger and higher than the others, and is supported by three rows of columns, and under those, on the three other sides of the court, which are narrower and lower, there are several small chambers for the soldiers of the guard. In the middle of the great gallery you see a niche in the wall to which the Emperor obtains access from his harem by a small concealed staircase, and when seated there he looks like a statue. He has no guards about him then, because he has nothing to fear; and because neither before nor behind, from the right nor from the left, can any one approach him. During the great heat he keeps only one eunuch by him, and most frequently one of his children, to fan him. The nobles of the court remain below in the gallery under this niche.

At the end of the court there is, on the left hand, a second gateway which gives entrance to another great court, which is also surrounded by galleries, under which there are also small rooms for some officers of the palace. From this second court you pass into a third, where the King's apartments are situated. Shāhjahān had intended to cover the arch of a great gallery which is on the right hand with silver, and a Frenchman, named Augustin de Bordeaux,[1] was to have done the work. But the Great Mogul seeing there was no one in his kingdom who was more capable to negotiate at Goa an affair with the Portuguese, the work was not done, for, as the ability of Augustin was feared, he was poisoned on his return from Cochin.[2] This gallery is painted with foliage of gold and azure, and the floor is covered with a carpet. There are doors under the gallery giving

would not have been admitted while Shāhjahān was imprisoned there from 1658 till his death in 1666.

[1] On his work at Agra see Smith's notes on Sleeman, *Rambles*, ed. 1915, 319 f. Tavernier's account of the building of the Tāj Mahall is discussed, ibid. 316.

[2] 'The assertion that Augustin was sent to Goa and poisoned is not corroborated from Portuguese sources'—*Journal Royal Asiatic Society*, 1910, p. 1345.

entrance into very small square chambers. I saw two or three of them which were opened for us, and we were told that the others were similar. The three other sides of the court are altogether open, and there is but a simple wall to the height of the support. On the side overlooking the river there is a projecting Dīvān or belvedere, where the Emperor comes to sit when he wishes to enjoy the pleasure of seeing his brigantines, and making his elephants fight. In front of this Dīvān there is a gallery which serves as a vestibule, and the design of Shāhjahān was to cover it throughout with a trellis of rubies and emeralds, which would represent, after nature, grapes green and commencing to become red; but this design, which made a great noise throughout the world, required more wealth than he had been able to furnish, and remains unfinished, having only two or three wreaths of gold with their leaves, as all the rest ought to be, and enamelled in their natural colours, emeralds, rubies, and garnets making the grapes.[1] About the middle of the court you see a great tank for bathing, of forty feet in diameter, and of a single piece of sandstone, with steps cut in the stone itself, both within and without.[2]

As for the tombs in Agra and its environs, there are some which are very beautiful, and every eunuch in the Emperor's harem is ambitious to have as magnificent a tomb built for himself. When they have amassed large sums they earnestly desire to go to Mecca, and take with them rich presents; but the Great Mogul, who does not wish the money to leave his country, very seldom grants them permission, and consequently, not knowing what to do with their wealth, they expend the greater part of it in these burying-places, and thus leave some memorial.

[1] We may compare the unfinished window in the palace of Alaeddin (Sir R. Burton, *The Book of the Thousand Nights and a Night*, ed. 1893, x. 108 ff.).

[2] The reference is apparently to the Bath or Cistern of Jahāngīr, now in the court opposite the Dīwān-i-'āmm. It is nearly 5 feet in height, 4 feet in depth, 8 feet in diameter, and 25 feet in circumference, with an inscription in Persian characters giving the date A. D. 1616, the year in which Jahāngīr married Nūrjahān (Syad Muhammad Latif, *Agra*, 79 f.).

Of all the tombs at Agra, that of the wife of Shāhjahān is the most splendid. He purposely made it near the Tasimacan,[1] where all foreigners come, so that the whole world should see and admire its magnificence. The Tasimacan is a large bazaar, consisting of six large courts all surrounded with porticoes, under which are chambers for the use of merchants, and an enormous quantity of cottons is sold there. The tomb of this Begam, or sultan queen, is at the east end of the town by the side of the river in a large square surrounded by walls, upon which there is a small gallery, as on the walls of many towns in Europe. This square is a kind of garden divided into compartments like our parterres, but in the places where we put gravel there is white and black marble.[2] You enter this square by a large gate, and at first you see, on the left hand, a beautiful gallery which faces in the direction of Mecca, where there are three or four niches where the Moufti[3] comes at fixed times to pray. A little farther than the middle of the square, on the side of the water, you see three great platforms raised one upon the other, with towers at the four corners of each, and a staircase inside, for proclaiming the hour of prayer. There is a dome above, which is scarcely less magnificent than that of the Val de Grace at Paris. It is covered within and without with white marble, the centre being of brick. Under this dome there is an empty tomb, for the Begam is interred under a vault beneath the first platform. The same changes which are made below in this subterranean place are made above around the tomb, for from time to time they change the carpet,

[1] The Tāj, known as Tāj-makān, 'Tāj-house,' Tāj-muqām, 'Tāj residence,' one of which is represented in Tavernier's Tasimacan, Tāj-mahall, 'Tāj palace,' or Tāj-ganj, 'Tāj bāzār', was erected as the tomb of Arjumand Bānū Begam, known as Mumtāz Mahall, 'exalted of the palace,' daughter of 'Āsaf Khān, Wazīr: born 1592, married to Shāhjahān 1612, died in childbed 1631. For the history of the building see Bernier, 294 ff.; Sleeman, *Rambles*, 312 ff.; Mundy, ii. 213 f.; Syad Muhammad Latif, 100 ff.

[2] For the Tāj garden see Mundy, ii. 214 f.; Sleeman, *Rambles*, 317 f.; and for gardens in mediaeval India see *Journal Anthropological Society, Bombay*, vii. 526 ff.; C. M. Villiers Stuart, *The Gardens of the Great Mughals*, 1913.

[3] Mufti, a Turkish title applied to the supreme exponent of the Law.

chandeliers, and other ornaments of that kind, and there are always there some Mollahs [1] to pray. I witnessed the commencement and accomplishment of this great work, on which twenty-two years have been spent, during which twenty thousand men worked incessantly; this is sufficient to enable one to realize that the cost of it has been enormous.[2] It is said that the scaffoldings alone cost more than the entire work, because, from want of wood, they, as well as the supports of the arches, had all to be made of brick; this has entailed much labour and heavy expenditure. Shāhjahān began to build his own tomb on the other side of the river, but the war with his sons interrupted his plan, and Aurangzeb, who reigns at present, is not disposed to complete it. A eunuch in command of 2,000 men guards both the tomb of the Begam and the Tasimacan, to which it is near at hand.

On one side of the town the tomb of King Akbar [3] is to be seen; as for those of the eunuchs they have but a single platform with small chambers at each of the four corners

When you reach Agra from the Delhi side you meet a large bazaar, close to which there is a garden where the King Jahāngīr, father of Shāhjahān, is interred.[4] Over the gate of this garden you see a painting which represents his tomb covered by a great black pall with many torches of white wax, and two Jesuit Fathers at the ends. One is much astounded at seeing that Shāhjahān, contrary to the practice

[1] More correctly Mullā.

[2] The facts have been collected by Smith in his edition of Sleeman's *Rambles*, 316 f.

[3] This was built by Jahāngīr at Sikandrā. For the best account of this building see E. W. Smith, *Akbar's Tomb, Sikandarah, Agra*. Allahabad, 1909; Sleeman, op. cit. 323, 354, 358.

[4] This is a mistake: Jahāngīr was buried at Shāhdara, Lahore. The difficulty is the identification of the building mentioned by Tavernier. Mr. R. Barkley-Smith, Magistrate of Agra, kindly referred the question to Father H. Hosten, who writes: 'I have always understood that the passage in Tavernier applies to Akbar's tomb at Sikandra. When I visited Sikandra in 1912 I looked carefully for the pictures which he mentions, but I could not see anything. Many Christian paintings existed in Jahāngīr's palace about 1608–9: in fact, his whole palace, I mean the public buildings, was covered with Christian paintings.' Tavernier, on his visit, could not have examined the place carefully.

of the Musalmāns, who hold images in abhorrence, has allowed this painting to remain, and it can only be explained because the Emperor his father and he himself had learnt from the Jesuits some principles of mathematics and astrology. But he had not the same indulgence for them in another matter, for on going one day to see a sick Armenian, named Cotgia,[1] ... whom he much loved, and whom he had honoured with splendid appointments, and the Jesuits, who had their house close to that of the Armenian, happening to ring their bell just then, the noise proved displeasing to the Emperor, and as he thought it might inconvenience the sick man, in a rage he commanded it to be removed and hung on the neck of his elephant; this was promptly done. Some days after, the Emperor seeing the elephant with this heavy bell suspended from its neck, thought that so great a weight might injure it, and he therefore ordered it to be carried into the office of the Couteval,[2] which is a sort of barrier where a provost administers justice to those of the quarter, and it has remained there ever since. This Armenian had been brought up with Shāhjahān, and, as he was very clever and an excellent poet, he was high in the good graces of the Emperor, who had given him valuable governorships, but had never been able, either by promises or threats, to induce him to become a Musalmān.

CHAPTER VIII

Route from Agra to Patna and Dacca, towns of the Province of Bengal; and the quarrel which the author had with Shāista Khān, uncle of the King.

I STARTED from Agra for Bengal on the 25th of November 1665[3] and halted the same day at a poor caravansarāī distant

[1] There is a hiatus here in the original, probably Tavernier was uncertain as to the name, Cotgia (for Khwāja, 'lord') being a title.

[2] Kotwāl, i. e. police-magistrate or provost.

[3] Tavernier, p. 301 ff. below, describes how he witnessed the Mogul's festival on the 4th to the 9th of November, and then saw the jewels. Soon afterwards he must have left Delhi so as to reach Agra for this start. (See *Joret*, op. cit., p. 193.)

3 coss[1] from Agra. The 26th [November] I reached Beruzabad, 9 coss. It is a small town, where, on my return, I received 8,000 rupees of the balance of the money which Ja'far Khān owed me for the goods which he had brought from me at Jahānābād.[2] The 27th [November] to Serail Morlides, 9 coss; 28th [November] to Estanja, 14 coss; 29th [November] to Haii-Mal, 12 coss; 30th [November] to Sekandera, 13 coss; 1st of December to Sanqual, 14 coss.[3]

On this day I met 110 wagons, each drawn by 6 oxen, and there was upon each wagon 50,000 rupees. It was the revenue of the Province of Bengal, which, all charges being paid and the purse of the Governor well filled, amounted to 5,500,000 rupees.[4] At one league on this side of Sanqual you cross a river called Sengar,[5] which flows into the Jumna, only at a distance of half a league. You cross this river Sengar by a stone bridge, and when you arrive from the Bengal side, to go to Sironj and Surat, if you wish to shorten the journey by ten days, when quitting the road to Agra you must come as far as this bridge, and cross the river Jumna by boat. Nevertheless the route by Agra is generally taken, because by the other there are five or six days' stony marches, and because one must pass through the territories of Rājās where there is danger of being robbed.

The 2nd [December] I came to a caravansarāï called Cherourabad,[6] 12 coss. Half-way you pass Jahānābād, a small town near which, about a quarter of a league on this side, you pass a field of millet, where I saw a rhinoceros eating stalks of this millet, which a small boy nine or ten years[7] old

[1] Mundy halted at Nūr Mahall kī Sarāī, 1 kos from Agra.

[2] See, for account of this purchase, p. 112.

[3] The route is: Fīrozābād; Sarāī Murlīdās; Etāwa; Ajītmall; Sikandra; Sanklā Jamwārā, 10 miles from Ghātampur. Mundy's stages were Fīrozābād; Shikohābād; Jaswantnagar; Etāwa; Bakhar Khānpur; Jānakī Sarāī; Sikandra; Bhognīpur; Shankar kī Sarāī; Ghātampur.

[4] Tieffenthaler places the revenue of Bengal at 13,006,590 rupees in Akbar's time, and he says that it was 40,000,000 rupees according to Manucci (ii. 414), in the time of Shāhjahān; subsequently it fell to 8,621,200 rupees (*Géog. de l'Ind.*, p. 443). See Bernier, 457; Elliot-Dowson, *Hist. of India*, vii. 138.

[5] Saingour in the original.

[6] Korā Jahānābād.

[7] Tame rhinoceroses, to which a good deal of freedom was allowed,

presented to him. On my approaching he gave me some stalks of millet, and immediately the rhinoceros came to me, opening his mouth four or five times; I placed some in it, and when he had eaten them he continued to open his mouth so that I might give him more.

The 3rd [December] I came to Serrail Chageada, 10 coss; the 4th, to Serrail Atakan, 13 coss; the 5th, to Aurangābād,[1] a large town, 9 coss. Formerly this town had another name, and it is the place where Aurangzeb, who reigns at present, gave battle to his brother Sultān Shujā', who held the government of the whole of Bengal. Aurangzeb having been victorious gave his name to the town, and he built there a handsome house with a garden and a small mosque.

The 6th [December] to Alinchan[2], 9 coss. About two leagues on this side of Alinchan you meet the Ganges. Monsieur Bernier,[3] Physician to the King, and a man named

were formerly not uncommonly kept by the Rājās. Sometimes, as at Baroda, they were performers in the fighting arena, and on such occasions were commonly painted with divers bright colours. Elsewhere Ball has shown that the Kartazon of Megasthenes and the 'Horned Ass' of Ktesias were probably this animal (J. W. McCrindle, *Ancient India as described by Megasthenes and Arrian*, 59); in the latter case the colours which have puzzled so many commentators were, he believed, artificial pigments applied to the hide of the rhinoceros seen by Ktesias, as they are on elephants at the present day (*Proceed. Roy. Irish Academy*, 2nd ser., vol. ii, no. 6, 1885). Chardin describes and figures a rhinoceros from Ethiopia which he saw at Ispahān. He says he did not know whether the animal was found in India (*Voyages*, Amsterdam ed., 1711, vol. viii, p. 133).

[1] The original name of the place was Khajuhā or Khajwā, which was changed to Aurangābād, 'place of the throne,' after the battle in which Shujā' was defeated, on January 5, 1659. See Jadunath Sarkar, *Hist. of Aurangzib*, ii. 143 ff. A Sarāī and hall (bāradarī) erected in honour of his victory, are fine buildings, which have been restored (*Imperial Gazetteer*, xv. 219 f.). The marches from Korā Jahānābād are Sarāī Shāhzāda, Hatgāon, Aurangābād.

[2] Alamchand.

[3] M. Bernier, the well-known historian of the Mogul Empire, was born at Joué-Etiau, in Anjou, in September 1620. In 1654 he went to Syria and Egypt, and from Cairo, where he remained for more than a year, he went to Suez and embarked for India, where he took service as physician to the Great Mogul (*Travels*, Introd. xxi). In 1668 he returned to France, and died in 1688. It is curious that he is not mentioned in the *Ency. Brit.* On his meeting with Tavernier see Bernier, Introd. xxi. 113. Bernier does not mention Rachepot.

hachepot, who was with me, were surprised to see that this river, so much talked about, is not larger than the Seine in front of the Louvre, it being supposed that it equalled in width, at the least, the Danube below Belgrade. There is actually so little water between the months of March and June or July, when the rains commence, that boats are not able to ascend it. On arrival at the Ganges, we each drank a glass of wine which we mixed with water—this caused us some internal disturbance; but our attendants who drank it alone were much more tormented than we were. The Dutch, who have a house on the banks of the Ganges, never drink the water of the river, except after it has been boiled; as for the native inhabitants, they have been accustomed to it from their youth; the Emperor even and all his court drink no other.[1] You see every day a large number of camels which do nothing else but fetch water from the Ganges.

The 7th [December] we came to Halabas,[2] 8 coss. Allāhābād is a large town built on a point of land where the Ganges and the Jumna meet one another. It has a fine castle built of cut stone, with a double ditch, and it is the dwelling of the Governor. He is one of the greatest nobles in India, and as he is troubled with bad health he employs some Persian Physicians, and he then also had in his service M. Claude Maille of Bourges,[3] who practised both surgery and medicine. It was he who advised us not to drink any of the Ganges water,

[1] When Akbar was at Agra or Fatehpur Sīkrī he used to get Ganges water from Soron in the Etah District, when in the Panjāb from Hardwār (*Āīn*, i. 55).

[2] Allāhābād, Ilāhābās of Akbar, at the junction of the Jumna and Ganges.

[3] M. Claude Maillé of Bourges. As we shall see (p. 231 below) a man of this name who had escaped from the Dutch service was, in the year 1652, a not very successful amateur gun-founder for Mīr Jumla; he had after his escape set up as a surgeon to the Nawāb, with an equipment consisting of a case of instruments and a box of ointments which he had stolen from M. Cheteur, the Dutch Ambassador to Golkonda. Tavernier does not mention his identity with this physician which, however, seems more than probable. He states that M. Cheteur left a surgeon named Pitre de Lan with the king of Golkonda. (See p. 241 below. Also see Smith's note on Sleeman, *Rambles*, ed. 1915, p. 560.) Manucci calls him Clodio Malier or Menolhaō (i. 86, iii. 173).

which would produce disturbance of the stomach, but to drink rather the water from wells. The chief of these Persian Physicians whom this Governor had in his pay, one day threw his wife down from the top of a terrace to the ground, impelled apparently to this cruel action by a freak of jealousy. He thought that she was killed, but she had only two or three ribs broken, and the relations of the woman threw themselves at the feet of the Governor to demand justice. The Governor summoned the Physician, and commanded him to withdraw, not wishing to keep him any longer in his service. He obeyed this order, and, having placed his disabled wife in a pallankeen, he departed with all his family. He was not more than three or four marches from the town when the Governor, finding himself unusually ill, sent to recall him, upon which the Physician stabbed his wife, four of his children, and thirteen female slaves, after which he returned to the Governor, who said nothing to him about it, and took him again into his service.

On the 8th I crossed the Ganges in a large boat, having waited from the morning till midday on the bank of the river, till M. Maillé brought a letter from the Governor giving us permission to cross. For on each side there is a Dārogha, who allows no one to pass without an order; and he takes note also of the kind of merchandise carried, each wagon being charged four rupees, and a chariot paying but one, without counting the boat, for which it is necessary to pay separately.

This day the halt was at Saudoul Serail, 16 coss; The 9th at Yakedil-sera, 10 coss; 10th at Bouraky-sera, 10 coss; 11th at Banarou,[1] 10 coss.

Benares [2] is a large and very well-built town, the majority of the houses being of brick and cut stone, and more lofty than those of other towns of India; but it is very inconvenient

[1] The halts are at inns on the road, and therefore difficult to fix. Probably his route was: Sa'adu-llā kī Sarāī; Jagdīs Sarāī; Ahīrbans kī Sarāī. The halts of Mundy (ii. 109) were: Barā Mahall ki Sarāī; Ahīrbans kī Sarāī; Jagdīs kī Sarāī; Mohan Sarāī.

[2] Benares is 74 miles distance to the east of Allāhābād, and 466 south-east of Delhi.

that the streets are so narrow. It has several caravansarāīs, and, among others, one very large and well built. In the middle of the court there are two galleries where they sell cottons, silken stuffs, and other kinds of merchandise. The majority of those who vend the goods are the workers who have made the pieces, and in this manner foreigners obtain them at first hand. These workers, before exposing anything for sale, have to go to him who holds the contract, so as to get the imperial stamp impressed on the pieces of calico or silk, otherwise they are fined and flogged.[1] The town is situated to the north of the Ganges, which runs the whole length of the walls, and two leagues farther down a large river [2] joins it from the west. The idolaters have one of their principal pagodas in Benares, and I shall describe it in Book II, where I shall speak of the religion of the Banians.

About 500 paces from the town, in a north-western direction, there is a mosque where you see several Musalmān tombs, of which some are of a very beautiful design. The most beautiful are placed each in the middle of a garden enclosed by walls which have openings of half a foot square, through which the passers-by can see them. The most considerable of all is like a great square pedestal, each face of which is about forty paces long. In the middle of this platform you see a column of 32 to 35 feet in height, all of a piece, and which three men could with difficulty embrace. It is of sandstone, so hard that I could not scratch it with my knife. It terminates in a pyramid, and has a great ball on the point, and below the ball it is encircled by large beads.[3] All the sides of this tomb are covered with figures of animals cut in relief in the stone, and it has been higher above the

[1] This custom of stamping cloth by officials, as a guarantee of its quality, prevailed in the time of the Mauryas, the mark known as 'the identity stamp' (*abhijnāna mudra* of the Indian writers, *σύσσημον* of the Greek travellers) being usually impressed on the bale with vermilion (Smith, *Oxford Hist. of India*, 58).

[2] This is probably the Barnā, as the Gūmtī is 16 miles off, and joins the Ganges at Saidpur in the Ghāzīpur District. The Barnā is not now a large river, but rather a small stream.

[3] The large beads are representations of the fruit of the emblic myrobalan (Skt. *āmalaka*), a favourite ornament in Hindu architecture.

ground than it now appears; several of the old men who guard some of these tombs having assured me that since fifty years it has subsided more than 30 feet. They add that it is the tomb of one of the kings of Bhutān, who was interred there after he had left his country to conquer this kingdom, from which he was subsequently driven by the descendants of Tamerlane. It is from this kingdom of Bhutān that they bring musk, and I shall give a description of it in Book III.[1]

I remained at Benares on the 12th and 13th, and during these two days there was continual rain; but it did not prevent me from resuming my journey, and on the evening of the 13th I crossed the Ganges with the passport of the Governor. They examine all travellers' baggage before embarking in the boat, personal property pays nothing, and it is only on merchandise that one must pay duty.

The 13th [December] I halted at Baterpour, 2 coss; 14th at Satragy-sera, 8 coss; 15th at Moniarky-sera, 6 coss. During the morning of this day, after having travelled two coss, I crossed a river called Carnasar-sou, and at three coss from thence one crosses another named Saode-sou, and both are crossed by fords. The 16th at Gourmabad, 8 coss.

It is a town on a river called Goudera-sou, and you cross it by a stone bridge. The 17th at Saseron, 4 coss.[2]

Sāsarām[3] is a town at the foot of the mountains, near to

[1] Tavernier seems to refer to the Buddhist remains at Bakariyā Kund, north-west of the city, part of the buildings having been subsequently utilized by the Musalmāns (Sherring, *The Sacred City*, 274 ff.; Greaves, *Kāshi*, 73 ff.). The pillar is one of Asoka's edict pillars which, according to the Chinese pilgrim, Hiuen Tsiang, stood north-east of the city. It was destroyed in a riot in 1809, and only the stump, known as Lāt Bhairon, survives (V. A. Smith, Hastings, *Ency. Religion and Ethics*, ii. 466). The mention of the tomb of the King of Bhutān may be due to confusion with Buddhism.

[2] The route was apparently: Bahādurpur; Sarāī Sīrsī; Mohaniā kī Sarāī; Khurramābād, now Jahānābād; Sāsarām. Mundy halted at Bahādurpur, Sarāī Sīrsī, Sāwant kī Sarāī, Khwāja kī Sarāī, Khurramābād, and Sāsarām. The rivers crossed were the Karamnāsā, Durgāvatī and Kudrā, for which see *Imperial Gazetteer*, xxii. 186 f.; *Āīn-i-Akbarī*, ii. 151.

[3] In the tank at Sāsarām are the tombs of Sher Shāh, the Afghān, who drove Humāyūn from his throne, and was killed in 1545 while directing the siege of Kālanjar, Bānda District, Bundelkhand. His son, Salīm

which there is a large tank. You see a small island in the middle, where there is a very beautiful mosque, in which there is the tomb of a Nawāb named Salīm Khān, who had it built during the time he was Governor of the Province. There is a fine stone bridge to cross into the island, which is all flanked and paved with large cut stones. On one of the sides of the tank there is a large garden, in the middle of which is another beautiful tomb of the son of the same Nawāb, Salīm Khān, who succeeded his father in the government of the Province. When you wish to go to the mine of Soulmelpour,[1] of which I shall speak in the last book of this narrative, you leave the main road to Patna, and turn straight southwards by Ekberbourg [2] and the famous fort of Rhodas, as I shall say in the same place. The 18th [December] I crossed, in a boat, the river Sonsou,[3] which comes from the mountains of the south ; and, after crossing it, those who have goods have to pay a certain duty. This day my halt was at Daoud-Nagar-Sera [4] where there is a fine tomb, 9 coss. The 19th to Halva-sera,[5] 10 coss ; 20th to Aga-sera, 9 coss. In the morning I met 130 elephants, both large and small, which were being taken to Delhi to the Great Mogul. The 21st to Patna, 10 coss.

or Islām Shāh, died at Gwalior in 1544, and was also buried at Sāsarām. For an account of the place see Buchanan, in Martin, *Eastern India*, i. 424, and a photograph in Smith, *Oxford Hist. of India*, 329.

[1] Soulmelpour, a misprint for Soumelpour (vol. ii, p. 63, where it is shown to have been situated in Palāmau). It is also mentioned by Tieffenthaler as Sommelpour, thirty milles SSE. of Rohtās. (*Géog. de l'Ind., traduit par Bernoulli*, Berlin, 1791, p. 433.)

[2] Ekberbourg, which is misprinted in the puzzling-looking form of Exberbourg in the English translation by John Phillips (1684), is undoubtedly identical with Akbarpur, a village at the foot of the hill upon which the remains of the old fort of Rohtās are still to be seen. A small portion has been restored and made habitable. Ball has described this neighbourhood in *Jungle Life in India*, p. 349. Of the substitution of the French *bourg* for the Indian *pur* these pages furnish several examples. Mundy (ii. 167) calls it Ecbarpore.

[3] The river Son, which rises in the west, near Amarkantak.

[4] Dāūdnagar in Gaya District. The tomb is not mentioned in *Imperial Gazetteer*, xi. 199.

[5] Arwal on the Son, formerly, as stated by Tieffenthaler, famous for its paper factory. The original village has been swept away by the river, and a new one bears the name. It is forty-one miles distant from Patna, so that the value of the coss is here also about two miles.

Patna is one of the largest towns in India, and is situated on the margin of the Ganges, on its western side,[1] and it is not less than two coss in length. The houses are not better than those in the majority of the other towns of India, and they are nearly all roofed with thatch or bamboo. The Dutch Company has an establishment there on account of the trade in saltpetre,[2] which is refined at a large village called Chaprā, situated on the right bank of the Ganges, 10 coss above Patna.

Arriving at Patna with M. Bernier, we encountered some Dutchmen in the street who were returning to Chaprā,[3] but who halted their carriages in order to salute us. We did not separate before we had emptied together two bottles of Shīrāz wine in the open street, regarding which there is nothing to remark upon in this country, where one lives without ceremony, and with perfect liberty.

I remained eight days in Patna, during which time an occurrence happened which will show the reader that unnatural crime does not rest unpunished by the Musalmāns. A Mimbachi[4] who commanded 1,000 foot disgraced a young boy who was in his service; . . . the boy, overwhelmed with grief, chose his time to avenge himself, and being one day out hunting with his master, and removed from the attendants by about a quarter of a league, he came behind him and cut off his head with his sword. He then rode immediately to the town at full speed, crying aloud that he had slain his master

[1] On the right bank.

[2] An account of the manufacture of saltpetre and the decadence of this once valuable trade will be found in the *Economic Geology of India*, 499; Watt, *Econ. Prod.*, 972 ff.; Bernier, 440. 'The Dutch have a Factory here [Patna] alsoe, for procureinge of Saltpeeter, but live with little freedom or Enjoyment of any worldly pleasure here, dareinge not to presume to Enter any of the Gates of the City without leave from some of the great Officers' (Bowrey, 225).

[3] Choupar in the original, Chaprā (Sœpra of Dutch writers), headquarters of Sāran District, Bengal; owing to the recession of the Ganges from it its importance has diminished. At the end of the 18th century the French, Dutch, and Portuguese had factories there, and the saltpetre of the district was specially famous. (*Imperial Gazetteer*, x. 175).

[4] Mimbachi, for Mīngbāshī, 'commander of 1,000.' Here Mīm stands for Mīng, Turkish for 1,000. (Yule, *Marco Polo*, i. 231.)

for such a reason, and came at once to the house of the Governor, who placed him in prison. But he left it at the end of six months, and although all the relatives of the deceased did what they could to procure his execution, the Governor did not dare to condemn him, as he feared the people, who maintained that the young man had acted rightly.

I left Patna by boat to descend to Dacca on the 29th of January (?),[1] between 11 o'clock and noon. If the river had been strong, as it is after the rains, I should have embarked at Allāhābād, or at the least at Benares. The same day I slept at Sera Beconcour,[2] 15 coss.

Five coss on this side of Beconcour you meet a river called Pompon sou,[3] which comes from the south and flows into the Ganges. The 30th [December] to Sera D'Eriia, 17 coss. On the 31st, after having gone 4 coss or thereabouts, you meet the river Kaoa, which comes from the south; 3 coss lower you see another called Chanon, which falls from the north; 4 coss farther you discover that called Erguga, which comes from the south; and again, 6 coss below, that of Aquera, which comes from the same quarter, and these four rivers lose their names in the Ganges.[4] All that day I beheld lofty mountains[5] on the south side and at a distance from the Ganges, some 10 coss and some 15 coss, and I came to a halt at Monger town, 18 coss.

The first day of January 1666, after having sailed two hours I saw the Gandak[6] enter the Ganges from the north. It is a large navigable river. This evening the halt was at Zangira[7] 8 coss. But as the Ganges twisted much during the day the distance is fully 22 coss by water. During the 2nd,

[1] This is a mistake for December, see below.

[2] Baikunthpur about 22 miles from Patna.

[3] Pūnpūn or Fatwā nālā, a river of South Behār, which rises in the south of the Gayā District. It joins the Ganges at Fatwā, and is crossed by the road from Bānkipur at 10 miles from that town.

[4] Compare Keul and Tiljugā rivers, and Kargariā, Bhāgmatī and Chāndū khāls or channels.

[5] Kharakpur hills and adjoining ranges. Monger is Monghyr (Mungīr: 25° 23′ N. Lat.; 86° 23′ E. Long.).

[6] Gandet in the original. This was the Būrh or Old Gandak river.

[7] Janjirā for Jahāngirhā of map, near Sultānganj.

between 6 o'clock in the morning and about 11 o'clock, I saw three rivers enter the Ganges, and they all three come from the north side. The first is called Ronova, the second Taè, and the third Chanan.[1] I slept at Baquelpour,[2] 18 coss.

The 3rd, after four hours' travelling on the Ganges, I encountered the river Katare,[3] which comes from the north, and slept this day at a village called Pongangel,[4] at the end of the mountains which abut on the Ganges, 13 coss.[5] On the 4th [January], one hour below Pongangel, I met a great river called Mart-nadi, which comes from the north, and I slept at Ragemehale,[6] 6 coss.

Rājmahāl is a town on the right bank of the Ganges, and when you approach it by land you find that for one or two coss the roads are paved with brick up to the town. It was formerly the residence of the Governors of Bengal, because it is a splendid hunting country,[7] and, moreover, the trade there was considerable. But the river having taken another course, and passing only at a distance of a full half league from the town, as much for this reason as for the purpose of restraining the King of Arakan, and many Portuguese bandits[8] who have settled at the mouths of the Ganges, and by whom the inhabitants of Dacca, up to which they made incursions, were molested—the Governor and the merchants who dwelt at Rājmahāl removed to Dacca, which is to-day a place of considerable trade.[9]

[1] These names probably represent sundry khāls. (Buchanan, in Martin, *Eastern India*, ii. 9 ff.)

[2] Bhāgalpur in Behār.

[3] Possibly the Kosī.

[4] Called Borregangel by De Graaf in 1669 (see *Histoire générale des Voyages*, La Haye, 1755, vol. xiii, p. 50, and Popangel in a map of 'Indostan' in the same volume). Its position corresponds with that of the modern Sikrīgali ghāt.

[5] This distance is much understated, being about 50 miles by land.

[6] Rājmahāl, a well-known town on the Ganges. Made the capital in 1592 (*Imperial Gazetteer*, xxi. 77). The Mart Nadī is possibly the Kālindrī.

[7] There is still a considerable amount of sport to be had in this neighbourhood, though the rhinoceros has become extinct since 1843.

[8] For Portuguese, at Noākhālī, see *Imperial Gazetteer*, xix. 130; and at Chatgāon (Chittagong), Jadunath Sarkar, *Hist. of Aurangzib*, iii. 19 and *Studies*, pp. 118 ff.

[9] This change was made in the time of Jahāngīr, according to Tieffenthaler, and now, owing to changes in the river, the remaining trade has gone to Sāhibganj (*Census Report Bengal*, 1911, vol. i. 25.)

On the 6th, having arrived at a great town called Donapour,[1] at 6 coss from Rājmahāl, I left M. Bernier, who went to Kāsimbāzār,[2] and from thence to Hugli [3] by land, because when the river is low one is unable to pass on account of a great bank of sand which is before a town called Soutiqui.[4] I slept this evening at Toutipour,[5] distant from Rājmahāl 12 coss. At sunrise I beheld a number of crocodiles asleep on the sand. The 7th I reached Acerat,[6] 25 coss.

From Acerat to Dacca, by land, there are still 45 coss. During this day I beheld so large a number of crocodiles that, at length, I became desirous to shoot one in order to ascertain if what is commonly said is true, namely, that a shot from a gun does not affect them. The shot struck him in the jaw and the blood flowed, but he did not remain where he was, and escaped into the river. On the 8th I again saw a great number of these crocodiles lying on the bank of the river, and I fired at two with two shots, each charge having three balls. Immediately they were wounded they turned over on the back, opening the mouth and dying on the spot. This day I slept at Douloudia, 17 coss. The crows were the cause of our finding a fine fish which the fisherman had concealed on the bank of the river in the reeds. For when our boatmen observed that there were a great number of crows which cawed and entered the reeds, they concluded that they must contain something unusual, and they searched so well that they found sufficient to make a good meal.

On the 9th [January], at 2 P.M., we encountered a river called Chativor which comes from the north, and our halt was at Dampour, 16 coss. The 10th we slept on the margin

[1] Donapur, situated on the farther bank of the Ganges at six milles east of Bakarpur, according to Tieffenthaler.

[2] Casenbazar in the original: Kāsimbāzār (Cossimbazar.) See p. 106 n.

[3] Ogouli in the original: Hugli. (See p. 108.) The Hugli factory was established in 1650, and became Head Factory of the Bay in 1657 (Temple on Bowrey, 168.)

[4] Sūti or Sooty in Murshidābād District, where the Bhāgirathī leaves the Ganges.

[5] Tartipur, which appears in Mīr Jumla's campaign against Sultān Shujā' (Jadunath Sarkar, *Hist. of Aurangzib*, ii. 273.)

[6] Acerat is identified by Professor Jadunath Sarkar with Hazrāhāt.

of the river in a place far removed from houses, and made this day 15 coss. On the 11th, having arrived towards evening at the spot where the Ganges divides into three branches, one of which goes to Dacca, we slept at the entrance of this channel, at a large village called Jatrapour,[1] 20 coss. Those who have no baggage can proceed by land from Jatrapour, to Dacca, and they shorten their journey very much, because the river winds about considerably. On the 12th, at noon, we passed before a large town called Bagamara, and slept at Kasiata, another large town,[2] 11 coss.

On the 13th, at noon, we met a river at 2 coss from Dacca called Laquia,[3] which comes from the north-east. Opposite the point where the two rivers join, there is a fortress with several guns on each side. Half a coss lower down you see another river called Pagalu,[4] over which there is a fine brick bridge, which Mīr Jumla [5] ordered to be built. This river comes from the north-east, and half a coss below you find another called Cadamtali, which comes from the north, and which you also cross by a brick bridge; [6] on both sides of the river you see several towers, where there are as it were enshrined many heads of men who have robbed on the high roads.[7]

[1] Jatrapore; Jātrapur, near Dacca, is mentioned in Hedges, *Diary*, iii. 220.

[2] So many changes in the courses of the rivers and the positions of the towns have taken place in this region, that it would require closer knowledge of the locality than the editors possess, and more detailed maps than we have had access to, to identify closely this portion of Tavernier's route. For the Dacca river, see *Imperial Gazetteer*, xi. 103. Kasiata is Qāzīhāt, the law officer's market.

[3] The Lakhya river is remarkable among Bengal rivers for its swift current.

[4] Pagla. This term, meaning 'fool,' is applied in deltaic regions in Bengal to branches or loops from rivers which derive their water not from an independent source, but from the river which they again rejoin. In the same way a river in Kāthiāwār is called Ghela, 'insane,' from its violent movements in the rainy season (Forbes, *Rās Mālā*, ed. 1921, p. 19.) The Bāvlī, or 'mad' stream in Rewa Kāntha, Bombay, once followed the Saint Mīrzā, and ran with butter instead of water (*Bombay Gazetteer*, vi. 170.)

[5] Mirza Mola in the original.

[6] Dacca stands on the north bank of the Būrhī Gangā, formerly the Padmā, 8 miles above its junction with the Dhaleswarī.

[7] For Skull pillars, see Fryer, ii. 245.

We arrived at Dacca [1] towards evening, and accomplished this day 9 coss. Dacca is a large town, which is only of extent as regards length, each person being anxious to have his house close to the Ganges. Its length exceeds 2 coss; and from the last brick bridge, which I have mentioned above, up to Dacca, there is a succession of houses, separated one from the other, and inhabited for the most part by the carpenters who build galleys and other vessels. These houses are, properly speaking, only miserable huts made of bamboo, and mud which is spread over them. Those of Dacca are scarcely better built, and that which is the residence of the Governor is an enclosure of high walls, in the middle of which is a poor house merely built of wood. He ordinarily resides under tents, which he pitches in a large court in this enclosure. The Dutch, finding that their goods were not sufficiently safe in the common houses of Dacca, have built a very fine house, and the English have also got one which is fairly good. The church of the Rev. Augustin Fathers is all of brick,[2] and the workmanship of it is rather beautiful.

On the occasion of my last visit to Dacca, the Nawāb Shāista Khān, who was then Governor of Bengal, was at war with the King of Arakan, whose navy generally consists of 200 galleys besides several other small boats. These galleys traverse the Gulf of Bengal and enter the Ganges, the tide ascending even beyond Dacca.

Shāista Khān, uncle of the King Aurangzeb, who reigns at present, and the cleverest man in all his kingdom, found means for bribing many of the officers of the King of Arakan's navy, and forty galleys, which were commanded by Portuguese, promptly joined him. In order to secure these new allies firmly in his service, he gave large pay to each of the Portuguese officers and to the soldiers in proportion, but the natives received only double their ordinary pay. It is most surprising to see with what speed these galleys are propelled by oars. Some are so long that they have up to fifty oars on each side, but there are not more than two men to each oar.

[1] Dacca in E. Bengal.

[2] 'There were many Christians [at Dacca], white and black Portuguese with a church served by a friar called Agostinho' (Manucci, ii. 26).

Some are much decorated, whereon the gold and blue paint have not been spared.[1]

The Dutch keep some of them in their service in which they carry their merchandise, and they occasionally have to hire some from others, thus affording a means of livelihood to many people.

The day following my arrival in Dacca, which was the 14th of January, I went to salute the Nawāb, and presented him with a mantle of gold brocade, with a grand golden lace of 'point d'Espagne' round it, and a fine scarf of gold and silver of the same 'point', and a jewel consisting of a very beautiful emerald. During the evening, after I had returned to the Dutch with whom I lodged, the Nawāb sent me pomegranates, China oranges, two Persian melons, and three kinds of apples.

On the 15th [January] I showed him my goods, and presented to the Prince, his son, a watch having an enamelled gold case, a pair of pistols inlaid with silver, and a telescope. All this which I presented, both to the father and to the young lord of about ten years of age, cost me more than 5,000 livres.

On the 16th I agreed with him as to the price of my goods, and afterwards I went to his wazīr to receive my bill of exchange payable at Kāsimbāzār.[2] Not that he was unwilling to pay me at Dacca, but the Dutch, who were more experienced than I, warned me that there was risk in carrying silver to Kāsimbāzār, where one cannot go except by re-ascending the Ganges, because the land route is very bad and full of jungle and swamps. The danger consists in this, that

1 With the aid of the Dutch and the partly enforced assistance of the Portuguese bandits, Shāista Khān captured Chittagong in 1666. For an account of this campaign see Jadunath Sarkar, *Hist. of Aurangzib*, iii. 220 ff.

2 Kāsimbāzār, a town in the Murshidābād District, was of great commercial importance before Calcutta was founded. It was situated on the Bhāgirathī river, which has changed its course, and now flows three miles from the town. The different European nations in succession monopolized the trade. The first English commercial agent was appointed in 1658. Its proximity to Murshidābād was a cause of constant danger, and it was often attacked by the Nawābs of Bengal. (See *Imperial Gazetteer*, xi. 52 f.)

the small vessels which are employed are very subject to be upset by the least wind, and when the sailors discover that one carries money, it is not difficult for them to wreck the boat, to recover the silver afterwards, at the bottom of the river, and appropriate it.

On the 20th I took leave of the Nawāb, who invited me to return to see him, and gave me a passport in which he described me as a gentleman of his household; this he had already previously done during the time that he was Governor of Ahmadābād, when I went to the army to meet him in the Province of Deccan, which the Rājā Sivajī [1] had entered, as I shall relate elsewhere. In virtue of these passports I was able to go and come throughout all the territories of the Great Mogul as one of his household, and I shall explain their tenor in Book II.

On the 21st [January] the Dutch gave a great banquet in my honour, to which they invited the English and some Portuguese, with an Augustin friar of the same nation. On the 22nd I went to visit the English, who had for Chief or President Mr. Prat,[2] and after that the Reverend Portuguese Father, and some other Franks. Between the 23rd and the 29th I made some purchases for 11,000 rupees, and all being embarked I went to bid farewell. On the 29th, in the evening, I left Dacca, and all the Dutch accompained me for two leagues in their small armed boats, and the Spanish wine was not spared on this occasion. Having been on the river from the 29th of January to the 11th of February, I left my servants and goods in the boat at Hazrāhāt, where I hired another boat which carried me to a large village called Mirdapur.

On the 12th [February] I hired a horse to carry myself, and not being able to hire another for my baggage, I was obliged to employ two women, who took charge of it. I arrived the same evening at Kāsimbāzār, where I was well received by M. Arnoul van Wachttendonk, Director of all the settlements of the Dutch in Bengal, who invited me to lodge with him.[3] On the 13th I passed the day agreeably

[1] Seva-gi in the original, see p. 147 below.

[2] Thomas Pratt, for whom see Irvine's note on Manucci, iv. 430 also Foster, *Eng. Factories, 1661–64*, pp. 294 and 393.

[3] Mr. W. Foster has kindly traced this Dutchman, Arnoldus van

with the Dutch gentlemen, who desired to enjoy themselves in honour of my arrival. On the 14th [February] M. Wachttendonk returned to Hugli, where the principal settlement is, and on the same day one of my servants, who had preceded me, came to give me notice that the people whom I had left in the boat with my goods had been in great danger on account of the strong wind, which had lasted two days, and which became stronger during the night.

On the 15th [February] the Dutch gave me a pallankeen to go to Murshidābād.[1] It is a great town, 3 coss from Kāsimbāzār, where the Receiver-general of Shāista Khān resided, to whom I presented my bill of exchange. After having read it he told me that it was good, and that he would have paid me if he had not on the previous evening received an order from the Nawāb not to pay me in case he had not already done so. He did not tell me the reason why Shāista Khān acted in this manner, and I returned to my lodging not a little surprised at this proceeding. On the 16th I wrote to the Nawāb to know what reason he had for ordering his Receiver not to pay me. On the 17th, in the evening, I left for Hugli in a boat with fourteen oars, which the Dutch lent me, and that night and the following I slept on the river.

On the 19th, towards evening, I passed a large town called Nadiyā,[2] and it is the farthest point to which the tide reaches. There arose so furious a wind, and the water was so high, that we were compelled to stop for three or four hours and draw our boat ashore.

On the 20th I arrived at Hugli, where I remained till the 2nd of March, during which time the Dutch made me welcome,

Wachtendonck, or Wagtendonck. He is mentioned in the 1663 Dagh-Register, Batavia, as upper merchant at Kāsimbāzār. A letter from Hugli of 22 June, 1665, N.S., states that on the death of Rogier van Heyningen, Wachtendonck had become provisional Chief (Directeur) (*Dagh-Register, Batavia*, 1665, p. 376). Evidently he was confirmed, as in succeeding volumes he is referred to as Directeur. He died at Hugli 30 August, 1668, N.S. (ibid., 1666–9, p. 184). He is apparently the Sieur Waikenton of vol. ii, p. 33.

[1] Madesou Bazarki in the original. Murshidābād, then also called Makhsūsābād or Makhsūdābād, and by the English Muxoodābād.

[2] Nandi in the original. Nadiyā, Nabadwīp, capital town of Nadiyā District, situated on the west bank of the Bhāgirathī. (*Imperial Gazetteer*, xviii. 261 f.)

and sought to give me all the amusement which the country could afford. We made several excursions on the river, and we enjoyed all the delicacies found in our European gardens, salads of several kinds, cabbages, asparagus, peas, and principally beans, the seed of which comes from Japan, the Dutch desiring to have all kinds of herbs and pulses in their gardens, which they are most careful to cultivate, but they have been unable, however, to get artichokes to grow.

On the 2nd of March I left Hugli and arrived on the 5th at Kāsimbāzār. The following day I went to Murshidābād to know if the Receiver who had refused to pay me had received another order from the Nawāb. For as I have above said, I immediately wrote to Shāista Khān to complain of his action and to know for what reason he did not wish my bills of exchange to be paid. The Director of the Dutch factories added a letter to mine, and pointed out to the Nawāb that I was too well known to him—having, formerly at Ahmadābād, at the army of the Deccan, and in other places, had many transactions with him—not to deserve favourable treatment; that he ought to remember that I, being the only person who often brought to India the choicest rarities of Europe, it was not the way to make me wish to return as he had invited me, if I should leave discontented; besides which, owing to the credit which I enjoyed, I should be easily able to dissuade those who intended to come to India with rare objects, by making them fear the treatment I had received. Neither my letter nor that of the Director produced the effect we had hoped, and I was in no wise satisfied with the new order which the Nawāb had sent to the Receiver, by which he ordered him to pay me with a rebate of 20,000 rupees from the sum which I ought to receive, and was carried by my bill of exchange, according to the price upon which we had agreed. The Nawāb added that if I was unwilling to content myself with this payment I might come to take back my goods. This action of the Nawāb had its origin in an evil turn played me by three rogues at the court of the Great Mogul. And this is the history of it in a few words.[1]

[1] In turning aside to relate what follows, Tavernier drops the thread of his narrative, and we are left to casual remarks from which to trace his route and his occupation from this time, namely, the beginning of

Aurangzeb, who reigns at present, at the solicitation of two Persians and a Banian, had a short time ago established a custom very injurious to merchants who come from Europe and other places to sell jewels at the Court. When they arrive, whether by sea or by land, the governors of the places where they arrive have orders to send them to the Emperor with their goods, either with their consent or by force;[1] this the governor of Surat did in the year 1665, and sent me to Delhi or Jahānābād where the Emperor was. There are in the employment of His Majesty, two Persians, and a Banian, whose duty it is to see and examine all the jewels which one wishes to sell to the Emperor. One of these two Persians is named Nawāb 'Ākil Khān,[2] i.e. the prince of wit, and it is he who has charge of all the Emperor's precious stones. The other is named Mīrzā Mu'azzam, whose duty is to tax each piece. The Banian, called Nihāl Chand,[3] has to see whether the stones are false and if they have any flaw.

These three men have obtained permission from the Emperor to see, before he does, all the foreign merchants bring to sell

March 1666 till his return to France in December 1668. Thus, on the 8th of April, he states he was at Mālda, and on the 12th of May he reascended the Ganges (vol. ii. 199); on the 2nd of July he witnessed an eclipse of the sun at Patna, where he had probably remained during the month of June (vol. ii. 192). Towards the end of this month, or beginning of August, we have casual mention of his having met the deputies of the French Company for Commerce in Agra (see Joret, op. cit., p. 201). He arrived at Surat by way of Sironj and Burhānpur on the 1st November (*Recüeil*, p. 117), and met there M. Thévenot, who returned then from Golkonda and Madras (*Recüeil*, p. 118). He makes two references to his having been in Surat in January, or the beginning of 1667 (see p. 118 below; and vol. iii. *Recüeil*, p. 118), where he relates an act of brutality by M. Berber. Shortly afterwards, or in February, i. e. within the sailing season, he probably embarked from Surat for Bandar 'Abbās (Gombroon). The above facts are partly derived from M. Joret's work, pp. 198–202.

[1] Marco Polo (ed. Yule, i. 379) reports that the Great Kaan used to treat in the same way merchants visiting his dominions.

[2] 'Āqil Khān, Mīr 'Askarī, was Aurangzeb's Wazīr, he died in A. D. 1695 (Beale, *Oriental Biographical Dict.* 76). See also bk. ii, ch. x, p. 314 f. For the legend of his love affair with the Princess Zeb-un-nissa, daughter of Aurangzeb, see Jadunath Sarkar, *Studies in Mughal India*, 79 ff., from which he appears never to have been Wazīr, though he rose to be Sūbahdār of Delhi, dying in 1696.

[3] This trio appears as Akel Kan, Mirza-Mouson, and Nali Kan, in the original.

to him, and afterwards to present them to him, and although they have sworn to take nothing from the merchant, they do not neglect to extort all they can in order to ruin him. When they see anything beautiful from which there is reason to hope for a large profit, they try to make him sell it to them for half its value, and if he refuses to let them have it, they are malicious enough to estimate the jewels when they are before the Emperor at half their value; besides which the Emperor Aurangzeb cares little for stones, and loves gold and silver much better. On the day of the Emperor's festival, of which I shall elsewhere speak, all the princes and nobles of the court make him magnificent presents; and when they are unable to find jewels to buy, they present him with golden rupees, of which the Emperor, as I have said, makes more account than the precious stones, although precious stones constitute a more honourable present than golden coins. It is at the approach of this festival that he sends out of his treasury numerous diamonds, rubies, emeralds, and pearls, which the controller of the jewels entrusts to several merchants for sale to the nobles, who are bound to make presents to the Emperor, and in this manner the Emperor receives both the money and his jewels together.

There is still another disadvantage for the merchant jeweller. It is that after the Emperor has seen any stones, a Prince or other noble who knows of it will never buy them, and besides, while these three valuers of the jewels are considering and examining them in their dwellings, where he is obliged to carry them, he meets several Banians who are experts, some for diamonds, others for rubies, for emeralds, and for pearls, who write down the weight, quality, perfection, and colour of each piece. And if the merchant afterwards goes to the Princes and Governors of Provinces, these people send them a memorandum of all that he carries, with the price, which they maliciously place at half the true value of the goods. These Banians are in business a thousand times worse than the Jews, and more cunning than they in all kinds of dodges and in malice when they wish for revenge.[1]

[1] Ralph Fitch (ed. Ryley, p. 101) says of the people of Bengal: 'they be a kind of craftie people, worse than the Jewes'. 'Those that are tradesmen are very ingenuous, and those that are accomplished Merchants

Observe then the bad turn which these three personages played me.

When I arrived at Jahānābād, one of them came and told me that he had the Emperor's order to see what I brought, before I would be permitted to exhibit it in his presence. They sincerely wished that the Emperor was not at Jahānābād, because they would have tried to buy all that I had for themselves, in order to profit by reselling it to the Emperor, and to the Princes when the opportunity should occur—this, nevertheless, they had never been able to induce me to do.

On the following day all three came to see me, one after the other, and they wished to get from me amongst other things a grand bouquet of nine large pear-shaped pearls, the largest of which weighed thirty carats and the least sixteen, with another single pear-shaped pearl of fifty-five carats. As for the bouquet, the Emperor took it; but with regard to the pearl, seeing that, notwithstanding all that they could say, I was unwilling to sell them anything, they so managed that before I had shown my jewels to the Emperor Ja'far Khān,[1] his uncle saw it, after which he did not wish to return it, saying that he would pay me as high a price for it as the Emperor, asking me not to mention it; for in fact he desired to present it to the Emperor.

After the Emperor had selected from among my jewels those which he desired, Ja'far Khān bought several pieces from me, and at the same time purchased the great pearl. Some days afterwards he caused me to be paid the amount agreed upon, with the exception of the pearl, upon which he desired me to rebate 10,000 rupees. The two Persians and the Banian had maliciously informed him that on my arrival they might, if they had wished, have had the pearl for 8,000 or 10,000 less than I had sold it to him for; this was wholly untrue, and Ja'far Khān having told me that if I would

are Very accute, and the most excellent arithmeticians in the world' (Bowrey, 24.)

[1] Ja'far Khān (not Zafar Khān as in the first edition) was appointed Wazīr by Aurangzeb about A. D. 1662, and died in 1670. He was son of Sādiq Khān, a cousin of Nūrjahān, who had married one of her sisters: hence his kinship to Aurangzeb (Bernier, 271: Beale, *Oriental Biographical Dict.*, 188.)

not accept the money which he offered me I might take it back, I took him at his word, assuring him that he would never see it again during his life. I kept to my word, and remained firm in my resolve. That which made me so fixed was because I desired to carry, if I could, something considerable to Shāista Khān, and if it had been permitted to me on my arrival at Surat to go to him first, I would not have gone to see the Emperor at Jahānābād, regarding which I had a great dispute with the Governor of Surat. For when I went to salute him, he immediately told me that I would not be treated as on my other journeys, and that the Emperor wished, absolutely, to be the first to see all that was curious which was brought into his kingdom.[1] I was more than four months disputing in vain with this Governor: at last I was obliged to go to visit the Emperor, and lest I should take another route they gave me fifteen horsemen to accompany me to Jalor.[2]

Having then started for Bengal, these three inspectors of jewels, incensed with spite, and urged on, no doubt, by Ja'far Khān, who was anxious to take his revenge for my refusal, wrote to Shāista Khān that I was taking some jewels to show to him, and among others a very beautiful pearl which I had sold to Ja'far Khān; but that he had returned it to me when he ascertained that I was trying to make him pay 10,000 rupees more than it was worth. They wrote similarly regarding the other jewels which I carried, and it was upon these false and malicious advices, which Shāista Khān did not receive till after he had delivered to me my bill of exchange, that the Prince wished to deduct 20,000 rupees from the total sum; this was reduced finally to a rebate of 10,000 rupees, with which I was obliged to content myself.

Since I have above spoken of the present which I made to Shāista Khān, I ought not to be silent regarding those which I was also obliged to make to the Emperor, to the Nawāb Ja'far Khān, to the eunuch of the Grand Begam,[3] sister of Aurangzeb, to the Grand Treasurer, and to the attendants of the treasury. For it should be stated that if any one

[1] See p. 324 below. [2] See p. 71.

[3] Jahāṇārā, who fills much space in Bernier and Manucci,

desires to have audience of the Emperor, they ask, before everything else, where the present is that he has to offer to him, and they examine it to see if it is worthy of being offered to His Majesty. No one ever ventures to show himself with empty hands, and it is an honour obtained at no little cost. On my arrival at Jahānābād I went to make my reverence to the Emperor on the 12th September 1665, and this is the present which I made him. Firstly, a shield of bronze in high relief thoroughly well gilt, the gilding alone costing 300 ducats of gold, which amount to 1,800 livres,[1] and the whole piece to 4,378 livres.[2] In the middle was represented the history of Curtius, who threw himself, on horseback and fully armed, into the gulf which opened in Rome, whence a mephitic vapour emanated. On the circuit of the shield was a clever representation of the siege of Rochelle. It was the *chef d'œuvre* of one of the most excellent workmen in France, and it had been ordered by M. le Cardinal Richelieu. All the great nobles who were then with the Emperor Aurangzeb were charmed with the beauty of this work of art, and they told him that he should place this rich piece on the grand elephant which carried the standard before His Majesty on the march.

I also presented the Emperor with a battle mace [3] of rock crystal, all the sides of which were covered with rubies and emeralds inlaid in gold in the crystal. This piece cost 3,119 livres.[4] Also a Turkish saddle embroidered with small rubies, pearls, and emeralds, which had cost 2,892 livres.[5] Also another horse's saddle with the housing, the whole covered with an embroidery of gold and silver, costing 1,730 livres.[6] The entire present which I made to the King amounted to 12,119 livres. Present made to Nawāb Ja'far Khān, uncle of the Great Mogul. Firstly, a table, with nineteen pieces to make a cabinet, the whole of precious stones of diverse colours representing all kinds of flowers and birds. The work had been done at Florence, and had cost 2,150 livres.[7] Also a ring with a perfect ruby which cost 1,300 livres.[8] To the

[1] £135.
[2] £328 7*s*.
[3] The Shushbur or Gurz of the *Āīn-i-Akbarī*, I, plate xii; list of plates i, p. x.
[4] £233 18*s*. 6*d*
[5] £216 18*s*.
[6] £129 15*s*.
[7] £161 5*s*.
[8] £97 10*s*.

Grand Treasurer a watch having a golden case covered with small emeralds, 720 livres.[1] To the attendants of the treasury of the Emperor, and to those who drew the money from the treasury, 200 rupees, which make 300 livres.[2] To the eunuch of the Grand Begam, sister of the Emperor Aurangzeb, a watch with a painted case which cost 260 livres.[3]

All the presents which I made, to the Great Mogul,[4] to Shāista Khān, and to Ja'far Khān, uncles of His Majesty, as also to the Grand Treasurers of the Emperor, to the stewards of the Khān's houses, to the captains of the palace gates, and further to those who on two occasions brought me the khil'at,[5] or robe of honour, on the part of the Emperor, and as often on the part of the Begam, his sister, and once on the part of Ja'far Khān—all these presents, I say, amounted to the sum of 23,187 livres.[6]

So true is it that those who desire to do business at the courts of the Princes, in Turkey as well as in Persia and India, should not attempt to commence anything unless they have considerable presents ready prepared, and almost always an open purse for divers officers of trust of whose services they have need.

I have said nothing in the former volume of the present which I also made to the bearer of the khil'at on the part of the King of Persia, to whom I presented 200 écus.[7]

CHAPTER IX

Route from Surat to Golkonda

I HAVE made several journeys to Golkonda, and by different routes, sometimes by sea, from Hormuz to Masulipatam, sometimes from Agra, and most frequently from Surat, which is the great threshold of Hindustān. I shall not speak in this chapter save of the ordinary route from Surat to Golkonda, in which I include that from Agra, which leads to Daulatābād,

[1] £54. [2] £22 10*s*. [3] £19 10*s*.

[4] Mogor in the original. [5] See p. 18.

[6] 23,187 livres at 1*s*. 6*d*. =£1,739 0*s*. 6*d*. Trade must have been profitable to have allowed such presents to be made. [7] £45.

as I shall describe in due course, only making mention, in order not to weary the reader, of two journeys which I made in 1645 and 1653.

I left Surat [1] on the 19th of January of the year 1645 and camped at Cambari, 3 coss; from Cambari to Barnoli, 9 coss; from Barnoli to Beara, 12 coss; from Beara to Navapour, 16 coss. This is the place where, as I have said, the best musk-scented [2] rice in the world grows. From Navapour to Rinkula, 18 coss; from Rinkula to Pipelnar, 8 coss; from Pipelnar to Nimpour, 17 coss; from Nimpour to Patane, 14 coss; from Patane to Secoura, 14 coss; from Secoura to Baquela, 10 coss; from Baquela to Disgaon, 10 coss; from Disgaon to Dultabat,[3] 10 coss.

Daulatābād [4] is one of the best forts in the empire of the Great Mogul; it is on a mountain which is scarped on all sides, the road to it being so narrow that only one horse or one camel can pass at a time. The town is at the foot of the mountain and has good walls, and this important place, which the Moguls lost when the Kings of Bījāpur and Golkonda revolted and threw off the yoke, was retaken under the reign of Jahāngīr by a subtle stratagem. Sultān Khurram, who was afterwards called Shāhjahān, commanded the army of the Emperor his father in the Deccan, and Asad Khān,[5] father-in-law of Shāista Khān, who was one of the generals, said something to the Prince, who was so enraged that, sending

[1] See for this part of the route, pp. 40–41 above.

[2] Scented rice, see p. 41 above.

[3] The stages, so far as they can be identified, seem to be: Surat, Khumbāriā, Viārā, Bardolī, Nārāyanpur, Pimpalner, Nāmpur, Patnā, Sakorā, Waklā, Deogāon, Daulatābād. But some places are doubtful: cf. Mundy's route, ii. 40 ff. For Pimpalner see p. 120, *n.* 1, below.

[4] Daulatābād. A town and fort in the Deccan, ten miles N.W. of Aurangābād, 170 miles N.E. of Bombay, and 28 miles N.W. of Haidarābād; also known by the name of Deogiri or Deogarh. 'The hill on which the fort stands rises almost perpendicularly from the plain to a height of about 600 feet, and it is entirely isolated, though commanded by several hills to the south.' The history of the changes of masters of this fort is too long for insertion here, but reference may be made to the *Imperial Gazetteer*, xi. 200 f., for information. The distance to Daulatābād from Nāmpur by these stages, measured on the map, is 94 miles, as against the 58 coss above. See for Daulatābād, Bilgrami & Willmott, *Sketch*, ii. 397 ff.

[5] Ast-Kan in the original.

at once for one of his paposhes or slippers, which are left at the door, he ordered him to receive five or six strokes with it on the head; this in India is the highest affront, after which it is impossible for a man to show himself.[1] All this was done through an understanding between the Sultān and the general, in order better to deceive the world, and especially the spies which the King of Bījāpur might have in the army of the Prince The rumour of the disgrace of Asad Khān being quickly spread, and he himself having gone to seek refuge with the King of Bījāpur, the latter, not having sharp enough eyes to perceive the ruse, gave him a good reception and promised him his protection. Asad Khān, finding himself so well received, asked the King to allow him for greater safety to take with him ten or twelve of his wives, and about as many servants, into the fortress of Daulatābād; this was granted to him.

He entered with eight or ten camels, the two kajāwas[2] which are carried on either side of the camels being well closed, according to custom, so that one cannot see the women who are inside. But instead of women they had put in them good soldiers, two in each kajāwa, all men of action;[3] of the same sort was each Shutari[4] who led his camel, so that it was easy for them to slaughter the garrison, who were not on their guard, and to make themselves masters of the place, which has ever since remained under the authority of the Great Mogul. There are, moreover, in this place numerous fine cannons,[5] and the gunners are generally English or Dutch. It is true that there is a small mountain higher than the fortress, but it is difficult of approach except by passing the

[1] On this incident see Bernier, 53; Manucci, i. 194.

[2] Cajavas in original, for kajāwas—panniers used for the conveyance of women on camels. For an illustration see Manucci, iv. 392.

[3] Sultān Khurram (i. e. Shāhjahān) imitated, if he did not take a hint, from the tactics of the siege of Troy. See Tod, *Annals of Rajasthan*, ed. 1920, i. 408.

[4] Chatre in original, for Shutarī, a camel driver.

[5] With reference to the early use of fire-arms, General Maclagan's article on Early Asiatic Fire Weapons is full of information. (See J.A.S.B., vol. xlv, 1876, p. 30.) For the artillery at Daulatābād, see Bilgrami & Willmott, ii. 431.

fortress. There was a Dutch gunner there, who after serving the Emperor for fifteen or sixteen years asked for his dismissal from him, and even the Dutch Company, which had placed him at the service of the Great Mogul, did all that it could to help him to obtain it; but it was never able to achieve this desire, because he was a very good gunner, and succeeded admirably with fireworks. The Rājā Jai Singh,[1] who is the most powerful of all the idolatrous princes of India, and who had most effectively aided Aurangzeb to ascend the throne, was sent as Commander-in Chief of the armies of that Emperor against the Rājā Sivajī, and when passing near the fortress of Daulatābād [2] this Dutch gunner went to salute him, and all the gunners of the army were Franks like himself. The Dutchman, taking advantage of the opportunity, told the Rājā that if he agreed to give him his dismissal he would promise to find him a means for mounting cannon on the mountain which commanded the fortress, and they had already surrounded the mountain with a wall, some soldiers having been placed within the enclosure to prevent any one taking possession of it. The Rājā, approving of the scheme, promised him that if he should be able to accomplish it he would obtain for him his dismissal from the Emperor with a liberal present. The matter having turned out successfully, to the Prince's content, he kept his promise to the Dutch gunner, and I saw the latter arrive at Surat at the beginning of the year 1667, whence he embarked for Batavia.

From Dultabat to Aurengabat,[3] 4 coss.

Aurangābād was formerly only a village, of which Aurangzeb

[1] Raja Jesseing in the original. For this appointment of Mīrzā Rājā Jai Singh see Grant Duff, *Hist. of the Mahrattas*, ed. 1921, i. 158.

[2] Daulatābād, see bk. ii, ch. xi., p. 326 below.

[3] Aurangābād, on the Kaum river, a tributary of the Godāvarī, is situated in the dominions of Haidarābād. It is 270 miles distant from the capital, and 68 miles from Ahmadnagar. The mausoleum resembles the Tāj at Agra, on a small scale. The tomb contains the body of Zainābādī, not the first wife, but concubine of Aurangzeb (Jadunath Sarkar, *Hist. of Aurangzib*, i, 65 f.). The caravansarāī referred to is still to be seen, and is described as being a vast stone building. The distance between Daulatābād and Aurangābād is 14 miles, so that the 4 coss is probably a misprint for 7. See *Imperial Gazetteer*, vi. 148 ff.; Bilgrami & Willmott, *Sketch*, ii. 322 ff.

has made a town which is not enclosed. He made this notable increase, both on account of a lake of about 2 coss in circuit, upon which the village was built, and in memory of his first wife, who died there, and who was mother of his children. She is buried at the end of the lake on the western side, where the King has built a mosque with a splendid tomb and a fine caravansarāī. The mosque and the tomb cost a large sum, because they are covered with white marble, which was brought by wagon from the neighbourhood of Lahore,[1] and was on the road nearly four months. One day, when going from Surat to Golkonda, I met, at five marches from Aurangābād, more than 300 wagons laden with this marble, the smallest of which was drawn by 12 oxen.

From Aurengabat to Pipeli, 8 coss ; from Pipeli to Aubar,[2] 12 coss ; from Aubar to Guisemner, 10 coss ; from Guisemner to Asti, 12 coss ; from Asti to Saruer, 16 coss ; from Saruer to Lesona, 16 coss ; from Lesona to Nadour,[3] 12 coss.

You must cross a river at Nander which flows into the Ganges, and pay 4 rupees per wagon, besides which, in order to cross, it is necessary to have a written order from the Governor. From Nadour to Patonta, 9 coss ; from Patonta to Kakeri, 10 coss ; from Kakeri to Satapour, 10 coss ; from Satapour to Sitanaga, 12 coss ; from Sitanaga to Satanagar, 10 coss. It is at Satanagar that you first enter the territories of the King of Golkonda. From Satanagar to Meluari, 16 coss ; from Meluari to Girballi, 12 coss ; from Girballi to Golkonda, 14 coss. This route from Surat to Golkonda amounts to 324 coss. And I made the journey in

[1] There must be a mistake as to the source of this white marble, as it could not have been obtained from the neighbourhood of Lahore. Probably it came from one of the known localities in Rājputāna in the States of Alwar, Jaipur, or Jodhpur. The Makrānā quarries in the last-named State furnished, it is said, the white marble of which the Tāj was built. See Sleeman, *Rambles*, 318 ; Watt, *Commercial Products*, 715.

[2] Thevenot (*Voyages des Indes*, p. 227) describes this route, and mentions a magnificent tank at Ambād.

[3] Nānder is situated on the north bank of the Godāvarī, which flows into the Bay of Bengal, and has no connexion with the Ganges, but the name Guenga (Ganges) was sometimes formerly applied to the Godāvarī itself. See p. 129 and Bilgrami & Willmott, ii. 688 ff. The route appears to be Aurangābād, Piprī, Gansargavī, Ashtā, Koalta, Lasonā, Nānder.

27 days.[1] I took 5 more on my journey in the year 1653, having followed a different road from Pimpalner,[2] where I arrived on the 11th of March, having parted from Surat on the 6th.

The 12th at Birgam; the 13th at Omberat; the 14th at Enneque-Tenque[3]—a good fortress; which bears the names of two Indian princesses. It is on a mountain scarped on all sides, and it has only a small path on the eastern side for the ascent. There is a tank inside the enclosure of this place, and they might sow sufficient to feed 500 or 600 men, but the Emperor does not desire to keep it garrisoned, and they have allowed it to fall in ruins.

The 15th [March], to Geroul. The 16th to Lazour, where there passes a river, upon which, at a cannon's shot from the eastern bank, there is one of the largest pagodas in the country, where a large number of pilgrims resort daily. The 17th [March] to Aurengabad; the 18th [March] to Pipelgan; the 19th [March] to Ember; the 20th [March] to Deogan; the 21st [March] to Patris; the 22nd [March] to Bargan; the 23rd [March] to Palam; the 24th [March] to Candear, a great fort, but commanded on one side by a mountain. The 25th [March] to Gargan; the 26th [March] to Nagouni; the 27th [March] to Indove; the 28th [March] to Indelvaï; the 29th [March] to Regivali. Between these two last places there is a small river which separates the territories of the Great Mogul from those of the King of Golkonda. The 30th [March] to Masapkipet; the 31st [March] to Mirel-mola-kipet; the 1st [April] to Golkonda.[4]

[1] The route, so far as the halts have been identified, is Nānder, Patantā, Karkhelī, Sāntāpur, Satulanagar, Shankarpallī, Golkonda.

[2] Pimpalner in Khandesh Dist., *Bombay Gazetteer*, xii. 465.

[3] Ankai and Tankai are distinct villages, the former being now a station on the Ahmadnagar Railway. The route is Vīrgāon, Umapurānā or Umiāna, Ankai, Tankai.

[4] Thévenot's route between Aurangābād and Golkonda, which he traversed about the year 1666, corresponds in parts with this one of Tavernier, but he appears to have left the regular line occasionally to visit pagodas, &c. (*Voyages des Indes*, pp. 235, 277.) The main line of his route is clear, but it is difficult to identify some of his intermediate stages: Aurangābād, Piprī, Ambād, Deogāon, Pathrī, Parthānī, Palam, Kandhār, Logāon, Indūr, Yellaredipetta, Massapet, Golkonda. The

To go from Agra to Golkonda it is necessary to go to Burhānpur by the route already described; from Burhānpur to Daulatābād, which is not more than five or six marches, and from Daulatābād to the other places which I have mentioned.

You may take still another route to go from Surat to Golkonda, that is to say, by Goa and Bījāpur, as I shall describe in the particular account of my journey to Goa. I come now to what I have been able to remark of greatest interest in the Kingdom of Golkonda, and to the late wars which it has had to undertake against the neighbouring States, during the time that I was in India.

CHAPTER X

Of the kingdom of Golkonda and the wars which it has carried on during the last few years.

THE Kingdom of Golkonda, speaking generally, is a rich country, abounding in corn, rice, cattle, sheep, fowls and other commodities necessary to life. As there are numerous tanks, there is also an abundance of good fish, and you find more particularly a kind of smelt, which has but one bone in the middle and is of very delicate flavour.[1] Nature has contributed more than art to make these tanks, of which the country is full. They are generally situated in somewhat elevated positions, where it is only necessary to make a dam[2]

small river dividing Mughal and Golkonda territories is apparently the Manjira. Kandhār or Kandahār is a famous old fort, 25 miles south-west of Nānder, both places mentioned in his account of Aurangzeb's invasion of Golkonda in 1656 (Jadunath Sarkar, i. 227; Bilgrami & Willmott, ii. 628 f.). Prof. Jadunath Sarkar identifies Bargan with Wuddagaon (Indian Atlas, sheet 56); Palam with Polliam; Nagouni, east of Komdelwaddy (not as Ball suggested, Hingānī); Mirel-mola-kī-pet with Mīr Jumla kī Pett. As to Indelvai cf. p. 127 *n.* below.

[1] Probably the so-called Chilwā or Chalwā fish, which are, as Dr. Francis Day states, Aspidoparia morar (*Fishes of India*, 565). They constitute the whitebait of India.

[2] Band is the native and Anglo-Indian term applied to these dams or embankments, which are thrown across valleys and hollows in order to form collecting areas for the drainage of the country.

on the side of the plain in order to retain the water. These dams are sometimes half a league long, and after the season of the rains is past they open the sluices from time to time in order to let the water run into the fields, where it is received in divers small canals to irrigate the lands of private individuals.

Bhāgnagar is the name of the capital town of this kingdom, but it is commonly called Golkonda, from the name of the fortress, which is only 2 coss distant from it, and is the residence of the King. This fortress is nearly 2 leagues in circuit, and requires a large garrison. It is, in reality, a town where the King keeps his treasure, having left his residence in Bhāgnagar since it was sacked by the army which Aurangzeb sent against it, as I shall relate in due course.

Bhāgnagar is then the town which they commonly call Golkonda, and it was commenced by the great grandfather of the King who reigns at present, at the request of one of his wives whom he loved passionately, and whose name was Nagar.[1] It was previously only a pleasure resort where the King had beautiful gardens, and his wife often telling him that, on account of the river, the spot was suitable for building a palace and a town, he at length had the foundations laid, and desired that it should bear the name of his wife, calling it Bhāgnagar, i.e. the Garden of Nagar. This town is in 16° 58′ of lat.[2] The neighbouring country is a flat plain, and near the town you see numerous rocks as at Fontainebleau. A large river [3] bathes the walls of the town on the south-west side, and flows into the Gulf of Bengal close to Masulipatam. You cross it at Bhāgnagar by a grand stone bridge, which

[1] Bhāgnagar, or the Fortunate City, was so called by Qutb Shāh Muhammad Kulī after a favourite mistress, whose name was, however, Bhāgmatī, not, as stated by our author, Nagar, which merely signifies town, and the name has no connexion with Bāgh, 'a garden'. It was founded in 1589, and became the seat of government instead of Golkonda, which is seven miles distant. By the Persians, according to Thévenot, it was already called Haidarābād, a title given by the King after the death of his mistress, but many Hindus still call it Bhāgnagar. See Ferishta, *Hist. of the Rise of the Mahomedan Power*, trans. J. Briggs, ed. 1910, iii. 451.

[2] The true latitude of Golkonda is 17° 22′ N., the longitude being 78° 27′ E.

[3] The Mūsi river, a tributary of the Kistnā.

is scarcely less beautiful than the Pont Neuf at Paris.[1] The town is nearly the size of Orléans, well built and well opened out, and there are many fine large streets in it, but not being paved—any more than are those of all the other towns of Persia and India—they are full of sand and dust; this is very inconvenient in summer.

Before reaching the bridge you traverse a large suburb called Aurangābād,[2] a coss in length, where all the merchants, brokers, and artisans dwell, and, in general, all the common people; the town being inhabited only by persons of quality, the officers of the King's house, the ministers of justice, and military men. From 10 or 11 o'clock in the morning till 4 or 5 in the evening the merchants and brokers come into the town to trade with foreign merchants, after which they return home to sleep. There are in these suburbs two or three beautiful mosques, which serve as caravansarāīs for strangers, and several pagodas are to be seen in the neighbourhood. It is through the same suburb that you go from the town to the fortress of Golkonda.

When you have crossed the bridge you straightway enter a wide street which leads to the King's palace. You see on the right hand the houses of some nobles of the court, and four or five caravansarāīs, having two storeys, where there are large halls and chambers, which are cool. At the end of this street you find a large square, near which stands one of the walls of the palace, and in the middle there is a balcony where the King seats himself when he wishes to give audience to the people. The principal door of the palace is not in this square, but in another close by; and you enter at first into a large court surrounded by porticoes under which the King's guards are stationed. From this court you pass to another of the same construction, around which there are several beautiful apartments, with a terraced roof; upon these, as upon the quarter of the palace where they keep the elephants,

[1] The Purāna Pul, or Old Bridge, built by Kulī Qutb Shāh in 1593. For an account of Haidarābād see Bilgrami & Willmott, ii. 522 ff.; Meadows Taylor, *Story of My Life*, Oxford, 1920, 44 ff., 70.

[2] The Kārwān suburb, Bilgrami & Willmott, ii. 584 ff.; Jadunath Sarkar, *Aurangzib*, i. 232.

there are beautiful gardens, and such large trees, that it is a matter for astonishment how these arches are able to carry such a weight;[1] and one may say in general terms that this house has all the appearance of a royal mansion.

It is about fifty years since they began to build a splendid pagoda[2] in the town; it will be the grandest in all India if it should be completed. The size of the stones is a subject for special astonishment, and that of the niche, which is the place for prayer, is an entire rock of such enormous size that they spent five years in quarrying it, and 500 or 600 men were employed continually on this work. It required still more time to roll it upon the conveyance by which they brought it to the pagoda; and they told me that it took 1,400 oxen to draw it.[3] I shall explain why the work is incomplete.[4] If it had been finished it would have justly passed for the noblest edifice in the whole of Asia.

On the other side of the town, from whence one goes to Masulipatam, there are two large tanks,[5] each of them being about a coss in circuit, upon which are some decorated boats intended for the pleasure of the King, and along the banks

[1] The idea of these elevated gardens was probably introduced by Persian immigrants. The gardens of Golkonda with their pavilions are still famous. The ultimate source of such gardens was Babylon. (*Ency. Brit.*, iii. 99.)

[2] This is the Mecca Masjid, commenced by Abdulla Qutb Shāh Kulī. (Bilgrami & Willmott, ii. 567.)

[3] Grandpré describes how these Megalithic structures were erected in India, and there is reason to believe the same method was followed in Egypt. After the first course was laid a slope of earth was placed against it up which the stones for the second course were rolled; when they were laid, more earth was added to raise the slope again, in order to roll up the stones for the third course, and so on. When completed the building was therefore surrounded by a mountain of clay, which had then to be removed (cf. *Voyage in the Indian Ocean, &c.*, i. 169, London, 1803). A very interesting account, with sketches and diagrams, of the means used by the Indians for moving large masses of stone will be found in the *Rurki Professional Papers on Indian Engineering*, 2nd Series, 1878, iii. 1; *Selec. Rec., N.W.P. Government*, New Series, v. 316; P. R. Gurdon, *The Khasis*, London, 1914, p. 154.

[4] See p. 132.

[5] The Husain Sāgar, area 8 square miles, and the Mīr Alam, 8 miles in circumference (*Imperial Gazetteer*, xiii. 311).

many fine houses which belong to the principal officers of the court.

At three coss from the town there is a very fine mosque where there are the tombs of the Kings of Golkonda;[1] and every day at 4 o'clock P.M. bread and pulão[2] are given to all the poor who present themselves. When you wish to see something really beautiful, you should go to see these tombs on the day of a festival, for then, from morning to evening, they are covered with rich carpets.

This is what I have been able to observe concerning the good order and the police which is maintained in this town. In the first place, when a stranger presents himself at the gates, they search him carefully to see if he has any salt or tobacco, because these yield the principal revenue of the King. Moreover, it is sometimes necessary that the stranger should wait for one or two days before receiving permission to enter. A soldier gives notice first to the officer who commands the guard, and he sends to the Dārogha[3] to give him notice also. But as it often happens that the Dārogha is engaged, or that he is taking exercise outside the town, and sometimes the soldier whom they have sent pretends not to have found him, in order to have an excuse for returning, and being much better paid for his trouble—the stranger is obliged to await the termination of all this mystery, and sometimes, as I have said, for one or two days.

When the King administers justice he comes, as I stated, into the balcony which overlooks the square, and all those who desire to be present stand below, opposite to where he is seated. Between the people and the wall of the palace three rows of sticks of the length of a short-pike are planted in the ground, at the ends of which are attached cords which cross one another, and no one, whosoever he may be, is allowed to pass these limits without being summoned. This barrier, which is not put up except when the King administers justice, extends the whole length of the square, and opposite the

[1] For a full account of these magnificent tombs see Bilgrami & Willmott, ii. 516 ff.

[2] Palāo or pulão, Hind., a dish of rice, meat, and spices.

[3] The Prefect or Superintendent of Police.

balcony there is an opening to allow those who are summoned to pass. Then two men, who hold by the ends a cord stretched across this opening, have only to lower it to admit the person who is summoned. A Secretary of State remains in the square below the balcony to receive petitions, and when he has five or six in hand he places them in a bag, which a eunuch, who is on the balcony by the side of the King, lowers with a cord, draws up, and presents them to His Majesty.

The principal nobles mount guard every Monday, each in his turn, and they are not relieved before the end of a week. Some of these nobles command 5,000 or 6,000 horse, and encamp under their tents around the town. When they mount guard each goes from his home to the rendezvous, but when they leave it they march in good order across the bridge, and thence by the main street they assemble in the square in front of the balcony. In the van ten or twelve elephants march, the number representing the rank of the officer who goes off guard. Some of them bear cages (howdahs) somewhat resembling the body of a small coach, while others carry only their driver, and another man who holds a sort of banner in place of the cage.

After the elephants the camels follow two by two, sometimes up to thirty or forty. Each camel has its saddle and on it is fixed a small culverin,[1] which a man. clad in a skin from head to foot, like a pantaloon, and seated on the crupper of the camel with a lighted match in hand, quickly turns from side to side before the balcony where the King is seated.

After them come the carriages, around which the servants walk on foot, after which the led-horses appear, and finally the noble to whom this whole equipment belongs, preceded by ten or twelve courtesans, who await him at the end of the bridge, leaping and dancing before him up to the square. After him the cavalry and infantry follow in good order. And as all that affords a spectacle, and has something of pomp

[1] Culverin, derived through Fr. Coulevrine, from Lat. Coluber, a serpent. It is a long slender gun which throws a ball to a considerable distance. The camel guns were known as Shutarnāl, 'camel-piece'; Zambūrak, 'hornet', Shāhīn, 'falcon' (Irvine, *Army of the Indian Moghuls*, 135 f.).

about it that amuses me, during three or four consecutive months which I have sometimes spent at Bhāgnagar, my lodging being in the main street, I enjoyed every week seeing these fine troops passing, which are more or less numerous according to the rank of the noble who has been on guard in his turn.

The soldiers have for their sole garment only three or four ells of cloths, with which they clothe the middle of the body before and behind. They wear the hair long, and make a great knot of it on the head as women do, having for their sole head-dress a scrap of three-cornered cloth, one corner of which rests on the middle of the head, and the other two are tied together on the nape of the neck. They do not wear a sabre like the Persians, but a broadsword like the Swiss, with which they both cut and thrust, and they suspend it from a belt. The barrels of their muskets are stronger than ours, and the iron is better and purer; this makes them not liable to burst.[1] As for the cavalry, they have bow and arrows, shield and mace, with helmet and a coat of mail, which hangs behind from the helmet over the shoulders.

There are so many public women in the town, the suburbs, and in the fortress, which is like another town, that it is estimated that there are generally more than 20,000 entered in the Dārogha's register, without which it is not allowed to any woman to ply this trade.[2] They pay no tribute to the King, but a certain number of them are obliged to go every Friday with their governess and their music to present themselves in the square in front of the balcony. If the King be

[1] The iron at Haidarābād, at a very early period, obtained a wide renown, being in fact the material which, when made into steel, afforded the source of supply for the manufacture of Damascus blades, the raw material having been exported to Persia and the Panjāb for that purpose (see *Journ. As. Soc. Bengal*, vol. xvi, pp. 417, 666; Yule, *Marco Polo*, i. 88). Two villages, situated to the north of Golkonda, namely Nirmal and Indore, are specially mentioned in the *Āīn-i-Akbarī* (ii. 230) as producing excellent iron and steel (Bilgrami & Willmott, i. 399 ff.). According to Thévenot, at Indelvai, i.e. Yédalvoi, four leagues from Indūr, quantities of swords, daggers, and lances were made and distributed thence throughout India (*Voyages des Indes*, p. 235).

[2] Compare the control of prostitutes at Vijayanagar (Elliot & Dowson, *Hist. of India*, iv. 111 f.; Abd-er-Razzak, *India in the Fifteenth Century*, Hakluyt Society, 29 f.).

there they dance before him, and if he is not, a eunuch signals to them with his hand to withdraw.

In the cool of the evening you see them before the doors of their houses, which are for the most part small huts, and when the night comes they place at the doors a candle or a lighted lamp for a signal. It is then, also, that the shops where they sell tārī [1] are opened. It is a drink obtained from a tree, and it is as sweet as our new wines. It is brought from 5 or 6 coss distant in leather bottles, upon horses which carry one on each side and go at a fast trot, and about 500 or 600 of them enter the town daily. The King derives from the tax which he places on this tārī a very considerable revenue, and it is principally on this account that they allow so many public women, because they are the cause of the consumption of much tārī, those who sell it having for this reason their shops in their neighbourhood.

These women have so much suppleness and are so agile that when the King who reigns at present wished to visit Masulipatam, nine of them very cleverly represented the form of an elephant, four making the four feet, four others the body, and one the trunk, and the King, mounted above on a kind of throne, in that way made his entry into the town.[2]

All the people of Golkonda, both men and women, are well proportioned, of good stature, and of fair countenances, and it is only the peasantry who are somewhat dark in complexion. The King of Golkonda who reigns at present is called Abdulla Qutb Shāh,[3] and I will inform the reader, in a few words, whence he derives his origin. Under the rule of Akbar, Emperor of India, father of Jahāngīr, the Moguls extended their authority southwards only to Narbeder, and the river which passes it and, coming from the south, flows

[1] Tārī, Anglicé toddy—the sap of Phoenix sylvestris.

[2] See a curious Indian picture in Fanny Parks, *Wanderings of a Pilgrim in Search of the Picturesque*, vol. ii, frontispiece; and Krishna on an elephant in J. L. Kipling, *Beast and Man in India*, ed. 1892, p. 334.

[3] Abdoul-Coutou-Cha in the original, for Abdulla Qutb Shāh; he succeeded his father Muhammad Kulī on the throne of Golkonda in A. D. 1611, and reigned till 1672.

into the Ganges, separated their lands[1] from those of the Rājā of Narsingha,[2] which extended to Cape Comorin, the other Rājās being, as it were, his subjects, and deriving their power from him. It is this Rājā and his predecessors who have always been at war with those who succeeded Tamerlane[3] in India, and they were so powerful that the last Rājā who was at war with Akbar had on foot four armies, commanded by as many generals.[4] The most powerful of the four had his quarters in the territories which to-day constitute the kingdom of Golkonda, the second held his in the country of Bījāpur, the third in the Province of Daulatābād, and the fourth in the region of Burhānpur. The Rājā of Narsingha dying without children, these four generals established themselves each in the country which he held with his army, and caused themselves to be recognized as kings—one of Golkonda, another of Bījāpur, another of Burhānpur, and the fourth of Daulatābād. Although the Rājā was an idolater, these

[1] This passage is obscure, owing to some jumble between the names Beder or Bidar and Narbeder (for Narbadā). The river of Beder which is referred to, and formed the boundary of the Mughal's ancient territory, was in reality the Godāvarī, which at one time was supposed to join the Ganges. Its real course, however, is to the Bay of Bengal, into which it flows below Coconada. See p. 119.

[2] The name of Narsingha (a prince of Telugu origin, who died 1508 A.D.) was applied by the Portuguese to the old kingdom of Vijayanagara. Its capital town, though it bore the same name, was called Bisnagar by them. It was an enormously wealthy city, and the ruins still to be seen on its site near the small village of Hampi, in the Bellary District, testify to the magnificence of its buildings (A. H. Longhurst, *Hampi Ruins described and illustrated*). See *India in the Fifteenth Century*, Hak. Soc., pp. 25, 39, &c. ; Barbosa, ed. Dames, i. 182 ; Yule, *Hobson-Jobson*, 618.

[3] Tamerlane or Tīmūr-lang (Temur-leng in the original), the ancestor of the Mogul emperors, invaded India in 1398 ; but Bābur was the actual founder of the dynasty (1526–30). For a good account of Tamerlane see Sir P. Sykes, *Hist. of Persia*, 2nd ed., ii. 118 ff., and for Bābur, *ibid.* ii. 142 ff. His *Memoirs* are published under the editorship of Sir Lucas King, Oxford [illegible].

[4] It was not in the time of Akbar, but in the reign of Mahmūd Shāh Bahmanī (1482–1518), that the provincial governors declared their independence and set up five separate kingdoms: the Imādshāhī dynasty of Berār ; the Nizāmshāhī of Ahmadnagar ; the Ādilshāhī of Bījāpur ; the Barīdshāhī of Bīdar ; and the Qutbshāhī of Golkonda.
5 See Smith, *Oxford Hist. of India*, 286 ff.

four generals were Musalmāns, and he of Golkonda was of the sect of Ali,[1] descended from an ancient family of Turkomāns, who inhabit the country of Hamadān in Persia.[2]

He was, as I have said, the most powerful of all; and a few days after the death of the Rājā of Narsingha they achieved a notable victory over the Mogul, after which there was nothing to prevent them from making themselves sovereigns. But since that time Jahāngīr, son of Akbar, conquered the kingdom of the new King of Burhānpur; [3] Shāhjahān, son of Jahāngīr, that of the King of Daulatābād; [4] and Aurangzeb, son of Shāhjahān, a part of the territory of Bījāpur.[5] As for the King of Golkonda, neither Jahāngir nor Shāhjahān made war upon him, and they left him undisturbed, on the condition that he should pay to the Moguls an annual tribute of 200,000 pagodas. These pagodas are gold pieces which are worth from 6 to 7½ francs [6] of our money, sometimes more and sometimes less. To-day the most powerful of the Rājās of this great peninsula south of the Ganges is the Rājā of Velou,[7] who extends his authority as far as Cape Comorin, and has succeeded to a part of the States of the Rājā of Narsingha; but, as there is no trade in his country, this Prince is little known, and strangers hardly ever go to it.

[1] Haly in original, for 'Alī, i.e. he was a Shī'a.

[2] Sultān Kulī Qutb Shāh was the first of the Qutb Shāhī kings. He reigned from 1512 to 1543, and was assassinated at the instigation of his son Jamshīd.

[3] Not quite correct as regards Burhānpur or Khāndesh as there were eleven princes of the Fārūqī dynasty; from its foundation in A. D. 1388 till A. D. 1601, when Asīrgarh was taken possession of by Akbar.

[4] Daulatābād, or Deogiri, was taken possession of in the year 1633 by Mahābat Khān, Shāhjahān's general.

[5] Bījāpur was not finally taken possession of by Aurangzeb till 1686, or subsequently to the date at which our author wrote, but he had partially subdued it some thirty years before. See Grant Duff, *Hist. of the Mahrattas*, Oxford, 1921, i. 165.

[6] Here we should read livres for francs, as in bk. II. ch. xviii, the value of the new pagoda is stated to be 3½ rupees or 5¼ livres, i.e. 7*s.* 10½*d.*: vol. ii. p. 70; and on p. 117 the old pagoda is said to be equal to 7½ livres, or 11*s.* 3*d.* Independent testimony (see Appendix) gives about the same values; so that 200,000 pagodas would be equal to about £100,000, more or less, in exchange value.

[7] Velou, Vellore in North Arcot, represents Vijayanagar; see Smith, *Oxford Hist.*, 299 ff.

The present King of Golkonda has no son; he has only three daughters, who are all married.

The eldest is married to one of the relatives of the Grand Shaikh of Mecca,[1] and the circumstances which preceded this marriage are sufficiently curious to occupy a place in my observations. The Shaikh having arrived at Golkonda in the garb of a mendicant, remained for some months at the gate of the palace, refusing to reply to sundry people of the Court who inquired why he had come. At length the matter being reported to the King, he sent his senior physician, who spoke Arabic well, to ascertain from the Shaikh what he wanted, and the reason of his coming. The physician, and some nobles of the Court who also spoke to him, immediately saw that he was a man of intelligence, and took him to the King, who was much pleased with his appearance and conversation. But at length the Shaikh having declared that he had come to marry the Princess, this proposition very much surprised the King, and was received by some of the Court as the proposal of a man who was not altogether in his senses. At first they merely laughed, but when they observed that he persisted in his demand, even threatening that a great calamity would befall the country if they did not give him the Princess in marriage he was cast into prison, where he remained for a long time.

The King, at length, considering that it would be better to send him back to his own country, made him embark at Masulipatam on one of the vessels which carry goods and pilgrims to Mocha, whence they travel by land to Mecca. About two years afterwards the same Shaikh returned to Golkonda, and managed so well on this occasion that he espoused the Princess and acquired great credit in the kingdom, which he now governs, and where he is all-powerful.[2]

[1] Chek of Mecque in the original; called Mīrzā Muhammad on p. 136. Ovington (p. 527) calls him Meera Mahmoed (? Mīr Ahmad), and he is possibly identical with the Sharīfu-l-Mulk, who surrendered to Shāh 'Ālam in 1685, and died in 1687 (Manucci, iv. 444). The question of his origin is fully discussed by Jadunath Sarkar, *Hist. of Aurangzib*, iv. 332 f., Grant Duff, *Hist. of the Mahrattas*, ed. 1921, i. 123.

[2] For another account of this marriage see Ovington, *Voyage to Suratt*, 527 ff.

It was he who prevented the King from yielding up the fortress of Golkonda, where he had taken refuge when Aurangzeb and his son entered Bhāgnagar, as I shall presently relate—throwing himself upon him, and threatening to kill him if he did not resolve to hold out without thinking more of delivering the keys to the enemy. This bold action was the reason why the King loved him the more, and made use of his counsel in all important affairs; and thus, not only as son-in-law of the King, but as Prime Minister, he is now the principal personage in the Court of Golkonda. It was he who caused the Great Pagoda[1] of Bhāgnagar to remain unfinished, because he threatened the kingdom with a great calamity if they persisted in completing it.

This Prince passionately loves all those who are proficient in mathematics, which he understands fairly well; hence, although he is a Musalmān, he favours all Christians who are learned in this science, as he particularly showed in the case of the Rev. Father Ephraim, a Capuchin,[2] when he was passing through Golkonda to go to Pegu, whither he was sent by his Superiors. He did all he could to induce him to remain in his country, and offered to build for him, at his own cost, a house and a church, assuring him that he would lack neither occupation nor parishioners, since some Christian Portuguese and many Armenians came every year for trade. But Father Ephraim, who had his orders to proceed to Pegu, was unable to accept his offer, and when he went to take leave of the Shaikh he received from him a khil'at of the most honourable kind, since it included the whole suit, namely the cap, the cabaye or grand robe, the arcalou[3] or cassock, two pairs of drawers, two shirts, and two girdles, with a scarf to be worn round the neck and upon the head for protection against the heat of the sun. The Reverend Father was astonished at this present, and told the Shaikh that he could

[1] Here used of the mosque at Bhāgnagar; see p. 124.

[2] Father Friar Ephraim of Nevers was Vicar of Madras from 1642 to his death in 1694 (Manucci, iv. 39).

[3] Cabaye, for qabā (-i-shāhī), i. e. royal robe. Arcalou, Turkish arqaliq, a coat with sleeves, a surtout, like the qabā, but having buttons, instead of strings, at the neck, breast, and waist. For this form of the khil'at see p. 18 above.

not wear it, but the latter pressed him to take it, and said that he might bestow it on one of his friends. Two months afterwards I received this present from Father Ephraim when I was at Surat, and I thanked him for it on the occasion of our first meeting.

The Shaikh, seeing that he could not detain the Father, and not wishing to allow him to travel on foot from Golkonda to Masulipatam, as he intended, compelled him to accept an ox which he gave him, with two attendants to conduct him; and not being able to force him to accept 30 pagodas[1] in addition, he directed the two attendants that on arrival at Masulipatam they should leave with the Capuchin Father both the ox and the pagodas. This order they did not fail to carry out in every particular, for otherwise on their return to Golkonda it would have cost them their lives. I shall complete the history of Father Ephraim, who afterwards experienced many misfortunes, when I describe Goa, which is the principal Portuguese possession in India.

The second daughter of the King of Golkonda was espoused to Sultān Muhammad, eldest son of Aurangzeb.[2] What led to the marriage was this: Mīr Jumla,[3] Commander-in-Chief of the army of the King of Golkonda, who had received from him much good service in establishing his throne, when he went to Bengal to deal with a Rājā's[4] affairs, left in hostage with the King, according to custom, his wife and children as pledge of his fidelity. He had many daughters, but only one son, who had a considerable following and made a great figure at Court.[5] The credit and the wealth which Mīr Jumla

[1] Say £15.

[2] Tavernier, probably correctly, styles him Sultān Muhammad: see p. 287 ff. below. He is also called Muhammad Sultān. The marriage took place in 1655–6 (Elliot & Dowson, *Hist.* vii. 118 f.). This prince died 3rd December 1676, aged 37 (Jadunath Sarkar, *Hist. of Aurangzib*, iii. 49 f.). See also Bernier, 21; Ovington, 527; Manucci, ii. 195.

[3] Mīr Jumla. Tavernier writes this name in five different ways—Mir Gimola, Mirza Mola, Mirgimola, Amir Jemla, and Mir Jemla. His son's name was Muhammad Amīn.

[4] Mīr Jumla was sent to Bengal by Aurangzeb in 1660, with instructions to deal with the rebellious zamīndārs of the province, especially those of Assam and Arakan (Jadunath Sarkar, *Hist. of Aurangzib*, iii. 178).

[5] This son, Muhammad Amīn, was a dissolute young man, who offended Abdulla Qutb Shāh, who found him asleep, in a state of intoxi-

had acquired made him enemies, who, jealous of such good fortune, sought to destroy it in his absence, and to injure him in the esteem of the King. They told him that Mīr Jumla's power should cause him to be suspected; that all his actions tended towards dethroning him and securing the kingdom of Golkonda for his son; that he ought not to wait till the evil was without remedy; and that in order to rid himself of an enemy—the more dangerous because he concealed himself—the shortest way was to poison him. The King, being easily persuaded, gave these persons an order to accomplish the deed; but having taken their measures clumsily three or four times in succession without being able to accomplish their object, the son of Mīr Jumla at length heard of it, and at once informed his father. It is not known exactly what command he got from his father; but after he had received his reply he went to the King, to whom he spoke out with boldness, taxing him with the services which his father had rendered him, and with the fact that without his aid he would never have come to the throne. This was true; but there was a Court intrigue which would take too long to describe. This young noble, somewhat carried away from his ordinary demeanour, used such sharpness of language to the King that His Majesty, offended by his insolence, rose in a rage, whilst the nobles of the Court, who were present, threw themselves on him and handled him roughly. At the same time, by order of the King, he was arrested with his mother and sisters, and put in prison, and this affair, which made a great commotion at Court, so much enraged Mīr Jumla, who soon had news of it, that, having forces at hand, and being beloved by the soldiers, he at once resolved to make use of these advantages to revenge himself for the injury. He was then, as I have said, deputed to Bengal, for the purpose of bringing to their allegiance some Rājās possessing territories on the Ganges; and Sultān Shujā', the second son of Shāhjahān,

cation on the masnad or royal throne-cushion. When the King refused to pardon him, on the appeal of his father, Mīr Jumla, the latter seized the opportunity of escaping service with the tottering Golkonda dynasty, and made overtures to Aurangzeb. See Bilgrami & Willmott, ii. 481 f.; Jadunath Sarkar, ii. 224 ff.; Grant Duff, *Hist. of the Mahrattas*, Oxford, 1921, i. 121.

who was then Governor of Bengal, was selected by him as most suitable to join forces with him against the King of Golkonda, whom he no longer regarded as his master, but as the greatest of his enemies. He accordingly wrote to the Prince that if he was willing to join him he would supply him the means of taking possession of the whole of the kingdom of Golkonda, and that he ought not to lose so good an opportunity of increasing the Mogul Empire, the succession to which affected him as well as the other princes, his brothers. But he did not receive a favourable reply from Sultān Shujā', who let him know that he did not trust the word of a man who was capable of betraying his King and might readily betray a strange prince whom he had attracted to his interests in order to accomplish his own revenge, and consequently he need not expect his aid. On receipt of this refusal of Sultān Shujā', Mīr Jumla wrote to Aurangzeb, who was then in his government of Burhānpur, and he, not being so scrupulous as his brother, accepted the offer which was made to him.[1]

While Mīr Jumla advanced his troops towards Bhāgnagar, Aurangzeb marched with his by long stages towards the Deccan, and the two armies having joined, they reached the gates of Bhāgnagar before the King had time to put his affairs in order. He only succeeded in taking refuge in the fortress of Golkonda, which Aurangzeb besieged after he had pillaged the town of Bhāgnagar [2] and removed all that was of much value from the palace. The King, seeing himself so hard pressed, believed that he would soon have to yield ; and in order to avoid this hurricane, which threatened his complete ruin, sent back his wife and children with every honour to Mīr Jumla. There is both virtue and generosity in India as in Europe ; and I shall give a noteworthy example of it in the person of the King of Golkonda. Some days after the enemy had laid siege to the fortress, a gunner perceiving Aurangzeb upon his elephant visiting the outworks, while

[1] For a correct account of the intrigues of Mīr Jumla see Jadunath Sarkar, *Aurangzib*, i. 219 ff.

[2] Bhāgnagar, the modern Haidarābād. On the campaign, *ibid.* i. 230 ff.; Grant Duff, *Hist. of the Mahrattas*, Oxford, 1921, i. 259.

the King was on the bastion, said to the latter that if His Majesty wished he could destroy the Prince with a cannon ball, and at the same moment he put himself in position to fire. But the King, seizing him by the arm, told him to do nothing of the sort, and that the lives of princes should be respected. The gunner, who was skilful, obeyed the King, and instead of firing at Aurangzeb, he killed the general of his army who was farther in advance, with a cannon shot.[1] This stopped the attack which he was about to deliver, the whole camp being alarmed by his death. Abd-ul-Jabbār Beg,[2] general of the army of the King of Golkonda, who was close by with a flying camp of 4,000 horse, having heard that the enemy were somewhat disordered by the loss of their general, at once took advantage of so favourable an opportunity, and going at them full tilt, succeeded in overcoming them; and having put them to flight he followed them vigorously for 4 or 5 leagues till nightfall.

A few days before the death of this general, the King of Golkonda, who had been surprised, seeing himself pressed, and supplies being short in the fortress, was on the point of giving up the keys; but, as I have above related,[3] Mīr Ahmad,[4] his son-in-law, tore them from his hands, and threatened to slay him if he persisted any longer in such a resolution; and this was the reason why the King, who previously had but little liking for him, thenceforward conceived a great affection for him, of which he daily gave him proofs. Aurangzeb having then been obliged to raise the siege, halted some days to rally his troops and receive reinforcements, with which he set himself to besiege Golkonda. The fortress was as vigorously attacked as it was vigorously defended; but Mīr Jumla, who still retained some regard for the King, and, as some persons say with good reason, without proclaiming it openly, did not wish to allow Aurangzeb to proceed to extremities, and by his diplomacy secured a suspension of hostilities for some weeks. Shāhjahān, father of Aurangzeb, had formerly

[1] Mīr Asadu-llāh Bukhārī, son of Aurangzeb's paymaster, Mīr Fazlu-llāh Bukhārī (Jadunath Sarkar, *op. cit.*, i. 239).

[2] Abdul Jaber Beg in the original. This officer has not been traced.

[3] See p. 132.

[4] Mirza Mahamed in original: v. 131.

received kind treatment from the King of Golkonda, with whom he had taken refuge when he had lost the battle with his elder brother against the Emperor Jahāngīr, their father.[1] Jahāngīr, having got the elder brother into his power, caused his eyes to be put out ; [2] but Shāhjahān, the younger brother, being better advised, took to flight, and the King of Golkonda, having received him with kindness, they bound themselves together in close friendship—Shāhjahān swearing to his host that he would never fight with him on any pretext. Mīr Jumla, who knew that it would not be difficult to bring two kings who were friends to an understanding, little as Aurangzeb was inclined to give way, and wishing, moreover, that that prince should find it advantageous to himself, communicated underhand to both of them what he planned in order to secure a lasting peace. He managed that the King of Golkonda should first write to Shāhjahān in very civil terms, praying him to become arbitrator between himself and Aurangzeb, placing his interests entirely in his hands, and promising to sign a treaty in whatever terms he pleased to frame it. With similar address Mīr Jumla persuaded Shāhjahān, on his side, to propose, as his response to the letter of the King of Golkonda, the marriage of the latter's second daughter to Sultān Muhammad, son of Aurangzeb, on condition that after the death of the King, the father of the Princess, his son-in-law should inherit the kingdom of Golkonda. This proposition having been accepted and the articles signed by the two kings, both the peace and the marriage were celebrated at the same time with much magnificence.[3] As for Mīr Jumla, he quitted the service of the King of Golkonda, and went to Burhānpur with Aurangzeb. Soon afterwards Shāhjahān created him first Minister of State and Commander-in-Chief of his armies, and he powerfully aided Aurangzeb to

[1] This was when Shāhjahān rebelled in 1623.

[2] Shahryār, who was blinded in 1627, was the youngest son of Jahāngīr. On the blinding of rivals to the throne see Fryer, iii. 38, and p. 268 below.

[3] The fine inflicted on the King of Golkonda amounted, it is said, to £1,000,000 as a first instalment of an annual tribute, but was in part remitted by Shāhjahān (Jadunath Sarkar, i. 238 ff.). The name of the princess was Pādshāh Bībī (Grant Duff, *Hist. of the Mahrattas*, Oxford, 1921, i. 209).

ascend the throne by defeating Sultān Shujā'. For Mīr Jumla was a man of great intelligence, who understood equally well both war and the affairs of State.[1] I have had occasion to speak to him several times, and I have admired the firmness and the promptitude with which he responded to requests presented to him, giving his orders in every direction, and signing several dispatches as if he had but one sole matter to attend to.

The third Princess of Golkonda was promised to Sultān Sa'īd, another Shaikh of Mecca,[2] and the matter had so far advanced that the day was named for the marriage. But Abd-ul-Jabbār Beg, general of the army, went to the King of Golkonda, with six other nobles, to turn him from his design; and they so managed it that the marriage was broken off, and the Princess was given to Mīrzā Abdul Hasan,[3] a cousin of the King, by which marriage there are two sons. This has entirely destroyed the claims of the son of Aurangzeb, whom his father now keeps in prison in the fortress of Gwalior, because he betrayed his interests in favour of Sultān Shujā', his uncle.[4] This Princess would have been given at first and with no difficulty to Mīrzā Abdul Hasan if he had not been a debauchee, but for this reason the King ceased to regard and respect him; since his marriage he has reformed.

At the present time the King of Golkonda does not so much fear the Moguls, because, as is the case in their dominions,

[1] He understood other matters also, for Thévenot says he possessed 20 mans, or 408 Dutch livres, weight of diamonds. He had acquired these riches when, at the head of the army of Golkonda, he made war with the King of Bījāpur against Bisnagar (*Voyages des Indes*, p. 306). And Bernier (p. 17) states that he acquired wealth in many ways, and 'caused the diamond mines, which he alone had farmed under many borrowed names, to be wrought with extraordinary diligence, so that people discoursed of nothing but of the riches of Emir Jemla, and of the plenty of his diamonds, which were not reckoned but by sacks'. For a review of the career of Mīr Jumla see Jadunath Sarkar, i. 216 ff.

[2] Sultān Sa'īd, or Sayyid, meaning a descendant of Muhammad.

[3] Mirza-Abdul-Cosing in the original. Called Miersa Abou-il-Hassan by Havart, who makes him out to have been a lineal descendant of Ibrāhīm, the second king of the dynasty: quoted in *Hist. gén. des Voyages*, vol. xiii, p. 425 *n.*

[4] See p. 287 ff. below.

money does not leave his country, and he has amassed much to carry on war. Besides, he is greatly attached to the sect of 'Alī, to the extent of not wearing a cap like the other Musalmāns, because they say that 'Alī did not wear one, but another kind of head-dress ;[1] and for this reason the Persians, who arrive in India in great numbers to seek their fortunes, prefer to go to the King of Golkonda rather than to the Mogul. It is the same with the King of Bījāpur,[2] whom the Queen, sister of the King of Golkonda, has been careful to bring up in the same sect of 'Alī, who attracts many Persians to his service.

CHAPTER XI

Route from Golkonda to Masulipatam[3]

THE distance from Golkonda to Masulipatam is counted to be 100 coss by the straight road ; but if you wish to go by way of the diamond mine called in Persian Coulour and Gani in the Indian language,[4] it is 112 coss, and the latter is the route which I ordinarily followed.

From Golkonda to Tenara,[5] 4 coss. Tenara is a fine place,

[1] The Persian tāj, or cap, was the mark of the Shī'a sect, and Shāh Tahmāsp Safavī, King of Persia, when Humāyūn took refuge in his territories, tried to induce him to wear it (W. Erskine, *Hist. of India under Baber and Humayun*, i. 281 f.).

[2] 'Alī II ('Adil Shāhī) 1656–72 : *Oxford Hist. of India*, 297.

[3] Masulipatam. Thevenot gives the distance as 53 leagues. The true distance is about 210 miles, and from Madras 285 miles.

[4] Kollūr is the modern name by which this famous site is known ; it is situated on the Kistnā river in Lat. 16° 42′ 30″, Long. 80° 5′. The identification was first traced out by means of the routes to it given by Tavernier here and in bk. II, ch. xviii. Although all memory was lost of the true position of this mine until it was recently rediscovered, and very wild suggestions have been made on the subject, its position is correctly indicated on several maps of the beginning of the eighteenth and end of the seventeenth centuries. The question of this identification has been fully discussed in the *Economic Geology of India*, p. 16. Gani is not a name, though so often quoted as such in works on precious stones. It is simply a Persian prefix, signifying ' Mine of ' (*Kān-i*), and is known to have been used in connexion with other mines.

[5] This place appears to be the same as Atenara, mentioned on p. 240 below. It is not given on modern maps. It is also mentioned by Thévenot as Tenara. By the kind influence of the Resident at Hyderābād,

where there are four very good houses, each having a large garden. That one of the four which is situated on the left of the high road is incomparably finer than the three others. It is built throughout of cut stone in two storeys, and contains large galleries, beautiful halls, and fine rooms. In front of this house there is a large courtyard, which resembles the Place Royale in Paris. On each of the three other sides there is a large entrance, and stretching from one side to the other a fine veranda which is elevated about 4 or 5 feet above the ground and well arched over; here travellers of the higher classes are accustomed to lodge. Over each entrance there is a grand balustrade, and a small chamber for ladies. When persons of position do not wish to occupy these dwellings, they can have their tents pitched in the gardens; but it should be remarked that only three of these houses may be thus used, for the grandest and finest of them is reserved for the Queen. When she is not there you may see it and walk through it, for the garden is very beautiful and contains many fine pieces of water. The whole area is laid out in a similar manner. There are small chambers destined for poor travellers, who every day, towards evening, receive a dole of bread, rice, or vegetables already cooked; and the idolaters, who eat nothing which has been prepared by others, are given flour to make bread and a little butter, and, as soon as their bread is baked like a cake, they cover it on both sides with melted butter.

From Tenara to Iatenagar, 12 coss; Iatenagar to Patengy, 12 coss; Patengy to Pengeul, 14 coss; Pengeul to Nagelpar, 12 coss; Nagelpar to Lakabaron, 11 coss; Lakabaron to Coulour or Gani (of which I shall speak in the account of the mines).[1]

Mr. Ghulam Yazdani, Superintendent, Archaeological Department, His Exalted Highness the Nizam's Government, has investigated the question. He identifies Tenara or Atenara with Sarūrnagar, because it is on the Masulipatam road; it is about 9 or 10 miles from Golkonda; there are several old Qutb Shāhī buildings and gardens which may be those described by Tavernier; and the next stage is Hayātnagar, the Jatenagar of Tavernier. He suggests that the word Tenara or Atenara is a corruption of Rāhatnagar, 'city of pleasure', Sarūrnagar having the same meaning.

[1] The route, as worked out by Mr. Dodwell of the Record Office, Madras, is as follows: Tenara, Sarūrnagar; Iatenagar, Hayātnagar;

The greater part of the road from Lakkāwurrum to Kollūr is rocky, especially towards Kollur, and in two or three places I was obliged to take my carriage to pieces, which can be quickly done. Wherever there happens to be a small quantity of good soil between the rocks cassia trees [1] flourish, the cassia produced from them being the best and most laxative in all India. This I know from the effect produced on my servants, who ate it as they walked along. Along the whole length of the town of Kollūr there runs a large river [2] which flows into the Bay of Bengal near Masulipatam.

From Coulour or Gani to Kah Kaly, 12 coss; from Kah Kaly to Bezouar, 6 coss. Close to Bezouar you recross the river.

From Bezouar to Vouchir, 4 coss; from Vouchir to Nilimor, 4 coss. Between Vouchir and Nilimor, about halfway, you cross a great river by means of a raft, there being no boat there. From Nilimor to Milmol, 6 coss; from Milmol to Maslipatan,[3] 4 coss.

Masulipatam [4] is a straggling town (*villace*), the houses in which are built of wood, and stand detached from one another. This place, which is on the sea shore, is renowned merely on account of its anchorage, which is the best in the Bay of Bengal, and it is the sole place from which vessels sail for Pegu, Siam, Arakan, Bengal, Cochin China, Mecca, and Hormuz, as also for the islands of Madagascar, Sumatra, and the

Patengy, Pantangi in Nalgonda District; Penguel, Pangal, about 4 miles N.E. of Nalgonda town; Nagelpar, Nagalpad, on the Mūsi river, about 20 miles E.S. of Nalgonda town; Lakabaron, Lacuaron; Coulour, Kōllūr, Guntūr District, Sattenapalle Taluk.

[1] Cassia fistula (Hind. amaltās) affords a valuable laxative; its long pods are familiar objects in Indian jungles. One of the native names for them is Bandar lāthī, or monkey's stick. (Watt, *Econ. Prod.*, 287 f.)

[2] The Kistnā. The 'great river' between Vouchir—Wouhir in original on p. 208 below—is one of its deltaic branches.

[3] The route, as worked out by Mr. Dodwell, is as follows: Coulour or Gani, Kōllūr, Guntūr District; Kah Kaly, Kākāni, 4 miles N. of Kōllūr, or possibly Karlapūdi, 29 miles S.E. by E. of Kōllūr; the river crossed is the Kistnā; Bezouar, Bezwāda; Vouchir, Vyyūru, 8 miles N.W. of Pāmarru; Nilimor, Pāmarru, 7 miles N.W. of Nidumōlu; Milmol, Nidumolu, 10 miles N.W. of Maslipatan or Masulipatam.

[4] See the accounts by the Dominican Fernandez Navarette, about 1670, and by the Dutch Minister, Philip Baldaeus, quoted in *Kistna Manual*, 1863, p. 90 f.; also Bowrey, 62, with other references, descriptions differing from that of Tavernier about the houses in the town.

Manillas. It should be remarked that wheel carriages do not travel between Golkonda and Masulipatam, the roads being too much interrupted by high mountains, tanks, and rivers, and because there are many narrow and difficult passes. It is with the greatest trouble that even a small cart can be taken. I have taken one to the diamond mines, but I was obliged to take it to pieces frequently in order to pass bad places. It is the same between Golkonda and Cape Comorin. There are no wagons in all these territories, and you only find there oxen and pack-horses for the conveyance of men, and for the transport of goods and merchandise. But, in default of chariots, you have the convenience of much larger pallankeens than in the rest of India; for one is carried much more easily, more quickly, and at less cost.

CHAPTER XII

Route from Surat to Goa, and from Goa to Golkonda by Bījāpur

TRAVELLERS can go from Surat to Goa partly by land and partly by sea, but the road is very bad by land, especially from Damān to Rājāpur. Most travellers prefer the sea route, and hiring an almadier,[1] which is a kind of row-boat, they go from point to point up to Goa, notwithstanding that the Malabaris, who are the pirates of India, are much to be feared along these coasts, as I shall presently describe.

The route from Surat to Goa is not counted by coss, but by gos, which are about equal to four of our common leagues.

From Surat to Daman, 7 gos; from Daman to Bassaïn, 10 gos; from Bassaïn to Chaoul, 9 gos; from Chaoul to Daboul, 12 gos; from Daboul to Rejapour, 10 gos; from Rejapour to Mingrela, 9 gos; from Mingrela to Goa, 4 gos. This makes in all, from Surat to Goa, 61 gos.[2]

The principal danger which has to be encountered on these coasts is, as I have said, the risk of falling into the hands of

[1] Almadier—from Arab. *al-maʿdīya*, a ferry-boat. Tavernier in his *Persian Travels* defines it as a small vessel of war. (Yule, *Hobson-Jobson*, 15 f.; Barbosa, ed. Dames, i. 14; Linschoten, i. 262.)

[2] The route is Surat to Damān, Bassein, Chaul, Dābhol, Rājāpur, Vengurla.

the Malabaris, who are fanatical Musalmāns and very cruel to Christians.[1] I once met a barefoot Carmelite Father who had been captured by these pirates. In order to extort his ransom speedily, they tortured him to such an extent that his right arm became half as short as the other, and it was the same with one of his legs. The commanders pay wages only to the value of two écus to each soldier for the six months they generally spend at sea, and do not share with them the prizes taken; but they allow them to keep as their perquisite the garments and food store of those whom they capture. It is true that the soldiers are permitted to leave then, and if the commanders desire to retain them they are obliged to make a new contract with them. They seldom venture farther to sea than from 20 to 25 leagues; whenever the Portuguese capture any of these pirates they either hang them straight off or throw them into the sea. These Malabaris number 200 and sometimes as many as 250 men on each vessel, and they set sail in squadrons of from ten to fifteen vessels to the attack of a big ship; they do not fear cannon. They at once come alongside and throw numbers of fire-pots on the deck, which cause much injury if care be not taken to provide against them. For as the habits of the pirates are well known, immediately they are seen all the scuttles on deck are closed and it is flooded with water, so that the fire-pots cannot take effect.

An English captain named Mr. Clerc,[2] when coming from Bantam to Surat, met, in the latitude of Cochin, a squadron of Malabaris, consisting of twenty-five or thirty vessels, which forthwith attacked him vigorously. Seeing that he could not withstand their first onset, he set fire to some barrels of gunpowder which he had time to prepare, and the deck being blown up, a great number of pirates who were on it were also blown into the sea. Notwithstanding this, the remainder did not lose courage, and continued to press on board. The English captain, seeing that no other resource was left, ordered all his crew into two boats and retired to his cabin, where the

[1] For the ravages of the Malabāri pirates, many of whom were fanatical Moplah or Māppilla Musalmāns, see Fryer, i. 164; J. Biddulph, *The Pirates of Malabar*, 1907.

[2] Walter Clark, Master of the Comfort, whose exploit is described by Rawlinson, *British Beginnings in Western India*, 104 f.

pirates could not reach him; he then set fire to a train which he had prepared, leading to a magazine containing a large quantity of powder. At the same time he threw himself into the sea, where he was picked up by his crew, and the vessel having caught fire, all the Malabaris who were on board jumped into the sea; but that did not prevent the two boats, which contained about forty Englishmen, being captured by the remaining Malabaris; and I was at breakfast at Surat with the English President, named Fremelin,[1] when he received a letter from Captain Clerc, which stated that he was enslaved by the Zamorin,[2] who is the most powerful king on the Malabar coast. This prince would not leave the English in the power of these savages, as they were in danger of their lives, because upwards of 1,200 women had become widows on the two occasions when the ship was on fire. He appeased them by promising them two piastres each [3] as recompense for the death of their husbands; this amounted to above 2,400 écus, besides 4,000 more required for the ransom of the captain and the other Englishmen. The President immediately sent the money, and I saw them return, some of them in good health, but others broken down by fever. The Malabaris are such superstitious people that they touch nothing dirty or unclean with the right hand; such service they reserve for the left, allowing the nails upon it, which serve as a comb, to grow, because they have long hair like women, which they twist round the head and cover it with a small three-cornered cloth.[4]

[1] William Fremlin, President of Surat, 1639–44. See Rawlinson, Index, for many references, and Mundy, ii. 24. In 1639, according to Mandelslo, Mr. Methwold, undoubtedly the Mr. Methold, whose visit to the diamond mines preceded Tavernier's (see bk. II, ch. xvi), resigned the Presidentship at Surat, and was succeeded by Mr. Fremling (*sic*): *Travels into the East Indies*, English Trans., London, 1669, p. 71. [Fremlen took over charge on Dec. 11 (not 27), 1638: note by Sir W. Foster referring to *Eng. Factories, 1637–41*, p, xv.]

[2] Samorin in the original. The title of the Hindu King of Calicut (Yule, *Hobson-Jobson*, 977 f.).

[3] Piastre = 4*s*. 6*d*.; the compensation for a husband was therefore about 9*s*.

[4] These are Moplah customs. Some Fakīrs grow their nails to a great length (Fitch, ed. Ryley, 102). Linschoten (i. 282) describes the careful purification of the Nāyars of Malabar. Musalmāns do not take food with the left hand, which is used in ablutions.

Having mentioned Damān,[1] I shall now describe in a few words how that town was besieged by Aurangzeb, who reigns at present. Many believe that elephants have a great effect in war; this is undoubtedly true, but not always in the way which is imagined, for it often happens that, instead of ravaging the ranks of the enemy, they turn upon those who drive them, and who are expecting an altogether different result, as Aurangzeb experienced at the siege of this city. He had been twenty days before Damān, and had arranged to make the assault on a Sunday, believing that Christians, like Jews, would not defend themselves on their Sabbath. The Commandant in Damān was an old soldier who had served in France, with three of his sons, whom he had with him then. There were in the place 800 men, both gentlemen and other brave soldiers, who had come from many places to take part in the defence and show their valour. For although the army of the Great Mogul consisted of more than 40,000 men, he was unable to prevent Damān being relieved from the sea, because he had no vessels and could not invest the place except by land. On the Sunday that he intended to make the assault, the Governor of Damān, in accordance with what had been settled at the council of war, caused mass to be said immediately after midnight, and then ordered a sortie to be made with all the cavalry and a part of the infantry, who were at first to attack on the side where there were 200 elephants. They threw a quantity of fireworks among them, which frightened them so much in the darkness of the night that, without knowing whither they went, and their drivers not being able to restrain them, they turned against the besiegers with such fury that in two or three hours half the army of Aurangzeb was destroyed, and three days after the siege was raised. Since that time the Prince has not cared to have anything more to do with Christians.[2]

I have made two journeys to Goa—the first was at the end

[1] Damān is situated in Lat. 22° 25′ N., Long. 72° 53′ E., about 100 miles north of Bombay. It was first sacked by the Portuguese in the year 1531, but it was rebuilt by the Indians, and was subsequently retaken in 1558 by the Portuguese, since which time up to the present it has remained in their possession.

[2] On the danger of elephants stampeding during a battle see Smith,
8 *Early Hist. of India*, 3rd ed., 69, with Pyrard de Laval, ii. 345.

of the year 1641, the second at the beginning of the year 1648. The first time I only remained seven days, and I returned to Surat by land. From Goa I went to Bicholly,[1] which is upon the mainland; from thence to Bījāpur, then to Golkonda, Aurangābād, and Surat. I could have gone to Surat without passing through Golkonda, but I was obliged to go there on business.

From Goa to Visapour,[2] which is generally accomplished in eight days, 85 coss. Visapour to Golkonda, which I travelled in nine days, 100 coss. From Golkonda to Aurangābād the stages are not so well defined, for sometimes it takes sixteen, sometimes twenty, or even twenty-five days. From Aurangābād to Surat the journey sometimes takes twelve days, but sometimes it is not accomplished in less than fifteen or sixteen.

Bījāpur is a large town which has nothing remarkable about it, either as regards public edifices or trade. The King's palace is large enough indeed, but badly built, and what causes the approach to it to be difficult is, that in the moat which surrounds it, and which is full of water, there are many crocodiles.[3] The King of Bījāpur has three good ports in his kingdom; these are Rājāpur,[4] Dābhol,[5] and Kare-

[1] This is the same as the Bicholi of vol. ii, p. 239, where it is stated to be on the Bījāpur–Goa frontier. At present Bicholim is the name of a district or subdivision of Goa territory (Fonseca, *Goa*, 1).

[2] Bījāpur, in Lat. 16° 49′ N., and Long. 75° 43′ E., is on the site of the ancient Vijayapura, which was called Visapour by early European travellers. Recently it has been made the head-quarters of the Kalādgi, now Bījāpur, District. It was taken possession of by Aurangzeb after Tavernier's time, namely in 1686. A full description of the ancient buildings which abound in Bījāpur will be found in Fergusson's *History of Indian and Eastern Architecture*, and H. Cousens, *Bījāpur and its Architectural Remains*, 1916. 'The vagueness and inaccuracy of his account seems to show that Tavernier did not carefully examine Bījāpur' (*Bombay Gazetteer*, xxiii. 587).

[3] On the guarding of the moats of Indian forts by means of crocodiles see Crooke, *Things Indian*, 111 f.

[4] Rājāpur, chief town in the subdivision of the same name in the Ratnāgirī District of Bombay. As a port it has deteriorated, and vessels of even moderate size cannot come within three miles of the quay (*Vide Imp. Gaz.* xxi. 67). Mandelslo describes it as one of the chief maritime cities of the kingdom of Konkan. On Bījāpur boundaries see Fryer, ii. 50, 67; Bowrey, 20 f.

[5] Dābhol or Dabul, a port in the Konkan, in Lat. 17° 34′. It is described by Mandelslo as being on the river Kalewacka (Anjanvel or

puttun.[1] The last named is the best of all, and the sea washes the foot of the mountain, where, close to land, there is from 14 to 15 fathoms of water. On the top of the mountain there is a fort with a natural supply of water, and although not commanded by anything and by nature impregnable, since the King has been at peace with the Portuguese he has abandoned it.

Kareputtun is only five days' journey from Goa northwards, and Rāībāgh,[2] where the King of Bījāpur disposes of his pepper, is about the same distance from Kareputtun to the east. The King of Bījāpur, like the King of Golkonda, was formerly a tributary of the Great Mogul, but is so no longer.

This kingdom has been in trouble for some time on account of the rebellion of Nāïr Sivajī,[3] who was, on the establishment of the King of Bījāpur, what we call in France, Captain of the Guards. His father had been guilty of misconduct, for which the King arrested him and put him in prison, where he remained for a long time till he died. The young Sivajī, his son, thereupon conceived so strong a hatred for the King that he became a chief of bandits, and as he was both courteous and liberal he had as many followers, both cavalry and infantry, as he cared for, and in a short time he got together an army, the soldiers, on the report of his liberality, coming to join him from all sides. He was thus in a position to undertake some enterprise, when the King of Bījāpur died without children, and accordingly, without any great difficulty, he became master of a portion of the Malabar coast, including Rājāpur, Rasigar,[4]

Vāsishti): *Travels into the East Indies*, Eng. Trans., London, 1669, p. 74. See for early references, Yule, *Hobson-Jobson*, 289.

[1] Crapaten in the original, Kareputtun of Map. The account of the port refers to Vijaydurg. The fort has been demolished (*Bombay Gazetteer*, x. 343).

[2] Rabaqué in the original; Rāībāgh, in Belgaum District.

[3] The original founder of the Marātha Confederacy was Shāhjī; he was succeeded by his son, Nāik Sivajī; born in 1627, died in 1680. By his valour and treachery he won for the Marāthas the suzerainty of Southern India. See for his life, Grant Duff, *History of the Mahrattas*, Oxford, 1921. In the text the title of Sivajī is Nāyar, a Malayāli term usually applied to the well-known caste of that name and meaning 'leader' (Skt. *nāyaka*). Nāik, of this same origin, is the more usual form of the word. His father, Shāhjī, died as the result of a hunting accident.

[4] Probably Rakshasagudda in Kānara District (*Bombay Gazetteer*, xv,

Kareputtun, Dābhol, and other places. It is said that during the demolition of the fortifications of Rasigar he found immense treasure, and with this he supported his forces, by whom he was well served because they were always very well paid.

Some years before the death of the King, the Queen, as she had no children, adopted a boy, upon whom she had bestowed all her affection, and she brought him up, as I have already said, with the greatest care in the doctrines of the sect of Ali.[1] On the King's death she caused this adopted son to be declared King, and Sivajī, as he then possessed an army, continued the war, and for some time caused trouble during the regency of the Queen. A treaty was concluded on condition that Sivajī should retain, as vassal of the King, all the country which he had taken, the King receiving half the revenue. When the young King was, by this peace, established on the throne, the Queen, his mother, undertook the pilgrimage to Mecca, and while I was at Ispahān she passed through on her return.

Returning now to the journey to Goa. When I left Surat for my second visit to Goa I embarked on a Dutch vessel called the *Maestricht*, which carried me to Vengurla, where I arrived on the 11th of January 1648.

Vengurla [2] is a large town, situated half a league from the sea, in the kingdom of Bījāpur. It has one of the best anchorages in all India, and the Dutch always came there for supplies when they blockaded Goa, and they still supply there the ships which they employ to trade in many parts of India, for excellent water and very good rice can be procured at Vengurla.

pt. 2, 80). For Sivajī s campaign see Grant Duff, *op. cit.* Prof. Jadunath Sarkar identifies Rasigar with Rājgarh.

[1] On the question of the parentage of 'Alī 'Adil Shāh II, see Jadunath Sarkar, i. 285 f.; Bernier, 197; Grant Duff, *History of the Mahrattas*, Oxford, 1921, i. 123; Fryer, ii. 55: on Shī'a influence in Bījāpur, Smith, *Oxford Hist. of India*, 291, 293.

[2] Mingrela in the original is Vengurla, a town and seaport, headquarters of a subdivision of the same name in the Ratnāgirī District of Bombay. The Dutch settlement was founded in 1638; in 1660 the town was garrisoned by Sivajī, and in 1664 it was burnt by him in consequence of a revolt; it was again burnt by Aurangzeb in 1675. A British settlement was established there in 1772, and in 1812 the town was ceded to the British (*Imperial Gazetteer*, xxiv. 306).

This town is also much renowned on account of its cardamoms,[1] which the orientals esteem as the best of spices, and as they are cultivated only in this country, are very scarce and dear. Coarse cotton cloths for home consumption are made there too, and a sort of matting called toti,[2] which is only used for wrapping up merchandise.

Hence it is not so much for commerce as for supplies which can be obtained at Vengurla, that the Dutch Company maintain an establishment there. For, as I have said, not only all the vessels which come from Batavia, Japan, Bengal, Ceylon, and other places, and those which sail for Surat, the Red Sea, Hormuz, Bassora, &c., both in going and returning, anchor in the roads at Vengurla, but also when the Dutch are at war with the Portuguese, and are blockading the bar at Goa, where they ordinarily keep eight or ten vessels, they send their small boats to Vengurla to obtain provisions. For they hold the mouth of the river during eight months of the year, so that nothing can enter Goa by sea during that time. It should be remarked in connexion with this subject that the bar at Goa is closed for a part of the year by sand, cast up by the south and west winds which precede the great rains, and to such an extent that there is only from a foot to a foot and a half of water for the passage of very small boats. But when the great rains begin to fall, the waters, which rise rapidly, soon remove the sands and open the passage to large vessels.[3]

[1] Cardamoms—the dried fruit of *Elettaria cardamomum* (Maton), a shrub belonging to the ginger family, much esteemed in the East as a spice, and largely exported to Europe for medicinal and other purposes. (Watt, *Commercial Products*, 511 ff.). Called *Cargamon* in the original.

[2] Tāt or Tānt, i. e. the fibre known as jute, with which gunny bags are made. It is produced from *Corchorus capsularis* (Linn).

[3] Aguada anchorage is virtually closed to navigation during the south-west monsoon, owing to the high winds and sea, and the formation of sandbanks in the estuary of the Mandāvī at this season (*Imperial Gazetteer*, xii. 250). On the Goa bar see P. della Valle, *Travels*, Hakluyt Society, i. 154, 158; *Commentaries of Afonso Dalboquerque*, Hakluyt Society, ii. 82, 170.

CHAPTER XIII

Remarks upon the present condition of the town of Goa

GOA is situated in latitude 15° 32″, on an island of six or seven leagues circuit, upon the river Mandāvī,[1] which two leagues farther down discharges itself into the sea. The island abounds in corn and rice, and produces numerous fruits, as mangues, ananas, figues d'Adam, and cocos; [2] but a good pippin is certainly worth more than all these fruits. All who have seen both Europe and Asia thoroughly agree with me that the port of Goa,[3] that of Constantinople, and that of Toulon, are the three finest ports in both the continents. The town is very large, and its walls are built of fine stone. The houses, for the most part, are superbly built, this being particularly the case with the Viceroy's palace. It has numerous rooms, and in some of the halls and chambers, which are very large, there are many pictures representing each of the vessels which come from Lisbon to Goa, and those which leave Goa for Lisbon, with the names of each vessel and that of the Captain, and the number of guns with which it is armed.[4] If the town were not so shut in by the mountains which surround it, it would without doubt be more numerously inhabited, and residence there would be more healthy than it is. But these mountains prevent the winds from refreshing it; this is the cause of great heat. Beef and pork afford the ordinary food of the inhabitants of Goa. They also have

[1] Mandoua in the original. It rises in the Parvar Ghāt, in the District of Satāra and is 38½ miles long. It is the most important stream in the territory.

[2] Mangoes, pine-apples, plantains, and coco-nuts. Most persons acquainted with Indian fruits will agree with Tavernier, though some might make an exception in favour of the mango.

[3] The best account of Goa is that of J. N. Fonseca, *Historical and Archaeological Sketch of the City of Goa*, 1878, condensed in the *Imperial Gazetteer*, xii. 249 ff.; also see Linschoten, i. 175 ff.; Pyrard de Laval, ii. 2 ff.; *Commentaries of Dalboquerque*, ii. 88 ff.; P. della Valle, i. 154 ff.; Fryer, *New Account*, ii. 10 ff.; Sir R. Burton, *Goa and the Blue Mountains*.

[4] For these pictures see Pyrard de Laval, ii. 50; Linschoten, ii. 14.

fowls, but few pigeons, and although they live close to the sea fish is scarce.[1] As for confectionery, they have many kinds, and eat a large quantity. Before the Dutch had overcome the power of the Portuguese in India, nothing but magnificence and wealth was to be seen at Goa, but since these late comers have deprived them of their trade in all directions, they have lost the sources of supply of their gold and silver, and have lost much of their former splendour. On my first visit to Goa I saw people who had property yielding up to 2,000 écus of income, who on my second visit came secretly in the evening to ask alms of me without abating anything of their pride, especially the women, who came in *pallankeens*, and remained at the door of the house whilst a boy, who attended them, came to present their compliments. You sent them then what you wished, or you took it yourself when you were curious to see their faces; this happened rarely, because they cover all the head with a veil. Otherwise when one goes in person to give them charity at the door, the visitor generally offers a letter from some religious person who recommends them, and speaks of the wealth she formerly possessed, and the poverty into which she has now fallen. Thus you generally enter into conversation with the fair one, and in honour bound invite her in to partake of refreshment, which lasts sometimes till the following day.[2]

If the Portuguese had not been occupied with guarding so many fortresses on land, and if, owing to the contempt they felt for the Dutch at first, they had not neglected their affairs, they would not be to-day reduced to so low a condition.

The Portuguese who go to India have no sooner passed the Cape of Good Hope than they all become Fidalgos [3] or gentlemen, and add Dom to the simple name of Pedro or Jeronimo by which they were known when they embarked; this is the reason why they are commonly called in derision 'Fidalgos of the Cape of Good Hope'. As they change their status so

[1] This is not the case at present (Fonseca, 13).

[2] The dissolute character of the women of Goa is remarked by Linschoten, i. 201, ii. 215; P. della Valle, i. 161; Fonseca, 162; Pyrard de Laval, ii. 113, 128.

[3] Fidalgues in the original. See Fryer, i. 191.

also they change their nature, and it may be said that the Portuguese dwelling in India are the most vindictive and the most jealous of their women of all people in the world. As soon as they entertain the least suspicion about their women they will, without scruple, make away with them by poison or the dagger. When they have an enemy they never forgive him. If they are of equal strength and dare not come to a struggle, they employ their black slaves, who blindly obey their master's order to kill any one; and this is generally accomplished with the stab of a dagger, or the shot of a blunderbuss, or by felling the man with a large stick of the length of a short pike which the slaves are accustomed to carry.[1] If it should happen that too long a time is spent in tracing the man they wish to murder, and they cannot find him in the fields or in the town, then without the slightest regard for sacred things they slay him at the altar; I have myself seen two examples of this—one at Damān, and the other at Goa. Three or four of these black slaves having perceived some persons whose lives they wanted to take attending mass in a church, discharged blunderbusses at them through the windows; without reflecting whether they might not wound others who had no part in the quarrel. It happened so at Goa, and seven men were slain near the altar, while the priest who was saying mass was seriously wounded. The law takes no cognisance of such crimes, because their authors are generally the first in the land. As for trials, they never come to an end. They are in the hands of the *Kanarins*,[2] natives of the country, who practise the professions of solicitors and procurators, and no people in the world are more cunning and subtle than they.

To return to the ancient power of the Portuguese in India, it is certain that if the Dutch had never come to India not a scrap of iron would be found in the majority of the Portuguese houses; all would have been of gold or silver, for they had to make but two or three voyages to Japan, to the Philippines, to the Moluccas,[3] or to China, to acquire riches, and to realize

[1] Pyrard de Laval, i. 131; Fryer, ii. 26.

[2] Canarins in the original, sometimes called Kanarese, the inhabitants of Kānara (Yule, *Hobson-Jobson*, 154).

[3] Moluques in the original.

on their return five or six fold, and even up to tenfold on the more important articles. Private soldiers as well as governors and captains acquired great wealth by trade. The Viceroy alone does not trade, or if he does, it is under the name of another ; and, moreover, he has a sufficient income without it. Formerly one of the most splendid posts in the world for a noble was to be Viceroy of Goa, and there are few monarchs who are able to bestow governments worth so much as those which depend upon this Viceroy. The first of these Governments is that of Mozambique, the appointment lasting for three years. In these three years the Governor makes a profit of 400,000 or 500,000 crowns [1] and sometimes more, if during the time he has no losses with the Cafres.[2] The Cafres are black people who come from many quarters of Africa to purchase cotton goods and hardware from the Commandant, who dwells on the Rio de Saine,[3] and is merely the agent of the Governor of Mozambique. These Cafres bring gold for the goods which they carry away, but if one of them happens to die when going or returning, all that has been entrusted to him is lost beyond remedy. The Governor of Mozambique trades also with the negroes who inhabit the length of the coast of Melinde,[4] and they generally barter for the goods which they require with ivory or ambergris.

On my last voyage to India the Governor of Mozambique, who then returned to Goa after having completed the three years of his government, procured a parcel of ambergris which was alone worth about 200,000 écus,[5] without counting the gold and ivory, which amounted to a larger sum.

[1] I. e. from £90,000 to £112,500. The enormous profits collected by the Portuguese Viceroys are detailed by Linschoten, i. 219 f., and by Pyrard de Laval, ii. 83. On their three years' term of office see Fryer, i. 189. Dalboquerque proposed to raise the period to eight years (R. S. Whiteway, *Rise of the Portuguese Power in India*, 174).

[2] Or Kaffir.

[3] The Zambezi, running past Sena (R. F. Burton, *The Lands of Cazembe*, 22).

[4] Malinda. An Arab town and kingdom on the east coast of Africa, from whence Vasco da Gama, on the occasion of his first voyage, struck across the sea to India (Yule, *Hobson-Jobson*, 566).

[5] £45,000.

The second valuable Government formerly was that of Malacca, on account of the dues which had to be paid there. For it is a strait through which all the vessels sailing from Goa to Japan, China, Cochinchina, Java, Macassar, the Philippines, and other places must pass. They can indeed pursue another route along the western coast of the island of Sumatra, and either traverse the Strait of Sonde,[1] or leave the island of Java to the north; but when they return to Goa they are required to show the free pass of the Malacca custom-house—this compels them to follow the first-named route.

The third Government in value was that of Hormuz,[2] on account of its great trade, and of the dues which all vessels had to pay, both when entering and leaving the Persian Gulf. The Governor of Hormuz also levied considerable dues from those bound for the island of Bahren to the pearl fishery, and if they omitted to take out a passport from him he promptly sent their vessels to the bottom by means of his galeasses.[3] The Persians levy this tax at present, and the English share a small part of it, as I have said in my accounts of Persia;[4] but although they treat the merchants roughly, nevertheless they do not derive nearly as much from this revenue as the Portuguese did. It is the same with the Dutch at Malacca, who experience difficulty in raising sufficient to pay for the garrison which they maintain there.

The fourth Government in value was that of Muscat, which also was one with a considerable income. For all vessels coming to India from the Persian Gulf, the Red Sea, and the coasts of Malinda must make the port of Muscat, and they generally take in water there. If any vessels failed to anchor there, the Governor sent to claim the custom, which was 4 per cent, and if any resistance was offered they ran the risk of being sent to the bottom by his galeasses.

[1] Sunda Strait, separating Sumatra from Java, to which the attention of the world was especially directed, in the year 1883, by the violent explosive eruption of the volcano of Krakatau or Krakatoa.

[2] Hormuz, see p. 3.

[3] A form of galley. See Yule, *Hobson-Jobson*, 361.

[4] The British grievance was that they did not receive their full moiety of the customs of Gombroon (Curzon, *Persia*, ii. 419 f.; Rawlinson, *British Beginnings in W. India*, 93).

The fifth Government was that of the island of Ceylon, to which all the places which the Portuguese had both on the coast of Malabar and on the Gulf of Bengal and other parts of India were subject, and the least of these petty Governments was worth 10,000 écus per annum.[1]

Besides these five principal Governments which were at the disposition of the Viceroy, he had also the patronage of a number of offices at Goa and other towns in India. The day upon which he makes his entry into Goa, his Captain of the Guards receives nearly 4,000 écus [2] of dues. The three offices of Engineer Major, Inspector of the Fortresses, and Grand Master of Artillery yielded 20,000 pardos [3] per annum, the pardo being worth 27 sols of our money. The Portuguese were then all rich—the nobles on account of the governments and other offices, and the merchants by the trade which they enjoyed before the English and Dutch came to cut the ground from under their feet. During the time they held Hormuz [4] they did not allow any merchant to travel to India by sea, all being compelled therefore to take the route by land through Kandahār. When the Turkish, Persian, Arab, Moscovite, Polish, and other merchants arrived at Bandar-'Abbās, they [5] constituted but one united body, and from it four of the most experienced were deputed to inspect all the different kinds of merchandise, and to ascertain the quality and price.

After their report to the others was made, the price was settled and the goods removed, and they were then distributed to each nation in proportion to the number of merchants who had come from the different countries. It is the custom throughout Asia that nothing is sold except in the presence

[1] £2,250. [2] £900.

[3] Pardao, a Portuguese name for a gold coin originally, afterwards applied to silver coins. If the sol may be taken as representing 0·9 of a penny (see p. 29), then the pardao of Tavernier's time was 2*s*., being less in value than the rupee of 30 sols, which has been shown to have been 2*s*. 3*d*. Kelly, in the *Universal Cambist*, gives the value of the pardao at 2*s*. 6*d*., and Sir H. Yule estimates it at the same figure in 1676, *vide* Yule, *Hobson-Jobson*, 672 ff.; Barbosa, ed. Dames, i. 191. This latter value would, however, proportionally raise the sol to upwards of a penny in value, and the rupee consequently to more than 2*s*. 9*d*.

[4] On the importance of Hormuz and its occupation by the Portuguese see Sir P. Sykes, *Hist. of Persia*, 2nd ed., ii. 185 ff.

[5] I. e. the Portuguese.

of a broker, and each class of goods has its own separate one.[1] These brokers pay the money to those who have sold, and receive it from those who have bought; there are certain classes of goods for which the fee due to them is 1 per cent, others for which it amounts to 1½ and even up to 2 per cent. Accordingly the Portuguese in those times made great profits and suffered no losses from bankruptcies. As to the pirates, the Viceroy took effectual steps, for when the rains were over and the season for embarkation had arrived, according to the number of vessels laden with goods, he gave a sufficient number of galiotes [2] to escort them to sea for from 25 to 30 leagues—the Malabaris not venturing farther from the coast than 15 or 20. The captains of the galiotes and even the marines did some little trade during the voyage, and as they paid no customs, they were able to gain something to maintain themselves in comfort during the rains, when they had to remain in quarters. There was also a good arrangement for the military, by which the soldiers were promoted, for all who had come from Portugal, after nine years of service, received some appointment at sea or on land, and if they did not wish to accept it they were permitted to travel as merchants. If there happened to be among them any one of intelligence, he did not fail to gain a fortune, as he had all the credit he could desire, and found numbers of people very willing to employ their money, lending it to him on the chance of 100 per cent. profit on his return from a journey. If the vessel was lost, those who had lent lost their money or their goods, but, when it arrived safely, for one écu they received three or four.

The people of the country, called Kanarese, do not hold any offices under the Portuguese save in reference to law as agents, solicitors, or scribes, and they are kept in subjection. If one of these Kanarese or black men struck a white or European, there was no pardon for him, and he had to have

[1] See Yule, *Hobson-Jobson*, s. v. Banyan; *Bombay Gazetteer*, vi. 193.

[2] This name is derived from Galeota of the Portuguese. In India it took the form Gallevat, which has been anglicized into jolly-boat, as is explained by Yule, *Hobson-Jobson*, 361. The Calcutta boatmen pronounce it *Jallybote*. Cf. p. 154.

his hand cut off.[1] Both Spaniards and Portuguese, especially the Spaniards, use them as receivers and men of business, and in the islands of Manilla or Philippines there are blacks so rich that some of them have offered the Viceroy up to 20,000 croisats [2] for permission to wear hose and shoes—this was not allowed them.[3] Certain of these blacks are to be seen with bare feet, though followed by thirty slaves, and superbly clad ; and if the Portuguese had permitted them to equip vessels, and appoint the captains and other officers according to their own wishes, the former would not have made so many conquests in India, or at least would not have made them so easily.

These blacks have much intelligence and are good soldiers, and the clerics have assured me that they learn more in the colleges in six months than the Portuguese children do in a year, whatever the science may be to which they apply themselves.[4] It is for this reason that the Portuguese keep them in subjection.

The Indians of the country about Goa are idolaters, and do homage to many kinds of idols, of which I have given likenesses in this book,[5] saying that the idols resemble those

[1] On these people see Pyrard de Laval, ii. 35 f. On the cruelty of the Portuguese to Indians, ibid. ii, Introd. xxvi ff.

[2] Croisart (of Genoa), so called on account of the cross on it ; it was worth about 6*s.* 6*d.*, and 20,000 = £6,500.

[3] The shoe question, we see, was in these early times as in latter days a burning one.

[4] The same may be said of the Indian youth of the present day, who far outstrip those of European parentage in the acquirement of learning before man's estate is reached.

[5] These engravings are not to be found in any of the editions of Tavernier with which Ball was acquainted. The statement in the text illustrates the prevalence of hero and ancestor worship. It may be remarked in this connexion that the worship of the Virgin Mary by Hindus is not uncommon in Western and Southern India. Khārva fishermen on the Bombay coast 'greatly revere the Roman Catholic saints, and offer flowers, oil, candles, and gold and silver ornaments in fulfilment of vows to the Virgin Mary and St. Francis Xavier' (Enthoven, *Tribes and Castes of Bombay*, ii. 204). Worship was done in Madras to a bust of the late Bishop Gell set up on an improvised altar, with a cast of Saraswati, goddess of learning above, and various members of the Hindu pantheon round her (Thurston, *Ethnographic Notes on Southern India*, 361).

who have done good works in former times, to whom they should offer homage by adoring their images. Many of these idolaters worship monkeys, and also, in many parts of India, as I have elsewhere said, pagodas have been built and endowed with provision to feed a certain number, besides others from outside, which come twice a week in order to obtain food.[1] In a village on the island of Salsette,[2] there was a pagoda in which the idolaters kept, in a kind of tomb made of silver, the bones and nails of a monkey which, they said, had rendered great services to their gods by the diligence with which he conveyed news and advice from one to the other,[3] when persecuted by some hostile princes, even to the extent of traversing the sea by swimming. People came from many parts of India in procession to this idol to make offerings to this pagoda; but the clergy of Goa, and especially the Inquisitor, one day carried away this relic and brought it to Goa, where it remained some time on account of the dispute which it occasioned between the ecclesiastics and the people. For when the idolaters offered a large sum to ransom their relics, the people were of opinion that it should be accepted, because they said it could be used to make war against their enemies or for assisting the poor; but the clergy held a contrary opinion, and maintained that for no reason whatever should this idolatry be permitted. At length the Archbishop and the Inquisitor on their own authority removed the relic, and, having put it on a vessel which sailed out about twenty leagues from land, it was thrown into the sea. They would have burned it, but that the idolaters would have then been able to collect the ashes, which would have served as material for some new superstition.

[1] See p. 85.

[2] This is not the island north of Bombay called Salsette, but a district of the same name in Goa territory (Linschoten, i. 177; Fonseca, 1).

[3] This refers, not as Ball suggested, to the monkey god Hanumān, but to the relic tooth of Buddha, which the Portuguese acquired in 1560, when they burnt it and threw the ashes into the Goa river (Yule, *Marco Polo*, i. 264 f.). Pyrard de Laval (ii. 145) follows the tradition accepted by Tavernier: 'They used to worship a monkey's tooth, and when that was taken by the Portuguese they wished to buy it back at the price of great riches, but the Portuguese would not restore it, and it was publicly burnt at Goa.' For the tooth in Ceylon see Tennent, *Ceylon*, 3rd ed., ii. 198 ff.; H. W. Cave, ***Ruined Cities of Ceylon***, 90, 117.

There are in Goa numbers of people connected with the Church, for besides the Archbishop and his clergy there are Dominicans, Augustins, Cordeliers, Barefoot Carmelites, Jesuits, and Capuchins, who are like the Recollects, with two houses of nuns, of which the Augustins are the Directors. The Carmelites, who are the last comers, are the best housed of all, and, although they are a little removed from the heart of the town, they have otherwise the advantages of enjoying fresh air, and of having the most healthy house in all Goa. It is on a fine elevation, where the wind blows about it, and is well built, with two galleries, one above the other.[1] The Augustins, who were the first comers in Goa, were well situated at the base of a small elevation, their church being on the main street with a handsome square in front.[2] But the Jesuits, having built a house, begged the Augustins to sell them the elevated ground, which was then unoccupied, under pretext of wishing to make a garden for the recreation of their scholars; and, having at length purchased it, they built a splendid college, which shut out the convent of the Augustins, and prevented it from receiving any fresh air. They have had great disputes with one another over this matter, but the Jesuits have at length gained their case.

The Jesuit Fathers are known at Goa by the name of Paulists, on account of their grand church dedicated to St. Paul.[3] They do not wear hats or three-cornered caps as in Europe, but a kind of cap which resembles, in form, a hat from which the brim has been removed, being somewhat like the caps of the slaves of the Grand Seigneur, which I have described in my account of the Seraglio. They have five houses in Goa, which are, the College of St. Paul, the Seminary, the Monks' House, the Noviciate, and the Bon Jesus.[4] The paintings of the ceiling of this last church are admirable. In the year 1663 the greater part of the College was burnt by an accident which happened in the night, and it cost them near 60,000 écus to rebuild it.

[1] For the Convent and Church of the Carmelites see Fonseca, 256 f.; Fryer, ii. 13. For the Recollects, *v.* p. 183 *n.*, below.

[2] Pyrard de Laval, ii. 57; Linschoten, i. 178; Fonseca, 311.

[3] Yule, *Hobson-Jobson*, 688; Mundy, iii, pt. 1, 163.

[4] Fonseca, 279 ff.

The hospital at Goa was formerly renowned throughout India ; and, as it possessed a considerable income, sick persons were very well attended to. This was still the case when I first went to Goa ; but since this hospital has changed its managers, patients are badly treated, and many Europeans who enter it do not leave it save to be carried to the tomb.[1] It is but a short time since the secret of treatment by frequent bleedings was discovered ; and it is repeated, according to need, up to thirty or forty times, as long as bad blood comes, as was done to myself on one occasion when at Surat ; and as soon as the bad blood is removed, which is like an apostume, the sick person is out of danger.[2] Butter and meat are to him as poison, for if he eats them he puts his life in danger. Formerly some small ragouts were made for the convalescent, but they must nowadays content themselves with beef-tea and a basin of rice. Generally all the poor people who begin to recover their health cry out from thirst, and beg for a little water to drink ; but those who wait upon them, who are at present blacks or Mestifs [3]—avaricious persons, and without mercy—do not give a drop without receiving something, that is to say, unless some money is placed in their hands, and to give colour to this wickedness they give it only in secret, saying that the physician forbids it. Sweets and confectionery are not wanting, but they do not contribute much to the establishment of health, which in a hot country rather requires nourishing food.

I forgot to make a remark upon the frequent bleedings in reference to Europeans—namely, that in order to recover their colour and get themselves into perfect health, it is prescribed for them to drink for twelve days three glasses of . . .[4] one in the morning, one at midday, and one in the evening ; but, as this drink cannot but be very disagreeable, the convalescent swallows as little of it as possible, however much he may desire to recover his health. This remedy has been learnt from the

[1] For the Royal Hospital at Goa in its best days see Pyrard de Laval, ii. 3 ff. It was afterwards removed, the site of the original building being included in the Arsenal (Fonseca, 228 ff.).

[2] Fryer (ii. 14) notices the excessive use of bleeding in Goa.

[3] Mesticos, Half-castes (see p. 166).

[4] Pissat de vache in orig.

idolaters of the country,[1] and whether the convalescent makes use of it or not, he is not allowed to leave the hospital till the twelve days have expired during which he is supposed to partake of this drink.

CHAPTER XIV

Concerning what the Author did during his sojourn at Goa on his last journey in 1648.

Two days before my departure from Vengurla for Goa I wrote to M. de Saint Amant, the chief engineer, to beg him to arrange to send me an armed boat, on account of the Malabaris who infest these coasts; this he immediately did. I departed from Vengurla on the 20th of January 1648, and arrived at Goa on the 21st. As it was late, I postponed till the morrow going to pay my respects to the Viceroy Dom Philippe de Mascaregnas, who had formerly been Governor of Ceylon.[2] He received me well, and during the space of nearly two months which I spent at Goa, on five or six occasions he sent a gentleman to conduct me to the Powderhouse,[3] outside the town, where he very often stayed. He took pleasure in showing me guns and other things of that nature, regarding which he asked my opinion; and, among several presents which I made to him on my arrival, he was specially pleased with a very curiously and richly decorated pistol. When passing Aleppo, the French Consul had given it to me, its fellow having been unfortunately lost. It was a present which the nation intended to make to the Pasha, who would have been able to boast the possession of a pair of the most beautiful and best made pistols in all Asia. The Viceroys of Goa do not permit any one, whoever he may be—not even their own children—to sit at their table; but in the hall where they

[1] Hindus have much respect for the five products of the sacred cow (*panchgavya*), of which this is one. See Mrs. S. Stevenson, *Rites of the Twice-born*, 166.

[2] Dom Filippe Mascarenhas, the 26th Viceroy, held office from 1646 to 1651 (Fonseca, 92). See Manucci, i. 232, and other references in the index; Bernier, 17 f.

17 [3] Casa de Polvora, at Panelim (Fonseca, 214.)

take their meals there is a small space partitioned off, where covers are laid for the principal officers, as is done in the Courts of the Princes of Germany.[1] On the following day I went to pay a visit to the Archbishop,[2] and I reserved the day after for that which I owed to the Inquisitor. But when I went to his house he sent one of his gentlemen to say that he much regretted that he was unable to see me that day on account of the dispatches under preparation for Portugal, for which were two vessels that were about to sail waited. Nevertheless, if it was in reference to a matter of conscience, he would leave everything in order to speak to me. Having informed the gentleman that I had only come to pay my respects, and proposing to withdraw at once, he begged me to tarry a moment; and after he had reported what I had told him to the Inquisitor, he returned to assure me, on the part of his master, that the latter was obliged to me, and that as soon as the vessels had started he would send to let me know, so that we might have our interview at leisure.

As soon as the vessels had left, the same gentleman came, on the part of the Inquisitor, to tell me that the latter would expect me at about two or three p.m. in the house of the Inquisition,[3] for he dwelt in another, and both houses are very magnificent. I did not fail to be at the place indicated at the prescribed hour; and on my arrival a page appeared, who conducted me into the great hall, where, after I had walked up and down for about a quarter of an hour, an officer came to conduct me into the room where the Inquisitor was. After passing through two grand galleries and some suites of rooms, I entered a small chamber where the Inquisitor awaited me seated at the end of a large table, made like a billiard table, and both the table and all the furniture in the room were covered with green cloth brought from England.

[1] 'The viceroy treats none with familiarity, nor ever goes to assemblies or banquets' (Pyrard de Laval, ii. 78). The President of Surat always dined alone, except on great occasions (Rawlinson, 122).

[2] Dom Fr. Francisco dos Martyres, 1636–52 (Fonseca, 72.)

[3] For the Inquisition at Goa see Pyrard de Laval, ii. 92 ff.; P. della Valle, ii. 421; Fonseca, 210 ff.; Grant Duff, *Hist. of the Mahrattas*, Oxford, 1921, i. 242.

As soon as I entered he told me I was welcome, and after I had presented my compliments he asked me what my religion was. I replied that I professed the Protestant religion. He then asked me whether my father and mother were also of the same religion, and I having replied that they were, he repeated that I was welcome, calling out to some persons who were close by to come in. At once a corner of the curtain was lifted, and I caught sight of ten or twelve persons who were in a small chamber at the side. The first who entered were two Augustin friars, and they were followed by two Dominicans, two Barefoot Carmelites, and some other ecclesiastics, to whom the Inquisitor straightway explained who I was, that I had no forbidden books with me, and that, being aware of the order to that effect, I had left my Bible at Vengurla. We conversed together for more than two hours about many things, particularly regarding my travels, all the company assuring me that they enjoyed hearing my account. Three days afterwards the Inquisitor invited me to dine with him at a fine house which is situated about half a league from the town, and belongs to the Barefoot Carmelites.[1] It is one of the most beautiful buildings in India, and I shall relate in a few words how these monks acquired possession of it. There was in Goa a nobleman whose father and grandfather had made much by trade, who built this house, which might be regarded as a splendid palace. He did not wish to marry, and, caring for nothing but religion, was frequently with the Augustins, for whom he manifested such affection that he made a will by which he bequeathed them all his wealth, provided that on his death they would inter him on the right side of the great altar, where they were to prepare for him a splendid tomb. According to common report this gentleman was a leper—a report which some persons diligently spread, seeing that he had given all his goods to the Augustins. It was said that the place on the right side of the altar was reserved for a Viceroy, and that it was not proper to place a leper there, to which the public generally and some even of the Augustins assented. Some Fathers of the convent having visited him and begged him to select some other

[1] Near the hill Nossa Senhora de Monte (Fonseca, 256 ff.): see Fryer, ii. 13.

place in the Church, he was so annoyed by the suggestion that he never returned to the Augustins, and went to his devotions with the Barefoot Carmelites, who received him with open arms, and accepted the conditions which the others had refused. He did not live long after he had made friends with these monks, who buried him with magnificence, and succeeded to all his property, including this superb mansion, where we were splendidly entertained with music during the repast.

I remained at Goa from the 21st of January to the 11th of March [1648], on the evening of which day I quitted it, after taking leave of the Viceroy. I also begged permission for the departure of a French gentleman named du Belloy,[1] which was granted me; but by his imprudence, this gentleman, who had not told me why he was at Goa, had a very narrow escape of being brought back, and I too of being carried along with him, before the Inquisition. This is the way he came to India, and his history as he told it to me: He had left his father's house in order to visit Holland, where, having spent more than he should, and not meeting any one who would lend him money, he resolved to go to India. He enlisted under the Dutch Company as a common soldier, and arrived at Batavia at the time when the Dutch were fighting with the Portuguese in the island of Ceylon.[2] As soon as he had arrived he was included among the recruits who were being sent to that island, and the General of the Dutch troops, seeing a reinforcement of brave soldiers commanded by a French captain named St. Amant,[3] full of courage and experience, resolved to lay siege to Negombo,[4] one of the towns in the island of Ceylon. Three successive assaults were made upon it, in which all the Frenchmen bore themselves bravely, especially St. Amant and Jean de Rose, who were both wounded.

The Dutch General, recognizing in these two men of courage,

[1] See p. 166, below.

[2] The war began with the arrival of Admiral Westerwold in 1638. There was an armistice in 1640 and Colombo was captured on 12th May 1656 (Tennent, *Ceylon*, ii. 42 ff.)

[3] Elsewhere called St. Amand.

[4] Negumbe in the original, it is Negombo, a town and fort about 20 miles north of Colombo in Ceylon (Tennent, *Ceylon*, ii. 630).

promised them as a reward that if Negombo were taken one of them would be made Governor of it. The place having at length been taken the General kept his promise to St. Amant, but when the news was sent to Batavia, a young man who had only recently arrived from Holland, a relative of the General, was appointed Governor of Negombo, to the prejudice of St. Amant, and came with orders from the Council at Batavia to displace him. St. Amant, finding himself thus treated, deserted with fifteen or twenty soldiers, the majority of whom were French, among them being MM. du Belloy, des Marests, and Jean de Rose, and joined with them the Portuguese Army. This small band of brave men, however, gave courage to the Portuguese, who advanced to the attack of Negombo, whence they had been driven, and they took it at the second assault.[1] At this time Dom Philippe de Mascarenhas was Governor of the island of Ceylon, and of all the places dependent on Portugal. He lived in the town of Colombo, and having received letters from Goa informing him of the death of the Viceroy, and conveying an invitation from the Council and all the nobility to take the vacant place, before leaving he desired to see St. Amant and those he had brought over with him and reward them. Dom Philippe was a gallant gentleman, and when he had seen them he resolved to take them with him to Goa, either because he thought he would have there the best opportunity of promoting them, or because he wished to have with him a body of resolute men on account of the Malabaris, who were lying in wait for him with about forty vessels, whereas he had but twenty-two. When near Cape Comorin the wind became so contrary, and so violent a tempest arose, that the whole fleet was dispersed, and many vessels were unhappily lost. Those who were in that of Dom Philippe exerted all their skill to bring it to land, but seeing they were unable to accomplish their object, and that it was breaking up, St. Amant, with five or six of his companions, including des Marests, du Belloy, and Jean de Rose, threw themselves into the sea with cords and pieces of wood, and managed so well that they saved Dom Philippe, and they themselves also escaped with him. To shorten this long story, on their arrival at Goa,

[1] For the capture and recapture of Negombo see Tennent, ii. 43 ff.

Dom Philippe, after he had made his entry as Viceroy, appointed St. Amant to the post of Grand Master of Artillery and Inspector-General of all the fortresses belonging to the Portuguese in India. Subsequently he arranged his marriage to a young girl, with whom he received a fortune of 20,000 écus. Her father was an Englishman, who had quitted the Company's service and had married the illegitimate daughter of a Viceroy of Goa. As for Jean de Rose, he asked the Viceroy to send him back to Colombo, where, with his permission, he married a young Mestive [1] widow, who brought him a large fortune. Dom Philippe, who had a very high opinion of des Marests, having witnessed his gallant deeds, and the many wounds which he received at the siege of Negombo, appointed him captain of his bodyguard, which was the best office at Court. It may be added that he was especially indebted for his own life to him, des Marests being the one who saved him from the wreck by taking him on his shoulders. Du Belloy asked to be permitted to go to Macao, and leave was granted to him. He had heard that some of the nobility retired thither after having acquired fortunes by trade, that they received strangers well, and that they loved gambling, which was du Belloy's strongest passion. He remained two years at Macao, greatly enjoying himself, and when his cash ran low these nobles willingly lent him some. One day, after winning about 6,000 écus,[2] and going back to play, he had the misfortune to lose all, and a considerable sum besides, which his friends had lent him. When he realized his loss, and that no one was willing to lend him more, he began to swear at a picture representing some holy subject, which was in the room, saying, in the rage which the majority of players feel, that this picture which was before his eyes was the cause of his loss, and that if it had not been there he would have won. Forthwith the Inquisitor was informed, for in all the towns in India which belong to the Portuguese there is one of these officials, whose power, however, is limited, for he has only authority to arrest the person who has said or done anything against religion, to examine the witnesses, and to send the offender with the informations by the first ship starting for Goa. There the

[1] Mestive, cf. Mestiços, half-castes, p. 160. [2] £1 350.

Inquisitor-General has the power to acquit him or condemn him to death. Du Belloy was accordingly put on board a small vessel of ten or twelve guns with his feet in irons, while the captain was warned to watch him well, and that he would be held personally answerable for him. But as soon as they got to sea, the captain, who was a gallant man, and knew that Du Belloy was of good family, ordered his irons to be removed, and even made him eat at his table, taking care to supply him with clean linen and clothes necessary for the voyage, which lasted some forty days.

They arrived at Goa on the 19th of February 1649, and the vessel had scarcely reached port when St. Amant came on board on the part of the Viceroy, both to receive letters and learn what was going on in China. His surprise was great on seeing du Belloy's condition, and learning that the captain would not allow him to land till he had delivered him to the Inquisitor. Nevertheless, as St. Amant at that time possessed great authority, by force of his entreaties he obtained permission from the captain for du Belloy to go with him to the town. Du Belloy purposely again put on his old clothes, which were all in rags and full of vermin, and St. Amant, who knew that it would not do to play with the Inquisition, went first to present him to the Inquisitor, who, seeing this gentleman in so poor a condition, took pity on him, and allowed him the run of the town as his prison till he should see what the advices regarding him were, on condition, however, that he should present himself when required to do so. After these proceedings St. Amant brought du Belloy to my lodging, just as I was on the point of going out to visit the Bishop of Mire (i.e. Myra in Lycia),[1] whom I had formerly known at Constantinople when he was guardian of the Franciscans of Galata. I asked them to await my return, and to dine with me, which they did, after which I offered board and lodging to M. du Belloy, who stayed with me, and I ordered three suits of clothes and whatever linen was necessary for his use.

I remained for eight or ten days longer at Goa, during which time it was impossible for me to induce M. du Belloy to put

[1] *Ency. Brit.*, xix, 113 f. On the religious importance of Myra see *Ency. Biblica*, iii. 3245 f.

on his new clothes. But he would never tell me why, while from day to day he promised me to wear them. Being on the point of departure I told him I was about to take leave of the Viceroy, and he besought me earnestly to try to obtain permission for him to go with me. I did so willingly and with success. We left the same evening in the vessel by which I had come, and immediately M. du Belloy began taking off his old clothes and putting on a new suit, threw his old ones into the sea, and continued swearing against the Inquisition without giving me any reason, for I was then unaware of what had passed. In my amazement at hearing him swear in this manner, I told him that he was not yet out of the hands of the Portuguese, and that he and I, with my five or six servants, would never be able to defend ourselves against the forty men who rowed our boat. I asked him why he swore in this way against the Inquisition, and he replied that he would tell me the whole story from beginning to end ; this he did when we reached Vengurla, where we arrived at eight o'clock in the morning. On landing, we met some Dutchmen with the Commander, who had come down to the seashore to eat oysters and drink Spanish wine. They asked me at once who it was I had with me. I told them that he was a gentleman, who came with the French Ambassador to Portugal, and embarked for India with four or five others, who were still at Goa, and that, as neither his residence in the town nor the manners of the Portuguese were pleasing to him, he asked me to help him to get back to Europe. Three or four days later I bought him a country mount, i.e. an ox,[1] to enable him to travel to Surat, and I gave him an attendant to serve him, with a letter to the Capuchin, Father Zenon, begging the Father to give him, through my broker, 10 écus a month for his expenditure, and to obtain from the English President permission for him to embark on the first opportunity. This, however, did not come about, for Father Zenon took him back to Goa when he went thither on the business of Father Ephraim his comrade, of which I shall speak in the next chapter. Father Zenon thought, no doubt, that du Belloy,[2] by showing himself to the Inquisi-

[1] See p. 35–6 above.

[2] M. de la Boullaye le Gouz is referred to on p. 179 as the person who

tion and asking pardon, would obtain it easily. It is true that he did obtain it, but only after two years spent in the Inquisition, when he came out wearing a brimstone-coloured shirt with a great St. Andrew's cross on the front of it. He had with him another Frenchman called Maître Louys de Bar-sur-Seine, who was treated in the same fashion, and they both had to go in procession with those who were led to torture. M. du Belloy had made a mistake in returning to Goa, and did much worse in showing himself at Vengurla, where the Dutch, who had learnt by the advices they had received from the Commander at Surat that he had previously escaped from their service, seized him immediately, and placed him on a vessel which was going to Batavia. They said they had sent him to the General of the Company to be disposed of as that officer should think proper. But I know on good authority that when the vessel was a short distance from land they put this poor gentleman into a sack and threw him into the sea. This, then, was the end of M. du Belloy, but that of M. des Marests had nothing tragical about it, as will be seen from his history, which I shall relate in a few words.

M. des Marests was a gentleman of Dauphiné, from the neighbourhood of Loriol, who, having fought a duel, and killed his man, fled into Poland, where he performed some gallant acts, which secured for him the esteem and affection of the General of the Polish Army. At this time the Grand Seigneur kept two Polish Princes as prisoners at Constantinople in the Castle of the Seven Towers, and the General, knowing the valour and skill of des Marests, who was enterprising, and a good engineer into the bargain, proposed to him to go to Constantinople to see if by any means he could manage to get the Princes out of prison. Des Marests accepted this commission very willingly, and would no doubt have had the good fortune to succeed if he had not been discovered by certain Turks, who accused him of having been seen examining the Seven Towers with too much attention, and, with pencil in hand, making a plan in order to accomplish some evil design. This had been sufficient to cause the destruction of this

accompanied Father Zenon to Goa, but the occasion was apparently different from this one. See Manucci, iv. 457.

man if M. de Cesi, the Ambassador of France, had not so arranged that the matter was promptly arranged by a present (this in Turkey is the most sovereign remedy in such troublesome matters), and by representing that he was a young gentleman who was travelling for his pleasure, and proposed going to Persia by the first opportunity. It was not, however, the intention of the Sieur des Marests to go further, and he was waiting his opportunity to return to Poland after having done all that was possible to get the Princes out of prison; but to escape from the hands of the Turks he was obliged to say that he was going to Persia, and to act moreover so that in fact he did go thither.

The Grand Seigneur had resolved never to give their freedom to these Princes, but they were lucky enough at length to find means of winning over a young Turk, son of the Captain of the Seven Towers, to whom his father generally entrusted the keys of the prison. On the night selected for their flight this young man pretended to lock certain doors, but left the padlocks open, and took the keys to his father; but he did not dare to do the same to the two principal doors—at one of which the captain with the main guard was stationed—for fear of being discovered. The young man, who was entirely devoted to the Princes had well considered his plans and made timely provision of rope-ladders in order to get over two of the walls. But for that purpose it was necessary to have some correspondent outside, and also some one inside who shared this important secret. As the severest rigour was not observed towards the Princes they were allowed to receive some dishes from the kitchen of the French Ambassador, and the groom of the kitchen, who was in the plot, sent them on different occasions some pastry filled with ropes, of which they made ladders to aid them in their escape. The matter was so well planned and so well carried out that it succeeded, and the young Turk followed the Princes into Poland, where he became a Christian, and received an ample reward in appointments and money. The others who had aided in the escape of the Princes were rewarded in like manner, and the latter, when they reached Poland, made ample acknowledgement of the services which had been rendered to them by each person.

In due course M. des Marests arrived at Ispahān, and first addressed himself to the Rev. Capuchin Fathers, who brought him to my lodging, where I offered him a room, with a place at my table. He made some stay at Ispahān, during which he became acquainted with the English and Dutch, who showed a high regard for him, as he indeed well deserved. But it happened one day that his curiosity made him undertake too rash an adventure, and he nearly brought destruction upon himself, and with himself upon all the Franks at Ispahān. Near the caravansarāī where we lodged is a large bath to which men and women go by turns on certain days,[1] and the Queen of Bījāpur, during her sojourn at Ispahān on her return from Mecca,[2] was very fond of going to converse with the wives of the Franks, because the garden of her house adjoined the bath where they generally went. The Sieur des Marests, eagerly desiring to see what passed among these women, satisfied his curiosity by means of a crevice which he had observed in the roof of the bath, where he went sometimes ; and mounting from outside upon this roof, which was flat, and such as I have described in my accounts of the Seraglio and of Persia—by a hidden way which adjoined the caravansarāī where we were dwelling, he lay down on his stomach and saw through this crevice, that which he so much desired to behold without being himself perceived. He went, in this way, ten or twelve times, and unable to restrain himself from telling me one day, I warned him against returning, and told him that he was risking his own destruction, and with himself the destruction of all the Franks.[3] But instead of profiting by my advice, he went again two or three times, and on the last occasion he was discovered by one of the female attendants of the bath, in charge of the sheets, who for the purpose of drying them upon the poles which project from the roof, had ascended by a small ladder which led to the top. Seeing a man stretched out there she seized his hat and began to raise an alarm ; but the Sieur des Marests, to extricate himself from so dangerous a scrape, and to hinder the woman from making

[1] For this custom see Lane, *Modern Egyptians*, 5th ed., ii. 36.

[2] See p. 148.

[3] On the danger of such prying see instances in Fryer, iii. 130.

more noise, made a sign to her to be silent, and promptly placed in her hands two tomāns,[1] which by good luck he had with him out of the money I had given him for his expenses. When he returned to the caravansarāī I saw he looked scared, and concluding that something unpleasant had happened to him, I pressed him to say what it was. With some reluctance he at length admitted that he had been discovered by the woman, but had tried to silence her with money. He no sooner made this confession than I told him he must at once take flight, and that the danger was very much greater than he supposed. The Dutch Commander, whom it was desirable to inform of what had occurred, in order that a quick remedy might be applied to an evil of which we feared the immediate results, advised his departure at once, and we gave him a mūle and as much money as he required to enable him to reach Bandar,[2] and to embark there on the first vessel sailing for Surat.

I gave him a letter of recommendation to the English President, who was a friend of mine, and asked him to advance him up to 200 ecus if he should require them. I spoke very well of him in my letter, and I mentioned the offer which the Dutch Commander had made him at Ispahān, to send him to Batavia with letters to the General, who would certainly employ him according to his merit; and, as a matter of fact, at this time, the Dutch being at war with the Portuguese in the island of Ceylon, a man of courage and intelligence like M. des Marests would be very useful to them. He was therefore strongly pressed to accept employment from them, they showed him great kindness and attention, and made him presents during his sojourn at Ispahān. But at length he told them that, not being of their religion, he felt some scruple in serving with them against the Portuguese, and that this was the only reason that prevented him from accepting the offers which they so kindly made him. The letters which I gave him for the English President contained an account of all this,

[1] Tomān, £3 9*s.*; see p. 20. The tomān was not a coin, as might be inferred from this, but a money of account. Yule, *Hobson-Jobson*, 928 f.

[2] i. e. Bandar 'Abbās, or Gombroon; see p. 3.

but the Sieur des Marests preferring to serve the Portuguese, the President, who wrote in his favour to the Viceroy, by whom he was much liked, laid stress upon the offer by the Dutch, in order to render this gentleman's services more acceptable. The Viceroy also gave him a good reception, and when the Sieur des Marests made known to him that he desired to go to the island of Ceylon and take service in the Portuguese Army, he left by the first opportunity with very favourable letters from the Viceroy for Dom Philippe de Mascarenhas, who was still Governor of all the places which the Portuguese possessed in the island and its neighbourhood. He arrived three days after they had lost Negombo, and when the Portuguese retook the place, as I have above said, the Sieur des Marests was one of those who received most wounds and acquired most glory. It was he also who did most to save Dom Philippe from the shipwreck ; and Dom Philippe, when he became Viceroy, thought that he deserved no less a recompense than the office of Captain of his Guards, in which he died three or four months afterwards. He was deeply regretted by the Viceroy, by whom he was much loved, and he left all his property to a priest with whom he had established a very close friendship, on condition that he paid me 250 écus which I had lent him ; this I had nevertheless much difficulty in obtaining from the priest.

During my sojourn at Goa I was told the history of a caravel[1] which had arrived a short time previously from Lisbon. When about to make the Cape of Good Hope she was caught by a storm which lasted five or six days, and so much confused the sailors that they knew not where they were. At length they entered a bay 30 leagues away from the Cape,[2] where they found many houses, and as soon as they had anchored they saw all the beach lined with men, women and children, who showed their astonishment at seeing white people, and a vessel like the caravel. The difficulty was that

[1] 'The Portuguese *caravel* is described by Bluteau as a round vessel (i. e. not long and sharp like a galley) with lateen sails, ordinarily of 200 tons burthen' (Yule, *Hobson-Jobson*, 162.)

[2] In vol. ii. p. 27, it is stated that this voyage was made in 1648, and that the distance was 18 or 20 leagues from the Cape !

they could understand one another only by signs, and after the Portuguese had given these Cafres tobacco, biscuits, and spirits, the latter brought in return on the following day many ostriches and other birds resembling large geese, but so fat that they had scarcely any lean upon them.[1] The feathers of these birds are very handsome, and those on the belly are good for stuffing beds. One of the Portuguese sailors who belonged to this vessel sold me a large cushion made with these feathers, and told me all that had happened in the bay, where the ship remained twenty-seven days. From time to time they made some presents to the Cafres, such as knives, hatchets, imitation coral and imitation pearls, in the hope of finding out if any trade could be established, and particularly whether gold was to be obtained,—for they noticed among these people some who had pieces of it in their ears, hammered on both sides, like nails (rivets) of a lock. They brought two of these Cafres to Goa, as I shall presently relate, and I saw one of them who had five or six of these pieces of gold in each ear. The sailor told me that some of the women wore them also at the tip of the chin and in the nostrils. Eight or nine days after the Portuguese arrived in the bay the Cafres brought them small pieces of ambergris, a little gold, and some elephants' tusks—but very small—ostriches and other birds, and some deer.[2] As for fish, they received a great quantity. They did all that they could by signs to ascertain where this ambergris, which was very choice, had been obtained. The Viceroy showed me a small piece of it which did not weigh half an ounce, but he told me he had never before seen any of such good quality. They also tried hard to discover from whence the gold was obtained,—for as regards the elephants' tusks they had no difficulty, seeing, as they did every morning, numerous elephants coming to drink at a river which discharged itself into the bay. At length the Portuguese, after a sojourn of

[1] These were penguins, of which one if not two species are still found near the Cape of Good Hope: *Ency. Brit.*, xxi. 89. See vol. ii. 302, 307; *Commentaries of Afonso Dalboquerque*, ii. Introd. xxxviii f.; Pyrard de Laval, i. 16, 97.

[2] Cerfs. These must have been antelope, as there are no deer in that part of Africa.

three weeks,[1] seeing that through inability to understand one another it was impossible to discover anything, resolved to make sail with the first favourable wind. There were always some of these Cafres on board the vessel, because the crew were liberal to them with tobacco, biscuit, and spirits, and two of them were carried off to Goa, in the hope that they would be able to learn Portuguese, or that some child who might be placed in their company would acquire their language. The sailor told me that when they set sail, the Cafres, observing that two of their people, who apparently were persons of consequence, were being carried off, tore their hair, striking themselves on the stomach like people in a frenzy, yelling and howling in a horrible manner. But, after their arrival at Goa, they never learnt the Portuguese language, and thus, as was expected, no information could be acquired about the country; whence the Portuguese carried away only two pounds' weight of gold and three pounds of ambergris, with thirty-five or forty elephants' tusks. One of these Cafres survived only six months, and the other but fifteen, both having died of sorrow and pining. All this information was obtained through M. de Saint Amant, Engineer and Inspector-General of all the Portuguese fortresses in India, who employed in his service the sailor who told me of this discovery.

From Goa I returned to Vengurla, whence I went to Batavia, as I shall elsewhere relate,[2] wishing to give a full account of all that occurred to me during the voyage thither and on my return by sea from Batavia to Europe. But I should not forget to mention one thing which happened at Vengurla during the nine days I spent there, before I departed for Goa in the vessel sent me by M. de Saint Amant. An Idolater having died, and the fire being ready in the pit to burn the body according to custom, his wife, who had no children, obtained the permission of the Governor and went to the pit with the priests and her relatives to be burnt with the body of her husband. While they made the three circuits which they are accustomed to make round the pit, suddenly such heavy rain fell that the priests, wishing to withdraw to shelter, threw the woman into

[1] In vol. ii. 27, fifteen days.

[2] See vol. ii. 298 ff.

the pit. But the rain was so heavy and lasted so long that it put out the fire, and the woman was not burnt. Rising at midnight, she knocked at the house of one of her relatives, where several Dutchmen and the Capuchin Father Zenon went to see her. She was in a frightful condition, hideous and disfigured, but the pain she had already suffered did not prevent her from going, attended by her relations, to be burnt two days later. I shall speak fully of this barbarous superstition in my discourse on the religion and ceremonies of the Idolaters.[1]

CHAPTER XV

History of Father Ephraim, Capuchin, and how he was cast into the Inquisition at Goa.[2]

THE Shaikh [3] who married the eldest of the Princesses of Golkonda was unable, as I have related, to induce the Rev. Father Ephraim to stay at Bhāgnagar, where he offered to build him a house and church, so he gave him an ox and two servants to convey him to Masulipatam, where he expected to embark for Pegu, according to the instructions received from his Superiors. But as he could not find any vessel in which he could embark, the English managed so well that they attracted him to Madras, where they have a fort named Fort St. George,[4] and a general office for all dependencies of

[1] See bk. iii, ch. ix. Escapes of widows from the pyre were not infrequent. Job Charnock is said to have married a woman he rescued (Hedges, *Diary*, ed. Yule, ii. 90); Sleeman, *Rambles*, 25; Manucci, ii. 157; Bernier, 313; Bowrey, 40.

[2] It is now unnecessary to annotate this chapter in detail, as the story is told, with Irvine's notes, in Manucci, iii. 428, iv. 31 ff.; W. Foster, *English Factories in India, 1651–1654*, Introd. xxviii. 92.

[3] See pp. 131 f.

[4] Madrespatan in original, Madras and Fort St. George. The first British settlement dates from 1639, when a site for a factory was granted to Mr. Francis Day by Sri Ranga Rāyal, Rājā of Chandragirī. Up to 1653 the settlement was subordinate to the Chief of Bantam in Java; but it was then raised to the rank of a Presidency. For its subsequent growth and development reference may be made to the *Imperial Gazetteer*, xvi. 368, and *Madras in the Olden Times*, by Talboys Wheeler, Madras, 188?.

the kingdom of Golkonda and the countries of Bengal and Pegu. They advised him that he would have a greater harvest to reap there than in any other part of India where he could go, and they built him a good house and a church. But in reality the English were not seeking the good of Father Ephraim so much as their own; and you must know why they wished to retain him among them. Madras is only half a league from St. Thomé,[1] a small maritime town on the Coromandel coast, fairly well built, and belonging at that time to the Portuguese.

Its trade was considerable, especially in cottons, and many artisans and merchants dwelt there, the majority of whom would have been very glad to settle with the English at Madras, but for the fact that there were opportunities at that time for the exercise of their religion in that place. But since the English built this church and kept Father Ephraim, many of the Portuguese left St. Thomé, attracted principally by the great care which this devout man took to instruct the people, preaching to them every Sunday and on all festivals, both in Portuguese and in the language of the country—a thing which was very unusual while they dwelt at St. Thomé. Father Ephraim came from Auxerre,[2] and was a brother of M. de Château des Bois, Counsellor of the Parliament of Paris, and he possessed a happy genius for all kinds of languages, so that in a short time he acquired both English and Portuguese in perfection. The ecclesiastics of St. Thomé, observing that Father Ephraim enjoyed a high reputation, and attracted by his teaching large numbers of their flock to Madras, conceived so much jealousy of him that they resolved to ruin him; and they made use of the following means to accomplish their object:—The English and Portuguese being such close neighbours, they naturally had occasional differences, and generally both nations employed Father Ephraim to settle these, because he was a man of peace and of good

[1] Saint Thomé, St. Thomas's Mount, a cantonment in the Saidapet division of Chingleput District, 8 miles south of Madras city and called by the Indians Parangi malai, or 'European hill' (*Madras Manual of Administration*, iii. 778; *Imperial Gazetteer*, xxi. 387.)

[2] Auxerre, in the northern part of the province of Burgundy, on the banks of the Yonne.

sense, and knew both languages perfectly. One day the Portuguese purposely picked a quarrel and beat some English sailors, whose ship was in the St. Thomé roads. The English President thereupon demanding satisfaction for this insult, strife began to kindle between the two nations, and would have ruined all the trade of the country if the merchants on both sides had not set themselves to arrange the affair, knowing nothing of the vile plot which certain persons were weaving to catch Father Ephraim. But all the mediation of these merchants availed nothing, and by the intrigues of the Portuguese ecclesiastics, it was so managed that the Father got mixed up in the matter, became the mediator, and undertook to conduct the negotiations between both sides—a part which he very readily undertook. But he had no sooner entered St. Thomé than he was seized by ten or twelve officers of the Inquisition, who placed him in a small armed frigate, which at once set sail for Goa. They put irons on his feet and hands, and during a voyage of twenty-two days they never permitted him to land, although the majority of those on the frigate slept on shore nearly every night, it being the custom to sail from place to place along these coasts. On arrival at Goa, they waited till dark to land Father Ephraim and conduct him to the house of the Inquisition, for they feared lest by landing him in the daytime the people might have wind of it, and make an attempt to release a person so venerated in all that part of India. The report spread however in many directions that Father Ephraim the Capuchin was in the hands of the Inquisition, and as many people arrived daily at Surat from the Portuguese territories, we were among the first to receive the news, which amazed all the Franks residing there. Father Zenon the Capuchin, who had formerly been a companion of Father Ephraim, was most surprised and most specially annoyed; and after consulting with his friends regarding the affair, he resolved to go to Goa at the risk of himself falling into the hands of the Inquisition. It was in truth a risk; for after a man is shut up in the Inquisition, if any one has the hardihood to speak for him to the Inquisitor, or to any member of his Council, he is himself immediately placed in the Inquisition, and is regarded as more criminal than the person on whose behalf he desired to speak. Neither the Archbishop of Goa nor the Viceroy himself dare interpose, they being the only persons over whom the Inquisition has no power. But even should they do anything which gives offence, the Inquisitor and his Council write to Portugal,[1] and, if it be so ordered by the King and the Inquisitor-General, when the answers arrive, proceedings are taken against these dignitaries, and they are remanded to Portugal.

Father Zenon was therefore not a little embarrassed, not knowing how to make the journey, as he had no friend to leave in his place nor any one to take with him, for it was then the season of contrary winds, and attacks of the Malabaris are always to be feared. He at length set out, travelling twenty-five or thirty days by land, and took as his companion M. de la Boullaye le Gouz,[2] of whom I have spoken in my account of Persia. The Father paid his expenses to Goa, for his purse had been a long time empty, and he would never have reached Surat but for the aid of the English and Dutch and other Franks, who gave him money at Ispahān.

On his arrival at Goa, Father Zenon was at first visited by some friends there, who, knowing the object of his journey, advised him to be careful not to open his mouth on behalf of Father Ephraim, unless he wished to be sent to keep him company in the Inquisition. Every one knows the strictness of this tribunal, and not only is it forbidden, as I have said,

[1] This passage has been rendered intelligible by collation with the French edition of 1713. In that of 1676 it is evidently incomplete, in consequence of the omission of a word. 'L'Inquisiteur et son Conseil en Portugal' should be 'l'Inquisiteur et son Conseil *écrivent* en Portugal,' &c.

[2] On p. 168 Tavernier has mentioned M. du Belloy as the person whom Father Zenon took with him to Goa from Surat, when he went there to obtain the release of Father Ephraim. His visit to Goa, when he was accompanied by Francis de la Boullaye le Gouz, was a different occasion. From Goa they went to Rājāpur, where they were imprisoned, and it was only on their return to Surat, or rather to Souali (i. e. Swally), that Father Zenon heard of the imprisonment of Father Ephraim. Tavernier writes the name Boulaye le Goût. Tavernier's statement about the poverty of le Gouz is also possibly incorrect, as the latter records that he refused an offer of money from the Viceroy of Goa. See his *Voyages*, Paris, 1653, and the *Biographie Universelle*, s.v. *Gouz (François de la Boullaye le)*.

to speak for a prisoner, but moreover the accused is never confronted with those who give evidence against him, nor even allowed to know their names. Father Zenon perceiving that he was unable to accomplish anything at Goa, advised M. de la Boullaye to return to Surat, and entrusted to him 50 écus which he was to give at Paris to the widow of M. Forest who had died in India. Accordingly, he left for Surat by the first opportunity, and Father Zenon went straight to Madras to find out more exactly all that had passed in connexion with the arrest of Father Ephraim. When he had ascertained the treachery practised upon Father Ephraim at St. Thomé, he resolved to get to the bottom of it, and without the knowledge of the English President confided his plan to the captain in command of the fort, who, like the soldiers, was much enraged at the outrage which had been perpetrated on Father Ephraim. Not only did the captain strongly approve of Father Zenon's plan but he promised to give it his support and to back him in its execution. The Father, by means of the spies whom he had placed in the country, ascertained that the Governor of St. Thomé went every Saturday, early in the morning, to say his prayers in a chapel half a league from the town, situated on a small hill dedicated to the Holy Virgin. He caused three iron gratings to be placed on the window of a small room in the convent, with two good locks on the door and as many padlocks, and having taken all these precautions he went to the captain of the fort, an Irishman of great personal bravery, who kept the promise he had made him to aid in the ambuscade which was laid for the Governor of St. Thomé. He himself headed thirty of his soldiers, and accompanying Father Zenon they all went out of the fort towards midnight, and concealed themselves till daylight in a part of the mountain upon which this chapel of the Holy Virgin was situated, where they could not be seen. The Governor of St. Thomé, according to his custom, did not fail to go to the chapel shortly after sunrise, and when he got out of his pallankeen and ascended the hill, which was rough, on foot, he was immediately seized by the Irish captain and his soldiers, who emerged from the ambuscade with Father Zenon, carried him off to Madras to the convent of the Capuchins, and imprisoned him in the chamber which had been prepared for him. The Governor, much surprised at finding himself carried off in this manner, protested strongly to Father Zenon, and threatened him with the resentment of the King of Portugal when he heard of this outrage against a Governor of one of his towns. This was his daily discourse during the time he was kept in the cell, and Father Zenon simply replied that he believed he was much more gently treated at Madras than Father Ephraim was in the Inquisition at Goa, whither he, the Governor, had sent him; that he had only to cause the Father to be brought back, and they would replace him at the foot of the hill where he had been seized with as much right as the others had to carry off Father Ephraim. However, for five or six days the St. Thomé road was crowded with people who came to beseech the English President to exercise his authority and release the Governor. But the President only replied that he was not in his hands, and that after their action towards Father Ephraim he could not in common justice compel Father Zenon to release a person who was one of the authors of the injury done to his companion. The President contented himself with asking the Father to have the goodness to permit his prisoner to dine at his table, promising to surrender him whenever he wished; this request he obtained easily, but was unable afterwards to keep his promise.

The drummer of the garrison, who was a Frenchman, and a merchant of Marseilles named Roboli, who was then in the fort, two days after the Governor of St. Thomé had entered it, offered him their services to aid him to escape, provided that they were well rewarded; this he promised them, and also that they should have a free passage on the first vessel sailing from Goa to Portugal. The agreement being made, on the following day the drummer beat the reveille[2] at an earlier hour than usual, and with great vigour, and at the same time the merchant Roboli and the Governor, tieing sheets together, let themselves down by the corner of the bastion, which was not high. The drummer at the same time left his drum and followed them quickly, so that St. Thomé being only a good half league[1] from Madras, they were all three inside

[1] See p. 177 n.

[2] 'Diane' in original.

it before anything was known of their departure.[1] The whole population of St. Thomé made great rejoicings at the return of the Governor, and immediately dispatched a boat to Goa to convey the news. The drummer and the merchant Roboli set sail forthwith, and when they reached Goa bearing the letters of the Governor of St. Thomé in their favour, every convent and wealthy house made them presents, and even the Viceroy himself, Dom Philippe de Mascarenhas, treated them kindly, and invited them to embark on his vessel intending to take them to Portugal with him ; but all three, the Viceroy and the two Frenchmen, died at sea.

I shall say in passing that there never was a Viceroy of Goa half so rich as Dom Philippe de Mascarenhas. He possessed a quantity of diamonds—all stones of great weight, from 10 to 40 carats ; two notably, which he showed me when I was at Goa. One of them was a thick stone, weighing 57 and the other 67½ carats, both being fairly clear, of good water, and Indian cut.[2] The report was that the Viceroy was poisoned on the vessel, and it was said that it was a just punishment for his having made away with many persons in the same manner, especially while he was Governor in the island of Ceylon. He always kept some of the most subtle poison to use when he wished his vengeance to be prompt ; and having on that account made many enemies, whom the fate of those he had murdered caused to fear a similar treatment for themselves, he was one morning hung in effigy at Goa, when I was there in the year 1648.

[1] 'To requite the affront of the Portuguese in betraying their French friar, they in February last [1651] seized the Padre governor, intending to detain him until the friar was released ; but on June 11 "in the dead of a darke night hee was conveyed over our walls with the laceing of a cott, and treachery of one Richard Bradbury, our drummer, who for that present had the round and charge of the watch ; and soe they escaped both to St. Thomey." However, with the help of representations from Surat and Bantam, the friar has been set at liberty.' Bradbury went to Macao in 1654, was wrecked and escaped to Macassar, when he was arrested by the English factors, but the Portuguese prevailed upon the King to insist on his release. Tavernier says wrongly that the drummer was a Frenchman and died on his voyage from Goa to Lisbon (W. Foster, *English Factories in India, 1651–1654*, p. 96 f.).

[2] Mir Jumla, from whom probably the diamonds came, was a great friend of the Viceroy (Manucci, i. 232.)

In the meantime the imprisonment of Father Ephraim made a great sensation in Europe. M. de Château des Bois, his brother, complained of it to the Portuguese Ambassador, who not feeling too sure of his position, wrote promptly about it to the King his master ; so that, by the first vessels which left for Goa, an order was sent that Father Ephraim should be released. The Pope also wrote saying that if he were not set free he would excommunicate all the clergy of Goa. But all these letters were of no avail,[1] and Father Ephraim had only the King of Golkonda, who loved him and who had done all he could to induce him to remain at Bhāgnagar, to thank for his liberty. The King had learnt from him some mathematics, like his son-in-law the Arab Prince, who had offered to build a house and church for the Father at his own expense.[2] This he had afterwards done for two Augustin clerics who had come from Goa. The King was then at war with the Rājā of the Province of Carnatica, and his army was close to St. Thomé ; as soon therefore as he heard of the evil trick which the Portuguese had played on Father Ephraim he sent an order to Mīr Jumla, the General of his troops, to lay siege to St. Thomé, and to kill and burn all if he could not obtain a definite promise from the Governor of the place that in two months Father Ephraim would be set at liberty. A copy of the King's order was sent to the Governor, and the town was so alarmed that nothing was to be seen but boat after boat setting forth for Goa in order to urge the Viceroy to take measures for Father Ephraim's speedy release. He was accordingly set free, and messengers came to tell him, on the part of the Inquisitor, that he might leave. But although the door was open to him he refused to quit the prison till all the clerics in Goa came in procession to bring him forth. This they promptly did, and after he came out he went to pass fifteen days in the Convent of the Capuchins, who are a kind of Recollects.[3] I have heard Father Ephraim many times say

[1] The Pope's mandates were often disobeyed by Jesuits in the East. (See *Memoirs of the Christian Church in China*, by Rev. R. Gibbings, B.D., Dublin 1862.)

[2] See p. 132.

[3] Members of an Observantine branch of the Franciscan Order, which originated in Spain in the end of the fifteenth century, and were

what distressed him most during his imprisonment was to witness the ignorance of the Inquisitor and his council when they examined him, and he believed that not one of them had ever read the Holy Scriptures. They had placed him in a cell with a Maltese, who was one of the greatest scoundrels under heaven. He did not speak two words without scoffing at God, and passed all the day and a part of the night smoking tobacco, which must have been most unpleasant to Father Ephraim.

When the Inquisition seizes any person he is at once searched, and all that is found in his house in the way of furniture and effects is inventoried to be returned to him should he be found innocent. But as regards gold, silver, or jewels, they are not recorded, and are never seen again, being taken to the Inquisitor for the expenses of the trial. The Rev. Father Ephraim when entering the Inquisition was searched, but there were only found, in the pocket which these monks have sewn to their cloaks in the middle of the back, a comb, an inkhorn, and some pocket handkerchiefs. The searchers forgot that the Capuchins have also a small receptacle in the mantle under the armpit, where some small requisites are carried, and Father Ephraim was not searched in that direction. This left him four or five lead pencils which are covered with wood lest they should be broken, and as the pencil is used you pare off the wood.[1] These pencils afforded a resource whereby Father Ephraim was less wearied during his imprisonment than he otherwise would have been, and that, squint-eyed as he was, he went out with a vision in which there appeared to be scarcely any defect. It is the custom in the Inquisition to ask the prisoners every morning what they wish to eat that day, and it is then supplied them. The Maltese cared for little besides tobacco, and he asked for it at morning, noon, and

so named from the detachment from creatures and recollection in God which the founders aimed at (*New English Dict.*, s.v.: W. E. Addis, T. Arnold, *A Catholic Dict.*, 774.)

[1] This description shows the rarity of lead pencils at the time. Possibly they were of metallic lead, not of graphite, the former having been first used, and having bequeathed its name to the latter. The first reference to the use of graphite for making pencils is in 1565 (*Ency. Brit.*, xxi. 86). Pencil writing is mentioned by Ben Jonson in his *Epicœne* (v. i), which appeared in 1609.

night, which were the times when food was taken to them. This tobacco was all cut and packed in white paper nearly of the size of a quarter of a page, for throughout all the East tobacco in powder, and all drugs and other wares which can be so treated, are wrapped in white paper ; this tends to the profit of the seller, who weighs the paper and the goods together. This is the reason why so much paper is used in Asia, and it is the principal article of trade of the people of Provence,[1] who export theirs even to Persia. I make these remarks in reference to Father Ephraim, who carefully collected all these pieces of white paper in which the tobacco brought to the Maltese was packed, and it was upon them he wrote with his pencil his daily thoughts in prison. This was partly the cause that his sight lost much of its natural defect, and when I beheld him again I had at first some difficulty in believing that he was the same Father Ephraim who had been much squint-eyed previously, as he appeared to be so no longer. The cell where he was confined had for sole window a hole 6 inches square, with bars of iron, and this hole was so placed that when Father Ephraim wished to write he could only have light on the side opposite to that where he ordinarily directed his sight ; and so it was that by degrees it became right ; thus he derived from this fact some advantage during his imprisonment.[2] The Inquisitor refused either to lend him a book or give him the end of a candle, and treated him as sternly as he did a criminal who had already twice gone out of the Inquisition with a sulphur-coloured shirt and the cross of St. Andrew on the front in company to execution with those who were to die, but who had entered it for the third time. It may be said to the glory of Father Ephraim that he showed in his prison as much patience as discretion and

[1] The word in the original is provençaux, which Ball rendered 'people of the provinces', but that would be *provinciaux*. For an account of paper-making in India see Watt, *Comm. Prod.* 861 ff. Nicolò Conti (1420–44) says that the people of Cambay alone used paper, all other Indians writing on the leaves of trees, of which they made beautiful books (R. H. Major, *India in the Fifteenth Century*, Nicolò Conti, 31).

[2] The interesting point in this story is altogether lost by the inaccuracy of the English translation of 1684 by John Phillips, which says that 'he lost the *sight* of one of his eyes through the darkness of the chamber'.

charity after he went out of it; and whatever evil the Inquisition had done to him, he was never heard to speak ill of it, nor even to make the least complaint, much less did he ever think of writing anything about it, which would have made public many things not tending to the glory of what the Portuguese call La Sanctissima Casa. Moreover, as I have said, all those who leave the Inquisition are made to swear to say nothing of what they have seen, nor of their examination, and, without breaking their oaths, they cannot speak or write concerning it.

Father Ephraim passed fifteen days at Goa in the Convent of the Capuchins, to regain some strength, after fifteen or twenty months spent in prison, and then set out to return to Madras; when passing Golkonda, he went to thank the King and the Arabian Prince, his son-in-law, for the kindness they had shown in interesting themselves so much in procuring his freedom. The King again begged him to live at Bhāgnagar, but perceiving that he wished to return to his convent at Madras, he gave him, as on the first occasion, an ox, attendants, and money for his conduct thither.[1]

[1] Ample testimony exists of the good repute in which these two French Capuchins, Fathers Ephraim and Zenon, lived in Madras. In the consultations of the Council, dated 4th April 1678, reference having been made to the troubles caused by Portuguese Popish priests, who meddled in the affairs of the town and were a cause of disturbance, it was resolved to remove some of them and to confirm the authority of Fathers Ephraim and Zenon, they being 'men that have ever behaved themselves with all due respect to the Government of the place and the English interest'.

Again, on Monday the 12th December 1715, the President, Edward Harrison, Esq., published a categorical statement of charges made in France against these Capuchins and others, and to the first article charging them with misbehaviour, &c., he replies: 'We are obliged to declare that the Capuchin Fathers above-named, who have had the care of this Mission in the city of Madras, from the first establishment thereof to the present time, by permission of our Right Honourable Masters, have always demeaned themselves in so humble a manner, both in spiritual and temporal affairs, as to give no just cause of complaint to us their representatives; their conduct has been regular and agreeable to their profession, nor have we ever heard of or remarked any action of theirs that could occasion the least scandal to their order.' (Talboys Wheeler, *Madras in the Olden Times*, pp. 59 and 338.)

CHAPTER XVI

Route from Goa to Masulipatam by Cochin, described in the history of the capture of that town by the Dutch.

AFTER the Dutch Company had deprived the Portuguese of all they possessed in the island of Ceylon, they cast their eyes on the town of Cochin, in the territory of which the variety of cinnamon called bastard [1] grows, as it had injured the sale of that of Ceylon. The merchants, finding that the Dutch valued their cinnamon at so high a price, began to buy that of Cochin instead, which they obtained very cheaply; and this cinnamon, as it gained a reputation, was carried to Gombroon, where it was distributed among the merchants who came from Persia, Great Tartary, Muscovy, Georgia, Mingrelia, and all the neighbourhood of the Black Sea. A large quantity of it was also taken by the merchants of Bassora and Bagdad, which supplied Arabia, and by those of Mesopotamia, Anatolia, Constantinople, Roumania, Hungary, and Poland. In all the countries just named much cinnamon is consumed, for either in pieces or in powder it is put into the majority of dishes to improve the flavour. When a dish of rice is served, especially in Lent among the Christians, it is so covered with powered cinnamon that one cannot recognize what it is, and the Hungarians exceed all other nations in this respect. As for the Turks and other Asiatics, they put the cinnamon in small pieces in their pulaos.

The army sent from Batavia to the siege of Cochin disembarked at a place called Belli-porto,[2] where there was a fort which the Dutch had built with palm trunks. It is close to Krānganur,[3] a small town which the Dutch had taken during the preceding year, without having conquered Cochin, upon

[1] This is the wild cinnamon (*Cinnamomum iners*), which is common in the forests of the Konkan and Travancore (Watt, *Commercial Products*, 310 ff.) See Dames, *Book of Duarte Barbosa*, ed. 1921, vol. ii. 112 f.

[2] This is probably Vaipur or Beypur (Yule, *Hobson-Jobson*, 90.)

[3] Cranganor in the original; Krānganur or Kodungalūr, see p. 189. It is a principality subordinate to Cochin (C. Achyuta Menon, *Cochin State Manual*, 381).

which they had made some attempt. When the army landed it advanced within range of the guns of Cochin, and a river lay between it and the town. The place where the Dutch encamped was called Belle Épine,[1] and having entrenched themselves as far as the nature of the place permitted, they placed some batteries in position which, however, could not injure the town, because they were too far from it. They remained in this position until reinforcements arrived, for only three ships had come, and the commander of these first troops was one of the bravest captains of his time. A few days after the Governor of Amboyna[2] arrived with two ships, and afterwards a Dutch captain brought a number of Chinglas,[3] i.e. the people of the island of Ceylon. For the forces of the Dutch in India would not be so considerable as they are if they did not employ the natives of the country, with whom they augment the troops from Europe. Those of the island of Ceylon are good for the trenches, but for an attack they are useless. Those of Amboyna are good soldiers, and 400 of those who arrived were left at Belle Épine. The bulk of the army re-embarked, and landed near Cochin in the vicinity of a church dedicated to St. André, where the Portuguese with some Malabaris awaited the Dutch with resolution.[4] When they saw that the enemy landed without manifesting any fear they fired a discharge and then fled, but as they only aimed at the boats the Dutch did not lose many men. The Dutch seeing some companies of Portuguese marching on the sea-coast, and others further inland in the direction of a church called St. Jean, ordered some horsemen to reconnoitre them, but the Portuguese had fled and had set fire to the church, abandoning all to the Dutch. The latter then approached the town, and a French soldier named

[1] Sir H. Yule identifies this place with the Vaypine of Baldaeus. It is Vaipin, or Vyepu of the A.S., an island close to Cochin (C. Achyuta Menon, *op. cit.*, 379 f.). This gives a full account of the campaign, p. 89 ff.

[2] Amboine in the original, Amboyna, an island in the Molucca Sea, with a population of 296,000. (See Crawfurd, *Dictionary*, 11; *Ency. Brit.*, i. 797.) The Governor was the Jacob Hustaart of p. 193 *n.* 1 below.

[3] Singalese (Linschoten, i. 77; Pyrard de Laval, i. 266.).

[4] Their commander was Ignatio Sermento. The Malabāris were Moplahs.

Christofle, who was in their pay, seeing a basket attached to a rope which was hung from a bastion, went boldly to see what it had inside, without fearing musket shots. But he was much surprised when he found that it was a poor famished infant which the mother had placed there in order to escape the sorrow of seeing it die of hunger,—for already some time had elapsed since the Dutch had begun the siege of Cochin, and since any food had entered the town. The soldier, smitten with compassion, took the infant and shared with it whatever food he had, at which the General of the army was so indignant, saying that the soldier should have left the infant to die, that he assembled the council of war, and proposed that he should be shot. This was very cruel, but the Council moderated the sentence, only condemning him to the lash.

The same day ten men of each company were ordered to go to one of the houses of the King of Cochin, but they found no one there, and the previous year it had been pillaged. The Dutch then slew four kings of the country and 1,600 blacks, and only an old Queen escaped, who was taken alive by a common soldier named Van Rez, whom the General of the army promoted as a reward to be a captain at once.[1] A company was left in this house, but the Queen remained there only six days, as she was given into the custody of the Zamorin,[2] who is the most powerful of the petty Kings of this coast, to whom the Dutch had promised that if they took the town of Cochin they would give him that of Krānganur,[3] provided he was faithful to them.

The Dutch then began to entrench themselves and erect

[1] See C. Achyuta Menon, *Cochin State Manual*, 91.

[2] Samarin in the original; Zamorin, or King of Calicut, see p. 144. It comes through a local vernacular rendering of Sanskrit *Sāmundri*, the Sea-king. (See Yule, *Hobson-Jobson*, p. 977.) But it is more likely to be a transliteration of the Malāyalam Sāmūtiri, itself a corruption of Swāmī-Srī, 'Lord Master': *Barbosa*, ii, p. 260 f.

[3] Krānganur, or, more properly, Kodungalūr, occupied by the Portuguese in 1523. They were expelled by the Dutch in 1661–2. The place has a remarkable history. According to tradition it was here that St. Thomas commenced his labours, in A.D. 52. The Jews claim to hold grants of land made to them there as early as A. D. 378, and the Syrian Church was firmly established there before the ninth century. The fort is now deserted. (See for further history *Imperial Gazetteer*, x. 343; C. Achyuta Menon, *op. cit.*, 381 ff.)

batteries, taking shelter under small forts made of palms, one laid upon another with clay. They erected one near the Church of St. Jean, which is close to the sea, and furnished it with four pieces of cannon ; and another in the neighbourhood of St. Thomas, where was the hospital for the wounded, and close by that for the sick. They also made a battery of seven pieces of cannon and two mortars in a quarter called Calvetti.[1] Sometimes they threw bombs, sometimes stones, but the stones did by far the most injury to the besieged. This was the spot where the Dutch lost most men, especially at a small river where they tried to make a bridge with sacks full of clay, in order to be able to cross under cover, on account of a point of the bastion which impinged directly upon the river. The Pepper House is a large store surrounded by the sea, and there was then no one inside it. But when the Portuguese perceived that the enemy entertained the design of assaulting it they placed some men there with two guns ; this resulted in the bridge scheme being given up and in other measures being adopted. Five weeks elapsed without anything important being accomplished, and when the Dutch delivered an assault at night they were vigorously repelled, and lost many soldiers through the fault of the Governor of Krānganur, who commanded them, and who was drunk when the attack was made.

He was also among the prisoners taken by the Portuguese, and the Dutch General promptly caused those soldiers who had survived the assault to withdraw in a boat. Two months later he resolved to make another assault on the place where the last attack had been made ; and he sent a large frigate

[1] Ċalivete in the original ; Calvetti Bazar, a quarter of Cochin inhabited by Moplas. The proper form of the name is Kalvetti, usually interpreted to mean 'a stone cutter' (*Madras Manual of Administration*, iii. 247.) But Mr. V. K. Raman Menon of Tripunittura, Cochin, who has kindly supplied an exhaustive note on the subject, writes that the name means 'Hangman's Canal or Island' (*kazhu ettuka*, 'to impale'), impalement, not hanging, being in ancient times the mode of execution. The Calvetti Canal, near which executions took place, separates the British from the native town of Cochin. In former times no Hindu lady, on the penalty of losing her caste, was allowed to cross into foreign territory, and this objection prevails at the present day. On punishment by impalement see Yule, *Hobson-Jobson*, 149, 432 f.

to fetch reinforcements who were encamped in the direction of Belle Épine. But by accident the frigate struck on a bank of sand and foundered, by which many men were lost. Those who could swim landed near Cochin, not being able to land elsewhere; they were in all about ten men, including soldiers and sailors, and the Portuguese made prisoners of them. The General did not on this account relinquish his intention to deliver an assault, and having disembarked all the sailors, he gave to some short pikes, to others hand grenades, and to some swords, with the intention of making an attack on the following night. But a French lieutenant, named St. Martin, representing that if they made a night assault they would in the darkness fall into the holes which the besieged might have made in the ramparts, and that by day they would run much less risk, his advice was followed and the General postponed the affair till the following day. As soon as the sun had risen he ranged his troops in battle order, and at about ten o'clock began the assault with four companies, each consisting of about 150 men. The Dutch lost many men in this last attack, and the Portuguese still more, for they defended themselves bravely, being aided by 200 soldiers of the Dutch Army who had deserted to them in revenge for having been kept out of six and a half months' pay, in consequence of the loss of Touan;[1] this made them unwilling to serve the Dutch Army longer. Without these soldiers, who constitued an important aid to the enemy, the town could not have held out for two months; and the ablest of the defenders was a Dutch engineer, who, on account of the bad treatment he had received on his own side, was constrained to pass over to that of the enemy.

The Dutch, who had entered Cochin on the Calvetti side, and were already masters of a rampart, remained all night under arms; and on the following day the town capitulated. The Portuguese came to carry off the bodies of some clerics who had been killed; but as for the others, the Dutch had

[1] Tuban, a town in north Java, about 50 miles east of Rambang, now included in the Netherlands Province of Rambang. It is described by Mandelslo (*Travels*, Eng. Trans., London 1669). See Crawfurd, *Dictionary*, 441; Pyrard de Laval, ii. 164. [But see Introduction.]

them all dragged to the river by the Chinese in their service—both the bodies of the Dutch as well as those of the Portuguese. The wounded were taken to the hospital, and those who had yielded embarked during the night with the engineer, passing without much noise between the Dutch ships, replying to those who asked them whence they came that they were commanded by the Dutch, and had orders for the ships to maintain a good look-out. This ruse served them well, and though the ships fired some cannon shots after them that did not prevent them from making their escape. The Portuguese, according to the terms of the capitulation, left Cochin with arms and baggage, but as soon as they were outside the gate of the town, where the Dutch troops were in order of battle, they were obliged to give up their arms and to lay them at the feet of the General, exception being made in the case of the officers, who retained their swords.[1] The General had promised the soldiers the loot of the town, but being unable to keep his promise for reasons which he explained to them, he led them to hope he would pay them six months' wages; this a few days afterwards was reduced to eight rupees each. The Zamorin then asked for the town of Krānganur, in accordance with the promise made to him, and it was indeed given to him; but first the General demolished all the fortifications and left him only the walls, at which the Zamorin was much displeased. The majority of those who were well were then commanded to march to one of the petty Kings of this coast known as the King of Porakād [2] to treat with him, and it was on this occasion that the Dutch General, who had formerly

[1] The capture of Cochin by the Dutch took place in the year 1663. The English factors who resided there retired to Ponnāni. The Dutch subsequently improved the place by erecting quays, building houses, &c. The Portuguese cathedral was made into a warehouse, and their churches were used for Protestant worship (*Imperial Gazetteer*, x. 355).

[2] Porca in the original stands for Porakād, formerly an important port in Travancore. The remains of a Portuguese fort and factory are now covered by the sea, being visible at low water. It is called Porcai by Varthema, who regarded it as an island, and the haunt of pirates in his time—1503–8. (See *Travels of Ludovico de Varthema*, edited by the Rev. Percy Badger, Hakluyt Society, p. 154; V. Nagam Aiya, *Travancore State Manual*, iii. 594 f.; Yule, *Hobson-Jobson*, 725; Barbosa, ed. Dames, vol. ii., 1921, p. 95 f.).

been, as I have said, a menial servant, showed himself to be of a cruel and barbarous nature. Four days had elapsed, during which the soldiers had been unable to buy any food, and two of them having stolen a cow and slaughtered it, the General, as soon as he knew of it, hung one of them forthwith, and intended to shoot the other, but the King of Porakād saved his life.

The treaty having been concluded with the King of Porakād, the Dutch General held a review of all the survivors, both sailors and soldiers, and the number amounted to about 6,000 persons, all the rest having died of disease or been slain. A few days afterwards he commanded some companies to lay siege to the town of Cannanore, which yielded at once without any resistance. When they returned the General had a crown made to place on the head of a new King of Cochin,[1] the former King having been driven away; and on the day selected for this grand performance he seated himself on a kind of throne, at the foot of which a Malabari called Montani, conducted by two or three captains, placed himself on his knees to receive the crown from his hand and to take possession of a kingdom of very limited extent—that is to say, some small territories in the neighbourhood of Cochin. This General when coming from Holland had been ship's cook, and this crowning of a miserable Malabari by the hands of a man who had more frequently brandished a pot-ladle than a sword, was without doubt a brilliant spectacle.

In the meantime the ships which had conveyed to Goa the Portuguese who had surrendered Cochin, returned laden with spoil. This was contrary to the terms of the capitulation, which provided that they should leave the place with arms and baggage, and be conducted to Goa without anything being taken from them. But as soon as they were at sea the Dutch took all that these poor people had, and having strictly searched both men and women, without the least respect for sex, returned laden with booty.

The General of the Dutch troops which came to the siege

[1] General Hustaart raised Prince Virakerala to the throne of Cochin, the treaty being concluded on 22nd March 1663 (C. Achyuta Menon, 95).

of Cochin having returned to Batavia, every one left, only a sufficient number of men remaining for the protection of the town. A Governor was sent from Batavia who overworked the soldiers in order to fortify the place, and he cut off the town from the gate of St. John to the Church of St. Paul, as also the whole quarter named Calvetti, because it was too extensive to be guarded. A short time after the siege, food became very cheap in Cochin, but that did not last long, for the Governor at once placed a duty on tobacco and various comestibles, so that there was only one dealer in them, and he fixed the price as he pleased. This Governor showed extreme severity towards the soldiers; he kept them shut up in the town, where they were, so to speak, in a prison; and they could drink neither wine nor suri[1] nor brandy, because the duties were excessive. This suri is a drink obtained from palms. While the Portuguese held Cochin one could live better on 5 sols than under the Dutch with 10 sols, because the Portuguese did not burden the town with taxes. This Governor, I say, was so severe that for the least fault he banished a man to the island of Ceylon, to the brickworks, sometimes for five or six years, and sometimes for life. But generally, however, when a man is sent there, although the committal is only for a few years, he never leaves it again.

There was in the garrison of Cochin a soldier of Aix in Provence named Rachepot, who, having failed to answer his name at roll-call, and having been late half a quarter of an hour, was sentenced to mount the wooden horse for three days. It is a common punishment for soldiers who are guilty of an offence, and is a very severe one. This horse is so sharp on the back that, with the great weight of the spurs which are placed on the feet of the victim, at the end of three or four hours he is severely torn and mutilated.[2] The poor Provençal, knowing that he had been sentenced to this

[1] From Sanskrit sura, a synonym with tārī, i. e. toddy, palm wine (see p. 128; Yule, *Hobson-Jobson*, 874).

[2] Also known as the Timber Horse. The remains of one existed on the Parade at Portsmouth about 1760 (*New English Dict.*, s. v. Horse; *Notes and Queries*, 9 Ser., v., 82, 253).

punishment not for three hours but for three days, and fearing that he would succumb, instead of surrendering at the guard-house, concealed himself at the house of a Frenchman, one of his friends, who had been but a short time married. The married soldiers sleep three times a week at their own houses, but the others are obliged to sleep every night in barracks. The Governor, seeing that the Provençal did not appear, ordered a drum to be beaten throughout the town, and proclamation to be made that whoever would disclose the place where he was concealed would receive a reward of 100 piastres, and also that whoever kept him concealed without making a declaration would be certainly hung with him. The Provençal having received intimation of this threat, and not wishing to ruin the Frenchman with whom he lodged, found means to entice five or six of his companions, who were not able to stand any more than he the severity of the Dutch General, and escaped with them successfully on the following night, which was dark and rainy. They passed very close to a sentry, by whom they were not seen, the darkness and rain being very favourable to them, and if he had said a word they were resolved to kill him. Having travelled all night, they came to a small river near Porakād, but when the tide ascends this river it is wide and deep; this obliged these poor soldiers to throw away their clothes, and to retain only their drawers, in order to swim across quickly, as they feared pursuit. Hunger beginning to oppress them, they realized at their leisure, which they had not done when taking flight, the danger of dying; for not only did they not understand the language of the country, but what was more vexatious, they had always to camp in the open, as the idolaters who inhabit all that part of India would not allow them even to touch the walls of their houses, through fear of being in consequence obliged to throw them down. The superstition of these idolaters goes so far that they dare not touch one another, except in time of war. When by accident they touch any one they are obliged to go immediately and bathe three times in the water, otherwise they dare not eat, drink, nor enter their houses.[1]

[1] Ball remarks that he met this dread of defilement in its most

The Provençal and his companions met a Portuguese Jesuit Father, who asked them whence they came, and they told him all their misfortunes. Rachepot was more inconvenienced than all the others, having received a musket-shot in the thigh at the last assault on Cochin; and the wound, which had not fully healed, having reopened on the road, it was impossible for him to travel before he was cured, as it had been insufficiently dressed; and the Jesuit Father could give him no other aid than to write a word on his behalf in the Malabar language, upon a piece of palm leaf, to the King of Godorme,[1] whom the Dutch had driven from his country before they took Cochin. Rachepot, followed by his companions, went to him by the road which the Jesuit Father had pointed out, and he was well received by him, and found a Malabari there who understood Portuguese. The King asked Rachepot if he would like to remain with him, and he replied that he was content to serve him, and that his companions, of whom he was, as it were, the chief, would serve him also, as they did not wish to be parted from one another. The King gave orders that the Provençal's wound should be carefully dressed, and a preparation of oil and butter was immediately applied, from which he experienced relief. The King made him visit him two or three times every day, sometimes to fire a musket, sometimes to

intense form in Orissa, where, as also in parts of the Madras Presidency, it exists to an extent hardly to be realized by those whose knowledge of the Indians does not extend south of the valley of the Ganges. The Nambūtiri Brāhmans of Malabar live in isolated houses in order to avoid contamination (Thurston, *Castes and Tribes of Southern India*, v. 172 ff.; A. K. Iyer, *Tribes and Castes of Cochin*, ii. 178 ff.; on pollution in India see Hastings, *Encyl. Religion and Ethics*, ix. 582). There are, however, few parts of India in which a European would be allowed to take shelter in an ordinary Hindu house. The dwellings of Rājās and wealthy men are sometimes provided with an antechamber to which a European may be invited; and of course there are some, but rare, individual exceptions to the rule which makes travelling in India so different from what it is in Persia.

[1] This place was Kottāyam, a town and State of some note, and the centre of the Syrian Christians; Lat. 9° 36′ N., Long. 76° 31′ E. A full account of these Christians is given in the *Imperial Gazetteer*, xvi, 6 f.; C. Achyuta Menon, 217 ff.; G. M. Rae, *The Syrian Church in India*, 1892; Hastings, *op. cit.*, xii. 167 ff.

wield a hand-pike, asking him much regarding the way war is conducted in Europe. Sometimes he took pleasure in making him sing, but the unhappy Provençal could sing but sadly in consequence of the poor cheer which he received; for the King had ordered so little for the support of himself and his companions, that it scarce sufficed to buy rice, and that of the blackest kind. But he was obliged to be patient, both to await the healing of his wound and in order to learn something of the Malabar language, without which it would be very difficult for them to reach Madras. For from Cochin up to the place where they then were, they had experienced much difficulty in making themselves understood by signs, and in their greatest hunger the people of the country offered them nothing to eat but coconuts, which were insufficient to satisfy them.

On the day of one of the local festivals the King summoned Rachepot and his companions, and in consequence of the festival presented them with four figs[1] each, which he desired them to eat in his presence. The Malabaris told them that the King did them a great honour; but the poor people, who had so little for their subsistence, would have preferred a measure of rice instead of these four figs. The people of that country go about quite naked, only wearing a cloth which covers their private parts. The King himself is in that respect like the least of his subjects, save that he wears some gold ornaments in his ears.

Rachepot having been completely cured at the end of forty days, resolved to pass on with his companions, and they left one night without saying farewell to any one. They took their road to the south-east for Madras,[2] where they wished to go; and it is easy to believe that, being without money and only knowing a few words of the language, they suffered much during their journey. They lived on the charity

[1] Plantains, or so-called Bananas, the fruit of *Musa sapientum*, commonly called Adam's figs by the Portuguese (Linschoten, i. 25; Pyrard de Laval, i. 113).

[2] Their position was probably to the south-west of Madras, hence they should have directed their course rather to the north-east. Had they done so they would not have reached so far south as they appear to have done (see p. 200).

bestowed upon them, and often when they arrived in the villages some of the idolaters fled from fear, because in these mountains they are not accustomed to see white men ; others, who were less timid, came near them and gave them the wherewithal to drink and eat , and those who were most friendly took them to their village in order to let their relatives and friends see them. When they had traversed these mountains [1] and began to enter the plain, they travelled in the forests for two and a half days without seeing any one ; and were convinced that they must die. To increase their misery in these forests they were attacked by great numbers of leeches which abound there, so that they were obliged to run in order to give the leeches less time to cling to their legs and thighs, where they assumed proportions larger than the hand. Thus they dared not rest in any place, but when they met a stream they plunged into the water, and removed the leeches on their bodies, whence much blood flowed in all directions; this made them weak and feeble, added to which, as I have said, they found no one to give them food. The leeches of this country are small and slender, and do not take to the water, but live in the grass.

These poor people having walked in the forests the first day till two or three hours after nightfall, found a little river in the middle of which was a small dry island, where they rested till daybreak not fearing the leeches there, because they were surrounded by water. On the following day they pursued their journey with the same annoyance from leeches, and slept at night close to a tree, where they found a kind of platform,[2] made of wood and elevated about 4 or 5 feet from the ground, which, without doubt, some one had made to protect himself from the attacks of the leeches. This platform served them as a camp for this second night, and, day having come, they were again on the road, and at length arrived by midday at a Pagoda,[3] where there were many Brahmans or Banian priests, who pitied their miserable

[1] Probably the hilly region between Travancore and Madura.

[2] Known in India as a machān, Hind.

[3] Possibly Trichinopoli, but more probably Madura, or some place still farther south (see p. 200).

condition, and having learnt from them that they had found nothing to eat for three days, gave them rice, fruit, and vegetables dressed with butter. But they gave it all from a distance, making a sign to them not to approach, as we do in Europe with the plague-stricken, to whom one throws charity on a handkerchief spread on the road, but standing aloof. As the soldiers had been nearly three days without eating they forthwith took so much food that all of them had fever on the following day, so that to cure themselves they had to fast afterwards, dieting being in India the sovereign remedy for all kinds of ills.

After having eaten they wished to pursue their way, but the Brahmans made them understand that the forest extended very far, and that the leeches would take their lives if they did not find some place to protect themselves from these insects,[1] so they advised them to remain there the whole night, and on the following day to start early. They followed their advice. During the night heavy rain fell, and one of the Banian priests made a sign to them to follow him to his house. Arriving there he made them enter a hole under the house, which he besought them not to touch; and though he brought them food, they would not eat it for fear of increasing the fever with which they were attacked. When it was quite dark these poor people came out of the hole, and went on the terrace of the house to sleep more at their ease. To avoid being caught there they did not fail to re-enter the hole at break of day, and the Brahman, master of the house, took them again to the Pagoda, where he ordered them to be supplied with food. He also made them rub their legs with a certain plant [2] the odour of which the leeches

[1] This was written long before naturalists had separated leeches from insects, and placed them in the class of the annelids.

[2] Sir G. Watt, who kindly investigated this question writes: 'I have no proof of the natives of South India actually using a decoction of the leaves of the very abundant wild plant, Adhatoda vasica, the Adatoda, Arusa, Rus, Bakas, &c.; but it is a powerful insecticide used all over the country, and I would be much surprised if it was not actually employed against leeches. In northern India it is used to kill the weeds and pests of the flooded rice fields, and the stems are used to line wells from which drinking water is drawn.' Col. L. A. Waddell (*Among the Himalayas*, 130)

could not bear, and gave each of them a cloth which contained a kind of chalk of the size of an egg, telling them that when the leeches attached themselves to their legs they need only touch them with this cloth, and that they would fall immediately. It has been proved that salt and fire have the same effect, and the natives of the country, when passing through the places where they know that there are leeches, always carry a lighted brand in their hands. The soldiers, with the preventative thus given to them, travelled with more comfort, and were not tormented by leeches as before. They reached open country at 4 p.m., and passed close to a fortress which belonged to the Banians, who gave them vegetables to eat and whey to drink—for water is not drunk in this country, as it is very unwholesome. The Banians pointed out to them, as well as they could, the road to Madras, which they had left in consequence of having kept too much, towards the south. By going more to the east they shortened their journey, and traversed a mountainous country, inhabited by Christians of St. John,[1] of the religion of which I have spoken in my account of Persia when describing Bassora.[2] In the year 1643 these Christians, both those of these mountains and those of Bassora, sent ambassadors to the Viceroy of Goa to obtain permission from him to be allowed to dwell in the island of Ceylon. They undertook to drive out the

guarded himself and his servants from leech-bites by dusting the stockings with tobacco-snuff and wearing putties, or thick woollen bandages round the legs. In Ceylon they used to carry knives to rid themselves of the leeches, 'which are so numerous, they would kill them if they did not so' (Dames, *Book of Duarte Barbosa*, ed. 1921, ii. 119). Friar Odoric in 1320 says the gem finders in Ceylon used lemon juice (*Hakluyt Voyages*, vol. ii, p. 58). Sir Joseph Hooker, who says he repeatedly took a hundred leeches at a time from his legs, and that they even found their way to his eyelids, adds: 'Snuff and tobacco leaves are the best antidote, but when marching in the rain it is impossible to apply this simple remedy. The best plan I found to be rolling the leaves over the feet, inside the stockings and powdering the legs with snuff' (*Himalayan Journal*, vol. ii, p. 42). Sir Emerson Tennent says the natives of Ceylon smear their bodies with oil, tobacco ashes, and lemon juice, to keep off the leeches (*Natural History of Ceylon*, p. 481; *Ceylon*, i. 302 ff.).

[1] Syrian Church—probably colonies from the central headquarters in Malabar (see p. 196 *n.*).

[2] *Persian Travels*, bk. ii, ch. viii, p. 222.

inhabitants of the country. But the Viceroy refused to grant what they asked except on condition that they became Catholics, and as they were unwilling to agree, the arrangement they proposed did not take effect.[1] A Jesuit Father was sent from Goa to these Christians to work for their conversion, but as he made no progress he preferred to devote his care to the idolaters, whose language he acquired so perfectly that he spoke it as if he had been born in the country. From time to time he converted some of them, whom he sent to Goa. This he was never able to accomplish with the Christians of St. John, who are thoroughly fixed in their views; as he passed nearly forty years with the idolaters, who were unwilling that any one should touch either their persons or their houses, it is easy to conclude that he suffered much during that time, and that no kind of life could be more austere than his. For he had to live like the idolaters, who eat nothing which has possessed life; and as he travelled from one place to another the food of these countries was insufficient to give him the strength necessary for the fatigues he had to undergo.[2]

Rachepot and his companions had one evening the good fortune to meet, on their road, this Jesuit Father, who on his part was much pleased to see them, and having asked them whence they came, they told him all that had happened at the siege of Cochin, the cruel treatment they had received from the Dutch, and the misadventures of their journey. The Father advised them to go back to Goa, where they might find opportunities to return to Europe by taking service on Portuguese vessels; but seeing they had resolved to go to Madras, he wrote down the route, not being able to indicate their stages beyond Gingi,[3] a small town inhabited

[1] Mr. J. P. Lewis, who kindly investigated this matter, has been unable to find any tradition of this proposed migration of the Syrian Christians to that island.

[2] Compare the rule of life practised by Abbé J. A. Dubois, *Hindu Manners, Customs, and Ceremonies*, Oxford, 1906, p. 201 f.

[3] Guinchy in the original, Gingi, in South Arcot District, a ruined hill-fort and village 50 miles south of Arcot. It was taken by Sivajī in 1677, from the Muhammadan Governor appointed from Bījāpur. It was for a time garrisoned by the French, 1750 to 1761. The place

by Musalmāns, except by the miserable hamlets which exist on this route.

On the following day, at their departure, he exhorted them to be of good courage, and gave them 24 measures of rice, which was sufficient for five or six days. On their arrival at Gingi, which is but two or three stages from the place where they left the Jesuit Father, they met four Portuguese who had escaped from Cochin, when they were about to surrender and hand over the town to the Dutch. These four unfortunates, who had become renegades, invited the newcomers to join the Musalmāns of Gingi, who asked them if they would serve them, offering them each three pagodas a month. In the extremity of their misery necessity would have compelled them to accept this offer, if they had not at the same time spoken of their being circumcised, and denying their faith; and fearing that they would be kept against their will, they left quietly, and followed their journey bravely to Madras, which is ten days' march from Gingi.[1] They still suffered much during so long a journey, living on the charity bestowed upon them, and not being able to communicate save by signs. They were received hospitably at Madras by the Rev. Fathers Ephraim and Zenon, French Capuchins, and as their bodies were all black and burnt by the sun, after five or six days of rest all the skin peeled off them, from which they suffered much.[2]

The English had the kindness to offer them a passage upon one of their vessels which was then returning to Europe, and Rachepot allowed his companions to go, but decided to return by land himself, after having rested nearly two months at Madras. During this time the Capuchin Fathers found means to enable him to earn more than 100 écus, and three suits of clothes with the necessary linen, by the sale of little rings of horse-hair, which he knew how to make very skilfully. He worked devices and letters on them, and these

is now deserted, and has the reputation of being one of the most unhealthy in the Karnatic (*Imperial Gazetteer*, xii. 242 ff.).

[1] The distance from Gingi to Madras is 82 miles.

[2] The story, in spite of the restrictions imposed by caste, gives a pleasant picture of the kindliness and charity of the people of southern India.

rings were much approved of by the Mestive[1] Portuguese, who never see anything of great value, so that some of them gave a gold ducat for each ring.

Rachepot having saved money, as I have said, went by land from Madras to Surat, from Surat to Agra, and from Agra to Delhi, where I arrived some time after on my last voyage to India. As I saw he was in want, I took him into my service, and I lent him, too, some money on my departure, which has never been repaid to me. From him I learnt all the details of the voyage which I have recounted, but I have also known fifteen or twenty other persons who have taken the same route when travelling from Goa to Cochin, and from Cochin to Madras.

It is fairly short, and there is no lack of food and good water, but it has otherwise, as I have said, many inconveniences, which are, that it is very little frequented; the almost inevitable annoyance from the leeches is one of the principal, and the superstition of the Banians, who do not allow any one to touch their persons nor their houses, is one of the most troublesome, and even if one takes water from their tanks they destroy them immediately,[2] and do not use them any more; for this reason some of the priests always guard them.

CHAPTER XVII

The Sea Route from Hormuz to Masulipatam[3]

I LEFT Gombroon for Masulipatam on the 11th of May 1652, embarking on a large vessel belonging to the King of Golkonda, which goes every year to Persia laden with muslins and chites or coloured calicoes, the flowered decoration of which is all done by hand, which makes them more beautiful and more expensive than when it is printed. The Dutch Company

[1] See pp. 160 and 166.

[2] The tank is not destroyed (see p. 225), but the water is let out and the tank is refilled, after purification by recital of sacred texts, and the water is mixed with some brought from a holy place of pilgrimage.

[3] See W. Foster, *English Factories in India, 1651–1654*, Introd. xxxviii f.

is in the habit of supplying a pilot and a sub-pilot and two or three gunners to the vessels belonging to the Kings or Princes of India, neither the Indians nor the Persians having the least knowledge of navigation.[1] On board the vessel upon which I embarked there were six Dutch, and about one hundred sailors of the country. We left the Persian Gulf with a soft and favourable wind, but made little way before meeting a rough sea and south-west winds so violent, though good for our course, that it was impossible to carry more than a small sail. On the day after, and those following it, the wind became more furious, and the sea more disturbed, so that, when we arrived at the 16th degree, which is the latitude of Goa,[2] the rain, thunder and lightning increased the hurricane, and we were unable to carry any sail except the simiane,[3] and that half furled, and thus we drove before the tempest for many days. We passed the Maldive islands without being able to see them, and our vessel made much water. For it had remained nearly five months in the roads at Gombroon during the hot season, and if care is not then taken to wet the timbers which are exposed above water they open; this is the reason why vessels make so much water when laden. The Dutch are careful to throw water all over theirs both morning and evening in order to preserve them, because without this precaution one runs risk of being lost in a tempest. We had

[1] 'Brave and victorious as the Persians have shown themselves at different epochs on land, no one has ever ventured so far to belie the national character as to insinuate that they have betrayed the smallest proficiency at sea' (Curzon, *Persia*, ii. 388). See also the account of the maritime ambitions of Nādir Shāh (*ibid.* ii. 390 ff.). For the invincible repugnance felt by Persians towards the sea, and the vain attempt of Nādir Shāh to organize a fleet, see Sir P. Sykes, *Hist. of Persia*, 2nd ed., i. 3 f., ii. 271. The Chinese, who were better navigators, not only visited India in early times, but continued to visit Hormuz up to the middle of the fifteenth century. Ships of Tchin, Matchin (South China), and Khanbalik (Pekin) are specifically referred to by Abd-er-Razzak (*India in the Fifteenth Century, Hakluyt Society*, pt. 1, p. 6).

[2] The latitude of Goa is 15° 30′ N.

[3] This word is the Persian shāmiyāna, which, however, signifies an awning, or a kind of tent without walls (Yule, *Hobson-Jobson*, 821). It must not be confounded with a kind of cloth called Samiano or Samānū, a fine stuff made at Samānā in the Patiāla State.

in our vessel fifty-five horses which the King of Persia was sending as a present to the King of Golkonda, and about 100 merchants, both Persians and Armenians, who were going to India for trade. During the whole of a day and night a cross wind blew with such violence that our vessel took in water on all sides, and the worst was that our pumps were no good. It fortunately happened that there was a merchant on board who was taking to India two bales of cow-hides, which we call Russian leather; these skins are much valued, because they are cool, for covering small beds on which one throws oneself during the day to sleep for an hour or two. There were also on board four or five shoemakers or saddlers, who understood how to stitch these skins and they did a good service to all in the vessel, and likewise to themselves, for we were in danger.[1] They made big buckets each consisting of four skins, and five large holes were cut in various parts of the lower deck, where some of the ship's company filled the skins, which were then hauled up through the holes. The skins held about a pipe of water each, and, in order to hoist them, a thick cable was extended from the mainmast to the foremast, to which as many pulleys were attached as there were buckets. To each bucket a sufficient number of passengers was allotted to hoist it, and so in less than an hour or an hour and a half we baled all the water out of the vessel. On this same day while the storm was so severe a strange thing occurred. Three thunderbolts struck our vessel. The first fell on the foremast, which it split from top to bottom, then leaving the mast at the level of the deck, it ran along the length of the vessel, killing three men in its course. The second fell two hours later, and, running from stem to stern, killed two more men on the deck. The third followed soon after, the pilot, sub-pilot, and I being together near the mainmast; and the cook coming just then to ask the pilot if he wished him to serve the supper, the thunderbolt made a small hole in the cook's stomach, and burnt off all his hair, as one scalds a pig, without doing him any other injury. But it is true that when this

[1] These skins were known as Bulgar leather, Persian *bulghār* (*ibid.* 125).

small hole was anointed with coconut oil he cried aloud and experienced acute agony.

On the 24th of June we sighted land in the morning, and when sufficiently near recognized that we were off Pointe de Galle,[1] the principal town of the island of Ceylon, which the Dutch took from the Portuguese. From this up to Masulipatam roads we had fairly good weather, and we arrived there on the 2nd of July, one or two hours after sunrise. Our pilot at once went on shore to salute the Dutch Commander, and when he told him that I was on board the vessel, with M. Louis du Jardin,[2] of whom I have spoken in my Persian narrative, he sent two horses to the landing-place, to enable us to visit him, for from thence to the house of the Dutch it is a good half-league's distance. The commander and the Dutch merchants received us with much civility, and prepared two rooms for us, and strongly pressed us to remain with them, which we accepted for this first night only. The following day we went to lodge with M. Hercules, a Swede by nationality, in the service of the Dutch Company; he, being married, had a house of his own in the town. In order to be free we lived *en pension* with him, and the Dutch Commander invited us often to dine at his house, where he very much pressed us to stay. We went two or three times to amuse ourselves with him in a beautiful garden which the Dutch have half a league from the town, and three of them being married, their wives generally took part in our amusements. We regaled them in our turn with many kinds of excellent fruits and good wine which we had brought from Persia; and M. du Jardin, who danced well and played the lute, strove on his own account to contribute to their amusement. The English also were present at our small parties, and they entertained us two or three times as pleasantly as they could, having baladines,[3] of whom there is no lack in this country, always in attendance after the repast.

[1] Ponte de Galle in the original. On another occasion Tavernier landed there (vol. ii. 246). For the Dutch and English Houses see Bowrey, 61 f.

[2] See vol. ii. 90, 125.

[3] Dancing-girls (see p. 71 *n.*).

On the 18th and 19th of June [1] we bought a pallankeen, three horses, and six oxen, to carry us with our servants and baggage. We had settled to go straight to Golkonda to the King, to sell him some of the pear-shaped pearls, of which the least weighed 34,[2] and the largest 35 carats ; and some other jewels, most of which were emeralds. But the Dutch told us that we should make a useless journey, and that the King would buy nothing rare or of high price which Mīr Jumla, who commanded his army and was the Prime Minister of his Court, had not first seen, and the Mīr was then engaged at the siege of Gandikota,[3] in the Province of Carnatic,[4] so we resolved to go in search of him, and the following is the route which we took in this journey.

CHAPTER XVIII

Route from Masulipatam to Gandikota, a town and fortress in the Province of Carnatic ; and the Author's transactions with Mīr Jumla, who commanded the Army of the King of Golkonda ; in which also there is included a full description of Elephants.

WE left Masulipatam on the 20th of June [5] [1652] at 5 p.m., and slept at a garden—which, as I have said, is only half a league from the town, and belongs to the Dutch, the chief of whom accompanied us, and we amused ourselves pretty well during a good part of the night. The following day being the 21st, after having taken leave of the Dutch, we

[1] As they arrived at Masulipatam on the 2nd of July, it is clear that the month should be July both in this passage and also in the next chapter.

[2] Probably a misprint for 24 (see p. 229).

[3] Gandicot in the original, for Gandikota (see p. 227).

[4] Carnatica in the original, for Carnatic or Kārnātaka. Its geographical limits have varied. At one time it corresponded with the kingdom of Vijayanagara, including Mysore and part of Telingana. It is now restricted to a region below the Ghāts. (See Yule, *Hobson-Jobson*, 164, and *Imperial Gazetteer*, ix. 301.)

[5] This should be July (see note [1]). On p. 212 the succeeding month is given as August, the year being 1652.

travelled 3 leagues, and slept at a place called Nilmol.[1] On the 22nd [July] we travelled 6 leagues to Wouhir,[2] another village, and before arriving there we crossed a river [3] on a raft. On the 23rd [July], after a march of six hours, we halted at Patemet,[4] which is but a poor village; on account of the rains we were obliged to remain there on the 24th, 25th, and 26th.

On the 27th [July] we arrived at a large borough called Bezwādā,[5] not having been able to accomplish this day more than a league and a half, on account of the quantity of water which flooded all the roads. We were obliged to halt till the 31st, as the rains had so much flooded the river that the boat could not hold its own against the swift current of the water, because they did not understand how to stretch ropes across the river. Besides which it required some time to enable the horses which the King of Persia was sending to the King of Golkonda to cross over; they were then reduced to fifty, five of them having died at sea.[6] They were being taken to Mīr Jumla, who was the Nawāb or Grand Wazīr,[7] because anything which he has not seen, or has not been approved by him, is not shown to the King, who buys nothing and receives no present except with the advice of his Prime Minister, who consequently must have the first view; and this, as I have said, was the reason which compelled us to go to the Nawāb at Gandikota.[8]

During the stay we made at Bezwādā [9] we visited many

[1] Nidumulu (see p. 141 *n.*). [2] Uyyuru (see p. 141 *n.*).

[3] One of the mouths of the Kistnā.

[4] Patamata, 3 miles ESE. of Bezwāda.

[5] Bezouart here, in the original (cf. p. 141 *n.*).

[6] Ball was told by a Calcutta horsedealer that the intelligent Arab horses adapt themselves much better to the sea-passage to India than do the rough and often unbroken Australian horses, which sometimes arrive in a very wretched condition, while in rough weather many are lost owing to injuries inflicted on one another in their excitement.

[7] i. e. of Golkonda. This was before his desertion of the King and his appointment as imperial Wazīr-i A'zam or secretary, which took place in 1657, when he presented to Shāhjahān the diamond now known as the Koh-i-nūr (Manucci, i. 237.)

[8] The preceding paragraph is omitted in John Phillips' translation of 1684.

[9] Bezwādā is noted for its antiquities, both of the Buddhistic and

pagodas, the country being full of them, there being more there than in any other part of India, because, with the exception of the Governors of the place and some of their servants, who are Musalmāns, all the people are idolaters. The pagoda in the town of Bezwādā is very fine, but it is not enclosed by walls. Fifty-two columns of 20 feet in height or thereabouts support a flat floor of large cut stones. They are ornamented by many figures in relief, which represent fearful demons and numerous animals—some of them being figures of demons with four horns, others with many legs and many tails, others which protrude their tongues, and others again in more ridiculous attitudes. There are similar figures carved in the stones of the floor, and in the intervals between each pair of columns the images of the gods are elevated on pedestals. The pagoda is in the middle of a large court, longer than it is wide, and the court is surrounded by walls which are enriched, inside and out, with the same figures as those on the pagoda. A gallery supported by sixty-six pillars, like a sort of cloister, runs all round the wall inside. This court is entered by a large gate, above which there are two great niches, one over the other, the first of which is supported by twelve pillars, and the second by eight. At the base of the columns of the pagoda there are old Indian inscriptions, which the priests of these idolaters have much difficulty in deciphering.

We went to see another pagoda, built on an elevation, and it is ascended by a staircase with 193 steps, each being 1 foot high.[1] The pagoda is square, with a dome on top; there are figures in relief around the wall like those in the Bezwādā pagoda. There is an idol seated in the middle, after the manner of the country, with crossed legs, and in this position it is about 4 feet in height. Its head is covered by a triple crown, from whence proceed four horns, and it

Hindu periods, the former consisting of rock-cut temples, and the latter of pagodas. By some authorities it is identified with the Dhanāka of Hiuen Thsiang, which others place at Amarāvatī. (See *Imperial Gazetteer of India*, viii. 18 f.; Beal, *Buddhist Records of the Western World*, ii. 221 ff.; *Journal Royal Asiatic Society*, N. S., xii. 98 ff.)

[1] There are remains on the east and west hills, but this building cannot
20 be clearly identified (Gordon Mackenzie, *Kistna Manual*, 1883, p. 218).

has the face of a man turned towards the east. The pilgrims who come to worship at these pagodas, when entering, join their hands together and carry them to their foreheads, then they approach the idol waving them and repeating many times (the words) Rām ! Rām ! i.e. God ! God ! When close to it they sound a bell thrice, which is suspended from the idol itself, different parts of the face and body of which have previously been smeared with various colours. Some carry bottles of oil, with which they anoint the idol, and they make offerings to it of sugar, oil, and other articles of food—the richest adding money. There are sixty priests in attendance at this pagoda, who live with their wives and children on the offerings brought to the idol. But that the pilgrims may believe the god takes them, the priests leave them before the image for two days, and on the evening of the third appropriate them. When a pilgrim goes to the pagoda to be cured of some malady, he takes, according to his means, a representation in gold, silver, or copper, of the diseased member, which he presents to his god ; [1] he then begins to sing, this all the others do also after their offerings. In front of the door of the pagoda there is a flat roof supported by sixteen pillars, and opposite is another supported by four, where food is cooked for the priests of the pagoda. Towards the south a great platform has been cut in the mountain, where shade is afforded by numerous beautiful trees, and there is also a very fine well there. The pilgrims come from great distances, and if there are any poor among them the priests feed them from the alms which they receive from the rich who come there

[1] In Gujarāt women offer to the smallpox goddess a tiny model of an umbrella, the sign of royalty, or a silver eye, when delivered from ophthalmia (Mrs. S. Stevenson, *Rites of the Twice-born*, 307). In Haidarābād Bhīls offer at Hanmant Nāik's tomb little wooden legs and arms to cure an aching limb (Bilgrami & Willmott, *Hist. Sketch*, i. 324). In Madras, if the eye, nose, ear, or any other organ be afflicted, they offer to the idols an image of it in gold or silver (Dubois, 600). In the Central Provinces, if a man kills a cat he offers a gold image of it to a Brāhman, and silver eyes are offered to the goddess Devī to save those of persons attacked by smallpox (Russell, *Tribes and Castes*, i. 121). Compare 1 Samuel, vi. 4 ; Hastings, *Encyl. Religion and Ethics*, vii. 112, xi. 97 ; Frazer, *The Golden Bough, The Magic Art*, i. 77 ; *Pausanias*, ii. 238, iii. 248 ff. ; Tylor, *Primitive Culture*, ii. 406.

to pay their devotions. The principal festival of this pagoda is held in the month of October, at which time there is a great assemblage of people from all quarters. When we were there we found a woman who had been three days in the temple without once leaving it, asking the idol from time to time, as she had lost her husband, how she should bring up her children and support them. We inquired from one of the priests why this woman had received no reply, and if she would receive one. He said that it was necessary that she should await the will of their god, and that he would then answer what she asked. I immediately suspected some deception, and, in order to discover what it was, resolved to enter the pagoda, especially as all the priests were absent, at their dinner, there being only one at the door, of whom I freed myself by asking him to go to fetch me some water at a fountain, which was situated two or three musket shots away from the place. I then entered the temple, when the woman, on catching a glimpse of me, redoubled her cries, for, as no light entered the pagoda except by the door, it was very dark inside. I entered, feeling my way in order to ascertain what took place behind the statue, where I found there was a hole through which a man could enter, and where, without doubt, the priest concealed himself and made the idol speak by his mouth.[1] I was not able to accomplish this before the priest whom I had begged to go to obtain water for me returned and found me still in the pagoda. He cursed me because I had profaned, as he said, his temple, but we soon became friends by means of two rupees which I placed in his hands, and at the same time he offered me betel.[2]

On the 31st we left Bezwādā and crossed the river,[3] which goes to the mine of Gani or Kollūr.[4] It was then nearly half a league wide, on account of the heavy rains which had fallen during eight or nine days. After having travelled

[1] Compare Bel and the Dragon, 1–22. The poet Sa'dī saw at Somnāth an image which could be moved by a hidden priest (*Bombay Gazetteer*, i, pt. 1, 189); cf. Bernier, 305; Tylor, *Primitive Culture*, ii. 171.

[2] Betlé in the original. The leaf of *Piper betel*, together with chopped areca nut and lime, constitutes what is here called betlé, for chewing. (See p. 229.)

[3] i. e. the Kistnā.

[4] See, for explanation of Gani or Kollūr, p. 139 above; also vol. ii, p. 73,

3 leagues on the other side of the river, we found a large pagoda built on a platform which is ascended by fifteen or twenty steps. There was an image there of a cow [1] in black marble, and numerous idols of 4 or 5 feet in height, which were all deformed, one having many heads, another many arms and many legs, another many horns, and the most hideous are the most adored and receive most offerings. At a quarter of a league's distance from this pagoda there is a large village. On this day we marched 3 leagues farther, and slept at another village called Kah Kali,[2] near which there is a small pagoda where there are five or six idols of marble fairly well made.

The first day of August, after a march of seven hours, we arrived at Condevir,[3] a large town with a double ditch, the bottom of which is lined with cut stone. It is entered by a road enclosed on both sides by strong walls, where at intervals there are round towers which afford but small defence. This town on the east impinges upon a mountain which is about a league in circuit, and surrounded above by high walls. At every 150 paces there is, as it were, a half moon; and within, in the walled enclosure, there are three fortresses, which have not been kept in repair.

On the 2nd [August] we travelled only 6 leagues, and halted at a village called Copenour.[4] On the 3rd [August], after having made 8 leagues, we reached Adanquige,[5] a fairly good village, where there is a very grand pagoda, with numerous chambers originally made for the priests of the Banians, but

[1] Siva's bull, Nandi.

[2] This is Kākānī, about 4 miles north of Guntūr, and 16 from Bezwādā. It is also mentioned on p. 141, being on the route from Golkonda to Masulipatam via the mine at Coulour (i. e. Kollūr).

[3] Kondavīdu or Kondavīr, 12 miles W. by S. of Guntūr. The fort, which is at an elevation of 1050 feet on a ridge of hills, is described by Mr. Boswell in the *Indian Antiquary*, i. 182. The town was built in the twelfth century by the Orissa Rājās. (*Madras Manual of Administration*, iii. 207.)

[4] Mr. F. W. Robertson suggests Kopporam, a village about 22 miles WSW. from Kondavīd, or Kondakavur; the identification is uncertain and there was no need for such a detour.

[5] Addanki, an important town, on the Gundla-Kamma river, 38 miles SSW. of Kondavīd (*Imperial Gazetteer*, v. 9).

to-day all is in ruins. There are still some idols in the pagoda, but all are mutilated, still these poor people do not cease to worship them. On the 4th [August] we made 8 leagues, and slept at the village of Nosdrepar.[1] Half a league on this side there is a large river, which contained but little water—the rains not having then commenced. On the 5th [August], after traversing 8 leagues of road, we slept at the village of Condecour.[2]

On the 6th [August] we marched seven hours and halted at another village called Dakijé.[3] On the 7th [August], after having travelled 3 leagues, we came to a town called Nelour,[4] where there are many pagodas, and having crossed a large river a quarter of a league farther on, we marched for 6 leagues and came to a village called Gandaron.[5] On the 8th [August], after a march of eight hours, we slept at Serepelé,[6] which is only a small village. On the 9th [August] we travelled 9 leagues, and slept at a good village called Ponter.[7] On the 10th [August] we marched eleven hours and halted at Senepgond,[8] another good village.

On the 11th [August] we only went as far as Palicate,[9]

[1] Nernūrupād, Kandukūr taluk, Nellore District, a mile south of the Musi, the large river referred to in the text.

[2] Kandukūr, headquarters of the taluk of the same name in Nellore District (*ibid.*, xiv. 379).

[3] Zakkepalli-Gūdūr, locally called Dakkipalli.

[4] Nellore. There is a temple on a hill near the town called Narasinha Kondu. Nellore is on the south bank of the Penner River, which, therefore, must have been crossed before the town was reached (*Imperial Gazetteer*, xix. 23 f.).

[5] Mr. Bateman would place this before Nellore, and identify it with Gandavaram, a large village in Kovūr taluk, Nellore District.

[6] Sarvēpale, a village in the Nellore taluk, 12 miles S. of Nellore, but, if so, the distances are wrong.

[7] Pūdēru, a village in the Pōlūr division, about 6 miles SE. of Naidupet railway station.

[8] Sunnapagunta, a large village in the Ponnēri taluk, Chingleput District, about 3 miles E. of Elāvūr railway station.

[9] Pulicat, in the Chingleput District of Madras. The town is on an island which separates the sea from a considerable lagoon or salt lake. It was the site of the first Dutch settlement on the mainland of India. In 1609 the fort referred to by Tavernier was built. The town was subsequently transferred to the English and back to the Dutch several times in succession. Orme gives a plan of this as well as of many of

which is but 4 leagues from Senepgond, and of these 4 leagues we marched more than one in the sea, our horses in many places having the water nearly to the saddle. There is also another road, but it is longer by 2 or 3 leagues. Pulicat is a fort belonging to the Dutch, who occupy the whole length of the coast of Coromandel; it is here they have their factory, and here the Chief of all those who live in the territory of the King of Golkonda resides. There are generally about 200 soldiers in garrison in this fort, besides many merchants who reside there for trade, and other persons who, after having served the Company for their full term, have retired to this place. Some natives of the country have by degrees also congregated here, so that Pulicat is to-day like a small town. Between the town and the fort a large open space is left, so that the fort is not incommoded by the town. The bastions are furnished with good guns, and the sea washes at the foot, but there is no port, and it is only a roadstead. We remained in the town till the evening of the following day, and the Governor would not allow us to dine elsewhere but at his table. He was the Sieur Pite,[1] a German of the town of Bremen. We received all kinds of attention from him, and he took us three times round the fort on the walls, where one could easily walk. The manner in which the inhabitants procure water for drinking is somewhat remarkable. When the tide is out they go on the sand as close to the sea as possible, and on making holes there, they find sweet water, which is excellent.[2]

On the 12th [August] at sunset we left Pulicat, and on the following day, at 10 o'clock A.M., arrived at Madras, otherwise called Fort St. George, which belongs to the English, and of which I have elsewhere spoken[3]—having travelled only

the other forts and towns mentioned by Tavernier (*Imperial Gazetteer*, xx. 241 f.). For a full note on Pulicat see Dames, *Book of Duarte Barbosa*, vol. ii., 1921, 129 ff.

[1] The French edition of 1713 has Pitre, but Laurens Pit (the elder) must be meant. Councillor Extraord. 1657–61 and Ordinary 1660–78.

[2] This method of obtaining fresh water is still followed in certain parts of the coast of India, and in the Persian Gulf by diving down to a considerable depth and then filling corked bottles. (See vol. ii, p. 84; Chardin, iv, p. 69; and *Persian Travels*, ed. 1676, p. 233.)

[3] Madras, see p. 176, 22 miles from Pulicat.

7 or 8 leagues this day. We went to stay at the Convent of the Capuchins, where we found the Rev. Father Ephraim of Nevers and the Rev. Father Zenon of Baugé, of whom I have also spoken in preceding chapters.[1] On the 14th [August] we went to the fort to visit the English President,[2] and we dined with him.

On the 15th [August] M. du Jardin [3] and I left in the morning to go to St. Thomé,[4] which, as I have said, is only a good half league from Madras. We first called on the Governor, who received us with much civility and kept us to dinner. The time after dinner was spent in visiting the Churches of the Augustin Fathers and the Jesuit Fathers; in the first there is the head of a lance, which is regarded as that with which St. Thomas [5] was martyred; and we also visited some Portuguese, who received us very well. In the cool of the evening we returned to Madras.

On the 16th [August] the Governor of St. Thomé and the Portuguese whom we had visited sent us a quantity of presents—hams, ox tongues, sausages, fish, water melons, and other fruits of the country. It took nine or ten men to carry these presents, and as we lodged with the Capuchins it was always believed that M. du Jardin was a bishop, and that, not wishing to make himself known, he had come to see the country in disguise. What confirmed them in this belief was that they knew that the Governor of Pulicat had treated us with great civility, and that he of Madras had done no less. Moreover, six months after our departure, no one could eradicate this belief, so strongly was it engrafted. On the 17th and 18th [August] we again went to dine with the

[1] See pp. 168, 178 ff., 202, above.

[2] Sir W. Foster states that the President at this time was Henry Greenhill (*English Factories in India, 1651–1654*, p. xxxix).

[3] See p. 206 above.

[4] St. Thomé, now a suburb of Madras (see p. 177 *n*, where the distance has been shown to be 8 miles. Tavernier doubtless meant 'a good league and a half').

[5] For a full discussion of this tradition, see *Imperial Gazetteer*, ii. 5 *n.*, 288; Linschoten, i. 83 ff.; Yule, *Marco Polo*, ii. 290 ff.; Smith, *Oxford Hist. of India*, 126; Dames, *Book of Duarte Barbosa*, vol. ii. 126 ff.

English President, and we passed the time with all the amusements which he could devise to remove from our bodies and minds the pains and fatigues we had incurred during so troublesome a journey. On the 19th [August] we visited some native Christians who dwell at Madras and live in tolerable comfort. They received us very well, and we heard that they are very generous to the Reverend Capuchin Fathers. On the 20th [August] the Christians whom we had visited also sent presents of some fruits of the country. On the 21st [August] we went to take leave of the English President and the chiefs of that nation, who had regaled us so well.

On the 22nd [August], in the morning, we left Madras, and, after having travelled 6 leagues, arrived at a large village called Serravaron.[1] On the 23rd [August], having travelled 7 leagues, we came to Oudecot.[2] This is a day's march through a flat and somewhat sandy country. On both sides there are groves of bamboo.[3] It is a kind of cane which is very tall, sometimes equalling in height our loftiest forest trees. Some of these forests are so thick that it is impossible for a man to enter them, and an enormous number of monkeys are found in them. Those on one side of the road are so hostile to those on the other, that none can venture to pass from one side to the other without running the risk of being at once strangled. While at Pulicat, the Governor told us that when we passed through these woods we should enjoy the opportunity, as he had done, of making the monkeys fight,[4] and this is the way which is employed to bring it about. Throughout all this country at every league the road is closed by gates and barricades, where a strict watch is kept, and all passers by are questioned whence they come and whither they are going, so that a traveller can without danger and in perfect safety carry his gold in his hand. In

[1] Chōlavaram, in the Chingleput District, where there is an old Saiva temple (*Madras Manual of Administration*, iii. 180).

[2] Ūttukkōttai, on the N. bank of the Arani river, 20 miles WSW. of Chōlavaram, in Ponnēri taluk, Chingleput District.

[3] Bambou in the original.

[4] A remarkable account of a battle between two troops of Langūr or Hanumān monkeys, which was witnessed by Mr. T. W. H. Hughes, F.G.S., will be found in the *Proc. As. Society Bengal*, for September 1884, p. 147; W. T. Blanford, *Mammalia of British India*, 29.

all these places rice can be bought, and those who wish to enjoy the amusement of making the monkeys fight place five or six baskets of rice in the road at forty or fifty paces distant the one from the other, and close to each five or six sticks, two feet long and an inch thick. The baskets being thus placed and uncovered, every one withdraws a short distance, and immediately the monkeys are to be seen on both sides descending from the bamboos and leaving the jungle to approach the baskets full of rice. They spend half an hour showing their teeth at one another before approaching the baskets; sometimes they advance, sometimes they retire, fearing to come to close quarters. At length the females, particularly those having young ones, which they carry in their arms as a woman carries her child, which are bolder than the males, approach the baskets, and when about to stretch out their heads to eat, the males of the other side of the jungle immediately advance to prevent them and bite them. Those of the other side then advance, and both parties becoming furious they take up the sticks near the baskets, and immediately a fierce combat ensues. The weakest being at length compelled to give way, withdraw into the jungle, some with broken heads, others maimed in some member, while those who remain masters of the field eat their fill of rice. It is true, however, that when they begin to be satisfied they allow some of the females of the other party to come and eat with them.

On the 24th [August], after having accomplished 9 leagues by a road similar to that of the preceding day, we arrived at Naraveron.[1] On the 25th [August], after a march of eight hours in a country of the same kind, finding gates at every two leagues, we arrived in the evening at Gazel.[2]

On the 26th [August] we travelled 9 leagues, and halted at Courua,[3] but could get no supplies, either for the men or

[1] Nārāyanavanam, 3 miles ESE. of Puttūr station, Madras–Bombay Railway, and 24 miles by road from Ūttukkōttai.

[2] Gāzulamandiyam, 3 miles SE. of Rēnigunta railway station, Madras-Bombay main line, 14 miles by road from Nārāyanavanam.

[3] The rock called Kuruva-bandalu, about a mile to N. of Settigunta-Bāhapalle. There is a forest Bungalow on the rock, which is in the Cuddapah District.

the mounts, whether oxen or horses, and ours had to content themselves with a little grass which was cut for them. Courua is renowned for its pagoda, and on arrival there we saw several companies of military marching, some with handpikes, others with guns, and others with sticks, going to join one of the principal captains of Mīr Jumla's army, on a hill near Courua, where he had pitched his tent. The place is very pleasant, and derives its coolness from numerous trees and fountains. As soon as we learnt that this officer was so near at hand, we set out in order to salute him, and found him in his tent with many nobles, chiefs of the country, all idolaters. After having saluted him and made him a present of a pair of pocket pistols decorated with silver, and two yards of Dutch flame-coloured cloth, he asked why we had come into the country, and we replied that we came to see Mīr Jumla, Commander-in-Chief of the King of Golkonda, to transact some business with him. At this reply he treated us kindly and having observed that he supposed us to be Dutchmen, we told him we were not of that country, but were Frenchmen. The captain, not having any previous knowledge of our nation, detained us a long time to acquaint himself with our forms of government, and the greatness of our King. While he kept us in this way the sufra [1] was spread, and then all the idolatrous nobles withdrew, as they do not eat anything cooked by Musalmāns. Having found that we had not the same scruples, he invited us to supper, but we declined, because it was late, and we wished to rejoin our people. But we had scarcely arrived at our tent when we saw three men, each with a large dish of pulão [2] on his head, which the captain had sent us. Before leaving him he invited us to remain for the following day to enjoy elephant-hunting, but as we did not wish to lose time we excused ourselves, and told him that our business compelled us to proceed. Six or seven days previously they had captured five elephants, three of which had escaped, and it was these which they were

[1] *Sofra* in the original: =tablecloth (see vol. ii.4). It is generally called Dastarkhān or Dastārkhwān; Pers. *dastār*, a fine muslin cloth, *khwān*, a tray

[2] Pulão (see p. 125.)

pursuing, and ten or twelve of the poor peasants who assisted in capturing them had been killed. We informed ourselves of the manner in which they hunt, and this is what we ascertained. Certain passages are cut in the jungle, in which holes are excavated and covered with branches with a little earth on top. The hunters, with shouts and the noise of drums, to which they add fire-darts, drive the elephant into these passages, when coming on the holes it falls in and is unable to get out again.[2] The hunters then place ropes and chains on it, which they pass under the belly, and bind the trunk and the legs, afterwards employing special machines to hoist the animal up. Nevertheless, out of five which had been taken three escaped, as I have said, although they had still some chains and cords about their bodies, and even on their legs. These people told us an astonishing thing, which is wonderful if one could believe it. It is, that elephants which have once been caught and have escaped, if driven into the jungle are always on their guard, and tear off a large branch of a tree with their trunks, with which they go along sounding everywhere before putting down their feet, to see if there are any holes, so as not to be caught a second time. It was this which made the hunters, who gave us this description, despair of being able to recapture the three elephants which had escaped. If we had been certain of witnessing this wonderful precaution of the elephant, no matter how pressing our business, we should have willingly waited for two or three days. This captain who had received us so well was a sort of Brigadier, and commanded 3,000 or 4,000 men who were stationed half a league off.

On the 27th [August], having marched two hours, we came to a large village, where we saw the two elephants

[1] This mode of capturing elephants is employed in Travancore (V. Nagam Aiya, *State Manual*, iii. 541), and in Bengal (F. Buchanan, Martin, *Eastern India*, ii. 502). In Malabar the system of catching elephants is to dig groups of pitfalls on their paths, or a little distance from them, a tree being felled to induce the animals to go round it, but a cautious old female will often suspect the trap (W. Logan, *District Manual Malabar*, i. 59). See Sir S. W. Baker, *Wild Beasts and their Ways*, 58; T. Williamson, *Oriental Field Sports*, ed. 1808, i. 151; Pliny, *Nat. Hist.*, viii. 8.

which had been captured. Each of these wild elephants was between two tame ones, and around the wild ones there were six men with fire-darts, who spoke to the animals when feeding them, saying in their language, 'Take that and eat it.' They gave them small wisps of hay, pieces of black sugar, rice cooked in water, and pounded peppercorns. When the wild elephant would not do what was ordered, the men told the tame elephants to beat him ; this they immediately did, one striking him on the forehead and head with his trunk, and if he attempted to revenge himself, the other struck him from his side, so that the poor elephant knew not where to turn ; this taught him to obey.

As I have insensibly drifted into a history of elephants, I shall add here some other remarks which I have made on the nature of these animals. Although the elephant does not approach the female after having been captured,[1] it happens nevertheless that he becomes in season sometimes. One day when Shāhjahān was out hunting on his elephant with one of his sons, who sat with him fanning him, the elephant became so much in heat that the driver was unable to control it, and he told the Emperor that to arrest the rage of the elephant, which might crush them among the trees, it was necessary that one of the three who were on the elephant should offer himself, and that with all his heart he sacrificed his life for the Emperor and his son, begging His Majesty to take care of his three children. Having said this, he threw himself under the elephant, and immediately the animal took him with his trunk, and crushing him under his feet, then became mild and tractable as before. The Emperor,

[1] This is still widely believed, but is not true ; not only are there well-authenticated instances of the birth of elephants in India, both the parents having been in captivity, but recently elephants appear to have been successfully bred in America (Blanford, *Mammalia of India*, 466). Some of the Indian instances just referred to are given in the *Asian* for the 5th of June 1883, and a case of congress was not only witnessed by a number of officers at Thaetmyo in Burmah, but was actually photographed. A lithograph taken from this photograph will be found in the manual of *The Elephant*, by Mr. J. H. Steel, V. S., Madras, 1885. Manucci (ii. 364) says that the Mughal Emperors held it to be unlucky that elephants should breed in captivity.

for this wonderful escape, gave 200,000 rupees to the poor, and promoted at court each of the sons of the man who had so generously given his life for the safety of his Prince.

I have to remark still that, although the skin of the elephant is very hard during life, when dead it feels like bird-lime in the hands.

Elephants come from many places in Asia—from the island of Ceylon, where they are the smallest, but the most courageous of all; from the island of Sumatra, the Kingdom of Cochin, the Kingdom of Siam, and the frontiers of the Kingdom of Bhutān towards Great Tartary. They come also from the coast of Malinda,[1] on the East coast of Africa, where they must be very abundant, according to a report which was made to me at Goa by a Portuguese captain who came from that region to make some complaint against the Governor of Mozambique. He told me that throughout that coast there are many enclosures fenced with elephants' tusks only,[2] and that some of them are more than a league in circuit. He added that the blacks of the country hunt the elephants, and eat the flesh, but for each elephant which they slay they have to give one of the tusks to their Chief.

I have described how elephants are captured in the territory of the King of Golkonda; the following is the method practised in the island of Ceylon for the capture of these animals. A long passage, enclosed on both sides, is prepared, so that when an elephant has entered he cannot turn either to the right or to the left. This passage is wide to begin with, but narrows gradually to the end, where there is only room for a female elephant, which is in season, to lie down. Although tame she is nevertheless bound with chains and strong cords, and by her cries she attracts the male, who comes to her

[1] This statement is of special interest if intended to mean that the African elephant was domesticated and exported to India. See vol. ii. 248; but Tavernier's statement does not seem necessarily to mean that they were imported from East Africa to India. On the use of elephants by the Greeks and Romans see Sir J. Frazer, *Pausanias*, ii. 105 ff.

[2] Ball refers to a statement by a comparatively recent African traveller that elephants' tusks are known to have been formerly so used for fences. (See vol. ii, p. 127.)

along the passage up to where it becomes narrow; and when he has passed that point, the men who are concealed close that portion of the passage by a strong barricade which they have in readiness; and when the elephant has advanced a short distance farther, and is close to the female, another barricade closes the passage in that direction. Then, with chains and ropes, thrown on the elephant, they bind his trunk and legs, and trap him so that he cannot escape. A nearly identical method is followed in the Kingdoms of Siam and Pegu, the only difference being that the peasants mount the female and go to the forests in search of the male. When they have found him, they tie up the female in the most convenient place they can find, after which they lay snares for the elephant, who approaches slowly on hearing her cries.

It is especially remarkable in the case of the female elephant that at certain seasons she collects all kinds of leaves and grass, with which she makes for herself a bed with a kind of bolster, elevated 4 or 5 feet from the ground, where, contrary to the nature of all other beasts, she lies to await the male, whom she calls by her cries.[1]

It is, moreover, peculiar to the elephants of Ceylon that only the first male produced by the female has tusks.[2] It is to be remarked also that the ivory from the islands of Ceylon and Achīn[3] has the peculiarity when it is worked that it never becomes yellow like that from the Peninsula and the

[1] This is a fable, repeated by Linschoten (ii. 4), though there appears to be some foundation for the belief that natural inequalities in the ground are availed of during the act of congress.

[2] 'While in Africa and India both sexes have tusks, with some slight disproportion in the size of those of the females, not one elephant in a hundred is found with tusks in Ceylon, and the few that possess them are exclusively males.' (Sir E. Tennent, *Nat. Hist. of Ceylon*, p. 78; *Ceylon*, ii. 273 f.). The same authority states that the desire for ivory is so great in Ceylon that when a tusker is known to be in a herd he is hunted till shot. This may have been going on for a very long period, and may account for the tuskless character of the breed. Thus the action of man may have prevented the operation of the law of the survival of the fittest, as those having tusks would otherwise hold possession of the herds of females.

[3] Achen in the original; it here stands for Sumatra. For the value of the different varieties of ivory see *Ency. Brit.*, xv. 92; T. P. Ellis, *Monograph on Ivory-work in the Panjab*, sect. 11.

West (*sic*) Indies;[1] this causes it to be more esteemed and dearer than the other.

When merchants are taking elephants anywhere to sell, it is amusing to see them pass. As there are generally both old and young, when the former have passed the children run after the little ones which follow behind, playing with them and giving them something to eat. Whilst these young elephants, which are then alone, are occupied in taking what is given, the children jump upon them, and it is then that the fun begins. The young elephants which remain behind to eat while their mothers have marched away, feeling themselves deserted, double their pace in order to rejoin them, flourish their trunks, and often dismount the children from their backs, without doing them any harm. This does not disperse this little crowd, which continues to follow them for some time, offering them food as before.

Notwithstanding all the research which I have made with much care, I have never been able to ascertain very exactly how long an elephant lives, and this is all the information that can be obtained from those who tend these animals. They cannot say more than that such an elephant has been in the charge of their father, grandfather, and great-grandfather, and by estimating the time that these people may have lived, it is found that an elephant's age sometimes amounts to 120 or 130 years.[2]

I observe that the majority of those who have written accounts of India say boldly that the Great Mogul keeps 3,000 or 4,000 elephants. When at Jahānābād, where the Emperor at present resides, I often inquired from the person

[1] Tavernier makes a slip if he alludes to elephant ivory, as there are no elephants in the West Indies.

[2] Mr. Sanderson says (*Thirteen Years among Wild Beasts in India*, 56), 'My own opinion is that the elephant attains at least to 150 years'. See Blanford, *Mammalia of British India*, 466. Sir Emerson Tennent gives evidence regarding a particular elephant, that it was found in the stables in Ceylon by the Dutch when they expelled the Portuguese in 1656, that it served the Dutch for upwards of 140 years, and passed into the hands of the British in 1799 (*Ceylon*, ii. 398). See also Sir S. W. Baker, *Wild Beasts and their Ways*, 20. The *Āīn-i-Akbarī* (i. 117 ff.) gives the natural duration of an elephant's life at 120 years.

who has charge of them, and who shows much friendship for the Franks, the number of elephants in his charge for the Emperor's service and he assured me that he had only 500,[1] called elephants of the household, because they are employed only to carry the women and the tents with all the rest of the baggage, and for war only 80 or at most 90. The most courageous of the latter has to be supported by the eldest son of the Emperor, and is allotted, both for food and for all other necessary expenses, 500 rupees a month, which amount to 750 livres. Some have only 50, others but 40, others 30, others 20 rupees; but the elephants which have 100 or 200 or 300 or 400 rupees a month have under them their horsemen to support, who share this pay, besides two, three, and up to six young elephants, who have to fan them during the great heat of the day. All these elephants do not remain in the town, as the majority go every morning to the country, where those who tend them take them into the jungles, where they eat branches of trees, sugar-canes, and millet, from which the poor peasants suffer much loss. This is profitable to those who tend these animals, because the more they eat in the country, the less food they consume in the town—the saving going into the pockets of the keepers.

This same day, the 27th of August, we travelled 6 leagues farther, and slept at a large town called Ragiapeta.[2] On the 28th, after having made 8 leagues, we came to Oudecour.[3]

On the 29th, after a march of nine hours, we arrived at

[1] The *Āīn-i-Akbarī* does not mention the number of elephants kept by the Great Mogul, but it gives a marvellous amount of details as to the classification, food, harness, capacities, and characteristics of the elephants in the establishment kept by Akbar, and states that he had 101 for his own use (i. 120). Pyrard de Laval (ii. 346) gives 30,000; Fitch (p. 95) 1,000; Bernier (p. 221) 800 or 900 at Delhi and Agra; Ovington (p. 191) 400 or 500. The number of elephants naturally varied from time to time, and was affected by their employment in campaigns or with the provincial governors.

[2] This is probably Anantarājupeta, a village about 4 miles NNW. of Kōdūru, on the way to Vontimitta on the railway line. There are several places called Rājupeta in its vicinity.

[3] Ūtukūr, about 2 miles SE. of Rājampet, the headquarters of the Pullampet tāluk, Cuddapah District.

Outemeda,[1] where there is one of the grandest pagodas in the whole of India. It is built of large cut stones, and has three towers whereon are many deformed figures cut in relief. It is surrounded by many small chambers for the dwellings of the priests of the pagoda, and 500 paces off there is a great tank, upon the borders of which there are many small pagodas of 8 or 10 feet square, and in each of them an idol in the form of a demon, with a Brahman,[2] who takes care that any stranger who is not of their faith does not come to bathe or draw water from the tank. If a stranger wants water some is given him in earthen pots, and if by chance the pot touches the vessel of the stranger the pot is broken. I am told, also, as I have elsewhere remarked, that if any one not of their faith bathes in the tank it becomes necessary to let out all the water which is then in it.[3] As for charity, they are very liberal, for to every traveller who is in want and asks alms, they give to eat and drink of whatever they may happen to have. You meet many women on these roads, some of whom always keep fire to light the tobacco of travellers, and to those who have no tobacco they even lend a pipe. Others go there to cook rice with quicheri,[4] which is a grain like our hemp-seed; others, too, cook beans, because the water in which they are cooked never causes pleurisy to those who are overheated. There are among these women some who have vowed to perform this charity for travellers during a period of seven or eight years; others for more or less time according to their convenience, and they give each traveller bean water and rice water to drink, and two or three handfuls of this cooked rice to eat. Other

[1] Vontimitta, an important place on the railway, 19 miles from Ūtukūr; see *Cuddapah District Gazetteer*, i. 237. There is a pagoda dedicated to Kodanandarā Swāmi, which, according to inscriptions at Gandikota, was built by a member of the Vijayanagar dynasty in the 14th century.

[2] Bramere in the original, Brahman.

[3] See p. 203 above.

[4] For khichari, Hind., a term applied to a dish of boiled rice and dāl, a kind of pulse (*Cajanus indicus*), flavoured with spices and onions; it is therefore not the name of a seed itself. (See p. 311 below, and Ja'far
21 Sharīf, *Islām in India*, Oxford, 1921, p. 320 f.)

women are to be seen on the high roads and in the fields following horses, oxen, and cows; these have vowed to eat nothing but what they find undigested in these animals' droppings.[1] As neither barley [2] nor oats are to be had in this country, the cattle are fed on certain large and hard peas,[3] which are first crushed between two grindstones and then allowed to steep for half an hour, for they are very hard and consequently difficult of digestion. The horses are given some of these peas every evening, and in the morning they receive about two pounds of coarse black sugar, which resembles wax, kneaded with an equal weight of flour and a pound of butter, of which mixture the grooms make pellets or small balls, and force them down the horses' throats; otherwise they would not eat them. Afterwards their mouths are washed, especially the teeth, which are covered with the paste, because this gives them a dislike to this kind of food. During the daytime the horses are given some grass which is torn up in the fields, roots and all, and is most carefully washed so that no earth remains.[4]

On the 30th [August] we made 8 leagues, and halted at Goulapali.[5] On the 31st, after a march of nine hours, we

[1] The Chief of Idar, in Akbar's time, used to feed on grain collected from the droppings of his cattle, 'a sustenance held in much esteem by the Brāhmans' (*Āīn-i-Akbarī*, ii. 241). At a more recent time the custom prevailed in western India (J. Forbes, *Oriental Memoirs*, 2nd ed., i. 51.) In the Central Provinces a sub-caste of Chamārs are called Gobardhua (*gobar*, cowdung) because they collect the droppings of cattle on the threshing-floors, and wash out and eat the undigested grain; in some places they fight for this perquisite (Russell, *Tribes and Castes, Central Provinces*, ii. 407 f., 422).

[2] Barley was known in the Vedic age, and it is now largely grown in India, but to a very small extent in Madras (Macdonell & Keith, *Vedic Index*, ii. 187; Watt, *Commercial Products*, 643).

[3] Bengal gram, the seed of Cicer arietinum, Linn., and horse gram of Dolichos biflorus, Lam., the former little grown in Madras and replaced by the latter (Watt, 300.)

[4] Dūb grass (Cynodon dactylon) is the kind of fodder still given to horses in India, but the clay is generally removed by beating not by washing. The daily preparation of this is the principal duty of the second attendant on a horse—the Ghasiyārā or grasscutter.

[5] This is probably Gollapalle, near the Gangyapalle railway station, about 13 miles NW. of Cuddapah, 5 miles W. of Chennūr, 22 miles by road from Vontimitta.

stopped at Gogeron.[1] On the first day of September we made only 6 leagues, and halted at Gandikota.[2] Only eight days had passed since the Nawāb had taken this town after a three months' siege, and he would not have taken it but for the aid of some Frenchmen who had quitted the Dutch service on account of the treatment they had received. He also had many English and Dutch gunners, with two or three Italians, who gave him great aid in the capture of the place.

Gandikota is one of the fortified towns in the Kingdom of Carnatic.[3] It is built on the summit of a high mountain, and the sole means of access to it is by a very difficult road, which is only 20 or 25 feet wide, and in certain parts only 7 or 8; the Nawāb was then commencing to improve it. On the right of the road, which is cut in the mountain, there is a fearful precipice, at the base of which runs a large river.[4] On the top of the mountain there is a small plain about a quarter of a league wide and half a league long. It is cultivated with rice and millet, and watered by many small springs. At the level of the plain to the south, where the town is built on a point, the limits are formed by precipices, with two rivers which bound the point at the base; so that, for access to the town, there is but one gate on the plain side, and it is fortified in that direction with three good walls of cut stone, the ditches at their bases being faced with the same stone. Consequently, during the siege, the inhabitants

[1] Possibly Goriganūr, a village on the N. bank of the Penner river, about 3 miles SE. of Jammalamadugu.

[2] Gandikota, a fort at an elevation of 1,670 feet above the sea in the Yerramalai Mountains of the Kadapa (Cuddapah) District, Lat. 14° 47′ N., Long. 78° 16′ E. According to Ferishta it was built in 1589. It was captured by the British under Captain Little in the first war with Tipu in 1791, and was thus again proved not to have been impregnable, having first yielded, as here related, to Mīr Jumla (*Imperial Gazetteer*, xii. 127). There is some doubt regarding the duration of the siege: W. Foster, *English Factories in India, 1651–1654*, p. 22 f. See also Grant Duff, *Hist. Mahrattas*, ed. 1921, i. 266.

[3] The Carnatic or Karnatic embraced Mysore and parts of Telingānā, and corresponded with the kingdom of Vijayanagar. (See p. 207 *n.* and, for use of the name at various periods, Yule, *Hobson-Jobson*, 164.)

[4] The Penner river.

had to guard a space of only 400 or 500 paces wide. They had only two iron guns—one a 12-pounder, the other 7 to 8; the first was placed on the gate, and the other on the point of a kind of bastion. Until the Nawāb found means to mount guns above he lost many men from the frequent sorties made by the besieged. The Rājā who was in the town was considered to be one of the best and bravest commanders among the idolaters, and the Nawāb, seeing at length that the place could not be taken unless guns were carried up to the heights, ordered all the Franks who were in the King's service as gunners to come to him, and promised each four months' wages in addition to their ordinary pay if they could find some means of conveying guns up to the heights. In this they were successful. They mounted four guns, with which they bombarded the place, and were so fortunate as to direct them against the gun mounted on the gate, which they soon rendered useless. When they had battered down half the gate of the town the besieged capitulated and evacuated the place under honourable conditions. On the day we arrived the whole army was encamped at the base of the mountain in a plain, where there is a very fine river,[1] and the Nawāb was just ending the review of the cavalry, which were very smart. An English gunner, with his comrade, an Italian, seeing M. du Jardin [2] and myself pass, and recognizing us to be Franks, as it was late, politely came to meet us, and invited us to spend the night with them. It was from them we heard that there was a French gunner then in the town, named Claude Maillé of Bourges,[3] and that he was engaged in casting some cannon which the Nawāb wished to leave in the fort.

On the following day, the 2nd of the month, we ascended to the town and stopped at the house of Maillé, whom I had known at Batavia, where he was in the Dutch service, being employed as gardener to the General. He received us with much joy, and having first notified our arrival to the Nawāb, he ordered them to provide immediately for lodging and

[1] The Penner. [2] See p. 206.

[3] For further particulars regarding this gun-founder and surgeon, see pp. 95 and 231.

necessary food, not only for ourselves, but also for our horses and oxen, during the stay that we were going to make at Gandikota.

On the 3rd [September] we went to call upon the Nawāb, who had caused his tents to be pitched on the summit of the mountain, in the quarter bordering the road cut in the rock. He received us kindly, asking us if we were comfortably housed, and whether we had been supplied with the food which he had ordered for ourselves and horses. Then he inquired the cause of our visit, and we replied that we had brought some goods sufficiently choice for the King, but that we had not gone to His Majesty before showing them to him—well knowing that the King bought nothing of high price without his advice, and that, in any case, we considered such deference to be due to him. The Nawāb assured us that our compliment had not displeased him, and after he had ordered betlé [1] to be presented to us we took our leave and returned to the town. We found all the gunners awaiting us, and we assembled at Maillé's house for supper, where the Nawāb sent us two bottles of wine—one Spanish, the other of Shīrāz—which is rare in this country.[2] As for brandy, they have no lack of it, for they make it of rice and also sugar, of which there is an abundance in all these parts of India.

On the 4th we again visited the Nawāb, and showed him the jewels which we hoped to sell to the King. They consisted of some pear-shaped pearls [3] of a weight, beauty, and size which were unusual—the least exceeding 24 carats. After having examined them well, and shown them to a number of nobles who were present with him, he asked us the price; which having heard, he returned them to us, and at the same time said he would consider it. He made

[1] Betlé, Port. The leaf of *Piper betel*, used as a masticatory together with areca nut and lime. In some parts of India, and by Europeans in India generally, it is called pawn (pān). See p. 211.

[2] For Shīrāz wine see Curzon, *Persia*, ii. 100 f., 504 ff., and for a graphic account of its manufacture, Wills, *Land of the Lion and the Sun*, 227 ff.

[3] The principal pearl was afterwards sold to Shāista Khān (see *ante*, p. 17).

us dine with him, and after the repast we returned to the town, where we remained till the 10th without seeing the Nawāb.

On the morning of the 10th [September] he sent to summon us, and as soon as we were seated in his tent, close to him, the attendants brought him five small bags full of diamonds, and each bag contained about as many as one could hold in the hand. They were all lasques,[1] but of very dark water and very small, and most of them were only 1 carat or half a carat in weight, but otherwise very clear. There were very few of them which weighed 2 carats. The Nawāb, showing us these stones, asked if such goods were saleable in our country. We replied that they might be sold provided the water was white, because in Europe we do not esteem diamonds if they are not clear and white, and we make no account of other kinds of water. When he first began to contemplate the conquest of this Kingdom for the King of Golkonda, he was told that it contained diamond mines, and he sent 12,000 men to work them, but in the space of a year they found only those which he had in the five bags. The Nawāb, seeing that they found only stones of very brown water, tending much more to black than white, rightly considered that it was loss of trouble, and, forbidding further mining, sent all these poor people back to tillage.[2] After the Nawāb had closed up his diamonds again, and we had dined with him, he mounted his horse, accompanied by many nobles, to go hunting, and desired to take us with him; but we begged him to excuse us, and we left without his speaking to us of our pearls.

[1] Lasques, a term applied by jewellers to flat and oval stones, such as are used in Indian jewellery, and derived from Pers. *lashk*, 'a bit, piece'. The 'table' was the original form in which diamonds were cut. The technical name of this is 'lasque', and small slabs in this form are still used for covering miniatures, and are then called portrait stones (Streeter, *The Great Diamonds of the World*, 283).

[2] The exact position of these mines (or washings ?) is unknown, but they were probably situated in the neighbourhood of the Penner river. The nearest of the Kadapa (Cuddapah) sites known in modern times was at Jammalamadugu, which is only 5 or 6 miles E. of Gandikota. There are a number of mines near Kadapa (see *Economic Geology of India*, p. 9). In vol. ii. 67, Tavernier says there were six of them. The mine at Wajrā-Karūr, in Bellary, was also taken by Mīr Jumla.

On the 11th [September] all the Frank gunners went to the Nawāb's tent, crying out that they had not been paid the four months' wages which had been promised, and that if they were not paid they would go to take service elsewhere, upon which the Nawāb put them off till the following day. On the 12th, the gunners having assembled at the tent of the Nawāb, he ordered them to be paid for three months, and promised to pay them the fourth at the close of the current month. They had no sooner received this money than they treated one another, and the baladines [1] received more than half of it.

On the 13th the Nawāb went to the town to inspect the foundry which Maillé had erected by his orders. Maillé, as I have said, was from Bourges, and enlisted at Amsterdam for India. When he arrived at Batavia, the General, perceiving that he was skilful and very intelligent, kept him in his personal service to make some grottoes and fountains in his garden. But Maillé, being neither satisfied with this employment nor with the rough treatment of the General, found means to attach himself to the suite of M. Cheteur,[2] who was sent from Batavia to the Nawāb, then engaged in the siege of Gandikota. This Envoy having finished his business with the Nawāb, and Maillé knowing that he would be leaving on the following day, took possession of the case and box of ointments belonging to the Ambassador's surgeon, and concealed himself until the Envoy had departed, without being able to find Maillé, in spite of all the search he could make, which had delayed his departure for some days. As soon as Maillé heard that the Envoy was gone, he was appointed to the service of the Nawāb as surgeon; and some time afterwards, having informed him that he was a good gunner and founder, he entered his service in that capacity. The Nawāb having taken Gandikota, and desiring to mount some cannon inside the fort, where it was very difficult to carry them, proposed to Maillé [3] to cast twenty pieces—ten

[1] Dancing-girls (see p. 71).

[2] The name of the ambassador was M. Steur, as Sir W. Foster points out.

[3] In 1665 Tavernier met a man with the same name installed as physician to the Governor at Allahabad, but does not allude to him

48-pounders, and ten 24-pounders; this Maillé undertook to do. He was supplied with copper for this purpose from all quarters, and the Nawāb collected a quantity of idols which had been removed from the pagodas which his army had visited. There is in Gandikota a pagoda [1] considered to be one of the principal in India, where there are many idols, some of gold and others of silver. Among these idols there were six of copper, three of which were seated on their heels, and the three others were about 10 feet high. After Maillé had made all preparations to melt the metals and the idols brought from different places, he accomplished the melting of all except the six large idols of the famous pagoda of Gandikota.[2] He was unable to melt them, no matter how much the Nawāb expended; and the latter went so far as to threaten the priests of the pagoda, whom he accused of having bewitched the idols. In short, Maillé did not succeed in making a single cannon, one being split, another incomplete; and so he relinquished all the work he had undertaken, and some time afterwards quitted the service of the Nawāb.

On the 14th we went to the Nawāb's tent to take leave and to hear what he had to say regarding the goods which we had shown him. But we were told that he was engaged examining a number of criminals, who had been brought before him for immediate punishment. It is the custom in this country not to keep a man in prison; but immediately an accused person is arrested he is examined, sentence is pronounced on him, and it is then executed without any delay. If the accused is found to be innocent he is released at once; and whatever the nature of the case may be, it is promptly concluded. We were told, moreover, that it would be difficult for us to see the Nawāb that day, because he intended to go down to the plain to review the greater part

expressly as being the same person, as he probably was. (See p. 95.)

[1] There are a fine mosque and two Hindu temples now in the fort (*Madras Manual of Administration*, iii. 334).

[2] Possibly these idols were made of iron and not of copper; this would account for the difficulty in melting them. Cast-iron was known in India in early times. The story may, however, be mythical.

of his army. We did not omit, however, to meet him at the door of his tent in the evening, where we dismounted. M. du Jardin and I saluted him, and he invited us to call upon him early on the following day.

On the 15th, at seven o'clock in the morning, we went to the Nawāb, and immediately we were announced he invited us to enter his tent, where he was seated with two of his secretaries by him. According to the custom of the country—where one goes with naked feet in slippers, without stockings, because wherever you enter you walk on a carpet, and sit in this country as in Turkey, and as our tailors do here—the Nawāb had the intervals between his toes full of letters, and he also held many between the fingers of his left hand. He drew them sometimes from his feet, sometimes from his hand, and sent replies through his two secretaries, writing some also himself. After the secretaries had finished the letters, he made them read them; and he then took them and affixed his seal himself, giving some to foot messengers, others to horsemen. But it should be remarked that in India all the letters which Kings, Generals of Armies, and Governors of Provinces send by footmen[1] go much faster than by horsemen, the reason being that at every two leagues there are small huts, where two or three runners are posted, and immediately when the carrier of a letter arrives at one of these huts he throws it to the others sitting at the entrance, and one of them takes it up and at once starts to run. It is considered unlucky to give a letter into the hand of the messenger; it is therefore thrown at his feet, and he must lift it up.[2] It is also to be remarked that throughout India the sides of most of the roads are planted with avenues of trees, and where there are no trees planted, at every 500 paces small pieces of stone are fixed, which the inhabitants of the nearest villages are bound to whiten from time to time, so that the letter carriers can distinguish the road on

[1] The Pattamārs (Yule, *Hobson-Jobson*, 687). For Akbar's post, *Āīn-i-Akbarī*, i. 252; on Persian couriers see Herodotus, viii. 98, with Rawlinson's note: *Encyl. Biblica*, iii. 3813.

[2] This was done because the courier was an outcaste, and merely touching him would convey pollution.

dark and rainy nights.[1] While we were with the Nawāb he was informed that four prisoners, who were then at the door of the tent, had arrived. He remained more than half an hour without replying, writing continually and making his secretaries write, but at length he suddenly ordered the criminals to be brought in; and after having questioned them, and made them confess with their own mouths the crime of which they were accused,[2] he remained nearly an hour without saying anything, continuing to write and to make his secretaries write. Then there entered into his tent many officers of the army who came to pay their respects with great humility, and to whose salute he replied only by an inclination of the head.

Among these four prisoners who were brought into his presence was one who had entered a house and had slain a mother and her three infants. He was condemned forthwith to have his feet and hands cut off, and to be thrown into a field near the high road to end his days. Another had stolen on the high road, and the N wāb ordered him to have his stomach slit open and to be flung in a drain. I could not ascertain what the others had done, but both their heads were cut off. While all this passed dinner was served, for the Nawāb generally eats at ten o'clock, and he made us dine with him. The sufra [3] having been removed, we took leave of the majority of the nobles who had also eaten with the Nawāb; and when only two or three persons remained with him, we inquired through his interpreter if he had any commands for us, and whether he thought that our goods should be shown to the King. He replied that we might

[1] The Great Kaan used to plant trees along the roads, to show the way at night, and also because the astrologers told him that whoever planted trees lived long; where trees would not grow he had landmarks, pillars or stones, erected, to show the way (Yule, *Marco Polo*, i. 394). Asoka planted trees and dug wells along the highways (Smith, *Asoka*, 3rd ed., 91). Akbar planted trees on the great northern road for 400 miles, and Coryat and Terry describe the avenue, which is marked in Bernier's map. (*Id.*, *Akbar, the Great Mogul*, 2nd ed., 413.)

[2] The criminal law of Islam is not satisfied until the accused makes confession of the crime.

[3] Sufra, Pers., tablecloth, see p. 218 above. The word properly means 'the food of the journey' (*safar*).

go to Golkonda, where he would communicate with his son on our behalf, and that his letter would arrive before us. He ordered sixteen horsemen to conduct us, and provide for us on the road whatever we required, up to a river 13 leagues from Gandikota, which no one is allowed to cross who does not bear the Nawāb's passport, so that the soldiers may not be able to desert.

CHAPTER XIX

Route from Gandikota to Golkonda

On the morning of the 16th [September 1652] we left Gandikota, accompanied by most of the gunners, who came with us to the first halt, carrying plenty of food with them; and this day we only made 7 leagues, and slept at Cotepali.[1]

On the 17th, after breakfasting with the gunners, who then returned to Gandikota, we pursued our way with the sixteen horsemen of the Nawāb, and having travelled 6 leagues we slept at a village named Coteen,[2] beyond the river, which was then very full. As soon as we had crossed it the sixteen horsemen took leave of us; and though we offered their chief some rupees to buy tobacco and betel, we could not induce him to accept anything. The boats employed in crossing this river are like large baskets,[3] covered outside with ox hides, at the bottom of which some faggots are placed, upon which carpets are spread to support the baggage and goods, lest they

[1] Cottapilly in A.S. No. 76; it is, however, 24 miles from Gandikota. Cotalpully and Gopalpilly are about 4 miles nearer.

[2] Not identified on the map. The exact route followed by Tavernier from Gandikota up to Gudimitta is very uncertain.

[3] Coracles, made of wicker-work and covered with bitumen, which are called Gufa or Kufa, are used on the Tigris and Euphrates (L. W. King, *Hist. of Babylon*, 178 ff.; Herodotus, i. 192; G. Maspero, *Dawn of Civilization*, 615). Jahāngīr, in his *Memoirs*, describes rafts made of bamboos and grass resting on inflated skins (Elliot & Dowson, *Hist. of India*, vi. 313). Such skin-rafts, called Senai, are still used on the Indus (F. St. J. Gore, *Lights and Shades of Hill Life*, 122). The Harigōlu, or coracles, used on the Kāvērī in Mysore, are circular baskets of stout wicker-work, composed of interlaced bamboo laths and covered with buffalo hides; similar coracles are used on the Haidarābād river (B. L. Rice, *Mysore*, 2nd ed., i. 6; Bilgrami & Willmott, *Descriptive Sketch*, i. 8).

should get wet. As for the coaches and carts, they are tied by the pole and wheels between two of these baskets, but the horses are made to swim across, a man driving his horse from behind with a whip, and another in the basket holding it by the halter. As for the oxen, which, according to the custom of the country, carry the baggage, as soon as they reach the bank of the river and have been unloaded, they are driven in, and cross the water without assistance. There are four men to each basket, one at each corner, who stand and row with paddles. Should one of them fail to keep equal stroke with the others, or if all do not keep time, the basket turns three or four times round, and, the current carrying it down, it descends much lower than the spot where it was intended to land.

On the 18th [September], after a march of five hours, we arrived at Morimol.[1] On the 19th we made 9 leagues, and halted at Santesela.[2] On the 20th we made 9 leagues more, and slept at Goremeda.[3] On the 21st, after six hours of marching, we passed the night at Kaman.[4] It was a frontier town of the Kingdom of Golkonda, before the conquest of the Carnatic by the army of Mīr Jumla, of which I have spoken in the preceding chapter.

On the 22nd we travelled 7 leagues, and slept at Emelipata.[5] About half-way we met more than 4,000 persons, men and women, and more than twenty pallankeens, each of which contained an idol. They were ornamented with gold, brocade of gold and velvet, with fringes of gold and silver, and some of these pallankeens were carried by four men, others by eight, and others by twelve, according to the size and weight of the idols. On each side of the pallankeens was a man with a large round fan about 5 feet in diameter, made of beautiful ostrich and peacock feathers of different colours. The handles of these fans were 5 or 6 feet long, and covered with gold and silver

[1] Recent inquiries show that Morimol is Poraimāmilla.

[2] Santesela is almost certainly Sancherla, in Cumbum tāluk, Karnūl District.

[3] Gudimitta.

[4] Kumbam, or Cumbum, 12 miles NW. of Gudimitta, an important town, headquarters of the tāluk of the same name.

[5] Vemulakota, in Mārkāpur tāluk, Karnūl District, 14 miles NW. of Kumbam.

nearly as thick as a French crown (écu). Every one strove to carry these fans in order to serve the idol by fanning it and preventing the flies alighting on its face. Another fan, somewhat larger, and without a handle, was carried like a shield. It was ornamented with feathers of different colours, ranged round little gold and silver bells. The person carrying it walked close to the pallankeen, on the sunny side, in order to shade the idol, for to close the curtains of the pallankeen would have made it too hot. From time to time the bearer of the shield shook it in order to ring the bells, so that the idol might be amused. All these people with their idols came from Burhānpur and its neighbourhood, and were going to visit their great Rām Rām, i.e. their great god, who is in a pagoda in the territory of the King of Carnatic. They had been fully thirty days on the road, and had to march fourteen or fifteen more before reaching the pagoda.[1] One of my attendants who came from Burhānpur, and belonged to the tribe of these same people, asked me to give him a holiday to go with them to accompany his gods, saying that a long time ago he had vowed to make this pilgrimage. I was obliged to give him leave, well knowing that if I did not give him the holiday he would take it himself, as he had many relatives in the troop. About two months later he rejoined me at Surat, and as he had served M. du Jardin and myself faithfully, I made no difficulty about re-employing him. When I asked him some questions about the pilgrimage which he had just made, he told me a story difficult to believe, but which happened, as he said, in this manner. Six days after having left me, all the pilgrims intended sleeping at a village; and before reaching it they had to cross a river, which during

[1] Tavernier (vol. ii. 191 below) describes meeting at Daulatābād a similar procession of 2,000 persons on their way to Tirupati pagoda from Tatta, in Sind. But all the details are different. Ball disagrees with M. Joret (*J.-B. Tavernier*, p. 131) in his identification of the two occasions, and does not see any difficulty in regarding each account as being distinct. Processions carrying idols, seldom seen in north India, but common in the Deccan and Madras, are a survival of Jainism, once powerful in these regions. Similar processions are described by Barbosa (ed. Dames, ii. 36) among Malabar Brāhmans, who carry their idol round a temple, and a procession, like that seen by Tavernier, by P. della Valle (ii. 279 ff.). The image of Mahāsū is carried in procession in the lower Himālaya.

the summer contains but little water and may be forded anywhere. But when it rains in India the water falls like a deluge, and in less than an hour or two small streams rise 2 or 3 feet in depth. The rain having surprised these pilgrims, this river increased so quickly that it was impossible to cross it that day. It is not necessary that those who travel in India should provide themselves with food beforehand, —especially is this the case with the idolaters, who do not eat anything which has had life—because even in the smallest villages rice, flour, butter, milk, beans, and other vegetables, sugar and other sweetmeats, dry and liquid, can be procured in abundance. This multitude of people, who had no food with them, were much astonished on reaching the bank of this river to see it so high and swollen, and at not being able to cross it to the village, which was on the other side, where they intended to make their halt. They had nothing to give their children to eat, and nothing was to be heard save lamentations among the crowd. In this extremity their chief priest sat down in the middle of them, and, causing himself to be covered with a large sheet, began to call those who wished for food to approach him. He asked each what he wanted, whether rice or flour, and for how many persons; and lifting the corner of the sheet, with a large ladle which he held he gave to all whatever they had asked for; so that this large number of people of 4,000 souls was satisfied.[1]

It was not only my servant who related this history, but having subsequently made many journeys to Burhānpur where I was known to the principal persons of the town, I made inquiry of many who had been on this pilgrimage, and

[1] It is perhaps not too much to say, that with the people of India the more *prima facie* incredibility there is in a story like this, the more likely is it to obtain their credence. Its resemblance to a certain Christian miracle is remarkable. In this connexion we may appropriately quote General Sleeman's remarks (*Rambles and Recollections*, 337): 'The miracles of Christianity exercise no influence on the imaginations of the Hindus, who can always tell of greater ones.' We may call to mind also the alleged miracles performed by sundry modern theosophists, and believed in by their disciples. The story is a variant of the well-known folk-tale of the inexhaustible pot or purse (Crooke, *Popular Religion and Folklore of N. India*, i. 214 f.).

all swore to me by their Rām Rām that it was true, which I nevertheless could not believe.

On the 23rd [September] we arrived at Doupar,[1] after having travelled 8 leagues, and crossed many torrents. On the 24th we made only 4 leagues, and came to Tripanté,[2] where there is a grand pagoda on a hill, the whole circuit of which forms a staircase and is faced with cut stone. The smallest stone of this staircase is 10 feet long and 3 feet wide, and in the pagoda there are many figures of demons. There is one, among others, which resembles a Venus standing upright, with many demons who surround her in lascivious attitudes, and this Venus and the demons are cut out of a single piece of marble, but the carving is very coarse. On the 25th we travelled 8 leagues, and halted at Mamli.[3] On the 26th we also travelled 8 leagues, and slept at Macheli.[4]

On the 27th we made only 3 leagues, because we had to cross a large river in baskets; this generally occupies half a day.[5] When we reached the margin of the water we saw neither basket nor any other means of crossing. A man came, with whom we bargained for our passage; and to test whether the money we offered him was good he made a large fire, and threw it into it.[6] He did the same with that of all the passengers. If amongst the money which he received he found a rupee which turned somewhat black, they had to give him another, which he also heated; then after he had proved that the money was good he called out to his comrades to bring the basket, which is generally concealed in some spot on the opposite side of the river. For these people are cunning, and seeing from afar off from which side the travellers are coming they send the basket to the other bank so as not to be

[1] Dūpād, a village in Mārkāpur taluk, about 20 miles N. of Vernulakota in the valley of the Gundhakamma river.

[2] Tripurāntakham, 7 miles NE. of Dūpād. It is the Tripparanticum of the Atlas Sheet.

[3] Marrivēmula, about 17 miles midway between Tripurāntakham and Mācherla.

[4] Mācherla, an important village in Gurujāla taluk, popularly called Palnād, in Guntūr District.

[5] The Kistnā, on which coracles are still used.

[6] See p. 25 above.

compelled to take any one across without being first paid. The money having been counted, and the man who had received it having called his comrades, they carry the basket on their shoulders to the edge of the water, and having launched it come across to fetch those waiting on the other side.

On the 28th, having made 5 leagues, we halted at a place called Dabir-pinta.[1] On the 29th, after a march of 12 hours, we slept at Holcora.[2] On the 30th we made 8 leagues, and passed the night at Peridera.[3] On Monday, the 1st day of October, after having made 10 leagues, we slept at Atenara.[4] It is one of the pleasure houses built by the Queen, mother of the King who reigns at present. It has many rooms for the accommodation of travellers, opening on a grand square in front of the house.

It should be remarked that in all the countries we have just passed through, both in the Kingdom of Carnatic and the Kingdoms of Golkonda and Bījāpur, there are hardly any physicians except those in the service of the Kings and Princes. As for the commonalty, when the rains have fallen and it is the season for collecting plants, mothers of families may be seen going out in the mornings from the towns and villages to collect the simples which they know to be specifics for domestic diseases. It is true that in good towns there are generally one or two men who have some knowledge of medicine, who seat themselves each morning in the market-place or at a corner of the street and administer remedies, either potions or plasters, to those who come to ask for them. They first feel the pulse, and when giving the medicine, for which they take only the value of two farthings, they mumble some words between their teeth.[5]

On the 2nd of October we were only 4 leagues distance from Golkonda. We halted at the house of a young Dutch surgeon

[1] Dabir-pinta appears to be the Debir Lake of Orme's map, but has not been clearly identified.

[2] Holcora, Huaticoor of Orme.

[3] Paraida.

[4] Ātenara or Tenara is Sarūrnagar: see Mr. Yazdani's note, p. 139–40 above.

[5] See the account of the methods of the Vaidyas, or native physicians of the Deccan, *Bombay Gazetteer*, xviii, pt. 3, p. 69 ff.

of the King, named Pitre de Lan, whom M. Cheteur, the Batavian Envoy, had left at Golkonda—the King having asked for him very earnestly.[1] This Prince suffered from a chronic pain in the head, and the physicians had ordered him to be bled under the tongue in four places; but he could not find any one willing to undertake it—because, as for surgery, the people of the country understand nothing about it.

Before de Lan entered the King's service he was asked whether he could bleed well, to which he replied that it was the least difficult operation in surgery. It was with great reluctance that the Batavian Envoy consented to leave him. But he did not like to disoblige the King, and de Lan received 800 pagodas as salary. Some days after the Envoy's departure the King summoned the surgeon and told him that he wished him to bleed him on the following day in four places under the tongue, as his physicians had directed, but that he should take care not to draw more than eight ounces. De Lan returned to the Court on the following day, was conducted into a room by two or three eunuchs, and four old women came to conduct him to a bath, where they undressed and washed him well, especially his hands, and anointed him with drugs and aromatics; in place of his own clothes, which were of European make, they gave him a garment made according to the fashion of the country. They then took him to the King, and brought basins of gold which the physicians who were present weighed; these were to receive the blood. He then bled the King under the tongue in four places, and he did it so skilfully that, on weighing the blood with the basins, he found that he had drawn eight ounces exactly.[2] The King was so satisfied with this operation that he gave him 300 pagodas, which are equal to nearly 700 écus. The young Queen and the Queen-dowager having heard of it, desired that he would bleed them also,

[1] Called Pieter de Lange in *Histoire générale des Voyages*, vol. xiii, p. 35. According to Valentyn he did good service to his country as their representative at the Court of Golkonda till 1656. He was succeeded by another surgeon, who died in 1660, after which the Dutch established a factory at Golkonda. On p. 231 we have been told that Claude Maillé of Bourges deserted M. Cheteur and set up as surgeon to Mīr Jumla.

[2] He was, therefore, successful under conditions somewhat similar to those from which Shylock recoiled.

but I believe it was more from the curiosity they had to see him than for any need they had to be bled, for he was a young and well-made man, and probably in their lives they had not seen a stranger at close quarters—for from a distance this is not impossible, since from the place where they stay they are able to see without being themselves seen. De Lan was then brought into a chamber, where the same women who had taken him to the bath before he had bled the King uncovered his arms, washed them well, and especially his hands, and anointed him with scented oil, as they had done when he went to bleed the King. That being done, they drew a curtain, and the young Queen putting out an arm through a hole, the surgeon bled her, and he afterwards did the same for the Queen mother. The former gave him a fee of 50, and the latter of 30 pagodas,[1] with some pieces of gold brocade.

Two days after our arrival we went to salute the son of the Nawāb, and were told that we could not speak to him that day. Next day we returned, and as the same thing occurred, some one told us that we might amuse ourselves in that manner for a long time, as he was a young noble who scarcely ever left the King's presence, and on leaving the palace he used to shut himself up in his harem with his women.[2] The surgeon, de Lan, seeing that our business might be delayed, offered to mention it to the first physician of the King, who was in his confidence, had shown much friendship for the Batavian Envoy and for de Lan himself, and could easily find an opportunity for obliging us. In short, as soon as de Lan had spoken to him he sent for us, to inquire what service he could render us. After he had saluted us, he caressed us a thousand times, invited us to be seated, and ordered some fruits of the country to be brought. He then inquired whence we had come, and upon what subject we desired to speak to the King; we told him that we had some choice pearls which

[1] About £25 and £15. See the accounts by Manucci (ii. 355, iv. 224) and Fryer (i. 326) of their experiences when they were called in to bleed or prescribe for Musalmān ladies.

[2] Muhammad Amīn Khān, son of Mīr Jumla, was an ill-conditioned, dissipated young man (Jadunath Sarkar, *Hist. of Aurangzib*, iii. 77; Bilgrami & Willmott, *Hist. Sketch*, i. 481 481); Bernier (p. 80) calls him Mahmet Emir-Kan.

we wished to show to His Majesty, and he asked us to show them to him the following day—this we did. After he had seen them, he told us to replace them in their little bags, desiring us to close them with our seal, because all things presented to the King should be sealed with the merchant's seal and when the King has seen it he affixes his, in order that there may be no fraud. Thus we left the whole sealed packet in his hands, and he promised to show it to the King, and render us a good account of the service which he had undertaken thus in order to oblige us.

The following morning, very early, we went to hunt with de Lan, and returning, at eight or nine o'clock a.m., we went to the river's bank to see how the elephants of the King and the great nobles are bathed. The elephant enters the water up to the belly, and lying down on one side takes water from time to time in its trunk, throws it upon the uncovered portion of its body and washes it well. The keeper then takes a kind of pumice-stone, rubs the skin and cleans it of all the dirt which has accumulated upon it. Some believe that when this animal lies on the ground it cannot get up by itself;[1] this is quite contrary to what I have seen, for as soon as the keeper has rubbed it well on one side he orders it to turn on the other, which the elephant promptly does, and after it is well washed on both sides it leaves the river and remains for some time on the bank to dry itself. Then the keeper brings a pot full of red or yellow paint, and paints lines on its forehead, around the eyes, on the chest, and on the back, afterwards rubbing it with coco-nut oil to strengthen the nerves, some keepers finally marking the forehead with false tinsel.[2]

On the 15th[3] [October] the chief physician sent for us at

[1] This old fable, though discountenanced by many writers, has had a wonderfully persistent existence (Sir T. Browne, *Works*, ed. 1880, i. 219 ff.; Blandford, *Mammalia of British India*, 466; Tennent, *Ceylon*, ii. 293).

[2] This sort of decoration, like the washing, is practised in India at the present day. Cf. Bernier, 261; J. L. Kipling, *Beast and Man in India*, 1892, p. 251, gives a good drawing of a decorated elephant.

[3] Thus in the edition of 1676, but in other editions this date is given as the 25th. M. Joret (*J.-B. Tavernier*, p. 130) concludes from the latter that Tavernier left for Surat on the 26th. But it appears probable that the

two o'clock p.m., and returned our pearls, carefully sealed with the King's seal, which His Majesty had ordered to be placed upon them after he had seen them. He asked us the price of each, which we told him, and, as he had a eunuch with him who noted all down, the latter, astonished at seeing pearls of such a price, remarked that we supposed the people of the court of the King of Golkonda to be without judgement or knowledge, and that he daily saw other precious things which were brought to the King. I replied sharply to the eunuch that I could well believe he knew the price of a female slave better than that of a jewel, and so saying we shut up our pearls, and taking leave of the physician, returned to our lodging. We had no sooner arrived there than we sent to hire two coaches, each of us having already a riding horse, and, on the following day, in the morning, we left Golkonda, but were not able to travel more than a league and a half that day, because the Portuguese, English, and Dutch gunners in the service of the King escorted us, and we spent our time in enjoying ourselves.

There is no need to repeat here what I have said at the beginning of this volume, as we returned from Golkonda to Surat by the same route as that from Surat to Golkonda, there being no other,—I have nothing to say except that, having left Golkonda immediately after the reply which I made to the eunuch, the King, who did not hear of it for two days after our departure, sent four or five horsemen after us with orders to bring us back to court if they found us. We had already made five marches from Golkonda, one of them being in the territories of the Great Mogul, when one of these horsemen came to us at sunset, while his companions remained on the frontier of the two kingdoms, rightly believing that as we had crossed the boundary we would be unwilling to return. This horseman showed us the order which he had received from the King, his master, who had told him that he would buy our pearls, and that he thought it very strange that we had left without saying anything. As we were no longer in the territory of Golkonda the horse-

25th is a misprint for the earlier date, i.e. the 15th. Hence his departure for Surat would have been on the 16th of October.

man could only urge us to return with him, giving us all possible assurances that we should be satisfied, and M. du Jardin almost yielded ; but I, knowing the atmosphere of the country better, told the horseman frankly that it was impossible, and after he had left I made my companion comprehend my reasons for being unwilling to return to Golkonda.

On arriving at Surat,[1] where a few days afterwards M. du Jardin died of an effusion of bile, as I have related in my account of Persia, I made arrangements to go to Agra to visit Shāhjahān, who was then on the throne. But the Nawāb Shāista Khān, the King's brother-in-law,[2] and Governor of the Province of Gujarāt, of whom I have elsewhere spoken, sent to me from Ahmadābād, where he resided, one of the principal officers of his household, to tell me that having heard I had some beautiful jewels to sell he would be much pleased if I went to him, assuring me that he would pay for them as liberally as the Emperor. I received this message during the illness of M. du Jardin, who died on the ninth day ; and after we had rendered him our last duties at Surat, I went to Ahmadābād, where I at once transacted some business with the Nawāb. As he understood all kinds of jewels well, we were at once agreed, and there was no difference between us save as to the nature of the payment. He gave me a choice of coins, and stipulated only that I should take golden or silver rupees ; but the Prince gave me to understand that he did not wish that so large a sum should be seen leaving his house, and suggested that I should take my payment in golden rupees, which would appear less. I agreed to what he

[1] As he left Golkonda on the 16th of October, and the journey from Surat took from twenty-one to twenty-six days, according to the route travelled, he should have reached Surat either on the 7th or the 12th of November. As stated in the previous note, M. Joret has been misled by a misprint to the conclusion that Tavernier started for Surat on the 26th. Further, he seems to mistake this record of the death of M. du Jardin for that of M. d'Ardilière his son. Tavernier's reference to the latter as being alive in 1653 is, therefore, not inconsistent, and further we have mention (*Persian Travels*, bk. ii, ch. x) of a Baron d'Ardilière being in Marseilles with our author in 1657, but Ball cannot say that he was the same person. See *Jean-Baptiste Tavernier*, by Joret, pp. 114 and 131.

[2] Shāista Khān was son of 'Āsaf Khān Wazīr, and brother of Shāh jahān's wife, Mumtāz Mahal (Bernier, 56 ; Manucci, i. 218.)

advised, and he showed me some very fine gold, namely, old rupees which apparently had not seen the light for a long time. But as the current price of the golden rupee is only 14 silver rupees,[1] and he wished to pass his for 14½, or at the least for 14¼, this almost ended the transaction, as I made him understand that upon so large a sum I could not consent to lose a quarter upon every golden rupee. Finally, in order to satisfy him, I was obliged to take them at 14⅛ rupees of silver; for the Prince, who was otherwise magnificent and generous, showed himself a stern economist in matters of purchase.[2]

During my residence at Ahmadābād he sent me every day, to the Dutch house where I lodged, four silver dishes from his table containing pulão and choice meats, and one day when the Emperor sent him ten or twelve men bearing apples, which had been received from Persia by way of Kandahār, he presented me with two dishes of them, which would have been worth at Ahmadābād, on account of their scarcity, 300 or 400 rupees. I gave a part of these fine fruits to the Dutch and to the ladies, and we amused ourselves well during my sojourn there. Moreover, Shāista Khān gave me a khil'at[3] complete, with sword and khanjar;[4] this was worth more than 1,000 rupees; and desiring to make me a further present of a horse, he asked me what kind I wished for. I replied that since he was pleased to give me my choice, I preferred a fresh and lively horse rather than an aged one. He gave me one from his stud, which I mounted forthwith and took to the Dutch house, but not without difficulty, for it only went by jumps, and was so fiery, that on my allowing a young Dutchman to mount it, he, who thought he could ride it better than I, found himself promptly out of the saddle, as he was unable to manage

[1] From this proportion, with the rupee at 2*s.* 3*d.*, the gold mohur was worth 31*s.* 6*d.* (See Appendix.)

[2] This transaction has already been described, with some difference in the details, on pp. 15 ff. In a paper, apparently written by Tavernier, which forms Appendix XLV of Raphael's *Estat de la Perse*, by Schefer (p. 352), the writer says that he took with him on one occasion five pear-shaped pearls to Ahmadābād, which he had purchased for 23,000 livres at Antwerp. He sold them to Shāista Khān for 64,000 livres.

[3] Khil'at (see p. 18.)

[4] Khanjar, i.e. dagger (see p. 82, ii. 281).

the horse. I told Shāista Khān that an older one would be more suitable for me, so he ordered his master of the horse to give me one which, although it had belonged to his father, was still fit for service, and had cost formerly more than 3,000 écus.[1] As I did not require it I sold it for 400 rupees to a Frenchman, whom at the same time I was able to place in the service of the Prince, where he might have saved much money if he had not squandered it in debauchery.

From Ahmadābād I returned to Surat, and from Surat I travelled[2] to Golkonda, and thence to the mine to make my purchase of diamonds. On my arrival at Surat I arranged to go to Persia, but experienced great difficulties, which were followed by a voyage in which I was exposed to dangers I might have foreseen, but did little to avoid, never having feared such dangers as travellers have to run both on sea and land, whenever it has been actually necessary for me to proceed forward.

CHAPTER XX

Return from Surat to Hormuz, and how the author found himself engaged in a very severe and dangerous naval combat, from which he escaped without accident.

WHILE on my return to Surat from my visit to the diamond mine, I learned that war had been declared between the English and Dutch,[3] and that the latter would not send any more vessels to Persia. The English also said the same, as they had already sent four which they expected to return every hour, and consequently I found the sea closed for my passage to Hormuz. I might have taken the land journey by Agra and Kandahār ; but the road was very long, and it was impossible, or at the least very difficult, to travel by it on

[1] £675. See p. 18 for another account of this transaction, which, as there pointed out in the footnote, varies the details.

[2] This was on the 6th March 1653. (See Introduction.)

[3] This was in the year 1654. War was proclaimed between England and Holland on 8th June 1652, and, on Dutch defeats at sea, ended in the peace of 1654.

account of the Kandahār war, and because the armies of Persia and India were in the field.[1] While afraid that I should be obliged to spend a long time in a place where I had no occupation, there arrived at Surat on the 2nd of January five large Dutch vessels from Batavia ; this rejoiced me exceedingly, as I was certain to obtain all I wanted from the Dutch Commander, who was a friend of mine. I may say, in passing, that in all my journeys there has never been one of these commanders—it is thus they call the chiefs of these settlements—who has not showed consideration for me, and has not been pleased at having an opportunity of doing me kindness. I have also sought on all occasions to serve them, especially when I went to the mine, by purchasing diamonds for them with private money of which they did not wish the Company to know anything, because they are forbidden to embark in private trade, and moreover they understood little about the purchase of precious stones. But although these small services which they asked me to render them had been without profit, that did not save me from being subjected later on, on account of one of them, to some unpleasantness at Batavia, from which I did not escape without trouble, as I shall describe hereafter in the sequel of my history.[2] I have also been very careful in all the places where the Dutch have settlements, and where I made any sojourn, to contribute as far as possible to the amusement of their ladies. As I never came from Persia to India without bringing good wine and fine fruits, and always had some one with me who understood cooking better than the Dutch in India, and knew how to make good soup and bake, I entertained them often with collations, where pigeons in pyramids, flavoured with pistachios, were not lacking. The amusements of the country, which I have sufficiently described, followed these small collations ; and the ladies gave me to understand that they were much pleased with these parties, to which I invited them with their husbands.

The Commander of Surat being, as I have said, a friend of

[1] Kandahār surrendered to the Persians in 1649, and was three times besieged ineffectually by the Mughals in 1649, 1652, 1653 (Smith, *Oxford Hist. of India*, 402 f.).

[2] See ii. 254 ff.

mine, offered me a passage upon one of the five vessels, whichever I pleased, which had arrived from Batavia ; but, on the other hand, he pointed out the risk I would run of meeting the English, and of being engaged, in that event, in a combat, which would be unavoidable. My friends also begged me to consider the great danger to which I exposed myself. But all that they could say to me was of no avail, and rather than lose the time uselessly at Surat, where I had nothing to do, I was firmly resolved to embark. As the Dutch vessels were men-of-war rather than merchant craft, the Commander ordered three to be unloaded as quickly as possible, and sent them in advance with instructions to seek the four English vessels which he knew ought to be on their return from Persia, laden with goods, and consequently less in a condition to fight than vessels which were empty. The two others followed three or four days afterwards, this interval being required by them in order to ship supplies for all five.

I embarked in one of the two vessels which left last, and having set sail on the 8th of January,[1] we arrived on the 12th before Diu,[2] where we found the three other vessels which had preceded us. Immediately a council of war was held to consider what direction we should take to meet the English, who we believed had already reached Persia ; but they had gone but a short distance, having left Diu only two days before the arrival of the three first Dutch vessels. It was settled that we should go to Sindi,[3] and that, with anchors up, each vessel, approaching Diu as near as it could, should fire off all its cannon at the town. As soon as the inhabitants perceived that we were sailing towards the town they took flight, only daring to fire two shots at us. After the discharge of all the guns, we set our course for Sindi, where we arrived on the 20th of the same month, and a boat was at once sent on shore, the English and Dutch each having a house there. Our Admiral was informed that the four English vessels, which were to embark about 200 bales of goods then ready on the seashore were expected daily ; and upon these tidings it was resolved to remain at anchor there till the 10th of February ; but that,

[1] This was in 1654. (See Introduction.)

[2] See p. 5.

[3] Scimdi in the original for Sindi (see p. 9).

if by that time they did not appear, we should put to sea again and seek for them in Persia.

On the 2nd of February, at break of day, we perceived some sails, but owing to their great distance were unable to make them out, and still less to go to meet them, the wind being contrary.[1] Some believed at first that they were fishing-boats, but little by little, as they approached, having the wind astern, we recognized that they were the English vessels, which advanced to attack us, upon the information they had received, as we subsequently learned, from some fishermen, that the Dutch vessels were simple frigates, of which they expected to make an easy capture. It is true they had not before seen such small Dutch vessels, and as they had been built expressly for fighting, they had not high bulwarks, and so appeared small externally, but were otherwise of great strength. Our 'Admiral' had forty-eight pieces of cannon, and in case of necessity was able to accommodate up to sixty, and had more than 120 men on board. Towards nine o'clock—the English, who advanced with all sails set, not being far off—in order not to lose time in raising the anchors, we cut cables and each one set himself to do his duty. But the wind, as I have said, being directly contrary, we could not approach the enemy. As they had thereby all the advantage of the wind, they came on in good order, and always stem on; and their Admiral and Vice-Admiral[2] at length came so close to the side of the Dutch Admiral that the English Admiral[3] was fouled by an anchor on the side of our Admiral. To tell the truth, our Admiral showed but little courage in this encounter, for instead of boarding then and there, the occasion being so favourable, he cut the cable in order to free his vessel. All the ports were

[1] See the account of this engagement in Rawlinson, *British Beginnings in Western India*, 115 ff.; W. Foster, *English Factories in India, 1651–1654*, Introd., xvii ff., 249 ff. The English squadron consisted of the *Endeavour*, *Welcome*, *Falcon*, and *Dove*. The *Falcon* was set on fire, as Tavernier says, by his lucky shot; the *Endeavour* holed, captured, and sunk. the *Dove* and *Welcome* sheered off in a disgraceful manner, and the Dutch towed the half-burnt *Falcon* in triumph to Surat.

[2] These terms are used both for the ships themselves and their commanders.

[3] The *Falcon*.

so well closed that from outside no one could say how many cannon she carried. But after the English had made their first discharge, and our Admiral had returned it, which was much more effective, the English, seeing the number of his guns and the crowd which appeared on deck, began to lose heart, and the wind proving favourable, drew off. However, the English Vice-Admiral having reloaded his guns, came skilfully against the vessel on which I was a passenger. Our Captain reserved his fire until we were nearly alongside one another, notwithstanding the loss of ten men which we had sustained. When we were not more than a pistol-shot off we let him have a discharge from all our guns, which broke his foremast. The two vessels coming in contact, our Captain was the first to board, being accompanied by many brave men with hatchets, who cut all the ropes. While the two vessels were close to one another the sub-pilot and I fired a cannon-shot so effectively into the cabin of the English Captain that the bullet set fire to some powder cartridges which had been placed there. This unforeseen fire caused the English to fear that the increasing conflagration would envelop all their vessel; and our Captain, who feared the same, commanded his crew to return into our vessel, where he ordered the English to follow ten by ten, and then immediately drew off. The courage of the crew being restored, they managed to extinguish the fire on the English vessel, in which ten or twelve of our sailors were left; but our Captain, who had acquired much glory in this action, died of his wounds after two or three days.

In the meantime another of our vessels had vigorously attacked a large English ship of about 30 guns [1] which held aloof, and had already damaged it badly, when the vessel on which I was went to assist in sending it to the bottom, by giving it a whole broadside, which completely disabled it from further defence. The English Captain, seeing himself lost, immediately ran up the white flag and asked for quarter, which was granted. The carpenters did their best to close up the holes made by the cannon, the vessel having been pierced in many places; but seeing themselves deserted by the sailors who rather than aid them preferred to drink the Shīrāz wine,

[1] The *Endeavour*.

of which there was a quantity in the bottom of the hold, before being taken by the Dutch, they left their work and went to drink with them. The Dutch, to the number of thirty or forty, manned their boats in order to take possession of the English vessel, and not seeing any one on deck, went below, where they found the sailors, who, not expecting death, which was closer than they supposed, drank each other's health. The Dutch being no wiser, and not knowing the condition of the vessel, which was on the point of foundering, began to drink with them, and some moments afterwards the vessel went to the bottom. All perished miserably together, both the victors and the vanquished, without any one being saved except the English Captain and two French Capuchins, who, seizing the opportunity while these brutes made themselves drunk, descended into a boat, and cutting the rope by which it was attached to the vessel, came to the one in which I was, where they were well received. Our master pilot then took charge, the Captain, as I have said, having been badly wounded, and he at once sent these prisoners to the Admiral, to dispose of them as might seem good to him. The following day the Admiral sent to invite me to his vessel, where all the Captains had to assemble to render thanks to God for the victory they had achieved over their enemies. We afterwards dined with him, and the Capuchin Fathers being of the company, he told me that, as they were of my country, they might, if they preferred it, go to the vessel in which I was, and he would issue orders that they should be well treated; this was done, and I took them with me the same evening, giving them, as far as I was able, whatever was necessary for their comfort.

The vessels which go from Persia to India are generally laden with wine and money, and that which went to the bottom carried more than the others; this was the reason why it held aloof, and did not join in the fray. This was a great loss, which might have been avoided if the Dutch had had more courage and more prevision; and the English Admiral, seeing the misfortune which had happened to one of his vessels, took flight with a second ship. For indeed, to say the truth, the want of enterprise on the part of the Dutch Admiral and the other Captains caused them to miss the certain capture of these fugitives, as it would have been an easy victory if they had known how to profit by their opportunities.

This combat was not finished without my life having been in jeopardy, more particularly from a cannon-shot which struck two Dutchmen who were close to me, and a splinter of the vessel cut open the head of another and carried away a part of my coat, so that I was covered with the blood of the Dutchmen who were slain at my side. The combat being over, we returned to the anchorage at Sindi; but a strong wind arose, and the sea being very high, we were obliged to go to moorings six leagues higher on the eastern coast, where we remained till the 20th of the same month ; [1] we occupied this time in the care of the sick, and many of the English died of their wounds there. At length we reached the anchorage at Sindi, both to obtain water and some stores, and also for the purpose of raising the anchors which we had left behind, and we remained there till the 28th, landing at Gombroon, after a pleasant cruise, on the 7th of March.

My first care when I was out of the vessel was to return thanks to God for having delivered me from this danger, and from many others which I had undergone in my previous travels, and I still offer Him my daily thanksgivings for the same.

[1] February 1654.

BOOK II

Historical and Political description of the Empire of the Great Mogul.

CHAPTER I

Account of the last wars in Hindostān, in which the present condition of the Empire and of the Great Mogul's Court is set forth.

I WRITE this history [1] without any commentary, and without describing how I became aware that these things happened during the sojourn which I made in the country.[2] I leave it to the reader, according to his pleasure, to make his own moral and political reflections. It is sufficient for me to give a faithful picture of the powerful Empire of the Moguls, in accordance with the sketch of it which I have taken on the spot, not wishing to increase this volume by any useless discussion.

This great and vast Empire, which forms the larger part of Hindostān,[3] and extends from the mountains upon this side of the river Indus to the other side of the Ganges, touches on the east the Kingdoms of Arakan, Tipperah, and Assam ;[4] on the west Persia and Tartary of the Usbegs ; on the south the Kingdoms of Golkonda and Bījāpur ; and on the north it reaches to the Caucasus, having on the north-east the Kingdom of Bhutān, from whence musk is brought, and to the north-west the country of Chegathay,[5] or the Usbegs.

[1] With reference to the historical chapters contained in this Book, there can be no attempt to correct or criticize all the author's statements, which occasionally conflict with those of other authorities. The story is fully told by Smith, *Oxford Hist. of India*, 407 ff.

[2] There is so much similarity between this account and that by Bernier in his *History of the late Rebellion in the States of the Great Mogul*, Oxford 1914, that it cannot but be supposed that that author supplied Tavernier with information, either when they were fellow-travellers or after Bernier had published his *History*.

[3] Here Hindostān, in the original Indostan, is used in the European sense as synonymous with India, not as the people of India use it, i. e. the country north of the river Nerbudda.

[4] Aracan, Tipra, and Assen in the original.

[5] Cathay originally meant Northern China ; subsequently, in the sixteenth century, it came to be regarded as a separate country north of China (Yule, *Hobson-Jobson*, 174). In the time of Kublai Khan 'the

As many persons have written about India itself, and of the genius of the Indians, I pass to subjects of more importance, but less well known, and I shall first speak of the family of the Kings of India, commonly known as the Moguls, that is to say whites, because the men who formerly conquered the country were white,[1] the native born Indians being brown or olive-coloured.

Aurangzeb, who reigns at present, is the eleventh in direct line of the descendants of the great Temurleng, commonly called Tamerlane, who by the extent and renown of his conquests from China to Poland surpassed the glory of the most renowned captains of previous ages. His successors succeeded in conquering the whole of India, between the two rivers,[2] thereby destroying many Kings, and Aurangzeb has to-day under his authority the Kingdoms of Gujarāt, Deccan, Delhi, Multān, Lahore, Kashmīr, Bengal, and many other countries, without mentioning many Rājās or Kinglets, who are his vassals and pay him tribute. The following is the succession of these Kings from Tamerlane to Aurangzeb, who reigns at present: I. Temur-leng,[3] named 'the cripple', because he had one leg shorter than the other, is buried at Samarkand in the country of Chegathay or Tartary of the Usbegs; it is also the place where he was born; II. Mīrān Shāh,[4] son of Temur-leng; III. Sultān Muhammad, son of Mīrān Shāh; IV. Sultān Abū Sa'īd Mīrzā,[5] son of Muhammad; V. 'Umar Shaikh Mīrzā,[6] son of Sultān Abū Sa'īd; VI. Sultān

Chagatai Khanate, or Middle Empire of the Tartars, with its capital at Almalik, included the modern Dsungaria, part of Chinese Turkestan, Transoxiana, and Afghanistan' (Yule, *Cathay and the Way thither*, Introduction, p. cxxi).

[1] Mughal is the same word as Mongol, meaning 'brave' (Howorth, *Hist. of the Mongols*, i. 27). 'These armies are composed either of natives, or of genuine Mogols and people who, though less esteemed, are called Mogols, because white men, foreigners, and Mahometans' (Bernier, 209).

[2] i. e. the Indus and Ganges.

[3] Commonly called Tamerlane, but Tavernier's rendering is closer to the real name, viz. Tīmūr-lang, i. e. Tīmūr the lame. See a full genealogy of the Houses of Tīmūr, N. Elias & E. D. Ross, *Hist. of the Moghuls of Central Asia*, 1898, p. 50.

[4] Miram-Cha in the original.

[5] Abousaïd-Mirza in the original.

[6] Hameth Schek in the original.

Bābur,[1] i. e. 'the brave Prince', son of 'Umar Shaikh, and the first of the Moguls who made himself all powerful in India. He died in the year 1532; VII. Humāyūn, which means 'happy', son of Sultān Bābur, died in the year 1552;[2] VIII. Ābu'l Fath[3] Jalāl-ud-dīn Muhammad, commonly called Akbar, that is to say, 'the mighty', son of Humāyūn, reigned fifty-four years, and died A. H. 1014, A. D. 1605; IX. Sultān Salīm, otherwise called Jahāngīr Pādishāh, i. e. Conqueror of the World, succeeded Akbar, his father, and died in the year 1627. He had four sons, the first named Sultān Khusrū, the second Sultān Khurram, the third Sultān Parwez, fourth Shāh Dāniyāl;[4] X. Sultān Khurram, the second of the four sons, succeeded Jahāngīr, his father, and was recognized as sovereign by the nobles of the Empire in the fortress of Agra, under the name of Sultān Shihāb-ud-dīn Muhammad, but he preferred to be called Shāhjahān, i. e. King of the World; XI. Aurangzeb, i. e. 'the Ornament of the Throne', is the Emperor who reigns at present.

The accompanying figure[5] shows the form of the coins which the Emperors cause to be thrown to the people when they ascend the throne. They bear the arms or seals of the Emperors whom I have just named. The largest seal, in the middle, is that of Shāhjahān, the tenth Emperor, for Aurangzeb, since he became Emperor, has not had any of these pieces

[1] Mīrzā Zāhir-ud-dīn Muhammad Bābur, born 15th February 1483. He invaded India in the winter of 1525, and died in 1530, not 1532 as above stated. The name Bābur has no connexion with the Persian *babur*, 'lion' or 'tiger', but has the same meaning.

[2] Humāyūn died in 1556.

[3] Abdul Feta in original.

[4] The sons of Jahāngīr were, in order: Khusrū; Parwīz; Khurram, who reigned under the title of Shāhjahān; Jahāndār; Shahriyār. Dāniyāl was a son of Akbar and brother of Jahāngīr.

[5] Tavernier's beautifully executed plate of these tokens is not reproduced. 'Among the coins of the Moghul Emperors, from Jahāngīr onwards, certain pieces of small size, bear the word *nisār*, which means "scattering". These coins were struck for the purpose of distribution among the crowd on the occasion of certain festivities, such as marriages, or progresses of state, and the like. They were in fact a species of Maundy Money. The custom is common in certain countries and survives to the present day.' (Stanley Lane-Poole, *The History of the Moghul Emperors of Hindustan illustrated by their Coins*, lxxxv ff.).

of bounty coined—these coins are nearly all of silver, a few only being of gold.

The Great Mogul is certainly the most powerful and the richest monarch in Asia ; all the Kingdoms which he possesses are his domain, he being absolute master of all the country, of which he receives the whole revenue. In the territories of this Prince, the nobles are but Royal Receivers, who render account of the revenues to the Governors of Provinces, and they to the Treasurers General and Ministers of Finance, so that this grand King of India, whose territories are so rich, fertile, and populous, has no power near him equal to his own.

CHAPTER II

Concerning the sickness and supposed death of Shāhjahān, King of India, and the rebellion of the Princes, his sons.

The revolutions which took place in the Empire of the Great Mogul on account of the supposed death of Shāhjahān are full of so many important and memorable incidents, that they deserve to be known throughout the whole world. This great monarch reigned more than forty [1] years, less as an Emperor over his subjects than as a father of a family over his house and children ; to such an extent was this the case that, during his reign, the police system was so strict in all things, and particularly with reference to the safety of the roads, that there was never any necessity to execute a man for having committed theft.[2] In his old age he committed an indiscretion ; and, moreover, used some drugs of so stringent a character that they brought on a malady which nearly sent him to the grave. This necessitated his shutting himself up for two or three months in his harem with his women, and during that time he showed himself to his people but rarely, and at long intervals ; this caused them to believe that he was dead. For custom requires these Kings to show themselves in public

[1] 30 years.

[2] This account of Shāhjahān's government is much too favourable. See the summary of Smith, *Oxford History of India*, 415 ff.

three times every week, or, at the very least, every fifteen days.[1]

Shāhjahān had six children, four sons and two daughters. The eldest of the sons was called Dārā Shāh; the second Sultān Shujā'; the third Aurangzeb, who reigns at present; and the last Murād Bakhsh. The elder of the two daughters was called Begam Sāhib, and the younger Raushanārā Begam.[2] All these names, in the language of the country, are titles of honour, as 'the wise', 'the brave', 'the accomplished', &c.; and we practise nearly the same in Europe by the use of the surnames which we give to our Princes, of 'just', 'bold', and 'affable', with this difference only, that these surnames are not given at birth, but after certain proof has been shown of the possession of the virtues which merit that their memories should pass to posterity under such fine names. Shāhjahān loved his four sons equally well, and had established them as Governors or Viceroys of four of his most considerable Provinces, or, if you prefer it, his four principal Kingdoms. Dārā Shikoh,[3] the eldest, remained near the person of the Emperor in the Empire of Delhi, and had the Government of Sindi,[4] where he placed a lieutenant in his absence; Sultān Shujā' had for his district the Kingdom of Bengal; Aurangzeb was sent to the Kingdom of Deccan; and Murād Bakhsh to that of Gujarāt. But much as Shāhjahān sought to give equal contentment to his four sons, their ambition was not satisfied by this allotment, and it overthrew all the projects that the good father had made to preserve peace between his children.

Shāhjahān having fallen sick, retired into the women's quarter without showing himself for many days. So the rumour spread that he was dead, and that Dārā Shikoh concealed his death in order to arrange his affairs and secure

[1] The Darshan or daily appearance at a Jharokhā, a window or balcony, was the custom of the Emperors (*Āīn-i-Akbarī*, i. 156 f.; Smith, *Akbar the Great Mogul*, 383). Aurangzeb abolished it because it savoured of the homage paid by Hindus to the image of their tutelary deity before beginning the day's work (Jadunath Sarkar, iii. 101).

[2] Called Rauchenara Begum in the original. Begam Sāhib. Jahānārā.

[3] Dara Cha (Shāh) in original. Dārā Shikoh: 'in majesty like Darius'.

[4] Sind. He was Viceroy of the Punjāb, and other provinces on the north and west, which he administered through deputies.

for himself the whole of the Empire. It is certain that the Emperor, believing that he was about to die and was near his last hour, ordered Dārā Shikoh to assemble all the Omrahs [1] or nobles of the Empire, and seat himself on the throne, which belonged to him as the eldest of all the brothers. He also told him that if God prolonged his life for some days he desired to see him, before he died, in the peaceable possession of his Empire; and his intention that his eldest son should succeed to the throne was undoubtedly right, because he had for some time observed that the three other Princes showed much less respect and affection for their father than Dārā Shikoh did. At this conversation with his son, Dārā Shikoh who honoured his father extremely and loved him tenderly, replied that he prayed to God for the life of His Majesty, which he hoped would be long, and that while God preserved it he would never dream of ascending the throne, but would consider himself always happy in being his subject. Indeed, this Prince did not absent himself for a moment from the presence of his father, so that he might be at hand to attend upon him during his sickness; and, wishing to be present at all times, he slept at night close to the Emperor's bed on a carpet spread on the floor.

However, upon the false report of the death of Shāhjahān, his three other sons straightway stirred themselves, and each laid claim to their father's throne. Murād Bakhsh, the youngest, who held the Government of the Province of Gujarāt, immediately sent troops to lay siege to Surat, the largest and most frequented port in all India. The city, which was without protection, made no resistance, for it has only weak fortifications, which are open in many places; but the citadel, where the treasure was stored, was defended vigorously; and this young, ambitious Prince, who had need of money, used all his powers to become master of it. Shāhbāz Khān,[2] one of his eunuchs, an industrious and energetic man, General of his army, conducted the siege with all the skill of an old commander.

[1] See p. 79.

[2] Chabas Kan in the original. See the account of the attack on Surat by Jadunath Sarkar, i. 323 ff. It occurred in November, 1657, not 1659, as in the original text.

Finding that he was unable to carry the place by storm, he ordered two mines to be excavated by a European. This plan was at once successful, and when the first mine was fired on the 29th of December 1657, it brought down a large portion of the walls, which filled the moat, and caused great alarm to the besieged. But they quickly plucked up courage, and, although they were few in number, defended themselves bravely for the space of more than forty days, during which time they did much injury to the army of Murād Bakhsh, and slew many of his soldiers. Shāhbāz Khān, irritated by this vigorous resistance, caused search to be made for the women and children, and relatives and friends of the artillerymen in the fortress, intending to place them in front of his soldiers during the attack ; and he also sent one of the brothers of the Governor of the city to parley with him, and to make an advantageous offer, if he would deliver it into his hands. But the Governor, a good servant of the Emperor, who had not received certain tidings of his death, replied that he recognized no other master than Shāhjahān, who had entrusted the place to him, and that he would not relinquish it save to the Emperor himself, or to whomsoever he pleased to order ; that he honoured Murād Bakhsh as Prince and son of the Emperor his master, but he refused to surrender the place even to him without receiving an express order from the Emperor.

The eunuch seeing the resolution of the Governor, made the most stringent threats to the besieged, swearing that he would kill all their relatives, their women, and their children, if they did not deliver themselves up to him on the following day. But these menaces had not, and could not have, any effect on the besieged ; and it was only the state of the breach, which they could not defend on account of the smallness of their numbers, and the fear of the second mine, that at length obliged the Governor to surrender under honourable conditions ; these were faithfully kept by Shāhbāz Khān, who seized the treasure, and carried it off to Ahmadābād, where Murād Bakhsh was occupied in oppressing the people in order to raise money.[1]

[1] The commander of the fort was Sayyid Tayyib. The keys reached Murād Bakhsh at Ahmadābād on 26th December 1657.

When the news of the capture of Surat reached the Prince, he immediately had a throne prepared, and having seated himself upon it on the day appointed for the ceremony, proclaimed himself Emperor not only of Gujarāt, but of all the dominions of Shāhjahān, his father. At the same time he had money coined, and dispatched new Governors to all the towns. But as his throne is badly founded it must quickly fall; and the Prince, the youngest of his brothers, is destined to end his days in prison because he claimed the succession to which he was not lawfully entitled.

Prince Dārā Shikoh was anxious to relieve Surat, but it was impossible for him to do so, for not only was he occupied in attending the Emperor, his father, during his sickness, but he had to watch his second brother, Sultān Shujā', who was much more powerful than Murād Bakhsh, and caused him far more trouble. He had already advanced into the Kingdom of Lahore,[1] and had entirely subjected that of Bengal. All that Dārā Shikoh was able to do was to dispatch with speed his eldest son, Sulaimān Shikoh,[2] with a powerful army against Sultān Shujā'. In the end, this young Prince defeated his uncle, drove him into the Province of Bengal, the frontiers of which he secured by strong garrisons, and then returned to Dārā Shikoh his father. In the meantime Murād Bakhsh, already recognized as King[3] in the Kingdom of Gujarāt, aspired to secure the Empire of India, to destroy his brothers, and establish his throne either in Agra or Jahānābād.

Meanwhile, Aurangzeb, as ambitious and more cunning than his brothers, allowed them to expend their energies, and concealed his design from them, which he intended to develop and to destroy them before long. He pretended to have no claims to the Empire, announcing that he had abandoned the world, and would live the life of a Darvish, or solitary devotee.[4] In order to play this part with greater success he informed

[1] Lahore is here a mistake for Behār. He could not have reached Lahore, and if he had, it would not have served his purpose.

[2] Soliman Cheko in the original. He was accompanied by Rājā Jai Singh. The engagement took place at Bahādurpur near Benares in February 1658.

[3] Tavernier means 'as Pādirhāh', i. e. Emperor.

[4] Aurangzeb did not turn hermit in a fit of religious devotion: his motive was political, not spiritual (Jadunath Sarkar, i. 76, 78).

his younger brother, Murād Bakhsh, that he perceived that he was desirous of reigning, and wished to aid him in his object, and that as he deserved the throne on account of his bravery, he would assist him with his armies and money to vanquish Dārā Shikoh, who was an obstacle in the way. The young Prince, having little judgement, and blinded by the prospect of his good fortune, was only too ready to believe Aurangzeb, and joining forces with him,[1] agreed to advance with him on Agra to take possession of it. Dārā Shikoh marched against them, and the battle was commenced, with the result as unfortunate for him as it was auspicious for the two brothers. The Prince, trusting too much to the principal officers in his army, and contrary to the advice of the General in command, who was his Prime Minister, and faithful to him, believed himself to be able to secure victory by attacking his brothers first, without giving them time to rest.[2] The first shock was rough and bloody, and Murād Bakhsh, full of fire and courage, fighting like a lion, received five arrows in his body, and the elephant upon which he was mounted was covered with them. Victory tending to the side of Dārā Shikoh, Aurangzeb retired ; but quickly turned his face when he saw the traitors in Dārā Shikoh's army coming to his aid, who had basely abandoned him after he had lost his best officers and their General. Immediately Aurangzeb took courage, and returning to the combat with Dārā Shikoh, the latter Prince, seeing that he was betrayed, and had no longer anything to hope for from the few adherents remaining with him, immediately beat his retreat, and returned to Agra, to the Emperor his father, who had already begun to amend. He advised his son to withdraw into the fortress of Delhi, and carry with him the treasure deposited in Agra ; [3] this he did without loss of time,

[1] This junction took place near Ujjain in Mālwā, whither Aurangzeb had marched from Burhānpur.

[2] The battle was fought at Dharmat, 114 miles SSW. of Ujjain on 15th April 1658. 'The disaster was due partly to the evils of divided command and jealousy between the Rājputs and the Musalmāns, and partly to the bad choice of ground made and the erroneous tactics pursued by Rājā Jaswant Singh of Mārwār', the general mentioned in the text (Smith, *Oxford History of India*, 410).

[3] According to Bernier (p. 223), Shāhjahān's treasure never amounted

accompanied by his most faithful attendants. Thus the victory of Aurangzeb and Murād Bakhsh was complete, and the latter before the end of the battle, weakened by loss of blood, retired to his tent to have his wounds dressed. It was easy for Aurangzeb to gain over these traitors, not only by means of the enormous treasure he had acquired, but because the Indians are ever inconstant and ungrateful. Moreover, the chiefs are generally emigrants from Persia, people of no birth and of little heart, who attach themselves to those who give most.[1]

Shāista Khān, son of 'Āsaf Khān,[2] who had betrayed the Prince Bulākī, as I shall relate, in order to obtain the throne for Shāhjahān, his brother-in-law—Shāista Khān, I say, uncle of the four Princes whose mother was his own sister, ranged himself on Aurangzeb's side, with the greater number of the principal officers of Dārā Shikoh and Murād Bakhsh, who abandoned their masters. Murād Bakhsh at last began to realize the mistake he had made in trusting Aurangzeb, who, seeing himself favoured by fortune, lost no time in carrying out his plans. Murād Bakhsh, who with reason entertained doubts as to his brother's loyalty to him demanded half the treasure which had been seized, that he might retire into Gujarāt, while Aurangzeb, in reply, assured him that he desired to aid him in ascending the throne, and that on that account he wished to consult with him. Murād Bakhsh, finding his wounds somewhat healed, visited his brother Aurangzeb, who received him kindly and praised his courage, which deserved, he said, the first Empire in the world.

The young Prince allowed himself to be deceived by these soft words; but his eunuch, Shāhbāz Khān, who had

to as much as 6 crores of rupees, which, at the rate of 2*s*. 3*d*., would be about £6,750,000. This was exclusive of the precious stones and throne.

[1] 'The Omrahs mostly consist of adventurers from different nations who entice one another to the Court; and are generally persons of low descent, some having been originally slaves, and the majority being destitute of education. The Mogul raises them to dignities, or degrades them to obscurity, according to his own pleasure and caprice' (Bernier, 212).

[2] 'Āsaf Khān was the brother of the famous Nūrjahān, wife of Jahāngīr; see p. 15 *n*.

conquered for him the best part of the Kingdom of Gujarāt, tried to excite his distrust, and make him realize the trap which had been set for him. But when Murād Bakhsh wished to profit by the advice of his eunuch it was then too late, as Aurangzeb had already taken measures to ruin him. He invited Murād Bakhsh to a feast, and the more he excused himself the more he was pressed to come. The young Prince, unable to refuse any longer, resolved to go in order that he might conceal his mistrust, although he feared that the day was to be the last of his life, and that some deadly poison had been prepared for him. He was mistaken, however, for Aurangzeb did not then aim at his life, and contented himself with securing his person ; so, in place of aiding him to ascend the throne, as he had promised, he sent him under safe custody to the fortress of Gwalior, to give him time to be cured of his wounds, and to take measures for the accomplishment of his designs.[1]

CHAPTER III

Concerning Shāhjahān's prison, and how he was punished by Aurangzeb, his third son, for the injustice he had done to Prince Bulākī,[2] his nephew, grandson of Jahāngīr, to whom, since he was the son of the eldest son, the Empire of the Moguls belonged.

JAHĀNGĪR, King of India, son of Akbar, and grandson of Humāyūn, enjoyed a very peaceable reign for the space of nearly twenty-three years, equally beloved by his subjects and his neighbours.[3] But his life was too long to suit the ambition of two of his sons, already advanced in years. The eldest[4] raised a powerful army at Lahore, with the object of surprising his father Jahāngīr, and seating himself by violence on the

[1] See the account of the betrayal of Murād Bakhsh in Jadunath Sarkar, ii. 91 ff.

[2] Dāwar Bakhsh, son of Khusrū, was called Bulākī because, probably to avoid the Evil Eye, a ring (*bulāq*) was inserted in the septum of his nose, in order to disguise him as a girl, who is believed not to be liable to fascination (R. C. Temple, *Proper Names of Panjābīs*, 28).

[3] For the correct view of his character see Smith, *Oxford History of India*, 387.

[4] Namely, Khusrū.

throne. The Emperor, becoming aware of the insolence of his son, resolved to chastise him, opposed him with a large army, and took him prisoner, with many of the chief nobles who followed him. But Jahāngīr, a generous Prince, who dearly loved his son, although he had him in his power was unwilling to sentence him to the death which he deserved; and contented himself with destroying his sight, by ordering a hot iron to be passed over his eyes [1] in the manner which, as I have described, is followed in Persia. The Emperor resolved ever after to keep this blind son about his person, intending that his eldest son, Sultān Bulāki, should some day reign; this Prince had already several other sons, all being under age. But Sultān Khurram,[2] who afterwards took the name of Shāhjahān, thinking that, as second son of Jahāngīr, he should be preferred to his nephew, resolved to use every effort to keep him from the throne, and to seat himself upon it, without waiting for the death of the Emperor. He, however, dissimulated, kept his real purpose concealed, and appeared at first entirely submissive to the will of his father, who always kept the children of his eldest son beside him. It was by this submission that Shāhjahān more easily attained his ends; in this manner he gained the goodwill of his father, and obtained permission from him to take with him the blind Prince his elder brother to his Government in the Kingdom of Deccan. He represented to the Emperor that it was advisable to remove from his sight an object which had become distressing to him, that the Prince, deprived of his eyes, would not in the future be other than a charge and trouble to him, and that he would pass the rest of his life with greater comfort in the Deccan. The Emperor, not penetrating the designs of Khurram, consented without difficulty to what he asked,

[1] Chardin relates how it came to pass, in the reign of Shāh 'Abbās II, that the custom of destroying the sight of Princes by means of a red-hot blade of copper passed over the eyes was replaced by the actual removal of the eyeballs themselves, in consequence of some of the Princes who had been operated on having been found to possess partial sight (*Voyages*, Amsterdam ed., 1711, vol. vi, p. 27). The eyes were destroyed either by piercing the eyes with a lancet, or using a heated plate or pencil of brass or iron (Erskine, *Hist. of India*, ii. 14).

[2] Courōm in the original.

but as soon as he had this poor Prince in his power he knew how to rid himself of him by the most secret means, and used the most plausible pretexts to conceal his crime from the view of men, not considering that he was unable to conceal it from the eyes of God, who did not leave this action unpunished, as we shall shortly see.[1]

After the death of the blind Prince, Sultān Khurram assumed the title of Shāhjahān, i. e. King of the World, and in order to support it raised an army to finish the task which his brother had begun, namely the dethronement of his father Jahāngīr and his succession to the Empire. The Emperor, much irritated by the death of his son and the outrage against his own person, sent considerable forces to chastise Khurram for so criminal an enterprise, and the rebel Prince, feeling himself too weak to resist them, quitted the Kingdom of Deccan, and wandered with some vagabonds who followed him, sometimes in one place, sometimes in another, until he arrived in Bengal, where he raised an army to give battle to the Emperor. Having crossed the Ganges, he directed his steps towards the Kingdom of Lahore,[2] and the Emperor in person confronted him with a more numerous and stronger army. But Jahāngīr, old and distressed by the troubles caused by his two sons, died on the road,[3] and left Shāhjahān free to pursue his designs. However, before he died this good Emperor had time to commend the care of his grandson, Sultān Bulākī,[4] to ʻĀsaf Khān, Commander-in-Chief of his armies and Prime Minister of State, who governed the whole Empire. He ordered all his officers to recognize Bulākī as Emperor and legitimate heir after his death, declaring Sultān Khurram a rebel, and incapable of succeeding him on the throne.

Moreover, he made ʻĀsaf Khān swear in particular that he would never suffer Bulākī to be killed, whatever the results

[1] Dāwar Bakhsh was permitted to escape to Persia, where he lived as a pensioner of the Shāh (Smith, *Oxford Hist.* 392 and pp. 271–2 below).

[2] As on p. 264, Lahore is here also a mistake for Behār. Smith, *op. cit.*, 386.)

[3] Jahāngīr died on the 28th October 1627. Tavernier's account is incorrect, as he died on his return journey from Kashmīr to Lahore at Chingiz Hatlī at the foot of the hills.

[4] Prince Dāwar Bakhsh, nicknamed Bulākī.

might be ; this oath ‘Āsaf Khān swore upon his thigh,[1] which bound him by his religion to save his life, but not to establish him on the throne, where he wished to place Shāhjahān, to whom he had given his eldest daughter in marriage. She was mother of the four Princes and the two Princesses to whom I have referred in the preceding chapter.

When the news of the Emperor's death was reported at Court, all appeared to be sorely afflicted, and immediately the nobles of the Empire proceeded to give effect to the will by recognizing Sultān Bulākī, still a youth, as Emperor. This Prince had two first cousins [2] who, with the King's consent, had become Christians, and had made public profession of the faith. The two young Princes, who were kind-hearted, observed that Āsaf Khān, father-in-law of Shāhjahān, and father of Shāista Khān, of whom I have often spoken, had evil designs against the new Emperor, to whom they speedily gave warning, and this warning cost them their lives and the Emperor the loss of his dominions. The young Emperor, who did not yet possess that prudence which can only be acquired by age, ingenuously told ‘Āsaf Khān what the two young Christian Princes, his cousins, had said to him in private, and asked him if it was true that he, as they had assured him, designed to make his uncle, Sultān Khurram, Emperor. ‘Āsaf Khān took care not to tell him the truth ; on the contrary, he accused those who had made the report of falseness and insolence, and protested that he would be faithful to his Emperor all his life, and that, in order to maintain him on the throne, he would shed his blood to the very last drop. Sultān Bulākī understood this to refer to himself, but ‘Āsaf Khān, when he promised to be faithful to his Emperor, really meant his own son-in-law, Shāhjahān, whom he desired to elevate to the throne—the consideration of affinity prevailing over that of justice. Seeing that his perfidy had been discovered, he averted the punishment which he began to apprehend, and obtaining possession of the two Princes, had them forthwith

[1] For swearing on the thigh compare Genesis xxiv. 2 ff., xlvii. 29.

[2] These were sons of Shāh Dāniyāl, named Tahmūras and Hoshang (*Āīn-i-Akbarī*, i. 309 f.). These seem to be the nephews of Akbar who became Christians (Bernier, 287).

murdered. As he was all-powerful both in the army and in the Empire, he had already secured, in the interests of Shāhjahān, the greater number of the officers and nobility of the Court; and the better to conceal his intention and to lull the suspicion of the young Emperor, who understood these affairs but imperfectly, he spread the report that Shāhjahān was dead, and that, as he desired to be interred near Jahāngīr, his father, his body was to be brought to Agra.[1] The stratagem was adroitly conducted. 'Āsaf Khān himself told the Emperor of this pretended death, and assured him that etiquette required that His Majesty should go from Agra to meet the body, when it came within a league or two of the city, such honour being rightly due to a Prince of the blood of the Moguls who was the brother of his father, and son of Jahāngīr. Accordingly Shāhjahān approached incognito, and when he was in sight of the army, near Agra, he got into a bier, where there was sufficient air for respiration. The bier was carried into a tent, and all the principal chiefs, who were in concert with 'Āsaf Khān, came as though to do honour to the dead Prince, the young Emperor, on his part, having left Agra to be present at the meeting. It was then that 'Āsaf Khān saw that the time had arrived for the execution of his design; he had the bier opened, and Shāhjahān raised himself and appeared before the eyes of all the army; he was saluted as Emperor by the generals and other officers, who took their cue, and at the same moment the name of Shāhjahān as Emperor was passed from mouth to mouth; the proclamation was made public, and the Empire of the Moguls was assured to him. The young Emperor hearing this news on the road, was so upset by it that he thought of nothing but flight, as he saw himself deserted by almost every one; and Shāhjahān, not thinking it prudent to pursue him, allowed him to wander for a long time in India as a sort of *Fakīr*. But at length, wearied with that kind of life, he took refuge in Persia, where he was magnificently received by Shāh Safavī,[2] who bestowed

[1] Jahāngīr was buried at Shāhdara, Lahore (*Imperial Gazetteer*, xvi. 108).

[2] Cha Sefi in the original. Shāh Safī, grandson of Shāh 'Abbās, King of Persia, whom he succeeded in 1629, after a reign characterized by cruelty, died in May, 1642 (Malcolm, *Hist. of Persia*, 2nd ed. i. 381 ff.).

upon him a pension worthy of a great Prince. He enjoys it still, and I had an opportunity of conversing with him during my travels in Persia, and drank and ate with him.[1]

Shāhjahān having usurped the throne in this way,[2] in order to secure himself and to stifle all the factions which might arise on behalf of the legitimate heir, whom he had unjustly despoiled of his Empire, by degrees murdered all those who showed affection for his nephew, and had made themselves suspects ; thus the early years of his reign were marked by cruelties which have much tarnished his memory. The end of his reign was in like manner unhappy, and as he had unjustly stolen the Empire from the legitimate heir to whom it belonged, so he was, during his lifetime, deprived of it by his own son Aurangzeb, who kept him a prisoner in the fortress of Agra ; and this, in a few words, is how it came to pass.

After Dārā Shikoh had lost the battle against his two brothers Aurangzeb and Murād Bakhsh, in the plain of Samonguir,[3] and was basely deserted by the principal officers of his army, he retired to the Kingdom of Lahore with as much of the royal treasure as he had been able to take in the confusion of his affairs. The Emperor, in the hope of resisting the impetuosity of his victorious sons, whose only thoughts were of reigning by depriving him of his throne, and possibly also of his life, shut himself up in the fortress of Agra to avoid arrest, and to see to what limits his sons would carry their insolence. Aurangzeb secured the person of Murād Bakhsh, as I have related in the preceding chapter, entered Agra and pretended to believe that Shāhjahān was dead, as an excuse for entering the fortress, which, as he said, was in possession of one of the Omrahs. The more Aurangzeb published the report that Shāhjahān was dead, the more Shāhjahān strove to publish the fact that he was alive ; but at length the Emperor perceived that he was no longer able to resist Aurangzeb, who had all the power and all the good luck on his side,

[1] He was seen also, according to Olearius (*Voyages and Travels*, &c., Eng. ed., p. 190), by the Holstein Ambassadors in 1633, and Dow's statement as to his murder by 'Āsaf Khān is incorrect.

[2] Shāhjahān ascended the throne on the 4th February, 1628.

[3] On the 29th May, 1658. Samūgarh, 8 miles east of Agra Fort.

and as the wells of the Agra fortress were dried up, he was compelled to provide himself with river water by a small postern which was the weakest part of the fortifications, and this Aurangzeb had already reconnoitred. He therefore sent Fāzil Khān,[1] the Grand Chamberlain, to assure Aurangzeb that he was alive, so that he should no longer pretend to be ignorant of the fact. Fāzil Khān was instructed to tell the Prince that the Emperor, his father, ordered him to return to the Kingdom of Deccan, the seat of his Government, without causing any more trouble, and that by showing this sign of obedience he would enable him to forget all that had passed. Aurangzeb, still firm in his resolve, replied to Fāzil Khān that he was convinced that the Emperor, his father, was dead, and that upon that ground he had fought for the throne, which he believed he deserved equally with his brothers, who naturally had no more right to it than he had; that if the Emperor was alive he had too much respect for him to have the least idea of doing anything to displease him, but that he might be convinced that he was not dead he desired to see him, and to kiss his feet, after which he would retire to his own Government, and obey his orders implicitly.

Fāzil Khān conveyed this reply to the Emperor, who answered that he was willing to see his son, and sent Fāzil Khān to say he would be welcome. But Aurangzeb more astute than Shāhjahān, assured Fāzil Khān that he would not venture into the fortress till the garrison which was in it was replaced by his own troops. The Prince feared, with good reason too, that if he entered except as master he might be served an evil turn and his person seized, and the Emperor when he knew his resolution, not being able to do any better, consented to all that his son demanded. Accordingly the garrison of Shāhjahān went out of the fortress, and that of Aurangzeb entered under command of Sultān Muhammad, the eldest of his sons, to whom he gave a command to secure the person of the Emperor his father. However, he postponed

[1] Fāzil Khān, Alāu-l-mulk, Tūnī, a Persian, native of Tūn in Khurāsān, a poet and of unblemished character, was Aurangzeb's first Wazīr; but he too enjoyed his new dignity only sixteen days, dying in June, 1663 (Jadunath Sarkar, *Hist. of Aurangzib*, iii. 73; *Studies in Mughal*
24 *India*, 52; Bernier, 200). [Cf. *Anecdotes of Aurangzib*, p. 40.]

the visit from day to day, awaiting an auspicious hour for this interview, and his astrologers not finding one, he withdrew to a country house 2 or 3 leagues distant from Agra; this displeased the people much, as they awaited with impatience the fortunate hour, which, by the visit of the son to the father, would terminate their disputes.

But Aurangzeb had no desire for this interview, but took the strange resolution to control his father's personal expenditure, and assume possession of all the treasures which Dārā Shīkoh had been unable to carry off in his precipitate flight.[1] He also caused the Begam Sāhib, his sister, to be confined in the fortress, that she might keep company with the King, whom she dearly loved.[2] And he also took possession of all the wealth which she had received from her father's liberality.

Shāhjahān, incensed at being treated in this manner by his own son, made some efforts to escape, and slew some of the guards who dared to oppose him; this caused Aurangzeb to order him into closer confinement. It is a most surprising thing, however, that not one of the servants of this great Emperor offered to assist him; that all his subjects abandoned him, and that they turned their eyes to the rising sun, recognizing no one as Emperor but Aurangzeb—Shāhjahān, although still living, having passed from their memories. If perchance there were any who felt touched by his misfortunes, fear made them silent, and caused them basely to abandon an Emperor who had governed them like a father, and with a mildness which is not common with sovereigns. For although he was severe enough to the nobles when they failed to perform their duties, he arranged all things for the comfort of the people, by whom he was much beloved, though they gave no signs of it at this crisis. Thus this great Emperor ended his days sadly in prison, and died in the Agra fort about the end of the year 1666,[3]

[1] For an interesting account of Muhammad Sultān, see Jadunath Sarkar, *Studies in Mughal India*, 72 ff. He died on 5th December, 1676, in the fort of Gwalior, where he had been imprisoned by his father, and was buried near the tomb of Qutbu-d-dīn, at Delhi. [2] See p. 276 below.

[3] 22nd January 1666. The estimate in the text is much too favourable as regards the character of Shāhjahān (Smith, *Oxford Hist. of India*, 415 f.).

during my last journey in India. During his reign he had commenced building the city of Jahānābād, which was not yet completed, and he wished to see it once more before he died. But for this purpose it was necessary to obtain the consent of Aurangzeb, his son, who held him prisoner, and he was quite willing to allow him to make the journey, and even to remain at Jahānābād as long as he wished, shut up in the castle, as he was in Agra, provided that he consented to travel up the river by boat, and return in one of the small painted and ornamented frigates which lie on the Jumna at the palace of Jahānābād. For Aurangzeb was unwilling to permit him to travel on his elephant by land, as he feared lest his father's appearance to the people might immediately raise a party in his favour, and that if he placed himself at their head, as people are inconstant, he might find means to recover the throne. Shāhjahān, perceiving the severity of his son, who wished to injure him in this way, gave up the idea of the journey, and the great displeasure he felt at such cruel treatment hastened his death.[1] As soon as Aurangzeb had news of it he came to Agra and seized all the jewels of the late King, his father, which he had not secured during his life. The Begam Sāhib also had a quantity of precious stones,[2] which he had not taken from her when he placed her in the fortress, as he was then satisfied with securing the gold and silver with which her chests were full. These jewels confirmed Aurangzeb's suspicions, the Princess, his sister, having already been suspected of having had improper relations with Shāhjahān and he found means to obtain them in a manner which appeared honest and reasonable, by treating the Begam Sāhib with much honour and attention; but he removed her to Jahānābād,[3] and I saw the elephant pass upon which she was mounted when she left Agra with the court, as I was entering it on my return from Bengal. In a short time after news was spread of the death of this Princess, and

[1] On 22nd January 1666.

[2] The delivery of the precious stones by the Begam Sāhib to Aurangzeb is described on p. 295 below.

[3] Here Jehanabad is in the original, though elsewhere generally Gehanabat. In the 1713 edition by a misprint it is Jehanabab.

all the world believed that it had been hastened by poison.[1] Let us now see what has become of Dārā Shikoh, and what has been the result of the war between the sons of the unfortunate Shāhjahān.

CHAPTER IV

Concerning the flight of Dārā Shikoh to the Kingdoms of Sind and Gujarāt; of his second battle with Aurangzeb; of his capture and death.

Dārā Shikoh having, on the advice of his father, carried off in haste some of the gold and silver which was in the fortress of Agra, retired to the Kingdom of Lahore, hoping to be able to place on foot, in a short time, a second army, to attack his brother Aurangzeb. His most faithful servants and friends had always accompanied him in his misfortunes, and his eldest son Sulaimān Shikoh was with Rājā Rūp [2] in his kingdom endeavouring to raise troops, having with him five millions of rupees (5,000,000),[3] which amount to seven million five hundred thousand (7,500,000) livres of our money, as an

[1] Jahānārā Begam died on 16th September, 1681. The rumour that she was poisoned is probably mere court gossip, spread by the partizans of Aurangzeb, as are also the tales of her relations with her father and other accounts of her licentiousness given by Bernier and other writers (Manucci, i. 217, ii. 255 f.; Bernier, 11 f.). She lies in the enclosure of the mausoleum of the Saint Nizāmu-d-dīn Auliya at Delhi, and her tomb bears the inscription: 'Let green grass only conceal my grave; grass is the best covering of the grave of the meek' (Fanshawe, *Delhi Past and Present*, 539; Sleeman, *Rambles*, 510). Tavernier's statement that she died 'a short time after' is incorrect.

[2] Roup in the original. Rājā Rūp Singh, a daughter of whom, although a Hindu, was married to Aurangzeb's son Mu'azzam, afterwards the Emperor Bahādur Shāh, in the year 1661. His mother was also a Hindu lady (Tod, *Annals*, i. 464). Rājā Rūp Singh was a landowner in the hills of Jammū in Kashmīr, who at first joined Dārā Shikoh when he was making military preparations at Lahore. Afterwards Aurangzeb induced him by promises to desert Dārā (Jadunath Sarkar, *History of Aurangzīb*, ii. 104, 111). The late Mr. W. Irvine supplied Ball with a translation of a passage in the *Ma'āsiru-l-umara* (printed texts, ii. 477) giving a full account of these transactions.

[3] £562,500.

inducement to attract soldiers more rapidly. But this large sum soon aroused Rājā Rūp's avarice, and he seized it for himself by a base and infamous act of treason. Sulaimān Shikoh fearing he would go further and seize his person also, withdrew promptly to the Kingdom of Srīnagar, under the protection of Rājā Nakti-Rānī,[1] who, by a still blacker act of treason, delivered him over to Aurangzeb some time afterwards.

Dārā Shikoh, having had notice of Rājā Rūp's treason and seeing all his friends abandoning him to join Aurangzeb, left Lahore intending to retire into the Kingdom of Sind. Before leaving the fortress he ordered all the gold, silver, and jewels in the treasury to be embarked on the river in the care of a strong escort, and sent them to Bukkur,[2] which is in the middle of the river Indus, where he took possession of a fort. He left there, as governor and guardian of his wealth, a faithful eunuch[3] and six thousand soldiers, and all the munitions necessary to sustain a siege, after which he went to Sind, where he left many heavy guns. He then went into the country of the King of Kachnagana,[4] who made him magnificent promises which came to no results; next he entered the

[1] Sireneguer in the original: in the French edition of 1713, Serenager, Srīnagar, in Pargana Dewalgarh, Garhwāl District, United Provinces. The Rājā of which place, with whom Sulaimān Shikoh took refuge, was Prithī Sāh (E. T. Atkinson, *Himalayan Districts of the N.W. Provinces* ii. 563 f., iii. 691 ff.; *Imperial Gazetteer*, xxiii. 105; Bernier, 59, 92; Elliot & Dowson, *Hist. of India*, vii. 230). His wife gained her title of Nāk-katī Rānī, 'the nose-cutting' Queen from her habit of cutting off the noses of her rebellious subjects, a custom infrequent in northern India, except when practised by jealous husbands on their unfaithful wives, but a common punishment inflicted in former days on enemies in southern India (Manucci, i. 216 *n.*, iv. 99, 460; L. Rice, *Mysore and Coorg from the Inscriptions*, 130). The principal deity of Bilāspur in the Central Provinces is Naktī Devī, the noseless goddess (Russell, *Tribes and Castes, Central Provinces*, ii. 231).

[2] Baker in the original, Bukkur or Bakhar. For the history of this island-fortress, which has always been a position of strategical importance, see *Imperial Gazetteer*, ix. 46 ff. It was the principal British arsenal during the Sind and Afghān campaigns.

[3] Basant Mewātī, whom Manucci calls Primavera, 'Spring' (i. 352, ii. 458), and see Bernier, 75.

[4] Cutch (or Kachchh).

Kingdom of Gujarāt, where he was received by the people with great acclamation as the legitimate Emperor and heir of Shāhjahān. He issued his commands in all the cities, and especially in Surat, where he established a Governor; but the Governor of the fortress, who had been appointed by Murād Bakhsh and was a Rājā, would not submit to Dārā Shikoh.[1] He protested that he would not give over charge of the place into the hands of any one except on the express order of Murād Bakhsh; and as he continued firm in this resolve, he was allowed to remain peaceably in the fortress, without, on his part, causing any trouble to the Governor of the town.

In the meantime, Dārā Shikoh got news at Ahmadābād that Jaswant Singh,[2] one of the most powerful Rājās in all India, had detached himself from Aurangzeb, and wished to join him. He was even invited by this Rājā to advance with his army, which was not large, and did not exceed 30,000 men when he arrived at Ahmadābād. Dārā Shikoh, confiding in his promise, followed his counsel, and went to Ajmer,[3] the appointed rendezvous, where he hoped to find him. But Jaswant Singh, who had been won by the arguments of the Rājā Jai Singh,[4] who was more powerful than he, and was wholly devoted to the interests of Aurangzeb, did not come to Ajmer on the day he promised, and only got there at the last moment, for the purpose of betraying this poor Prince. The armies of the two brothers met, the combat commenced, and the battle lasted for three days; but during the course of the engagement Jaswant Singh, with manifest treachery, passed over to the side of Aurangzeb, and when Dārā Shikoh's soldiers saw him, they lost courage and took to flight.[5] There

[1] As already explained on page 6 the governorship of the fort at Surat was a distinct post from that of the governor of the town. One of Dārā Shikoh's officers took peaceful possession of Surat from Aurangzeb's governor (Jadunath Sarkar, ii. 165).

[2] Jaswant Singh—Jessomseing in the original. He was Rājā of Jodhpur or Mārwār, and died in 1678.

[3] Emir in the original.

[4] Jesseing in the original, Mīrzā Rājā of Jaipur.

[5] The battle was fought at the Pass of Deorāī, south of Ajmer, 12–14th April, 1659. See Jadunath Sarkar (*History of Aurangzīb*, ii. 171 ff.), who gives 11–12th March as the date of the battle.

had been much bloodshed on both sides ; Shāh Nawāz Khān,[1] father-in-law of Aurangzeb, was left on the field, and there were on both sides 8000 or 9000 men slain, without counting the wounded, the number of whom was still greater. Dārā Shikoh had no other resources, and fortune had been against him in all his enterprises ; so fearing lest he should fall into the hands of his enemies, he took flight in a pitiable conveyance with his wives, some of his children, and his most faithful followers. As he approached Ahmadābād, Monsieur Bernier,[2] a French physician, on his way to Agra to visit the Court of the Great Mogul, and well known to all the world as much by his personal merit as by the charming accounts of his travels, was of great assistance to one of the wives of this Prince who was attacked with erysipelas in one leg. Dārā Shikoh, learning that an accomplished European physician was at hand, sent immediately for him, and Monsieur Bernier went to his tent, where he saw this lady and examined her ailment, for which he gave a remedy and quick relief. The poor Prince, much pleased with Monsieur Bernier, strongly pressed him to remain in his service, and he might have accepted the offer if Dārā Shikoh had not received news the same night that the Governor whom he had left at Ahmadābād had refused to allow his quarter-master to enter the town, and had declared for Aurangzeb. This compelled Dārā Shikoh to decamp quickly in the darkness of the night, and take the road to Sind, fearing some new treachery, which he could not defend himself from in the unhappy condition into which he had fallen.

Dārā Shikoh arrived in Sind, intending to pass into Persia, where Shāh 'Abbās II awaited him with a magnificent outfit, and was resolved to aid him with men and money. But the Prince unwilling to entrust himself to the sea, and fearing that the uncertainty of a voyage would subject him to some new reverse of fortune, believed that by going by land he would secure greater safety for himself, his women and children. However, he deceived himself, for when passing through the country of the Pathāns, on the road to Kandahār,

[1] Chanavas Kan in the original. See Bernier, 73.

[2] François Bernier. See his *Travels*, p. 90, where he says that the lady had a bad wound in her leg.

he was again shamefully betrayed by one of the chieftains of the country named Juin Khān,[1] who had been an officer of the Emperor his father, and having been condemned to death by them for his crimes, and sentenced to be thrown under the feet of an elephant, obtained forgiveness through the intercession of Dārā Shikoh, to whom, therefore, he owed his life. To augment his affliction Dārā Shikoh, before reaching the house of Juin Khān, received by a foot messenger the sad intelligence of the death of his most beloved wife who had accompanied him during all his misfortunes. He heard that she had died of heat and thirst, not being able to find a drop of water in the country to assuage her thirst.[2] The Prince was so affected by this news that he fell as though he were dead, and when, by the assistance of those who were with him, he came to himself, in the excess of his grief he rent his garments; this is a custom of great antiquity in the East, as David rent his at the news of the death of Absalom, his son.

The unhappy Prince had always appeared to be unmoved by evil fortune, but this grief overwhelmed him, and he refused all the consolation offered by his friends. He clad himself in mourning garments, and in place of a turban (sesse) he wrapped a piece of coarse cloth round his head.[3] It was in this miserable costume that he entered the house of the traitor Juin Khān, where he lay on a camp-bed to rest, only to wake to learn of fresh misfortunes. Juin Khān attempted to seize Sipihr Shikoh,[4] the second son of Dārā Shikoh, but the young Prince, though but a child, resisted the traitor with courage, and with his bow and arrow laid three men low on the ground. But being alone he was unable to resist the traitors, who

[1] This was Malik Jīwan Aiyūb, whose real name was Jiand, an Afghān of Dādar, near the Bolān Pass, who, for his treachery, received the honorific title of Bakhtyār ('fortunate') Khān. (Jadunath Sarkar, ii. 206; Manucci, iv. 427; Elliot & Dowson, *Hist.*, vi. 245 f.; Bernier, 95.)

[2] Dārā Shikoh's wife, Nādirā Begam, died from diarrhoea on the way to Dādar (Jadunath Sarkar, ii. 206).

[3] Orthodox Musalmāns do not, as a rule, make any alteration in their dress in time of mourning (E. Lane, *Modern Egyptians*, 5th ed. ii. 271). But Dārā Shikoh was admittedly unorthodox.

[4] Sepper Chekour in the original, third son of Dārā Shikoh, who was imprisoned at Gwalior, where he died in 1708.

secured the doors of the house, and did not allow any one of those who might have aided him to enter. Dārā Shikoh, awakened by the noise which these ruffians made when they seized the little Prince, then saw before his eyes his son, whom they brought in with his hands tied behind his back. The unhappy father, unable to doubt any longer the black treason of his host, could not restrain himself from launching these words against the traitor Juin Khān: 'Finish, finish,' said he, 'ungrateful and infamous wretch that thou art, finish that which thou hast commenced; we are the victims of evil fortune and the unjust passion of Aurangzeb, but remember that I do not merit death except for having saved thy life, and remember that a Prince of the royal blood never had his hands tied behind his back.' Juin Khān being to some extent moved by these words, ordered the little Prince to be released, and merely placed guards over Dārā Shikoh and his son. At the same time he sent an express to Rājā Jaswant Singh and to 'Abdullah Khān to inform them that he had captured Dārā Shikoh and his followers.[1] On receipt of this intelligence they hastened to share in the spoliation of the Prince, but before they arrived Juin Khān had time to seize Dārā Shikoh's most precious possessions, and he also treated his wives and children with the greatest barbarity. When the Rājā and 'Abdullah Khān arrived, they made Dārā Shikoh and his son travel on one elephant, and his wives and children on others; and with this equipage, very different from that with which they had before appeared at Jahānābād, they travelled thither, and entered the city on the 9th of September. All the people hastened to witness this spectacle, desiring to see the Prince whom they had wished to be their Emperor. Aurangzeb ordered him to be taken through the principal streets, and all the bazars of Jahānābād, so that no one might entertain any doubt as to his capture, and as though he himself were glorified by the treachery he had

[1] Jai Singh, the Kachhwāhā Rājā of Jaipur, not Jaswant Singh of Jodhpur, and Bahādur Khan were the officers to whom Dārā Shikoh surrendered. They brought him to Delhi on 23rd August 1659, and he was paraded through the city on the 29th (Jadunath Sarkar, ii. 211; Bernier, 98).

shown towards his brother, to whom he allotted the fortress of Asser [1] as a prison. But of all those who crowded to see this Prince, and were not ignorant of the fact that he was really their legitimate Emperor, and even then desired to see him on the throne, not one had the courage to aid him. There were only some generous soldiers formerly in the Prince's service who, as they had received many benefits, thought themselves bound on this occasion to give him some mark of their fidelity. Unable to deliver their legitimate Prince from the hands of those who held him captive, they flung themselves with fury on the traitor Juin Khān,[2] who was indeed delivered from them for the moment, but in a short time afterwards he suffered the penalty due to his crime, and was slain while traversing a forest on his return to his own country.

Aurangzeb, however, being a good politician and an extraordinary dissembler, caused it to be noised abroad that he had not ordered the seizure of the person of Dārā Shikoh, but only that he should be persuaded to depart out of the Empire. As Dārā had been unwilling to do so, Juin Khān had, without authority, unworthily seized his person, and instead of honouring the royal blood, had shamefully tied behind his back the hands of the young Prince, Sipihr Shikoh, son of Dārā Shikoh. That this criminal action, which was an offence against His Majesty, deserved a severe punishment, and that it had in part been avenged by the death of Juin Khān and his accomplices. But this story which Aurangzeb ordered to be spread among the people was only for the purpose of deception ; for if he truly had such consideration for the royal blood and any love for his elder brother, he would not have ordered his head to be cut off, as was immediately done in the following manner.

Dārā Shikoh, left Jahānābād with his guards to go to the place of his imprisonment, and when he had reached a pleasant spot where he thought he was to sleep, his tent in which he was to lose his head was prepared.[3] After he had eaten, Saif

[1] Asser. Asīrgarh in the Nīmār District, Central Provinces. Bernier (p. 97) says it was proposed to send him to Gwalior ; but the Council called by Aurangzeb decided that he should die.

[2] Bernier, 99 ; Jadunath Sarkar, ii. 216.

[3] The murder took place in Dārā Shikoh's prison at Khizrābād, in Old Delhi.

Khān,[1] who had been in his service, came to announce to him the order for his death. Dārā Shikoh, seeing him enter, welcomed him and said that he was rejoiced to see one of his most faithful servants. Saif Khān replied that it was true that he had formerly been in his service, but that he was now the slave of Aurangzeb, who had commanded him to return with his head. 'Am I to die then ?' said Dārā Shikoh. 'It is the order of the Emperor,' replied Saif Khān, 'and I am here to carry it out.' Sipihr Shikoh, who was sleeping in an antechamber of the tent, awakened by this conversation, endeavoured to seize some weapons which had been taken from him, and made an effort to aid his father, but he was prevented by those who accompanied Saif Khān. Dārā Shikoh also tried to resist, but perceiving it would be useless, merely asked time for prayer, which was granted. In the meantime Sipihr Shikoh was drawn aside, and, whilst they amused him, a slave cut off Dārā Shikoh's head ; and Saif Khān took it to Aurangzeb, who thought that by the death of his brother he would establish his throne. After this bloody tragedy the afflicted Sipihr Shikoh was conveyed to the fortress of Gwalior to keep company with his uncle, Murād Bakhsh.[2] As for the wives and daughters of Dārā Shikoh, they were given quarters in the harem of Aurangzeb, who, in order to fix himself firmly on the throne of the Moguls, now thought only of the destruction of his other brother, Sultān Shujā', who was in Bengal. There he was assembling forces to come to the release of the Emperor his father, who still lived in the fortress at Agra, where Aurangzeb kept him a prisoner.

[1] Seif Kan in the original.

[2] This was in July, 1659. According to Bernier (p. 101) the murderer of Dārā Shikoh was Nazar Beg, a slave, who acted under Saif Khān's orders. In the 16th year of his reign Aurangzeb released Sipihr Shikoh from the prison of Gwalior, and married him to his daughter, Badru-n-nissa.

CHAPTER V

How Aurangzeb seated himself upon the throne and had himself declared Emperor; and concerning the flight of Sultān Shujā'.

It was not difficult for Aurangzeb, after the imprisonment of his father Shāhjahān and of his brother Murād Bakhsh, and his eldest brother's cruel execution, to whom by right the Empire belonged, to resolve to have himself declared Emperor, especially as fortune favoured it and all the nobles of his dominions approved. As it is the custom, at this ceremony, to sit upon the throne, not much time was required to prepare it, since Shāhjahān, before he was imprisoned, had completed the throne which the great Tamerlane had commenced; it is the richest and most superb throne which has ever been seen in the world. But as it was necessary that the Grand Kāzī[1] or Chief Officer of the Law should proclaim the new Emperor, it was in this direction that Aurangzeb encountered the first obstacle. The Grand Kāzī openly opposed his design, and said that the Law of Muhammad and the law of nature equally prevented him from proclaiming him Emperor during the lifetime of his father; added to which, in order to ascend the throne, he had murdered his eldest brother, to whom the Empire belonged after the death of Shāhjahān, their father. This vigorous resistance of the Kāzī troubled Aurangzeb, and in order not to appear unjust, he assembled the doctors of the Law, to whom he represented that his father was incapable of reigning on account of his great age and the infirmities with which he had been overwhelmed; and as for Dārā Shikoh, his brother, he had put him to death because he was not zealous in obeying the Law; that he drank wine, and favoured infidels. These reasons, mingled with menaces, caused his 'Council of Conscience' to pronounce that he merited the Empire, and that he ought to be proclaimed Emperor—to which, nevertheless, the Grand Kāzī persistently objected. There was, therefore, no other remedy but to depose

[1] Cadi in the original.

him from his office as a disturber of the public peace, and elect another who would be zealous for the honour of the Law and the good of the Empire. This was forthwith done. The person selected by the Council was afterwards appointed by Aurangzeb, and in recognition of this act of grace, he proclaimed him Emperor on the 20th of October 1660.[1] This proclamation having been made in the Mosque, Aurangzeb seated himself on the throne, where he received the homage of all the nobles of the Empire, and there were great rejoicings that day in Jahānābād. At the same time orders were sent throughout the Empire to celebrate his accession to the throne. This was carried out with great splendour, and lasted for many days.

Aurangzeb did not consider his throne secure nor his Empire well established so long as Sultān Shujā', his brother, was engaged in raising a powerful army in Bengal with the design of setting Shāhjahān at liberty. He thought that it behoved him to anticipate him, and sent considerable forces against him under the command of Sultān Muhammad, his eldest son, to whom he gave as lieutenant Mīr Jumla,[2] one of the greatest captains who had ever migrated from Persia to India. His good judgement and courage would have made him revered by posterity if he had only been faithful to the Princes whom he served. But he first betrayed the King of Golkonda,[3] with whom he made his fortune, and afterwards Shāhjahān, whose protection had so maintained it that there was scarcely

[1] Aurangzeb was crowned twice; once, informally, on 21st July 1658; the formal coronation took place on 5th June 1659 (Jadunath Sarkar, ii. 107, 289 ff.). The account of the resistance of the Grand Kāzī is not confirmed from other sources (Khāfī Khān, in Elliot & Dowson, *History of India*, vii. 229; Manucci, ii. 3 f.)

[2] Although previously called Mir Jimola or Mir Gimola, his name is here given in the nearly correct form of Emir Jemla. For an estimate of his character see Jadunath Sarkar, iii. 71, 203, 206; for his influence, W. Foster, *English Factories in India, 1651–1654*, p. 12.

[3] His desertion of the King of Golkonda seems to have been justified by the action of that King, as described by Tavernier on pages 134 *et seq.*, or due to his desire to quit a dynasty, then in decay; but his son, Muhammad Amīn, brought the family into disgrace by his imprudence and misconduct at the King's Court. See Jadunath Sarkar, iii. 71, 77: Elliot & Dowson, *Hist.* vii. 108 f.

another noble in the whole of India more powerful or richer than he was.

Moreover, he was both feared and beloved by the army, and he thoroughly understood the art of war as it is carried on in this country. Having then deserted the interests of Shāhjahān, he attached himself to the side of Aurangzeb, and if Sultān Shujā' had not been opposed by so brave and able a commander he would, no doubt, have given more trouble to his brother, and might possibly have conquered him. The two armies met several times, victory was sometimes on one side, sometimes on the other; Sultān Muhammad, assisted by the advice of his lieutenant, seeing that this war was protracted, resolved to change his methods and to combine ruse with force in order to accomplish the destruction of Sultān Shujā'. He treated secretly with the majority of the officers of his uncle's army, and made them magnificent promises, urging them so strongly to follow Aurangzeb—whom he called the pillar and protector of the Muhammadan Law—that he secured the principals, to whom he afterwards made considerable presents, to assure himself better of their support. This was a mortal stroke against Sultān Shujā', which he was unable to parry; for those who followed him being mercenaries, and of that kind of people who declare for those who give most, they concluded that they had nothing more to hope from the Prince, whose finances were expended, and they would find it more profitable to declare for Aurangzeb, whom fortune favoured in every way, and who was master of all the treasures. Thus it was easy for Aurangzeb to bribe the whole army of his brother, who in the last battle which was fought found himself deserted by all and compelled to fly with his wives and children. The traitors, ashamed of their baseness, did not pursue the unfortunate Prince, as they might have done; and, like mean folk, as soon as he had taken flight busied themselves with the destruction of his tents, and the pillage of his baggage. They were allowed to do this by Mīr Jumla as a reward for their treachery. Sultān Shujā' having embarked with his family in boats, crossed the Ganges, and some time afterwards withdrew to the Kingdom of Arakan on the confines of Bengal, where we must leave him to take breath, in order to discuss the doings of Sultān Muhammad, eldest son of Aurangzeb, and Sultān Sulaimān Shikoh eldest son of Dārā Shikoh, who still caused trouble to Aurangzeb.[1]

CHAPTER VI

Concerning the prison of Sultān Muhammad, son of Aurangzeb, and of Sultān Sulaimān Shikoh, eldest son of Dārā Shikoh.

ALTHOUGH Aurangzeb was considered a great politician, and was so in fact, still he allowed himself to be deceived in entrusting a powerful army to his son under the conduct of a great captain, but one whose betrayal, as I have said, of two Kings, his masters,[2] ought to have made Aurangzeb fear similar treatment. This Prince, who had mounted the throne by means of many crimes, and had supplanted his father, whom he held a prisoner, and also his two brothers, one of whom he had executed, and the other he had put to flight, was always justly alarmed lest Heaven should inspire his own son to avenge his grandfather. As it had been reported to him that Sultān Muhammad was extraordinarily pensive and melancholy, he firmly believed that he was meditating plans to ruin him, and in this belief he sought to draw some explanation from Mīr Jumla. He wrote to him that having heard that Sultān Muhammad had had some secret communications with his uncle, Sultān Shujā‘, it was advisable that he should arrest him and send him to court. The letter was accidentally seized by Sultān Muhammad's guards, and brought to the Prince; he being a man of sense, concealed the matter from Mīr Jumla, fearing that he might have received other more precise orders from his father concerning his life. So he resolved to cross the Ganges, and throw himself into the arms of his uncle Sultān Shujā‘, from whom he hoped for more kindness than from his father.[3] With this resolve he pretended to go fishing, and,

[1] For the campaign against Shujā‘ see Jadunath Sarkar, ii. 237 ff.

[2] Namely, the King of Golkonda and Shāhjahān.

[3] The real object of his affection, and possibly the cause of his going over, was Sultān Shujā‘'s daughter Gulrukh Bānū, 'Lady Rose-cheek' to whom he was soon after married (Jadunath Sarkar, ii. 260 ff.).

having speedily prepared boats on the Ganges, crossed with many of his officers to the camp of Sultān Shujā', who was on the other side of the river, and who had found means for assembling some troops during the time he had been meditating his retreat to the King of Arakān. Sultān Muhammad on reaching his uncle's presence, threw himself at his feet, and asked his pardon for having taken up arms against him, a course to which he had been forced by his father, adding that he was not ignorant of the injustice with which the latter had seized the throne. Although Sultān Shujā' might have thought that the arrival of Muhammad in his camp was only a ruse of Aurangzeb, who had possibly sent him to spy out his condition and discover his weakness, nevertheless, being a good and generous Prince, and seeing his nephew at his knees, he immediately raised him, and embracing him, assured him of his protection against Aurangzeb. Some days afterwards the two Princes made an attempt, recrossed the Ganges, and made a long detour to surprise the army of the enemy, who did not expect them. They attacked with vigour, and slew many; but when they saw that the enemy began to recover from this sudden attack, they contented themselves with the advantage gained, and recrossed the Ganges, being afraid of being surrounded, and of not being able to withdraw when they wished.

Mīr Jumla had already informed Aurangzeb of the flight of his son, at which the Emperor displayed considerable displeasure, though he dared not show it to the Mīr, lest it might cause him to do likewise, and betray him as he had betrayed Shāhjahān, his father, and the King of Golkonda. Aurangzeb merely wrote to him that he confided entirely in his prudence, and delicate tact to restore to his duty Sultān Muhammad, who was still young; and that this escapade was due only to his youthful enthusiasm and love of change. The confidence Aurangzeb showed towards Mīr Jumla induced that general to use all possible means to withdraw Muhammad from the hands of Sultān Shujā'. He informed the Prince that the Emperor, his father, had the best intentions regarding him, and was always ready to receive him with open arms, provided he would make good use of his refuge with Sultān

Shujā', which he might make serviceable to Aurangzeb, who would love him the more, and would have an opportunity of praising his prudence and affection. The Prince allowed himself to be easily persuaded ; and by the same way that he went to the camp of his uncle Sultān Shujā', he returned to that of his father Aurangzeb, where Mīr Jumla received him with honour, and great demonstrations of joy.[1] He advised him to tell his father as soon as he saw him, that he went to Sultān Shujā' merely for the purpose of spying out his forces and the condition of his army, and that he would repair with speed to Aurangzeb, to tell him what he had done in his service, and receive his reward. It was also the command of Aurangzeb that his son should be sent to him ; and Muhammad, whether willingly or by compulsion, set out for Jahānābād, where he arrived accompanied by the guards Mīr Jumla had sent with him. Their commander having announced to the Emperor the arrival of his son, His Majesty assigned a lodging for him outside his palace, and would not allow him to come to kiss his hands. He ordered him to be told he was indisposed ; and whilst this lodging served him as a prison until he was transferred to the fortress of Gwalior,[2] let us see what happened to Sultān Sulaimān Shikoh, eldest son of the unfortunate Dārā Shikoh, whose head Aurangzeb had cut off.

Sultān Sulaimān Shikoh, having been betrayed by Rājā Rūp, as I have above related,[3] remained in the country of Srīnagar,[4] under the protection of Naktī Rānī,[5] its ruler. The Prince, who was courageous as well as unfortunate, was compelled to pass a wild life in the mountains in order not to fall into the hands of Aurangzeb, who with all his forces was unable to harm him there. On the other hand, Naktī Rānī assured him by an oath, accompanied by all the ceremonies which could render it solemn and inviolable, that he would lose his kingdom rather than allow Aurangzeb to do any violence

[1] Jadunath Sarkar, ii. 275.

[2] Sultān Muhammad died 5th (or 3rd, cf. p. 133 *n.*) December, 1676, in his 38th year. His wife, the daughter of Shujā', was with him in prison.

[3] See pp. 276–7.

[4] Serenaguer in the original, Srīnagar, in Garhwāl.

[5] For Naktī Rānī see p. 277.

to a suppliant under his protection. He went for this purpose to a river which runs through his country, to bathe as a testimony of the purity of his soul; and being thus purified, he made his promise to Sulaimān Shikoh never to abandon him, took his gods as witnesses to the purity of his intentions, and gave the Prince no ground for doubting his promises. Sulaimān Shikoh, after that, thought of nothing but amusing himself and his followers with the chase, and they, on their part, tried to amuse him to the utmost of their power, while he devoted himself entirely to pleasure.

Aurangzeb ordered troops to advance towards the mountains of Srīnagar to compel Rājā Naktī Rānī to surrender Sulaimān Shikoh. But the Rājā being able with 1000 men to defend all the passes to his country, which are narrow and difficult, against 100,000, this rendered all Aurangzeb's efforts futile, and he thereupon had recourse to treachery, seeing that force availed nothing. He sought at first to treat with the Rājā, but in vain, for the Rājā would not violate his oath; and moreover his priests assured him that Aurangzeb would be deprived of the Empire, and that Sulaimān Shikoh would reign in a short time; this made him treat the Prince with all possible kindness.

Aurangzeb seeing that his army was unable to advance into the country of the Rājā, set himself to make war of another kind in order to secure the son of Dārā Shikoh. He forbade commerce between his subjects and those of the Rājā; this was very prejudicial to the latter, who inhabit a country of mountains and rocks, and are constrained to import from outside whatever they want. They immediately began to murmur at the protection given to Sultān Sulaiman Shikoh and cried out that it was to the prejudice of the public welfare. Their priests also began to doubt the truth of their oracles, and to believe that it was desirable to interpret them otherwise. At last they began to arrange for the ruin of the poor Prince; and what completed it was that Rājā Jaswant Singh,[1] who had betrayed Dārā Shikoh, as I have above related, sent to Rājā Naktī Rānī secretly to advise him that it was for his own safety and that of his country to yield to the will of Aurangzeb, and

[1] Rājā Jai Singh of Jaipur.

give up his nephew into his hands. This advice of Jaswant Singh sorely embarrassed the Rājā, for on the one side he had made a solemn oath, and sworn by *Rām Rām* to protect Sulaimān Shikoh at the risk of his country and his life, on the other he feared a revolt in his kingdom and the prospect of losing it.

Uncertain what to do, he consulted the Brahmans, who pronounced that he was bound to protect his people and his faith, which would be destroyed if the country became subject to Aurangzeb, who was a Musalmān, rather than to protect a Prince from whom he could never receive any benefit. These councils having been held without Sulaimān Shikoh's knowledge, his destruction was settled at a time when he believed himself to be in the greatest safety. The Rājā Naktī Rānī thinking to shield his honour and conscience, replied to Jaswant Singh's messenger that he was unable to bring himself to betray the Prince, but that Aurangzeb might seize him, and so save his reputation; and that Sulaimān Shikoh was in the habit of going to hunt in certain mountains in his country, taking only a few people with him, and that it would be easy for Jaswant Singh to send a number of soldiers to take him prisoner, and hand him over to Aurangzeb.

Immediately on receipt of this reply, Jaswant Singh gave orders to his son [1] to execute the design as it had been arranged, so that when on a certain day Sulaimān Shikoh on going to hunt at the usual place, was attacked by a strong party in ambuscade, he at once saw that he was betrayed, and put himself in a position of defence with his followers, who were all slain on the spot. The Prince defended himself bravely, and with his own hand slew nine of his assailants; but he was borne down by numbers, and was carried to Jahānābād. When he came into Aurangzeb's presence, the Emperor asked him how he felt. 'As your prisoner,' replied the Prince, 'who does not expect from you different treatment from that which my father has received.' The Emperor replied that he had nothing to fear, that he would not put him to death, but only assure himself of his person. Aurangzeb then inquired what had become of the treasures he had carried away; he replied

[1] This was Kunwar Rām Singh, son of Rājā Jai Singh.

that he had employed a portion to raise troops to make war against him and destroy him, if good fortune had been on his side ; that another portion had been retained by Rājā Rūp, whose avarice and perfidy were sufficiently well known ; and that the traitor Rājā Naktī Rānī had seized the remainder when delivering him treacherously to his enemies, despite his promise and pledged honour. Aurangzeb was surprised and much moved by the noble courage of his nephew, but ambition closed his eyes and stifled in him all the sentiments of justice which a true remorse of conscience might arouse ; and in order to secure his throne he directed that Sultān Muhammad, his son, and Sulaimān Shikoh, his nephew, should be conducted to the fortress of Gwalior, to keep company with their uncle, Murād Bakhsh and some other Princes who were in prison. This was done on the 30th of January 1661.[1]

Sultān Shujā‘, who still lived, although in a miserable condition, was the last thorn which remained in the foot of Aurangzeb, and it was the King of Arakan, with whom he had been compelled to take refuge, who extracted it, and relieved him of this unfortunate Prince whom he had still reason to fear. As Shujā‘ saw that there was now no more hope of aid for him, he resolved to make a pilgrimage to Mecca, and thence to travel into Persia to seek an asylum with the King. For this purpose he hoped to obtain a ship from the King of Arakan or of Pegu to take him to Mocha, but he was unaware that neither of these Kings had other than long and narrow much decorated demi-galleys, which they use on their rivers, and that they had no vessels capable of traversing the ocean. Consequently Sultān Shujā‘ was obliged to remain with the King of Arakan, who is an idolater, and in order the better to secure his protection, asked for one of his daughters in marriage ; his request was granted, and he had a son by her. But this, which should have been a strong bond of friendship between father and son-in-law, soon became a cause of division and hatred ; and some nobles of the country, who had already shown jealousy towards Sultān Shujā‘, caused

[1] For another account of this interview, which occurred on 5th January, 1661, see Bernier, 105 f. ; Manucci, i. 380. Sulaimān Shikoh was dosed with pōst, or infusion of poppy-heads, and died in May 1662, aged 30.

him to be regarded with suspicion by the King of Arakan, as though he desired, in consequence of his marriage with his daughter, and of the son which he had by her, to depose him from his throne.[1] This pagan King, in whose country several Musalmāns were settled, easily believed what was told him, namely, that this Musalmān Prince might readily induce all who were in his country, under the pretext of zeal for religion, to form a conspiracy, and place himself on the throne of Arakan, in exchange for that which his younger brother had seized. These doubts were not altogether ill-founded, for in truth Sultān Shujā‘, who still had quantities of golden rupees and many jewels, easily bribed a number of these Musalmāns of the Kingdom of Arakan, and with about 200 men who remained of those who had followed him from Bengal after the defeat of his army, he planned an enterprise of much boldness, and at the same time less an indication of bravery than of despair.

He appointed a day with his own party for forcing an entry into the palace, when, after he had put to death all the royal family, he intended to have himself forthwith proclaimed King of Arakan. But this great plot having been discovered the day before it was to have been executed, Sultān Shujā‘ and Sultān Bangue, his son, had no other resource left but to take flight, hoping to escape to the Kingdom of Pegu.[2] But the high, nearly inaccessible mountains, and the thick jungles full of tigers and lions [3] through which they had to travel, and where there was scarcely any road, made their flight useless, in addition to which the enemy gave them but little

[1] Bernier (p. 109 ff.) does not say that Shujā‘ married the daughter of the King of Arakan, but that the latter demanded to receive a daughter of the former as his wife, and was exasperated by Shujā‘'s refusal.

[2] There is some doubt as to the identity of Sultān ‘Bangue’, whom Bernier calls ‘Banque’ (p. 109), and says he was eldest son of Shujā‘. The two sons of Shujā‘ who accompanied him to Arakan were his younger sons, Buland Akhtar and Zainu-l-ābidīn. The former of these may have been nick-named ‘Bang’ or Bangālī, in consequence of Shujā‘'s connexion with that province. (Manucci, i. 309, iv. 427; Jadunath Sarkar, ii. 279.)

[3] There are no lions in these regions, nor is there the slightest reason for supposing that they ever ranged so far to the east as Arakan, it being beyond the limits of their so far ascertained geographical distribution in prehistorical, as well as in historical times.

time to get away before they followed on their tracks. Sultān Bangue, who marched last, to resist those whom he believed the King would surely send to seize them, and to give his father, and his family who accompanied him, a chance to escape, defended himself bravely against the first assailants, but at length he was overcome by numbers, thrown down, and carried off together with his two younger brothers, his mother, and sisters. All the members of this unhappy family were placed in prison, where they were at first treated with great harshness; but some time afterwards, the King being inclined to marry the eldest sister of Sultān Bangue, they were given a little more liberty. They would have enjoyed it longer, but for the impatience of the young Prince, who, having an active and ambitious spirit, made a new plot against the King, which proved to be the cause of their total ruin. For the plot having been precipitated without success, the King, roused to anger, commanded that the whole family should be straightway exterminated, even including the young Princess whom he had espoused, although she was enceinte.

As for the end of Sultān Shujā', who was the foremost in the flight, the accounts of his fate vary so much that one does not know which to believe. But, if all vary in the circumstances, they agree so far in the fact that he is no longer alive, and that he died either by the hands of the soldiers who were sent to seize his person, or that he was torn to pieces by tigers or lions, which abound in the jungles of these countries.[1]

This, then, is what I have been able to ascertain concerning this famous war which lasted six years, and I have not met with any other version of it at Surat, Agra, Jahānābād, or in Bengal, where I was precisely informed by those who were present at the principal events, having been myself a witness of a portion of them, as I have related in this account. Let us now see what were the first acts of the reign of Aurangzeb, and what was the fate of his father Shāhjahān.

[1] He is said by some writers to have been taken out in the river in a canoe, which was scuttled; his captors, escaping in another canoe, left him to drown. It is possible that he was killed by the Magh tribe as recorded by the Dutch authorities; the Muhammadan records give no definite information (Manucci, i. 374 ff.; Jadunath Sarkar, ii. 286 ff.).

CHAPTER VII

Concerning the beginning of Aurangzeb's reign, and the death of his father, Shāhjahān.

I HAVE mentioned in the fifth chapter that Aurangzeb ascended the throne[1] as soon as he had disposed of his brother, Dārā Shikoh, and I shall add here some details which preceded this ceremony, and are sufficiently worthy of record. Some days previously Aurangzeb boldly sent to present his compliments to his father, Shāhjahān, which he well knew would be displeasing to him. He begged him, as he was about to ascend the throne in a few days, to have the kindness to send some of his jewels to be used on that day, so that he might appear before his people with the same magnificence as the other Emperors, his predecessors, had done. Shāhjahān became so enraged at this demand of Aurangzeb, which he regarded as an insult levelled at him in his prison by his son, that for some days he was like a madman, and he even nearly died. In the excess of his passion he frequently called for a pestle and mortar, saying that he would pound up all his precious stones and pearls, so that Aurangzeb might never possess them.[2] But the Begam Sāhib, his eldest daughter, who had never left him, threw herself at his feet, and besought him not to proceed to such an extremity, and as she had full power over him in consequence of the intimate relations which existed between them, she appeased him, rather with the object of keeping the precious stones for herself than to give pleasure to her brother, her mortal enemy

[1] See p. 285 *n.*

[2] Shāhjahān appears to have subsequently relented, though it is not so stated by Tavernier; but Bernier says, 'that of his own accord he sent some of those jewels, which before he had told him of, that hammers were ready to beat them to powder, the first time he should again ask for them' (pp. 127, 166). Ultimately, on Shāhjahān's death in 1666 when Aurangzeb entered the Seraglio at Agra, the Begam Sāhib presented him with a large golden basin full of jewels (*Vide ante*, p. 275, p. 317 below, and Bernier, 198 f.). Thévenot relates the same story as Bernier, and adds that the Peacock throne was in Shāhjahān's possession in prison, but this latter statement is incorrect (*Voyages des Indes*, p. 101).

who might one day become their possessor. Thus, when Aurangzeb ascended the throne he had only one jewel on his cap (*toque*); [1] but if he had desired more he did not lack them, as I have elsewhere said, and he asked for the stones from his father only with the intention of retaining them permanently. This cap, as I have related in my account of Persia, cannot be called a crown, neither, consequently, can the ceremony be called a coronation.[2]

From the moment that Aurangzeb took possession of the throne, he would eat neither wheaten bread, flesh, nor fish. He sustained himself with barley bread, vegetables, and sweetmeats, and would not drink any strong liquor. This was a penance which he imposed on himself for the many crimes he had committed; but his ambition and the desire to reign are still strong, so much so that he is resolved not to renounce the throne during his life.[3]

When Aurangzeb was settled on the throne, and all Asia had heard the news, there arrived at different times at Jahānābād many ambassadors, who came to salute the new Emperor on the part of their masters, to offer him their service and ask for his friendship. The Usbeg Tartars were the first,[4] afterwards the Cherif [5] of Mecca, the King of Hyeman,[6] or

[1] Possibly the topaz referred to at pp. 318, ii. 102, 348, and also by Bernier, who says, 'The King appeared seated upon his throne at one extremity of the great hall of the 'Ām khās splendidly attired, his garment being of white flowered satin embroidered, his turband of gold cloth having an egret worked upon it, the feet of which were studded with diamonds of extraordinary lustre and value, and in the centre was a beautiful Oriental topaz of matchless size and splendour shining like a little sun.' (*Travels in the Mogul Empire*, 268.)

[2] This very trivial point as to whether the term coronation was strictly applicable or not, was the subject of some sharp controversy between Chardin and our author. (See Chardin, *Voyages*, Amsterdam edition, 1711, vol. ix, p. 85, and *Persian Travels*, bk. v, ch. i, p. 524.)

[3] On the puritanical habits of Aurangzeb see Manucci, ii. 332; Jadunath Sarkar, iii. 98 ff.; Smith, *Oxford Hist. of India*, 445.

[4] A previous embassy from the Usbeg Tartars to Shāhjahān brought him boxes of choice lapis lazuli, camels, fruit, &c. Lapis lazuli is a product of Badakhshān. (See Bernier, 133, who says that the first embassy which arrived was that of the Sharīf.)

[5] Sharīf, Arab., a descendant of Muhammad. On the Sharīfs of Mecca see *Ency. Brit.*, ii. 267, xvii. 952.

[6] The province of Yemen, S.W. corner of Arabia.

Arabia Felix, the Prince of Bassora, and the King of Ethiopia sent theirs. The Dutch also sent M. Adrican,[1] Commander-in-Chief of the factory at Surat, who was very well treated, and was quickly received out of respect for the European nation. For these Emperors of India consider that it enhances their dignity if foreigners remain at Court for a considerable time. All these Ambassadors, according to custom, made presents to Aurangzeb, of whatever was most rare in their respective countries, and this Prince, who desired from the first to spread a good reputation for himself throughout Asia, took care to send them back well satisfied.

Some months before the death of Shāhjahān, Aurangzeb sent an Ambassador to Persia, who was at first magnificently received,[2] as I have stated in the first part of my travels. When he arrived the talk for a month was all of feasts and hunting parties, and every night he was entertained with fireworks. The day upon which he was to make the present on behalf of the Great Mogul, the King of Persia appeared upon his throne, superbly clad, accepted what the Ambassador had to give and contemptuously distributed the whole of it among the officers of his house, retaining for himself only a diamond weighing nearly 60 carats. Some days afterwards he sent for the Ambassador, and asked him, after some conversation, whether he was a Sunni [3]—that is to say, of the

[1] Dirk van Adrichem, chief of the Dutch factory at Surat, 1662–65 (Bernier, 127, 138). [The ed. of 1678 has 'Commandeur ou Chef.'] Cf. also *Eng. Factories, 1661–64*, p. 121.

[2] The results of Aurangzeb's embassy to Shāh 'Abbās, under Tarbīyat Khān, in 1663, are described by Manucci, ii. 128 ff. The ambassador sent by Shāh 'Abbās in 1661 was Budāq Beg (Jadunath Sarkar, iii. 121 ff.). Chardin says that Negef Coulibec (Najaf Quli Beg) was sent by the King of Persia as Ambassador in the year 1664, simply in order to report the safe arrival of the Mogul's Ambassador in Persia, and to convey a present of melons and other fruits. The Great Mogul received him well, and sent him back with presents; but news having arrived, two days after his departure, of the bad treatment of the Mogul's Ambassador by the King of Persia, the Mogul had Najaf brought back, and ordered all the fruit to be flung into the house where he lodged (Chardin, *Voyages*, Amsterdam edition, 1711, vol. viii, p. 213).

[3] Sonnis in the original. The distinctive characteristics of the Sunnis and Shī'as are set forth in bk. iv, ch. vii, of the Persian Travels. (See also vol. ii, pp. 137–9 ff.; Ja'far Sharīf, *Islām in India*, 14; Hughes, *Dict. Islām*, s.vv. *Shī'ah, Sunnī*.)

sect of the Turks; the meaning of this has been sufficiently explained elsewhere. The Ambassador in reply having allowed some smart remark to escape him against the Prophet 'Alī, whom the Persians revere, the King again asked him his name. He replied that his Majesty Shāhjahān had given him the name of Baobhāk Khān,[1] *i.e.* lord of a free heart, that he had received great bounties from him, and had been honoured by one of the first officers in his Court. 'Thou art then a villain', said the King with an angry countenance, 'to have abandoned, after so many favours, thy Emperor in his need and to serve a tyrant who keeps his father in prison, and has murdered his brothers and nephews. How is it', continued the King, 'that he dares to assume the stately titles of 'Alamgīr Aurang Shāh,[2] the King who holds the universe in his hand, since he has as yet conquered nothing, and all he possesses is derived from murders and treason? Is it possible', added the Prince, 'that thou art one of those who have counselled him to shed so much blood, to be the executioner of his brothers, and to hold his father in prison; thou who hast acknowledged having received so much honour and so many benefits? Thou art not worthy', said the King, 'to possess the beard that thou wearest', and straightway he ordered him to be shaved, which is the greatest affront that can be done to a man in that country.[3] The Ambassador, who little expected to be so treated, at the same time received orders from the King of Persia to return, and the King gave him as a present for Aurangzeb, his master, 150 beautiful horses, with a quantity of gold and silver carpets, pieces of gold brocade, rich sashes, and other beautiful stuffs; this

[1] In the original 'Baubec Kan'. Various suggestions have been made to account for the name Būbāk, in Persian 'an old dotard', or Bebāk, 'fearless'. But the true explanation has been recently suggested by Prof. Jadunath Sarkar; that Tavernier confounded Tarbiyat Khān, Shāhjahān's ambassador to the Persian court, with Budāq Khān, the Persian ambassador to Shāhjahān; see *Hist. of Aurangzīb*, iii. 121 ff.

[2] 'Ālamgīr, 'world-conquering'; Aurangzeb, 'ornament of the throne.'

[3] On the respect Orientals pay to the beard see Lane, *Modern Egyptians*, 5th ed., i. 35; Ja'far Sharif, *Islām in India*, Oxford, 1921, p. 304; 2 Samuel x. 4.

was worth much more than the present which Aurangzeb had sent him, although that was valued at near two millions.[1]

When Baobhāk Khān returned to Agra, where the King was staying, Aurangzeb, enraged at the affront done to himself by the King of Persia, in the person of his Ambassador, ordered the 150 horses to be taken, some to the centre of the city, and others to the corners of the streets, and had it proclaimed throughout the city that the followers of 'Alī could not mount these horses without becoming Nagis,[2] *i.e.* unclean, since they came from a King who did not observe the true Law, and with whom they could have no communion. This done, he ordered the 150 horses to be slain, and all the rest of the present to be burned, while he used most abusive language towards the King of Persia, by whom he considered himself to be mortally insulted.

At length when Shāhjahān died in the Agra fort towards the end of 1666,[3] Aurangzeb had no longer before his eyes a troublesome object which reproached him constantly with his tyranny, and he began to enjoy more fully the pleasure of reigning. He received the Begam Sāhib, his sister, into his favour soon afterwards, restoring all her governments to her, and commanding, moreover, that she should bear the title of Princess Queen.[4] It is true that she has notable qualities, and is capable of governing the whole Empire. If, at the commencement of the war, her father and her brothers had only trusted her, Aurangzeb had never been Emperor, and affairs would have worn a totally different aspect. As for Raushanārā Begam, his sister, she had always supported Aurangzeb, and when she heard that he had taken up arms she immediately sent him all the gold and silver she possessed. He promised her, in recognition of her good services, that when he became Emperor he would give her

[1] The coin not being mentioned, whether rupees, livres, or some Persian coin, the statement is vague. In the English translation of 1684 the passage is judiciously rendered ' to a vast value '.

[2] *Najis,* Persian for ' unclean '. (See Vambéry, *Life,* p. 57, for an example of its use.)

[3] Shāhjahān died on 22nd January O.S., 1666.

[4] Bādshāh Begam (Manucci, ii. 127).

the title of Shāh Begam, and would seat her on a throne.[1] He kept his word, and they were always much attached. Nevertheless, the last time I was at Jahānābād I heard that their friendship had somewhat cooled. The cause, as I was assured, was that the Princess had conveyed into her apartments a handsome young man, and wishing to get rid of him at the end of fifteen or twenty days, when she was tired of him, the thing could not be accomplished without the news reaching the Emperor. The Princess, in order to anticipate the disgrace and reproach which she feared, hastened with assumed terror to the Emperor, and told him that a man had entered the harem, even her own chamber, that she was certain his intention was either to slay or rob her, that such a thing had never before been seen, that the safety of his royal person was involved, and that His Majesty should severely punish all the eunuchs who were on guard that night. The Emperor himself, with a number of eunuchs, immediately hastened to the spot, and in this extremity the poor young man could not do otherwise than leap from the window into the river which flows below.[2] Thereupon a crowd assembled from all quarters to seize him, the Emperor calling out to them to do him no injury, but take him to the Chief Judge. Since then no more has been heard of the matter, and it is not difficult to imagine that strange things take place in the enclosure where these women and girls are shut up.

[1] Some writers consider that this amounted to a promise that he would marry her himself, although she was his sister. Whatever truth there may be in the reputed incest of Shāhjahān, Aurangzeb was not guilty of that crime. The scandalous tales told about her by Bernier (132 f.) and Manucci (ii. 189 f.) are discredited by Jadunath Sarkar (iii. 68). In later years she fell into the background, and died on 11th September, 1671, aged 56.

[2] Bernier (p 132) says that the eunuchs hurled him from the top of the palace walls.

CHAPTER VIII

Concerning the preparations which are made for the festival of the Great Mogul, when he is solemnly weighed every year. Of the splendour of his thrones and the magnificence of his Court.

AFTER finishing all my business with the Emperor, as I have related in the first Book,[1] when I went to take leave of His Majesty on the first of November 1665, he told me he was unwilling that I should depart without having witnessed his fête, which was then at hand, and that afterwards he would give orders that all his jewels should be shown to me.[2] I accepted, as in duty bound, the honour he conferred on me; and thus I was a spectator of this grand festival, which commenced on the fourth of November and lasted five days. It is on the anniversary of the Emperor's birthday that they are in the habit of weighing him,[3] and if he should weigh more than in the preceding year, the rejoicing is so much the greater. When he has been weighed, he seats himself on the richest of the thrones, of which I shall speak presently, and then all the nobility of the kingdom come to salute him and offer presents. The ladies of the court also

[1] See p. 112. [2] See p. 314.

[3] Aurangzeb evaded the custom of distributing his weight in money, and did not have tokens coined, like his predecessors, to celebrate the occasion of his coronation. Sir T. Roe describes in rather contemptuous terms the scramble for thin pieces of silver, made to resemble different fruits. The Mogul, Jahāngīr, presented to him a basin full of them; but while he held them in his cloak the nobles snatched most of them from him. He estimates that the amount distributed did not exceed £100 in value (ed. Foster, i. 252, ii. 411 f.). Terry, his chaplain, also describes the scene (*Voyage*, ed. London 1777, p. 376; Bernier, 270; Ovington, 178 f.). For Akbar's practice see *Āīn-i-Akbarī*, i. 266 f.; Hindu Rājās adopted the practice (Thurston, *Castes and Tribes of Southern India*, vii. 202 ff.). For further references to the custom see J. Fryer, *New Account of East India and Persia*, Hakluyt Society, i. 206; iii. 194; Ja'far Sharīf, *Islām in India*, 191. Sivajī having been weighed against gold, the amount of which was distributed to Brāhmans, obtained a high rank among Rājputs, from whom the Brāhmans tried to prove his descent (Grant Duff, *Hist. Mahrattas*, ed. 1921, i. 207).

send gifts and he receives others from the Governors of Provinces and other exalted personages. In diamonds, rubies, emeralds, pearls, gold and silver, as well as rich carpets, brocades of gold and silver, and other stuffs, elephants, camels, and horses, the Emperor receives in presents on this day to the value of more than 30,000,000 livres.[1]

Preparations for this festival which lasts five days commence on the 7th of September, about two months before the event; and the reader should remember the description which I have given of the palace of Jahānābād in the sixth chapter of Book I.[2] The first thing done is to cover in two large courts of the palace from the middle of each up to the hall, which is open on three sides. The awnings covering this great space are of red velvet embroidered with gold, and so heavy that the poles which are erected to support them are of the size of a ship's mast, and some of them are 35 to 40 feet in height; there are thirty-eight for the tent of the first court, and those near the hall are covered with plates of gold of the thickness of a ducat. The others are covered with silver of the same thickness, and the cords which sustain these poles are of cotton of different colours, some of them of the thickness of a good cable. The first court is, as I have elsewhere said, surrounded by porticoes with small rooms connected with them, and here it is that the Omrahs stay while they are on guard. For it should be remarked that one of the Omrahs mounts guard every week.[3] He disposes, both in the court as also about the Emperor's palace or tent when he is in the field, the cavalry under his command, and many elephants. During this week the Omrah on guard receives his food from the Emperor's kitchen, and when he sees from afar the food which is being brought to him, he makes three obeisances in succession, which consist in placing the hand three times on the ground, and as often on the head,[4] at the same time praying to God to preserve the Emperor's health, and that He will give him long life and power to vanquish his enemies. All these Omrahs, who

[1] 30,000,000 livres, at 1*s.* 6*d.* to the livre = £2,250,000.
[2] See p. 79.
[3] Sir T. Roe, i. 172; Bernier, 214.
[4] The Taslīm (*Āīn-i-Akbarī*, i. 158; Bernier, 214).

are the nobility of the kingdom and Princes of the blood royal, regard it as a great honour to guard the Emperor; and when mounting or leaving guard, they don their best clothes; their horses, elephants, and camels are also richly clad, and some of the camels carry a swivel-gun with a man seated behind to fire it. The least of these Omrahs commands 2,000 horse, but, when a Prince of the blood royal is on guard, he commands up to 6,000.[1]

It should be stated that the Great Mogul has seven magnificent thrones, one wholly covered with diamonds, the others with rubies, emeralds, or pearls.[2] The principal throne, which is placed in the hall of the first court, resembles in form and size our camp beds; that is to say, it is about 6 feet long and 4 wide. Upon the four feet, which are very massive, and from 20 to 25 inches high, are fixed the four bars which support the base of the throne, and upon these bars are ranged twelve columns, which sustain the canopy on three sides, that which faces the court being open. Both the feet and the bars, which are more than 18 inches long, are covered with gold inlaid and enriched with numerous diamonds, rubies, and emeralds. In the middle of each bar there is a large balass [3] ruby, cut en cabuchon, with four emeralds round it, forming a square cross. Next in succession, from one side to the other along the length of the bars

[1] Bernier, 212. [2] *Ibid.*, 269.

[3] Balet in the original, for balass, &c. Ball has elsewhere referred to this word as being probably derived from Balakhshān, a form of the name Badakhshān (see *Economic Geology of India*, 430). Yule (*Hobson Jobson*, 52, and Marco Polo, i. 149, 152, ii. 298) however, establishes this view beyond question of doubt by quotations from Ibn Batuta, iii. 59, 394, Barbosa, &c. The stones from this locality, which is on the banks of the Shignān, a tributary of the Oxus, are not, however, rubies, but spinelles; at the same time it would appear that according to some authorities the term balass has been transferred to true rubies of a particular shade of colour—hence a considerable degree of confusion has arisen in this branch of the nomenclature of precious stones. After Ibn Batuta's testimony, derivations from Bálūchistān and Baluchin—an old name for Pegu?—need perhaps only be mentioned in order to be dismissed; but with reference to the latter, Chardin, *Voyages*, tome iv, p. 70, Amsterdam ed. of 1711, says:—'On l'appelle aussi Balacchani, Pierre de Balacchan, qui est le Pegou, d'où je juge qu'est venu le nom de Balays qu'on donne aux Rubis couleur de rose.'

there are similar crosses, arranged so that in one the ruby is in the middle of four emeralds, and in another the emerald is in the middle and four balass rubies surround it. The emeralds are table-cut, and the intervals between the rubies and emeralds are covered with diamonds, the largest of which do not exceed 10 to 12 carats in weight, all showy stones, but very flat. There are also in some parts pearls set in gold, and upon one of the longer sides of the throne there are four steps to ascend it. Of the three cushions or pillows which are upon the throne, that which is placed behind the Emperor's back is large and round like one of our bolsters, and the two others placed at his sides are flat. Moreover, a sword, a mace, a round shield, a bow and quiver with arrows, are suspended from this throne, and all these weapons, as also the cushions and steps, both of this throne and of the other six, are covered over with stones which match those with which each of the thrones respectively is enriched.[1]

I counted the large balass rubies on the great throne, and there are about 108, all cabuchons, the least of which weighs 100 carats,[2] but there are some which weigh apparently 200 and more. As for the emeralds,[3] there are plenty of good colour, but they have many flaws; the largest may weigh 60 carats, and the least 30 carats. I counted about 116; thus there are more emeralds than rubies.

The underside of the canopy is covered with diamonds and pearls, with a fringe of pearls all round, and above the canopy, which is a quadrangular-shaped dome, there is a peacock with elevated tail made of blue sapphires and other coloured stones, the body of gold inlaid with precious stones, having a large ruby in front of the breast, whence hangs a pear-shaped pearl of 50 carats or thereabouts, and of a somewhat yellow water. On both sides of the peacock there is a large bouquet of the same height as the bird, con-

[1] V. p. 80 above.

[2] Rubies of good quality weighing 100 carats would be worth more than diamonds of equal weight, but it is probable that these were not perfect in every respect. See Linschoten, ii. 151 ff.

[3] For the source whence the emeralds were obtained, see bk. ii, ch. xix, in vol. ii. 81 f.

sisting of many kinds of flowers made of gold inlaid with precious stones. On the side of the throne opposite the court there is a jewel consisting of a diamond of from 80 to 90 carats weight, with rubies and emeralds round it, and when the Emperor is seated he has this jewel in full view. But in my opinion the most costly point about this magnificent throne is that the twelve columns supporting the canopy are surrounded with beautiful rows of pearls, which are round and of fine water, and weigh from 6 to 10 carats each. At 4 feet distance from the throne two umbrellas are fixed, on either side, the sticks of which for 7 or 8 feet in height are covered with diamonds, rubies, and pearls. These umbrellas are of red velvet, and embroidered and fringed all round with pearls.

This is what I have been able to observe regarding this famous throne, commenced by Tamerlane and completed by Shāhjahān; and those who keep the accounts of the King's jewels, and of the cost of this great work, have assured me that it amounts to 107,000 lakhs of rupees,[1] which amount to 160,500,000 livres of our money.

[1] There is certainly some mistake here; the figure should stand at 107,000,000, namely, 1070 lakhs, which at two-thirds of the rupee to the livre would be equal to 160,500,000 livres, or £12,037,500, the rupee being 2*s.* 3*d.*, and the livre 1*s.* 6*d.* Thevenot says that the throne was reported to be worth 20,000,000 in 'gold' (mohurs ?), but he adds that a true estimate could only be arrived at by a careful examination of the precious stones with which it was adorned (*Voyages*, Paris ed., 1684, p. 123). Bernier says 4 crores of rupees, or about 60,000,000 French livres, say £4,500,000 (*Travels in the Mogul Empire*, 268). Elsewhere (p. 223) he fixes the value at 3 crores. A recent estimate of the value of this throne as it stands in the Shāh's palace at Teherān at present is 13,000,000 dollars, say £2,600,000 (S. G. W. Benjamin, *Persia*, 73). More is now known about the Peacock Throne than when the first edition of this work was prepared. Lord Curzon, who inspected it at Teherān, writes: 'The Takht-i-Taous [Peacock Throne] is not an Indian work at all. It was constructed by Mohammed Husein Khan, Sadr [High Priest, if that term may be used of Musalmāns] of Ispahan, for Fath Ali Shah [1793-1847] when the latter married an Ispahani young lady, whose popular sobriquet, for some unexplained reason, was Taous Khanum, or the Peacock Lady. The King is further said to have been so much delighted with the throne that it was made a remarkably prominent feature in the ceremonies that commonly ensue upon marriage.
28 . . . The original Peacock Throne of Nadir Shah (i. e. the survivor of the

Behind this grand and magnificent throne a smaller one stands, in the form of a bathing-tub. It is of oval shape, about 7 feet in length and 5 in breadth, and the outside is covered with diamonds and pearls, but it has no canopy.

In the first court, on the right hand, there is a special tent under which, during the Emperor's festival, the principal baladines of the town are obliged to attend to sing and dance while the Emperor is seated on his throne.[1] To the left there is another place, also covered by a tent, where the principal officers of the army and other officers of the guard and of the Emperor's household are in attendance.

In the same quarter, during the time the Emperor remains seated on his throne, thirty horses are kept, all bridled, fifteen on one side and fifteen on the other, each held by two men.[2] The bridles are very narrow, and for the most part enriched with diamonds, rubies, emeralds, and pearls, while some have only small gold coins. Each horse has upon its head, between the ears, a bunch of beautiful feathers, and a small cushion on the back with the surcingle, the whole embroidered with gold; and suspended from the neck

two facsimiles) was discovered in a broken-down and piecemeal condition by Agha Mohammed Shah [Āghā Muhammad Khān Qājār, 1785–97] who extracted it, with many of the conqueror's jewels, by brutal torture from his blind grandson Shah Rukh at Meshed, and then had the recovered portions of it made up into the throne of modern shape and style, which now stands in the palace at Teheran. . . . In this chair, therefore are to be found the sole surviving remnants of the Great Mogul's Peacock Throne' (*Persia*, i. 321 f.). See for an account of the present so-called Peacock Throne, *ibid.*, i. 317 ff., with an illustration, p. 319; and for the duplicates of it made by Nādir Shāh, *ibid.*, i. 320 f. In 1919 a rumour spread that the Great Mogul's Peacock Throne was at Constantinople, and might be purchased from the Turks and sent to Delhi. Lord Curzon, in a letter to *The Times*, 10th September 1919, repeated the above facts, adding that when the Turks attacked the Persians, two years before the murder of Nādir Shāh, they suffered a crushing defeat, and could not have gained possession of this trophy. It is impossible to reconcile the accounts of the cost of the throne. An account of the throne based on Indian contemporary authorities will be found in Jadunath Sarkar, *Studies in Mughal India*, 18 ff.

[1] Aurangzeb prohibited singing and dancing at the Court (Elliot & Dowson, *Hist.*, vii. 283; Jadunath Sarkar, iii. 95).

[2] Bernier, 363.

there is a fine jewel, either a diamond, a ruby, or an emerald. The least valuable of these horses costs from 3,000 to 5,000 écus, and there are some worth 20,000 rupees, i. e. 10,000 écus.[1] The Prince, who was then only seven or eight years old, rode a small horse, the height of which did not exceed that of a large greyhound, but it was a very well-made animal.[2]

Half an hour, or, at the most, one hour after the Emperor is seated on his throne, seven of the bravest elephants, which are trained to war, are brought for his inspection. One of the seven has its howdah ready on its back, in case the Emperor wishes to mount; the others are covered with housings of brocade, with chains of gold and silver about their necks, and there are four which carry the royal standard upon their backs; it is attached to a hand pike which a man holds erect. They are brought, one after the other, to within forty or fifty paces of the Emperor, and when the elephant is opposite the throne it salutes His Majesty by placing its trunk on the ground and then elevating it above its head three times. On each occasion it trumpets aloud, and then, turning its back towards the Emperor, one of the men riding upon it raises the housing in order that the Emperor may see whether the animal is in good condition or not, and has been well fed. Each has its own silken cord, which is stretched round its body in order to measure whether it has increased in girth since the previous year. The principal of these elephants, of which the Emperor is very fond, is a large and fierce animal which has 500 rupees *per mensem* for its expenses.[3] It is fed with the best food and quantities

[1] The écu being equal to 4*s.* 6*d.* the prices of the horses would be £875 to £1,125 and £2,250. Pyrard de Laval says that Arab horses were worth about £104 or £112 each at Goa; while Linschoten doubles this estimate.

[2] The Prince, aged 7, was Muhammad Akbar, fourth son of Aurangzeb, He was born on 11th September 1657 (O. S.); as he lost his mother, Dilras Bānū, when he was a month old, he was much petted by his father, and other members of the family (Jadunath Sarkar, *Hist. of Aurangzīb*, iii. 58 f.; *Studies in Mughal India*, 91 ff.).

[3] £56. The ordinary Government allowance for all expenses connected with the keep of an elephant is, or was a few years ago, about 30 rupees a month in Northern India. Saunderson gives it at only 24 rupees in Bengal, and 48 rupees in Madras (*Thirteen Years, &c.*, 100).

of sugar, and is given spirits to drink. I have elsewhere spoken of the number of elephants kept by the Emperor,[1] to which I add here that when he rides out on his elephant the Omrahs follow him on horseback, and when he rides a horse the Omrahs follow on foot. After the Emperor has inspected his elephants he rises, and accompanied by three or four of his eunuchs enters his harem by a small door which is behind the oval-shaped throne.

The other five thrones are arranged in a superb hall in another court, and are covered with diamonds, without any coloured stones. I shall not give a minute description of them for fear of wearying the reader, not forgetting that one may become disgusted with the most beautiful things when they are too often before the eyes. These five thrones are disposed in such a manner that they form a cross, four making a square, the fifth being in the middle, but somewhat nearer to the two which are placed furthest away from the people.

After the Emperor has remained about half an hour in his harem, he comes out with three or four eunuchs to seat himself in the middle one of the five thrones, and during the five days of the festival, sometimes his elephants are brought, sometimes his camels, and all the nobles of his Court come to make their accustomed presents. All this is done with much magnificence, and with surroundings worthy of the greatest monarch in the East, the Great Mogul being in power and wealth in Asia what the King of France is in Europe, but having nothing comparable with him in might if he waged war with a valiant and clever people like our Europeans.[2]

For the food given by Akbar to his elephants see *Āīn-i-Akbarī*, i. 124. Commissariat elephants in India get daily 15 lbs. of flour, 600 lbs. green fodder, and 1 lb. ghī or butter, with coarse sugar and salt. Sir S. W. Baker doubled the allowance of flour for elephants employed in sport (*Wild Beasts and their Ways*, 24).

[1] See p. 223 above.

[2] On the inferiority of Indian as compared with European armies, see Bernier, 55, and p. 311 below.

CHAPTER IX

Concerning other details of the Great Mogul's Court.

SINCE Aurangzeb, who reigns at present, has occupied the throne of the Moguls, which he usurped from his father and brothers, he has imposed on himself, as I have said, a severe form of penance, and eats nothing which has enjoyed life. As he lives upon vegetables and sweetmeats only, he has become thin and meagre, to which the great fasts which he keeps have contributed. During the whole of the duration of the comet of the year ——,[1] which appeared very large in India, where I then was, Aurangzeb drank only a little water and ate a small quantity of millet bread; this so much affected his health that he nearly died, for besides this he slept on the ground, with only a tiger's skin over him, and since that time has never enjoyed perfect health.[2]

I remember seeing the Emperor drink upon three different occasions while seated on his throne. He had brought to him on a golden saucer, enriched with diamonds, rubies and emeralds, a large cup of rock-crystal,[3] all round and smooth,

[1] This comet, if, as we may suppose, it appeared in 1665, was first seen in Europe at Aix, on the 27th of March of that year. It lasted four weeks, and had a tail 25° long. Its orbit was computed by Halley (*vide* Chambers's *Astronomy*, 'Catalogue of Comets', No. 64). Terry refers to two great comets which appeared while he was at the Mogul's Court in the month of November 1618. They were followed by drought and famine. (See *A Voyage to East India,* London, 1777, p. 393.) For Newton's comet of 1680, see Fryer, iii. 174.

[2] At one period this Emperor subsisted on the proceeds of the sale of caps which he had embroidered with his own hands. He also wrote and sold extracts from the Korān for his daily bread. (See Chardin, *Voyages,* Amsterdam ed., 1711, vol. viii, p. 91.) He is said on one occasion, when urged to found hospitals, to have replied that he would make the country so prosperous that there would be no more mendicants to be seen in it. (Chardin, *Voyages,* Amsterdam, ed., 1711, vol. viii, p. 86.).

[3] Vessels made of rock-crystal were much esteemed by the Emperors. Ball saw some very fine examples of large size which were found in the palace at the capture of Delhi after the Mutiny. Possibly some of the fine specimens preserved in the Green Vaults at Dresden came from India. See Watt, *Commercial Products,* 561: *Ency. Brit.,* xxiii. 433.

the cover of which was of gold, with the same decoration as the saucer. As a rule no one sees the Emperor eat except his womenkind and eunuchs, and it is very rarely that he goes to dine at the house of any of his subjects, whether it belongs to a Prince or to one of his own relatives. While I was on my last journey, Ja'far Khān, who was his Grand Wazīr, and moreover, his uncle on his wife's side, invited the Emperor to visit him and inspect the new palace which he had had built for himself. This being the greatest honour His Majesty could do him, Ja'far Khān and his wife, in testimony of their gratitude, made him a present of jewels, elephants, camels, horses, and other things, to the value of seven lakhs of rupees (700,000), which amount to one million and fifty thousand (1,050,000) livres of our money.[1] This wife of Ja'far Khān is the most magnificent and the most liberal woman in the whole of India, and she alone expends more than all the wives and daughters of the Emperor put together; it is on this account that her family is always in debt, although her husband is practically master of the whole Empire. She had ordered a grand banquet to be prepared for the Emperor, but His Majesty, as he did not wish to dine at Ja'far Khān's house, returned to the palace, and the Princess sent after him the dishes she had destined for him. The Emperor found all the dishes so much to his taste that he gave 500 rupees to the eunuch who brought them, and double that amount to the cooks.

When the Emperor goes to the mosque in his pallankeen one of his sons follows on horseback, and all the Princes and officers of the household on foot.[2] Those who are Musalmāns wait for him upon the top of the steps to the mosque, and when he comes out they precede him to the gate of the palace. Eight elephants march in front of him, four carrying two men each, one to guide the elephant, and the other,

Some splendid examples of modern work in rock-crystal are illustrated in *Country Life*, 16th April 1921, p. lxxii.

[1] £78,750. See vol. ii. 100. The wife of Ja'far Khān, sister of Shāista Khān, was a notable woman: see the anecdotes regarding her told by Manucci (iii. 418) and Jadunath Sarkar (iv. 88). She is mentioned below, p. 313.

[2] Cf. Bernier, 280.

seated on its back, bearing a standard attached to a hand pike. Each of the four other elephants carries a seat or kind of throne [1] on its back, one of which is square, another round, one covered, and another closed with glass of many kinds. When the Emperor goes out he has generally 500 or 600 men with him for his bodyguard, each man armed with a kind of hand pike. Fireworks are attached to the iron blade; these consist of two rockets crossed, each of the thickness of the arm, and a foot in length; when ignited they will carry the hand pike 500 yards.[2] The Emperor is also followed by 300 or 400 matchlock men, who are timid and unskilful in firing, and a number of cavalry of no greater merit. One hundred of our European soldiers would scarcely have any difficulty in vanquishing 1,000 of these Indian soldiers; [3] but it is true, on the other hand, that they would have much difficulty in accustoming themselves to such an abstemious life. For the horseman as well as the infantry soldier supports himself with a little flour kneaded with water and black sugar, of which they make small balls; and in the evening, whenever they have the necessaries, they make khichari,[4] which consists of rice cooked with a grain of the above name in water with a little salt. When eating it they first dip the ends of their fingers in melted butter, for such is the ordinary food of both soldiers and poor people. To which it should be added that the heat would kill our soldiers, who would be unable to remain exposed to the glare of the sun throughout the day as these Indians do. I should say en passant that the peasants have for their sole garment a scrap of cloth to cover those parts which natural modesty requires should be concealed; and that they are

[1] Howdah.

[2] Rockets were used, and often proved most effective, in battle. It is said that the cause of Dārā Shikoh's descending from his elephant at the critical moment when engaged at Samūgarh with Murād Bakhsh and Aurangzeb (p. 265) was that the elephant had been struck by a rocket, which rendered it unmanageable. See Jadunath Sarkar, ii. 58.

[3] See p. 308 above.

[4] See p. 225. Khicharī is the term for rice boiled with pulse (*dāl*), usually that of arhar, *Cajanus indicus*; See Ja'far Sharīf, *Islām in India*, 320 f.

reduced to great poverty, because if the Governors become aware that they possess any property they seize it straightway by right or by force.[1] You may see in India whole provinces like deserts, from whence the peasants have fled on account of the oppression of the Governors. Under cover of the fact that they are themselves Musalmāns, they persecute these poor idolaters to the utmost, and if any of the latter become Musalmāns it is in order to escape work; they become soldiers or Fakīrs, or people who make profession of having renounced the world, and live upon alms; but in reality they are all great rascals. It is estimated that there are in India 800,000 Musalmān Fakīrs, and 1,200,000 among the idolaters, of whom I shall speak further on.[2]

Once a fortnight the Emperor goes out to hunt, and while *en route*, and also while the chase lasts, he is always mounted on his elephant. All the animals which he shoots are driven within musket range of his elephant. Ordinarily these are lions, tigers, deer, and gazelles—because, as for wild boars, he as a good Musalmān does not wish to see them. On his return he uses a pallankeen, and there is the same guard and the same order as when he goes to the mosque, save that during the chase there are 200 or 300 horsemen who ride before him in confused ranks.[3]

The Princesses, whether they are the Emperor's wives, his daughters, or his sisters, never leave the palace except when they go to the country for a few days' change of air and scene. Some of them go, but rarely, to visit the ladies of the nobles, as for example the wife of Ja'far Khān, who is the Emperor's aunt. This is not done except by the Emperor's special permission. The custom here differs from that in Persia where the Princesses make their visits only at night, accompanied by a great number of eunuchs, who drive away all persons whom they meet on the road.[4] But at the court of the Great Mogul the ladies generally go out at nine o'clock in the morning, and have only three or four eunuchs to accompany them, and ten or twelve female slaves who act as ladies

[1] See Bernier, 225 ff.; Smith, *Oxford History of India*, 418.
[2] See Bernier, 316 ff. [3] *Ibid.*, 374 f.
[4] This was known as the Qurq, see Fryer, iii. 41.

of honour. The Princesses are carried in pallankeens covered with embroidered tapestries, and every pallankeen is followed by a small carriage which contains only one person. It is drawn by two men, and the wheels are not more than a foot in diameter. The object in taking these carriages is, that when the Princesses arrive at the houses they are going to visit, the men who carry the pallankeens are allowed to go only to the first gate, where the eunuchs compel them to retire; the Princesses then change into the carriages, and are drawn by the ladies of honour to the women's apartments. For, as I have elsewhere remarked, in the houses of the nobles the women's apartments are in the centre, and it is generally necessary to traverse two or three large courts and a garden or two before reaching them.

When the Princesses are married to nobles of the Court they become the rulers of their husbands, who, if they do not live as they desire, and do not act according to their commands, as they possess the power of approaching the Emperor whenever they wish, they persuade him to do what they please, to the disadvantage of their husbands; most frequently asking that they be deprived of their offices.[1] As it is the custom that the firstborn, although he be the son of a slave, succeeds to the throne, when the Princesses in the imperial harem become aware that there is one among them with child, they immediately use all conceivable methods to cause a miscarriage. When I was at Patna in the year 1666, Shāista Khān's surgeon, who is a half-caste (mestice) Portuguese, assured me that the Princess, wife of Shāista Khān, in one month had caused miscarriages to eight women of his harem, as she would not permit any children but her own to survive.[2]

[1] Bernier says that the princesses were rarely married, 'no man being considered worthy of royal alliance; an apprehension being entertained that the husband might thereby be rendered powerful, and induced perhaps to aspire to the throne' (p. 12). 'The Great Mogoll's or King's daughters are never supposed to marry' (Mundy, ii. 202 f.). For marriages of Aurangzeb's daughters see Jadunath Sarkar, iii. 69.

[2] On the frequency of abortion in India see N. Chevers, *A Manual of Medical Jurisprudence in India*, 712 ff.

CHAPTER X[1]

The Great Mogul orders all his jewels to be shown to the Author.

On the first day of November 1665 I went to the palace to take leave of the Emperor, but he said that he did not wish me to depart without having seen his jewels, and witnessing the splendour of his fête.[2]

Early in the morning of the next day five or six of the Emperor's officers and others on behalf of Nawāb Jaʿfar Khān, announced that the Emperor wished to see me. Immediately on my arrival at the Court the two custodians of the royal jewels, of whom I have elsewhere spoken,[3] accompanied me into the presence of His Majesty; and after I had made him the customary salutation, they conducted me into a small apartment, which is at one of the ends of the hall where the Emperor was seated on his throne, and whence he was able to see us. I found in this apartment 'Ākil Khān,[4] chief of the jewel treasury, who, when he saw us, commanded four of the imperial eunuchs to bring the jewels, which were carried in two large wooden trays lacquered with gold leaf, and covered with small cloths made expressly for the purpose—one of red and the other of green brocaded velvet. After these trays were uncovered, and all the pieces had been counted three times over, a list was prepared by three scribes who were present. For the Indians do everything with great circumspection and patience, and when they see any one who acts with precipitation, or becomes angry, they gaze at him without saying anything, and smile as if he were a madman.

[1] This very important chapter and the next are altogether omitted in the English translation by John Phillips, 1684.

[2] Joret (*J.-B. Tavernier*, p. 190) sees an inconsistency between this statement and that at the beginning of chap. viii, p. 301. The words as he quotes them support this view, but they are not Tavernier's. Ball, as he understands Tavernier, sees no inconsistency. Prof. Joret quotes, it should be added, as from chap. ix, but that is a misprint for chap. x.

[3] See p. 110 above.

[4] *Ibid.*

The first piece which 'Ākil Khān placed in my hands was the great diamond, which is a round rose, very high at one side.[1] At the basal margin it has a small notch and flaw inside. Its water is beautiful, and it weighs 319½ ratis, which are equal to 280 of our carats—the rati being ⅞th of our carat. When Mīr Jumla, who betrayed the King of Golkonda, his master, presented this stone to Shāhjahān, to whose side he attached himself,[2] it was then in the rough, and weighed 900 ratis, which are equivalent to 787½ carats; and it had several flaws.

If this stone had been in Europe it would have been treated in a different manner, for some good pieces would have been taken from it, and it would have weighed more than it does, instead of which it has been all ground down. It was the Sieur Hortensio Borgio,[3] a Venetian, who cut it, for which he was badly rewarded; for when it was cut he was reproached with having spoilt the stone, which ought to have retained a greater weight; and instead of paying him for his work, the Emperor fined him 10,000 rupees, and would have taken more if he had possessed it. If the Sieur Hortensio had understood his trade, he would have been able to take a large piece from this stone without doing injury to the Emperor's jewel, and without having had so much trouble in

[1] A resume of all the information regarding this important stone, the so-called 'Great Mogul', will be found in an appendix. Ball has proved that this was the Koh-i-Nūr. It may be mentioned here that this allusion to the form of the stone as a 'rose' appears to have given rise to the erroneous idea with one author, and those who have followed him, that it had a roseate tinge.

[2] Bernier's reference to this incident (p. 22) is as follows: 'At first he (Mīr Jumla) presented to him (Shāhjahān) that great diamond which is esteemed matchless, giving him to understand that the precious stones of Golkonda were surely more deserving of his consideration than the rocks of Kandahār, whither the Mogul was about to lead an army: his military operations in that Kingdom ought not to cease, he said, until the conquest of his arms extended to Cape Comory.'

[3] Bernier (ed. Constable, 269) mentions but does not name a jeweller who took refuge at the Mogul's Court after having cheated all the monarchs of Europe with his 'doublets'. He was, however, a Frenchman, said to be La Grange, while Hortensio was an Italian, and therefore King is probably mistaken when he suggests their identity. [The ed. of 1678 has Borgis, but Ortencio Bronzoni had espoused Suzana, widow of Nicolao Borges: Manucci, iii, 214.]

grinding it; but he was not a very accomplished diamond cutter.[1]

After I had fully examined this splendid stone, and returned it into the hands of 'Ākil Khān, he showed me another stone, pear-shaped, of good form and fine water, and also three other table diamonds, two clear, and the other with some little black spots. Each weighed 55 to 60 ratis, and the pear 62½. Subsequently he showed me a jewel set with twelve diamonds, each stone of 15 to 16 ratis, and all roses. In the middle a heart-shaped rose of good water, but with three small flaws, and this rose weighed about 35 or 40 ratis. Also a jewel set with seventeen diamonds, half of them table and half rose, the largest of which could not weigh more than 7 or 8 ratis, with the exception of the one in the middle, which weighed about 16. All these stones are of first-class water, clean and of good form, and the most beautiful ever found. Also two grand pear-shaped pearls, one weighing about 70 ratis, a little flattened on both sides, and of beautiful water and good form. Also a pearl button, which might weigh from 55 to 60 ratis, of good form and good water. Also a round pearl of great perfection, a little flat on one side, which weighs 56 ratis. I ascertained this to be the precise weight, and that Shāh 'Abbās II, King of Persia, sent it as a present to the Great Mogul. Also three other round pearls, each of 25 to 28 ratis, or thereabouts, but their water tends to yellow.

[1] Ball remarks that he cannot understand this statement in the light that Mr. King seems to have done, namely, that Hortensio might have defrauded the Mogul by taking off a large piece. It simply means, he thinks, that Hortensio might with advantage have cleaved the stone instead of grinding it; the pieces so cleaved would then have been the property of the Mogul, not the perquisite of Hortensio. (See *Natural History of Precious Stones*, Bohn's ed., 1870, p. 78 *n.*) In an appendix Ball has dealt with the stories which, to have any reasonable possibility, must have referred to the breaking up of the original large stone, as, after Tavernier's time, the stone of 280 carats could not, as is often stated, have been made to break up into three whose united weights were equal to more than twice that amount; but the statement in the text here is clearly against the supposition that the large stone was otherwise treated than by grinding down from 787½ to 280 carats. That the Indians knew how to cleave diamonds is abundantly proved in ii. 45, where Tavernier says they understood the art better than Europeans.

Also a perfectly round pearl of 36½ ratis, of a lively white, and perfect in every respect. It is the only jewel which Aurangzeb, who reigns at present, has himself purchased on account of its beauty, for the rest either came to him from Dārā Shikoh, his eldest brother, he having appropriated them after he had caused his head to be cut off,[1] or they were presents made to him after he ascended the throne. I have elsewhere remarked that the Emperor has no great regard for jewels, priding himself only on being a great zealot of the law of Muhammad.[2]

'Ākil Khān also placed in my hands, for he allowed me to examine all at my ease, two other pearls, perfectly round and equal, each of which weighed 25¼ ratis. One is slightly yellow, but the other is of a very lively water, and the most beautiful that can be seen. It is true, as I have elsewhere said, that the Prince of Arabia, who has taken Maskat from the Portuguese, possesses a pearl which surpasses in beauty all others in the world ; for it is perfectly round, and so white and lively that it looks as though it was transparent, but it only weighs 14 carats. There is not a single monarch in

[1] This statement is important, as we know that Shāhjahān, who was still alive at this time in prison, had with him a great number of his precious stones, which were not handed over to Aurangzeb till after Shāhjahān's death, when Jahānārā Begam presented him with a gold basin full of them (see pp. 274 and 275). According to Bernier, however, some had been previously given to Aurangzeb by Shāhjahān during his lifetime. Moreover, Aurangzeb, in a letter written to Shāhjahān at the time when he arrested him, acknowledged the gift (!) of Dārā Shikoh's jewels by letter. Dārā Shikoh was left about £4,000,000 worth of gold and jewels by his grandfather, Āsaf Khān, who passed over his own sons Shāista Khān and Nawāz Khān—perhaps because the Mogul, according to custom, might have declared himself the heir, so that they would have derived no benefit. But Āsaf Khān consoled himself with the reflection that he left his sons in good and highly lucrative positions, which was a better provision for them (Bernier, 70, 127 ; Manucci, i. 310, 326, 354). 'Besides the mansion which he had built in Lahore, and on which he expended twenty lacs of rupees, he [Āsaf Khān] left money and valuables to the amount of two krors and fifty lacs of rupees. There were 30 lacs of rupees in jewels, besides other property.' (Elliot & Dowson, *History of India*, vii. 68 f.).

[2] On the prohibition by the Law of Islām against the wearing of ornaments by men see T. P. Hughes, *Dict. of Islām*, 448.

Asia who has not asked the Prince of Arabia to sell him this pearl.[1] Also two chains, one of pearls and rubies of different shapes pierced like the pearls ; the other of pearls and emeralds, round and bored. All the pearls are round and of diverse waters, and from 10 to 12 ratis each in weight. In the middle of the chain of rubies there is a large emerald of the 'old rock',[2] cut into a rectangle and of high colour, but with many flaws. It weighs about 30 ratis. In the middle of the chain of emeralds there is an oriental amethyst,[3] a long table, weighing about 40 ratis, and the perfection of beauty. Also a balass [4] ruby cut en cabochon, of fine colour and clean pierced at the apex, and weighing 17 melscals.[5] Six melscals make one once (French). Also another cabochon ruby of perfect colour, but slightly flawed and pierced at the apex, which weighs 12 melscals. Also an oriental topaz [6] of very

[1] See below (ii. p. 86).

[2] Precious stones were denominated 'of the old rock' (*rocca velha*), when they exhibited more or less perfect crystalline forms, being considered more developed than those with amorphous forms. (Linschoten, ii. 137 ; Fryer, i. 96 ; Bernier, 148).

[3] The 'oriental' amethyst is a purple sapphire, and when perfect is of great beauty.

[4] Balet in the original. (See p. 303, *n.*)

[5] Melscals = mishkāls. (See Appendix, p. 333.) In 1836, when Baron Charles v. Hügel visited Ranjit Singh at Lahore, the pommel of one of the Mahārāja's saddles was decorated with a ruby two inches square, bearing the name of Jahāngīr. Nūrjahān objected to the injury to the stone, but Jahāngīr replied : 'This jewel will assuredly hand down my name to posterity more than any written history. The house of Tīmūr may fall, but as long as there is a King, this jewel will have its price.' Ahmad Shāh, who had found it on the Peacock Throne, also inscribed his name on it. It had been stolen from Tīmūr in 1398 and repurchased by Jahāngīr (*Travels in Kashmir and the Panjab*, 1845, p. 303.) Shāh Rukh of Persia refused to deliver the famous ruby of Aurangzeb to the brutal eunuch; Āghā Muhammad, until a circle of paste had been fixed on his head and molten lead poured on it (Sir P. Sykes, *Hist. of Persia*, 2nd ed. ii. 294.)

[6] The oriental topaz is a yellow sapphire (corundum). According to Strabo (xvi. 770) it was found only in the Ophiodes island off the Troglodytic shore of the Red Sea. It was probably this topaz which Aurangzeb wore at his coronation. (See p. 296 and ii. 102 *n.*) It is also mentioned by Bernier (p. 268). Its weight, as given on page 102, vol. ii, was $181\frac{1}{8}$ ratis, or $157\frac{1}{4}$ carats (should be $158\frac{1}{2}$ carats), hence these should = 6 melscals, and the melscal = $30\frac{3}{16}$ ratis, or $26\frac{5}{12}$ carats. To the mishkāl of Babur

high colour cut in eight panels, which weighs 6 melscals, but on one side it has a small white fog within.

These, then, are the jewels of the Great Mogul, which he ordered to be shown to me as a special favour which he has never manifested to any other Frank; and I have held them all in my hand, and examined them with sufficient attention and leisure to be enabled to assure the reader that the description which I have just given is very exact and faithful, as is that of the thrones, which I have also had sufficient time to contemplate thoroughly.

CHAPTER XI[1]

Terms of the passport which the Nawāb Shāista Khān sent to the Author, with some letters which he wrote to him, and the replies to them, in which the style of these countries manifests itself.

I COME now to the passport which the Nawāb Shāista Khān gave me, and the letters which I wrote to him in reference to my affairs, as both by these letters and by the replies to them the reader will be enable to comprehend the style and manner of writing among the Indians. I also received a passport from the Emperor himself, which His Majesty had already given me through Ja'far Khān,[2] his uncle, to whom I returned it after having read it, because it was not couched

a weight of 40 ratis is attributed, so that either Babur's mishkāl must have weighed absolutely one-third more than Tavernier's, or Tavernier's rati must have exceeded Babur's by one-third. The latter will be shown to be the case. (See Appendix.) Ball believed that this topaz is probably that figured, together with the Koh-i-nūr, by Miss Eden, and mentioned also by Osborne as being in the possession of Ranjīt Singh.

[1] This chapter is omitted in the English translation by John Phillips, 1684.

[2] Giafer Kan in the original. He was brother of Arjumand Begam, afterwards called Mumtāz-i-Mahall, the lady for whom the Tāj was built by her husband, Shāhjahān. There is frequent mention of Ja'far Khān in these pages, though he is not often referred to in other histories of India.

in the language I approved. I desired it to be without restriction, equally full and in the same style as that which I had received from the King of Persia, in virtue of which I had been exempt from all dues both in going and coming, whether I sold or did not sell; because the passport offered me on the part of the Great Mogul was limited, and in the event of sale it required that I should pay custom dues on whatever I had sold. Although Ja'far Khān assured me that it was the most favourable passport of the kind which the Emperor had ever given, and that according to custom it could not be otherwise, nevertheless I was unwilling to accept it, and contented myself with that which I had held for some years from Shāista Khān, which sufficed for me, and was as much esteemed as that of the Emperor, or more so. It is true that the Emperor did not require me to pay any duty on account of what I sold to him, and that the matter was done graciously.

Copy of the letter which the Author wrote to Shāista Khān, uncle of the Great Mogul, on the 29th of May 1659.

The least of the servants of your Highness, who prays to God for the prosperity of your Greatness, Jean-Baptiste Tavernier, a Frenchman, presents a request to your liberal bounty. You who are the Lieutenant of the Emperor, who govern as his kinsman all the Kingdoms which are subject to the rule of His Majesty, who has placed under your direction the most important affairs of his Crown, the Prince invincible, Shāista Khān, whom may God keep in his care.

It is now some years since I had the honour of presenting to your Highness, then Governor of the Kingdom of Gujarāt, and residing in Ahmadābād, some large pearls and other rarities, which were deemed worthy of your treasury, for which I received a just payment and magnificent liberality. At the same time I received your instructions to return to Europe, to search for other rarities and bring them to you:[1] this I have done during the five or six years which I have spent traversing many European countries, where I have met with many beautiful objects and rare curiosities, which are

[1] These commands were given in 1654.

worthy of being presented to your Highness. And as I heard, when at the Court of the King of Persia, that wars were in progress in India, I sent by one of my servants the aforesaid effects and rarities by way of Masulipatam; and when I reached Surat some days ago, I received intelligence of the safe arrival of all.[1] If his Highness is willing to buy the aforesaid rarities, and desires that I should bring them into his presence, I beg to be given an order by which I shall be able to travel to him without any one causing me trouble *en route*. But if your Highness does not wish me to go to you I shall proceed elsewhere. However, I await your orders at Surat, praying God that He will keep you always in all kinds of prosperity.

Translation of the first letter which Shāista Khān wrote to the Author in reply to the above.

GREAT GOD—[2]

To the beloved of fortune, support of virtue, Monsieur Tavernier, Frenchman, my dear friend, know that your letter has been delivered to me, by which I have learnt of your return to Surat, and that you have brought with you what I asked. I have carefully considered all that you have written to me, with which I am much contented; wherefore, on receiving this, you should arrange to come to me, with those things which you have brought; and be assured that I will render you all possible courtesy, and all the aid and profit that it is possible for you to wish for. Moreover, I send you the passport you have asked from me, recommending

[1] What the postal arrangements could have been between places so distant as Masulipatam and Surat we can only guess—probably letters between the factories were conveyed mainly by sea. Tavernier sent the letters by his own servants. 'The Indians in sending their letters abroad have not learnt the conveniences of the quick Dispatches of our Posts: A Pattamar, i. e. a Foot Messenger, is generally employ'd to carry them to the remotest Bounds of the Empire. So that whenever the English are under a necessity of writing to Bengal, Maderas, or any other part of Indostan, a Person is sent on purpose upon the Errand' (Ovington, 251). Special runners were employed by the Indian Princes.

[2] Shāista Khān used at the beginning of his letter the usual Musulmān formula: *B'-ism 'Illāhi 'r-rahmāni 'r-rahīm*: 'In the Name of God, the Compassionate, the Merciful!'

you to come quickly in order that I may see the things described in your letter. The quicker you are able to come the better, wherefore write more? The 11th of Chouval,[1] in the year of Muhammad 1069 [A. D. 1661].

This which follows is written in Shāista Khān's own hand :—

The chosen one among my most beloved, your request has been delivered to me. God bless you and reward you for having held to your word and kept your promise. Come quickly to me, and be assured that you will receive all sorts of contentment and profit from me.

This which follows is contained round his seal :—

The Prince of Princes, the servant of the Emperor, victorious Aurangzeb.

Translation of the passport which Shāista Khān sent to the Author.

GREAT GOD—[2]

To all the agents and officers of the customs and tolls, to all the guardians of the roads, both great and small, between the port of Surat and the Court of Jahānābād. As Monsieur Tavernier, Frenchman, the most exalted and beloved of us, who is a servant of my household, comes to me from the port of Surat, let no one, whosoever he may be, or on any pretext, interrupt his way or his journey, or cause him inconvenience or trouble, but permit him to pass in all safety, so that he may be able to come into my presence with comfort; and let each of the abovenamed see that he is accompanied through their respective jurisdictions, so as to facilitate his journey. I charge you specially with this matter, and let no one act otherwise. Done the 11th of Chouval,[3] in the year of Muhammad 1069.

Translation of the second letter written by Shāista Khān to the Author.

To the most expert of engineers and the cream of good fellows, Monsieur Tavernier, Frenchman, know that I regard

[1] Shawwāl, the tenth month. [2] See p. 321 *n.* 2, above.

[3] See note 1 above.

you as one of my dearest favourites and well beloved. As I have before written to you to come to Jahānābād and to bring with you the rarities which you have for me, now, by the favour and grace of the Emperor, I have been appointed his Viceroy and Governor in the Kingdom of Deccan.[1] Immediately on the receipt of his Majesty's orders I set out, on the 25th of the month of Chouval; for this reason it is no longer desirable that you should come to Jahānābād, but rather that you should make your way as soon as possible to Burhānpur, where, with God's assistance, I shall arrive in the course of two months or thereabouts. I trust you will act in accordance with what I now write to you.

Reply of the Author to this second letter.

He who prays to God for your Highness, and for the increase of your greatness and prosperity, Jean-Baptiste Tavernier, Frenchman, &c. [as in the first letter]. I have received the honour of the commands which your Highness has deigned to bestow on the least of your servants. Salutation to the Nawāb, the Prince of Princes. I gave myself the honour some days past to write by the messenger of your Highness, that after the rains I should not fail to go to your presence at Jahānābād. Now that you direct that our meeting is to be at Burhānpur, I shall follow your orders and carry with me all the rarities which I have destined for your Highness's service. Done the 10th of the month Huge.[2]

Translation of the third letter written by Shāista Khān to the Author.

The most beloved of my favourites, Monsieur Tavernier, Frenchman, know that I keep you fresh in my memory. The letter which you wrote me by my messenger has been received, and I have read it word by word. You write that the rains and bad roads have prevented your coming, and that after the winter you will come to seek me. Now that

[1] Shāista was appointed Viceroy of the Deccan in July, 1659, relieving Muhammad Mu'azzam, afterwards the Emperor Bahādur Shāh I, second son of Aurangzeb.

[2] Zī-l-hajja, the last month of the Musalmān year.

the rains are over,[1] and that I hope that in twenty-five or twenty-six days I shall be at Aurangābād, on receipt of this hasten to come to me. I believe you will not fail. Done the 5th of Sefer,[2] in the first year of the reign of Aurangzeb.[3]

This which follows was in the hand of the Nawāb :—

Dear friend, you will not fail to act according as I have written.

Reply of the Author to this third letter.

The least of the servants of your Highness, Jean-Baptiste Tavernier, Frenchman, prays God for the prosperity of your person, you who are the Lieutenant of the Emperor, the channel by which his favours are distributed, of whom the title is venerable and full of respect, who are the near relative of the Emperor, the Governor-General of his Kingdoms, to whom he refers the accomplishment of all matters of importance. To you who are the Prince of Princes, I the servant of your Highness present this petition. Having arrived in this country in obedience to your orders, I have wholly trusted in your favour; and when I believed myself to be most laden with your bounty, I fell into the nets of Mīrzā Arab, Governor of Surat, for, having received the latest orders of your Highness, I went to take leave of him to go to make my salutation to you. He replied that he had written to the Emperor in reference to my person [and that in consequence he could not give me permission to depart till he had received the reply of His Majesty. I represented to him that, having nothing with me, and at my arrival in this port not having been found possessed of any merchandise of importance passing through the customs, I was astonished

[1] i.e. the rainy season or south-east monsoon.

[2] The month Sefar or Safer, is the second month of the Persian lunar year.

[3] Tavernier (p. 285 above) says Aurangzeb ascended the throne in 1660, and hence Prof. Joret remarks that consequently he would have remained in Surat on this occasion more than fifteen months, which is inadmissible, as on p. 325 he says six months. This, adds Prof. Joret, is an almost insoluble difficulty. There is, however, a simple solution, namely, that Tavernier was in error in giving 1660 as the year of Aurangzeb's coronation, it having in fact been 1659.

that he had written to the Empero in reference to my person].[1] He disregarded all my arguments, did not alter his decision, and refused to give me permission to leave Surat. Now all is in the hands of your Highness, to whom it is due that I should obey his commands, and that a person like Mīrzā Arab should not be able to oppose his wishes with so formal a resistance.

Besides, not having my effects with me, as I have written to your Highness, my delay in Surat causes me considerable loss, which must give you displeasure. Moreover, it will prevent merchants from coming to this port, and that will inflict considerable injury on the Empire. As for myself, I am resolved to burn my effects or throw them into the sea rather than allow any one but your Highness to see them. I trust that the great authority of your Highness will relieve me speedily from my trouble, and will enable me to go to pay you my respects. And I hope that the news of the favours which I have received from your Highness, when it shall reach France, will cause many great merchants to do business in this country, and then India will know that the rare goods of the French and their precious curiosities put to shame all that has hitherto appeared in the country. This is what I deemed it necessary to write to your Highness. Dated at Surat the 25th of the month Rabi and Auel.[2]

All these letters and replies explain the reason why I delayed nearly six months[3] at Surat. At length there came an express order from the Nawāb to the Governor of the town to allow me to depart, or otherwise he would have to resign his office. The Governor of Surat was so much annoyed at being baffled that when I took leave of him he did not deign to look at me, of which I willingly absolved him.

In consequence of the news which I had received that the Nawāb had departed from Aurangābād, I found him

[1] The portion between brackets is omitted in the edition of 1713, though given in those of 1676 and 1679.

[2] Rabī'ul-awwal, the third Musalmān month.

[3] Tavernier's account of this same visit on p. 27 seems somewhat inconsistent with this, as he implies there that no delay occurred, while the contents of these letters bear out his specific statement here of six months spent at Surat.

with the army in Deccan, where he had besieged Chākan,[1] one of the towns of Rājā Sivājī. I sold him what I had intended for him, and during the time I remained with him he gave orders that I should lack nothing, neither for my own mouth nor the feed of my horses. Every day four trays of meat and two of fruit and sweetmeats were brought to me; these for the most part fell to the share of my servants, because I was seldom permitted to eat in my tent.

The Nawāb gave orders that five or six Rājās or idolatrous Princes who were in his army should entertain me in their own manner. But their rice and vegetables, which constitute, as I have said, all their dishes, were so full of pepper, ginger, and other spices that it was impossible for me to eat them, and I left the repast with a very good appetite.

During this time the Nawāb fired a mine, which so much alarmed the inhabitants of Chākan that they yielded by agreement, on which account the soldiers, who thought to take the town by assault, were much annoyed, seeing themselves deprived of the hope of the loot which they had anticipated. On my departure the Nawāb wanted to pay me, but I represented to him that I had to pass through a disturbed country, and had to fear the followers of both armies, so I asked him to allow me to draw the money at Daulatābād;[2] this he willingly granted, and on an order which he gave me I was paid on the day following my arrival in that town. The treasurer who counted out the money to me said that he had received the advice four days previously by express, and that the Nawāb had commanded him to pay me promptly; this shows the great precision of the Indians in matters of trade to satisfy debts without delay.[3]

[1] Choupar in the original, on p. 26 written Choupart. It is Chākan, 18 miles north of Poona: not Sholāpur, as suggested by Ball.

[2] Dultabat in the original, for Daulatābād, also called Deogir (see p. 130). Bernier describes this town as the capital of Deccan

[3] According to the statement on p. 28, this payment was made at Aurangābād, and by no means promptly, or with satisfaction to Tavernier. This is but another inconsistency in the narrative.

APPENDIX

On the values of Coins, Weights, and Measures referred to by Tavernier.

I LIMIT myself here mainly to an interpretation of the values given by our author, not having space for any wider discussion of the question. He has been quoted as an authority, not always correctly, as I believe, in support of particular views, especially as to the value of the rupee. I think it can be demonstrated from the numerous relations which he gives between Indian coins and various European ones that it cannot have had a less average value than 2*s.* 3*d.* Sometimes, however, the evidence tends in the direction of a greater and sometimes of a less value.

The discrepancies are in part due to the varying values of coins bearing the same names in different provinces, and partly to the fact that European coins in Oriental countries, and Oriental coins in countries not their own, had two values—one the intrinsic, which was ascertained at the mints, and sometimes by actual conversion into the coin of the country, and the other the exchange value of the coins themselves when used as a means of purchasing in the marts.

This Appendix is supplementary to the foot-notes, but is at the same time intended to give a general and connected view of the subject.

French Money.

12 Deniers (money of account) = 1 Sol (Sous Tournois).
20 Sols = 1 Livre (money of account).
60 ,, or 3 Livres = 1 Écu.

2 Louis d'or, old = 16*s.* 9*d.*, new = £1 0*s.* 6*d.*; both according to Sir Isaac Newton. (*Assays, &c., of Coins at London Mint, before 1717.*)

It is of the utmost importance to establish beyond question of doubt the value of the above as they were employed by Tavernier. Sir Isaac Newton's estimate of the value of the écu in 1717 was 4*s.* 6*d.*, and the very frequent relations given between it and various other European coins by Tavernier clearly indicate, as will be apparent in speaking of them, and as has been shown already in the foot-notes, that a less value cannot be ascribed to it. Whence it follows that what Tavernier understood as the livre, or ⅓*d* of an écu, had a value of 1*s.* 6*d.*, and the same value is indicated by its relations to other well-known coins—as, for instance, the Dutch guilder (florin). From this again we obtain the deduction that the sol, as he uses it, which, from its small value, gives that of other coins with great nicety, was worth 0·9 of a penny; in other words, 10 sols=9*d.*[1]

Spanish Money.

The piastre and reale or real, as determined by Sir Isaac Newton, and as valued by Tavernier, were of equal value with the écu, being therefore worth 4*s.* 6*d.* Tavernier states that the former was equal to two rupees (*Persian Travels*, p. 238), i.e. 4*s.* 6*d.* also. The double pistole or Frederic d'or was worth from £1. 12*s.* 6½*d.* to £1 13*s.* 3*d.*, the latter being Sir Isaac Newton's estimate. The single pistole he valued at 16*s.* 9*d.*

Portuguese Money.

Crusado.—According to Sir Isaac Newton, in 1717, the crusado = 2*s.* 10*d.* Other authors place its value as low as 2*s.* 3*d.*, and there are various intermediate valuations. For its value in 1518 see *Barbosa*, ed. Dames, i. 65, 118, who estimates it to be worth about 10*s.*

Italian Money.

Croisart of Genoa and Sequin of Venice. The croisart is once mentioned by Tavernier, p. 157 above; its value seems to have been about 6*s.* 6*d.* The sequin, according to Sir Isaac Newton, was worth 9*s.* 5·7*d.*, and according to Yule, *Hobson-Jobson*, p. 193, 111*d.*, or 9*s.* 3*d.*

German Money.

Gulden, Rixdollars,[2] properly Reichsthalers (Richedales of Tavernier, p. 19 above), and Ducats. The gulden, of which there were several different kinds, ranged from about 2*s.* 2*d.* to 2*s.* 4*d.*, the double gulden being equal to about twice that amount. The rixdollars, of which there were many kinds, averaged, according to Sir Isaac Newton, about 4*s.* 7*d.* in intrinsic value; being, therefore, worth slightly more than the écu, or French crown. The ducats averaged about 4*s.* 9*d.*

Dutch Money.

Gulden (gulde of Tavernier, vol. ii) or florin.—Its value in currency seems to have been about 1*s.* 9*d.* to 1*s.* 9½*d.*, and to the livre it bore the proportion of 5 to 6, which gives a value for the latter of very nearly 1*s.* 6*d.*

[1] The above computations, as well as those of the values of Indian and Persian coins, although made independently, agree exactly with those which are given in a table in the English translation of Tavernier, by J. Phillips, dated 1684.

[2] The rixdollar was also a money of account in several different countries.

Indian Money.

50–80 Cowrie (corie of Tavernier, p. 23 above), shells (*Cypraea moneta*), = 1 paisā.

35–40 Bādām (baden of Tavernier, p. 23 above), bitter almonds (*Amygdalus communis*, var. *amara*) = 1 paisā.

46–56 Paisā (pecha of Tavernier) = 1 rupee (p. 23) above.

14–14¼ Rupees = 1 gold rupee or gold mohur.

Also

Fanam (fano of Tavernier, vol. ii, 118) = 4½*d.*; but some, of which six only went to the écu, were worth double, or 9*d.*

Pardao = 27 sols.

Pagoda, new = 3½ rupees; old = 4½ rupees and 2⅓ écus.

Passing the bitter almonds and cowries, we come to the paisā (or pecha of Tavernier). He says that it was worth about 2 French liards, but that there were coins of half a paisā, 2 and 4 paisā. At Surat 49 to 50, and sometimes only 46, paisā went to the rupee; and at Agra, nearer the copper mines, 55 to 56. Taking it at the average of 50, therefore, this coin was worth the 50th part of the rupee,[1] and it was also worth the 20th part of the mahmūdī. If the rupee, as shown below, was worth 2*s.* 3*d.*, then Tavernier's paisā was worth 0·54 of a penny; but with the mahmūdī at 9*d.* its value would be only 0·45*d.* The former appears to be the safer figure to adopt, owing to the various relations given by Tavernier from which we can determine the value of the rupee.

The Rupee.—The simplest of these relations (pp. 22, 305 above) is 2 rupees = 1 écu, or 4*s.* 6*d.*[2] ∴ 1 rupee = 2*s.* 3*d.* Tavernier frequently repeats his calculations in rupees, separately also in livres; these always indicate a ratio of 2 to 3, and, as we have shown his livre to have been equal to 1*s.* 6*d.*, the rupee would again be 2*s.* 3*d.*[3]

In terms of the Spanish reale, 100 of which = 213 to 215 rupees, the latter must have had the intrinsic value of at least 2*s.* 1½*d.*, and in terms of the rixdollar or reichsthaler, 2*s.* 1½*d.* These alone prove an absolute intrinsic value of upwards of 2*s.* 1*d.* The relations with Persian coins, to which reference has been made in the foot-notes, and the values of which are discussed below, support the ascription of values of from 2*s.* 1*d.* to 2*s.* 3*d.* for the rupee.

[1] Thévenot and Mandelslo make somewhat similar statements, but contradict themselves in other passages.

[2] Bernier (p. 200) says the same.

[3] Terry gives the value of 2s. 3d. for ordinary rupees, and 2s. 9d. for the best (*Voyage, &c.*, London, 1777, pp. 67, 113, 167). Fryer and Mandelslo also give the value at 2s. 3d. Mr. Keene's ascription of only 1s. 3d. to the rupee seems to be based on an incorrect valuation of the livre, for which Tavernier cannot be held responsible. (See *History of Hindustan*, p. 211).

The gold rupee, or gold mohur.—All the evidence goes to show that this coin, as known to Tavernier, was worth at least from 31*s*. 6*d*. to 32*s*.; its equivalent was 14 to 14¼ rupees, hence we may again deduce a value of at least 2*s*. 3*d*. for the rupee.

The fanam is of no importance in so far as Tavernier's calculations are concerned.[1]

Pardao.—In two places (pp. 155 above, and vol. ii. 109) Tavernier gives for the pardao the value of 27 sols=2*s*. 0·3*d*.; this is less than what is ascribed to it about this period in Yule (*Hobson-Jobson*, p. 672 ff.) namely, 2*s*. 6*d*.

Pagoda.—Tavernier gives a number of different values for this coin. Thus, New P.=3½ rupees, say 7*s*. 10½*d*. (vol. ii. 101); Old P.=4½ rupees (vol. ii. 71), say 10*s*. 1½*d*.; also=7½ livres)=11*s*. 9*d*., or 2⅓ écus (p. 241 above)=10*s*. 6*d*. In the table in the English translation referred to in p. 328 *n*. the pagoda=the demi-pistol, or 8*s*. 3*d*. The average value was therefore about 9*s*.[2]

Persian Money.

2 shāhīs=1 mahmūdī.
2 mahmūdīs=1 'abbāsī.
5 'abbāsīs=1 ' or ' ? (money of account).
50 'abbāsīs=1 tomān (money of account).

Shāhī (chaez of Tavernier).—According to Tavernier (p. 20 above), 200 shāhīs=29½ rupees, so that with the rupee at 2*s*. 3*d*. the value of one shāhī would be 3·98*d*., say 4*d*. As he elsewhere states the relation to French money to be 10 shāhīs =46 sols and 1 liard, ∴ 1 shāhī=4½*d*., and Mandelslo (*Voyages*, English translation, p. 8) gives the value of one shāhī to be nearly 5*d*., I conclude, although the value is given at only 2⅓*d*. by Kelly in the *Universal Cambist*, that in Tavernier's time its value was from 4*d*. to 5*d*., say 4½*d*.

Mahmūdī (mamoudi of Tavernier, p. 21 above).—Hence the mahmūdī would be worth between 8*d*. and 9*d*. Both Tavernier and Fryer represent it, however, as being worth ⅖ of a rupee, so that with the latter at 2*s*. 3*d*. its value would be 10⅘*d*.; and Mandelslo (English ed., pp. 13 and 68) gives it the value of 1*s*., which would make the rupee 2*s*. 6*d*. Its range in value, therefore, was from 8*d*. to 1*s*.

'Abbāsī.—Tavernier, in his account of Persian money, says 1 'abbāsī=18 sols 6 deniers, which would be about 1*s*. 4·65*d*. Mandelslo (p. 8) says 3=1 écu, and as we must give a value of at least 4*s*. 3*d*. to the écu, the 'abbāsī would be worth 1*s*. 6*d*.;

[1] See Yule, *Hobson-Jobson*, 348.

[2] For a full account of the various kinds of pagodas and their values see *Madras Manual of Administration*, iii. 643.

so confirming the intermediate values of the shāhī (chaez) ($4\frac{1}{2}d.$) and of the mahmūdī (9*d.*) above given.

In his *Persian Travels*, 1st ed., 1676, p. 122, Tavernier states that 1 or=5 'abbāsīs, or about 6*s.* $11\frac{1}{4}d.$ with the 'abbāsī at 1*s.* 4·65*d.*, or 7*s.* 6*d.* with the 'abbāsī at 1*s.* 6*d.* The or may have been a name used by the Franks much as we use the slang term ' tin ' ; it corresponded to the Persian zar, which simply means money,[1] but Tavernier here gives it a definite value.

Tomān.—Though generally regarded as a money of account, it is sometimes spoken of as though it had actually been a coin. At 50 'abbāsīs, as above, its value was £3 15*s.* ; but Tavernier states that in India its value was $29\frac{1}{2}$ rupees, which at 2*s.* 3*d.* would be only £3 6*s.* $4\frac{1}{2}d.$ Tavernier also states that the tomān=46 livres, which at 1*s.* 6*d.*=£3 9*s.* Mandelslo gives it as=5 pistoles, i.e. about £4 3*s.* 9*d.* Fryer says £3 6*s.* 8*d.*; and Tavernier, in his *Persian Travels*, p. 122, says it=15 écus, which at 4*s.* 6*d.*=£3 7*s.* 6*d.* Probably about £3 9*s.* would be a fair average estimate, In 1821, according to Kelly (*Universal Cambist*), it only represented a value of £1 16*s.*

Tonne of Gold.—According to Tavernier (vol. ii, 320), the tonne was equal to 100,000 gulden (or Dutch florins), or 120,000 livres ; and as these were worth 1*s.* 9*d.* and 1*s.* 6*d.* respectively, the value of the tonne would be about £9,000. The ton or tonne of gold equalled 100,000 gulden.[2]

It is unnecessary to describe other Persian coins here, as they are not mentioned by our author in the Indian portion of his travels.

Chinese Money.

A money of account=600 livres=£45 (see vol. ii. 111, 238, and *Persian Travels*) is referred to by Tavernier as a pain, i.e. a loaf or cake ; probably it was represented in bullion by an ingot, to which the English applied the term ' shoe ' (Yule, *Hobson-Jobson*, 830 ; N. Elias & E. D. Ross, *History of the Moghuls of Central Asia*, 256, note 3).

Weights.

French Weights.

1 grain =·819 of a grain troy.
24 grains=1 denier.
72 ,, (=3 deniers)=1 gros.
579 ,, =1 once=472·187 grs. troy.
16 onces =1 livre= 1 lb. 4 oz. 1 dwt. 13 gr. troy, or 1 lb. 1 oz. $10\frac{1}{5}$ dr. av.

[1] Comp. Chardin, *Voyages*, Amsterdam, 1711, vol. iv, 277.
[2] Bernier, Introd., xxix.

Indian Weights.

Ghungchi (gongy).—The name of the seed of *Abrus precatorius*. 3=1 vāl ∴ 1=1·91 to 1·94 grs. troy (see vāl); but this value is too high for the ordinary rati, and too low for Tavernier's rati (see under rati on next page).

Carat.—In order to determine the value of Tavernier's carat, we may have recourse to one particular diamond of which he makes mention, namely, that belonging to the Grand Duke of Tuscany, which he figures and states weighed 139½ carats. From the foot-notes in bk. II, ch. xxii, it will be seen that it is practically certain that this stone is the same as the one now known as the 'Austrian Yellow', which weighs, according to Schrauf, 133⅓ Vienna carats, or 133⅗ modern French carats, the latter differing very slightly from English carats. Hence we deduce that Tavernier's carats were about 4 per cent. lighter than the modern French carat.

If we could be quite sure that the melscal of Tavernier was the orthodox Persian mishkāl, weighing about 74 grains troy, we should also have a means of testing the value of his carat, because he gives the weight of Aurangzeb's celebrated topaz in one place as 6 melscals, and in another as 181⅛ ratis, or 157¼ carats (more properly, as the proportion of 8 to 7, it should be 158½ carats), the equivalent of which would be 72·187 grs. troy, and a rati consequently would be equal to 2·66 troy grains, and a carat to 2·98 troy grains, or ·19 less than the modern carat. Tavernier's melscal, however, seems to have been equal to from 78·698 to 80·5 grs. troy (see below), and the carat calculated from the latter equals 3·05 grs. troy—a very close approximation indeed to the modern Florentine carat. From both the above we may conclude that Tavernier's carat differed but slightly, if at all, from the Florentine carat of to-day.

The Rati.—Tavernier, however, further says that 6 melscals =1 once, and, therefore, as the French once=472·687 grs. troy, the rati would be 2·66 grs. troy,[1] which is an approximation to its value (see bk. II, ch. xviii), and a still closer approximation, namely 2·74, if we regard, as above, Tavernier's carat as being 4 per cent. less than the modern carat. The average of these three gives a value of 2·72, which I conclude may have been about the value of the rati uniformly used by Tavernier, but I shall employ the 2·66 grs. as a definitely arrived at sum in future calculations. This was the pearl rati, equal, as he himself tells us, to the 'abbās (see bk. II, ch. xxi, and *Persian Travels*, p. 238), which was used in Persia for weighing pearls. The value of the 'abbās, as given by Kelly

[1] The carat, calculated in the same way, would be similarly enhanced, and would amount to 3·043 troy grains, or within ·127 of the modern value.

in the *Universal Cambist*, is 3·66 diamond, or 2·25 troy grains. This proportion is, I think, incorrect, as 3·66 diamond grs. = 2·9 troy grains, or 1 diamond grain = ·7925 gr. troy.

The ordinary rati (the seed of the *Abrus precatorius*) varied from 1·75 up to 1·9375, the mean of which is 1·843 grs. troy. Mr. Thomas [1] has finally adopted 1·75 in his calculations. The above mean is identical with the value derived from the tolā of Bābur of 177 grs. = 96 ratis. From the mishkāl of Bābur Prof. Maskelyne has deduced values of 1·8425 to 1·85 grs. troy for the rati. General Cunningham [2] and Mr. Laidlay, by weighment of the seeds, obtained 1·823 and 1·825 grs. troy,[3] or only about $\frac{2}{3}$ of the rati of Tavernier. Another weighment by Mr. Blackie in the Bellary District gave an average of 2·142 grs.—the seeds in the south being larger.[4]

Mangelin.—Seed of *Adenanthera pavonina*, L.; it varied as follows;

		If Florentine carat grains.	If ordinary French grains.
In Ramalakota (Raolconda)	= 7 gr.	= 5·38 gr. troy	5·73 gr. troy.
,, Golkonda and Bījāpur	= $5\frac{1}{2}$,,	4·18 ,,	4·5 ,,
,, Goa	= 5 ,,	3·8 ,,	4·095 ,,

Yule, (see *Hobson-Jobson*, 776 f.), gives the average result of the weighment of 50 seeds of *Adenanthera pavonina* as 4·13 grs. troy; selected seeds gave 5·02 to 5·03 grs. troy.

Vāl (from Sanskrit valla) = 3 seeds of *Abrus precatorius*.
32 vāls = 1 tolā (tole) ∴ 1 = 5·733 grs. troy nearly (see tola).
81 ,, = 1 once Fr. ∴ 1 vāl = 5·83 grs. troy.

Melscal of Tavernier.[5] Arabic mithkāl (or mitskāl).

1 melscal = $\frac{1}{6}$ of an once, or 78·698 grs. troy.
6 ,, = $181\frac{1}{8}$ ratis, or $157\frac{1}{4}$ (rather $158\frac{1}{2}$) carats.
∴ 1 ,, = $30\frac{3}{16}$ ratis, or $26\frac{5}{12}$ carats.
$30\frac{3}{16} \times 2{\cdot}66 = 80{\cdot}2$ grs. troy; $26\frac{5}{12} \times 3{\cdot}05 = 80{\cdot}5$ grs. troy.

The average of these, say 83·7 grs. troy, is considerably in excess of the ordinary Persian miskhāl of from 73·69 to 74 grs. troy; but it must nevertheless be accepted as representing approximately the melscal known to Tavernier.

Tolā (tole of Tavernier).—1 tole = 9 deniers 8 grains = 224 French grains = 183·456 troy grains.

[1] *Numismata Orientalia*, new ed., Pt. I, pp. 13–14.

[2] Royal Institution of Great Britain, March, 1860. Cf. V. A. Smith, *Journ. As. Soc. Bengal*, Part I, 1884, p. 147.

[3] *Num. Chron.*, vol. xiii, N.S., 1873, pp. 196–7.

[4] *Proceed. As. Soc. Bengal*, 1887, p. 222. Further inquiry caused Ball to modify his views regarding his value of the rati and carat; see vol. ii, p. 347.

[5] See Barbosa, ed. Dames, i. 157.

The modern British Indian tolā = 180 grs. troy.

Seer or Ser (serre of Tavernier).

In Surat	42 seers	= 34½ livres, bk. II, ch. xii.	
,,	40 ,,	= 34 ,, ,,	
,,	1 seer	= ¾ livre, bk. I, ch. ii.	
Agra	60 seers	= 51¾ livres, bk. II, ch. xii.	
Bengal	1 ,,	= 72 ,,	bk. III, ch. xv.
,,	1 ,,	= for amber, &c. = 9 oz.	

From the above indications of the value of the Surat ser, we may conclude that it averaged nearly 13 French onces, and that the Agra ser was equal to 13·6 French onces. In reference to the Bengal ser, the value 72 livres is possibly a copyist's mistake, and is certainly a blunder (see notes in bk. III, ch. xv). The small Patna ser of 9 onces is probably right.

Thévenot, p. 52, gives the equivalent of the Surat ser at 14 onces, or 35 tolās; and Mandelslo, English ed., p. 67, says 40 sers = 30½ livres, therefore 1 = 12·2 onces. To the Agra seer Thévenot gives the value of 28 onces.

Maund, man, Hind. (mein and men of Tavernier).

Tavernier's ordinary maund		= 69 livres.
Indigo ,,		53 ,,
Surat ,,		42 sers.
,, ,,		40 ,,
,,	(Mandelslo)	40 ,,
,,	(Thevenot)	40 ,,
,,	(Fryer)	42 pounds.

We may therefore conclude that the Surat maund contained about 40 sers, at about 13 French onces to the ser, or 35·5 English pounds avoirdupois.

The maund of Agra contained 60 sers of 13·6 onces, or about 57 lb. av. English, which corresponds approximately with a value of 55 lb. given by Hawkins in 1610.

Measures of Length.

French.

The French lieue is generally given by Tavernier as the equivalent of the coss, but as he recognizes the variability of the latter, it must be considered that the adoption of the European term was determined rather by convenience than by any positive identity having been established by actual measurement. The old lieue de poste of France was equal to 2 miles and 743 yards.

Indian Measures.

The Indian measures which we have to investigate are the tasū (tassot of Tavernier), cubit, coss, and gos.

24 tasūs (tassots) = 1 cubit (aune of Tavernier).
(5000 ?) cubits = 1 coss (cosse [1] of Tavernier).
4 coss = 1 gow (gos of Tavernier).

The tasū (tassot) of Surat, as graphically represented in bk. II, ch. xii, and in *Observations sur le Commerce, &c.*, in the 'Recueil', is exactly equal to 1⅛ in. English. The cubit of Surat was equal to 24 times that amount, in other words to 27 in. In bk. I, ch. ii (see p 32), the ⅛ of a Surat cubit as represented would indicate a cubit of about ½ an inch less, but the same figure is said to be equal to only $\frac{1}{10}$ of the Agra cubit, which would therefore be about 32¾ in. This is very near the Ilāhī gaz of Akbar, namely 33 in. The tasū of Agra was, therefore, about 1⅓ in. English.

The Coss.—As stated above, Tavernier regarded the coss and the lieue as equivalent values, frequent illustrations of which are pointed out in the foot-notes. In bk. I, ch. iv, he speaks of the coss between Surat and Burhānpur as short, a cart being able to traverse one in an hour; but between the latter and Sironj the coss were longer, a cart taking up to five quarters of an hour; between Sironj and Agra they were common coss, of which there were 106; the true distance is about 220 miles. In general, I have found that the true distances indicate a value of 2 miles, approximately, for Tavernier's coss. Thus, between Golkonda and Masulipatam the distance is given as 100 coss, the true distance being about 210 miles. Thévenot speaks of the coss as being equal to half a league; but his lieue must have been a double one, since, in the particular instance just quoted, he represents the distance as being 53 lieues.[2]

The Gos of Tavernier appears to have been the same as the gow (Hind. gau) of some other authors, and this term is at present in use locally both in parts of India and Ceylon; but in the latter country it represents a smaller value than it does in the Peninsula, as stated in the note on page 39. In three different places, bk. II, chap, xii, and in bk. II, ch. xviii, the value of the gos is stated to be 4 lieues; in other words, 4 coss, or say from 8 to 9 miles, which is the value of the gau in S. India at present. According to Tavernier it was the unit of measurement between Surat and Goa, and was also used between Golkonda and the Diamond Mines.

[1] Misprinted coste for cosse in Tavernier's first edition of 1676, and repeated in other editions, but corrected in the errata.

[2] 'They told us the way to the City was seven *Cos* or *Corà* (for 'tis all one) and every *Cos* or *Corrà* is half a *Ferseyna*, or league of *Persia*; so that it answers to little less than two English Miles' (P. della Valle, i. 23). Actual measurements between pillars or Kos-minār, near Delhi, gave a mean of 2 miles, 4 furlongs, 158 yards to the Kos (Bernier, 289).

Travels in India *by* Jean-Baptiste Tavernier

Baron of Aubonne

In 2 Vols.
(Bound in 1)

Vol. 2

Jean-Baptiste Tavernier, Baron d'Aubonne, in 1676 at the age of 74

CONTENTS OF VOL. II

ILLUSTRATIONS

PLATES IN THE ORIGINAL NOT REPRODUCED

Figures of three Rubies belonging to His Majesty.

The Animal which produces Musk.

Cobra di capello.

Banyan Tree and Fakirs.

A Penitent.

Canjare (Khanjar), or Dagger.

Marks on Batavian Reales.

Note.—The Dutch Edition (see ante, p. xi) contains some additional Plates.

PREFACE BY DR. V. BALL

VOL. II

In the course of the preparation of a work of so diversified and complex a character as this, it is almost certain to be the case that, even up to the last moment before publication, matter bearing upon the subject comes to hand. The present occasion, so far from forming an exception to the rule, exemplifies it in a very remarkable degree. The subjects upon which additional information has been acquired during the progress of the printing of these volumes are many ; but there are some in particular which deserve special notice, to which it may therefore be well to call attention here.

Through the kindness of Prof. Joret I have received a pamphlet, written by himself, entitled *Le Voyageur Tavernier (1670–89)*, in which he has pursued his investigations as to the events of the last twenty years of Tavernier's life. As some of these confirm while others modify the conclusions set forth in the Introduction to vol. i, it is desirable to notice them briefly.

Prof. Joret describes his examination of the original manuscripts of Tavernier's *Memoirs*, which are in the possession of M. Schefer at his Château of St. Alban near Chambéry. Without entering into details, it may be said that they completely confirm the view expressed in the Introduction, that the material made use of by Chappuzeau was largely documentary ; that it could have been communicated orally by dictation, the internal evidence, as it appeared to me, sufficiently disproved.

Chappuzeau's work consisted in giving a literary style, such as it was, to Tavernier's simple and rough notes ; but in this work Tavernier himself very possibly assisted. These MS. *Memoirs* contain some details not included in the *Travels*, such as personal expenses and other minor day-to-day notes. The death of M. Ardilière, a subject of some confusion (see vol. i, 25 *n.*), is fixed by the original record as having taken place on the 12th December 1652. And Tavernier's arrival at

Ispahān in 1654 was on the 9th of July, not in May as previously supposed.

It is hoped that this original text may be published, as it would seem, from the glimpse of it thus given by Prof. Joret, that it would to a great extent aid in co-ordinating various statements in the published *Travels* which are now contradictory.

The suggestion that J.-B. Tavernier had been imprisoned in the Bastille on the 13th January 1686 is now shown [1] to be a mistake, and that it was a namesake of his, a Tavernier of Villiers-le-Bel, who was so incarcerated.

Passing the important additional information obtained as to Tavernier's relations with the Elector of Brandenburg, we find that Prof. Joret has reason for concluding that the discovery of the supposed tombstone of Tavernier at Moscow is of a somewhat mythical character; but, be that as it may, an important letter from the Swedish Resident at Moscow, dated 8th March 1689, has been discovered, by which the Swedish Chancellor was informed that Tavernier had died three weeks previously, not at Moscow, but at Smolensk, when on his journey to Moscow.

When in the course of these pages reference was made to the Grand Duke of Tuscany's diamond, it was supposed that the weight given by Schrauf for this diamond, which is now in the Imperial Treasury in Austria, was to be accepted as more correct than Tavernier's; but an examination of Schrauf's original papers shows that he really confirms Tavernier's weight for the stone in a very remarkable way. The present weight is 133⅕ Vienna carats, which are equal to 139¼ of the lighter Florentine carats; and as Tavernier gives the weight at 139½ carats we are justified in concluding that in this case he used, and that in general he was probably in the habit of using, the Florentine carat = 0·1972 grams,[2] or 3·04 grs. troy, *i.e.* 4 per cent. less than the English carat. The previous estimate of the value of the pearl rati given in Appendix, vol. i, having been calculated on the basis of ⅞ths of a modern

[1] M. Douen in *Bulletin de la Société du Protestantisme Français*, vol. xxxiv, 1887, p. 95.

[2] Prof. Church, *Precious Stones*, p. 50, gives the value as 0·1965 grams.

English or French carat, amounted to 2·77 grs. troy; but as $\frac{7}{8}$ths of a Florentine carat only amounts to 2·66 grs. troy, it seems probable that that would more closely approximate to the value of the pearl rati which was used in the weightment of jewels by Tavernier. From the discussion on the weight of Bābur's diamond given in Appendix I (p. 332) of this volume, it will be seen that there is independent testimony by Ferishta in favour of the view that 2·66 approximates more closely to the true value of the rati known to Tavernier and Ferishta. Other confirmatory evidence of this having been the value of the pearl rati will be found in the same Appendix.

A partial and preliminary notice of Tavernier's work has been referred to on p. 100 as having appeared in the *Philosophical Transactions*, to which it should be added that in the same journal abstracts of the contents of the first two volumes were subsequently published.[1]

The reader's attention is invited to the curious facts brought out in Appendix VI, from which it would appear that Chappuzeau obtained access to some of Tavernier's *Memoirs* while the latter was still absent on his last voyage. So far as I can ascertain it has never before been recognized that the *Histoire des Joyaux* and the English version of it, *The History of Jewels*, were founded on Tavernier's original *Memoirs*. This work serves to clear up several points commented on in the footnotes.

During a recent visit to Holland I ascertained that, as stated in the Bibliography (see vol. I, p. iii). there is but one edition of Tavernier's Travels in the Dutch language. It was translated by J. H. Glazemaker, and published at Amsterdam in 1682. A copy of it which I obtained contains a number of engravings by Jan Luyken in addition to copies of the original plates in the French editions.

It is hoped that the present edition of Tavernier's Indian Travels, by drawing attention to the work, will hereafter lead to the further elucidation of many points of interest; and the Editor desires to intimate here, to those who may be willing to assist, that he will gratefully acknowledge all contributions on the subject which he may receive from readers of these volumes.

[1] No. 129, Nov. 20, 1676, p. 711; No. 130, Dec. 14, p. 751.

TABLE OF THE BOOKS AND CHAPTERS

BOOK II (*Continued*)

Historical and Political Description of the Empire of the Great Mogul

BOOK III

APPENDICES

TRAVELS IN INDIA

CHAPTER XII[1]

Concerning the articles of merchandise yielded by the Empire of the Great Mogul and the Kingdoms of Golkonda and Bijāpur and other neighbouring territories.

I CAN easily believe that those who have previously written accounts of the condition of the Empire of the Great Mogul did not feel themselves called upon to give full lists of all the articles of merchandise which it furnishes to foreigners. This I shall endeavour to do from the information I have acquired during the many years I have passed in different journeys in these countries. The reader will, doubtless, cheerfully approve of this research which I have made with so much care, particularly if he is connected with commerce, and desires to know what curiosities art and nature produce, in different places, for the enjoyment of the human race.

It is necessary to remember here, what I have stated at the commencement of the first book, regarding the weights and measures used in India, where I have spoken of the maund and of the ser.[2] It is still necessary to say a word about the cubit.[3]

The cubit is a measure for all goods which can be measured by the ell, of which there are different kinds, as we have different kinds of ells in Europe. It is divided into 24 tasūs,[4] and as the greater part of the Indian merchandise is

[1] In the English translation by John Phillips of 1684, this chapter is numbered x, the two preceding ones having been omitted.

[2] See Appendix, vol. i.

[3] Cobit in the original. According to the figure given by Tavernier of an eighth of a cubit, overleaf, its length must have been 27½ inches. The ordinary hāth of India, measured from the top of the middle finger to the elbow, is 18 inches, but is sometimes increased by the width of the hand or of three fingers.

[4] Tassots in the original. The tasū is properly the breadth of the second and third fingers. At present the Surat gaz, or yard, known as the tailors' yard, is divided into 24 tasū, or in all 28 inches, about 31 tasū equalling the English yard (*Bombay Gazetteer*, ii. 209).

delivered at Surat, there is represented on the margin, a figure of the eighth part of a cubit of the town of Surat, divided into three tasūs.

I ought to commence this list of goods with the most precious of all, namely diamonds and coloured stones ; but, as that subject is somewhat extensive, and is the most important of my accounts, I shall give it separate treatment, and mention is this chapter only silks, cloths, cottons, spices, and drugs, which five classes include all the kinds of merchandise obtained from India.

Concerning Silks.

Kāsimbāzār,[1] a village in the Kingdom of Bengal, can furnish about 22,000 bales of silk annually, each bale weighing 100 livres. The 22,000 bales weigh 2,200,000 livres at 16 onces to the livre. The Dutch generally took, either for Japan or for Holland, 6,000 to 7,000 bales of it, and they would have liked to get more, but the merchants of Tartary and of the whole Mogul Empire opposed their doing so, for these merchants took as much as the Dutch, and the balance remained with the people of the country for the manufacture of their own stuffs. All these silks are brought to the Kingdom of Gujarāt, and the greater part come to Ahmadābād and Surat, where they are woven into fabrics.

Firstly, carpets of silk and gold, others of silk, gold, and silver, and others altogether of silk, are made in Surat. As for the woollen carpets, they are made at Fatehpur,[2] 12 coss from Agra.

[1] Kasembazar in original, elsewhere Cosenbazar, for Kāsimbāzār. The decay of Kasimbāzār, in the Murshidābād District, Bengal, dates from the beginning of the nineteenth century, when its climate, once celebrated for its salubrity, underwent an unexplained change for the worse, so that the margin of cultivation receded and wild beasts increased (*Imperial Gazetteer*, xi. 23). The trade in Indian silk has recently declined according to the figures given by Watt (*Commercial Products*, 1024 ff.).

[2] Vettapour in the original, Fatehpur Sīkrī, which is 23 miles W.S.W. of Agra. See vol. i, p. 73. It was founded as the Metropolis of the Mogul Empire by Akbar in 1570. Previously it bore the name of Sīkrī. Its magnificence is testified by the ruins of palaces and mosques, which still attract many visitors. Its industries were numerous, including silk-spinning, weaving, and stone-cutting. At present the carpets produced there are of an inferior and coarse kind. For the building of

In the second place, satins with bands of gold and silver, some with bands of different colours, and some all uniform are made there, and it is the same with the taffetas.

Thirdly, patoles,[1] which are stuffs of silk, very soft, decorated all over with flowers of different colours, are manufactured at Ahmadābād. They vary in price from 8 to 40 rupees the piece. This is one of the profitable investments of the Dutch, who do not permit any member of their Company to engage in this private trade. They are exported to the Philippines, Borneo, Java, Sumatra, and other neighbouring countries.

As for crude silks, it should be remarked that none of them are naturally white except that of Palestine, of which even the merchants of Aleppo and Tripoli experience difficulty in obtaining but a small quantity. Thus the silk of Kāsimbāzār is yellow, as are all the crude silks which come from Persia and Sicily. But the people of Kāsimbāzār know how to bleach theirs with a lye made of the ashes of a tree which is called Adam's fig,[2] which makes it as white as the silk of Palestine. The Dutch carry their silks and the other goods they obtain in Bengal by the canal [3] which connects Kāsimbāzār with the Ganges; this canal is nearly 15 leagues long. There remains an equal distance to descend by the Ganges to Hugly, where their goods are shipped on board Dutch vessels.

Fatehpur Sīkrī see Smith, *Akbar the Great Mogul*, 104 ff.: for its trade in carpets *Āīn-i-Akbarī*, ii. 181; *Imperial Gazetteer*, xii. 86.

[1] This is from the Kanarese pattuda, 'a silk cloth' (Yule, *Hobson-Jobson*, 686). Terry calls them pintadoes, and extols the art displayed in stitching together 'fresh coloured taffata and pintadoes, and taffata and satin, with cotton wool between, to make quilts'. (*A Voyage to East India*, ed. 1777, 127.) The pintado was properly a chintz. In Bombay the term patolā is applied to the robe worn by a bride (T. N. Mukharji, *Art Manufactures of India*, 360).

[2] Adam's fig is a translation of the Portuguese name for the plantain, Musa paradisiaca. The Musalmāns believe that its leaves were used by Adam and Eve to clothe themselves with in the Garden of Eden. Hence the name. The ash of the plantain resembles that of the potato, as it contains both potash and soda salts, and the percentage of phosphoric acid and magnesia is said to be about the same in both. Ashes of the leaves and roots of the plantain are still used in Bengal for this purpose (Watt, *Dict. Economic Products*, v. 296; F. Buchanan, in Martin, *Eastern India*, iii. 964).

[3] Tavernier has 'canal', probably 'channel'.

Concerning Cotton Cloths, and first of the painted fabrics called Chites.[1]

The chites or painted cotton cloths which are called calmendar,[2] that is to say, painted with a brush, are made in the Kingdom of Golkonda, and particularly in the neighbourhood of Masulipatam ; but the quantity turned out is so small that when one makes requisition on all the workers who manufacture these cotton cloths it is with difficulty that he can obtain as much as three bales. The chites made in the Empire of the Great Mogul are printed, and are of different degrees of beauty, according to the printing and the fineness of the cotton cloth. Those made at Lahore are the coarsest of all, and consequently the cheapest. They are sold by corges,[3] a corge consisting of 20 pieces, and costing from 16 to 30 rupees. The chites made at Sironj are sold at from 20 to 60 rupees the corge or thereabouts.[4] All the chites I am about to speak of are printed cotton cloths, of which bedcovers are made, and also sufras [5] or tablecloths, according to the custom of the country, pillowcases, pocket-handkerchiefs, and especially waistcoats for the use of both men and women, principally in Persia. The chites of bright colours are manufactured at Burhānpur. They are made into handkerchiefs, which are at present much used by those who take snuff, and a sort of veil called ormis,[6] which the women throughout Asia use to put on their heads and wrap about their necks.

[1] Chintzes.

[2] Properly qalamdār, derived from qalam, Hind., a pen or brush. The Persians use the form *qalamkār* (Curzon, *Persia*, ii. 525). Prof. Jadunath Sarkar notes that the correct form of the word, as used in India, is *būqalamūn*, 'of various hues, variegated'. Bernier (p. 270) describes the canopies at the Dīwān-i-'āmm at Delhi : 'the outside of this magnificent tent was red, and the inside lined with elegant Masulipatam chintzes, figured expressly for that very purpose with flowers so natural and colours so vivid, that the tent seemed to be encompassed with real parterres'. For an account of this work see Sir G. Watt, *Indian Art at Delhi*, 1903, p. 259 ff.

[3] Undoubtedly, Sir W. Foster writes, from kōrī, Hind., a score.

[4] The trade at Sironj in Tonk State, Rājputāna, has disappeared (*Imperial Gazetteer*, xviii. 39).

[5] Sufra means literally 'the food of the traveller' ; then 'the receptacle for food', 'a tablecloth

[6] Orhnīs (see i. 43).

The bāftas,[1] or cotton cloths required to be dyed red, blue, or black, are taken uncoloured to Agra and Ahmadābād, because these two towns are near the places where indigo is made, which is used in dyeing. They cost from 2 rupees the piece up to 30 or 40 rupees, according to the fineness and the amount of gold at the ends, and in some also at the sides. The Indians know how to pass some of these cloths through a certain water which causes them to appear like a waved camlet, and these pieces are the dearest.

These kinds of cotton cloth, which cost from 2 to 12 rupees the piece, are exported to the coast of Melinde,[2] and they constitute the principal trade done by the Governor of Mozambique, who sells them to the Kafir who carry them into the country of the Abyssins and the Kingdom of Saba,[3] because these people, who do not use soap, need only simply rinse out these cloths. Those costing 12 rupees and upwards are exported to the Philippines, Borneo, Java, Sumatra, and other islands. The women of these islands have for their sole garment a piece of this cotton cloth, of which, without cutting, one end serves as a petticoat, the remainder being wound round the waist and head.

White Cotton Cloths.

White cotton cloths come partly from Agra and the vicinity of Lahore, partly from Bengal, and some from Baroda, Broach, Renonsari,[4] and other places. They come in a crude condition to Renonsari and Broach, where they have the means of bleaching them in large fields, on account of the quantity of lemons growing in the neighbourhood, for cotton cloths can never be well bleached if they are not steeped in lemon juice.

[1] Bastas in the original, for Bāftas (see vol. i. 54).

[2] Melinda, properly Malinda, an Arab town on the east coast of Africa in S. Lat. 3° 9′ (Yule, *Hobson-Jobson*, 568).

[3] Abyssinia; Saba which was probably the Saboea of Strabo, occupies a large portion of Southern Arabia (*Ency. Brit.*, xxiii. 955 ff.).

[4] With reference to this place, Sir H. Yule states that it is Navsārī or Navasārī in Baroda, and that van Twist, in his *General Description of India* (1638), says that it was 6 Dutch miles (24 English) to the south of Surat, and produced much coarse cloth (*Imperial Gazetteer*, xviii. 425 f.). Only coarse cloths are now made at Navsārī (*Bombay Gazetteer*, vii. 568).

The cotton cloths brought from Agra, Lahore, and Bengal are sold by corges, and cost from 16 up to 300 or 400 rupees and even more, according as the merchant directs them to be made. The cotton cloths from Renonsari and Broach are 21 cubits long when crude, but only 20 cubits when bleached. Those from Baroda are 20 cubits when crude, and 19½ when bleached. The cotton cloths or bāftas from these three towns are of two kinds; for there are both broad and narrow kinds; it is the narrow of which I have just spoken, and they are sold at from 2 to 6 mahmūdīs each. The broad bāftas are 1⅓ cubit wide, and the piece is 20 cubits long. They are commonly sold at from 5 to 12 mahmūdīs, but the merchant on the spot can have them made much wider and finer, up to the value of 500 mahmūdīs the piece. In my time I have seen two pieces of them sold, for each of which 1,000 mahmūdīs were paid. The English bought one and the Dutch the other, and both were 28 cubits long. Muhammad 'Alī Beg, when returning to Persia from his embassy to India, presented Cha Sefi II [1] with a coco-nut of the size of an ostrich's egg, enriched with precious stones; and when it was opened a turban was drawn from it 60 cubits in length, of a muslin so fine that you would scarcely know what it was that you held in your hand.[2] When returning from one of my voyages, I had the curiosity to take with me an ounce of thread, of which a livre's weight cost 600 mahmūdīs,[3] and the late Queen-Dowager, with many of the ladies of the Court, was surprised at seeing a thread so delicate, which almost escaped the view.

Concerning Spun Cotton.

Both spun and unspun cotton come from the Provinces of Burhānpur and Gujarāt. The unspun cottons are not sent to

[1] Shāh Safī or Safavī II (1629–42). Tavernier describes him in the *Persian Travels*, Paris ed., 1676, p. 524. Muhammad 'Alī Beg was treasurer of Shāh 'Abbās and Shāh Safī (Malcolm, *Hist. of Persia*, 2nd ed., i. 365; Manucci, iv. 433).

[2] This must have been like the famous Dacca muslins, upon which such names as ābrawān, 'flowing water', were conferred (Mukharji, *Art Manufactures of India*, 318 ff.; cf. vol. i. 47). It is said that a pair of the kid gloves, formerly made at Limerick, could be enclosed in a walnut shell (*Notes and Queries*, 11th Ser., ii. 297).

[3] i.e. about £22 10*s*.

Europe, being too bulky and of too small value ; they are exported only to the Red Sea, Hormuz, Bassora, and sometimes to the islands of Sonde [1] and to the Philippines. As for the spun cottons, the English and Dutch Companies export large quantities to Europe, but they are not of the finest qualities ; of the kinds exported the maund weight is worth from 15 to 50 mahmūdīs.[2] These are the kinds which are used to make the wicks of candles, and stockings, and to mix with the web of silken stuffs. As for the finest qualities, they are of no use in Europe.

Concerning Indigo.

Indigo comes from different localities of the Empire of the Great Mogul, and in these different localities it is of various qualities, which increase or diminish its price.

In the first place some comes from the territory of Biānā, from Indoua, and from Corsa, one or two days' march from Agra [3] ; this is considered to be the best of all. It is also made at eight days' march from Surat, and at two leagues from Ahmadābād, in a village called Sārkhej.[4] It is from thence indigo cake comes, and some of the same kind and nearly of the same price also comes from the country of the King of Golkonda. The maund of Surat, which is 42 sers, or 34½ of our livres, is sold at from 15 to 20 rupees. Some of the same quality as this last is also made at Broach. As for that from the neighbourhood of Agra, it is made in small pieces like hemispheres, and it is, as I have said, the best in India. It is sold by the maund, and the maund in these regions weighs 60 sers, which are equal to 51¾ of our livres. One generally pays for it from 36 to 40 rupees. Indigo is also produced at 36 leagues from Burhānpur on the road to Surat at a large village called Raout,[5] and other small villages in its neighbourhood ;

[1] Sunda archipelago, in the Sunda straits, where the volcano of Krakatoa is situated. (See vol. i. 154.)

[2] i.e. the maund of 34 livres is worth 11*s.* 3*d.* to £1 17*s.* 6*d.* with the mahmūdi at 9*d.*

[3] Bayānā in Bharatpur State ; Hindaun in Jaipur State ; Khurjā in Bulandshahr District, United Provinces : cf. Mundy, ii. 222 ; Bernier, 292 ; and see W. Foster, *English Factories in India, 1651–1654,* p. 51.

[4] Sarquesse in the original. (See vol. i. 59 *n.*)

[5] Raout, identified by Sir W. Foster with Arāvad in Chopra subdivision, East Khāndesh District, Bombay : see Intro.

and the people there generally sell more than 100,000 rupees worth of it every year.

There is lastly the indigo of Bengal, which the Dutch Company conveys to Masulipatam ; but this indigo and that of Burhānpur and Ahmadābād can be bought cheaper by 30 per cent. than that of Agra.

Indigo is prepared from a plant [1] which is sown every year after the rains ; before preparation it much resembles hemp. It is cut three times in the year, the first cutting taking place when it is about 2 or 3 feet high ; and it is then cut to within 6 inches of the ground.[2] The first leaf is certainly better than those which follow, the second yielding less by 10 or 12 per cent. than the first, and the third 20 per cent. less than the second. It is classified by the colour, determined when a morsel of the paste is broken. The colour of the indigo made from the first crop is of a violet-blue, which is more brilliant and more lively than the others, and that of the second is more lively than that of the third. But besides this difference, which causes a considerable effect on the price, the Indians manipulate the weight and quality, as I shall elsewhere explain.

After the Indians have cut the plant they throw it into tanks made of lime,[3] which become so hard that one would say that they were made of a single piece of marble. The tanks are generally from 80 to 100 paces in circuit, and when half-full of water, or a little more, they are filled up with the cut plant. The Indians mix it and stir it up with the water every day until the leaf—for the stem is of no account—becomes reduced into slime or greasy earth. This done, they allow it to rest for some days, and when they see that all has sunk to the bottom and that the water is clear above, they open the holes made round the tank to allow the water to escape. The water having been drawn off, they then fill baskets with the slime, after which, in a level field, each man sits near his basket, takes this paste in his fingers, and moulds it into

[1] The indigo plant, Indigofera tinctoria, Linn.

[2] This is known as Jarī, or 'root', indigo, because it grows from the plants sown the previous year, as contrasted with Naudhā, 'new sown', that planted annually and ploughed up after the stalks have been cut.

[3] The indigo vats are faced with chunam or lime, which, especially when made from shells, produces a marble-like surface.

pieces of the shape and size of a hen's egg cut in two—that is to say, flat below and pointed above. But the indigo of Ahmadābād is flattened and made into the shape of a small cake.[1] It is to be particularly remarked, that the merchants, in order to escape paying custom on useless weight, before sending the indigo from Asia to Europe are careful to sift it, so as to separate the dust attached to it, which they afterwards sell to the people of the country, who make use of it in their dyes. Those who are employed to sift the indigo observe great precautions, for while so occupied they hold a cloth in front of their faces, and take care that all their orifices are well closed, only leaving two small holes in the cloth for the eyes, to see what they are doing. Moreover, both those who sift the indigo and the writers of sub-merchants of the Company who watch them sifting, have to drink milk every hour, this being a preservative against the subtlety of the indigo. All these precautions do not prevent those who are occupied for eight or ten days, sifting indigo, from having all that they expectorate coloured blue for some time. I have indeed on more than one occasion observed that if an egg is placed in the morning near one of these sifters, if it is broken in the evening, it is found to be altogether blue inside, so penetrating is the dust of indigo.

As the men take the paste from the baskets with their fingers steeped in oil, and mould it in pieces, they expose them to the sun to dry. When the merchants buy the indigo they always burn some pieces in order to see if there is any sand mixed with it. For the peasants who take the paste out of the baskets to separate it into pieces, after they have dipped their hands in oil, place it in the sand, which mingles with the paste and makes it heavier; but when burnt the indigo is reduced to ashes and the sand remains entire. The Governors do all they can to stop this fraud, but there are always some who practise it.[2]

[1] For a similar account of indigo manufacture see Mundy, ii. 221 ff. It will be noticed that there is no reference to the boiling of the precipitated dye after its removal from the vats, a common practice in Northern India, but not essential (Yule, *Marco Polo*, 1st ed., ii. 312, 317; Garcia da Orta, *Simples and Drugs of India*, 51; Watt, *Dict. Economic Products*, iv. 443).

[2] Adulteration of indigo still occurs in some places (Watt, *Dict Econ. Prod.*, iv. 435).

Concerning Saltpetre.

Saltpetre comes in abundance from Agra and from Patna, a town of Bengal; that which is refined costs three times as much as that which is impure. The Dutch have established a depot at Chaprā,[1] which is 14 leagues above Patna; and the saltpetre refined there is sent by river to Hugly. The Dutch imported boilers from Holland, and employed refiners to refine the saltpetre for themselves; but have not succeeded, because the people of the country, seeing that they wished to deprive them of the profits of refining, would not supply them any longer with whey, without the aid of which the saltpetre cannot be bleached, for it is worth nothing at all if it is not very white and very transparent. A maund of saltpetre costs 7 mahmūdīs.[2]

Concerning Spices.

Cardamom, ginger, pepper, nutmegs, mace, cloves, and cinnamon are the several kinds of spices which are known to us. I place cardamom and ginger first, because cardamom grows in the Kingdom of Bījāpur and ginger in that of the Great Mogul, while the other kinds of spices are imported from abroad to Surat, where they constitute an important article of commerce.

Cardamom is the best kind of spice, but is very scarce, and as but a small quantity is grown in the place I have indicated, it is only used in Asia at the tables of the nobles. 500 livres of cardamom are sold at from 100 to 110 reals.[3]

Ginger comes in large quantities from Ahmadābād, where

[1] Choupar in the original (vol. i. 100), Bernier, 440. The crude saltpetre is obtained in India by lixiviation of the soil on deserted and even occupied village sites. It consists of the potash nitrate, and a simple explanation may be given of the chemical reaction which produces it. The nitrogenous waste of the village being brought into contact with potash derived from wood-ash, the ammonia is converted into nitric acid, which combines with the potash, and the salt so formed permeates the soil. A century ago most of the saltpetre of the world which was used for gunpowder came from India. Now there are other sources of supply. See the full account in Watt, *Commercial Products*, 972 ff.

[2] i. e. 5*s.* 3*d.* for 34 livres.

[3] i. e. with the real at 4*s.* 6*d.*, £22 10*s.* to £24 15*s.* On cardamom see Watt, *Commercial Products*, 511 ff.

it grows in greater abundance than in any other part of Asia, and it is difficult to realize the quantity which is exported in a candied condition to foreign countries.[1]

Pepper is of two kinds, one of small size, and the other much larger; these are respectively known as small and long pepper.[2] The long kind is chiefly from Malabar, Tuticorin, and Calicut being the towns where it is purchased. Some comes also from the Kingdom of Bījāpur, and is sold at Rājāpur,[3] a small town of that kingdom. The Dutch who purchase it from the Malabaris do not pay for it in cash, but exchange for it many kinds of merchandise, such as cotton, opium, vermilion, and quicksilver, and it is this long pepper which is exported to Europe. As for the small pepper which comes from Bantam, Achīn, and other places eastwards, it is not exported from Asia, where much is consumed, especially by the Musalmāns. For in a pound of small pepper there are double the number of seeds that there are in a pound of the long; and it is more used in the pulaos, into which it is thrown by the handful, besides which the large pepper is too hot for the mouth.[4]

This small pepper, when delivered at Surat, has in some years been sold at the rate of 13 or 14 mahmūdīs the maund;[5] I have seen it bought at this price by the English, who export it to Hormuz, Bassora, and the Red Sea. As for the long

[1] Zingiber officinale is cultivated all over the warmer and moister parts of India; it grows in great perfection at Kaira and Baroda, as Tavernier says (Watt, *op. cit.*, 1139 ff.). Barbosa (ed. Dames, i. 1918, 25) speaks of ginger in Madagascar, and for Southern India see Yule's note in *Marco Polo*, ii. 316 f. At Calicut 'for the propagation of ginger, they plant a piece of small fresh root, about the size of a small nut, which at the end of a month grows large: the leaf resembles that of a wild lily' (Hieronimo di Santo Stefano, *India in the Fifteenth Century*, Hakluyt Society, iv, p. 4 f.).

[2] See Watt, *Commercial Products*, 896 ff.

[3] Regapour in the original is Rājāpur in the Ratnāgirī District. As a port its importance has much diminished, it being now inaccessible for large vessels by the creek which connects it with the sea, 15 miles distant. In 1660–1 and 1670 it and the English factory were sacked by Sivajī. (See *Imperial Gazetteer*, xxi. 66 f.; cf. vol. i. 146.)

[4] It may be remarked that the whole-pepper obtained in the bazars, and commonly used in cookery in India, is a much smaller, less pungent, and generally inferior seed to that which comes to Europe.

[5] 9*s.* 9*d.* to 10*s.* 6*d.* per 34 livres, with the mahmūdī at 9*d.*

pepper which the Hollanders fetch from the coast of Malabar, 500 livres [1] of it yield them only 38 reals, but on the merchandise which they give in exchange they gain 100 per cent. It can be bought for the equivalent in money of 28 or 30 reals cash, but to purchase it in that way would be much more costly than the Dutch method. As for long pepper, without going beyond the territories of the Great Mogul there is enough to be obtained in the Kingdom of Gujarāt; it is generally sold at the rate of from 12 to 15 mahmūdīs the maund.[2] The wood of long pepper costs but four mahmūdīs.

Nutmeg, mace, clove, and cinnamon are the only spices which the Dutch have in their own hands.[3] The three first come from the Molucca Islands, and the fourth, i.e. cinnamon, comes from the island of Ceylon.

There is one remarkable fact about the nutmeg, namely, that the tree is never planted. This has been confirmed to me by many persons who have dwelt for many years in the country. They have assured me that when the nuts are ripe certain birds which arrive from the islands to the south swallow them whole, and reject them afterwards without having digested them, and that these nuts, being covered by a viscous and sticky substance, fall to the ground, take root, and produce trees, which would not happen if they were planted in the ordinary way.[4] I have here a remark to make upon the subject of the Bird of Paradise. These birds, which are very fond of the nutmeg, assemble in numbers in the season to gorge themselves with it, and they arrive in flocks as flights of

[1] i. e. £6 6*s*. to £6 15*s*.

[2] 9*s*. to 10*s*. 6*d*. for 34 livres.

[3] Most of the cloves of commerce now come from Zanzibar and Pemba, where the tree was introduced early in the nineteenth century: see Barbosa, ed. Dames, vol. i, 1918, p. 28.

[4] This is so far true as regards the fact that the great fruit-eating pigeons are able to swallow large fruits, the stones of which they afterwards reject. These pigeons belong to the genera Carpophaga and Myristicivora, and Ball had often been amazed at the wide gape and the mobility of the articulation of the jaws of these birds. When wounded he had seen them disgorge very large fruits. Several species occur in the Andaman and Nicobar Islands, and other allied species in the Malayan Archipelago. That these birds aid in propagating plants in remote islands by conveying the seeds cannot be doubted. But it is now raised from seed (Watt, 791).

field-fares do during the vintage. As the nut is strong it intoxicates the birds and causes them to fall dead upon the spot, and immediately the ants which abound in the country eat off their feet. It is on this account that it is commonly said that a Bird of Paradise with feet [1] has never been seen. This is, however, not precisely true, for I have seen three or four with their feet intact, upon which the ants had not had time to operate. A French merchant, named Contour, sent one which had feet, from Aleppo, to King Louis XIII, who prized it much for its beauty.

But notwithstanding all the Dutch can do to prevent it, cloves can be obtained at Macassar, in the Isle of Celebes,[1] without the spice passing through their hands, because the islanders buy in secret from the captains and soldiers of the Dutch forts at the places where the cloves grow, giving them in exchange rice and other necessaries of life, without which, being miserably paid, they would be unable to subsist. Whilst commerce was vigorously pushed by the English, they acted as though their object was to destroy that of the Dutch. Having bought a parcel of cloves at Macassar they sent them to all the places where the Dutch were accustomed to deal, and selling them at a cheap price, sometimes even at a loss, by this means they ruined the clove trade of the Dutch. For it is an established custom in India that the first who fixes the price of any article of merchandise constrains all others, by his example, to sell at the same rate during the year. It is for this reason that the Dutch established a factory at Macassar, where their officers raise the price of cloves as high as they can when the King of the Island opens the sale. They make considerable presents to the King in order to induce him to uphold the price, which neither the English nor the Portuguese, in the miserable state in which their affairs are to-day, are able to prevent.[2]

[1] As is well known, the true origin of this fable about the apodas is, that the natives who prepare the plumes of the Birds of Paradise for decorative purposes remove the feet from the skins, and as the birds were in early times only known by these dried and stitched-up skins, the idea spread that they had no feet. Tavernier's explanation shows the tenacity of the myth (*Ency. Brit.*, iii. 978; Linschoten, i. 118; Pinkerton, *Voyages*, ix. 625).

[2] See the account of cloves in Linschoten, ii. 81 ff.

Whenever the people of Macassar have any cloves they pay for the goods brought to them with that spice; payment is also made with tortoiseshell, which is in great demand in all the Empire of the Mogul and in Europe: it is also made with gold dust, by which there is 6 or 7 per cent. to be gained instead of its being lost on the money of the island, although it be gold, because the King alloys it so much. The four places where cloves grow in abundance are the land of Amboine, the land of Ellias, the land of Seram, and the land of Bouro.[1]

The islands of Banda, which are six in number, known as Nero, Lontour, Pouleay, Roseguin, Polleron, and Grenapuis,[2] yield nutmegs in great abundance. The island of Grenapuis is about 6 leagues in circuit, and culminates in a peak from whence much fire issues. The island of Damne,[3] where the nutmeg also grows in great abundance and of large size, was discovered in the year 1647 by Abel Tasman, a Dutch commander.

The prices of cloves and nutmegs, as I have seen them sold to the Dutch in Surat in certain years, were as follows: The maund of Surat is equal to 40 sers, which make 34 of our livres at 16 onces to the livre. A maund of cloves was sold for 103½ mahmūdīs. A maund of mace was sold for 157½; of nutmegs for 56½ mahmūdīs.[4] All the cinnamon comes at present from the island of Ceylon.[5] The tree which produces it closely resembles our willows and has three barks. The first

[1] Amboyna, Gilolo, Ceram, and Boeroe (or Buru), islands in the Molucca Sea.

[2] Pulo Neīrā (i.e. island of palm wine); Lontor (the name of a palm); Pulo Ai or Pulo Wai (i.e. water-island); Rosingen (Rosolanguim of De Barros); Pulo Run (or Rung, i.e. chamber island); and Gunongapi (fire-mountain or volcano). These, with four others, constitute the Banda group. (Crawfurd, *Dict.* 33 ff.; *Ency. Brit.*, iii. 310.)

[3] Tasman discovered Van Diemen's Land, but nutmegs can hardly grow there; possibly Tavernier has made some mistake. The reference is possibly to the Dama Archipelago off the west coast of Cochin-China.

[4] Equal respectively to £3 17*s.* 6*d.*, £5 18*s.* 1½*d*, and £2 2*s.* 4*d.* per 34 livres.

[5] Tennent, *Ceylon*, ii. 161 f.; Watt, *Commercial Products*, 313 ff. On the strange tale of the mode of collecting cinnamon, in Arabia, resembling the way in which Sindbad the Sailor found diamonds, see Herodotus, iii. 111; Sir R. Burton, *Book of the Thousand Nights and a Night*, ed. 1894, iv. 357 ff.

and second only are removed, the latter being considered to be much the best. As for the third, it is not touched, for if the knife cuts it the tree dies. This is an art which the natives learn from their youth. Cinnamon costs the Dutch more than is generally believed. For the King of the island of Ceylon, otherwise called the King of Kandy,[1] from the name of the capital town, being a sworn enemy of the Dutch because they did not keep their promise with him, as I have elsewhere related, sends troops every year with the intention of surprising them when they go to collect the cinnamon. It is for this reason that the Dutch are obliged to have 1500 or 1600 armed men to defend an equal number while engaged in removing the bark of the cinnamon, and they are obliged to feed these labourers for the remainder of the year in addition to the expenditure on the garrisons in several parts of the island. These great outlays enhance the price of the cinnamon; it was not so in the time of the Portuguese, who did not incur this expenditure, but placed all to profit. The cinnamon tree bears a fruit like an olive, but it is not eatable. The Portuguese used to gather quantities of it, which they placed in cauldrons with water together with the small points of the ends of the branches, and they boiled the whole till the water was evaporated; when cooled the upper portion of what remained was like a paste of white wax, and at the bottom of the cauldron there was camphor. Of this paste they made tapers, which they used in the churches during the services at the annual festivals, and as soon as the tapers were lighted the church was perfumed throughout with an odour of cinnamon. They have often been sent to Lisbon for the King's chapel. Formerly the Portuguese procured cinnamon from the countries belonging to Rājās in the neighbourhood of Cochin.[2] But since the Dutch have taken this town, and have become masters of the coast of Ceylon, where the cinnamon grows, they find that what comes from the neighbourhood of Cochin injures the trade, because, being not so good as that of Ceylon, it was sold at a low price, and they destroyed all the places where it grew; thus there is no cinnamon now but that of Ceylon,

[1] Or Candy, as in the original.

[2] Bastard cinnamon. (See vol. i, p. 187.)

which is altogether in their hands. While the Portuguese held this coast the English bought cinnamon from them and usually paid them 50 mahmūdīs for a maund.[1]

Concerning the drugs obtainable at Surat, and those imported from foreign countries, with the price of each, per maund.

Sal Ammoniac costs per maund according to the ordinary price	20	mahmūdīs.
Borax, like the preceding, is brought from Ahmadābād[2] without being refined, and costs per maund	35	,,
Gum-lac,[3] of which I shall speak below .	$7\frac{1}{2}$	,,
,, washed	10	,,
,, in sticks of sealing-wax . .	40	,,
Some kinds cost 50 and 60 mahmūdīs per maund, and even more when musk is added to it		
Saffron[4] of Surat, which is only used for colours	$4\frac{1}{2}$	,,
White Cumin[5]	8	,,
Black Cumin	3	,,
Arlet,[6] small	3	,,
Incense,[7] from the Arabian coast . .	3	,,
Mirrha.[8] The good quality called Mirrha-gilet	30	,,

[1] £1 17*s.* 6*d.*

[2] Probably brought to Ahmadābād from Tibet, but Ball had seen a statement as to its occurrence in Kāthiāwār, which, however, requires confirmation. (Vide, *Economic Geology of India*, p. 498.) There is no evidence of its discovery in Kāthiāwār, but it has been found mixed with common salt in certain lakes in the Panjāb (Watt, *Economic Dict.*, i. 505).

[3] Shellac, produced on certain trees by the Coccus lacca.

[4] Saffron consists of the stigmas of Crocus sativus, L., which was an article of trade at the time the Periplus (ch. 24) was written, and has been cultivated in the East ever since. All the Kashmīr saffron is produced at the village of Pampur, where it causes violent headaches among the people (Elliot & Dowson, *Hist.*, vi. 304 f., 375 ; *Āīn-i-Akbarī*, ii. 357).

[5] The fruit of Cuminum cyminum, L., a small annual indigenous to the Upper Nile regions, spread by cultivation to Arabia, India, China, &c. (Hanbury and Flückiger, *Pharmacographia*, 295.)

[6] Perhaps harlā, the black myrobolan.

[7] The gum resin (olibanum) of Boswellia carterii, Endl. See Barbosa, ed. Dames, 1918, vol. i, p. 65 f.

[8] The precise nature of the trees yielding myrrh is somewhat doubtful.

Mirrha-Bolti, from Arabia	15	mahmūdīs
Cassia [1]	2	,,
Sugar-Candy	18	,,
Asutinat,[2] a kind of grain which is very hot .	1	,,
Fenoüil [3] (Fr.), large	3½	,,
,, small and very hot	1½	,,
Oupelote,[4] root	14	,,
Cointre,[5]	5	,,
Auzerout,[6] from Persia	120	,,
Aloës sucotrin,[7] from Arabia	28	,,
Reglisse [8] (Fr.)	4	,,
Vez-Cabouli,[9] a kind of root	12	,,
Aloe-wood,[10] in large pieces	200	,,
,, in small pieces	400	,,
There is a sort of aloe-wood which, if very oily, costs per maund .	4000	,,

Two varieties from Africa are called Heera Bol (true myrrh) and Bissa Bol (an inferior variety). Arabian myrrh is obtained to the east of Aden (see Hanbury and Flückiger, *Pharmacographia*; Watt, *Commercial Products*, 401).

[1] The fruit of Cassia fistula, L. (Watt, 287).

[2] Mr. Longworth Dames, with much probability, identifies this with Persian a*sbatān* or i*sbatān*, seeds of the wild rue, still used as bazar medicine in the Panjāb (Stewart, *Punjab Plants*, Lahore, 1869, p. 381).

[3] The fruit of Pimpinella anisum, L., cultivated in India (Watt, 887).

[4] Costus or kostus, the root of Aucklandia costus.

[5] Possibly kundur, i. e. frankincense, obtained from Boswellia floribunda carterii, but that has already been enumerated.

[6] For Anzarūt, a gum-resin once known to Europeans as a drug under the name sarcocolla. According to Ainslie (*Materia Medica*, vol. i, p. 381) it is derived from Penœa mucronata, Linn., which yields it by spontaneous exudation; it is a native of Africa. It was used by the Arabs for healing wounds, and by Mesue it was believed to have cathartic properties. According to Dymock's *Vegetable Materia Medica*, 2nd ed., Bombay 1885, it is still largely used by the natives of Western India. Sir H. Yule made the two last identifications.

[7] Socotrine aloes, prepared from the juice of *Aloe perryi*, Linn. (Watt, 59), see Barbosa, ed. Dames, vol. i, 1918, p. 61.

[8] Liquorice, glycyrrhiza (Watt, *Economic Dict.*, iii. 512).

[9] Possibly for bish, Sanskrit visha, i. e. poison, Aconite root (Watt, *Commercial Products*, 20 ff.).

[10] Bois d'aloës. This is the Lignum Aloes of Latin writers and the Aloes-wood of the Bible, quite distinct from the modern aloes, being the inside of the trunk of Aquilaria ovata and A. Agallochum, which contain a fragrant resinous substance of dark colour (Watt, 72 ff.). It was formerly generally used both for incense and for medicinal purposes,
3 but is now only esteemed in the East. From the Portuguese term agila

I shall now make some special remarks about gum-lac, sugar, opium, tobacco, and coffee.

Gum-lac [1] for the most part comes from Pegu, but it also comes from the Kingdom of Bengal; and it is dearer in the latter place because the inhabitants of the country extract from it that beautiful scarlet colour [2] which they use to dye and paint their cotton cloths. Nevertheless, the Dutch buy it to export to Persia, where it is used to produce the colour which the Persians employ in their dyes. That which remains after the colour is extracted is used only to embellish toys [3] made in the lathe, of which the people are very fond, and to make sealing-wax; and be it for the one or the other purpose, they mix whatever colour they desire with it. That which comes from Pegu is the cheapest, though it is as good as that of other countries; what causes it to be sold cheaper is that the ants, making it there on the ground in heaps, which are sometimes the size of a cask,[4] mix with it a quantity of dirt.

or aguila has come the popular name 'eagle-wood'. There is an account of it in Royle's *Illustrations*, &c., and Garcia da Orta devotes his 30th Colloquy to it under the title Linaloes (251 ff.). It is described very concisely in Yule, *Hobson-Jobson*, 335. It is used in the manufacture of the incense-sticks from Burma, which are now well known in Europe. See *Ency. Biblica*, i. 120 ff.

[1] Ball has elsewhere identified the Ἤλεκτρον of Ktesias with shellac. (See 'On the Identification of the Animals and Plants of India, which were known to Early Greek Authors', *Proc. Royal Irish Academy*, 2nd series, vol. ii. No. 6, p. 331, but this is not certain; see Watt, 1054 ff.; *Ency. Biblica*, i. 134 ff. The classical references are collected by Sir J. Frazer, *Pausanias*, iii. 548 f. In the *Revue d'Ethnographie et de Sociologie*, ii. 5, de Morgan points out that electrum, a compound of gold and silver, was collected from the nuggets and dust obtained by washing, and that as the process of separating the metals was unknown, the first Greek coins contained as much as fifty per cent. of silver (Sir P. Sykes, *Hist. of Persia*, 2nd ed. i. 99, note 2) and for an account of the production and manufacture of shellac in Bengal, see Ball, *Jungle Life in India*, 308; McCrindle, *Ancient India as described by Ktesias*, 70.)

[2] The dye consists of the bodies of the female coccus which alone secretes the lac.

[3] Such as the Benares toys, nests of boxes, &c., of the present day. The coloured lac is applied in sticks to the wood surfaces as they revolve in the lathe, after which they require only to be burnished (Mukharji, *Art Manufactures*, 249; Watt, 1063).

[4] Ball suggests that this description may be due to some confusion about white ants' nests. But he failed to find any peculiarity ascribed to the Burma lac which would explain the passage.

On the other hand, in Bengal, the district whence they bring the lac being a kind of jungle full of shrubs, the ants secrete it round the ends of branches, which makes it fair and clean, and it is consequently dearer. The inhabitants of Pegu do not use it as a dye because they receive their cotton cloths ready dyed from Bengal and Masulipatam; and, moreover, they are so uncivilized that they do not engage in any art.[1] There are many women at Surat who gain their livelihood by preparing lac after the colour has been extracted. They give it whatever colour they wish, and make it into sticks like Spanish wax. The English and Dutch Companies export about 150 chests annually. Lac in sticks does not cost more than 10 sols the livre, and it is worth 10 sols the once in France, though it be half mixed with resin.

Moist sugar is exported in quantity from the Kingdom of Bengal, and there is great traffic in it at Hugly, Patna, Dacca, and in other places. During my last visit to India I penetrated very far into Bengal, even up to the frontiers of the neighbouring States. I was told a fact by many old people of the country which should be recorded. It is that sugar kept for thirty years becomes a poison, and that there is nothing more dangerous or rapid in producing this effect.[2] Loaf-sugar is made at Ahmadābād, where the people understand how to refine it; it is called on this account royal sugar. These loaves of sugar generally weigh from 8 to 10 livres.

Opium comes from Burhānpur, a good mercantile town between Surat and Agra. The Dutch buy it there and exchange it for their pepper.

Tobacco[3] also grows abundantly in the neighbourhood of

[1] Tavernier probably knew very little of Pegu, which he never visited. Had he done so he would have found certain arts flourishing there. It is used as a dye in Upper Burma (Scott & Hardiman, *Gazetteer of Upper Burma*, part i, vol. ii, p. 394).

[2] It is not unlikely that there may be still a belief to this effect in India. Ball remembered having heard something of the same kind about rice when kept beyond a certain time. Possibly they both originate in some proverbial saying having reference to storing up articles of food too long.

[3] The practice of smoking tobacco, which was first learnt by the Spaniards from the Cuban Indians in the year 1492, was introduced into Turkey, Egypt, and India about the end of the 16th century; and it spread steadily, though opposed by the severest enactments of both

Burhānpur; and in certain years I have known the people neglect harvesting it because they had too much, and they allowed half the crop to decay.

Coffee grows neither in Persia nor in India.[1] Nevertheless, as some Indian vessels load up with it on their return from Mecca, I give it place here amongst the drugs. The principal trade in it is at Hormuz and Bassora, where the Dutch, when returning empty from Mocha, load up as much as they can, as it is an article which they can sell well. From Hormuz it is exported to Persia, and even to Great Tartary; and from Bassora it is distributed in Chaldee, in Arabia along the course of the Euphrates, in Mesopotamia, and other Turkish provinces —for as for India, it is but little used there. Coffee, which means wine in the Arabian tongue, is a kind of bean which grows at eight days' journey from Mocha, on the road to Mecca. Its use was first discovered by a hermit named Shaikh Siadeli (Sayyid ʿAlī), some 120 years ago or thereabouts; for before him there is no author, ancient or modern, who has mentioned it.[2]

Christian and Muhammadan governments. (See Hanbury and Flückiger, *Pharmacographia.*) For its early use in India see Elliot & Dowson, *Hist.*, vi. 155; Smith, *Akbar the Great Mogul,* 407 f.; Watt, *Commercial Products,* 795 f.

[1] It is perhaps needless to point out that this was written two centuries before the cultivation of coffee became an important industry in Ceylon and Southern India. The history of its introduction into India is very obscure (Watt, 367).

[2] Coffee was first mentioned in European literature in 1573 by Ruwolf. Seventy years later a sample of it was brought from Constantinople to Marseilles by Thévenot. It was first brought to Aden by Shaikh Shihābuddīn Dhabhāni, who died in 1470, hence it is concluded that its introduction was about the middle of the fifteenth century. Niebuhr states that it was first brought from Kaffa in Abyssinia to Yemen by Arabs. It appears to have been cultivated principally at Jabal, whence it was conveyed to Mocha. The Arabic name is *qahwa*, pronounced *kahveh* by the Turks. The plant itself is called *bun*. As Tavernier says, the name *qahwa* was originally applied to wine. (*Vide*, Yule, *Hobson-Jobson,* 232.) Terry's account of the use of coffee in India in his time is of sufficient interest to be quoted in full: 'Many of the people there who are strict in their religion drink no wine at all; but they use a liquor, more wholesome than pleasant, they call coffee, made by a black seed boiled in water, which turns it almost into the same colour, but doth very little alter the taste of the water. Notwithstanding, it is very good

All goods arriving from Agra at Surat, for dispatch of bills of exchange at 5 per cent., for packing, carriage, and customs, according to their classes, are charged with from 15 to 20 per cent.

All gold and silver, whether in ingots or coin, pays 2 per cent. on entering Surat.[1] The merchant does what he can to avoid this charge ; nevertheless, when caught, he is let off with paying double and nothing more. The Princes would like to confiscate the whole sum, but the judges are opposed, and maintain that Muhammad forbade all custom dues and interest on money.[2] I have spoken fully in the second chapter of the first book of the custom dues, the money, both gold and silver, and the weights and measures of India, to which I refer the reader.

CHAPTER XIII

Concerning the frauds which can be practised in manufactures, either by the roguery of the workers or the knavery of the brokers and buyers.

I SHALL follow in this chapter the same order as I have observed in the preceding, with the object of making plain, for the benefit of the merchant, all the frauds which can be effected in silk, cotton cloths, cotton, and indigo, for there are none in the case of spices and drugs.

Frauds in Silken Stuffs.

Silken stuffs vary in breadth, length, and quality. The length and breadth are ascertainable by measurement, the quality depends upon whether the stuffs are uniformly woven, whether the weight is right, and whether there is any cotton introduced into the web, as the Indians very often introduce it.

to help digestion, to quicken the spirits, and to cleanse the blood.' (*A Voyage to E. India*, ed. 1777, pp. 100–1.) The facts are given more fully by Watt, 364 ff.

[1] See vol. i, p. 7.

[2] 'They who swallow down usury shall arise at the Last Day only as he ariseth, whom Satan has infected by his touch' (*Korān*, ii. 276, and other texts collected by Hughes, *Dict. of Islām*, 656 f.).

The Indians, not knowing the art of gilding silver,[1] insert in their striped stuffs threads of pure gold; on this account it is necessary to count the number of threads to see if the stuff contains the requisite quantity, and the same should be done in the case of stuffs striped with silver. As for taffetas, it is only necessary to see whether they have a uniform fineness, and next to unfold some of them to see if they contain any foreign substance to increase the weight, after which each piece should be weighed separately, in order to ascertain whether it is of proper weight.

In Ahmadābād, as I have said, an abundance of these stuffs is made of gold and silk, silver and silk, and of silk alone; and carpets [2] of gold and silver and silk, but the colours of these carpets do not last so long as those of the carpets made in Persia. As for the workmanship, it is equally beautiful. It is for the eye of the broker to observe the size, beauty, and fineness of the work in the carpets worked with gold and silver, and he should judge if it is good and rich. Finally, in the case of carpets, and in other stuffs worked with gold and silver, it is necessary to withdraw some threads to prove them, and to see if they are of the standard which they ought to reach.

Frauds in Cotton Cloths, and, firstly, in White Cloths.

All cotton cloths, both fine and coarse, which the Dutch company order to be made in the Provinces of the Empire of the Great Mogul, are brought in bales to the storehouse at Surat, and delivered to the broker about the months of October and November.

The frauds commonly perpetrated are in respect of the fineness, the length, and the breadth.[3] Each bale contains

[1] The art is now well known in India. For the methods employed see Mukharji, *Art Manufactures*, 226 ff.; Baden Powell, *Handbook of Manufactures and Arts of the Punjab*, 157 ff.

[2] The word in the original here is *tapis*, which should perhaps be translated otherwise than carpet, though that is the ordinary signification of the word. Perhaps table-covers are meant. [See also Index, *s.v.*] For the Alcatifa, 'carpet with long pile', see Yule, *Hobson-Jobson*, 11.

[3] 'It must be observed that all Indian weavers, who work for common sale, make the woof of one end of the cloth coarser than that of the other, and attempt to sell it to the unwary by the fine end, although

about 200 pieces, among which five or six and up to ten pieces may be inserted of less fine quality, thinner, shorter, or narrower than the sample of the bale ; this cannot be ascertained without examination piece by piece. The fineness is judged by the eye, the length and breadth by measurement. But a still greater refinement is practised in India, which is to count the number of the threads which ought to be in the breadth according to the fineness of the sample. When the number is lacking it is thinner or narrower or coarser. The difference is sometimes so imperceptible to the eye that it is difficult to discern it without counting the threads,[1] nevertheless this difference amounts to a considerable sum in the price of a large quantity, for it requires but little to abate an écu or even two écus on a piece when the price is from 15 to 20 écus the piece. Those who bleach these cloths, in order to save something for their own profit out of the quantity of lemons which are required, beat the cloths on stones, and when fine the beating does them much injury and diminishes their price.[2]

It should be remarked that the Indians, when making their cloths, if the piece is worth more than 2 écus, insert at either end threads of gold and silver, and the finer the cloth, the more of these threads do they insert, the price of which amounts to nearly as high a figure as that of the cloth itself. It is for this reason that it is necessary to forbid the workers to insert these threads of gold in cloths ordered to be made for export to France—the gold and silver, which the Indians insert as an ornament in their own cloths and garments, being of no use to the French. But for the cloths ordered for Poland and Muscovy, it is necessary to have the gold and silver in the Indian style, because the Poles and Russians will have nothing to do with the cloths if they have not got the threads of gold and silver. It is necessary also to take care that they do not

every one who deals with them is perfectly aware of the circumstance, and although in the course of his life any weaver may not ever have an opportunity of gaining by this means.' (F. Buchanan, in Martin, *Eastern India*, i. 355.)

[1] The Manchester goods of the present day are subjected to the same examination in India. It is a matter of some notoriety that fraud in connexion with them is not unknown.

[2] The destructive methods of the modern Dhobi or washerman are familiar to all Anglo-Indians.

become black, because people in these countries are unwilling to buy cloths when the gold and silver are black.

As for cloths dyed with indigo, either violet or black, it is necessary to take care that the workers do not blacken the threads of gold at the ends of the pieces, and that they do not beat the pieces too much after being folded, because, in order to make them smooth, they sometimes beat them so much that when one comes to unfold them he finds them broken at each fold.

It should also be remarked that upon the fag end of pieces of cloth the Indians print with a seal and gold leaf an Arabesque flower, which extends the whole width of the piece. But if the pieces are destined for France, it is necessary to forbid the workers to impress this flower, which costs half a piastre, in order to save this sum on the price of the piece. But if it is for exportation to the Indian islands, anywhere in Asia, or even to a certain part of America, it is necessary that the flower should be on the fag end of the pieces, and that it should be preserved entire, otherwise one is unable to sell them.

As for coloured and printed cloths, they are coloured and printed while crude, and it is necessary to take care that the work is finished before the end of the rains, because, when they are washed, the more the waters are disturbed, so much the more do the colours applied with a brush or printing block remain vivid.[1]

It is easy to distinguish the cloths which are printed from those done with a brush, and if the broker is intelligent he will distinguish the difference in the beauty of one painted cloth from another by the cleanness of the work. But for the fineness and other qualities of the stuff, they are more difficult to distinguish than in the case of white cloths, and consequently it is necessary to observe more precaution.

Frauds practised in Cottons.

Cottons are the goods which are always first to be manufactured and the earliest to be delivered in the stores of Surat, because they are all spun in the Province of Gujarāt.

[1] In vol. i, p. 46, this is differently stated, but apparently it is so through an error in the mode of expression.

The frauds possible with them are in weight and quality. The fraud in weight can be effected in two ways, the first by putting the cotton in a damp place, and by inserting in the middle of each skein some substance which increases the weight; the second in not weighing it truly when the broker[1] receives it from the worker or from the merchant who delivers it.

The fraud in the quality is accomplished in only one way, which is by inserting in every maund three or four skeins of worse quality than that at the top, and in a large quantity that may amount to something considerable, for there is a variety of cotton thread which costs up to 100 écus the maund. As these two frauds are practised very often on the Dutch Company, the precaution they are obliged to adopt is this. It is to weigh, in the presence of the Commander and his counsel, and to examine carefully, each maund, skein by skein, to see if there is any fraud in the weight or quality. When that is done the Vice-Commander and those who are appointed under him to make this examination are obliged to attach to each bale a statement of the weight and quality; and when the bale is opened in Holland, if anything is wanting in either of these respects, those who have signed the statement are obliged to pay the loss.

Frauds practised in Indigo.

I have said[2] that the natives withdraw the paste from the baskets containing the indigo, and mould it into pieces with the fingers steeped in oil, and the cakes are then exposed in the sun to dry. The Indians who wish to cheat the merchants lay the cakes on the sand to dry, so that the sand attaches itself and the indigo then weighs more. They also sometimes lay the paste on damp ground, which makes it moist and consequently heavier. But when the Governor of the place discovers these frauds, he inflicts a heavy fine. Such frauds are easily discovered by a broker and Commander experienced in the trade in this kind of merchandise by burning some morsels of indigo, after which the sand which remains becomes visible.

I have still to make a somewhat curious remark regarding

[1] Courtier in original. [2] See p. 9, above.

the brokers of India. These brokers are commonly, as it were, chiefs of their families, for whom they hold all the joint property in trust to turn it to account. For that reason those qualified by years and experience are selected, so that they may be able to secure benefit to all the kinsmen, being both the depositaries and the guardians of their goods. Every evening, when they return from business, and, according to the custom of the Indians, who do not sup, eat some sweetmeats and drink a cup of water, the oldest of the kinsmen assemble at the house of the broker, who renders an account of what he has done during the day, and they hold counsel together as to what should be done in the future. He is especially exhorted to take care of their business, and if possible to defraud rather than be defrauded.[1]

CHAPTER XIV

Concerning the Methods to be observed for establishing a new Commercial Company in the East Indies.[2]

SHOULD any nation desire to establish a Commercial Company in the East Indies, before all things it ought to secure a good station in the country to be in a position to refit its ships, and to lay them by during the seasons when they cannot go to sea. The want of a good harbour is the reason why the English Company has not progressed so well as it might have done, because a vessel cannot last for two years without being refitted, as it is liable to be attacked by worms.

As the route from Europe to the East Indies is long, it is desirable that the Company should have some place at the Cape of Good Hope for watering and obtaining supplies of

[1] See an interesting account of the customs of the Hindu brokers at Goa by Caesar Fredericke, Marchant of Venice, in his *Voyage and Travell* (R. Hakluyt, *Principall Navigations*, Everyman's Library, iii. 206 f.). As regards rights of property mentioned above, 'the normal state of every Hindu family is Joint. Presumably every such family is Joint in food, worship, and estate' (J. D. Mayne, *Hindu Law and Usage*, 2nd ed., 242 f.).

[2] This chapter is also introduced into the supplementary volume of Tavernier's travels entitled *Recüeil de plusieurs relations et traitez singuliers et curieux*, &c., where it is somewhat modified in details.

food, both when going and returning from the Indies, especially when returning, because, the vessels being then loaded up, they cannot carry a supply of water sufficient for a long voyage. In the meantime the Dutch have put this advantage out of the reach of other nations, by means of the fort which they have built at the Cape,[1] and the English have done the same thing at St. Helena,[2] although, by the law of nations and the general consent of the people of Europe, liberty to use these two places of refreshment has been for many years free to the whole world. Nevertheless, there may still be some mouth of a river near the Cape where another fort might be constructed, and this position would be worth more than all that can be made in the island of Daufine,[3] where there is no trade except in the purchase of cattle for their hides. But this trade is so insignificant that it would quickly ruin any Company, and the French have hitherto engaged in it without any advantage to themselves.

My reason for making this suggestion is the fact that in the year 1648 two Portuguese vessels coming from Lisbon to India, desiring to touch at the Cape to take in water, made their observations incorrectly, and the sea being very high, entered a bay 18 or 20 leagues from the Cape on the western side. They found in this bay a river, the water of which is very good, and the negroes of the country brought them supplies of all kinds of river-birds, fish, and beef. They remained there about fifteen days, and before leaving took two of the inhabitants to Goa, intending to teach them Portuguese, and endeavour to draw from them some information as to the trade which could be carried on there.[4] The Dutch

[1] In 1652 Jan van Riebeck built a fort at Table Bay, and in 1671 the Dutch purchased land from the Hottentots and founded the colony: cf. *n.* 5 on p. 305 below (*Ency. Brit.*, v. 237).

[2] The English appropriated the island after the departure of the Dutch in 1651, and built a fort in 1658 (*ibid.*, xxiv. 8). [See Introd.]

[3] The 'Daufine island' of the original stands for the Fort of Dauphin, on the south-east coast of Madagascar. It was held by the French for some years, but was afterwards abandoned (*ibid.*, xvii. 276).

[4] The details in vol. i, p. 173, differ from those here given. The distance is there stated to be 30 leagues from the Cape; the only conclusion which can be drawn is that this bay was a part of, or in the vicinity of, Table Bay. Or he may mean Saldanha Bay; see Pyrard de Laval, i. 22.

Commander at Surat asked me to go to Goa, and ascertain what the Portuguese had learnt from these two negroes ; but a French engineer named Saint Amand,[1] who had the supervision of the forts at Goa, told me that they had not been able to teach them a single word of the language, and had only guessed from their signs that they knew ambergris and elephant's tusks. The Portuguese, nevertheless, did not doubt that they would find gold if they were able to trade with the interior. The revolution in Portugal and the wars with Spain [2] have prevented them from examining this coast more particularly, and it would be well that the Company should examine it carefully without giving offence to the Dutch, or allowing them to suspect its object.

Moreover, it is necessary that the Company should have a port near Surat to lay by and refit its vessels, when delayed by the rainy season. The reason is, that during this bad weather, when it is almost impossible to withstand the violence of the sea, the Mogul, for fear of danger to his fortress at Surat, does not allow any foreign vessel into the river, where otherwise, when unladen, they might remain protected from the destructive storms which last for nearly five months.[3]

The only place suitable for harbouring the vessels of the Company is the town of Diu,[4] which belongs to the Portuguese. The advantages of its position are considerable for many reasons. The area of the town includes nearly 400 houses, and is capable of affording dwellings sufficiently numerous, where the crews of the vessels would find all they required. It is situated on the coast of Gujarāt, at the point of the Gulf of Cambay, facing towards the south-east. Its shape is nearly circular, and more than half the circle is surrounded by the sea. It is not commanded by any heights, and the Portuguese have built some fortifications on the land side which might be easily completed. It has numerous wells of good water, and also a river which falls into the sea near the town, the water

[1] Called St. Amant in vol. i, p. 164, and elsewhere.

[2] 1640–88.

[3] Aurangzeb specially favoured local Musalmān interests, because he regarded Surat as the Gate of Mecca (*Bombay Gazetteer*, ii. 88).

[4] Diu, see vol. i, p. 5.

of which is better than that of Surat and of Suwālī,[1] and the shelter is very commodious for vessels.

The Portuguese, on their first establishment in India, kept a fleet at Diu composed of galleys, brigantines, and smaller vessels, with which they made themselves, for a very long time, masters of all the commerce of the places about to be enumerated, so that no one was able to trade without taking out a passport from the Governor of Diu, who franked it in the name of the Viceroy of Portugal at Goa. The revenue he obtained from these passports sufficed to support the fleet and garrison, and the Governor, who was only appointed for three years,[2] did not omit to accumulate wealth for himself during that time.

Thus, according to the force established in this place, great benefit would result. The Portuguese, feeble as they are at present, do not fail to profit by not having to pay duty for the money they convey into the Kingdoms of the Great Mogul and the King of Bījāpur, nor for the goods which they take there.

When the rainy season is over, the wind being nearly always north or north-east, one can go from Diu to Surat in light boats in three or four tides, but if large vessels are laden, it is necessary for them to coast all round. A man on foot going by land to a small borough named the Gauges,[3] and from thence crossing the end of the Gulf, can go from Diu to Surat in four or five days, but if the season prevents him from making this passage, he cannot reach Surat from Diu in less than seven to eight days, because he must then make the circuit of the Gulf.

The town does not possess any territory outside the boundaries, but it would not be difficult to arrange with the Rājā, or Governor of the Province, and obtain from him as much as may be required for the convenience of the inhabitants. The soil of the neighbourhood is not fertile, and the population around is the poorest in all the Empire of the Mogul. Never-

[1] Suwāli or Swālly, see vol. i, p. 5. No important river falls into the sea at Diu.

[2] See i. 153 above.

[3] Gogo or Gogha on the western side of the Gulf of Cambay (Barbosa, ed. Dames, i. 134 f.: *Imperial Gazetteer*, xii. 301 f.).

theless, there is an abundance of cattle in the jungles, with which the country is covered, so that a buffalo or a cow does not cost more than 2 piastres.[1] The English and Dutch use these cattle to feed their people, in order to save the provision of their vessels during their sojourn at Suwālī.

It is well to remark that experience has shown that the flesh of buffaloes[2] often causes dysentery, which is considered most injurious to crews, but cow beef never gives rise to it.

The Rājā who rules the country bears the title of Governor for life; and this is the case with nearly all the Rājās in the Empire of the Mogul, who were the nobles of the Provinces where their descendants only have the title of Governors.[3] He treats the Portuguese well, because their position as neighbours brings him in money by the sale of his corn, rice, and vegetables, and for the same reason he treats the French still better.

After the establishment of such a position, which should be the principal basis of the trade of the Company, there is nothing more important than to select two men, marked by their wisdom, rectitude, and intelligence in trade, and there should be no regard for economy in their allowances. These two men are intended to serve the Company, one in the position of Commandant or Commander, as the Dutch entitle them, with a council of a certain number of persons for his assistance; the other for the office of broker or merchant, who should be a native of the country, an idolater and not a Musalmān, because all the workmen with whom he will have to do are idolaters. Good manners and probity are above all things necessary in order to acquire confidence at first among these people. It is well to secure like qualities in the private brokers, who are under the direction of the Broker-General,

[1] i. e. about 9*s*.

[2] Both the flesh and milk of buffaloes are at times, if not always, considered unwholesome (Fryer, i. 296). At the present day buffalo beef is thought, and rightly, to be coarse, unpalatable, and liable to breed maggots; it is eaten by none but the lowest classes of the population.

[3] Bernier (p. 210 f.) accurately describes the relations of the Rājās or Chiefs to the Imperial Government. From the context, Tavernier seems to refer to the numerous petty Chiefs of Gujarāt and Kāthiāwār.

in the provinces where the offices of correspondents are established.[1]

Intelligence is not less necessary for these two men, in order that they may detect any adulteration in the manufacture of the goods. It arises, as I have said, either from the trickery of the workmen and merchants or from the connivance of the sub-brokers with them. This adulteration may cause so much injury to the Company that private brokers profit by it sometimes from 10 to 12 per cent. If the Commander and the Broker-General conspire together it is very difficult for the Company to guard against this fraud, but if they are both faithful and wise it will be easy to remedy it by changing the private brokers.

The way in which these officers are able to defraud a Company is this. When a vessel arrives in port, the letters of the Company and bills of lading are handed to him who commands on shore for the particular nation. This Commander assembles his Council, and sends for the broker and gives him a copy of the bill of lading. The broker communicates it to two or three of the merchants who are in the habit of buying wholesale. If the broker and the Commander conspire together to profit, the broker, instead of expediting the sale as he ought, tells the merchants privately that they have only to keep firm and offer such a price. Then the Commander sends for the broker and the two or three merchants. He asks them in the presence of his Council what they offer for the goods mentioned in the bills of lading which have been communicated to them. If the merchants persist in saying that they will only give so much, the Commander postpones the sale for fifteen days, more or less, according as he has reason for being pressed to sell. He causes the merchants to come many times, merely for the look of the thing, and he then takes the advice of the Council in order also to save appearances, and for his own protection; after which he orders the goods to be sold at the merchants' prices.

But although the temptation is great for these two officers,

[1] Some of the contemporary writers describe the importance of the Broker to the Factory (Fryer, i. 127 f.; Ovington, 401; Rawlinson, *British Beginnings in Western India*, 127).

on account of their power, the frequent opportunities, and the absence of their superiors from whom it is easy to conceal the truth, a Company is able to remedy this evil, by making a careful selection of these two officers, and by removing the pretext which the Dutch Commanders and brokers urge, which is that they are constrained to sell quickly to the merchants, wholesale, to avoid the costs of delay.

The fault the Dutch make is, that their officers order all the goods they wish to export from the Mogul Empire, to be made on credit from year to year according to the instructions they have received from Batavia. The cost of this advance is sometimes 12, sometimes 15 per cent., so that as soon as their vessels, laden with merchandise, arrive at the port where they are due, the goods must be sold promptly at the price which the wholesale merchants offer to the brokers, in order to obtain immediate funds to repay the advances made for the preparation of the goods which their vessels carry away, and to obtain credit for the manufacture of the following year.

It is this which gives an opportunity for the understanding between the Commanders and their brokers with the merchants, who profit by the necessity which forces the sales, and besides, this private profit diminishes that of the Company, and a part of the clearest gain is expended in paying the interest of the loan of which we are about to speak. For this interest mounts, from time to time, more or less, according as the Commander and the broker agree to make it increase. In the event of French vessels carrying the same goods as the Dutch, they should carry in addition money for the advances to the artisans who work in the provinces, and for a part of the price of the goods which are being made for the following year. The Company by making this advance escapes payment of the high interest on the loan, namely 12 to 15 per cent., which the Dutch pay ; and it will obtain the very best goods at the lowest price. All the artisans will work more willingly for it on account of this ready money.

The cargo for the vessels should be in readiness before they arrive in port. Being quickly laden they will be able to seize the good season for their return. The Company will not be compelled by necessity to sell at a low price to three or four local wholesale merchants who have made themselves masters of the trade, but its brokers will be able to await the arrival of foreign merchants who will come to carry away its goods, or rather, because they will have the means to have them exported to the places where they will themselves be able to dispose of them.

It should be remarked, besides, that it is profitable to carry gold and silver to India in bullion rather than in coin, because gold and silver are not valued in India except by their standard, and because there is always a deduction on coined money on account of the cost of minting.[1]

Should the broker be unfaithful, he is, moreover, able to come to an understanding with the master of the Mogul's mint, established in every port in the Empire, and to value the gold or silver, coined or in bars, at a lower standard than it really is, by telling the Commander and his Council that in the assay which has been made at the mint it is found to be only of such a standard. But it is easy to prevent this fraud, provided the Commander is upright and intelligent, if he sends for one of the native refiners of gold and silver, who can easily be found, and who understand how to assay metals perfectly, and if he sees it done in his own presence.[2]

This is what the Sieur Waikenton[3] did for the Dutch Company, in whose name he managed a factory at Kāsimbāzār, where he received each year from 6,000 to 7,000 bales

[1] See vol. i, p. 7.

[2] Ball received from Mr. J. Twigg of the N. W. P. Civil Service, the following account of the operations of one of these native assayers, as witnessed by himself. The object assayed was an ornament consisting of an alloy of gold and silver, which was first hammered out thin; it was then heated in nitric acid, the vessel used being a broken glazed English tea-cup; after some time, the silver being then dissolved out, the thin plate of gold was removed and fused with borax, the furnace being an old clay potsherd, and the fuel charcoal burnt under a mouth blow-pipe. The resulting gold button was then weighed, and the silver was precipitated by means of a piece of copper thrown into the solution. The nitric acid had been prepared by distillation of a mixture of saltpetre and iron sulphide (Pyrites). See *Diary of Samuel Pepys*, ed. Wheatley, iii. 103 ff.; *Ency. Brit.*, ii. 776 ff. For modern Indian methods Sir E. D. Maclagan, *Monograph on the Gold and Silver Work of the Panjab*, 4 p. 16 f.

[3] See vol. i. 107.

of silk. He ascertained by this test that his broker, having an understanding with the master of the mint, cheated him of 1½ or 2 per cent. on the quality of the gold and silver which was brought to him from Japan, either in bar or in coin, and that the Company had been defrauded of considerable sums.

The broker is also able to defraud by having an understanding with the master of the mint, or with the person who weighs the gold and silver in bars, coin, or dust by employing too heavy weights, or scales which are not true. It is easy to prevent this fraud if the Commander, assisted by his Council, has them weighed in his presence with a scale and weights proved and stamped, which he keeps by him for the purpose.

One of the most important observations that is to be made on the commerce of the proposed Company and the discipline of its factors is this :—It should forbid the merchants, sub-merchants, the scribes, and sub-scribes, who serve under the Commanders, and the brokers, and also these superior officers, from doing any trade on their own private accounts, because having communication with all the artisans, and obtaining by the correspondence from the other factories information as to the articles of merchandise which will be saleable in the following year, they do not fail to purchase them on their own account, and ship them on the vessels of the Company to the addresses of their correspondents, who share the gain.

The Commander being himself interested, either by closing his eyes, or by a too great laxity, permits them to make this profit on account of their poor salaries.[1] The captain of the vessel is in league with them, because he secretly derives some advantage for allowing them to load and unload. And inasmuch as these officers have little capital, and desire to receive the price on the return of the vessel, they direct their correspondents to sell at from 8 to 10 per cent. below market price, which they can easily do, because, as I shall explain further on, they do not pay custom dues either at Surat or at Gombroon, and because they gain by this means about 26 per cent. ; and so this causes a considerable injury to the Company, and particularly to foreign merchants.

To remedy this disorder it is requisite to profit by the mistake

[1] See p. 37.

of the Dutch, and follow the rule which they have adopted since they realized the extent of this injury after an experience of many years. For, in fine, the Commander is not ignorant of the profit which there is for officials of the house when they load the goods of foreigners on the vessels of the Company, be it for Hormuz, for Bassora, for Mocha, or other places. With respect to Mocha on the Red Sea, the merchants who trade there are allowed one bale free of customs; it is for this reason that among their bales they have always one five or six times larger than the others, which ten or twelve men have difficulty in carrying.[1]

The freight of some vessels amounts to 60,000 rupees, and when the Commander and broker are in league, they sometimes make a third, and even as much as a half, as their profits, besides which a vessel never leaves without the Commander and his wife presenting some rewards to their most faithful servants and slaves of both sexes. To one they give permission to ship six bales, to another eight, and to another ten, more or less, and as the bales in these countries pay freight according to the value of the goods, when a merchant has any bale of great value, amounting sometimes to 20,000 rupees, he agrees for the freight at the best price he is able, and abates one half, at least, in the case of one of these servants or slaves who has received this free permission from his master or mistress.

The pursers also take part in it, but as for the merchants and sub-merchants, they generally disdain these small profits, and content themselves with their own shipments. Another trick is played, when a merchant has some bales of rich goods, such as Deccan caps, which are sometimes worth as much as 400 écus, or the ornis[2] of Burhānpur, of which I have spoken above, which serve to make veils for the ladies of Persia, Constantinople, and other places in Asia and Europe—when, I say, a merchant has some bales of such valuable goods

[1] The early records of the East India Company abound in complaints against the Interlopers, as they are called, who interfered with the Company's monopoly (Yule, *Hobson-Jobson*, 438), and against the trickery of officials (*Court Minutes of the East India Company, 1660–1663*, Index. s.v. Trade, Private).

[2] Orhni (see vol. i: 43).

which should pay high duty to the Prince of the place where they are to be loaded, as soon as they are on board, the purser and captain, who are in league with the merchant, place on each the Company's mark, and after reaching the store of the place where they have been landed with the goods of the Company, they are removed at night in secret to the house of the merchant.

These people are able, moreover, to employ still another artifice. If the merchant is a friend of the Commander he settles with him, and pretending to have bought the bales of merchandise from the Company, which is free from all custom, he is released by paying the 2 per cent., the same as all those who have bought goods from the Company.[1]

The following is the remedy which can check this irregularity. It is necessary to establish in the principal factory a fiscal counsellor to act in the name of the King and by his authority. He should be independent of the General of the Company, in order that he may have the right to keep an eye upon his actions as upon those of the least of the officers.

A man of position is required for this post, who will be resolute and watchful, and has under him a representative at each factory. Each of these representatives, in the exercise of his duties, should observe what is indicated in the following articles :—As soon as he sees a vessel belonging to the Company in the offing, he should go at once, or sometimes, according to the season, he should wait till it has cast anchor. Then the captain of the vessel should deliver no letter to any other person, but should place all in the hands of the representative, who will deliver those of the Company to the Commander. He should take two or three person with him, who will remain on the vessel until it is unloaded, to see that all that is landed belongs to the Company. It is especially necessary that he should take care that the people whom he takes with him do not get drunk, for it often happens on these occasions that the officers of the vessel purposely intoxicate them when they have some contraband goods to send off the vessel, and secretly convey them to the fishing boats which bring them fish and other supplies ; this is done generally at night.

[1] The preceding four paragraphs are omitted in the reprint of the *Recüeil.*

If it is a place where there are islands in the offing, as the time is approximately known when the vessels ought to arrive, the representative of the Fiscal Counsellor should send beforehand, as far out as he can, two or three small boats, to be on the look-out round these islands, and as soon as they have discovered the vessel, they should join her, to prevent any contraband goods being landed on the islands, to which bribed persons might come to carry them secretly to the person to whom they are addressed. He should confiscate all that he discovers in the vessel which does not bear the mark of the Company, or does not belong to foreign merchants. He should have power to dismiss from his post the officer to whom the goods belong, if a subaltern ; but if it be one of the superiors he should give notice to the Chief of the Factory, who, with his Council, may degrade him from his office and confiscate his salary. He may order all letters of private persons to be opened to detect contraband trade and the parties engaging in it. This is why the captain of the vessel is obliged to hand letters over to him ; but he may not open the Company's letters. The proceeds of this confiscation of goods should be applied, one third to the poor of the nation, another third to the Company, and the remainder to the Fiscal and his officers, as is the custom of the Dutch. He will also represent the King in all criminal and civil processes which come before the Commander and his Council, and he will be able to requisition and take part in the name of His Majesty in all kinds of actions. Provided always that this officer is vigilant and a man of integrity, he will be able to render considerable service to the Company.

If the English had established such an official in their factories, they would have had greater profit ; but the officers of that nation pretend that there is no superior power capable of withdrawing the privilege from them after they have once completed their apprenticeship in London, and hold the certificate of their master of having served him well for seven years.[1]

[1] The salaries of the English Company's officials at this period, as stated by Fryer (i. 216), were so small that one would suppose that they could have hardly subsisted without having some private oppor-

This injunction against private trade cannot be too strictly imposed. It is observed to-day with so much strictness amongst the Dutch that when a vessel of that Company is ready to leave Amsterdam, a Burgomaster administers to the captain and all on board a solemn oath that they will content themselves with their wages, two months of which are given in advance, and that they will not trade on their own account; but the conduct of the Company in respect to their wages compels them, in spite of their oaths, to aid themselves by secret traffic in order they may subsist while in their employment.

This is the artifice which they make use of to satisfy their consciences. When they have arrived in India, and see a prospect of obtaining some good employment, they marry as quickly as possible, and trade secretly in their wives' names; this is not always permitted. They imagine that in this way their conscience is relieved. But they are sometimes caught, and I shall give a somewhat amusing example of it, from among many others which I could recount.

The captain of a vessel,[1] a rich man, who troubled himself little about making court to the wives of the Chiefs of the Company, became a butt for their attacks, and was one day stung by some remarks made by Madame la Générale, who was talking to him at Batavia in the presence of many ladies. Without saying a word then, and well knowing all their intrigues, he resolved to revenge himself on the first occasion, which offered itself in this manner.

tunities for trade. The writers had to serve five years at £10 per annum, factors had £20 for three years, merchants £40 during their stay in the service, besides free food and lodging. The President received £500 a year, of which half was reserved at home to be confiscated in case of misdemeanour, in addition to his bond of £5,000. On the rates of pay of the Company's officials in the early period of its operations see Ovington, *Voyage to Suratt*, 392 f.; *Diary of William Hedges*, ii. 11, iii. 189; and the summary by Rawlinson, *British Beginnings in Western India*, 125 f. But it must be remembered that they received diet and lodging gratis from the Company, were allowed profits, often large, from private trade, and to accept presents from merchants and others who had dealings with the Company.

[1] This story is also told in the *Histoire de la Conduite des Hollandois en Asie*, chap. vi, where the [Governor] General is called Matsuker [Maatsuiker, to be quite correct] and the captain or ship Lucifer!

When this captain was about to return from Pulicat to Batavia, the wife of the Governor of the former place, who was in league with Madame la Générale in some private trade, believing that the captain was one of her friends, begged him to ship secretly eight bales of very valuable goods, and to take particular care that they were not wetted, in order to convey them to Batavia; this the captain promised to do, and he placed the bales in a separate place.

On his arrival at Batavia, he first went according to custom, to salute the General and to hand him the letters belonging to the Company. The General is in the habit of keeping the captains to dinner or to supper, according to the hour of their arrival. Some Councillors of India are always present on these occasions, to hear the news, and remain to dine with the General.

At the close of dinner the General asked the captain what news he had from Pulicat, and if the Governor and his wife had not asked for anything to be done for them. 'Nothing,' replied the captain coldly, 'except that Madame, the Governor's wife, specially charged me with eight bales of goods, articles of great value, asked me to keep a good eye on them, so that they should not get damp, and to deliver them on my arrival into the hands of Madame la Générale.' This unexpected reply much surprised the General and those of the Council who were dining with him, and still more Madame la Générale, to whom the Governor,[1] turning, asked somewhat rudely if she carried on trade with the wife of the Governor of Pulicat, which, according to the laws of the Company, would have been criminal. Madame la Générale stoutly defended herself, and protested that she knew nothing of what the captain had said. The General then told the latter that he must be mistaken, and there and then ordered the Fiscal to go and seize the bales, and expose them on the quay to see if they would be claimed by any merchant. After they had remained there for some days without any claimant appearing, they were confiscated; and thus, without scandal, the captain had his revenge for the ill treatment he had received at the hands of Madame la Générale.[2]

[1] [-General].

[2] The previous four paragraphs are omitted in the *Recüeil*.

All the subaltern officers of the Factories should be promoted by grades, from that of the post of sub-writer to that of Commander, so that the expectation of this promotion should encourage them to live decently, and acquire all the niceties and details of the Indian trade which qualify for the highest posts.

It is of the greatest importance not to show any favour in this, and that interest should not give advancement to anyone who has not passed through all the grades ; for one of the things which does most injury to the Dutch trade is that for some years back the higher classes in Holland have sent their sons to India to seek for the posts which secret trade makes so profitable. The access which they obtain to the principal officers or to their wives, whose power is great in this country, causes them to be preferred to those who have no other recommendation than that of long service when any post becomes vacant.

It is true that some years ago the General at Batavia and his Council, seeing the injury this did to the Company, wrote to the Directors that they might send people to India of any quality they please, but that they should not send any more with recommendations ; that in the future these would be of no avail, but would rather injure the advancement of their friends, because it was not fair that favour should precede merit ; that the General and his Council had sufficiently good eyes to recognize the fitness of those sent, and would employ them according as they were worthy and as it was considered proper.

These are all the remarks which I have been able to make in reference to the discipline of the Factories and the methods that a new Company ought to observe for its establishment in the East Indies.

But I was forgetting one thing, which is of importance for a commercial Company, and to which it should pay attention. Up to this hour the Dutch observe this precaution, that they send to India neither captain nor pilot who has not passed through all grades, from a simple ship's boy up to the most important charge, and does not know how to take observations, and is not thoroughly acquainted with the coasts. Moreover, these captains are not of delicate constitutions, and content themselves with a piece of cheese or a slice of beef which has been in pickle for two or three years. And truly they are to be imitated in that respect. It is altogether different with some other nations, who often place on vessels captains who have never seen the sea, and whom favour alone immediately elevates to this post. In addition to which, when they embark they generally require elaborate cuisine appliances, plenty of sheep, calves, fowl, and turkeys, which consume much water, and soil the vessel with their droppings. Economy is the great support of commercial Companies, and it is an article to which those who are Directors should give their particular attention.

CHAPTER XV

Concerning diamonds, and the mines and rivers where they are found; and especially of the Author's Journey to the Mine of Rammalakota.[1]

THE diamond is the most precious of all stones, and it is the article of trade to which I am most devoted. In order to acquire a thorough knowledge of it I resolved to visit all the mines, and one of the two rivers where diamonds were found; and as the fear of dangers has never restrained me in any of my journeys, the terrible picture that was drawn of these mines, situated in barbarous countries to which one could not travel except by the most dangerous routes, served neither to terrify me nor to turn me from my intention. I have accordingly been at four mines,[2] of which

[1] This is Raolconda in the original; for its identification with the modern Ramulkota, properly Rammalakota, see p. 43 below.

[2] The four mines appear to have been—1, Rammalakota (Raolconda); 2, Kollūr (Coulour or Gani); 3, Soumelpour; and 4, the locality on the Kistnā between Rammalakota and Kollūr, which, as pointed out on p. 61, may have been a deserted mine near Damārapād and Malawaram. The point is not quite clear, as in chap. xviii two mines near Rammalakota are mentioned, but there cannot be said to be descriptions of more than three mines in the text. There is ample reason for believing that the diamond mines existing in India in Tavernier's time were far more numerous than he had any conception of (see *Economic Geology of India*, pp. 1–50, and Appendix to this volume). The two rivers he mentions

I am about to give descriptions, and at one of the two rivers whence diamonds are obtained, and I have encountered there neither the difficulties nor the barbarities with which those imperfectly acquainted with the country had sought to terrify me. Thus I am able to claim that I have cleared the way for others, and that I am the first European who has opened the route for the Franks[1] to these mines, which

seem to be—1, the Penner River, below Gandikota, probably in the neighbourhood of Chenūr (see vol. i, 230); and 2, the river he did not visit, which was in Borneo (see p. 359 below).

[1] Tavernier was not aware that he had been preceded by other European visitors to the mines, e.g. Cæsar Fredericke and Methold (see p. 56 *n.*), and, as stated in the previous note, he was probably mistaken as to these being the only mines in India which were known in his time; besides many in Southern India, those at Pannā in Bundelkhand, Sambalpur on the Mahānadī, and Wairāgarh—the Bairagarh of the *Āīn-i-Akbarī* (ii. 230)—were almost certainly open then. We have, too, evidence of the working of a mine by a European at an earlier date. A paper presented by the Earl Marshal of England to the Royal Society (*Phil. Trans.*, vol. xii, 1677, p. 907) states that about the commencement of the seventeenth century (say 1610) a Portuguese gentleman went to Çurrure, i.e. Wajrā Karūr in the Bellary District, and expended a large sum of money, namely 100,000 pagodas or £45,000 in searching for diamonds without success. He then sold everything he had with him, even to his clothes, and on the last day when he could pay the wages of the workmen he had prepared a cup of poison which he intended to take that night if no diamonds were found. In the evening a fine stone of 26 pagodas' weight was brought to him by the workmen. The figures given in the paper indicate a value of 53 troy grains for the pagoda; at that rate 26 pagodas would be equal to 1,378 troy grains, or 434·7 carats. The recognized equivalent of the pagoda is something less, namely 52·56 troy grains (Kelly, *Universal Cambist*). In the same mine, we are told, diamonds of a seize (? ser) weight, namely 9 ounces troy, or 81½ pagodas, i.e. 1362·6 carats, had been found; and as Mīr Jumla took possession of this mine, together with the Carnatic, one cannot help suggesting that it may have been here that the Great Mogul's diamond was found, although Kollūr is particularly mentioned by Tavernier as the mine which produced it. To return to the above-mentioned Portuguese, he took the stone with him to Goa, and to commemorate its discovery put up a stone tablet, on which the following lines were engraved in the Telugu language:—

'Your wife and children sell, sell what you have,
Spare not your clothes, nay, make yourself a slave,
But money get, then to Çurrure make haste,
There search the mines, a prize you'll find at last.'

For further information regarding the early history of diamond mining in India see Watt, *Economic Dictionary*, iii. 93 ff.

are the only places in the world where the diamond is found.[1]

The first of the mines which I visited is situated in the territory of the King of Bījāpur in the Province of Carnatic, and the locality is called Rammalakota,[2] situated five days journey from Golkonda,[3] and eight or nine from Bījāpur. The fact that the two Kings of Golkoṇḍa and Bījāpur were formerly subject to the Mogul, and were then only Governors of the Provinces which they acquired by their revolt, caused it to be said, and to be still said by some people, that the diamonds come from the Empire of the Great Mogul. It is only about 200 years since this mine of Rammalakota was discovered, at least so far as I have been able to ascertain from the people of the country.[4]

All round the place where the diamonds are found the soil is sandy, and full of rocks and jungle, somewhat comparable to the neighbourhood of Fontainebleau. There are in these rocks many veins, some of half a finger and some of a whole finger in width ; and the miners have small irons, crooked at the ends, which they thrust into the veins to draw from them the sand or earth,[5] which they place in vessels ; it is in this earth that they afterwards find the

[1] He here forgets Borneo (see p. 359 f. below).

[2] Raolconda in the original. The proper form of the name, Rammalakota, means in Telugu ' precious stone hill fort '. By means of the route given on p. 73 this locality has been identified with Rammalakota, about 20 miles south of Karnūl (Kurnool), where excavations are to be seen to this day (*Economic Geology of India*, p. 15). The position is fairly indicated on the small map of India which accompanies the Revised French edition of Tavernier's Travels, published at Rouen in 1713. The identification both of it and Coulour have foiled many investigators both in this and the last century. But it is needless to refer here to the various suggestions as to their identification, as the question is now fully set at rest by the identification of the stages on the routes to these mines.

[3] On p. 73 the distance is given as being 17 gos or 68 French leagues. The true distance by the direct route is about 120 English miles.

[4] This evidence for the antiquity of the mine is of but little value, and cannot be relied on.

[5] This description and what follows indicate that the mining was carried on in the rock, not in detrital beds. It is, indeed, now known that the matrix at Rammalakota is an old pebble conglomerate belonging to the ' Karnūl ' series.

diamonds. But as the veins do not always run straight, as some ascend, while others descend, they are obliged to break the rocks, always following the direction of the veins. After they have opened them out, and have removed the earth or sand which may be in them, they then commence to wash it two or three times, and search it for whatever diamonds it may contain. It is in this mine that the cleanest and whitest-watered diamonds are found; but the evil is that in order to extract the sand more easily from the rocks the miners strike such blows with a heavy iron crowbar that it fractures the diamonds, and gives rise to flaws. This is the reason why so many thin stones come from this mine, for when the miners see a stone in which there is a flaw of some size, they immediately cleave it, that is to say split it, at which they are much more accomplished than we are. These are the stones which we call thin (*foible*), which make a great show. If the stone is clean they do not do more than just touch it with the wheel above and below, and do not venture to give it any form, for fear of reducing the weight. But if it has a small flaw, or any spots, or small black or red grit, they cover the whole of the stone with facettes in order that its defects may not be seen, and if it has a very small flaw they conceal it by the edge of one of the facettes. But it should be remarked that the merchant prefers a black point in a stone to a red one. When there is a red one the stone is roasted, and the point becomes black. I learned this trick at length so well that when I examined a parcel of stones which came from this mine, and saw that there were facettes on any of them, especially small facettes, I was certain that there was some speck or flaw in the stone.

There are at this mine numerous diamond-cutters, and each has only a steel wheel of about the size of our plates. They place but one stone on each wheel, and pour water incessantly on the wheel until they have found the 'grain' of the stone.[1] The 'grain' being found, they pour on oil

[1] The word in the original is chemin, or 'way' of the stone. It refers to the discovery of the position of the lines of cleavage, which determines the method to be adopted in the treatment of the stone. For some

and do not spare diamond dust, although it is expensive, in order to make the stone run faster, and they weight it much more heavily than we do.

I have known them to weight a stone with 150 livres of lead. It is true that it was a large stone, which weighed 130 carats after it had been cut, and that the mill was like ours, the large wheel of which was turned by four blacks. The Indians do not agree with us in believing that weighting them causes flaws in the stones. If theirs do not receive any it is because they always have a small boy who holds in his hand a very thin wooden spoon, with which he anoints the wheel incessantly with oil and diamond powder. Besides this their wheel does not go so fast as ours, because the wooden wheel which causes the steel one to revolve is seldom more than 3 feet in diameter.

The Indians are unable to give the stones such a lively polish as we give them in Europe ; this, I believe, is due to the fact that their wheels do not run so smoothly as ours. For, being made of steel, in order to grind it on the emery, of which it has need every twenty-four hours, it has to be taken off the tree, and it cannot be replaced so as to run as evenly as it should do. If they possessed the iron wheel like ours, for which not emery but the file is required, it is not necessary to remove it from the tree in order to file it, and they could give the stones a better polish than they do. I have stated that it is necessary to rub the wheel with emery or to file it every twenty-four hours, and it is desirable that this should be done every twelve hours if the workman is not lazy. For when the stone has run a certain time, the part of the wheel where it has pressed becomes polished like a mirror, and if the place be not roughened by emery or the file, the powder does not stick to it. When it does adhere more work can be done in one hour than in two when there is none on the wheel.

Although a particular diamond may be by nature hard,

details of the methods of Indian lapidaries see Mukharji, *Art Manufactures of India*, 267 ff. ; Baden Powell, *Handbook of Manufactures and Arts of the Punjab*, 193 f. ; on the European methods, *Ency. Brit.*, xvi. 198 f.

having, so to speak, a kind of knot,[1] such as is seen in wood, the Indian diamond-cutters would not hesitate to cut such a stone, although our diamond-cutters in Europe would experience great difficulty in doing so, and as a general rule would be unwilling to undertake it; but the Indians are paid something extra for their trouble.

I come to the government at the mines. Business is conducted with freedom and fidelity. Two per cent. on all purchases is paid to the King, who receives also a royalty from the merchants for permission to mine. These merchants having prospected with the aid of the miners, who know the spots where the diamonds are to be found, take an area of about 200 paces in circumference, where they employ fifty miners, and sometimes a hundred if they wish the work to proceed rapidly. From the day they commence mining till they finish the merchants pay a duty of 2 pagodas[2] per diem for fifty men, and 4 pagodas when they employ a hundred men.

These poor people only earn 3 pagodas[3] per annum, although they must be men who thoroughly understand their work. As their wages are so small they do not show any scruple, when searching the sand, in concealing a stone for themselves when they can, and being naked, save for a small cloth which covers their private parts, they adroitly contrive to swallow it.[4] The chief of all the merchants who embark in mining

[1] Certain points of a stone are often found to be exceptionally hard, as, for instance, when a facet is cut on the angle where two cleavage planes meet, or, so to speak, across the grain of the stone. (See p. 44 *n.*) A difficulty of this nature is mentioned by Messrs. Garrard as having been experienced when the Koh-i-Nūr was recut. (See Professor Tennant's lecture *On Gems and Precious Stones*, Society of Arts, 1852, p. 86.)

[2] Say 16*s*.

[3] Equal to about one rupee or 27 pence per mensem, or less than a penny a day. The rupee is now (1922) worth about 1*s*. 4*d*. In some remote parts of India labour can still be obtained at about that rate, or from 3 pice to an anna, i.e. 1⅛*d*. to 1½*d*.; but wages have greatly increased in recent years.

[4] Owing to the belief which exists in India that diamond dust is a poison (Tod, *Annals of Rajasthan*, ii. 1074; *Āīn-i-Akbarī*, i. 510 note) it is thought by some persons that native miners would not swallow diamonds. I have seen several authentic records of their having done so; Garcia da Orta, (*Simples and Drugs of India*, 343) for instance,

one day pointed out to me one of these miners, who had worked for him for many years, and who had stolen a stone from him which weighed a mangelin, i. e. nearly two of our carats.[1] He had concealed it in the corner of his eye, but it was taken from him as soon as the theft was discovered. In order to prevent these knavish tricks there are always twelve to fifteen watchmen employed by the merchants to see that they are not defrauded. If by chance a stone is found which weighs above 7 to 8 mangelins, it is taken to the master of the mine, who by way of recompense gives a sarpo,[2] which is a piece of cotton cloth to make a turban, of the value of 25 to 30 sols,[3] and generally with it half a pagoda in silver, or else a pagoda,[4] when rice and a plate of sugar are not given.

The merchants who visit the mine to buy, remain in their dwellings, and every morning at from 10 to 11 o'clock the masters of the miners, after they have dined (for the Banians never leave their houses till they have washed and eaten),[5] take their diamonds to show to them. If the parcels are large, and contain many stones of the value of from 2,000 up to 15,000 or 16,000 écus,[6] they entrust them to the foreign merchant for seven or eight days or more in order that he may examine them with care. When the stones have been examined, and are returned by the merchant, if they suit him he should conclude the transaction at once, otherwise the owner of the stones wraps them in a corner of his waist-

refers to cases as evidence that the diamond is not poisonous. Once a diamond had been smuggled away from the mines, its possessor was not only safe, but if it was of large size, and he offered it to the King, either of Golkonda or of Bījāpur, he had every chance of selling it well, and being presented with a robe of honour. (See the *Account of the Diamonds, &c.*, presented to the Royal Society by the Earl Marshal of England, *Phil. Trans.*, vol. xii, 1677, p. 907.)

[1] See Appendix, vol. i.

[2] Sar-o-pā, a complete dress of honour, from head to foot. (See Yule, *Hobson-Jobson*, 808.)

[3] 1*s.* 10½*d.* to 2*s.* 3*d.*

[4] About 8*s.*, if new pagodas.

[5] This may be illustrated by the practices of the Srāvak or Jain Vāniā traders of Western India, who are careful not to eat food which may be contaminated by the presence in it of any animal life (Jagmanderlal Jaini, *Outlines of Jainism*, 69; *Bombay Gazetteer*, ix, part i, 93 ff.).

[6] £450 to £3,600.

band, his turban, or his shirt, and departs, so that one never sees the same stones again, or at least they are mixed with others, when the miner returns with another parcel. When the transaction is concluded the puchaser gives an order for payment on the Shroff or person who issues and receives bills of exchange. If you have agreed to pay in three or four days, and delay longer, you have to pay interest at the rate of 1½ per cent. per month. Most frequently, when the merchant is known to be solvent, a bill of exchange on Agra, Golkonda, or Bījāpur is preferred, but more especially one upon Surat, where, as it is the most famous port in India, the dealers desire to purchase the commodities which come in vessels from foreign countries, and are suitable for their wants.

It is very pleasant to see the young children of these merchants and of other people of the country, from the age of ten years up to the age of fifteen or sixteen, assemble every morning under a tree which is in the town square. Each has his diamond weights in a little bag suspended on one side, and on the other a purse attached to his waistband, which contains as much as 500 or 600 gold pagodas. They seat themselves there awaiting the arrival of anyone who wishes to sell diamonds, either brought from this or from some other mine. When anyone brings a stone he places it in the hands of the eldest of the children, who is, so to speak, the chief of the band ; he looks at it and passes it on to him who sits next. Thus it goes from hand to hand till it returns to the first one without anyone saying a word.

He then asks the price of the specimen, wishing to purchase, if possible ; and if by chance he buys at too high a price he is responsible. In the evening these children count up what they have purchased, and after examining the stones separate them according to their water, weight, and cleanness. Next they price each as they expect to dispose of them to strangers ,and by this they see how far the value exceeds the cost of purchase. They then carry them to the great merchants who always have a number of parcels to match, and all the profit is divided among the children, save only that their chief receives a quarter per cent. more than the others. Young as they are, they know the value of all the stones so well that if one of them has bought a stone and is willing to lose a half per cent., another gives him cash for it. You can seldom show them a parcel of a dozen stones, among which they will not discover four or five with some flaw, point, or defect at the angles.[1]

It remains to be said that these Indians have a high regard for strangers, and especially for those whom they call Franks.[2] Immediately on my arrival at the mine I went to call upon the Governor of the place, who also rules the Province on behalf of the King of Bījāpur. He is a Musalmān, who embraced me and assured me I was welcome—not doubting that I had brought gold with me—for at all the mines of Golkonda and Bījāpur they speak but of new pagodas,[3] which are golden coins—and that I had only to place it in my lodging, where it would be safe, and he would be responsible for all I had. Besides the servants I brought with me he allotted me four others, and commanded them to keep watch on my gold by day and night, and to obey all my orders. Shortly after I had left him he recalled me, and on my return: 'I sent to seek you', he said, 'in order to assure you again that you have nothing to fear—eat, drink, and sleep, and have a care for your health. I have forgotten to tell you to be careful not to defraud the King, to whom 2 per cent. is due on all your purchases. Do not attempt', he continued, 'to do as some Musalmāns did, who came to the mine and combined with the merchants and some brokers to withhold the royalties of the King—saying that they had only purchased to the value of 10,000 pagodas, while they had invested more

[1] 'The Gentoo merchants too use the same method with their children, initiating them, with the first dawn of their reason, into all the mysteries of their trade and contracts, insomuch that it is not uncommon to see boys of ten or twelve years of age so acute and expert that it would not be easy to over-reach them in a bargain.' (J. H. Grose, *A Voyage to the East Indies*, 1757, p. 238.) For the method by which children of the Bania or mercantile castes are trained in mental arithmetic see Russell, *Tribes and Castes, Central Provinces*, ii. 128.

[2] Fringuis for Franguis in the original, for Franks, i.e. Europeans. (See vol. i, 5.)

5 [3] They were worth about 8*s*., more exactly 3½ rupees. (See vol. i, p. 329.)

than 50,000.' I then commenced to purchase, and saw that there was a sufficiently large profit to be made, all being 20 per cent. cheaper than at Golkonda, in addition to which, one sometimes, by chance, met with large stones.

One evening a Banian, poorly clothed, having indeed only a band round his waist and a miserable handkerchief on his head, came towards me politely and seated himself by my side. In this country one pays no attention to dress, and a person who has but a miserable ell of calico about his loins may sometimes have a good parcel of diamonds concealed. I, on my part, treated the Banian with civility, and after he had been seated by me for some time he asked me through my interpreter [1] if I wished to buy some rubies. The interpreter told him to show them to me, upon which he drew a number of small rags from his waistband, in which he had about a score of rings mounted with rubies. After I had examined them I said that they were too small for my purpose and that I sought large stones. Nevertheless, when I remembered that I had been asked by a lady at Ispahān to bring her a ruby ring of the value of about 100 écus, I bought one of his rings which cost me nearly 400 francs. I knew well that he did not value it at more than 300 francs, but willingly risked the additional 100 francs in the belief that he had not sought me to sell the rubies only, and because I understood from his manner that he desired to be alone with me and my interpreter in order to show me something better. As the time of prayer of the Musalmāns approached, three of the servants appointed by the Governor left, and I found an excuse for getting rid of the fourth, who stayed behind to wait on me, by sending him to buy bread, where he remained a sufficiently long time. For all the people of this country being idolaters, content themselves with rice, and do not eat bread, and when a person wishes for it it is necessary to have it brought from a distance, from the fortress of the King of Bījāpur, where the Musalmāns reside. The Banian, seeing that he was alone with me and the interpreter,

[1] From this and other similar references we learn that Tavernier did not acquire a knowledge of Eastern languages. The fact is indeed referred to contemptuously by some of his critics, especially Chardin.

with a good deal of mystery, removed his headdress and untwisted his locks, which, according to the usual custom, were bound round his head. Then I observed a small rag appearing amidst his hair, in which there was concealed a diamond, weighing 48½ of our carats, of beautiful water and of cabuchon[1] shape, three-quarters of the stone clear, save for a small flaw on one side which appeared to penetrate some distance into the stone. The remaining quarter was full of flaws and red spots.

While I examined the stone, the Banian, seeing the attention which I gave to it, said, 'Do not trouble yourself now, you will see it to-morrow morning at your leisure when you are alone. When a fourth of the day has passed', it is thus that they speak,[2] 'you will find me outside the town, and if you wish for the stone you will bring the price of it with you,' and he then stated the amount he wanted for it. For it should be stated *en passant* that after this quarter of the day the Banians, both male and female, disappear into the city or town where they dwell, both to satisfy the ordinary necessities of nature and bathing, as well as to say the prayers which their priests require them to repeat. The Banian having named this hour—because he did not wish anyone to see us together—I did not fail to go in search of him, and carried with me the price he asked, less by 200 pagodas, which I kept apart, in reserve. But in the end, after we had bargained for a short time, I gave him 100 pagodas extra. On my return to Surat I sold the stone to a Dutch captain, and I earned a fair profit from the transaction.

Three days after I had bought this stone a messenger arrived from Golkonda who had been sent by an apothecary, named Boëte, whom I had left at Golkonda to receive and take care of a part of my money, and in the event of the Shroff paying in rupees, he was to change them into golden pagodas. The day after he had received payment, he was attacked by so serious a disorder in the stomach that he

[1] A cabuchon diamond is one merely polished, not cut (*New English Dict. s.v.*).

[2] The day is divided into four pahars which terminate at 9 a.m., 12 m., 3 p.m., and 6 p.m.

died in a few days. He informed me by letter of his sickness, and that he had received my money, which was all in my chamber in sealed bags ; but, as he did not believe that he would survive two days, he exhorted me to hasten my return, because he did not think that my money would be safe in the hands of the servants whom I had left with him. Immediately on receipt of this letter I waited on the Governor to take leave of him, at which he was astonished, and inquired if I had expended all my money. I replied that I had not spent half of it, and that I had still upwards of 20,000 pagodas.[1] He then said that if I wished he would afford me an opportunity of investing it, and that I should certainly not lose upon what he would enable me to buy. He further asked if I was willing to show him my purchases, although he was not ignorant of their extent, since those who sold were obliged to make a return of all to him, on account of the charge of 2 per cent. duty which is due to the King by those who buy. I showed him then what I had bought, and told him what they had cost me. This agreed with the book of the Banian who received the King's dues. At the same time, I paid him the 2 per cent. for the King's dues, on which he remarked that he perceived that the Franks were persons of good faith. He was the more persuaded of this, however, when, drawing forth the stone of 48½ carats, I said, 'Sir, this is not in the Banian's book, and there is no one in the town who knows that I have bought it, nor would you yourself had I not told you. I do not wish to defraud the King of his rights—here is what is due to him on account of the price paid by me for this stone.'[2] The Governor appeared surprised and much edified by my proceeding ; he praised me much, and said that this was an action worthy of an honest man, and that there was not another merchant in the country, either Musalmān or Hindu, who would act in the same manner if he believed that no one was aware of what he had purchased.

[1] i.e. about £8,000, which shows the extent of our author's transactions. At the same time we know that he bought largely on commission for the Dutch officials.

[2] Unlike his usual habit of giving prices, Tavernier carefully omits all mention of what he paid for this stone.

Upon this he summoned the richest merchants of the place, told them the facts, and ordered them to bring with them the best stones they possessed. This was done by three or four of them, and thus I expended my 20,000 pagodas in one or two hours. The transaction having been completed and the money paid, he told the merchants that as they had dealings with an honest man they ought to present me with a souvenir. This they did with a good grace, giving me a diamond worth nearly 100 écus.[1] As for the Governor himself, he gave me a turban and waistband.

I have to record a rather singular and curious account of the manner in which the Indians, whether they are idolaters or Musalmāns, make their sales of all kinds of commodities. All passes in complete silence and without any one speaking.[2] The seller and the buyer sit facing one another, like two tailors, and one of the two opening his waistband, the seller takes the right hand of the buyer and covers his own with his waistband, under which in the presence of many other merchants, who occupy themselves sometimes in the same manner, the sale is completed secretly without any one having cognizance of it. For the seller and buyer talk neither by means of their lips nor their eyes, but only by the hand, which they manage to do in the following manner: When the seller takes the whole hand of the buyer that means 1,000, and as many times as he presses it so many thousands of pagodas or rupees, according to the coin which may be in question. When he takes only five fingers that means 500, and when he takes only one it means 100. By taking only the half up to the middle joint, 50 is meant, and the

[1] £22 10*s*.

[2] This system of selling by means of secret signs has often been described by Indian travellers. For a recent account of it reference may be made to the *St. James's Gazette*, January 20, 1887; and for early notices see Yule, *Hobson-Jobson*, 849 f. The subject has been fully dealt with by Sir P. J. H. Grierson, *The Silent Trade*, Edinburgh, 1903. An early instance is recorded by Pliny (*Nat. Hist.*, vi. 22 (241)) for Ceylon, and by Marco Polo (ii. 416), of laying out goods and allowing the purchaser to leave the value in their place—a variant of the custom described by Tavernier. The form of bargaining noted in the text is recorded by Pyrard de Laval (ii. 179), and is familiar to all who have been present at horse or cattle fairs in India.

end of the finger up to the first signifies 10. This is the whole mystery employed by the Indians in their sales, and it often happens that, in a place where there are many people, a single parcel will change hands five or six times without those present knowing for how much it has been sold on each occasion. As for the weight of the stones, one need not be deceived if he does not buy in secret. For when one buys them in public there is a man specially employed by the King to weigh diamonds, who receives no fees from private persons. When he names the weight, both buyer and seller accept his statement, since he has no interest in favouring either party.

Having completed my business at the mine, the Governor gave me six horsemen, that I might traverse, with greater security, the tract under his authority, which extends up to a river [1] separating the Kingdom of Bījāpur from that of Golkonda. The transit of this river is very difficult, because it is wide, deep, and rapid, and there is neither bridge nor boat. In crossing it the same contrivances are used as those of which I have elsewhere spoken for the passage of certain Indian rivers, for men, for their goods, carriages, cattle, and horses. A round vessel of 10 or 12 feet in diameter made of branches of osier, like our hampers, and covered outside with ox hides, serves in place of a boat,[2] and I have described in the same place how the passengers arrange themselves. Good boats or a bridge over this river might be provided, but the Kings of Golkonda and Bījāpur do not allow this, because the river serves to separate the two Kingdoms. Every evening the boatmen on both banks are obliged to report to the two sub-governors, who reside on either side, at about a quarter of a league from the river, an exact statement of the people, beasts of burden, and merchandise which have crossed during the day.

When I arrived at Golkonda, three days had elapsed since

[1] The Kistnā with its tributary the Bhīmā, which separated the ancient Kingdoms.

[2] Coracles (see i. 235 and 239). Tavernier is probably not correct in saying that they were made of osiers or willow; more probably they were made of bamboo.

the death of Boëte, the apothecary, and the room where I had left him had been sealed with two seals—one that of the Kāzī, who corresponds to the Chief Justice, and the other that of the Shāhbandar, who is the Provost of the merchants. An officer of justice watched the door of the chamber together with the servants whom I had left with the deceased. Immediately on my arrival the fact was announced to the Kāzī and the Shāhbandar, and forthwith they sent for me

After I had saluted them, the Kāzī asked me whether the money which was in the chamber of the deceased was mine, and how I could prove it. I said I had no better proof to show him than the letters of exchange which I had given to the Shroff, and that since my departure he had by my orders paid the sum to the deceased ; that I had instructed the latter in case the Shroff paid in silver to change it into golden pagodas, and forward them to me. Upon this reply, they sent to call the two Shroffs who had paid my bills, to know if it was true, and as they agreed that it was, the Kāzī forthwith ordered his lieutenant to open the door of the room, and see if the seals were intact on all the bags. He did not leave till he had my assurance that I had found the full sum, and that nothing was wanting. I returned with him to make the same declaration to the Kāzī and the Shāhbandar, and to thank them for their trouble, and it ended by my signing a document which they had written in Persian, in which I testified my satisfaction.

The lieutenant told me that I must pay the charges of the burial of Boëte, those due to the persons who had placed the seals, and to the officer who had kept guard at the door of the chamber. These all amounted to but 9 rupees, or 4½ écus of our money.[1] One would not have got off so easily in most places in Europe.[2]

[1] i.e. £1 0*s*. 3*d*.

[2] The story gives the impression that the affairs of the Local Government were well administered.

CHAPTER XVI

Journey of the Author to the other Mines, and concerning the method of searching for Diamonds.

SEVEN days' journey east of Golkonda there is another diamond mine, called Gani in the language of the country, and Coulour in the Persian tongue.[1]

It is close to a large town on the same river which I crossed

[1] This mine has been identified in the *Economic Geology of India*, by the routes in vol. i. 140 and vol. ii. 73 with Kollūr on the Kistnā, where, according to a MS. map by Col. Mackenzie, there was a mine in 1798. The word Gāni is equivalent to the Persian Kān-i, signifying 'mine of'. It is found in use by writers of the present century in connexion with another mine, namely Gani-Partiāl. It is the title for this mine most commonly used in works on mineralogy and precious stones, sometimes considerably modified in spelling, as Garee, &c. But it cannot be correctly used as the name of the mine where the Great Mogul or any other diamond was found. The date assigned to the discovery of this mine by Tavernier, namely about the middle of the sixteenth century, is of no value any more than the period assigned for the discovery of the Rammalakota mine. One hundred years, the native estimate, means a long time,. that is all. Somewhere about the year 1622, William Methold, together with Andreas Socory and Adolf Thomason, visited from Masulipatam certain diamond mines, which the first-named describes as being situated 'at the foot of a great mountayne, not far from a river called Christena', the mining town being 2 miles off, and distant 108 English miles, or 12 Gentine leagues (gows, or gos ?) from Masulipatam. In all respects, save as regards the distance, the description of the mines and the methods of working correspond with Tavernier's account of Coulour or Gani, i.e. Kollūr. The distance given by Tavernier is 36 coss, or 72 miles from Masulipatam—the true distance is about 100 miles. In the *Histoire générale des Voyages*, vol. xiii, p. 20, Methold is misquoted as though he said the mines were but 2 leagues from Golkonda, whereas he says 2 miles from the temporary town, containing 100,000 persons, which had grown up in connexion with the mines. He says that they were closed for a time, in consequence of a demand made by the Mogul for a vyse (i.e. 3 lb. English, Tamil Visai) of the finest diamonds. The farmer paid the King 300,000 pagodas, say £120,000, per annum for the mine, the King retaining all stones above 10 carats. This sum is possibly an exaggeration—*vide Purchas His Pilgrimage*, 1626, vol. v. 1002. There is, as already stated, an account of the diamond mines of Golkonda and Bījāpur in the *Phil. Trans.*, vol. xii, No. 136, 1677. Ruins of houses, &c., and old mines are still to be seen at Kollūr. (See *Kistna Manual*, pp. 170, 244.)

when coming from the other mine,[1] and at a league and a half from the town there are high mountains in the form of a cross. The space between the town and the mountains is a plain where the mine is situated and the diamonds are found. The nearer one searches towards the mountains the larger the stones which are found, but when one ascends too high nothing is found.[2]

It is only about 100 years since this mine was discovered when a poor man, digging a piece of ground where he purposed to sow millet, found a pointe naïve [3] weighing nearly 25 carats. This kind of stone being unknown to him, and appearing remarkable, he carried it to Golkonda, and by good luck addressed himself to one who traded in diamonds. The trader having ascertained from the peasant the place where he had found the stone, was much surprised to see a diamond of such a weight, especially because the largest that had hitherto been seen did not exceed 10 or 12 carats.[4]

The rumor of this new discovery quickly spread abroad throughout all the country, and some persons of wealth in the town commenced to mine in this land, where they found, and where they still find, large stones in greater abundance than in any other mine.[5] There are found here at

[1] i.e. the Kistnā, crossed on the route from Raolconda (i.e. Rammalakota) to Golkonda (see p. 54).

[2] The probable explanation of this is that the diamond-bearing strata do not extend far up the slope.

[3] This term (Latin *nativus*) was applied to natural octahedra and other modifications of the cube which the diamond assumes. 'In this Roca Velha [old rock], there are Diamonds founde that are called Nayfes ready cut, which are naturall, and are more esteemed than the rest, specially by the Indians themselves' (Linschoten, ii. 137); cf. Fryer, ii. 143.

[4] This statement is quite incorrect, as will be seen in Appendix I.

[5] In the paper in the *Phil. Trans.*, which has just been referred to, the largest diamonds are said to have been obtained at the mine of Currure, i.e. Wajrā Karūr in Bellary, where some of a seize (ser ?) weight = 9 ounces troy, or 81½ pagodas, were reported to have been discovered. This mine, though unknown to Tavernier, had been taken possession of by Mīr Jumla about the year 1640. Probably there is some mistake in the weight. In the same paper this Kollūr mine is called Quolure, and it is said to have been the first mine excavated in the Kingdom, but it was then nearly exhausted. Many of the diamonds found there were well formed and pointed, and of good lively white water, others were

present, I say, many stones from 10 up to 40 carats, and sometimes indeed much larger; among others the great diamond which weighed 900 carats before cutting, which Mīr Jumla presented to Aurangzeb,[1] as I have elsewhere related.

But if this mine of Kollūr is of importance on account of the number of large stones which are found there, it is a misfortune that, as a rule, these stones are not clear, and that their water contains indications of the quality of the soil where they are found. If the soil is marshy and humid, the stone tends to blackness; if it is reddish, it tends to red, and so with the other conditions, sometimes towards green, sometimes towards yellow, just as there is diversity of soil in the area between the town and the mountain. Upon the majority of these stones, after they are cut, there always appears a kind of grease which necessitates one always carrying a handkerchief in the hand in order to wipe them.[2]

As regards the water of the stones, it is to be remarked that instead of, as in Europe, employing daylight for the examination of stones in the rough (*brutes*), and so carefully judging their water and any flaws which they may contain, the Indians do this at night; and they place in a hole which they excavate in a wall, one foot square, a lamp with a large wick, by the light of which they judge of the water and the cleanness of the stone, as they hold it between their fingers. The water which they term 'celestial'[3] is the worst of all, and it is impossible to ascertain whether it is present while the stone is in the rough. But though it may not be apparent

yellow, brown, &c., and had a greenish transparent skin. The weights ranged from 6 to a mangelin up to 5 or 6, and even rarely 10, 15, or 20 mangelins each. In consequence of its exhaustion, the King permitted the mine at Melwillee, i.e. Mulavilly or Mulēlī, to be regularly worked in the year 1673.

[1] This statement contains two mistakes. The stone was presented by Mīr Jumla to Shāhjahān, not to Aurangzeb, and in three other places Tavernier gives its weight as 900 ratis or upwards, 787½ carats; the latter misprint has unfortunately often been quoted. (See Appendix I.)

[2] 'Diamond possesses a brilliant "adamantine" lustre, but this tends to be greasy on the surface of the natural stones and gives the rounded crystals the appearance of drops of gum' (*Ency. Brit.*, viii. 158 f.).

[3] Persian *āb-i-āsmānī*, Hind. *pānī āsmānī*.

on the mill, the never-failing test for correctly ascertaining the water is afforded by taking the stone under a leafy tree, and in the green shadow one can easily detect if it is blue.

The first time I was at this mine there were nearly 60,000 persons working there, including men, women, and children, who are employed in diverse ways, the men in digging, the women and children in carrying earth, for they search for the stones at this mine in an altogether different manner from that practised at Rammalakota.

After the miners have selected the place where they desire to work, they smooth down another spot close by, of equal or rather greater extent, round which they erect an enclosing wall of two feet in height.

At the base of this little wall they make openings, at every two feet, for the escape of the water, which they close till it is time for the water to be drawn off. This place being thus prepared, all who are about to engage in the search assemble, men, women, and children, together with their employer and a party of his relatives and friends. He brings with him a figure in stone of the god whom they worship, which is placed standing on the ground, and each person prostrates himself three times before it, their priest, however, offering up the prayer.[1] This prayer being finished, he makes a particular kind of mark upon the forehead of each one with a paste composed of saffron and gum, in order that it may sustain seven or eight grains of rice, which he places upon it.[2] Then they wash their bodies with the water which each of them carries in a vessel, and sit down in ranks to eat that which is presented at the feast given by their employer at the beginning of their work, in order to give them courage and induce them to acquit themselves faithfully. This feast merely consists of a portion of rice to each, which is distributed by the Brahman, because every idolater can eat what is

[1] The prayer is an appeal for protection from the mine spirits, which are much dreaded (Crooke, *Popular Religion and Folk-lore of Northern India*, i. 282 f.),

[2] The sectarial mark, known as tilak or nāma, of which see an illustration in Russell, *Tribes and Castes, Central Provinces*, ii. 102. (See Monier-Williams, *Brahmanism and Hinduism*, 4th ed. 66 f.; Linschoten, i. 255.)

served to him by the hands of the priests. Some among them are so superstitious that they will not eat what is prepared even by their own wives, and prefer to cook for themselves.[1] The plate upon which the rice is placed is made of the leaves of a tree pinned together ; to some extent they resemble our walnut leaves.[2] To each there is also given about a quarter of a pound of melted butter in a little cup of copper, with some sugar.

When dinner is finished, each starts work, the men to excavate the earth, and the women and children to carry it to the place which has been prepared as I have said above. They excavate to 10, 12, or 14 feet in depth, but when they reach water there is nothing more to hope for. All the earth is carried to this place, men, women, and children draw water with pitchers from the hole which they have excavated, and throw it upon the earth which they have placed there, in order to soften it, leaving it in this state for one or two days, according to the tenacity of the clay, until it becomes like soup. This done, they open the holes which they made in the wall to let off the water, then they throw on more, so that all the slime may be removed, and nothing remain but sand. It is a kind of clay which requires to be washed two or three times. They then leave it to be dried by the sun, which is quickly effected by the great heat. They have a particular kind of basket made something like a winnowing fan, in which they place the earth, which they agitate as we do when winnowing grain. The fine part is blown away, and the coarse stuff which remains is subsequently replaced on the ground.

All the earth having been thus winnowed, they spread it with a rake and make it as level as possible. Then they all stand together on the earth, each with a large baton of

[1] This is due to fear of pollution and witchcraft. In South India it is only at the marriage ceremonial eating, or confarreatio, that husband and wife eat together (J. E. Padfield, *The Hindu at Home*, 133, and compare Sir J. G. Frazer, *Pausanias*, iv. 117).

[2] In northern India and the Deccan these are the leaves of the Sāl, Shorea robusta, Gaertn., the giant creeper, Bauhinia vahlii, W. and A., or the Dhāk or Palās, Butea frondosa, Roxb. ; in Western India plantain leaves, or those of the nymphaea lotus are used (Russell, *op. cit.*, ii. 204 ; Forbes, *Oriental Memoirs*, 2nd ed., i. 52 ; Mrs. S. Stevenson, *Rites of the Twice-born*, 240).

wood like a huge pestle, half a foot wide at the base, and pound the earth, going from one end to the other, always pounding each part two or three times; they then place it again in the baskets and winnow it, as they did on the first occasion, after which they spread it out again and range themselves on one side to handle the earth and search for the diamonds, in which process they adopt the same method as at Rammalakota. Formerly, instead of using wooden pestles for pounding the earth, they pounded it with stones, and it was that method which produced so many flaws in the diamonds.

As for the royalties which are paid to the King, the annual wages to the miners for their work, and the presents which are given to them when they find any large stone which they carry to the master whom they serve, all are the same as at the Rammalakota mine.[1] No one hesitated formerly to purchase diamonds which had a green crust on the surface, because when cut they proved to be white and of very beautiful water.

About 30 or 40 years ago a mine situated between Kollūr and Rammalakota[2] was discovered, but the King ordered it to be closed on account of fraud, as I shall explain in a few words. Stones were found in it which had this green crust, beautiful and transparent, more beautiful even than the others, but when one attempted to grind them they broke in pieces. Whenever they were ground by another stone of the same quality which had been found in the same mine they submitted to the grinding without breaking, but were unable to bear the wheel, upon which they immediately flew into pieces. It is on this account that one is careful not to buy those which have been ground in this way, through fear of their breaking, and it is, as I said, on account of the deceptions which have been practised with these stones that the King ordered the mine to be closed.[3]

[1] *Vide ante*, p. 46.

[2] Ball suggests (see *Economic Geology of India*, p. 16) that this mine was situated near Damārapād and Malāwaram on the Kistnā in Lat. 16° 35′, Long. 79° 30′, where old excavations are still to be seen.

[3] A little-known but very important paper on the diamond mines of Golkonda, of which twenty-three are named, and of Visapore, i. e. Bījāpur, of which fifteen are named, is to be found in the *Phil. Trans.*, No. 136, June 25, 1677, vol. xii, p. 907. The anonymous author must have been

While the Messrs. Fremlin and Francis Breton [1] were Presidents at Surat on behalf of the English Company, a Jew named Edward Ferdinand, a free merchant, that is to say not subject to any Company, combined with these two gentlemen, a short time after the mine was discovered, to purchase a stone. This stone was clean and of good form, and weighed 42 carats.[2] Edward went to Europe, and Messrs. Fremlin and Breton placed the stone in his hands to sell to the best advantage, and render an account to them. On his arrival at Leghorn [3] he showed it to some Jew friends, who offered him 25,000 piastres [4] for it. But as he asked 30,000 he was unable to let them have it, and took it to Venice to get it cut. It was well cut, without any injury, but upon being put upon the wheel it immediately broke into nine pieces. I myself was on one occasion deceived by one of these stones, which weighed 2 carats; it broke into small pieces on the wheel when it was only half finished.

CHAPTER XVII

A continuation of the Author's Journeys to the Diamond Mines.

I NOW come to the third mine, which is the most ancient of all, and is situated in the Kingdom of Bengal. You may call it by the name Soumelpour,[5] which is a large town near

in that part of India within ten or fifteen years of Tavernier's last visit. Ball discovered this paper too late, unfortunately, to make use of it in the footnotes to his translation. It contains names, he remarks, which had long puzzled him, owing to the confused way in which they have been introduced into the literature of the subject. Full use has now been made of it in revising Ball's notes, e. g. it has been referred to on pp. 42 and 56–7 above and will be found freely cited by Ball himself in App. II to this volume.

[1] William Fremlin was President of Surat 1638–44, and was succeeded by Francis Breton, who died in 1649 (Rawlinson, *British Beginnings in Western India*, 108 ff.). For 'Ed. Ferdinand' see *Eng. Factories, 1642–1645*, p. xv.

[2] The extent to which investments in diamonds for themselves and their friends in England were made by English officials at a later period is very fully brought out in the letters published by Colonel Yule in his account of the Pitt diamond (see Hedges' *Diary*, Hakluyt Society, iii. 125 ff.).

[3] Ligorne in the original.

[4] Say £5,625.

[5] Among a host of writers of the last century, so far as known, Karl Ritter (*Erdkunde Asien*) and Francis Buchanan (in Martin's *Eastern*

to which the diamonds are found, or rather by the name Koel, which is that of the river in the sand of which they are found. The country through which this river has its course belongs to a Rājā who was formerly a tributary of the Great Mogul, but withdrew from his allegiance during the wars between Shāhjahān and Jahāngīr his father. Immediately on his coming to the throne Shāhjahān sent to demand tribute and arrears of it from this Rājā, and the Rājā, as his property was not sufficient to discharge the whole, quitted the country and took refuge with his subjects in the mountains. Upon the news of the Rājā's first refusal, Shāhjahān, who did not know that he purposed to abscond, but believed that he intended to defend himself, sent an army into his country, where he was persuaded that he would find an abundance of diamonds. It happened otherwise, however, for those who were sent into the country of the Rājā found neither diamonds, inhabitants, nor food, as the Rājā had ordered all the grain which his subjects could not carry with them to be burnt, and this was so effectually done that the greater portion of Shāhjahān's army perished of famine. The final result of the matter was, that the Rājā returned to his country on agreeing to pay a light annual tribute to the Great Mogul.[1]

India, i. 535) alone suggested that this locality was not to be identified with another diamond locality, Sambalpur on the Mahānadī, in the Central Provinces. Ball has been able to show that it was situated in the District of Lohārdagā and subdivision of Palāmau in Chota Nāgpur, and that the Gouel river, as Tavernier calls it, is identical with the Koel, which traverses that District (*Imperial Gazetteer*, xix. 335). It joins the Son not far from the fortress of Rohtās, and so its waters find their way northwards to the Ganges. It is probable that both Sambalpur and Soumelpour derive their names from the Samul tree (*Bombax malabaricum*), and about the site assigned to the latter there are the remains of an old town called Sema—Lat. 23° 35′ N., and Long. 84° 21′ E. As the available details regarding these long-forgotten mines are too long for a footnote, they will be found in an Appendix at the end of this volume. Much information on this chapter will be found in Jadunath Sarkar, *Hist. of Aurangzib*, vol. iii, especially pp. 35 ff.; *Journal, Bihar and Orissa Research Society*, vol. i.

[1] Shāhjahān came to the throne in 1628, but the reference seems to be to the campaign of 1641–2, when Shāista Khān attacked the Chero tribe in Palāmau (L. L. S. O'Malley, *Palāmau Gazetteer*, 20 ff., quoting H. Blochmann, *Journal, Asiatic Society Bengal*, xi, part i, 1871).

The following is the route to be followed from Agra to this mine: From Agra to Halabas, 130 coss; Halabas to Banarous, 33 coss; Banarous to Saseron, 4 coss.

From Agra to Sāsarām [1] you travel eastwards, but between Sāsarām and the mine you turn to the south and come first to a large town—21 coss. This town is that of the Rājā of whom I have just spoken, to whom the country belongs which is traversed by the river in which the diamonds are found.

After this town the traveller reaches a fortress called Rohtās [2]—4 coss. It is one of the strongest places in Asia, situated upon a mountain having six great bastions and twenty-seven pieces of cannon, with three trenches full of water in which there are good fish. There is but a single path by which to ascend the mountain, where there is a plain of half a league or so in area, on which corn and rice are cultivated. There are more than twenty springs which irrigate the soil, and all about the mountain from the base to the top there are precipices covered for the most part with jungle. The Rājās ordinarily held this fortress with

[1] This route is also given in vol. i, pp. 92–9, but the details are very different. Here the stages are Agra; Allahābād; Benares; Sāsarām. In the first place Sāsarām and the large town are here misplaced. The latter is probably the Gourmabad, i.e. Khurramābād or Tilothū of p. 98, but the distance, which there amounts to 27 coss, is here stated to be only 21 coss. The true distance is about 58 miles. After Khurramābād, not before it, Sāsarām comes as the next stage, distant 4 coss, the true distance being 12 miles; but after it again the distance to Rohtās is understated at 4 coss, it being really about 24 miles. These discrepancies may be explained by the fact that Tavernier does not appear to have gone to Rohtās from Sāsarām. If he visited it and the diamond mine, as is probable, he almost certainly did so from Patna, in which neighbourhood he was for some time in 1640 and again in 1665–6.

[2] Rodas in the original—Rohtāsgarh, Lat. 24° 27′ 30″, Long. 83° 55′ 50″. (See *Imperial Gazetteer*, xxi. 322 ff.; Hunter, *Statistical Account of Bengal*, xii. 209–212.) There are also detailed descriptions and plans by F. Buchanan in Montgomery Martin, *Eastern India*, i. 432 ff.; Mundy, ii. 168 f. The capture of the fortress by Mīr Jumla has not been traced. It was captured by Sher Shāh in 1539, but the present buildings were completed by Mān Singh, Viceroy of Bengal and Bihār, in 1654. In 1644 the Governor protected the family of Shāhjahān while he was in rebellion against his father. For Sher Khān's attack see Erskine, *Hist. of India*, ii. 147.

from 700 to 800 men, but at present it belongs to the Great Mogul, who acquired it by skill of that great Captain Mīr Jumla of whom I have so often had occasion to speak. The last Rājā left three sons who betrayed each other; the eldest was poisoned, the second attached himself to the court of the Great Mogul, who gave him the command of 4,000 horse, and the youngest maintains his position in the country by paying tribute like his father. All the Kings of India, successors of Tamerlane, have besieged this place without being able to take it, and indeed two of these Kings died in the city of Sasarām.[1]

From the Fortress of Rohtās to Soumelpour it is 30 coss. Soumelpour [2] is a large town with houses built only of clay, and thatched with the branches of the coco-nut tree.[3] Throughout this march of thirty coss there are jungles which are dangerous, because the thieves, who know that merchants do not visit the mine without carrying money, attack them and sometimes murder them.[4] The Rājā lives half a coss from the town, and in tents placed on an eminence. The Koel passes the fort, and it is in this river that the diamonds are found. It comes from the high mountains to the south and loses its name in the Ganges.[5]

This is the manner in which diamonds are sought for in this river. After the great rains are over, that is to say usually in the month of December, the diamond seekers

[1] Sher Shāh, killed at Kālanjar, his father Hasan Shāh Sūrī, and Islām or Salīm Shāh, son and successor of Sher Shāh, who died at Gwalior, are buried at Sāsarām.

[2] This name is left in its original form in the text, as its identification with Sema, although most probable, has not been absolutely proved.

[3] The coco-nut has been observed nearly as far inland as this locality, but it is possible that the leaves of the Tāl palm (*Borassus flabelliformis*, Linn.) are meant.

[4] Descendants of the thieves belonging to the Dom tribe, especially of the Maghaiya branch, still roam about Palāmau. Out of three occasions when Ball's camp was robbed during seventeen years' travelling in India, two were in this district and the third not very far from its limits.

[5] It joins the Son, which flows into the Ganges. It is possible that Pliny's mention of the Ganges as yielding precious stones may be connected with this fact; but the statement (*Nat. Hist.*, xxxvii. 1, 9) is vague.

await the conclusion of the month of January, when the river becomes low, because at that time, in many parts, it is not more than two feet deep, and much of the sand is left uncovered. Towards the end of January or commencement of February, from the town of Soumelpour and also from another town 20 coss higher up the same river, and from some small villages on the plain, about 8,000 persons of both sexes and of all ages capable of working assemble.

Those who are expert know that the sand contains diamonds, when they find small stones in it which resemble those we call 'thunder stones'.[1] They commence to search in the river at the town of Soumelpour and proceed up-stream to the mountains where it takes its rise, which are situated about 50 coss from the town.[2] In the places where they believe there are diamonds they excavate the sand in the following manner. They encircle these places with stakes, fascines, and clay, in order to remove the water and dry the spot, as is done when it is intended to build the pier of a bridge. They then take out the sand, but do not excavate below the depth of two feet. All this sand is carried and spread upon a large space prepared on the banks of the river and

[1] It is to be noted in reference to these 'pierres de tonnerre', which Ball takes to be ferruginous concretions (but the term is often applied to stone implements), that in the *Tuzūk-i-Jahāngīrī* as translated by Blochmann (J. A. S. B., vol. xl, p. 114) there occurs the following passage: 'When the river contains little water, tumuli and hollows are formed. The diamond diggers know from experience that those tumuli contain diamonds over which insects (?), called by the Hindus jhinga, hover.' Ball thought it just possible that the term chikā or jhingā (shrimps) might in this instance have been applied technically to the particular kind of pebbles which Tavernier denominated as above, and that Blochmann was unaware of the technical application of the term. But this suggestion is very doubtful; see the translation in Elliot & Dowson, *Hist.*, vi. 344 f.

[2] The distance of the source of the river is here very much overstated, but by crossing the watershed, the Sānkh river is met with, and in it diamonds used to be found. (*Vide* map in Appendix III.) The sources of these rivers are close to one another, and there the diamond stratum should be looked for. Unfortunately Ball had not made this identification of Tavernier's site when traversing that part of the country, and there is, so far as he knows, no local tradition of diamonds having been found in the Koel.

surrounded by a low wall a foot and a half high, or thereabouts. They make holes at the base, and when they have filled the enclosure with as much sand as they think proper, they throw water upon it, wash it and break it, and afterwards follow the same method as is adopted at the mine which I have above described.

It is from this river that all the beautiful points come which are called pointes naïves [1] (natural points), but a large stone is rarely found there. It is now many years since these stones have been seen in Europe, in consequence of which many merchants have supposed that the mine has been lost, but it is not so; it is true, however, that a long time has elapsed since anything has been obtained in this river on account of the wars.[2]

I have spoken elsewhere of another mine of diamonds in the Province of Carnatic, which Mīr Jumla, General-in-Chief and Prime Minister of State of the King of Golkonda, commanded to be closed,[3] not wishing that it should be worked further, because the stones from it, or rather from these six mines—for there are six of them, close to one another—were all black or yellow, and not one of good water.

There is, finally, in the Island of Borneo [4] the largest of

[1] i. e. diamonds having crystalline facets and angles. (See p. 57.)

[2] From this circumstantial account it would seem probable that Tavernier visited this locality himself during his stay at Patna in 1640 or in 1666. The statement on p. 41 that he had visited the four mines which he describes and one of the two river washings is puzzling, because, if Gandikota is to be classed as one of the mines, then he describes none of the river washings, as he calls Soumelpour the third 'mine' on p. 62.

[3] This appears to be a different case from that mentioned on p. 61, where the green crust and friability of the diamonds caused the mines to be closed. It is probably the one which Mīr Jumla told Tavernier of at Gandikota (vol. i, p. 230).

[4] In 1609 Captain John Saris found a considerable trade being carried on at Soekadana in the diamonds which he says were found in great abundance there and in the river Lave. He says they were obtained, as pearls are, by diving. In a footnote to Linschoten's *Travels* (Hakluyt Society, vol. ii, p. 137 f.), Mr. Tiele gives an explanation of a statement, first made, it is believed, by Garcia da Orta (p. 343), that diamonds were found at Taniapura in Malacca. Here Malacca, it seems, means Borneo, and Taniapura stands for Tandjongpura. There is hardly a work on

all the islands in the world, a river called Succadan, in the sand of which beautiful stones are found, which have the same hardness as those of the river Koel, or of the other mines of which I have made mention.

General Vandime once sent me at Surat six of them, of 3 to 4 carats each, from Batavia, and he believed that they were not so hard as those from other mines, in which he was mistaken, because there is no difference in that respect; it was in order to ascertain the fact that he sent them to me. When I was at Batavia one of the chief officers of the Company showed me a point naive of 25½ carats, a perfect stone, obtained in this river of Succadan. But at the price which he told me it had cost him he had paid more than 50 per cent. than I should have been willing to give for it. It is true that I have always heard that these stones are very dear. The principal reason which has prevented me from going to this river of Borneo is that the Queen of the Island does not allow foreigners to carry away the stones, and there are great difficulties in conveying them thence—the insignificant number which are carried away secretly are sold at Batavia. I shall be asked, without doubt, why I only mention the Queen of Borneo, and not the King. The reason is that in this Kingdom it is the women who govern and not the men, because the people are so particular about having for their sovereign a legitimate heir to the throne that, the husband not being certain that the children which he believes he has had by his wife are his very own, and the wife being, on the contrary, quite certain that the children are hers,

precious stones which does not erroneously cite Malacca as a diamond locality. Mr. D. F. A. Hervey states that Tanjongpura is situated about 30 miles up the river Pāwan in the northern portion of the Mātang District adjoining Soekadana, according to De Carubee's Netherlands India Maps. The question of the distribution and mode of occurrence of diamonds in Borneo, though now well understood, is too large to enter upon here. Probably the best account is by Dr. Theodor Posewitz. (Vide *Mith. a. d. Jahrb. d. Kgl. Ung. Geolog. Anst.*, Bd. vii, 1885; see Appendix.) On diamonds at Soekadana see Purchas, *Pilgrimes*, ed. 1625, i. 223, 393. 'Borneo is amazingly rich in minerals, gold, silver, coal, iron, and even diamonds being won from it, mostly by the industrious Chinese' (*The Times*, 24 May, 1921).

they prefer to have a woman for their ruler, to whom they give the title of Queen, her husband being her subject, and not having more power than that which she chooses to confer upon him.[1]

CHAPTER XVIII

The different kinds of Weights for weighing Diamonds at the Mines; the kinds of Gold and Silver in circulation; the routes by which one is able to travel; and the rule in use for the estimation of the Prices of Diamonds.

I COME now to some details as to the traffic in diamonds and in order that the reader may understand this easily believing that no one has previously written of this matter[2] I shall speak in the first instance of the different kinds of weights which are in use, both at the mines and in other places in Asia.

At the mine of Rammalakota they weigh by mangelins, and the mangelin is equal to 1¾ carats, that is to say, 7 grains.[3] At the mine of Gani[4] or Kollūr the same weights are used. At the mine of Soumelpour in Bengal they weigh by ratis, and the rati is ⅞ths of a carat, or 3½ grains.[5] This last weight is used throughout the whole of the Empire of the Great Mogul. In the Kingdoms of Golkonda and Bījāpur mangelins are also used, but the mangelin in these places is only 1⅜

[1] Descent by the mother's side obtains in some other Oriental countries, and is observed among the Nāvars of Malabar. This is one of the many incidents connected with the widely spread legends of the Kingdom of Women. The belief was current that Achīn was always ruled by a woman. On the death of the King in 1641 a Queen did reign long enough to give rise to the story: v. 294 below. (See Temple's note on Bowrey, i. 295; Fryer, i. 121.)

[2] In this Tavernier was mistaken, several Portuguese writers having treated of this subject before his time.

[3] Seven modern diamond grains = 5·55 grains troy, the proportion being 3·17 troy grains to the carat of 4 diamond grains.

[4] See p. 56 for meaning of Gani.

[5] This (= 2·77 troy grains) was the pearl rati, much greater than the ordinary ratī, which varied from 1·75 to 1·84 grains troy, or even more. (See on this point vol. i, Appendix.)

carats.[1] The Portuguese use the same weight name in Goa, but it is then equal to only 5 grains.[2]

I come now to the kinds of money with which diamonds are purchased in India.

Firstly, in the Kingdom of Bengal, in the territories of the Rājā of whom I have spoken, as they are included in the dominion of the Great Mogul, payment is made in rupees. At the two mines [3] in the Kingdom of Bījāpur, in the neighbourhood of Rammalakota, payment is made in the new pagodas which the King, being entirely independent of the Great Mogul, coins in his own name. The new pagoda does not always bear the same value, for sometimes it is valued at 3½ rupees,[4] sometimes more and sometimes less, according as it is raised or lowered by the state of trade, and according as the moneychangers arrange matters with the Princes and Governors. At the mine of Kollūr or Gani, which belongs to the King of Golkonda, payment is made in new pagodas of equal value with those of the King of Bījāpur. But one has to buy them sometimes at from 1 to 4 per cent. premium, because they are of better gold, and because the merchants do not accept others at this mine.

These pagodas are made by the English and Dutch, who have obtained from the King, either by agreement or by force, permission to manufacture them, each in their own fortress. And those of the Dutch cost 1 or 2 per cent. more than those of the English, because they are of better quality, and the miners also much prefer them. But as the majority of the merchants are influenced by the false reports that the people at the mine are unsophisticated and almost savages, and that, moreover, the routes from Golkonda to the mines

[1] i.e. 4·36 troy grains. Mangelin in Tamil Manjādi, Telugu Manjali, the seed of the Adenanthera pavonina, or red sandalwood (Yule, *Hobson-Jobson*, 553; Watt, *Economic Dict.*, i. 107 f.). These weights and their modern equivalents are discussed in vol. i, Appendix. Elsewhere Tavernier seems to imply that, Rammalakota being in Bījāpur, this mangelin was used there.

[2] i. e. 3·962 troy grains.

[3] The second mine here referred to was possibly the one mentioned as having been closed. (See p. 61 *n.*)

[4] I.e. 7*s.* 10½*d.*

are very dangerous, they generally remain at Golkonda, where those who work the mines have their correspondents to whom they send the diamonds. Payments are made there with old pagodas, well worn, and coined many centuries ago by different Princes, who reigned in India before the Musalmāns gained a footing in the country. These old pagodas are worth 4½ rupees,[1] i. e. 1 rupee more than the new, although they do not contain more gold, and consequently do not weigh more; this will be a cause of astonishment if I do not explain the reason. It is that the Shroffs or Changers, in order to induce the King not to have them recoined, pay him annually a large sum, because they themselves thereby derive a considerable profit; for the merchants never receive these pagodas without the aid of one of these Changers to examine them, some being defaced, others of low standard, others of short weight, so that if one accepted them without this examination he would lose much, and would have the trouble to return them, or perhaps lose from 1 to even 5 or 6 per cent., in addition to which he must pay the Shroffs ¼th per cent. for their trouble. When you pay the miners, they will also receive these pagodas only in presence of the Changer, who points out to them the good and bad, and again takes his ¼th per cent. But to save time, when you desire to make a payment of 1,000 or 2,000 pagodas, the Changer, when receiving his dues, encloses them in a little bag, on which he places his seal, and when you wish to pay a merchant for his diamonds you take him, with the bag, to the Changer, who, seeing his own seal intact, assures him that he has examined all the coins, and will be responsible if any do not prove good.

As for rupees, the miners take indifferently those of the Great Mogul and those of the King of Golkonda, because those coined by this King would have been the coinage of the Great Mogul if these monarchs had remained on good terms.

The natives of India have more intelligence and subtlety than one thinks. As the pagodas are small, thick pieces

[1] i. e. 10*s*. 1½*d*. Much information on the various kinds of pagodas is collected in *Madras Manual of Administration*, iii. 642 f.

of gold of the size of the nail on the little finger, and as it is impossible to clip them without it being apparent, they bore small holes in them all round, from whence they extract 3 or 4 sols value of gold dust, and they close them with such skill that there is no appearance of the coins having been touched. Moreover, if you buy anything in a village, or if when you cross a river you give the boatmen a rupee, they immediately kindle a fire and throw the rupee into it, from whence if it comes out white they accept it, but if black they return it ; for all the silver in India is of the highest quality, and that which is brought from Europe has to be taken to the mint to be recoined. I say also that those are very much deceived (as a merchant tried to make me believe on my first journey) who imagine that it answers to take to the mines spices, tobacco, mirrors, and other trifles of that kind to barter for diamonds ; for I have fully proved the contrary, and am able to assert that the merchants at the mine who sell the diamonds require good gold, and the best too.

Now let us say something as to the routes to be followed to the mines. Some modern rather fabulous accounts represent them to be, as I have said, dangerous and difficult, and frequented by tigers, lions,[1] and barbarous people ; but I have found them altogether different from what they were represented to be—without wild beasts, and the people full of good will and courtesy to strangers.

As for Golkonda, one need know but little of the map to be aware of its position ; but from Golkonda to Rammalakota, where the principal mine is, the route is less known, and this is the one which I followed. The measure of distance in this country is the gos, and a gos is equal to 4 French leagues.[2]

From Golkonda to Canapour, 1 gos ; Canapour to Parquel, 2½ ; Parquel to Cakenol, 1 ; Cakenol to Canol-Candanor, 3 ; Canol-Candanor to Setapour, 1 ; Setapour to the river, 2.[3]

[1] Lions are not likely to have occurred so far south in India in Tavernier's time (Blanford, *Mammalia of British India*, 57).

[2] i. e. to, say, about 8 miles. (See vol. i, Appendix, p. 335.)

[3] This route cannot be accurately determined. The stages possibly

This river is the boundary between the Kingdoms of Golkonda and Bījāpur.

From the river to Alpour, $\frac{3}{4}$ gos; Alpour to Canol, $\frac{3}{4}$; Canol to Raolconda, where the mine is, $2\frac{1}{2}$. Thus in all it is 17 gos, or 68 French leagues from Golkonda to the mine.[1]

From Golkonda to the mine of Coulour, or Gani,[2] it is $13\frac{3}{4}$ gos, which amounts to 55 of our leagues. From Golkonda to Almaspinde, $3\frac{1}{2}$ gos; Almaspinde to Kaper, 2; Kaper to Montecour, $2\frac{1}{2}$; Montecour to Nazelpar, 2; Nazelpar to Eligada, $1\frac{1}{2}$; Eligada to Sarvaron, 1; Sarvaron to Mellaserou, 1; Mellaserou to Ponocour,[3] $1\frac{3}{4}$.

Between Ponocour and Coulour or Gani (Kollūr) there is only the river [4] to cross.

I come now to an important subject which is little understood in Europe.

Rule for ascertaining the proper price of a Diamond of whatsoever weight it may be, from 3 up to and above 100 carats.

I do not mention diamonds below 3 carats, their price being sufficiently well known.

are: Golkonda; Konador; Burgal; Koyalconda; Kandanūl; Saidupur; the river here crossed is the Kistnā.

[1] This route is: Kistnā river to Alampur; Alampur to Karnūl; Karnūl to Rammalakota. It crossed two rivers, namely the main stream of the Kistnā and its tributary the Tungabhadra, Alampur being situated in the fork between, and Karnūl being on the south bank of the Tungabhadra. The total of these distances, as printed, is $14\frac{1}{2}$ gos, which at 4 leagues to the gos would be equal to 58 leagues. The true distance by this route would be about 135 miles, which is equal to the 17 gos, or 68 leagues. Hence some of the stages must be understated.

[2] See p. 56 where it is shown that Gani (Kān-i) is only a Persian prefix signifying 'mine of', and that Coulour is identified with Kollūr on the Kistnā.

[3] The total of these distances is $15\frac{1}{4}$ (not $13\frac{3}{4}$) gos, which, as above, would be equal to 61 leagues. The distance of the first stage is evidently wrong, being in reality only about 10 miles. The distance by the route given in bk. i, ch. xi, is 76 coss. Here, again, the route is uncertain. As worked out by Ball, the stages are; Almāsguda; Munugudu, Nagulpad (Naglepar in ed. of 1678); Lingalla; Sarawaram; Mailacheru.

[4] The river here mentioned is the Kistnā, and Ponocour must have been in the position of Vellutar. Vellatoor, lower down the Kistnā, is quite distinct.

It is first necessary to ascertain the weight of the diamond, and next to see if it is perfect, whether it is a thick stone, square-shaped, and having all its angles perfect; whether it is of a beautiful white water, and bright, without points, and without flaws. If it is a stone cut into facettes, which is ordinarily called 'a rose', it is necessary to observe whether the form is truly round or oval; whether the stone is well-spread, and whether it is not a lumpy stone; and, moreover, whether it is of uniform water, and is without points and flaws, as I described the thick stone.

A stone of this quality, weighing 1 carat, is worth 150 livres[1] or more, and supposing it is required to know the value of a stone of 12 carats of the same degree of perfection, this is how it is to be ascertained: Square the 12, this amounts to 144; next multiply 144 by 150, i. e. the price of 1 carat, and it amounts to 21,600 livres—12 × 12 × 150 = 21,600.[2] This is the price of a diamond of 12 carats.

But it is not enough to know the price of only perfect diamonds, one must know also the price of those which are not so; this is ascertained by the same rule, and on the basis of the price of a stone of 1 carat. This is an example: Suppose a diamond of 15 carats which is not perfect, the water being not good, or the stone badly shaped, or full of spots or flaws. A diamond of the same nature, of the weight

[1] Say £11 5s., at 1s. 6d. to the livre. Thévenot gives 15 to 16 écus as the price of stones of 1 or 2 mangelins, but those of 3 mangelins were worth at the rate of 30 écus the mangelin. (*Voyages des Indes*, Paris, ed. 1684, p. 289.) As Thévenot gives the value of a mangelin at 1·6 carats, 3 would be equal to 4·8 carats, and the price of 90 écus, or £20 5s., while Tavernier's valuation for a stone of 4·8 carats would be 4·8× 4·8× 150 = 3,456 livres = £259 4s. This enormous discrepancy must be due to a mistake by Thévenot.

[2] i. e. £1,620. Whatever may have been the case, it is now apparent that no hard and fast rule can be given to determine the selling value of diamonds, as it is subject to very great variations. Among other formulae, however, the following may be mentioned:

$$\frac{m}{2}(m \times 2)\,a \text{ where } m = \text{the number of carats, and } a \text{ the value of 1.}$$

This is given in *Handbuch der Edelstein*, A. Schrauf, Vienna. A stone of 12 carats, similar in quality to that above given, so calculated, would be worth £945.

of 1 carat, would not be worth more than 60 or 80 or 100 livres at the most, according to the beauty of the diamond. You must then square the weight of the diamond, i.e. 15 carats, and next multiply the product 125 by the value of the stone of 1 carat, which may for example be 80 livres, and the product, which is 10,000 [1] livres, is the price of the diamond of 15 carats.

It is easy to see from this the great difference in value between a perfect stone and one which is not so. For if this stone of 15 carats had been perfect, the second multiplication would be by 150, which is the price of a perfect stone of 1 carat, and then it would amount not to 10,000 livres, but to 33,750 livres, i.e. to 23,750 [2] livres more than an imperfect diamond of the same weight.

According to this rule, the following is the value of the two largest among the cut stones in the world—one of them in Asia belonging to the Great Mogul, the other in Europe belonging to the Grand Duke of Tuscany—as will be seen by the subjoined figures.

The Great Mogul's diamond weighs $279\frac{9}{16}$ carats, is of perfect water, good form, and has only a small flaw which is in the edge of the basal circumference of the stone. Except for this flaw the first carat would be placed at 160 livres, but on that account I do not estimate it at more than 150, and so calculated according to the above given rule it reaches the sum of 11,723,278 livres, 14 sols, and 3 liards. If this diamond only weighed 279 carats, it would have been worth 11,676,150 livres only, and thus these $\frac{9}{16}$ths are worth 47,128 livres, 14 sols, 3 liards.[3]

[1] £750. But this calculation, though represented graphically as a sum in figures, in the original, is wholly incorrect, as 15 × 15 = 225, not 125, and the product of its multiplication by 80 is 18,000 instead of 10,000 livres; the value of the diamond consequently would be £1,350. In the edition of Tavernier of 1678, this sum is correctly worked out to 18,000 livres.

[2] i.e. £2,531 5*s.*, and £1,781 5*s.* The former is correctly calculated, but the latter should be 33,750—18,000 livres = 15,750 livres = £1,181 5*s.*

[3] These amounts are equivalent to £879,245 18*s.* 1½*d.*, £875,711 5*s.*, and £3 534 13*s.* 1½*d.*—the livre being 1*s.* 6*d.*, and the sol 0·9*d.*

The Grand Duke of Tuscany's diamond weighs 139½ carats, is clear, and of good form, cut on all sides into facettes, and as the water tends somewhat to a citron colour,[1] I estimate the first carat at only 135 livres, from which the value of the diamond ought to be 2,608,335 livres.[2]

In concluding the remarks which I have made in this chapter, I should say that in the language of the miners the diamond is called iri;[3] that in Turkish, Persian, and Arabic it is called almās,[4] and that in all the languages of Europe it has no other name than diamond.

This, then, in a few words is all that I have been able to discover with my own eyes in regard to this subject during the several journeys which I made to the mines; and if by chance some other has written or spoken of them before me, it can only have been from the reports which I have made of them.[5]

[1] This description and that in ch. xxii, as also the figure of the stone, correspond in all important respects with the 'Austrian yellow', once in the possession of the Emperor of Austria. Its weight is 133⅛ Vienna carats according to Schrauf, which would amount to about 134 French carats, the proportion in milligrams being 206·13 : 205·5, and not to 139½ as stated in the work quoted below. The value of the stone has been variously estimated at £40,000, £50,000, and even £155,682. (See E. Streeter, *The Great Diamonds of the World*, p. 161 ff., and Murray, *On the Diamond*, second edition, London, 1839.) The figure which the latter gives of the Mātan diamond is really of Tavernier's 'Grand Duke', not so the figure purporting to be of itself.

[2] The equivalent of 2,608,335 livres is £195,625 2*s.* 6*d.*

[3] Linschoten (ii. 136) has iraa, both are from the Sanskrit hira, the term now used in Hindustani, and some other languages in India.

[4] Almās is believed to be closely related with the adamas of the Greeks and Romans—the latter term, however, does not appear to have been originally applied to the diamond, but to corundum or steel. (See *New English Dict.*, s. v.)

[5] It has already been shown that Methold had actually visited the mines before Tavernier. (See p. 56, *n.*) And it is probable that Caesar Fredericke had been at Rammalakota, which he describes, about the year 1570. (See Hakluyt, *Voyages*, Everyman's Library, iii. 216.)

CHAPTER XIX

Concerning Coloured Stones and the places where they are obtained.

THERE are only two places in the East where coloured stones are obtained, namely in the Kingdom of Pegu and in the island of Ceylon. The first is a mountain twelve days journey or thereabouts from Siren [1] in a north-east direction, and it is called Capelan.[2] It is the mine from whence is obtained the greatest quantity of rubies, spinelles or mothers of rubies, yellow topazes, blue and white sapphires, hyacinths, amethysts, and other stones of different colours. Among these hard stones others which are soft are found and are called bacan [3] in the language of the country. These are not considered to be valuable.

Siren is the name of the city where the King of Pegu resides, and Ava is the port of the Kingdom.[4] From Ava to Siren you ascend the river in large flat-bottomed boats, and the voyage lasts about sixty days. You cannot travel by land on account of the jungles, which abound with lions,[5] tigers, and elephants. It is one of the poorest countries in the world; nothing comes from it but rubies, and even they

[1] Siren is here a mistake for Ava. Siriam or Syriam is a port on the Pegu river 6 miles E. of Rangoon. It was famous in connexion with Portuguese dealings with Pegu, and was the site of an English factory in the seventeenth century. (See Yule, *Hobson-Jobson*, 886.) In the second reference below it would seem that the names Siren and Ava are transposed, as Ava was the capital and Syriam the port.

[2] Kyatpyen. Its distance from Ava is about 70 miles. (See Map in vol. i, and Appendix on Burma ruby mines.) 'Caplan is the place where they finde the rubies, saphires, and spinelles; it standeth six dayes iourney from Aua in the kingdome of Pegu' (R. Fitch, ed. Ryley, 172 f.; Varthema, 219).

[3] Bacan. This is possibly the Persian pākand or bākand, which signifies ruby.

[4] It is a strange statement that Ava is the port of Pegu; Barbosa (ed. Dames, ii. 1921, 159), a century and a half before, knew more of the geography.

[5] Lions here, as elsewhere, must be understood as a figure of speech, since there are none in Burma.

are not so abundant as is generally believed, seeing that the value does not amount to 100,000 écus [1] per annum.

Among all these stones you would find it difficult to meet with one of good quality, weighing 3 or 4 carats, because of the strict injunctions against allowing the removal of any which the King has not seen ; and he retains all the good ones which are found among them. This is the reason why in all my journeys I have earned a sufficiently large profit from taking rubies from Europe into Asia ; and I very much doubt the story of Vincent le Blanc where he says that he has seen rubies in the King's palace as large as eggs.[2]

The following is the price of some rubies which might pass as of good quality. During my several journeys I saw them sold by merchants who came from the mine, while I was at Masulipatam and Golkonda. All rubies are sold by the weight called rati, which is $3\frac{1}{2}$ grains or $\frac{7}{8}$th of a carat ; [3] and payment is made in the old pagodas, of which I have spoken in the preceding chapter :

A ruby of 1 rati was sold for 20 pagodas ; $2\frac{1}{8}$ ratis was sold for 85 pagodas ; $3\frac{1}{4}$ ratis was sold for 185 pagodas ; $4\frac{5}{8}$ ratis was sold for 450 pagodas ; 5 ratis was sold for 525 pagodas ; $6\frac{1}{2}$ ratis was sold for 920 [4] pagodas. When a ruby

[1] £22,500. In the year 1855 the revenue from the mines was estimated at from £12,500 to £15,000. Since the conquest of Upper Burma these mines have, as is well known, been let for a term of years to an English company. Further information will be found in an Appendix to this volume. For the Ruby Mines District see *Imperial Gazetteer*, xvi. 333 f. ; Scott & Hardiman, *Gazetteer, Upper Burma*, Part ii, vol. iii. 18 ff. ; *Ency. Brit.*, xxiii. 812 f. ; Barbosa, ed. Dames, 1921, vol. ii. 161 f.

[2] This statement does not appear in the Paris edition of Le Blanc's *Voyages*, 1648. Sir T. Roe speaks of a ruby weighing 13 tolas, or about $5\frac{1}{4}$ oz., which was offered to Jahāngīr for 5 lakhs of rupees by the Portuguese, but he would give only one lakh for it. (See *Journal*, ed. Foster, i. 183.)

[3] Namely the pearl rati = 2·66 grains troy. (See Appendix to vol. i.)

[4] In other words, a ruby of 18 grains troy was sold for about £465 15*s.*—the rati being equal to 2·66 grains troy, and the pagoda to 10*s.* $1\frac{1}{2}$*d.* (See vol. i, Appendix.) According to Mr. Streeter (*Precious Stones*) rubies over a carat in weight vary in value from £20 to £100 per carat at present, but he adds that no definite price can be given to aid the purchaser. According to Barbosa, the King of Ceylon used to put a ruby in a fierce charcoal fire, and if it stood the test it became much more

exceeds 6 ratis, and is perfect, it is sold for whatever is asked for it.

All the other coloured stones in this country are called by the name ruby, and are only distinguished by colour.[1] Thus in the language of Pegu the sapphire is a blue ruby, the amethyst a violet ruby, the topaz a yellow ruby, and so with the other stones.

The dealers are so particular about their profit in trade that they will not show you a parcel of rubies, although they may be fine, unless you promise beforehand that in case you do not buy you will make them a small present—such as a turban or a waistband ; and when you act with some liberality to them they show all their stock, and you can then transact some business with them.

The other place in the East whence rubies and other coloured stones are obtained is a river in the island of Ceylon.[2] It flows from high mountains which are in the middle of the island, and as the rains greatly increase its size—three or four months after they have fallen, and when the water is lowered, the poor people go to search the sand, where they find rubies, sapphires, and topazes. The stones from this river are generally more beautiful and cleaner than those of Pegu.

I forgot to remark that in the mountains which run from Pegu towards the Kingdom of Camboya [3] some rubies are

perfect in colour (Dames, *Book of Duarte Barbosa*, vol. ii, ed. 1921, 126).

[1] A very legitimate system of nomenclature, as they are all of the same chemical composition, viz. alumina or corundum.

[2] In Ceylon sapphire is the variety of corundum most commonly found, but rubies are also sometimes met with. The annual average value of precious stones found in Ceylon is said to be about £10,000 at present. 'Stones of inferior kinds are found in the beds of streams about Kandy, Nuwara-Eliya, Badulla, and some of the small rivers in the south ; but the more precious stones, such as the ruby, sapphire, topaz, alexandrite, and catseye, must be sought within a radius of 30 or 40 miles from Ratnapura (the City of Gems), the capital of Saffragam, a district of the Western Province, though occasionally rubies are found in Uva.' (Tennent, *Ceylon*, i. 36.)

[3] The mode of occurrence of rubies in Cambodia and Siam is not very well understood, but Ball had met with some references to the fact,

found in certain places, but more balass rubies [1] than others, many spinelles, sapphires, and topazes. There are gold mines in these mountains, and rhubarb [2] also comes from these places, which is highly esteemed, because it does not spoil so quickly as that which grows in other parts of Asia.

There are also in Europe two places from whence coloured stones are obtained, viz. Bohemia and Hungary. In Bohemia there is a mine where pebbles of different sizes are obtained, some being as large as an egg, others the size of the fist, and on breaking them some of them are found to contain rubies [3] as hard and as beautiful as those of Pegu. I remember being one day at Prague with the Viceroy of Hungary, in whose service I then was, as he washed his hands with General Wallenstein, Duke of Friedland, before sitting down at table, observing on the General's hand a ruby he admired for its beauty. And he admired it much more when Wallenstein told him that these stones came from Bohemia; and, in fact, at the Viceroy's departure the General presented him with about 100 of these pebbles in a basket. When we returned to Hungary the Viceroy had them all broken, and out of the whole of the flints rubies were found only in two, one of them weighing about 5 carats and the other about 1 carat.

which appears to be undoubted. Thus Crawfurd says they are found in hills at Chan-ta-bun in Lat. 12° on the east side of the Gulf. They constitute a rigidly-guarded royal monopoly, but are much inferior in quality to the Ava stones. (*Embassy*, 4to., London, 1828, p. 419.) No recent account of rubies in Cambodia has been traced. 'Rubies are found in Siam, at several localities in the provinces of Chantabon and Krat,' and at Moung Klung (*Ency. Brit.*, xxiii. 812).

[1] The distinction made by our author between 'balass' rubies, and spinels indicates that already in his time the name had been transferred from its true original application to spinels—to rubies of a particular shade of colour, probably light, and resembling the spinel. (See vol. i, p. 303 *n.*)

[2] This was probably China rhubarb, which thus found an outlet to Europe. Afterwards it mainly came through Russia. A very interesting account of the rhubarb trade from the earliest times, though Cambodia is not mentioned there, will be found in Hanbury's and Flückiger's *Pharmacographia*, Art. 'Rhubarb'; Watt, *Commercial Products*, 912 f.; Yule, *Marco Polo*, ii. 144; Bernier, 425; Barbosa, ed. Dames. i. 93 f.

[3] These rubies, so called, were doubtless only garnets.

As for Hungary, it has a mine whence opals [1] are obtained; they are not found in any other place in the world.

Turquoise occurs only in Persia, and it is obtained in two mines. One of them which is called 'the old rock' is three days' journey from Meshed towards the north-west and close to a large town called Nichabourg; [2] the other, which is called 'the new', is five days' journey from it. These stones from the new are of an inferior blue, tending to white, and are little esteemed, and one may purchase as many of them as he likes at small cost. But for many years the King of Persia has prohibited mining in 'the old rock' for anyone but himself, because there are no gold workers in the country except those who work in thread, who are ignorant of the art of enamelling on gold, and without knowledge of design and engraving, and he uses for the decoration of swords, daggers, and other work, instead of enamel, these turquoises of 'the old rock' which are cut and arranged in patterns like flowers and other figures which the jewellers make. This catches the eye and passes as a laborious work, but it is wanting in design.

As for the emerald, it is an ancient error of many people to suppose that it was originally found in the East [3] [because

[1] There are early references to the occurrence of opal in India, at Poona, Bījāpur, and Sītābaldī (Watt, *Economic Dict.*, ii. 175), but Ball had never been able to identify any local source there. Hungary still retains pre-eminence in this respect, but very beautiful opals are now found in Australia.

[2] Nishapur in Meshed is the classic locality for the true turquoise. Its mode of occurrence there will be found described in a paper by Mr. A. H. Schindler published in the *Records of the Geol. Survey of India*, vol. xvii, 1884, p. 132. Vambéry, *Life*, 290, also describes these mines. Turquoise has been found in some other places in Asia, as for instance in the province of Ferghana at Mount Karumagar, 24 miles NE. of Khojend. It occurs there in veins in a decomposed felspar porphyry. It is also found in South America. The best account of the Nishapur mines is that of Lord Curzon (*Persia*, i. 264 ff.). He could find only inferior stones at Meshed, near Nishapur, all the best being exported; the poor stones are kept in damp earthenware pots, until they are sold, when they turn to a sickly green colour (*ibid.*, i. 167, 267; *Russian Central-Asia*, H. Lansdell, 515).

[3] Tavernier appears to have been wholly unaware of the true source of the emerald in early times. Although common beryl is abundant in

before the discovery of America they could not believe otherwise][1], and the majority of jewellers and artisans, when they see an emerald of high colour inclining to black, are still accustomed to call it an oriental emerald, in which they are mistaken [since the East has never produced them]. I confess I have not been able to find the places in our Continent from whence these kinds of stones are obtained. But I am assured that the East has never produced them, either on the mainland or on the islands; and having made a strict inquiry during all my journeys, no one has been able to indicate any place in Asia where they are found. It is true that since the discovery of America some few rough stones have often been carried by the Southern Sea from Peru to the Philippine Islands, whence they have been exported in due course to Europe; but that does not justify these being called 'oriental', nor support the view that their source is in the East, since both before this discovery and this passage there was no want of emeralds for disposal throughout the whole of Europe, and because at present, having left this route, they are all conveyed by the North Sea (Atlantic) to Spain.[2] In the year 1660 I saw 20 per cent. less price

India the emerald, though highly esteemed, and well known at a very remote epoch, does not appear to have been found there. All records, and indeed many might be quoted since the times of the Ptolemies, point to certain mines in Egypt, especially at Mount Zabara on the Red Sea, as having afforded the supply. Prof. Maskelyn, *Edin. Rev.* 1866, p. 244, records that when this locality was visited by Sir G. Wilkinson he found several emeralds of pale and poor quality (Wilkinson, *Ancient Egyptians*, ed. 1878, i. 33). The matrix was mica schist. Among other authors who have mentioned Egypt as supplying emeralds to India, the following are the principal: Pliny, the Monk Cosmas, *circa* A.D. 545, Masūdī, and the Muhammadan travellers of the ninth century. The emeralds of Siberia do not appear to have been discovered before the present century. F. Leguat (*Voyage*, ii. 269) denies that they are found in Java.

[1] The passages in square brackets do not occur in the 1678 edition of Tavernier, but are in that of 1713.

[2] The foregoing passage is thus recast in the edition of 1713: 'I believe that long before that part of the world which is called the West Indies had been discovered, emeralds were carried from Asia into Europe; but they came from mines in the Kingdom of Peru. For the Americans, before we had knowledge of them, trafficked in the Philippine

given in India for emeralds than they would be sold for in France.

But concerning this commerce by sea between America and the Philippine Islands, it should be remarked that when the Americans arrive at these islands,[1] the people of Bengal, Arakan, Pegu, Goa, and other places, carry thither all sorts of cloths, and a quantity of worked stones, such as diamonds and rubies, with many manufactured articles of gold and silver, silken stuffs, and Persian carpets. But it should be added that they are unable to sell anything directly to these Americans, but only to those who reside in the Manillas, and that they resell them again when the former have left. Similarly, if any one obtained permission to return from Goa to Spain by the Southern Sea he would be obliged to pay 80 or 100 per cent. for transmitting money as far as the Philippines, without being allowed to buy anything, and to do the same from the Philippines as far as New Spain.

[This then was the course of trade in emeralds before the West Indies were discovered, for they came to Europe only by this long way and tedious journey. All that were not fine remained in this country, and all those that were passed on into Europe.] [2]

Islands, where they carried gold and silver; but more silver than gold, as there was more profit on the one than the other, on account of the abundance of gold mines in the East. To-day this trade still continues, and the people of Peru go annually to the Philippines with two or three vessels, whither they only carry silver and a small quantity of rough emeralds, and indeed for some years they have ceased to carry the emeralds, sending them all to Europe by the Northern Sea.'

[1] This early traffic between Peru and the Philippine Islands, by which our author strives to explain the source of the emeralds, is corroborated by recent researches by Prof. Elliot Smith and others. It is curious to note that the agreement between the Spaniards and the Portuguese, that the former should extend their conquests only to the west and the latter to the east of Europe, was disturbed when vessels first crossed the Pacific from South America to Manilla. The Spaniards, so far as is known with certainty, probably first carried Peruvian emeralds to the Eastern nations.

[2] Interpolated in the edition of 1713.

CHAPTER XX

Concerning Pearls and the places where they are fished for.

PEARLS are found in the eastern and western seas, and although I have not been in America, both for the satisfaction of the reader and so as to avoid omitting anything important, I shall mention all the places where there are pearl-fisheries, commencing with those in the East.

In the first place, there is a pearl-fishery round the island of Bahrein,[1] in the Persian Gulf. It belongs to the King of Persia, and there is a good fortress there, where a garrison of 300 men is kept. The water drunk in this island and that used on the coast of Persia is salt, and has an unpleasant taste, and it is only the people of the country who can drink it. As for strangers, it costs them not a little to obtain good[2] water, for they have to get it out at sea from half a league distance from the island up to nearly two leagues. Those who go in boats for it should number five or six, one or two of whom dive to the bottom of the sea, and hang from their waistbands a bottle or two, which they fill with water and then cork them well. For at the bottom of the sea, for about two or three feet in depth, the water is fresh, and the best that can be drunk. When those who dive to the bottom of the sea to get this water, pull a small cord which is attached

[1] Bahrein Island, the well-known centre of the pearl-fishery in the Persian Gulf.

[2] See vol. i, p. 214. 'Bahrein . . . is still noted for the fresh springs which rise from the earth under the sea, and from which the Arabs contrive to water their ships by placing over the spot a vessel with a syphon attached to it' (J. Morier, *A Journey through Persia, Armenia, and Asia Minor*, 52). At Bahrein freshwater springs bubble up from the bottom of the sea, even at a depth of 18 feet, and some miles from the shore (Curzon, *Persia*, ii. 457). Cases of water-springs flowing from under the sea are reported in many places. At Anavolo in Greece a body of fresh water rises from the sea, 50 feet in diameter, about a quarter of a mile from the narrow beach under the cliffs (Sir J. Frazer, *Pausanias*, iii. 306, and for a similar case, *ibid.*, iv. 198 f.). For the pearl-fishery see *Journal, Royal Asiatic Society*, xii. 189 ff.; Varthema, 94 ff.

to one of those who remain in the boat, it is the signal to their comrades to haul them up.

While the Portuguese held Hormuz and Muscat, each terate [1] or boat which went to fish was obliged to take out a licence from them, which cost 15 'abbāsīs,[2] and many brigantines were maintained there, to sink those who were unwilling to take out licences. But since the Arabs have retaken Muscat, and the Portuguese are no longer supreme in the Gulf, every man who fishes pays to the King of Persia only 5 'abbāsīs,[3] whether his fishing is successful or not. The merchant also pays the King something small for every 1,000 oysters.

The second pearl-fishery is opposite Bahrein, on the coast of Arabia Felix, close to the town of Al Katīf,[4] which, with all the neighbouring country, belongs to an Arab Prince.

The pearls fished in these places are for the most part sold in India, because the Indians are not so particular as we are. All pass easily, the baroques [5] as well as the round; each has its price, all being saleable. Some of them are taken also to Bassora. Those which go to Persia and Russia are sold at Bandar-Congo,[6] two days distance from Hormuz. In all the places which I have named, and in other parts of Asia, the water tending slightly to yellow is preferred to the white,[7] because it is said that pearls the water of which

[1] Spelt terrade in *Persian Travels*, p. 232, Paris edition, 1676. Various forms of the word, which means a galley or a small ship of war, occur in Portuguese, Spanish, and Arabic, but its etymology is uncertain. Dalboquerque (*Commentaries*, Hakluyt Society, i. 105) speaks of Terradas, explained as 'Shore boats'.

[2] Or, allowing 1*s*. 6*d*. for the 'abbāsī, £1 2*s*. 6*d*.

[3] 7*s*. 6*d*. [not 3*s*. 9*d*. as in 1st ed.]

[4] This is Catifa in the original. Al Katīf, on the Persian Gulf, is a considerable Arabian town, with a district of some extent (Curzon, *Persia*, ii. 454).

[5] The term baroques, which is sometimes written barocche, is from the French baroque, Span. barruco, Port. barroco signifying irregular or uncouth: it is applied to irregularly-shaped pearls. They are much used for grotesque figures. Castellani says they are specially esteemed in Spain and Poland. (*History of Gems*, p. 172.)

[6] Kongūn, on the Persian Gulf, 100 miles west of Gombroon. Bandar-Congo is mentioned as a port for Lār in the *Persian Travels*, pp. 232–4 (Curzon, *Persia*, ii. 408; Yule, *Hobson-Jobson*, 246).

[7] The statement at the end of this chap. (xx) contradicts this.

is slightly golden retain their brightness and never change, but that when they are white they do not last for thirty years without losing their brightness, and, on account both of the heat of the country and the perspiration of the body, they assume a vile yellow colour.

Before leaving the Gulf of Hormuz I shall speak a little more fully than I have done in my account of Persia [1] of that splendid pearl which is possessed by the Arab Prince who took Muscat from the Portuguese. He then assumed the name of Imenhect, Prince of Muscat, having been previously called Asaf bin Ali,[2] Prince of Norenuaé. This is but a petty Province, but the best in Arabia Felix. All

'Generally speaking, the Bahrein pearls are not so white as Ceylon pearls, but are larger and more regular in shape, while they are said to retain a lustre for a longer period' (Curzon, *Persia*, ii. 457).

[1] The account in the *Persian Travels* is that the pearl belonged to the Amīr of Vodana, who showed it to M. Constant and our author at Hormuz; it was perfectly round and transparent, and weighed 17 'abbās, or 14⅞ carats, the 'abbās being equal to ⅞ of a carat. On behalf of the Governor of Surat, the latter, on a subsequent occasion, offered 60,000 rupees, say £6,750, to the owner for it, but he refused to sell it (*Persian Travels*, bk. ii, ch. ix.).

[2] Aceph Ben-Ali in the original. Mr. E. Heawood has kindly investigated the question of Vodana and Norenuaé. Ptolemy is evidently the source of the Vodana of Ortelius and others, but as in bk. vi, ch. 7 the position assigned to it is in the very centre of Southern Arabia, it can hardly be connected with the actual Wadām. Yet even in D'Amville's Atlas Vodana still appears in 'Omān, but there it is placed as a Wadī debouching not, as in Ortelius, on the Persian Gulf, but on the outer coast. Regarding Norenuaé nothing has been discovered, save the suggestion that it may represent some honorific title. The first syllable may be Persian *nūr*, 'bright', as Nūr-chashmī, 'light of the eyes', a beloved daughter. Imenhect may represent some title like Shaikh Imām. As regards the capture of Maskat, Nāsir-bin-Murshid was succeeded by his cousin, Sultān-bin-Saif, who determined to drive the Portuguese from Maskat. He was repulsed several times, but finally the place was captured by the treachery of a Banian, Narūtam, who induced the commandant, Pareira, to empty the water-tanks, clear out the provisions, and remove the gunpowder. This seems to have occurred in 1651–2 (G. P. Badger, *History of the Imāms and Seyyids of 'Omān*, Introd., xxvi f., 79 ff., 89 note). For another account see A. Hamilton, *A New Account of the East Indies*, in Pinkerton's *Collection of Voyages and Travels*, viii. 284 f. Maskat was captured by the Imām of 'Omān in 1650 (Sir P. Sykes, *Hist. of Persia*, 2nd ed., ii. 194).

that is necessary for the life of man grows there, and more especially splendid fruits, and in particular excellent grapes, from which very good wine can be made. This Prince possesses the most beautiful pearl in the world, not by reason of its size, for it only weighs $12\frac{1}{16}$ carats, nor on account of its perfect roundness; but because it is so clear and so transparent that you can almost see the light through it. As the Gulf opposite Hormuz is scarcely 12 leagues wide from Arabia Felix to the coast of Persia,[1] and the Arabs were at peace with the Persians, the Prince of Muscat came to visit the Khān of Hormuz, who entertained him with magnificence, and invited the English, Dutch, and some other Franks, in which number I was included, to the festival. At the close of the feast the Prince took this pearl out of a small purse which he carried suspended from his neck and showed it to the Khān and the rest of the company. The Khān wished to buy it, to present to the King of Persia, and offered up to 2,000 tomāns,[2] but the Prince was unwilling to part with it. Since then I crossed the sea with a Banian merchant whom the Great Mogul was sending to this Prince to offer him 40,000 écus [3] for this pearl; but he refused to accept that sum.

This account proves that fine jewels ought not always to be taken to Europe,[4] but rather from Europe to Asia, as I have done, because both precious stones and pearls are esteemed there very highly when they have unusual beauty;

[1] According to Yule's map (*Marco Polo*, i. 108) the distance from Jerum, or New Hormuz, to Old Hormuz on the Persian coast, is about 40 miles. Badger, in his note on Varthema (p. 95), says that the channel between Hormuz and the mainland, directly opposite, is only 4 miles broad; between the island and Bandar 'Abbās it averages between 11 and 12.

[2] About £6,900.

[3] i. e. £9,000. Its value is stated to have been £32,000. (See Streeter, *Precious Stones and Gems*, 3rd. edition, part iii, p. 14.)

[4] Ball recalled a case in India a few years since illustrative of this, which gave rise to a trial. One or two persons residing at Simla bought some stones as a speculation and sent them to England, where they were valued at a lower price than had been given for them. The purchasers thereupon sought by an action to recover their money from the native jewel merchant, but lost their suit

but an exception must be made in the case of China and Japan, where they are not valued.[1]

The other locality in the East where there is a pearl-fishery is in the sea near a large town called Manār, in the island of Ceylon.[2] The pearls found there are the most beautiful, both as regards water and roundness, of all the fisheries; but one is rarely found which exceeds 3 or 4 carats in weight.

Moreover, on the coast of Japan, there are pearls of very beautiful water and good size, but they are very imperfect; nevertheless they are not fished for, because, as I have said, the Japanese do not esteem jewels.

Although the pearls which are found at Bahrein and at Al Katīf tend somewhat to yellow, they are esteemed as highly as those of Manār, as I have remarked, and throughout the East it is said that they are mature or ripe, and that they never change colour.

I come now to the fisheries of the West, which are all situated on the great Gulf of Mexico, along the coast of New Spain, and there are five of them which succeed one another from east to west.

The first is near the island of Cubagua,[3] which is only 3 leagues in circuit, and is distant about 5 from the mainland. It is in 10° 30 of N. Lat., and 160 leagues from S. Dominique[4] in the Isle of Spain. It is a very barren land, wanting in

[1] The Chinese prefer to invest their money in porcelain, lacquer, and other works of art, and ridicule the craze for precious stones: but both Chinese and Japanese women wear jade, gold, and pearl necklaces (Pyrard de Laval, ii. 173; *Ency. Brit.*, vi. 173; Chamberlain, *Things Japanese*, 3rd ed. 116). Ornaments are less worn by the Chinese than by other Asiatics (S. W. Williams, *The Middle Kingdom*, 4th ed. ii. 37).

[2] The best account of the pearl-fisheries in the Gulf of Manaar will be found in the Report by Prof. Herdman (Royal Society, London, 1903–6). In 1905 the fisheries realized 25 lakhs of rupees, and have since that time been leased for £20,000 per annum (Watt, *Economic Products*, 557 f.; *Ency. Brit.*, xxi. 24 ff.). For early accounts of the fisheries see Dames, *Book of Duarte Barbosa*, ed. 1921, vol. ii. 115, 123. Small pearls are found in the Thāna creek, Bombay, and being ground and mixed with lime juice, are used as a nerve tonic (*Bombay Gazetteer*, xiii, part 1, 55).

[3] Cubagua is one of the Antilles group. It lies between the isle of Margarita and the coast of Cumana, and belongs to Venezuela. It was formerly a centre of the pearl-fisheries (*Ency. Brit.*, xxvii. 989).

[4] San Dominique, also one of the Antilles.

all things, and especially water, which the inhabitants are obliged to obtain from the mainland. This island is renowned throughout the west, because here the most considerable pearl-fishery is situated, although the largest pearls do not exceed 5 carats. The second fishery is in the island of Marguerite, that is to say, the island of pearls, at 1 league from Cubagua, which it surpasses much in size. It produces all that is necessary to life except that, like Cubagua, it lacks water, which has to be sent for to the river Cumana, near New Cadiz.[1] This fishery is not the most abundant of all the five in America ; but it is considered the principal, because the pearls which are found there surpass the others in perfection, both as regards water and size. One of the latter which I possessed, of well-formed pear shape, and of fine water, weighed 55 carats, and I sold it to Shāista Khān, uncle of the Great Mogul.[2]

Many are astonished to learn that pearls are taken from Europe to the East, whence they come in abundance, but it should be remarked that in the Oriental fisheries they are not found of as great weight as in those of the West, added to which all the kings and great nobles of Asia pay much better than do people in Europe, not only for pearls, but for all kinds of jewels—when they are out of the common run—excepting only the diamond.

The third fishery is at Comogote,[3] near the mainland. The fourth is at Rio de la Hacha,[4] along the same coast. The fifth, and last, is at Sainte Marthe, 60 leagues from Rio de la Hacha. All these three fisheries produce pearls of good weight ; but generally they are ill-formed and are of a leaden-coloured water.

Finally, as for the pearls of Scotland, and those which are found in the rivers of Bavaria,[5] although necklaces are

[1] The positions of Marguerite and Cumana are indicated in the previous note.

[2] See vol. i. (112 f.) for details of the sale, and the quarrel it gave rise to.

[3] Comogote is not marked in ordinary maps, but it is near Cubagua.

[4] Rio de la Hacha, a province and its chief town, is in Columbia.

[5] Obtained from the Unio and Anodonta, freshwater mussels (*Ency. Brit.*, xxi. 26 ; *Notes and Queries*, 2nd Ser. v. 400 f.). Pearl-fishing has

made of them which are worth up to 1,000 ecus [1] and beyond, they cannot enter into comparison with those of the East and West Indies.

It is possible that none of those who have written before me concerning pearls have recorded that some years back a fishery was discovered in a certain part of the coasts of Japan, and I have seen some of the pearls which the Dutch brought from there. They were of very beautiful water, and some of them of large size, but all baroques. The Japanese, as I have said above, do not esteem pearls. If they cared about them it is possible that by their means some banks might be discovered where finer ones would be obtained.[2]

Before concluding this chapter I shall make a very important remark in reference to pearls and the differences in their waters, some being very white, others tending to yellow, and others to black, and some which are, so to speak, lead-coloured. As for the last, they are found only in America, and this colour is caused by the nature of the bottom, which is muddier than in the East. In a return cargo which the late M. du Jardin,[3] the well-known jeweller, had in the Spanish galleons, there were included six perfectly round pearls, but black as jet, which weighed altogether 12 carats. He gave them to me with some other things to take to the East, to see if they could be disposed of, but I brought them back again, as I found no one who would look at them.[4] As for the pearls tending to yellow, the colour is due to the fact that the fishermen sell the oysters in heaps, and as the merchants wait sometimes as long as fourteen or fifteen days till the shells open of themselves, in order to extract the pearls, some of these oysters lose their water during this time, decay, and become putrid, and the pearls become yellow by contact. This is so true that in all oysters which have

been resumed on the river Ugie in north-east Aberdeenshire; in former times this was a lucrative industry (*The Sunday Times*, 26th March 1922).

[1] £225.

[2] The Japanese have recently started the industry of producing pearls in oysters by artificial means.

[3] See p. 125, below.

[4] Black pearls do not suit dark complexions so well as the lighter kinds.

retained their water the pearls are always white. They are allowed to open of themselves, because if they are opened by force, as we open our oysters in the shell, the pearl may be damaged and broken. The oysters of the Manār Strait open of themselves, spontaneously, five or six days sooner than those of the Gulf of Persia, because the heat is much greater at Manār, which is at the 10th degree of North Latitude,[1] while the island of Bahrein is at about the 27th. And consequently among the pearls which come from Manār there are few yellow ones found. Finally, all the Orientals are very much of our taste in matters of whiteness, and I have always remarked that they prefer the whitest pearls,[2] the whitest diamonds, the whitest bread, and the whitest women.

CHAPTER XXI

Concerning the manner in which Pearls originate in Oysters how they are fished for and at what Seasons.

I AM aware that according to the testimony of some ancient authors, who were not well instructed in these matters, it was commonly believed that the pearl originates from the dew of heaven, and that but one is found in each oyster;[3] but experience proves the contrary. For, as regards the first, the oyster does not stir from the bottom of the sea, where the dew cannot penetrate, and sometimes it is necessary to dive for them to a depth of 12 cubits, as we shall see presently; and as for the other, it is common to find as many as six or seven pearls in a single oyster, and I have seen one in which there were ten or so in process of formation. It is true that they are not all of the same size, because they are produced in the oyster in the same manner as eggs are in a fowl: as the largest egg advances towards the orifice and goes out

[1] The true Latitude of Manār, a gulf or arm of the sea between Ceylon and Southern India, is about 8° to 9° N. Lat., and of Bahrein about 27° as stated.

[2] On p. 85 it was stated that slightly yellow pearls have the preference.

[3] Pliny, *Nat. Hist.*, ix. 54; Fryer, ii. 362 f.

first, while the small eggs remain inside to complete their formation ; so the largest pearl advances first, and the other smaller ones, not having arrived at their full perfection, remain under the oyster at the bottom of the shell until they have attained the size which nature gives them.[1] But it cannot be said that there are pearls in all oysters, and many may be opened in which none are found.

Moreover, it should not be supposed that a great profit is earned by those who fish for pearls ; for if the poor people who engage in it had anything else to do they would leave the fishing, which merely saves them from dying of hunger.[2] I have remarked in my account of Persia, that from Bassora up to Cape Jasque,[3] on both coasts of the Gulf of Persia, the land produces nothing. The people there are so poor, and live in so miserable a way, that they never have any bread or rice, and only dates and salt fish for their food, and you must travel nearly 20 leagues inland before finding grass.

This fishing in the Eastern seas takes place twice in the year, the first being in March and April, and the second in August and September, and the sale lasts from the month of June till November, but this fishing does not take place every year. For those who fish like to know beforehand whether it will pay. In order not to be deceived they send to the fisheries seven or eight boats, each of which brings back about 1,000 oysters, which are opened, and if there is not found in every thousand oysters the value of 5 fanos of pearls—that is to say a half écu of our money [4]—it is accepted as a proof that the fishing will not be good, and that these poor people will not recover the outlay which they have had

[1] This physiological explanation will hardly receive acceptance at the present time. (Cf. Pliny, *Nat. Hist.*, ix. 55, 57.)

[2] Diamond and gold washing have always, likewise, been the most miserably requited trades in India.

[3] Cape Jask, or the Rās Jāshak of the Arabs, is 'a point on the eastern side of the Gulf of 'Omān near the entrance to the Persian Gulf, and 6 miles south of a port of the same name. The latter was frequented by the vessels of the English Company whilst the Portuguese held Hormuz. After the Portuguese were driven out of Hormuz (1622) the English trade was moved to Gombroon' (Yule, *Hobson-Jobson*, 453).

[4] Or 2*s.* 3*d.* The écu being worth 2 rupees, or 4*s.* 6*d.*, therefore these fanos were worth 5·4*d.* each.

to incur. For both on account of their outfit and for their food during the time of the fishing they borrow money at the rate of from 3 to 4 per cent. per month. Accordingly, if, at the worst, 1,000 oysters do not yield 5 fanos worth of pearls, they do not fish during that year. The merchants buy the oysters on chance, and content themselves with what they find inside. It is a great piece of good fortune when large pearls are found, but it rarely occurs, especially at the Manār fishery which produces no large ones, as I have said, the majority being only pearls to be sold by the ounce and ground into powder.[1] Only a few among them weigh half a grain or a grain, and it is a great event when any of 2 or 3 carats are found. In some years the 1,000 oysters contain as much as 7 fanos worth, and the whole fishing yields 100,000 piastres and over.[2] While the Portuguese were masters of Manār they levied toll from every boat, and the Dutch, who have taken possession of it from them, now levy 8 piastres from each diver, and sometimes up to 9; this yields them a revenue in the best years amounting to 17,200 reals. The reason why the Portuguese took this revenue from these poor people, and why the Dutch take it still, is that they are obliged to protect them against their enemies, the Malabaris, who come with armed boats to capture and enslave the fishers.

Whilst the fishing lasts the Dutch always keep two or three armed boats at sea on the quarter whence the Malabaris come, these precautions being taken so that the work may proceed in safety. The fishermen are for the most part idolaters, but there are also Musalmāns who have boats of their own. They never mingle with one another, and the Dutch levy more from the latter than from the others. For the Musalmāns, besides having to pay as much as the idolaters, have also to give one day's take, the particular day being left to the choice of the Dutch.

The heavier the rainfall in the year, the better is the pearl-fishery. But since many think that at the greatest depths

[1] The term aljofar was applied by the Portuguese to seed pearls said to be from *al-jauhar*, Arab., (the) jewel. (Yule, *Hobson-Jobson*, 12.)

[2] With the piastre at 4*s*. 6*d*. this would be equal to £22,500.

at which the oyster is found, the pearl is whitest, because the water is not so hot there, and the sun has more difficulty in penetrating to the bottom, it is necessary to correct this error. The fishing is carried on in from 4 to 12 cubits depth on the banks, where there are sometimes up to 250 boats. In the majority of the boats there is but one diver, and in the largest only two. These boats sail from the coast every day before sunrise, with a land wind which never fails and lasts till 10 a.m. In the afternoon they return with a wind from the sea, which succeeds the land-wind, and does not fail to blow at 11 or 12 o'clock, as soon as the other has ceased. The banks are 5 or 6 leagues out to sea, and when the boats have arrived there the oysters are fished for in the following manner :—

A cord is tied under the arms of those who dive, which those who remain in the boats hold by the end. A stone of 18 to 20 pounds weight is attached to the diver's great toe which those who remain in the boat also hold by a rope. They have a net made like a sack, the mouth of which is surrounded by a hoop to keep it open, and this net is attached like the rest. Then the diver plunges into the sea, and as soon as he reaches the bottom, which he does quickly, on account of the weight of the stone attached to his great toe, he removes the stone, and those who are in the barque draw it up. For as long as the diver is able to hold his breath he puts oysters into the net, and as soon as he feels that he is unable to hold out longer, he pulls the cord which is tied under his arms ; this is the signal for him to be drawn up, which those who are in the boat do as quickly as they can. The people of Manār are better fishers, and remain for a longer time under the water than those of Bahrein and Al Katīf, for they do not place any clips on their noses nor cotton in their ears to keep the water from entering, as is done in the Persian Gulf.

After the diver has been drawn into the boat the nets containing the oysters are hauled up, and it requires about seven or eight minutes to lift the oysters and to give the diver time to regain breath, after which he returns to the bottom as before ; this he does many times during ten or twelve hours, and then returns to land. Those who are in want of money sell what they have taken, at once, but those who have what they require to live on, keep the oysters until the whole fishing is finished. The oysters are left unopened, and as they decay open of themselves. There are some of these shells which are four times as large as those of our Rouen oysters, but as the flesh of this kind of oyster, of which we speak, is poor and of bad flavour, it is not eaten but thrown away.

To conclude the discourse on pearls, it should be remarked that throughout Europe they are sold by carat weight, which is equal to 4 grains, the same as the diamond weight, but in Asia the weight is different. In Persia the pearls are weighed by the 'abbās, and an 'abbās is an eighth less than our carat. In India, and in all the territories of the Great Mogul and the Kings of Golkonda and Bījāpur, they are weighed by ratis, and the rati is also an eighth less than the carat.[1]

Goa was formerly the place where there was the largest trade in all Asia in diamonds, rubies, sapphires, topazes, and other stones.[2] All the miners and merchants went there to sell the best which they had obtained at the mines, because they had there full liberty to sell, whereas, in their own country, if they showed anything to the Kings or Princes, they were compelled to sell at whatever price was fixed. There was also at Goa a large trade in pearls, both of those which came from the island of Bahrein in the Persian Gulf, and those fished for in the straits of Manar on the coast of the island of Ceylon, as also of those which were brought from America. It should be known then, that in Goa and in all the other places which the Portuguese hold in India, they have a particular weight for pearls which is not used in the other places where there is a trade in pearls, neither in Europe, Asia, nor America. I do not include Africa, because this trade is unknown there, and because in that part of the

[1] Kelly in the *Universal Cambist*, i, p. 278, gives the value of the Persian 'abbās as 3·66 diamond grains = 2·25 (2·9 ?) troy grains. But it has been shown that the pearl rati of our author was equal to 2·77 troy grains. (See vol. i, Appendix, p. 333.)

[2] Cf. Linschoten, i. 225, and on the great trade of Goa, Pyrard de Laval, ii. 212 f.

world the women content themselves, in lieu of jewels, with pieces of crystal, beads of false coral, or yellow amber, of which they make necklaces and bracelets to wear on their arms and legs.

The Portuguese, then, in all the places in India where they are in authority, sell pearls by a weight which they call chegos, but buy them of the merchants, according to the places from whence they bring them, by carats, ʿabbās, or ratis. The table which follows shows the ratio between these chegos and carats.

Carats.	Chegos.	Carats.	Chegos.	Carats.	Chegos.	Carats.	Chegos.
1	5	11	84	21	306	31	667¼
2	8	12	100	22	336	32	711
3	11½	13	117	23	367¼	33	756¼
4	16	14	136	24	400	34	802¾
5	21	15	156	25	430	35	850½
6	27	16	177¾	26	469¼	36	900
7	34	17	200½	27	506¼	37	950⅛
8	44	18	225	28	544½	38	1002¾
9	56	19	250½	29	584	39	1056
10	69	20	277¾	30	625	40	1111¼ [1]

[1] With such an extraordinary table of equivalents one may easily understand the difficulty that is experienced in reconciling statements about weights and measures. If 1 carat equals 5 chegos, it might be supposed that 20 carats would equal 100 chegos, and 40 carats 200; but it will be seen that the equivalents above given are 277¾ and 1111¼ respectively.

This table has been explained by Mr. A. Rambaut, Assistant Astronomer Royal for Ireland. For the first six equivalents the equation $y = 3 + 1\frac{3}{4} x + \frac{3}{8}x^2$, represents the relation when y = the number of chegos and x the number of carats, subject, however, to the condition that wherever an uneven number of eighths of a carat occurs, one is rejected. If this table is followed the precise figures of Tavernier's table are obtained. From 7 carats onwards a very simple rule is followed to obtain the number of chegos. It is to multiply the number of carats by 10, divide by 12, and square the result—thus $36 \times 10 \div 12 = 30$, which squared $= 900$. There is one exception to this rule in the case of 25 carats, which in the table is given equal to 430 chegos, whereas it ought to be, when calculated as above, 434·05 chegos. This discrepancy is probably due to a misprint, so that the table should be corrected accordingly.

On the difficult word Chego Mr. M. Longworth Dames writes: "I find that the word Chego is in Dalgado's *Glossario Luso-Asiatico.* It appears to be an ingenious method of combining weight with size, according to Ficalho in his note on a passage in his edition of Garcia da Orta's *Collo-*

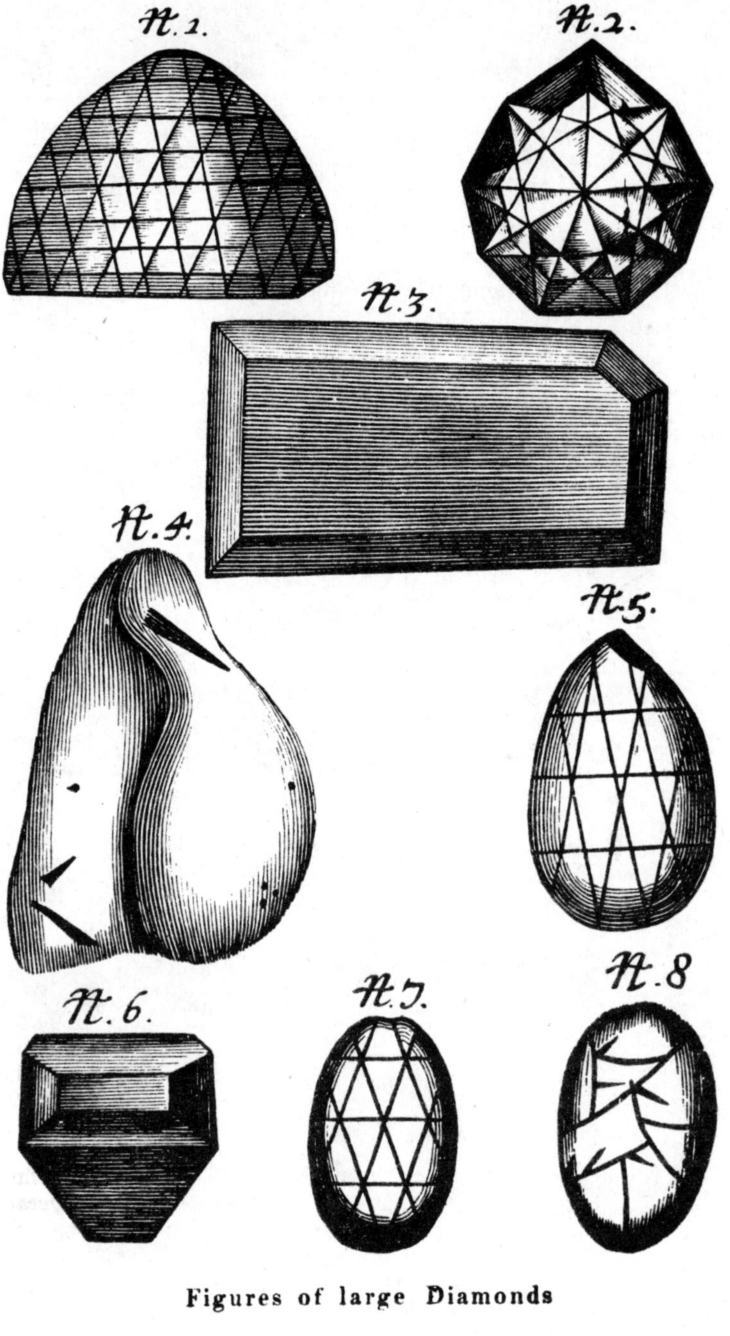

Figures of large Diamonds

CHAPTER XXII

Remarks upon the largest and most beautiful Diamonds and Rubies which the Author has seen in Europe and Asia, the figures of which are here given, together with those of large Stones which he sold to the Emperor on his return from his last Journey to India, with a representation of a magnificent Topaz, and the largest Pearls in the World.

I SHALL follow the order of the figures as they are arranged [in Pl. II] by their numbers, and I shall commence with the heaviest diamond of which I have any knowledge :

No. 1. This diamond [1] belongs to the Great Mogul, who did me the honour to have it shown to me with all his other jewels. You see represented here its form after having been cut, and, as I was allowed to weigh it, I ascertained that it weighed 319½ ratis, which are equal to $279\frac{9}{16}$ of our carats. When in the rough it weighed, as I have elsewhere said, 907 ratis, or $793\frac{5}{8}$ carats. This stone is of the same form as if one cut an egg through the middle.[2]

quios, quoted by Dalgado. Orta does not use the word Chego, although he describes the process of passing the pearls through a sieve. The earliest mention appears to be that in Teixeira (see Ferguson's note on p. 179 of the Hakluyt Society ed., 'The Kings of Ormus'). He says 'the reckoning and weighing is by Chegos, by a method not easy, but very subtle and ingenious'. The system appears to have been used for seed-pearls mainly or only in the Ceylon fishery. Dalgado says the word is not now in use, and he has not been able to trace its origin."

The relationship between the real weight called the mangelin in Madras, and the nominal weight called chow, though it does not elucidate this table, throws some light on the subject. *Rule*—Square the number of mangelins, and divide three-fourths of this product by the number of pearls. The quotient is the number of chows. *Example*—To find value of 21 pearls weighing 16 mangelins at 12 pagodas per chow, $16 \times 16 \times \frac{3}{4} = 192$, $192 \div 21 = 9$ chows $9\frac{1}{7}$ = parts, which at 96*s*. per chow = £43 17*s*. 8¼*d*. (See Kelly, *Universal Cambist*, p. 92.)

[1] For full discussion of all the facts connected with the Great Mogul's diamond, see Appendix I.

[2] This operation may be performed in either of two ways; from the figure given by Tavernier he evidently means transversely. The Koh-i-Nūr as it was when brought to England might be described as of the shape of half an egg, cut longitudinally, but this difference of form,

No. 2 represents the form of the Grand Duke of Tuscany's diamond, which he has had the goodness to show me upon more than one occasion. It weighs 139½ carats, but it is unfortunate that its water tends towards the colour of citron.[1]

No. 3 is of a stone [2] weighing 176⅛ mangelins, which amount to 242 5/16 of our carats. The mangelin, as I have said, is the weight used in the Kingdoms of Golkonda and Bījāpur and it amounts to 1⅜ of our carats. When at Golkonda in the year 1642, I was shown this stone, and it is the largest diamond I have seen in India in the possession of merchants. The owner allowed me to make a model of it in lead, which I sent to Surat to two of my friends, telling them of its beauty and the price, namely 500,000 rupees, which amount to 750,000 livres of our money.[3] I received an order from them, if it was clean and of fine water, to offer 400,000 rupees, but it was impossible to purchase it at that price. Nevertheless, I believe that it could have been obtained if they would have advanced their offer to 450,000 rupees.

No. 4 represents a diamond which I bought at Ahmadābād for one of my friends. It weighed 178 ratis, or 157¼ of our carats.[4]

No. 5 represents the shape of the above mentioned diamond after it had been cut on both sides. Its weight was then 94½

as will be explained, was the result of the mutilation to which it was subjected. (See Appendix I.)

[1] For identification of this stone with the Austrian yellow, once the property of the Emperor of Austria, and known as the Florentine, see Index. Its weight, as recently determined by Schrauf, is 133⅕ Vienna carats, or 27·454 gramms. His figure of it corresponds with that given by our Author. The figures of the Austrian yellow given by Murray, and following him by Emanuel, erroneously represent a distinct stone.

[2] It is not known whether this stone still exists in the form it had when seen by Tavernier. Mr. Streeter (*Great Diamonds*, 88 ff.) devotes a chapter to it under the title 'The Great Table'. Ball could not ascertain the source whence the story which he gives as to its discovery by a Bhīl Chief is derived. What has become of it is not known; it has most probably been broken up. Prof. Maskelyne has suggested that it is the Daryā-i-Nūr, or Ocean of Light, but it is difficult to compare them, as we are ignorant of the thickness of the stone described by Tavernier. The Daryā-i-Nūr is said to be ⅜ inch in thickness.

[3] £56,250.

[4] The equivalent should be 155¾ carats.

carats, the water being perfect. The flat side, where there were two flaws at the base, was as thin as a sheet of thick paper. When I had the stone cut I had all this thin portion removed, together with a part of the point above, where a small speck of flaw still remains.[1]

No. 6 represents another diamond which I bought in the year 1653 at the Kollūr mine. It is beautiful and pure, cut at the mine. It is a thick stone, and weighs 36 mangelins, which are equal to 63⅜ of our carats.[2]

Nos. 7 and 8. The two pieces represented are from a cleaved stone, which, when whole, weighed 75⅝ mangelins, or 104 carats.[3] Although of good water, there appeared so much impurity inside it, that, as it was large and high-priced there was no one among the Banians who dared to purchase it. At length a Dutchman named Bazu ventured to do so, and, having had it cleaved, he found inside it about 8 carats weight of impurity like decomposed vegetable matter.[4] The small piece was clean, save for a nearly imperceptible flaw; but as for the other, where the flaws traversed right through, it had to be divided into seven or eight pieces. The Dutchman risked much in cleaving this stone, and it was a great piece of good luck for him that it did not break into a hundred fragments. Still, for all that, it did not repay him; this makes it sufficiently plain that where the Banians refuse to bite there is nothing to be hoped for by the Franks.

[1] Mr. Streeter (*Great Diamonds*, 140 ff.) heads a chapter with this, the 'Ahmadābād Diamond', but, so far as the stone is concerned, all that can be said is that nothing is certainly known of its subsequent history. It may have been disposed of in Persia.

[2] The equivalent of 36 Kollūr or Golkonda mangelins, in carats at 1⅜, is 49½ carats, and in Rammalakota mangelins at 1¾ (see p. 69) = 63 carats. Nothing further is known of this stone.

[3] Strictly $103\frac{63}{64}$ carats, in round numbers therefore 104, the mangelins being those of Golkonda at 1⅜ carats in this case.

[4] This case has been quoted in connexion with investigations into the nature and origin of the diamond. Mr. Streeter devotes a chapter to this diamond. (See *Great Diamonds*, ch. xxx, p. 218.) Bazu, on his return to Europe, sold a number of diamonds and pearls to Louis XIV.

Figures of twenty Diamonds which the Author sold to the King on his return from his last Voyage to India. The figures before the Reader show the weight, the extent, and thickness of each Stone.[1] [Pl. III.]

Here [in Pl. IV] are the figures of the most beautiful rubies in the world, and of the topaz of the Great Mogul, in the order in which they are arranged here by numbers.

No. 1. Figure of a ruby which belongs to the King of Persia. It is of the thickness and shape of an egg, is bored through and of very high colour, beautiful and clean, with the exception of a small flaw at the side. The custodians refuse to say what it cost, as is also the case with the pearl belonging to the same King, which is represented further on; they are likewise unwilling that any one should know the weight of either. Those who keep the registers of the King of Persia's jewels merely say that this ruby has been in the possession of the King for many years.

No. 2 represents a large stone believed to be a ruby, and sold as such to Ja'far Khān, the Great Mogul's uncle, who bought it for the sum of 95,000 rupees, which amount to 1,425,000 livres.[2] He presented it to the Great Mogul, with

[1] The violet-blue diamond A, and the two rose-coloured diamonds B and C, which are here figured, are referred to in 'A Note about some unusual Diamonds', published in the *Phil. Trans.* for 27th April 1674, No. 102, p. 26, as being in a representation of a considerable number of diamonds, which were sold by Tavernier to the King of France. Louis XIV paid 220,000 livres for it. Hence it would seem that this plate reached the Royal Society in London before the publication of the travels in 1676. The adamantine hardness of the stones, in spite of their unusual colours, caused them to be admitted to be diamonds. The history of the blue diamond is well told in Mr. Streeter's work on *The Great Diamonds*. The blue diamond which belonged to Mr. Hope, weighing 44¼ carats, is believed to be a fragment of this stone, which was stolen from the Garde Meuble in 1792.

[2] There is here a mistake on one side or the other; a cipher should either be added to the rupees or subtracted from the livres. See vol. i, p. 310, where the total value of a present made by Ja'far Khān is put at 1,050,000 livres, hence perhaps it may be concluded that the figure here should be 142,500 livres, but it is not certain that the occasions referred to were identical. Bernier (p. 271) says that it was valued at 40,000 crowns, but 'Chah-Jehan, who understood better than any man the

nany other precious things, on the King's festival, that is to say, the day whereon he is weighed, as I have elsewhere said. This stone having been priced at a little less than it cost, there happened to be present at that time an old Indian who had previously been chief jeweller to the King, but had been dismissed from his charge through jealousy. Having taken this stone in his hands, he maintained that it was not a balass [1] ruby, that Ja'far Khān had been cheated, and that the stone was not worth more than 500 rupees. The King having been informed of the discussion, summoned the old Indian, with all the other jewellers, who maintained on their side that the stone was a balass ruby. As in the whole Empire of the Great Mogul there was no one more proficient in the knowledge of stones than Shāhjahān, who was kept as a prisoner at Agra by Aurangzeb, his son, the latter sent the stone to the Emperor, his father, asking for his opinion. After full consideration he confirmed the verdict of the old jeweller, and said that it was not a balass ruby, and that its value did not exceed 500 rupees. The stone having been returned to Aurangzeb, he compelled the merchant who had sold it to take it back and return the money he had received.

Nos. 3 and 4 are figures of a ruby which belongs to the King of Bījāpur. No. 4 shows the height of the stone above the ring, and No. 3 the circuit of the chaton.[2] It weighs 14 mangelins, which equal $17\frac{1}{2}$ of our carats, the mangelin at Bījāpur being 5 grains.[3] It is hollowed from beneath, [i. e. cut *en cabuchon*] clean, and of the first quality. The King of Bījāpur bought it in the year 1653 for the sum of 14,200 new pagodas, the pagoda being then worth $3\frac{1}{2}$ rupees, this, in our money, would be equal to 74,550 livres.[4]

value of every kind of precious stone, discovered it to be worth less than five hundred, to the great confusion of the principal Jewellers, who in this instance had been completely deceived.'

[1] Ballet in the original, for balass. (See vol. i. 303 *n.*)

[2] The chaton is the bezel of a ring which holds a jewel in position.

[3] On p. 98 the Bījāpur mangelin is said to be equal to $1\frac{3}{8}$ carats (i. e. $5\frac{1}{2}$ diamond grains), and 14 mangelins should therefore be equal to $19\frac{1}{4}$ carats.

[4] £5,591 5*s.*

No. 5 is the figure of a ruby which a Banian merchant showed me at Benares during my last visit to India. It weighs 58 ratis, or $50\frac{3}{4}$ [1] carats, and is of the second quality. Its form is of an almond cabuchon somewhat hollowed beneath, and bored near the point. I was willing to give 40,000 rupees for it, which make 60,000 livres,[2] but the merchant to whom it belonged asked 55,000 rupees. I believe I could have got it for 50,000 rupees.[3]

No. 6 is the figure of the large topaz of the Great Mogul. I did not see him wear any other jewel during the time I remained at his Court on my last visit to India. This topaz weighs $181\frac{1}{8}$ ratis, or $157\frac{1}{4}$ carats.[4] It was bought at Goa for the Great Mogul, for the sum of 181,000 rupees, or 271,500 livres of our money.[5]

No. 7. These grand monarchs of Asia are not the only ones in the world who are in possession of beautiful stones. I have not seen as large rubies in any of the thrones of the Great Mogul as are those represented in the plate Nos. 7, 8, and 9, which belong to our great King, the most powerful and magnificent, in all respects, among the Monarchs of the earth !

[1] At the rate of one *rati* = $\frac{7}{8}$th of a carat. [2] £4,500.

[3] £5,750. The following reference to two great rubies may be quoted : 'In the aforesaid island of Sylen [Ceylon] is a very potent King, who hath precious stones of every kind under heaven, in such quantity as to be almost incredible. Among these he hath two rubies, of which he weareth one hung round his neck, and the other on the hand wherewith he wipeth his lips and his beard ; and each is of greater length than his breadth of four fingers, and when held in the hand it standeth out visibly on either side to the breadth of a finger. I do not believe that the universal world hath two stones like them, or of so great a price, of the same species' (Friar Jordanus, *Wonders of the East*, ed. Yule, p. 30 ; cf. Yule, *Marco Polo*, ii. 254, 256).

[4] $181\frac{1}{8}$ ratis = $158\frac{1}{2}$ carats nearly. In vol. i, p. 319, it was said to weigh 6 melscals = 1 Fr. once. It was probably the stone referred to in vol. i, p. 296. Bernier, already quoted, alludes to it as a 'beautiful oriental topaz of matchless size and splendour, shining like a little sun' (*Travels in the Mogul Empire*, 268).

[5] £20,412 10*s*.

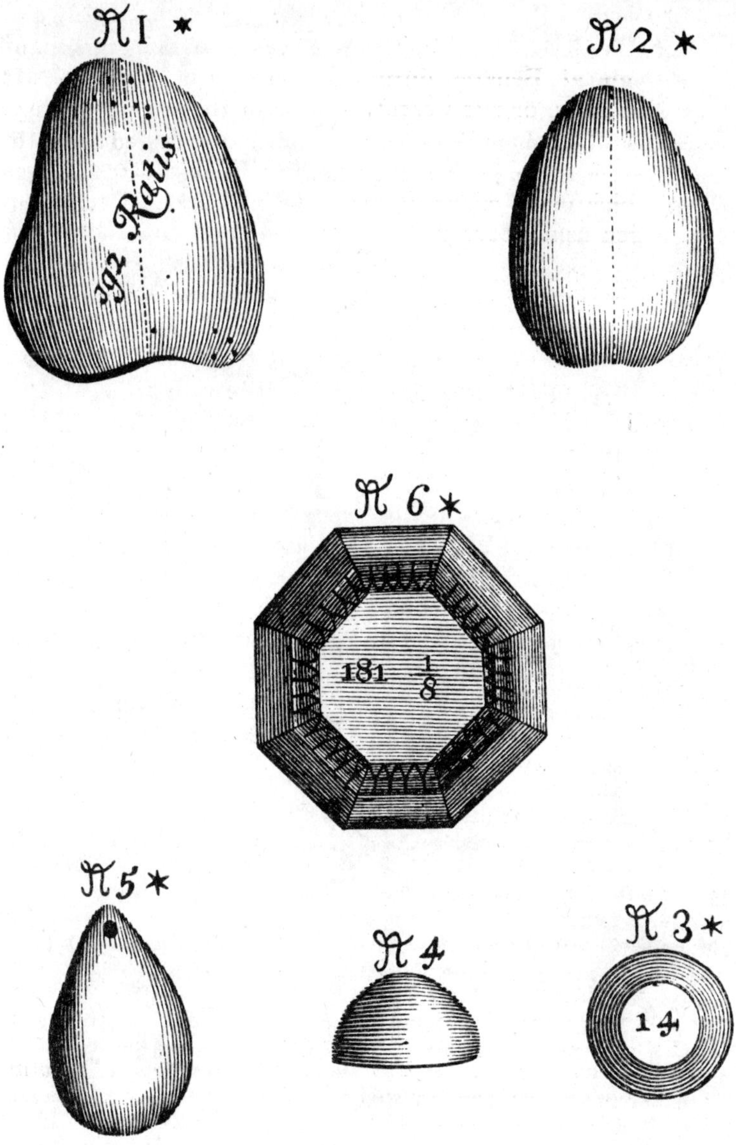

Figures of Rubies and Topaz

Iere again [in Pl. V] *are figures of the largest pearls of which we have knowledge, in the order of their numbers.*

No. 1 is the figure of a pearl which the King of Persia bought in the year 1633 from an Arab who had just received it from the fisheries at Al Katīf. It cost him 32,000 tomāns, or 1,400,000 livres of our money at the rate of 46 livres and 6 deniers per tomān.[1] It is the largest and most perfect pearl ever discovered, and it has not the least defect.

No. 2 is the figure of the largest pearl which I saw at the Court of the Great Mogul. It is suspended from the neck of a peacock made of precious stones, and rests on the breast, and this peacock surmounts the throne.

No. 3 is the figure of a pearl which I sold, on my last journey, to Shāista Khān,[2] uncle of the Great Mogul and Governor of Bengal. It weighs 55 carats, but the water is somewhat dead; it is the largest pearl which has ever been taken from Europe to Asia.

No. 4 is the figure of a large pearl perfect both as regards its water and its form which is like that of an olive. It is in the middle of a chain of emeralds and rubies that the Great Mogul sometimes wears round his neck, and it hangs down to his waist.

No. 5. As a round pearl of perfect form, this is the largest I know of, and it belongs to the Great Mogul. Its equal has never been found, for which reason the Great Mogul has not worn it, but has left it with other jewels which are unmounted. For if a match for it had been found, the pair might have been used as ear pendants, and each of the two pearls would have been placed between two rubies or two emeralds, in

[1] 32,000 × 46*l*. 6*d*. = 1,472,800 livres = £110,460, and 32,000 tomāns at £3 9*s*. = £110,400. Ainslie, referring to this in his chapter on pearls as a drug, erroneously states that Tavernier himself paid the enormous sum of £110,000 for this pearl. (*Materia Medica*, vol. i, p. 294.) A value of £64,000 for this pearl is mentioned by Streeter (*Precious Stones and Gems*, 3rd edition, part iii, p. 14), but that sum appears to have been derived from an underestimate of the equivalent values of the livre and tomān, as known to Tavernier.

[2] See for the incidents connected with the sale of this pearl, vol. i, p. 113. It was the cause of serious disagreement between Tavernier and Shāista Khān. Tavernier states that it came from the American pearl fishery.

conformity with the custom of the country, every one, rich or poor, in proportion to his means, wearing in each ear a pearl set between two coloured stones.

CHAPTER XXIII

Concerning Coral and Yellow Amber and the places where they are found.

ALTHOUGH coral does not rank among precious stones in Europe, it is nevertheless held in high esteem in the other quarters of the globe, and it is one of the most beautiful of nature's productions, so that there are some nations who prefer it to precious stones. I shall set down here, in a few words what I have been able to ascertain about the places where it is fished for, and of the manner in which it is obtained.

I shall say in the first place that there are three fisheries on the coast of Sardinia. That obtained at Arguerrel[1] is the best and the most beautiful of all, the second locality is called Boza,[2] and the third is close to the island of St. Pierre.[3] There is another fishery on the coasts of the island of Corse,[4] and the coral found there is slender but beautiful in colour. It is found at two other places on the coast of Africa—one near the Bastion de France,[5] and the other at Tabarque;[6] the coral from this locality is fairly thick and long, but the colours are pale. There is a seventh fishery on the coast of Sicily, near Trapano;[7] the coral there is slender, but of good colour. There is still another locality on the

[1] Alghero, near Cape Caccia, on west coast of Sardinia.

[2] Boza, on the west coast of Sardinia, about 5 miles from Cagliari. The coral fishery, mainly on the west coast, has now lost its importance (*Ency. Brit.*, xxiv. 212).

[3] St. Pierre is probably some small islet not on ordinary maps.

[4] Corsica.

[5] The Bastion de France was one of the forts belonging to France on the coast of Algiers before the nineteenth century. It was near La Callé, which in 1594 belonged to France, and was the centre of a coral fishery. It is now destroyed.

[6] Tabarka, a rocky islet on north coast of Tunis, near La Callé.

[7] Trepani, the Drepanum of the ancients, 18 miles north of Marsala.

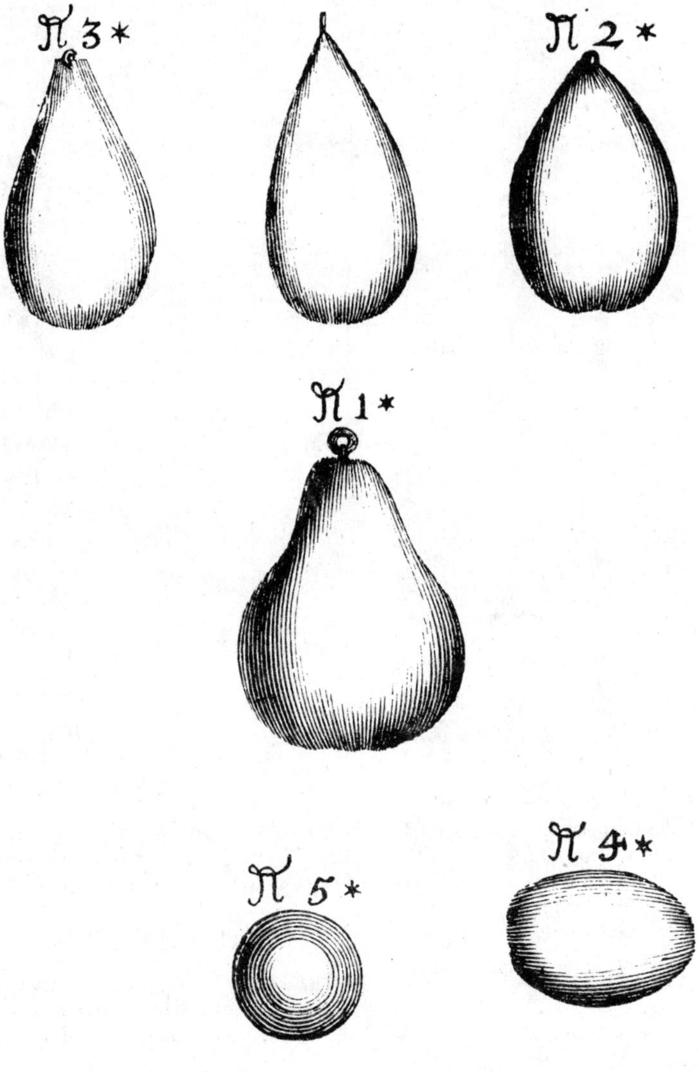

Figures of Pearls

coast of Catalogne, towards Cape de Quiers;[1] the coral there is of excellent colour and thick, but the branches are very short. There is, moreover, a ninth fishery in the island of Majorque,[2] of the same nature as that of the island of Corse; and these are all the places in the Mediterranean where there are coral fisheries,[3] for there are none in the Ocean.[4] The following is the method of fishing for it.

As coral grows under hollowed rocks where the sea is deep, the following device is used in order to obtain it. The fishers bind two rafters together in the form of a cross, and place a large lump of lead in the centre to make them sink to the bottom. They then bind tufts of hemp about the rafters, and twist them irregularly to the size of the thumb, and attach the wood by two ropes, one of which hangs from the bow and the other from the stern of the boat. They then allow the wood to drift with the current across the rocks, and the hemp becoming entangled about the coral, it sometimes requires five or six boats to hoist the rafters; and when exerting the great strain necessary, if one of the cables breaks all the rowers are in danger of perishing; it is a very risky trade. When dragging up the coral thus, by force—for as much as is drawn out an equal quantity falls back into the sea, and the bottom being generally very muddy—the coral is injured from day to day, as our fruits on the earth are, by worms, so that the sooner it is extracted from the mud the less is it deteriorated. In reference to this I may say that

[1] Catalonia, in Spain; Cape de Quiers, possibly C. Servère,

[2] Majorca. The fact of there being so much variation in the characters of the coral from these different localities should be of some interest to naturalists.

[3] 'The most important fisheries extend along the coasts of Tunis, Algeria, and Morocco, but red coral is also obtained in the vicinity of Naples, near Leghorn and Genoa, and on the coasts of Sardinia, Corsica, Catalonia, and Provence. [It is said that it attains greater perfection in the East than in the South, and that it is rarely found in a western, and never in a northern aspect.]' (*Encyclopædia Britannica*, vii. 131.) In 11th ed. the passage in brackets is omitted.

[4] This is now known to be not correct, since 'red or precious coral occurs at San Jago and also at St. Vincent . . . It occurs in about 100 or 120 fathoms, and is dragged for with swabs as in the Mediterranean.' (H. N. Moseley, *Notes of a Naturalist on the Challenger*, 65.)

I have seen, at Marseilles, something wonderful in a shop where coral was worked. There was a piece as big as the thumb, and as it was somewhat glassy it was cut in two, and a worm was found inside, which I saw wriggle ; it had been kept alive for some months by shutting it up in its hole. For it should be remarked that among some branches of coral there grows a sort of sponge similar to our honey-combs, where small worms ensconce themselves like bees—in such ways does nature delight to diversify her works. Some persons believe that coral is soft in the sea, but, as a matter of fact, it is hard. It is, however, true that in certain months of the year one can express from the ends of the branches a kind of milk as from the breast of a woman.[1] This may be the seed which, falling upon whatsoever it meets with in the sea, produces another branch of coral—thus, for instance, it has been found on a human skull, upon the blade of a sword, and upon a grenade which had fallen into the sea, where it was interlaced in the branches of coral to the height of six inches ; and I have had the grenade in my hands.

The coral fishery lasts from the beginning of April to the end of July, and generally 200 boats are engaged in it, some years more and some less. They are built on the Genoa river,[2] and are very light. They carry much sail in order to sail fast, there is no other part of the Mediterranean where boats carry so much, and there are no galleys able to outstrip them. There are seven men to each boat, with a boy to attend on them. The fishing is carried on from 25 to 40 miles from the land, where it is believed there are rocks, the boats not advancing farther to sea for fear of pirates, from whom they escape, when they meet them, by swift sailing.

I have to make a remark here about coral in reference to certain nations of the East. The Japanese, as I have said, esteem neither pearls nor precious stones,[3] but they value

[1] This refers to the ova of the coral polypes.

[2] [Surely 'Genoese Riviera'.]

[3] See vol. ii, p. 88 above. It is also remarkable that red coral seems to have been little used as an ornament in Egypt and Phoenicia, but the material may have crumbled away, or been dissolved (Hastings, *Dict. Bible*, i. 478 and cf. *Ency. Biblica*, i. 895 f.).

beautiful beads of coral, which serve to close their bags; these bags are made, as they were formerly, in France. It is for this purpose that they use the largest beads of coral, to run on a silken cord which closes the bag; so that if you are able to offer them one of the size of an egg, beautiful and clean, without any spot upon it, they will pay whatever you ask. The Portuguese, who formerly did a large trade in Japan, have often assured me that they could obtain for one as much as 20,000 écus.[1] It is much to be wondered that the Japanese give so much money for a fine piece of coral, since they have a contempt for jewels, caring only for things which are little thought of elsewhere. They attach great value to the skin of a particular fish, which is rougher than shagreen; this fish has on the back, as it were, six small bones, and sometimes eight, which are elevated and form a circle, with another in the middle, resembling a rose of diamonds.[2] They make sword scabbards of these fish-skins and the more symmetrically these small bones form the rose and are arranged, the more money is given for them—sometimes up to 10,000 écus,[3] as the Dutch have assured me. To return to coral and to finish the discourse about it, it should be added that the common people wear it and use it as an ornament for the neck and arms throughout Asia, but principally towards the north in the territories of the Great Mogul, and beyond them, in the mountains, of the Kingdoms of Assam and Bhutān.[4]

[1] £4,500.

[2] This appears to have been the skin of some kind of shark or ray. Ball had seen, but could not refer to, figures of it in some of the old Dutch and Portuguese travels. A common kind of it is still to be seen on the handles of the Japanese swords, of which such large numbers have been recently imported. In his chapter on the *Conduite des Hollandois en Asie*, published in the *Recũeil*, ed. 1679, p. 17, Tavernier gives a further account of it. He says a perfect skin was worth up to 10,000 écus, an ordinary one being obtainable for 1 écu. The fish, he adds, occurred in the Persian Gulf (*Ency. Brit.*, xxiv. 769).

[3] The French editions of 1679 and 1713 have 1,000 écus.

[4] The reason for the preference shown for coral is probably to be attributed to the way its tints adapt themselves to set off a dark skin, and also look well with a white garment. It is much worn in the Himalayas (Yule, *Marco Polo*, i. 162; Baden Powell, *Economic Products of the Punjab*, 48).

Yellow amber is not found except on a particular coast of Ducal Prussia, in the Baltic Sea,[1] where the sea during certain winds throws it from time to time on the sand. The Elector of Brandenburg, who is the proprietor of it, farms out all this coast for from 18,000 to 20,000 écus a year, and sometimes up to 22,000 écus ; and the farmers employ watchmen, who traverse the length of the shore, the sea throwing the amber sometimes on one side and sometimes on the other, so that no one can steal it ; and whoever ventures to do so receives corporal chastisement.

Amber is nothing more than a congelation of a species of gum which forms in the sea. This experience sufficiently proves, because numerous pieces are to be seen which contain flies and other insects congealed in them.[2] I have had many such pieces, and one, among others, which had four or five small flies inside it.

As I have made a remark about coral in reference to Japan, I shall make another about amber in reference to China. It is a custom among the Chinese that when any great noble gives a feast, his reputation for grandeur and magnificence depends upon his having brought in, at the close of the repast, three or four perfume-pans and his having thrown into each of them a large quantity of amber, sometimes to the value of 1,000 écus and upwards, in consideration of the fact that the more he burns, and the larger the pieces, the more magnificent is the entertainment regarded, for a piece weighing one livre is worth 200 to 300 écus.[3] They use amber for this purpose because they adore fire, and because amber, thrown in the fire, yields a certain odour which is not unpleasing to the Chinese ; as it contains a kind of oil it gives out a flame

[1] The source of amber in Upper Burma in the Hukung valley was not known to Tavernier. (See *Economic Geology of India*, p. 57 ; Watt, *Economic Products*, 64 ; Scott & Hardiman, *Gazetteer*, Part i, vol. ii. 289 ff. for a description of the mines there.)

[2] Tavernier had therefore an approximately correct idea as to the true nature and origin of amber as a fossilized vegetable production.

[3] i. e. £45 to £67 10*s*. per livre. This use of amber has not been traced in modern authorities, but that of incense sticks is common (J. D. Ball, *Things Chinese*, 4th ed., pp. 64, 74, 551, 553, 643; Hastings, *Ency. Religion and Ethics*, vii. 204 f.).

exceeding most other flames. This profusion and waste explain the reason why amber is one of the best articles of merchandise that one could carry to China if trade had been open to foreigners, but the Dutch Company strictly reserve to themselves the trade in it—the Chinese coming to buy it from them at Batavia.

I am unwilling to finish this chapter without making some remarks on ambergris also. We do not very well know either how it is formed or where it is found; but it would appear as though it can only be in the seas of the East, although it has sometimes been found on the English and other European coasts.[1] The largest quantity of it is found on the coast of Melinda, principally towards the mouths of the rivers, and especially at the mouth of that which is called Rio di Sena.[2] When the Governor of Mozambique returns to Goa at the close of three years, the term of his government, he generally brings with him about 300,000 pardos' worth of ambergris, and the pardo, as I have elsewhere said, amounts to 27 sols

[1] Ambergris, as is now well known, consists of the fæces of the Cachelot or Sperm whale, Physeter macrocephalus, which inhabits the Indian Ocean. Multitudes of small cuttlefish are swallowed whole, and their horny beaks are not digested. This causes irritation, which produces ambergris (Dr. C. F. Sonntag, London Zoological Society; cf. *Daily Mail*, 10th May 1922). Garcia da Orta (*Drugs and Simples of India*, 24) in his chapter on ambergris speaks of ambergris containing beaks of birds. These were no doubt the beaks of the cuttlefish upon which these whales feed. A form of this story is told by Barbosa (ed. Dames, ii. 107), who says ambergris is the guano of birds which has been swallowed and voided by whales. Chardin (iv. 47) doubts the connexion with birds, but mentions a number of alternative myths as to its origin. Ainslie and Watt (*Materia Medica*, i. 15–17; *Commercial Products*, 64) give an interesting account of it, and refer to a vegetable ambergris yielded by a tree in Guiana. Ainslie says, like many other authors, that the best ambergris was obtained on the coast of Madagascar. (See *Voyage of F. Leguat*, Hakluyt Society, ii. 152 ff.) In the *Daily Press* there once appeared a paragraph headed 'An Ambergris King', in which one William A. Atkins, the owner of a fleet of Cape Cod whalers, is described as having the monopoly of the ambergris trade of America—the ambergris being for equal weight worth more than gold. Owing to ambergris being called *ambra* by some nations, very erroneous statements occur in many authorities as to the distribution in the East of true amber, for which it has been mistaken. (See *Economic Geology of India*.)

[2] The Zambezi, see p. 126 below.

of our money.[1] Sometimes pieces of ambergris of considerable size and weight are found. In the year 1627 a Portuguese vessel sailing from Goa to the Manillas, after it had passed the Straits of Malacca was overtaken by a tempest which lasted many days and nights; the sky was always concealed, and it was impossible for the pilot to take observations. Meanwhile the rice and other articles of food began to be exhausted, and the crew discussed whether they should not throw the blacks who were in the vessel into the sea in order to preserve the food for the white men. They were about to carry this plan into execution, when one morning the sun showed itself, and disclosed an island tolerably near, but they were unable to anchor till the following day, the sea being high and the wind unfavourable. There were in the vessel a Frenchman, named Marin Renaud, of Orleans, and his brother, who on going on shore found a river and, together with two Portuguese corporals and a sergeant, went to bathe at its mouth. One of the corporals when bathing perceived in the water a large mass which floated near the shore, and which he concluded, on going near it, was a sort of spongy stone. So he left it without another thought, as did the four others, who also went to look at it and handled it without being able to make out what it was. When he returned to the vessel the corporal reflected during the night what this object, of which he had been unable to ascertain the nature, could be, and having heard ambergris spoken of, began to think that it might be it, in which he was not mistaken. The following day, without saying anything to his comrades, he took a sack and got himself put on shore, and going to the river as though he wished to bathe again, found the piece of ambergris and carried it secretly to the vessel, where he placed it in his box. He could not help communicating the fact the same evening to Marin Renaud, who was unwilling to believe at first that it was really ambergris, but having well considered it thought at length that the corporal was right. Taking all chances, he offered the piece to Marin for two pains of Chinese gold, and the golden

[1] 27 sols = 2*s*. ·03*d*., or say 2*s*. 300,000 pardos therefore = £30,000. On the finding of ambergris in the Indian Ocean see Linschoten, ii. 92 f.

pain is equal to 600 livres[1] of our money; but Marin was only willing to give one; the other held out on his side and kept the piece in his box. A few days afterwards, either spite at not being able to get the piece of ambergris for what he had offered caused Marin to speak, or the matter was discovered in some other way; the report, however, was spread throughout the vessel that the corporal had a big piece of ambergris in his box, which he had found by chance on the shore of the island near which the Portuguese were at anchor, and the sailors and soldiers then insisted on having their share. Marin Renaud out of petty revenge set the ball a-rolling and taught them their lesson. They told the corporal that, being all comrades and all running the same risks, it was just that they should all share in common the benefits which fortune offered them; and, moreover, that he was not the only one to whom she had disclosed this piece of ambergris, which should consequently be divided between all the crew. The corporal defended himself as well as he could, and as there were some who took his part, in the hope of having a better share of the piece if there were few pretenders to it, the dispute became so hot that at length it gave rise to a disturbance, which the captain of the vessel at once prudently sought to allay. He pointed out to the sailors and soldiers that this large piece of ambergris, which, when it was weighed in their presence, proved to be 33 livres in weight, being a rare piece and worthy of being presented to the King, it was a pity to break it into so many small pieces; that they would find it pay them better to keep it till their return to Goa, where if it was presented to the Viceroy, he would not fail to pay handsomely for it, and by this means they would each receive much more. This suggestion of the captain was generally approved. They pursued their voyage to the Manillas, and on their return the piece of ambergris was taken to the Viceroy. The captain told him beforehand how the matter stood, and they concerted together how they could secure the ambergris without it

[1] Literally 'loaves'. The English name for the ingots of gold used in currency by the Chinese was 'shoes'; the equivalent value here would be £45. See vol. i, p. 331; Yule, *Hobson-Jobson*, 830.

costing the Viceroy anything. Those who presented it to him on the part of the sailors and soldiers were thanked for it, and the Viceroy told them that he recognized their goodwill by so splendid a present which he would send to the King, who at that time was Philippe the Fourth,[1] to whom Portugal was still subject. Thus all the pretenders to the piece of ambergris were defrauded of their expectations, and neither from the Viceroy nor the King himself, to whom the ambergris was sent, did they receive any gift.

I shall say one other word concerning a piece of ambergris weighing 42 livres. In the year 1646 or 1647 a Zealander, of one of the best families of Middlebourg, who commanded for the Dutch Company in the Island of Maurice, which is to the east of that of St. Laurens,[2] found this piece on the shore and sent it to the Company. As these people always have enemies, and there being a mark on the piece as if some one had broken a portion off, the Commander was accused of having stolen half, but he cleared himself of this charge at Batavia. But the suspicion, however, dwelt in the minds of many persons, and the Commander seeing that they would not give him another appointment, returned to Zealand on the same vessel on which I was a passenger.

CHAPTER XXIV

Concerning Musk and Bezoar and some other medicinal stones.

MUSK and bezoar being included among the rarest articles of trade, and the most precious which Asia furnishes us with, I have considered it appropriate to devote a chapter to them, and present the reader with some remarks about these two articles.

The best kind and the greatest quantity of musk come

[1] Philip IV, King of Spain, 1605–65.

[2] Mauritius and Madagascar, the latter having been known to the Portuguese as St. Lorenzo. Some say the Portuguese landed there first on the festival of the Saint, others that it was discovered by Lorenzo de Almeyda in 1506. (Varthema in Hakluyt Soc. ed., 296; Pyrard de Laval, i. 29; Fryer, i. 54.)

from the Kingdom of Bhutān, whence it is conveyed to Patna, the principal town of Bengal, to be sold to the people of that country. All the musk sold in Persia comes from there, and the merchants who sell musk prefer to receive in exchange yellow amber and coral, rather than gold and silver, because they make great profits out of these two commodities. I had the curiosity to take to Paris[1] a skin of this animal, which is here represented.

After this animal has been killed, the bladder, which is situated under the belly, is cut off—it is of the size of an egg, and is closer to the genital parts than to the navel. The musk is then extracted from the bladder which contains it—it is then like coagulated blood. When the peasants wish to adulterate it, they insert some of the liver and the blood of the slaughtered animal mixed together, instead of the musk which they have withdrawn. This mixture generates in the bladders certain small worms which eat the good musk, so that when one opens them he finds that much has gone bad. Other peasants, when they have cut the bladder and have drawn as much musk as they can without its appearing to be excessive, put in its place small pieces of lead to make up the weight. The merchants who buy it and transport it into foreign countries prefer this fraud to the other, because it does not generate these little worms. But it is still more difficult to discover the fraud when they make small purses of the skin of the animal's stomach, which they sew up with threads of the same skin, so as to resemble the true bladders; these purses are filled with what has been removed from the good bladders, together with the fraudulent mixture which is added to it, so that it is difficult for the merchants to discover anything.[2] It is true that if they bind the bladder directly

[1] The figure in the original, which it is needless to reproduce here, is a tolerable representation of the musk deer, *Moschus moschiferus* (Linn.). The trade now recognizes three grades of musk; Cabardien or Russian; Tonquin or Chinese; and Assam, including all the Indian varieties, reaching Europe via Calcutta (Watt, *Economic Products*, 786, and see Linschoten, ii. 94 f.; Fitch, ed. Ryley, 189).

[2] A still more remarkable method of adulteration is that mentioned by Barbosa, which consists, in short, in putting leeches on the living animal, after the musk has been removed, and then allowing them to

they cut it, without letting the air get to it, and without giving time to the odour to lose some of its strength by evaporation while they take out what they want to remove, if this bladder should be held to any one's nose, blood would immediately issue from it in consequence of the pungency of the odour, which for this reason must be tempered to render it agreeable and prevent it from injuring the brain. The odour from the skin of this animal, which I took to Paris, was so strong that it was impossible to keep the skin in my rooms, as it caused headache to all the people in the house, and it was necessary to put it in a garret, where at length my servants cut off the bladder, but this did not prevent its always retaining some of the odour. You do not begin to meet with this animal till about the 56° of latitude; but at 60° it is in great abundance, the country there being well wooded. It is true that in the months of February and March, after these animals have suffered from famine in their own country on account of the snow, which falls in abundance to depths of 10 or 12 feet, they come south to 44° and 45°, to eat the corn and new rice, and it is at this time that the peasants entrap them, in snares which they set, and kill them with arrows and blows of sticks. Some persons have told me that the deer are so thin and feeble in consequence of the hunger from which they have suffered, that many allow themselves to be captured by coursing. There must be an enormous number of these animals, as each has but one bladder, the largest of which is ordinarily of the size of a hen's egg, and only yields half an ounce of musk. It sometimes requires even three or four of these bladders to make an ounce.[1]

gorge themselves with the blood, after which they are dried in the sun and pounded, and the substance so prepared is placed in counterfeit pods made of the skin of the animal. (*The Book of Duarte Barbosa*, ed. Dames, ii. 1921, 161.) Linschoten says that the Chinese adulterated it with the livers of cattle, dried and beaten to powder (ii. 95). According to Varthema (p. 102), the test of true musk is to take a bladder of it in the morning fasting, let three or four men smell it, and if it is genuine it will make their noses bleed.

[1] 'The musk deer is found throughout the Himalayas, always at great elevations, and in summer rarely below 8,000 feet, and as high as the limits of forest. It extends through the Himalayas to Central and

The King of Bhutān, of whom I shall speak in the following Book, in the description which I shall give of his Kingdom, fearing that the fraud done in musk might stop the trade, especially as musk is also obtained in Tonquin or Cochin-China, but is much dearer because it is not so abundant there—this King, I say, fearing lest this falsification of goods might divert the trade from his territories, some time ago ordered that the bladders should not be stitched, but should be brought open to Bhutān, which is his place of residence, to be examined and sealed with his seal. Those which I bought were of this kind; but notwithstanding all the King's precautions, the peasants open them secretly, and place small pieces of lead in them, as I have said; this the merchants tolerate, because the lead does not spoil the musk, and causes no injury, save in the weight. On one of my journeys to Patna I bought 7,673 bladders, which weighed 2,557½ ounces, and 452 ounces without the bladders.[1]

Bezoar [2] comes from a district of the Kingdom of Golkonda,

Northern Asia as far as Siberia. A good musk pod is valued at from 10 to 15 rupees. One ounce is about the average produce of the pod.' (Jerdon, *Mammals of India*, 268; Blanford, *Mammalia*, 552 f.; Yule, *Marco Polo*, i. 242, 245.) Adulteration, as it is described by Tavernier, appears to be still practised.

[1] Barbosa (ed. Dames, 1921, vol. ii, p. 159) says that musk was abundant in Ava. From this, with similar statements about other commodities, we see that Tavernier did not limit his mercantile transactions to precious stones and he shows the abundance of the animal in his time. On p. 201 below, he again refers to this purchase (?), and says he bought 26,000 rupees' worth—a Fr. ounce in the capsule costing 4 livres and 4 sols, i. e. about 6*s*. 3*d*., and out of the capsule 8 francs, or say 6*s*. 8*d*., or if livres are intended, 12*s*. But at these prices the quantity here mentioned falls far short of making the total sum of 26,000 rupees. This, supposing the occasions to be identical, as appears to be the case, is a characteristic Tavernier discrepancy.

[2] Bezoar is from Persian *pādzahr*, Arabic *bāzahr*, *bādizahr*, 'counter-poison, antidote' the name given to intestinal calculi. It was formerly so highly esteemed in the East as a drug that the early European travellers all seemed to believe in its efficacy, and accounts of it are to be found in the writings by many of them. (See note 1, on p. 119; Yule, *Hobson-Jobson*, 90.) It has at present no medicinal value (See *Ency. Brit.*, i. 668, xi. 418; Blanford, *Mammalia*, 503); Garcia da Orta (*Colloquies on the Simples and Drugs of India*, ed. Sir C. Markham, p. 362 ff.) has much to say on the subject.

towards the north-east. It is found in the fodder in the paunches of goats which browse on a tree, the name of which I have forgotten. This plant bears little buds, about which, and also on the tips of the branches, which the goats eat, the bezoar concretes in the bellies of these animals. It assumes a form according to the shape of the buds and the ends of the branches, and this is why one finds it in so many different shapes. The peasants, by feeling the belly of the goat, know how many bezoars it contains, and they sell the goat for a price in proportion to the number which are therein. In order to ascertain this, they run both hands under the belly of the goat and beat the paunch along both sides, so that all the stones fall to the middle, and they then estimate exactly, by touch, how many bezoars are in it. The value of bezoar depends on the size, although the small possess no less virtue than the large. But in this respect one is often deceived by the fact that there are people who enlarge the bezoar with a kind of paste made of gum and other materials of the same colour as the bezoar. They understand, even, how to give as many coats as the natural bezoar ought to have. One can detect this fraud easily by two methods. The first by weighing the bezoar and placing it to steep for some time in lukewarm water; if the water does not change its colour, and if the bezoar does not lose weight, it has not been adulterated. The other means is to touch the bezoar with a pointed hot iron; if the iron enters it and makes it fry, it is a sign that it is a mixture, and that it is not genuine.[1] For the rest, the larger the bezoar the higher the price, which rises in proportion like that of the diamond. For if 5 or 6 bezoars weigh an ounce, the ounce will be worth from 15 to 18 francs, but if it is a bezoar of one ounce, the ounce will be worth fully 100 francs. I have sold one of $4\frac{1}{4}$ ounces for as much as 2,000 livres.[2]

I had the curiosity to investigate all that can be ascertained regarding bezoar,[3] having already made several visits

[1] Fryer recommends touching it with a hot iron, or rubbing the stone on paper smeared by the application of chalk, when, if it leaves an olive colour, it is good (ii. 141). [2] £150.

[3] Bezoar is the Jadah stone of Central Asia, often alluded to by Bābur, and said to be able to produce rain and snow; the word has no

to Golkonda, which is the place where there is the most considerable sale, without being able to ascertain in what part of the body of the goat it is found. On my fifth journey some persons who were in the services of the English and Dutch Companies, and who dared not trade on their own account, were indebted to me because I purchased about 60,000 rupees' worth of bezoar for them. The merchants who sold it, wishing to show their gratitude, and make me some present, I refused, and told them I had never taken anything from anyone for a service which I was able to render. But I let them know that I would be able to serve them again in the approaching monsoon, and that they would oblige me, on their part, if they would get three or four of these goats which produce the bezoar for me, promising to pay them for them whatsoever they were worth. The merchants appeared much surprised at this demand, and replied that the prohibition was so strict that if any one dared to remove the goats out of the Province he would be executed without fail. I saw plainly that this request troubled them, for on the one side they feared punishment and on the other they were afraid lest I might prevent them from making another sale; this would have been a great loss to these poor people, who, whether they do or do not sell, are obliged to pay the King, for the farm, 6,000 old pagodas, which amount to 45,000 livres of our money.[1] Fifteen days or so afterwards, when I had thought nothing further about them, three of them knocked at my door before daylight. As soon as they entered my chamber, where I was still in bed, they asked me if all my servants were foreigners. As I had none from the town, and they were all either Persians or from Surat, I told them they were all foreigners, upon which they withdrew without replying. Half an hour afterwards they returned with six of these goats, which I examined at my leisure. It should be said that they are beautiful animals,

connexion with Jade (N. Elias & E. D. Ross, *Hist. of the Moghuls of Central Asia*, 1898, p. 32, note 4).

[1] There may be some mistake here, as 6,000 old pagodas are only equal to 45,000 livres when the pagoda is taken at 5 rupees, whereas Tavernier in general gives the old pagoda the value of only 4½ rupees, 45,000 livres = £3,375.

very tall, and having fine hair, like silk. As soon as the goats were safely in my hall, the eldest of the three merchants who had brought them, began by paying me a compliment, and told me that since I had not been willing to take the present which they wished to make me, for having procured the sale of so large a parcel of bezoar, at the least I would not refuse these six goats which they gave me with their whole hearts; but as I did not wish to take them entirely as a gift, as they desired, I asked what the value of them was; and, after having made great difficulty about telling me, I was at length much surprised and thought they were joking when they said that one of the goats which they pointed out was worth three rupees, that each of the two next were worth four rupees, and each of the three which remained four and a quarter rupees. Upon which I asked them why some of the goats were dearer than others, and I learnt that it was because one had only one bezoar in the stomach, and the others had two or three or four of them; this they made me see for myself, forthwith, by tapping the belly, as I have above described. These six goats had 17 bezoars, and a half one, like the half of a nut. The inside was like the soft dropping of a goat, as these bezoars grow amongst the food in the belly of the goat. Some have told me that bezoars originate close to the liver, others maintain that it is close to the heart, but I was never able to ascertain the truth.[1]

Both in the East and West there are an abundance of bezoars obtained from cows, and there are some which weigh up to 17 or 18 ounces, such an one having been given to the Grand Duke of Tuscany. But nothing is thought of this kind of bezoar, six grains of the other having a greater effect than thirty of it.

As for the bezoar obtained from monkeys, as some believe, it is so strong that two grains of it do as much as six from that of the goat; but it is very rare, and it is found particu-

[1] That Tavernier was not well versed in anatomy is sufficiently apparent from this passage, but at the period at which he wrote it, more than two centuries ago, such references to the heart and liver, and their communication with the stomach, would probably have passed without criticism.

larly in the species of monkeys which live in the Island of Macassar. This kind of bezoar is round, while the other is of diverse forms, according to the shapes of the buds and ends of branches which the goats have eaten. As these stones, which it is believed come from monkeys, are much rarer than the others, they are also much dearer and much more sought after; and when one is found of the size of a nut it is valued at more than 100 écus. The Portuguese, more than other nations, attach great value to bezoar, because they are always on their guard, one against the other, fearing that an enemy may wish to poison them.[1]

There is still another much esteemed stone which is called the porcupine stone, which this animal has in its head, and is more efficacious against poison than bezoar. When it is placed to steep in water for a quarter of an hour, the water becomes so bitter that there is nothing in the world to equal it in bitterness.[2] This animal has also sometimes, in its belly, a stone which is of the same nature and equally good as that which comes from the head, except with this difference, that it loses nothing of its weight or size by steeping in water, while there is diminution of the other. During my life I have bought three of these stones. One cost me 500 écus, and I disposed of it subsequently with advantage to the Ambassador Dominico de Santis,[3] of whom I have spoken in my accounts of Persia. I paid 400 écus for another, which I still

[1] Garcia da Orta (*Drugs and Simples*, 362 ff.), who devotes a chapter to bezoar, highly extols its merits as a medicine in cases of ague, measles, as an antidote to poison, and in the treatment of abscesses; he mentions that it was supposed, moreover, to possess aphrodisiac properties. It is not now believed to have any therapeutic value—to be, in fact, neutral.

[2] It seems probable that the substance supposed to be obtained in the head of the porcupine was a vegetable drug, to which that mythical origin was ascribed (Garcia da Orta, 470 f.). Castanheda mentions a stone obtained in the head of an animal called bulgoldorf, which was exceedingly rare, and was said to be an antidote against all kinds of poison (Kerr, *Voyages and Travels*, ii. 439). A. Hamilton (in Pinkerton, viii. 450) says that at Lingen, near Johore, he has seen pieces of porcupine bezoar as big as, and shaped like, a walnut, valued at 600 pieces of eight.

[3] See *Persian Travels*, Paris, 1576, bk. ii, ch. v, p. 181. He was an ambassador from the Venetian Republic.

keep; and the third was sold to me for 300 écus, and I made a present of it to a friend.

I shall finally make mention of the snake-stone, which is nearly of the size of a double,[1] some of them tending to an oval shape, being thick in the middle and becoming thin towards the edges. The Indians say that it grows on the heads of certain snakes, but I should rather believe that it is the priests of the idolaters who make them think so, and that this stone is a composition which is made of certain drugs.[2] Whatever it may be, it has an excellent virtue in extracting all the poison when one has been bitten by a poisonous reptile. If the part bitten is not punctured it is necessary to make an incision so that the blood may flow; and when the stone has been applied to it, it does not fall off till it has extracted all the venom which is drawn to it. In order to clean it it is steeped in woman's milk, or, in default of it, in that of a cow; and after having been steeped for ten or twelve hours, the milk, which has absorbed all the venom, assumes the colour of matter. One day, when I dined with the Archbishop of Goa, he took me into his museum, where he had many curiosities. Among other things he showed me one of these stones, and in telling me of its properties assured me that but three days since he had made trial of it, and then he presented it to me. As he traversed a marsh on the island of Salsette, upon which Goa is situated, on his way to a house in the country, one of his pallankeen bearers, who was almost naked, was bitten by a serpent and was at once cured by this stone. I have bought many of them; it is only the Brahmans who sell them, and it is that which makes me think that they make them. You employ

[1] Doubloon? A Spanish gold coin, formerly worth 33*s*. or 36*s*., now £1.

[2] Thévenot says that they were made of the ashes of the root of a certain plant, mixed with a particular kind of clay (*Voyages*, p. 94). Some snake-stones appear to have been made of charred bone. (See for an exhaustive account of this subject Yule, *Hobson-Jobson*, 847; Tennent, *Ceylon*, i. 197; Fryer, 138 f.; *Voyage of F. Leguat*, ii. 234.) The belief in their efficacy is still very general in India; by some they are supposed to be found in the head of the adjutant bird (see Ball, *Jungle Life in India*, 82; Prof. W. R. Halliday, *Folk-lore*, xxxii. 262 ff., xxxiii, 118 f.).

two methods to ascertain if the snake-stone is good, and that there is no fraud. The first is by placing the stone in the mouth, for then, if good, it leaps and attaches itself immediately to the palate. The other is to place it in a glass full of water, and immediately, if it is genuine, the water begins to boil, and small bubbles ascend from the stone which is at the bottom, to the top of the water.

There is still another stone which is called 'stone of the hooded snake.' [1] It is a kind of snake which has, as it were, a hood which hangs behind the head, and it is behind this hood that the stone is found, the smallest being of the size of a hen's egg. There are snakes in Africa and in Asia of an enormous size,[2] and up to 25 feet in length, as was that one whose skin is preserved at Batavia. This snake had swallowed a girl of eighteen years, of which fact I have elsewhere given an account.[3] You find these stones only in snakes which are, at the least, two feet in length. The stone, which is not hard, when rubbed against another stone yields a kind of slime which, when dissolved in water and drunk by a person who has some poison in his body, has the property of driving it out at once. These snakes are only to be found on the coasts of Melinda, and you can obtain the stones from Portuguese sailors and soldiers on their return from Mozambique.

CHAPTER XXV

Concerning the places from whence gold is obtained in Asia and Africa.

JAPAN consists of many islands to the east of China trending northwards; some even believe that Niphon, which is the largest of them, is, as it were, in contact with the mainland; it is the region of all Asia which furnishes the greatest quantity

[1] Cobra di capello—*Naja tripudians.* The figure referred to is a spirited one of a cobra, but is not reproduced here.

[2] Pythons. Marco Polo's great snakes were probably alligators (ii. 45, 49). For pythons nearly 30 feet long see *Ency. Brit.*, xxii. 704.

[3] Ball could not find the account to which Tavernier refers.

of gold, but it is thought that the principal part of it comes from the island of Formosa, from whence it is carried to Japan. Since the Dutch have held Formosa they have been unable to develop the trade of the particular locality where they believe the gold to occur.[1] Gold also comes from China, and the Chinese exchange it for the silver taken to them, for, price for price, they prefer silver to gold, because they have no mines of silver. This gold is of one of the lowest standards of any found in Asia.

The island of Celebes or Macassar[2] also produces gold, which is obtained from the rivers, where it occurs mingled with the sand. In the island of Achīn or Sumatra,[3] after the rainy season, and when the waters in the streams have subsided, veins of gold are found in the pebbles of different sizes which the rains have carried down from the mountains facing the north-east. On the west coast of the same island, where the Dutch go to ship pepper, the peasants bring an abundance of gold, but it is of very low standard, even inferior to the gold of China. Towards Tibet, which is identical with the Caucasus of the Ancients, in the territories of a Rājā beyond the Kingdom of Kashmīr, there are three mountains, close to one another, one of which produces gold of excellent quality, another grenat, and another lapis.[4] Finally, gold

[1] The occurrence of gold in China, Japan, and Formosa is not a subject that can be treated of exhaustively in these notes. That mines occur in China and Japan is well known, but Ball was not able to find conclusive evidence with reference to Formosa. See *Ency. Brit.*, x. 670. There is little in Japan (*ibid.*, xv. 197). Ainslie (*Materia Medica* i. 516) quotes the *Asiatic Journal* for December 1824 in support of the statement that the island abounds in gold. From a cursory examination of Mr. Locke's great work on gold, it seems to contain no reference to Formosa. For gold in China see *Ency. Brit.*, vi. 178.

[2] Gold occurs in the rivers of the northern and south-western peninsulas of Celebes. (Crawfurd, *Dictionary*, 144; *Ency. Brit.*, v. 578.)

[3] According to Crawfurd a small gold coin called mas (worth 1*s.* 2*d.*) from the Malay name of the metal, has been coined at Achīn. Gold dust, however, was the common medium of exchange. The Achinese have learnt the use of the touchstone from Telugu settlers. The gold filigree work of the Malays of Sumatra is very beautiful. A total of £1,000,000 worth of gold was considered by Crawfurd to cover the annual yield of all the Malayan islands in 1856.

[4] This indication as to the three mountains is somewhat vague. In all probability the grenat mine may be identified with the ruby, or

comes from the kingdom of Tippera,[1] of which I shall give a description in the following Book, but this gold is of bad quality, being of about the same standard as the gold of China.

These are all the places in Asia [2] whence gold comes, and I shall now say something of the gold of Africa, and of the region where it is obtained in greatest abundance.[3]

It should be remarked, under this head, that the governor

rather spinel mine, which is situated on the banks of the Shignān, a tributary of the Oxus in Badakhshān. As pointed out in vol. i, p. 303 *n.*, the name balass was derived from this locality. The lapis mine is near Firgāmu, also in Badakhshān, Lat. 36° 10′ Long. 71°. (Yule, *Marco Polo*, i. 150, 153.) The Tibet gold mines, famous since the days of Herodotus, are somewhat numerous. Each of these localities will be found described in the *Economic Geology of India*, pp. 213, 430, 529, where, also, an explanation of the myth of the gold-digging ants is suggested. See Watt, *Dict. Economic Products*, iii. 529. Khoten is famous for its gold, of which there are several mines under the mountains near Kiria to the east of Khoten (R. Shaw, *Visits to High Tartary, Yārkand, and Kāshghar*, 476). For Mīrzā Haidar's account of Tibetan gold mines see N. Elias & E. D. Ross, *Hist. of the Moghuls of Central Asia*, 409, 411 f. On various explanations of gold guarded by griffins or dug by ants in Sir J. Frazer, *Pausanias*, ii. 328 f. Sir T. Holdich (*Tibet the Mysterious*, 2 f.) points out that the myth is based on the practice of Tibetan miners, covered with blankets, who excavate gold by means of deer horns. The subject is fully discussed in *Indian Antiquary*, iv. 225 ff. The stone most frequently associated with Media was the highly-prized lapis lazuli, said to be found in Mount Demavand. But nothing is known of the locality of this mine, which must have been one of the most ancient in the world (Sir P. Sykes, *Hist. of Persia*, 2nd ed. i. 33).

[1] Tipra in the original. Ball did not know of any evidence for the occurrence of gold in Tippera; possibly what was brought thence in Tavernier's time was received from Assam, China, or Burma, in exchange for other commodities. Our Author devotes ch. xvi of bk. iii to a description of this Kingdom, which see.

[2] It is strange that Tavernier should have been unaware of the occurrence of gold in any part of the Indian Peninsula, there being so many localities where it is obtained, some of which were most probably worked in his time. (*Vide* for distribution of gold *Economic Geology of India*, ch. 'Gold'.) For gold-mining in neolithic times at Maski in the Nizam's Dominions see *The Foote Collection of Indian Prehistoric and Protohistoric Antiquities*, Madras, 1916, ii. 29, 125.

[3] Of the existence of gold in Eastern Africa there is abundant evidence. Of that which reaches the coast, however, a large proportion probably comes from afar off in the interior. Alluvial gold has long been collected in the Zambezi watershed (Sir H. H. Johnston, *British Central Africa*, 463).

of Mozambique has subject to him the commanders of Sofāla[1] and of Shupanga.[2] The first of these two small governments is on the river Sena 60 leagues from its mouth, and the other is 10 leagues higher up. From the mouth of the river up to these places on both sides there are many settlements of negroes, each of which is commanded by a Portuguese. These Portuguese have for a long time been masters of the country, and act like petty princes, making war against one another on the smallest pretext, there being some among them who have as many as 5,000 Cafres, who are their slaves. The Governor of Mozambique, to whom these petty princes are subject, furnishes them with cloth and other necessary goods, each of which he sells according to its market value. When the Governor of Mozambique[3] leaves Goa to assume charge of his government, which is the best of those subject to the Viceroy, he takes with him a great quantity of goods, and especially calicoes dyed black. His correspondents at Goa also send him every year two vessels laden with the same goods, which he forwards to Sofāla and Shupanga, and up to the town of Monomotapa,[4] capital of a Kingdom of the same name, otherwise called Voubebaran—the town being about 150 leagues distant from Shupanga. The ruler of all

[1] The position ascribed to Sofāla is incorrect, as it was not on the river named, but some two degrees, or say 70 leagues, to the south of the Delta of the Zambezi, on which the town of Sena is situated. A very interesting collection of notices referring to Sofāla and its gold is given in Yule, *Hobson-Jobson*, 849 f. Tavernier calls the river '*Sene*'.

[2] Chepon-Goura in the original. The modern Shupanga on the Zambezi is probably Tavernier's Chepon-Goura; it is between Sena and the coast.

[3] Castanheda says that the Moors took from India to Mozambique 'silver, linen cloth, pepper, ginger, silver rings, many pearls and rubies, and from a country inland they procured gold'. He also states that much gold was brought from the interior to Sofāla. (See Kerr, *Voyages and Travels*, ii. 317, 427.)

[4] The name is spelt Monomopata and Monomotapa in the original. Monomotapa is the old name of an extensive region on the Zambezi, and to the south of it. The meaning is uncertain, one explanation being that it means 'lord of the hippopotamus'. Its capital was Zumubany, a corruption of Zimbabwe, the Voubebaran of the text. See a full account in *Ency. Brit.*, xviii. 731 f.; Sir H. H. Johnston, *British Central Africa*, 56; Barbosa, ed. Dames, i. 9 ff.; Sir R. Burton, *Lands of Cazembe*, 22; Linschoten, i. 26.

this country takes the name of Emperor of Monomotapa, and his authority extends up to the confines of Preste Jan.[1] It is from these territories of Monomotapa whence the purest and finest African gold comes, and it is extracted without great difficulty by excavating in the ground to a depth of only 2 or 3 feet. In certain places in this country which are not inhabited, because there is no water there, gold is found on the surface of the ground in nuggets of all kinds of shapes and weights, and there are some of these nuggets which weigh an ounce. I have had, as curiosities, some pieces which I have presented to my friends, and some of them weighed as much as 2 ounces. I still have one of them weighing an ounce and a half or thereabouts.[2] When at Surat with M. d'Ardilière,[3] son of M. du Jardin, of whom I have made mention in my account of Persia, an Ambassador from the King of Abyssinia arrived, whom we went to salute. I presented him with a pair of pocket pistols decorated with silver, and when he invited us to dine with him he showed us the presents which he was carrying to the Great Mogul on behalf of the King, his master. They consisted of fourteen

[1] i.e. Abyssinia. The name Prester John was given to the ruling monarch by the Portuguese. (Varthema, Hakluyt Society, 63; Barbosa, ed. Dames, i. 39; Yule, *Marco Polo*, i. 205 ff.)

[2] For the Portuguese gold trade from Monomotapa, see Linschoten, i. 30 ff.

[3] The references to M. du Jardin and his son are very perplexing. In the *Persian Travels*, bk. ii, ch. vi, Tavernier says he started on his fourth journey from Paris with M. d'Ardilière, son of M. du Jardin. When landing at Masulipatam he refers to his companion as M. Louis du Jardin (vol. i, p. 206). He again mentions him as being with him at Madras (vol. i, p. 215), and on p. 245 he records his death in the year 1652. In vol. ii, p. 191, he speaks of being in M. d'Ardilière's company on the road from Golkonda to Surat in 1653. From all of which it would seem to be the legitimate conclusion that both father and son travelled with him in India, as is suggested on pp. 336 and 690. However, it is due to M. Joret to say that he may be right in treating these notices as all referring to the same person, and consequently the date 1653 must be wrong, if du Jardin died in 1652: *J.-B. Tavernier*, pp. 131, 114. But it should be added that this present notice seems to contradict that view, as M. du Jardin died within a few days of their arrival at Surat. Fryer in 1671 mentions M. Jordan (? Jardin) as having, with M. Rezin, succeeded Tavernier in the trade of carrying diamonds to and from Europe (i. 226, with the editor's note).

beautiful horses, which were all that remained out of thirty he had taken from his country, the others having died in the vessel when crossing the sea from Mocha to Surat. Also a number of young slaves of both sexes; and finally, this being the most important and worthy to be admired, there was a tree of gold 2 feet 4 inches high, and about 5 or 6 inches round the stem.[1] It had ten or twelve branches, some of which were nearly half a foot long and an inch broad, others being smaller. In some parts of the large branches there was to be seen some roughness, which in a manner resembled buds. The roots of this tree which had been thus naturally formed, were small and short, the longest not being more than 4 or 5 inches.

The people of this Kingdom of Monomotapa, knowing the time that the calicoes and other goods arrive at Sofāla[2] and Shupanga, come punctually to provide themselves with what they require. Many Cafres from other Kingdoms and Provinces also come, and the Governors of these two towns sell them calicoes and other things of which they have need, trusting for the payment which they undertake to make the following year by bringing gold, to the amount agreed upon; for if the Governor did not trust them thus there would be no trade between the Portuguese and the Cafres. It is almost the same with the Ethiopians who every year carry gold to Cairo, of which I have spoken in my account of the Seraglio of the Grand Seigneur. These people of Monomotapa do not live a long time on account of the bad water in their country. At the age of twenty-five years they begin to be dropsical, so that it is considered a marvel when they exceed forty years in age. The Province where the river Sena rises is called Moukaran,[3] and belongs to another King, commencing at 100 leagues or thereabouts above

[1] This description suggests a manufactured article, but it is possible that it was really, as Tavernier supposed, a natural arborescent nugget.

[2] Sofāla, a district and town on the East African coast, the most remote settlement towards the south made on that coast by the Arabs (Yule, *Hobson-Jobson*, 849; Barbosa, ed. Dames, Hakluyt Society, i. 6 ff. Shupanga is situated on the lower Zambezi (*Ency. Brit.*, xxviii. 952).

[3] Sir H. H. Johnston kindly writes: 'Sena is the lower Zambezi: Moukaran is probably the country of Karana or Karanga'.

Shupanga. The people of this Province find much gold dust in several rivers which join the Sena ; but this gold is inferior to the other kind, and it is also taken to Shupanga and Sofāla. The country is very healthy, and the inhabitants live as long as those of Europe. In certain years Cafres arrive there from much farther than the Province of Moukaran, and even from the neighbourhood of the Cape of Good Hope. The Portuguese know of the country and its name, but have not induced the Cafres to reveal more than that their country, called Sabia,[1] is governed by a King, and that they generally spend four months on the road to Sofāla. The gold which they bring is excellent, and is in nuggets, like that of Monomotapa ; they say that they find it on high mountains, where they only have to excavate the ground for it to the depth of 10 or 12 feet. They also bring an abundance of elephants' tusks, and say that there are so many elephants in the country that they are to be seen in troops in the fields, and that all the palisades of the fortresses and parks are made of elephants' tusks ; this I have also observed elsewhere.[2] The ordinary food of these Cafres is the flesh of this animal, and four of them, with their assegais,[3] which are a kind of short pike are able to bring an elephant to the ground and kill it. All the water in their country is very bad, which is the reason why they have swollen legs, and it is a marvel when any one escapes this disease.

Above Sofāla there is a country commanded by a King called the King of Baroé. In some part of his country there grows a root which is an inch thick, and of a yellow colour. It cures all kinds of fever by causing vomiting ; but as very little of it is found the King forbids, under severe penalty, any of it to be carried out of his Kingdom. While Dom Philippe de Mascarenhas was Viceroy of Goa the King of

[1] Sabia, Sir H. H. Johnston writes : 'is almost certainly the basin of the upper Sabi'.

[2] See vol. i, p. 221.

[3] Ageagayes in the original, for assegais, the well-known hurling spears used in Africa. The word is from the Berber zaghāya, with the Arabic article prefixed. It occurs commonly in travellers' accounts of other countries besides those included in Africa. (See Yule, *Hobson-Jobson*, p. 38.)

Baroé sent him a piece of this root [1] about 3 feet long, garnished with gold at both ends, and with rings of gold in the middle. The Viceroy having received it made great account of it, and causing it to be cut up into several pieces presented them to certain of his friends. He sent two to Surat to Mr. Fremlin, the English President, who showed them to me, and when I placed a piece of the root on my tongue I found the taste very bitter.

As for silver mines, there are none in the whole of Asia,[2] save only in the Kingdom of Japan. Some years ago very rich mines of tin were discovered at Delegore, Sangore, Bordelon, and Bata; [3] this has done some injury to the English, because there is no longer need of their tin as formerly, sufficient being now produced in Asia. Tin is only used in this country to tin cooking-pots, kettles, and other copper utensils.[4]

CHAPTER XXVI

Account of a notable act of perfidy done to the author when he was about to embark at Gombroon for Surat.

In the month of April 1665, I was about to leave Gombroon, and on the point of embarkation for Surat in a vessel belonging

[1] De Lacerda speaks of the Baroé, probably the Barue of Livingstone, to the west of Sena and north of Māniça, the Bambire or people of Baroé (Sir R. Burton, *Lands of Cazembe*, 44).

[2] Tavernier is here in error, as there are undoubted sources of silver in India and on the confines of Assam and Burma, which have been largely worked. (See *Economic Geology of India*, ch. iv, 'Silver'; Watt, *Dict. Economic Products*, vi. part iii, 239 f.) Silver certainly occurs also in other parts of Asia. (See pp. 212, 220, below.) For its occurrence in Burma see Scott & Hardiman, *Gazetteer, Upper Burma*, part i, vol. ii, p. 303 f.

[3] Ball identified these places with Delhi, Salangor, Billiton, and Banka. But Col. G. E. Gerini (*Journal Royal Asiatic Society*, 1904, p. 720 f.) points out that Delegore is Ligor; Sangore, Senggora or Singora; Bordelon, P'hattalang; Bata, Pate, on the east coast of the Malay Peninsula, between Siam and Patāni.

[4] The artificer is known as the Qala'igar. Copper vessels, to be safely used, must be tinned at least once a month, the vessel to be heated and the tin (qala'ī) applied by means of sal-ammoniac (W. Hoey, *Monograph on Trades and Manufactures of Northern India*, 162 f.).

to the broker of the Dutch Company, and commanded by Captain Hans, when the Agent of the English gave me a packet of letters, which had arrived by express from England, to deliver to the President of Surat. This packet was very large, because, besides the Company's letters, he had included in it those which were addressed to private persons in Surat and other parts of India. I received the packet from him, on the evening of my embarkation, in presence of M. Casembrot, a Dutchman, who had come to Persia by land, and was related to M. Henry Van-Wück, Commander at Gombroon.[1] Casembrot managed to accompany me on all occasions when I went to see the English Agent, and Van-Wück asked me at each visit which I paid him, whether the Agent had not entrusted me with letters for Surat. I replied ingenuously that he had told me that he would give me some, without suspecting anything of the evil intention of both these men. Their object, as appeared subsequently, was to obtain possession of this packet in consequence of the rumour which was in circulation of a rupture between England and Holland,[2] and because they thought that the English had received definite news of it, as some days previously an Arab had arrived by the desert route and had brought a packet to the English Agent; this caused the Commander Van-Wück much anxiety.

As soon as I had received the packet from the Agent, Casembrot, who was always on the watch, and was looking on, as it was put into my hands, reported it to Van-Wück, and told him of its form and size. I pledged the Agent in a glass of wine which he offered me when wishing me a good passage, and went to take leave of Van-Wück, who would not allow me to go till after I had supped with him. He kept me, as it were by force, in order to have more time to accomplish his coup. He excused himself for being unable

[1] Henrik van Wijk, at this time Chief in Persia (1663–5). He is mentioned in W. Foster's *English Factories in India, 1651–1654*, p. 181, who refers, for this incident of the packet entrusted to Tavernier, to Report (1913) of the Hist. MSS. Commission on the Finch MSS., vol. i, p. 439. Tavernier spells his name Van-Wück in the ed. of 1678.

[2] War between England and Holland was declared on 14th March 1665, and ended with the Peace of Breda, signed on 31st July 1667 N. S.

to accompany me on account of the arrival of three vessels which cast anchor while we were at table, and lent me his own boat to go on board, together with four or five of the principal officers of his staff, whom he sent with me, under pretext of escorting me, and with them the captain of the vessel also, to whom he gave the word. As soon as we were on board the captain offered me his own cabin, where he had already directed my bed to be placed by my servants, who had been on board for two days before, and on my making a difficulty about accepting it, he told me that the Commander had ordered him to do so; to which I replied that I would not accept his cabin, except on the condition that I should only occupy half of it, while he took the other. This having been arranged, I drew the packet of English letters from the pocket of my greatcoat, and giving it to one of my servants to place in my boucha,[1] which is the valise of these countries, he put the boucha between the side of the vessel and the head of my bed. There had come with us to the ship two small boats, bringing more than sixty bags of silver, some of 50 and others of 100 tomāns,[2] all the bags being made in Persia in that manner. Immediately the boats were alongside, the crew commenced to hoist the bags, one after the other, into the vessel, but did so very slowly, with the object of delaying us the whole night, and compelling me to go to bed. But as they observed that I was unwilling to retire, the captain, the pilot, and the Company's Broker, to whom, as I have said, the vessel belonged, consulted with the Dutch, and all together conspired to let a bag of 100 tomāns fall into the sea when hoisting it into the vessel; this was done in order to have time to accomplish their design. As soon as the bag fell into the sea they sent a boat to Gombroon to fetch a diver, who reached the vessel by daybreak, to dive for the sack. Seeing then that the vessel could not leave before the following day at two or three o'clock, I went to lie down, my boucha being all the time in the same place, half under the head of my bed and half outside. My servants went to rest in the gunner's cabin, and while I slept alone

[1] Pers. *buqcha*, *bughcha*, 'a knapsack, wallet, bundle'.
[2] Tomān (see i. p. 331).

in that of the captain my boucclia was quietly drawn out, and from it the packet of letters was taken, and another well sealed and of similar form and size, which contained only white paper was put in its place. The bag which they had purposely allowed to fall into the sea in order to accomplish this wicked coup having been pulled up, we made sail, and arrived at the port of Surat on the 5th of May of the same year. The Dutch Commander did me the honour to send a barque 2 or 3 leagues out to sea to fetch me, and immediately on landing, which was about midnight, as I specially desired to pay my respects to him, I asked two Capuchin Fathers, who were at the port on our arrival, to deliver to the English President the packet which I had taken out of my bouccha, a service they willingly undertook. But they told me that, as it was an unseasonable hour, and that the President, who was gouty, might be then asleep, they did not consider it proper to awake him, and would wait till the morrow to accompany me, when I should be able to deliver the packet to the President myself. But the gout from which he suffered not permitting him to sleep much, it was delivered to him the same hour. The President opened the packet in presence of the chief officers of his staff, but they found only white paper folded like letters inside it. When this was reported to me, I realized at once the bad turn which Van-Wück and his accomplices had played me. What confirmed me further as to this perfidy was, that on going to examine my bouccha I found that a jewel which I had tried to sell to the Governor of Gombroon had also disappeared. As I was unable to agree with him as to the price, he returned it to me some hours before I embarked for Surat, and I had placed it in haste with the packet of letters in my bouccha, where I did not find it on my arrival at Surat.

The theft of this packet of letters, thus accomplished, incensed the President against me so much that he refused to allow me to justify myself, and I was moreover subjected to the displeasure of many private Englishmen affected by the loss of the letters in the packet, which were addressed to them. They went so far on different occasions as to attempt my life, as I am able to prove by the evidence and affidavits of many men of honour, and particularly of M. Hartman, who was then the second officer in the factory at Surat. So, to protect myself from snares which were set for me, I was obliged to be constantly accompanied by many people, and I was even unable to go to Golkonda, where there is a great trade in diamonds, as I was warned by my friends that ten or twelve English awaited me in that part of the world to do me some injury. The treachery which was thus done to me disturbed all my plans and caused me considerable loss; besides which I was obliged to carry back to Persia a large sum of money, in consequence of my not being able to invest it in India.

This is a copy of the letter which I sent on this subject to Batavia, to the General of the Dutch Company and the members of his Council, dated Surat, the 16th May 1665.

'GENTLEMEN—I take the liberty to write to you these lines in order to testify the displeasure I have experienced at the affront done me by Commander Henri Van-Wück at Gombroon, who has ignored the letters of recommendation which I received from the Ambassador to the States, an Officer of my King, addressed, one to the Chief Officer of the Company at Ispahān, another to the Commander at Gombroon, and a third to the Commander in this town of Surat, asking all three to assist me as much as possible, except in so far as the Company was interested. But M. Henri Van-Wück has disregarded that addressed to him, and has done me the most signal affront that a man of honour, as I, an Officer of his Royal Highness, the brother of my King, could ever receive, which was to have my baggage opened, in which there were many jewels, some of which have been lost, and to have ordered a large packet of letters to be taken which the Agent of the English at Gombroon entrusted to me to deliver to the President of the English in this town of Surat, having had another packet containing blank paper placed in its stead. I leave you to reflect what kind of esteem the President and all the English hold me in at present, and whether I have not good cause for making my complaints and asking justice from you. And, if it should please you gentlemen to send me permission to wait upon you at Batavia, in order to testify, by word of mouth, the displeasure which I feel on account of what M. Van-Wück has done to me in order to accomplish a crime of this nature, and to inform you in detail of the manner in which all this affair has happened, you would oblige me much. At the least, I ask you to give me some satisfaction in respect to the author of the theft, in default of which I shall not fail, as soon as I have, by the grace of God, returned to France, to make my complaints through the King my master, who has honoured me with his protection, and through his Royal Highness, his only brother, to MM. the States, and to their Ambassador, to obtain satisfaction, at whatever cost, from the said Van-Wück, and by this means re-establish my honour. Moreover, if I return by Ispahān, I shall not neglect to bring it to the notice of the King of Persia, and shall tell him that, after all the honour His Majesty has done me, and notwithstanding all the passports which I have had from him, the said M. Van-Wück has treated me in this fashion. I believe also that His Majesty will not be pleased to hear that all the patterns of jewels, which I was to buy and have made for him both in India and Europe, were lost when the packet of letters was stolen. I can also advise him of the plots and conspiracies which M. Van-Wück has carried on at Gombroon with a Prince, an enemy of Persia, who came to that place in disguise. Finally, I know enough to make him receive an equal or greater affront than he has done me; and by his receiving it the Company will receive it also. This, Gentlemen, is what I am resolved to do if you do not decide to give me complete satisfaction, though I believe I shall not have that trouble. Hoping that you will not omit to do me justice before I leave this country to return to Europe, where as in all other places I shall always be, Gentlemen, your very humble, &c.'

It is rare to see treason unpunished, and the principal actors in this plot all had miserable ends.

In the following monsoon the vessels which arrived from Surat at Gombroon spread in that region the tidings of the black villany which had been done to me; and a short time after, when M. Van-Wück was attacked by a kind of fever, the Rev. Father Balthasar, Carmelite Monk, went to see him, and sought to get him to speak of this affair in which he was so prominently involved. He strongly defended himself against the charge, and making use of an equivocation, said, that if it was true that he had taken the letters, he wished to die without speaking, and not to live three days. He had not in truth committed the theft, but he had arranged for its being done ; and he died at the end of three days, and without speaking. His Lieutenant, named Bozan, one of those whom he had sent to escort me to the vessel, and who apparently had opened the bouccha and committed the theft, after a great debauch, lay down on the terrace of the house to sleep in the fresh air, and as these terraces have neither parapet nor anything to prevent a fall, on moving and rolling in his sleep, he fell over, and on the following day was found dead on the seashore. As for the Captain of the vessel, who was also in the plot, four or five days after his arrival at Surat, as he pursued his way, a Musalmān, jealous of his wife, whom he had beaten, and excited to rage against some Franks who separated them, believing this Captain, whom he found alone, to be a member of the band, stabbed him five or six times with a dagger, upon which he fell dead on the ground. Such were the miserable ends of all these people.

BOOK III

Concerning the religion of the Musalmāns and that of the Idolaters of India: the voyage of the Author by sea from Surat to Batavia, and from Batavia to Holland; and of many peculiarities in different Kingdoms of the East.

CHAPTER I

Concerning the religion of the Musalmāns in the East Indies.

The diversity which exists among the Musalmāns consists not only in the different explanations which they give of their Korān,[1] but also in the different opinions which they entertain regarding the first successors of Muhammad. From this cause two sects, entirely opposed to one another, have sprung; the one calling itself the Sunnīs is followed by the Turks, the other the Shī'as,[2] which is the sect of the Persians. I shall not delay here to say more as to the difference between these two sects, which divide the Musalmān world, having spoken sufficiently of them in my accounts of Persia, and I shall only describe the present condition of this false religion, both in the Empire of the Great Mogul and in the Kingdoms of Golkonda and Bījāpur.

At the first establishment of Islām in India the Christians [3] of the East were very ostentatious [estoient fort superbes] but not very devout, and the Idolaters were effeminate people unable to make much resistance. Thus it was easy for the Musalmāns to subject both by force of arms. This they did with so much success that many Christians and Idolaters embraced the Law of Muhammad.

The Great Mogul with all his Court followed the sect of

[1] Alcoran in the original.

[2] Sounnis and Chias in the original, and Sunnis and Schiais in the *Persian Travels*, bk. iv, ch. vii. The former revere the direct successors of Muhammad, and the latter maintain that 'Alī and his sons Hasan and Husain are the true successors to the caliphate. Sunnīs predominate in the Musalmān population of India, but there are also many Shī'as there, some of them being descendants of Persian immigrants. (See *Islām in India*, Oxford, 1921, ch. i.)

[3] M. Thévenot states that about the year 1665 some believed that there were 25,000 families of Christians in Agra, but all were not agreed as to this estimate (*Voyage des Indes*, 102). Colonel Sleeman, who refers to this, adds that he himself came upon a colony of 2,000 in the year 1814 in Bettiah in Tirhūt (*Rambles and Recollections*, ed. 1915, pp. 11 ff.; Smith, *Akbar, The Great Mogul*, 136 ff.).

the Sunnīs, the King of Golkonda that of the Shī'as, and the King of Bījāpur had in his territories both Sunnīs and Shī'as.[1] The same might also be said of the Court of the Great Mogul, on account of the number of Persians who came to serve in his armies. It is true that although they regard the Sunnīs with horror they nevertheless follow, in outward show, the religion of the Monarch, believing that to make or secure their fortune they may conceal their true belief, and that it suffices for them to cherish it in their hearts.[2]

As for the Kingdom of Golkonda, Qutb Shāh, who reigns at present [1625–72], maintains with great zeal the law of the Shī'as, and as the nobles of his Court are nearly all Persians, they observe the customs of the sect of the Shī'as with the same strictness and the same freedom from restraint as in Persia.

I have elsewhere remarked that among the native Musalmān subjects of the Great Mogul there are but few in positions of command; this is the cause why many Persians, oppressed by want, or ambitious of better fortune than they can hope for in their own country, go to seek for it in India. Being clever they are successful in finding means to advance themselves in the profession of arms, so that in the Empire of the Great Mogul, as well as in the Kingdoms of Golkonda and Bījāpur, the Persians are in possession of the highest posts.[3]

[1] It is curious that half of the Bījāpur Kings were Sunnī and half Shī'a—the Sunnī being Ibrāhīm I, Ibrāhīm II, and his son Mahmūd, and probably Sikandar, the last of the dynasty; while 'Alī 'Ādil Shāh, Yūsuf, and Ismāīl were Shī'as (*Bombay Gazetteer*, xxiii. 413 note 4).

[2] This is the Shī'a doctrine of Taqīa, whereby he believes that he is justified in smoothing down or in denying the peculiarities of his religious belief, in order to save himself from religious persecution (Hughes, *Dict. of Islām*, 628).

[3] On the Persian adventurers who crowded out the Courts of the Mughal Emperors and the Musalmān Kingdoms of Southern India see Erskine, *Hist. of India*, ii. 24 f.; Smith, *Akbar, The Great Mogul*, 357, 362. Persian influence is strong at Haidarābād even at the present day. Also see Bernier, 209: 'The court itself does not now consist, as originally, of real Mogols; but is a medley of Usbecs, Persians, Arabs, and Turks, or descendants from all these peoples, known, as I said before, by the general appellation of Mogols.'

Aurangzeb, especially, shows great zeal for the Sunnī sect, of which he is so faithful a follower that he surpasses all his predecessors in external observance of the Law, which has been the veil by means of which he has concealed his usurpation of the kingdom. When he took possession of the throne he proclaimed that it was with the design of insisting upon the Law of Muhammad being observed in all its strictness, as it had been relaxed during the reigns of Shāhjahān his father and Jahāngīr his grandfather. To show himself still more zealous for the Law he became a Dervish or Fakīr, i. e. a professional beggar, and under this false mantle of piety cleverly made his way to the Empire. Although he had, as I have said, numerous Persians in his service, he did not allow them to celebrate the festival of Hasan and Husain,[1] sons of 'Alī, who were killed by the Sunnīs, as I have mentioned in my account of Persia ; and they themselves, to please the Emperor and advance their own fortunes, made no scruple about conforming themselves outwardly to the cult and customs of the Sunnīs.

CHAPTER II

Concerning Fakīrs or Musalmān beggars in the East Indies.[2]

It is estimated that there are in India 800,000 Musalmān Fakīrs, and 1,200,000 among the idolaters, which is an enormous number.[3] They are all vagabonds and idlers, who blind the eyes of the people by a false zeal, and lead them to believe that all that falls from their own mouths is oracular.

There are different kinds of Musalmān Fakīrs ; some are almost naked, like the Fakīrs of the idolaters, who have no

[1] Hosen and Heussin in the original. The observance of the Shī'a Muharram festival was prohibited in 1669 (Jadunath Sarkar, *Hist. of Aurangzib*, iii. 104). On Aurangzeb becoming a Fakīr see i. 264.

[2] See *Islām in India*, the *Qānūn-i-Islām* of Ja'far Sharīf, Oxford, 1921, pp. 283 ff.

[3] The numbers of Fakīrs, Hindu and Musalmān, are great, but no exact figures are available, because at recent enumerations it has been found impossible to distinguish them from ordinary beggars.

regular dwellings, and abandon themselves to all kinds of impurity without any shame. They persuade simple souls that they are privileged to do all kinds of evil without sin.

There are other Fakīrs who are clad in garments of so many pieces of different colours that one is unable to say what they are. These robes extend half-way down their legs and conceal the miserable rags beneath. These Fakīrs generally travel in companies, having a chief or superior over them who is distinguished by his garment, which is poorer and made up of more pieces than those of the others. He, moreover, drags a heavy iron chain attached to one leg; it is 2 cubits long and thick in proportion. When he prays it is with a great noise, which he makes with this chain and a loud voice; this is accompanied by an affected gravity, which attracts the veneration of the people.[1] The people, however, bring him and his followers food to eat, which is served to him in the place where he halts, generally a street or public place. His carpets are spread by his disciples, and he seats himself on them while he gives audience to those who wish to consult him. Moreover, his disciples proclaim throughout the country the great virtues of their master and the favours he receives from God, Who reveals to him the most important secrets, and confers upon him the power to aid afflicted persons with good advice. The people give him easy credence, regard him as a holy man, approach him with great devotion, and when one of them comes close to him, he removes the shoes off his feet, prostrates himself before the Fakīr and kisses his feet. Then the Fakīr, in order to show his humility, extends his arm and gives his hand to be kissed, after which he makes those who come to consult him sit near him, and listens to each in turn. He boasts of possessing a prophetic spirit, especially for indicating to women who are sterile the way in which they may obtain children, and how to constrain anyone they wish to manifest love for them.

Some Fakīrs have more than 200 disciples, whom they assemble by the sound of the drum and with a horn similar

[1] Bernier (p. 317) notes the habit of Fakīrs dragging chains, of which there are many modern instances; cf. *Islām in India*, 289 f.

to those of our huntsmen. When marching, the disciples carry their standard, lances, and other arms, which they plant in the ground near their master when he halts to rest anywhere.[1]

The third class of Fakīrs of the East Indies consists of those who, being born of poor parents, and wishing to know the Law thoroughly, in order to become Mullās or doctors, take up their abode in mosques, where they live on charity bestowed upon them. They occupy their time in reading the Korān, which they learn by heart, and when they are able to add to this study some little knowledge of natural things, with the example of a good life, according to their ideas, they become heads of mosques, and reach the dignity of Mullās and judges of the Law.[2] Fakīrs of this class marry wives, and some of them through piety and their great desire to imitate Muhammad, take three or four of them, believing that they render to God signal service, by becoming fathers of many children who will follow the Law of their Prophet.

CHAPTER III

Of the Religion of the Gentiles or Idolaters of India.

THE idolaters of India are so numerous that for one Musalmān there are five or six Gentiles.[3] It is astonishing to see how this enormous multitude of men has allowed itself to be subjected by so small a number, and has readily submitted to the yoke of the Musalmān Princes. But astonishment ceases when one remembers that the idolaters have no union among themselves, and that superstition has introduced

[1] Ja'far Sharīf gives a full account of the organization of these bands (*ibid.*, 169 ff.). P. della Valle describes them as begging and sounding a trumpet (i. 94).

[2] For a good account of the qualifications and duties of the Mullā and other Muslim officials see *Bombay Gazetteer*, ix, part. 2, 132 ff. A man who knows the Korān by heart is called Hāfiz. Mosque schools, as described in the text, still exist.

[3] At the Census of 1911 Hindus numbered 217 millions and Musalmāns 66 millions, the proportions to the total population being respectively 69 and 21 per cent.

so strange a diversity of opinions and customs that they never agree with one another.[1] An idolater will not eat bread nor drink water in a house belonging to anyone of a different caste from his own, unless it be more noble and more exalted than his; thus they can all eat and drink in the houses of the Brāhmans,[2] which are open to all the world. Among these idolaters a caste is, so to speak, what a tribe was among the Jews, and although it is commonly believed that there are seventy-two of these castes, I have ascertained from the most accomplished of their priests that they can be reduced to four principal castes from which all others derive their origin.[3]

The first caste is that of the Brāhmans, the successors of the ancient Brachmanes or philosophers of India, who specially studied astrology. Their ancient books, in the reading of which the Brāhmans generally occupy themselves, still exist and they are so skilled in their observations that they do not make a mistake of a minute in foretelling eclipses of the sun and moon. In order to preserve this science among themselves, they have a kind of university in a town called

[1] This has ever been the strength of those who have conquered India.

[2] Bramines in the original. Brāhmans' houses are certainly not now open to all the world; the very reverse is the case. The accuracy of this statement, even in Tavernier's time, may be doubted. True as it is that a man of lower caste may eat from the hand of a Brāhman, a Brāhman has, himself, to guard against defilement by contact with men of lower caste. Dubois, who allows that Brāhmans permit no stranger to enter their kitchens, was admitted into their houses by Brāhmans (*Hindu Manners, Customs, and Ceremonies*, ed. 1906. Introd. x. 181, 201 f.) and Mrs. Stevenson was admitted to eat in Brāhman houses in Kāthiāwār (*Rites of the Twice-born*, 240). But tnese cases are exceptional.

[3] The number of castes at the present day is enormous; see the list in the *Census Report, India*, 1911, vol. i, Part 2, pp. 177 ff., and Sir E. A. Gait's analysis of the Statistics in Part 1, ch. xi. He remarks that earlier writers 'accepted his view that the classes [Tavernier's four castes] had gradually developed into castes. It has, however, been shown by Senart and others that the division into castes has no direct relation with the division into classes. The castes came into existence independently, without regard to the classes.' The best short summary of the question will be found in Sir E. A. Gait's article 'Caste' in Hastings, *Encyclopædia of Religion and Ethics*, vol. iii, p. 230 ff.

Benares,[1] where they study astrology principally, but they also have doctors who teach the Law, which is observed with very great strictness. This caste is the most noble of all, because it is from among the Brāhmans that the priests and ministers of the law are selected. But as they are very numerous and cannot all study in their university, the majority of them are ignorant and consequently very superstitious, those who pass as the most intellectual being the most arrant sorcerers.

The second caste is that of the Rājputs or Ketrīs,[2] i. e. warriors and soldiers. These are the only idolaters who are brave, and distinguish themselves in the profession of arms. All the Rājās, of whom I have often spoken, are of this caste. They are like so many petty kings, whose disunion has made them tributaries to the Great Mogul; but as the majority are in his service, they are highly recompensed for the small tribute which they pay him by the large and honourable salaries which they receive from him. These Rājās, and the Rājputs their subjects, are the most firm supports of the Great Mogul's kingdom; and it was the Rājās Jaisingh and Jaswantsingh who placed Aurangzeb on the throne. But it should be remarked that this second caste does not exclusively consist of people who follow arms as a profession. It is only the Rājputs who go to war, and who are all cavaliers; but as for the Ketris they have degenerated from the bravery of their ancestors, having quitted arms for merchandise.[3]

The third caste is that of the Banians,[4] who attach them-

[1] Benarez in the original, elsewhere written Benarow or Banarous.

[2] Kshatriya, Chhatrī.

[3] He refers to the Khatrī caste of Northern India, who claim Kshatriya descent, but are merchants (Rose, *Glossary of Tribes and Castes, Panjab*, ii. 501 ff.).

[4] Tavernier spells this word Baniane, which has been altered in the text to Banian. It is otherwise, and perhaps more properly, spelt Banyan, or Vānya in Western India. It signifies a trader or merchant, especially in Gujarāt. In Calcutta it is a title still used for the Indian brokers attached to houses of business. It is derived from Vānya (Gujarāti Vāniyo), and that from the Sanskrit Vanij, a trader. Our author's testimony as to the astuteness of the men of this caste is borne out by many authors, notably P. F. Vincenzo de Maria, who says to make one it takes three Chinese, and three Hebrews to make a Chinese,

selves to trade, some being Shroffs, i. e. money-changers or bankers, and the others brokers, by whose agency the merchants buy and sell. The members of this caste are so subtle and skilful in trade that, as I have elsewhere said,[1] they could give lessons to the most cunning Jews. They accustom their children at an early age to shun slothfulness, and instead of letting them go into the streets to lose their time at play, as we generally allow ours, teach them arithmetic, which they learn perfectly, using for it neither pen nor counters, but the memory alone, so that in a moment they will do a sum, however difficult it may be. They are always with their fathers, who instruct them in trade, and do nothing without at the same time explaining it to them. These are the figures which they use in their books, both in the Empire of the Great Mogul, as well as in other parts of India,[2] although the languages may vary. If anyone gets in a rage with them they listen with patience, without replying, and withdraw coldly, not returning to see him for four or five days, when they anticipate his rage will be over. They never eat anything which has enjoyed sentient life, and they would rather die than slay the least animal, not even excepting an insect or vermin, being in this respect very zealous observers of their Law. It is sufficient to add that they never strike one another, and that they never go to war, and can neither eat nor drink in the houses of the Rājputs, because they slay animals and eat meat, with the exception of that of the cow, which is never eaten.

The fourth caste is called Charados or Soudra.[3] Like that of the Rājputs, it occupies itself with war; but with this difference, that the Rājputs serve on horse, and the Sūdras on foot. Both glory in dying in battle, and a soldier, whether of the cavalry or foot, is esteemed for ever infamous

therefore a Banian ought to possess the subtlety of nine Jews. (Yule, *Hobson-Jobson*, 63.)

[1] Vol. i. 24. 'The chief Pleasure of the Gentiles, or Banyans, is to Cheat one another, conceiving therein the highest Felicity' (Fryer, i. 281).

[2] These figures are not reproduced here.

[3] Sanskrit Sūdra. Tavernier confines the name to infantry in the Indian armies, perhaps with reference to the Nāyars of Malabar, who, by an extension of the term, rank as Sūdras.

if, in the moment of combat, he runs away. It is regarded as an eternal disgrace in his family, and in this connexion I shall relate a story which was told me in the country. A soldier who loved his wife passionately, and by whom he was equally beloved in return, fled from the field of battle, not out of fear of death, but simply on account of his wife's sorrow in case she might find herself a widow. When she heard the cause of his flight, as she saw him approach the house she closed the door, and told him she was unable to recognize as a husband a man who had preferred the love of a woman to honour; that she did not wish to see him any more, to avoid leaving a blot on the reputation of her family, and to teach her children to have more courage than their father. This woman remained firm in her resolution. The husband, to regain his reputation and his love, returned to the army, where he performed noble actions which redounded to his credit, and having splendidly repaired his fault, the door of his house was opened to him, and his wife received him with pleasure.[1]

The remainder of the people, who do not belong to either of these four castes, are called Pauzecour.[2] They all occupy themselves with mechanical arts, and do not differ from one another except in the trades which they follow from father to son; so that a tailor, although he may be rich, is unable to advance his children, except in his own calling, nor to marry them, be it a son or a daughter, to others than those of his trade. So also when a tailor dies all those of his calling go to the place where his body is burnt, and the same custom is observed among all the other artisans.

Among the special castes there is one that is called Halāl-

[1] Tod and Bernier tell a similar story about Jaswant Singh, who was so treated by his wife on his return from the battle of the 17th April 1658. (Tod, *Annals of Rajasthān*, ed. 1920, ii. 724; Bernier, 40 f.; A. Hamilton, in Pinkerton, *Voyages*, viii. 311.)

[2] The origin of the name is uncertain. Tavernier may have heard of the Panchama, a general name for a class of artisans or menials in Madras, and may have confounded them with the Pānchgaur, or Panchagauda, a term applied to the five classes of the northern Brāhmans (Thurston, *Castes and Tribes of Southern India*, vi. 43 f.; J. Wilson, *Indian Caste*, ii. 124 ff.).

khor,[1] who engage only in cleaning houses, each house paying them something monthly, according to its size. If a man of quality in India, whether a Musalmān or an idolater, has ifty servants, not one of them will use a broom to clean the house, for he would consider himself contaminated by it, and one of the greatest insults that one can do to a man in India is to call him Halālkhor. It is proper to remark here that each of these servants has his own special duty, the one to carry the vessel of water for drinking by the way, another to have the pipe of tobacco ready, and if the master asks one to perform the service for which the other is employed, that service will not be performed, and the servant remains as though he were immovable. As for slaves, they have to do whatever their master orders. As the caste of Halālkhors is only occupied in removing the refuse from houses, it gets the remains of what the others eat, of whatever caste they may be, and it does not make any scruple about eating indifferently of all things. It is the people belonging to this caste. alone, who make use of asses, to carry the sweepings from the houses to the fields; while all other Indians will not touch this animal. It is otherwise in Persia, where asses are used both for baggage and for riding. It is also the Halālkhors in India who alone feed pigs and use them for food.[2]

[1] Alacors in the original. The name Halālkhor signifies an eater of lawful food, or rather, one to whom all kinds of food are lawful, euphemistically applied to the Sweepers, to whom all things are lawful. (Yule, *Hobson-Jobson*, 409; Ovington, 382.)

[2] Dhobīs, or washermen, use asses to convey clothes backwards or forwards from a river or tank, and Kumhārs, or potters, employ the asses for carrying clay, but both these castes are held in low esteem. Many menial castes, besides Halālkhors, or sweepers, keep swine, such as the Chamārs, or leather-dressers; Kumhārs and Dhīmars, or fishermen and palanquin-bearers of the Central Provinces, breed pigs, which they sell to people of low caste to be used in sacrifice (Russell, *Tribes and Castes, Central Provinces*, iv. 8).

CHAPTER IV

Concerning the idolatrous Kings and Princes of Asia.

It is necessary to place in the front rank of the idolatrous Kings of Asia, the King of Arakan, the King of Pegu, the King of Siam, the King of Cochinchina, the King of Tonquin, and, as for the King of China, we know that he was an idolater before the irruption of the Tartars into his territories; but since that time one can say nothing certain about him, because these Tartars, who are now the masters of the country, are neither idolaters nor Musalmāns, being, rather, both combined.[1] In the principal islands, firstly, the King of Japan, next the King of Ceylon, and some small Kings of the islands of the Moluccas, and, finally, the Rājās, both of the Empire of the Great Mogul and of the neighbourhoods of the Kingdoms of Bījāpur and Golkonda, are all idolaters. In general, all the common people, whether in the territories subject to the Great Mogul, or the Kings of Golkonda and Bījāpur, and the islands of Achīn, Java, and Macassar, the Kings of which, as I have elsewhere said, are Musalmāns,—all the common people, I say, of these countries are idolaters.

I have stated that the King of Ceylon[2] is an idolater, and it is true. But it is true also that about fifty years ago a King of Ceylon became a Christian, and received at his baptism the name of Jean, having been previously called the Emperor Priapender.[3] As soon as he embraced Christianity, the

[1] Tavernier knew little about the Chinese.

[2] The ruler of Ceylon at this period was the merciless tyrant, Rājāsingha II, who being unable to resist the Dutch in the low country, practised ruthless cruelty against his subjects in the hills (Tennent, *Ceylon*, ii. 49).

[3] Although the period of his reign was somewhat more remote than Tavernier states, it seems probable that this Emperor Priapender was Don Juan Dharmapāla, who was raised to the throne in 1542 by the Portuguese, and reigned thirty-nine years. He was baptized by Wilponte Alphonso Perera, who went to Ceylon from Goa for the purpose. A number of his chiefs and people also became Christians at the same time. He was opposed throughout his reign by Rājā Singha, who ultimately superseded him (Forbes, *Eleven Years in Ceylon*, ii. 315). Ribeiro calls him Paria Pandar, which is like Tavernier's form of the name (Damer'

Princes and priests of the country established another King in his stead. He did what he could to induce all his people to imitate him, and for this purpose assigned to the Jesuit Father twelve of the largest villages which were around Columbo, so that from the revenue of these places they might support the children of the country in colleges, where, being well instructed, they would afterwards be able to teach others. For the King represented to these Fathers that it was impossible for them to learn the language of the country well enough to preach to the people, and in effect they found that the youth of Ceylon were so quick and intelligent that they learnt, in six months, more Latin, philosophy and other sciences, than Europeans acquire in a year, and they questioned the Fathers with such subtlety, and so deeply, that they were amazed.

Some years after the King had become a Christian, a very accomplished man and good native philosopher, named Alegamma Motiar,[1] as one might say master of the philosophers, after having conversed some time with the Jesuit Fathers and other priests at Columbo, was inspired to become a Christian. With this object he went to see the Jesuit Fathers, and told them that he desired to be instructed in the Christian faith, but he inquired what Jesus Christ had done and left in writing. He set himself then to read the New Testament with so much attention and ardour that in less than six months there was not a passage which he could not recite, for he had acquired Latin very thoroughly. After having been well instructed, he told the Fathers that he wished to receive holy baptism, that he saw that their religion was the only good and true one, and such as Jesus Christ had taught, but what astonished him was, that they did not follow Christ's example, because, according to the Gospel, he never took money from anyone, while they on the contrary took it from everyone, and neither baptized nor buried anyone without it. This did not prevent him

Book of Duarte Barbosa, ed. 1921, vol. ii, p. 114; see Tennent, *Ceylon*, ii. 14 f.).

[1] Mudaliyar, a Cingalese title, meaning a headman. Alegamma has not been identified (Yule, *Hobson-Jobson*, 569 f.).

from being baptized, and from working for the conversion of the idolaters afterwards.

Such is the present condition of the idolaters throughout Asia. I come now to those of India in detail and to their gross errors, after which I shall speak of their customs and of the penances of their Fakīrs.

CHAPTER V

Concerning the belief of the Idolaters with respect to the Deity.

THE idolaters of India yield to creatures like the cow, the ape, and different monsters, honours which are only due to the true Deity, although it is certain that they acknowledge one infinite God, all-powerful and all-wise, Creator of the heavens and the earth, who is omnipresent. They call him in some places Permesser, in others Peremael,[1] as, for example, towards the coast of Malabar; and Vvistnou [2] in the language of the Brahmans who inhabit the coast of Coromandel. As the idolaters have perhaps heard that the circle is the most perfect of all figures, they have thought to improve upon it by saying God is of an oval figure, and it is for this reason that they generally keep in their pagodas an oval pebble, which they obtain from the Ganges,[3] and adore as God. They

[1] Perumāl, 'great man', is the most common title of Vishnu in the Tamil country (B. Ziegenbalg, *Genealogy of the South-Indian Gods*, Madras, 1869, p. 83); Permesser in the text represents Paramesvara, 'Supreme Lord'.

[2] Vishnu, the preserver, one of the Hindu triad. He is represented as a dark man with four arms—one hand holds a club, another a shell, the third a chakra, or metal quoit, and the fourth the lotus.

[3] This is the so-called Sālagrām stone. The Son river supplies some which are, it is believed, silicious pebbles derived from the basalt; others are obtained from the Himalayas, and these are said to include fossils, ammonites. The Sālagrām is connected with the worship of Vishnu, but it may be worshipped as representing for the time being any god. According to Ward (*History of the Hindus*, ed. 1815, ii. 221 ff.; Sleeman, *Rambles*, ed. 1915, p. 121; Dubois, *Hindu Manners*, ed. 1906, p. 648 f.) the Sālagrām is black, hollow, and nearly round, and is obtained from the Gandak river. As much as 2,000 rupees was given for one of the

are so strongly fixed in this foolish idea that the wisest among the Brahmans will not listen to any argument against it, and thus it is not to be wondered at if a people who have such evil guides fall into this gross and monstrous idolatry. There is a caste so superstitious about this, that those who belong to it keep these oval stones suspended from their necks, and press them against their bodies while they pray.

In this gross and pitiable ignorance the idolaters, like the ancient pagans, regard their gods as men, and even bestow wives upon them, thinking that they love the same things as those in which men take pleasure. Thus they regard their Rāma as a great deity on account of the wonders which they believe he performed during his life. The following are the fables which they relate regarding him, as I have learnt from the most accomplished among their Brahmans :—

Rāma was the son of a powerful Rājā, who called himself Deseret,[1] and the most virtuous of many children which he had by two legitimate wives. He was particularly beloved by his father, who had destined him to be his successor. The mother of Rāma having died, the other wife of the Rājā, who possessed entire control over her husband, induced him to drive Rāma and his brother Lakshman [2] from his house and territories ; this was done, and by the exclusion of these two brothers, the son of this other wife was declared to be heir to the Rājā. Rāma and his brother having then received an order to depart, obeyed the command of their father, and as they were about to leave, Rāma went to bid farewell to his wife Sītā, whom these idolaters regard as a goddess. She was unwilling to part from him, and protested that she would follow him everywhere, and so they all three left the house of the Rājā, to seek their fortunes. They were unlucky

first class. Vast sums of money are sometimes expended on the festivities connected with the marriage of the Sālagrām to the Tulsī plant (*Ocymum sanctum*). But Tavernier may confuse it with the Lingam worn by the Lingāyat sect.

[1] Rāma, son of Dasaratha, King of Ayodhya. What follows is a tolerably correct version of the Rāmāyana epic, for a popular abstract of which see J. C. Oman, *The Great Indian Epics*, 1899, and for criticism, Hastings, *Ency. Religion and Ethics*, x. 574 ff.

[2] Lokeman in the original.

at first, for while passing through a forest, Rāma went in pursuit of a bird, and remained a long time absent, when Sītā, fearing that some disaster had happened to her husband, by force of her entreaties obliged Lakshman to go in search of him. He strongly objected, because Rāma told him not to leave Sītā, having foreseen by a spirit of prophecy what would happen if she remained alone. Nevertheless Lakshman, moved by the earnest prayers of his sister-in-law, went to seek his brother Rāma. In the meantime Rāvana,[1] another god of the idolaters, appeared to Sītā in the garb of a Fakīr and asked alms of her. Rāma had told Sītā not to go beyond the spot where he had left her; this being well known to Rāvana he refused to receive the alms which Sītā offered him unless she left the place. Sītā either by mistake or forgetting the command of Rāma, passed beyond the limits which he had prescribed, and then Rāvana seized her and took her into the depths of the forest where his followers awaited him, with whom he departed to his territories. When Rāma returned from the chase, and missed Sītā, he fell senseless from grief, but Lakshman his brother brought him to his senses, and they went together to search for Sītā, who was tenderly beloved by her husband.

When the Brāhmans recount this ravishment of their goddess Sītā they do so with tears and demonstrations of excessive grief,[2] and they add to the story a multitude of ridiculous fables, extolling the great bravery of Rāma in the pursuit of the ravisher of Sītā. All the animals were employed in order to discover her, among which the monkey Hanumān[3] alone had the good fortune to be successful. He crossed the sea with a bound, and arrived in the gardens of Rāvana, where he found Sītā in the deepest affliction, and she was much surprised on beholding a monkey, who spoke on behalf of her husband. At first she was not willing to give credence to such an ambassador, but the monkey, to authenticate

[1] Rhevan in the original. Rāvana was the demon king of Lankā or Ceylon.

[2] This is done at the Rāmlīlā or mystery play, describing the adventures of Rāma and Sītā, who are impersonated by boys, performed in Northern India in September–October. See Oman, *The Great Indian Epics*, 75 ff.

[3] Harman in the original.

his mission, handed her a ring which her husband had given her, but which she had left in her baggage. She had much difficulty in believing such a miracle, and that Rāma her husband had been able to make a beast give her news of him, and such certain indications of his love. The monkey Hanumān did wonders at this interview, and being recognized as a spy by the servants of Rāvana, who wished to burn him, he made use of the fire which they had prepared for him to set alight the palace of Rāvana, which was consumed almost entirely, by means of the rags which they tied to his tail and body and set on fire. He threw himself immediately among the straw and other combustible matter, which caused a great conflagration in the palace. The monkey realizing that he would not escape from Rāvana if he again fell into his power, promptly retraced the road by which he had come, and having bathed himself in the sea, which he recrossed at a single bound, he gave Rāma an account of his adventures, and told him of the affliction in which he had found Sītā, who was in despair at finding herself so far removed from her husband. Rāma, touched by the affection of his wife, resolved at any cost to deliver her from the hands of Rāvana. This was accomplished, the monkey serving him as guide, and with the aid of forces which Rāma had collected from different places. With much difficulty he approached the palace of Rāvana, which was still smoking, so great had been the fire; and the subjects of this Prince having been dispersed, it was easy for Rāma again to see his beloved Sītā, whom Rāvana abandoned and fled in fear to the mountains. Rāma and Sītā experienced infinite joy at seeing one another again, and did much honour to the monkey Hanumān, who had rendered them so great a service.

As for Rāvana, he passed the remainder of his days as a poor Fakīr, his country being altogether ruined by the troops of Rāma, who avenged the injury he had received, and it is from this Rāvana that this incredible number of Fakīrs, whom one sees in peregrination throughout India, have taken their origin.[1] These Fakīrs lead a life of such

[1] Tavernier was possibly misinformed. Sir G. Grierson, who has kindly made inquiries, has failed to trace any legend connecting Rāvana

austerity that their penances amount to prodigies, and I have had the curiosity to collect several pictures of them, some of which I shall show to the reader in the following chapter.

CHAPTER VI

Concerning Fakīrs, or the professional Mendicants of India, and their penances.[1]

THE Fakīrs, as I have just said, take their origin from Rāvana, whom Rāma despoiled of his kingdom; on that account he felt so much remorse that he resolved to wander like a vagabond throughout the world, poor and bereft of all property, and completely nude. He soon found many people to follow him in this kind of life, which afforded them all kinds of license. For being reverenced as saints, they had abundant opportunities of doing whatever evil they wished.

Fakīrs ordinarily travel in troops, each of which has its Chief or Superior. As they go perfectly nude, winter and summer, always lying on the ground, and since it is sometimes cold, the young Fakīrs and other idolaters who are the most devoted, go in the afternoon to search for the droppings of

with any of the mendicant or ascetic Orders. Many legends about him are told at Gokaru in Kānara (*Bombay Gazetteer*, xv, part 2. 290). The story in the Rāmāyana tells that Rāma, mounted on Indra's chariot, slew Rāvana with an arrow forged by Brahmā. Ovington (p. 360) tells the same story: 'The Original of these Holy Mendicants is ascrib'd, according to their Account, to a certain Prince named *Revan*, who quarell'd with *Ram*, a Knowing and Victorious Prince'. Russell, however (*Tribes and Castes, Central Provinces*, iii. 155 f.) describes an Order of Gosāīns, called Rāvanvansī, or 'of the race of Rāvana'. When Rāma left his wife, Sītā, in the forest, Rāvana disguised himself as a beggar and begged alms from her. She told him to come within the magic circle which Rāma had cast round her, but he refused, and induced her to leave the circle, whereupon he seized her and carried her to Lankā or Ceylon. This Order claims descent from him.

[1] The subject of Fakīrs and their austerities attracted much attention from the earlier writers; for example, Ovington, 363 ff.; Mundy, ii. 176 ff; Bernier, 316 ff.; Fryer, i. 257 ff. Though at the present day the clothing of a Fakīr is scanty, absolute nudity is prohibited by the police and municipal regulations.

cows and other animals, which are dried by the sun, and with them they kindle fires. They seldom use wood through fear lest it may contain some living animal which would be killed—that which is used to burn the dead is a kind of drift-wood which does not engender worms. These young Fakīrs, having collected a quantity of these droppings mingled with dry earth, make many large fires according to the size of the troop, and ten or twelve Fakīrs seat themselves around each fire. When sleep overtakes them, they let themselves fall on the ground, upon which they spread ashes to serve as a mattress, and they have only the heavens for a covering. As for those who perform the penances, of which I shall presently speak, when they lie during the night in the same position as one sees them during the day, fires are kindled for them on either side, without which they would be unable to withstand the cold; this will be seen at the end of this chapter in the illustrations which I give of the penances. Wealthy idolaters consider themselves happy, and believe that their houses receive the blessings of heaven, when they have as guests some of these Fakīrs, whom they honour in proportion to their austerity; and the glory of a troop is to have someone in it who performs a notable penance, like those of which I shall hereafter speak.

These troops of Fakīrs assemble in numbers to go on pilgrimage to the principal pagodas, and to the public bathing-fairs which are held on certain days of the year, both in the river Ganges, which they specially esteem, as also in that which separates the territories of the Portuguese at Goa from those of the King of Bījāpur.[1] Some of the most austere Fakīrs dwell in miserable huts near their pagodas, where they are given food, for the love of God, once in every twenty-four hours.

The tree, of which a picture will be seen at the end of this chapter, is of the same kind as that near Gombroon, of which I have given a description in the accounts of Persia.[2] The

[1] The Kistnā, though it may be doubted if the authority of Portugal extended so far to the east and north-east.

[2] Namely the Banyan, *Ficus Indica*, Linn. The reference is to Book V, ch. xxiii, of the *Persian Travels*. See Curzon, *Persia*, ii. 421.

Franks call it the tree of the Banians, because, in places where there are any of these trees, the idolaters sit under them and cook their food there. They reverence them specially, and generally build their pagodas either under or close to one of these great trees. The one which the reader will see depicted further on is at Surat,[1] and in its trunk, which is hollow, a monster is represented like the head of a deformed woman, which is said to be the representation of the first woman, whom they call Mamaniva.[2] Every day a large number of idolaters assemble there to adore this monster, near whose shrine there is constantly some Brāhman detailed for its service, and to receive the offerings of rice, millet, and other grains made to it. On all those who have prayed in the pagoda, both men and women, the Brahman makes a mark on the middle of the forehead with a kind of vermilion, with which the idol is also painted. With this mark on them they do not fear that the devil will injure them, because they are, as they say, under the protection of their God.

I give here the explanation of the figures represented under the tree of the Banians, marked by the numbers 1, 2, 3, etc.[3]

Another example with its numerous stems is the famous Kabīr bar on an island in the Narbadā 12 miles above Broach. At one time it covered an area of 2,000 feet in circumference, and had upwards of 3,250 separate stems. It has afforded shelter to 7,000 men at a time, but is now much reduced in size (Yule, *Hobson-Jobson*, 277). The particular tree at Gombroon referred to by our author is also mentioned by Mandelslo, Valentijn, and della Valle. The Persian name for the tree is lūl. This is a species distinct from the famous Bo tree (*F. religiosa*) of Ceylon, one of which, having a known history, recorded in full detail by Sir Emerson Tennent (*Ceylon*, ii. 613), was planted 288 B.C.

[1] The tree at Surat has frequently been described; Fryer, i. 265; Mundy, ii. 34; and see Yule, *Hobson-Jobson*, 65 ff.

[2] It has been suggested that this word is a corruption of Māriamma, the 'death mother', who, in Southern India, controls epidemic disease (B. Ziegenbalg, *Genealogy of the South Indian Gods*, 138 ff.; G. Oppert, *Original Inhabitants of Bharatavarsa or India*, 471 ff.; B. L. Rice, *Mysore*, 2nd ed. i. 456). But, as the reference is to a goddess at Surat, the term probably represents Mahāmāi, or Māmā Devī, the mother of the gods. But Tavernier, working through an interpreter, confuses names of this kind, not connected with his business. For Māmā Devī see Tod, *Annals of Rajasthan*, ii. 781.

[3] This plate is not reproduced here or in Ball's edition, being rudely drawn and of no great interest or importance.

1. Is the place where the Brāhmans dress up a representation of some one of their idols, as Mamaniva, Sītā, Madedina,[1] and similar images which are very numerous. 2. Is the figure of Mamaniva which is in the pagoda. 3. Is another pagoda close to the preceding. It has a cow at the door, and inside a representation of the god Rāma. 4. Is another pagoda, where Fakīrs betake themselves for penance. 5. Is a fourth pagoda dedicated to Rāma. 6. Is the form of a grave into which several times during the year a Fakīr retires, where he gets no light except through a very small hole. He sometimes remains there nine or ten days without drinking or eating, according to his powers of devotion—a thing which I could not easily have believed if I had not seen it. Curiosity led me to go to see this penitent in company with the Dutch Commander of Surat, who ordered a watch to be set in order to see whether he did not receive something to eat by day or night. The watch were unable to discover that he received any nourishment, and he remained seated like our tailors without changing his position either by day or night. He whom I saw was not able to remain more than seven days out of the ten which he had vowed to spend, because the heat stifled him on account of the lamp in the grave.[2] The other kinds of penance, of which I am about to speak, would still further exceed human belief if thousands of men were not witnesses of them. 7. Is the position of a penitent who has passed many years without ever lying down either by day or night. When he wishes to sleep he leans on a suspended cord, and in that position, which is very strange and inconvenient, the humours descend to the legs, which become thereby

[1] Mahādeva ?—another name for *Shiva*.

[2] Ibn Batuta (ed. Lee, p. 159) speaks of Jogīs who used to allow themselves to be buried for months, or even for a whole year on end, and were afterwards revived, upon which Col. Yule remarks, 'This art, or the profession of it, is not yet extinct in India'. A very curious account of one of its professors will be found in Major-General A. H. E. Boileau's *Personal Narrative of a Tour through the States of Rajwara*: Calcutta, 1837, 41–4. (See *Cathay and the Way Thither*, 413; *post*, p. 173; N. Chevers, *Manual of Medical Jurisprudence in India*, 656; Carpenter, *Human Physiology*, 4th ed. 1103; J. Braid, *Observations on Trance or Human Hybernation*, 1850.)

swollen.[1] 8. These are the positions of two penitents who, till death, keep their arms elevated in the air, so that the joints become so stiff that they are never able to lower them again. Their hair grows below the waist, and their nails equal their fingers in length. Night and day, winter and summer, they remain stark naked in this position, exposed to the rain and heat, and to the stings of mosquitoes, without being able to use their hands to drive them away. With regard to the other necessities of life, as drinking and eating, they have Fakīrs in their company who wait on them as required. 9. Is the position of another penitent, who stands for several hours daily on one foot, holding in his hands a chafing-dish full of fire, upon which he throws the incense which he offers to his god, at the same time fixing his eyes on the sun. 10 and 11. These are the postures of two other penitents, seated, who have their hands elevated in the air. 12. Is the position in which the penitents sleep without ever lowering their arms; this without doubt is one of the greatest torments which the human body can suffer. 13. Is the position of another penitent, whose weakness has caused his hands to fall behind his back, not being able to lower his arms, which are dried up from lack of nutrition.

There are an infinity of other penitents, some of whom assume positions altogether contrary to the natural attitude of the human body, turning their eyes always towards the sun; others who have their eyes directed to the ground, without ever looking anyone in the face, or saying a single word; and the diversity is so great that it would be sufficient to form the subject of a long discourse.

In order to give more satisfaction to the curious, and to enable them to understand matters more distinctly, I shall add here other pictures of these same penitents, which I have drawn, on the spot, after nature. Modesty has compelled me to conceal the parts which they have no shame about exposing to view, for at all times, both in the country and in the towns, they go about altogether as naked as they came from their mothers' wombs; and although the women

[1] Cf. Bernier, 317; M. Monier-Williams, *Brahmanism and Hinduism*, 4th ed. 88.

approach them out of devotion in order to do what cannot be named for shame, you do not see in them any sign of sensuality; but on the contrary, as they pay no attention to anyone, and roll their eyes terribly, you would say they are absorbed in abstraction.

CHAPTER VII

Concerning the belief of the Idolaters touching the condition of the soul of man after death.

It is one of the articles of belief of the idolaters that the souls of men on leaving their bodies after death are presented to God, who, according to the life the owners have led, allots them other bodies to inhabit, so that the same person is several times reborn into the world. And God sends the souls of men of evil life, degraded in their habits and plunged in all kinds of vices, after being separated from the bodies, into the bodies of inferior animals, such as asses, dogs, cats, and others, in order that they may perform penance for their crimes in these infamous prisons. But it is believed that the souls which enter the bodies of cows are supremely happy, because these animals are regarded as divinities. If a man dies with a cow's tail in his hand, that will suffice, it is said, to render him altogether happy in a future life.[1]

As the idolaters believe in this passage of human souls into the bodies of animals, they abhor the slaughter of any kind of animal, through fear of being guilty of the death of some one of their relations or friends who may be doing penance in one of these bodies.[2]

If these men, during their lives, perform virtuous actions, such as pilgrimages and the giving of alms, it is believed that after death their souls pass into the bodies of some powerful

[1] For the doctrine of Metempsychosis or transmigration of souls see Manu, *Laws*, xii. 1 ff.; Dubois, *Hindu Manners*, 556 ff; Mrs. S. Stevenson, *Rites of the Twice-born*, 195 f., 198 f., 225, 436 ff. For notices by early travellers, P. della Valle, i. 79; Ovington, 283 f.; Fryer, i. 95.

[2] The doctrine of Ahimsa, or veneration for animal life, exemplified in Buddhism (V. A. Smith, *Asoka*, 27 ff. E. W. Hopkins. *Religions of India*, 199 f.).

Rājās or other rich persons, who enjoy the pleasures of life as a reward for the good deeds they had done in other bodies.

This is the reason why the Fakīrs, of whom I have spoken in the preceding chapter, perform such horrible penances; and as all men are not able to bring themselves to suffer so much in this world, they seek during their lives to make up by good works for the want of penances, and by their wills direct their heirs to give alms to Brāhmans, to the end that, by the power of the prayers which they order them to say, God may assign them the body of some grand personage. In the month of January of the year 1661 the Shroff or money-changer of the Dutch Company, named Mondās Parek,[1] died at Surat. He was a rich man and very charitable, and bestowed much alms during his life on the Christians as well as on the idolaters; for the Rev. Capuchin Fathers[2] of Surat used to live for a part of the year on the rice, butter, and vegetables which he sent to them. This Banian was ill only for four or five days, and during that time, as well as for eight or ten days after his death, his brothers distributed 9,000 or 10,000 rupees, and burnt his body, adding to the ordinary wood much sandal and aloes, believing that by this means the soul of their brother, on passing into another body, would become a great noble in some other country. There are some among them who are foolish enough to bury their treasures during their lifetime, as, for instance, nearly all the rich men of the Kingdom of Assam, so that if they enter, after death, the body of any poor and miserable mendicant, they can have recourse to the money which they have buried in order to draw from it at necessity.[3] This is the reason why so much gold and silver and so many precious stones are buried in India,[4] and an idolater must be poor indeed

[1] His name was perhaps Mohandās, 'slave of the captivating one', Krishna: pārakh, 'a money-tester'.

[2] Manucci (i. 62) speaks of 'a little church', at Surat, 'belonging to the French Capuchin Fathers, whose superior was the famous priest Brother Ambrozio'. Cf. Fryer, i. 225.

[3] See p. 219 below.

[4] The enormous absorption of gold by India and its disappearance, is explained by many writers in the same way. Bernier, (p. 223) among others may be mentioned, but the subject is too extensive to be entered

if he has no money buried in the earth. I remember one day buying in India, for 600 rupees, an agate cup 6 inches high and of the size of one of our silver plates.[1] The seller assured me that more than forty years had elapsed since it was buried in the earth, and that he preserved it to serve his need after death, as it was a matter of indifference to him whether he buried the cup or the money. On my last voyage I bought from one of these idolaters sixty-two diamonds weighing about 6 grains apiece, and on expressing my astonishment at seeing so fine a parcel, he replied that I need not be surprised seeing that it took nearly fifty years to accumulate them for his wants after death; but his affairs having changed, and having need of money, he had been obliged to dispose of them. These buried treasures were once of great service to the Rājā Sivajī, who took up arms against the Great Mogul and the King of Bījāpur. This Rājā having taken Callian Bondi,[2] a small town of the Kingdom of Bījāpur, by the advice of the Brāhmans, who assured him that he would find a considerable amount of buried treasure, he ordered

on here. See *Imperial Gazetteer*, iii. 269. Not many years ago about £5,000,000 of hoarded treasure, including precious stones, was taken from pits and wells sunk in the palace zenāna at Gwalior.

[1] This was probably of the kind known to the Romans as the Murrhine cups. The custom of roasting the agates to develop the colours doubtless gave rise to the idea that the material was some form of porcelain; while the suggestion that they were made of fluor-spar may be rejected, as that mineral is not known in India, and there is no trace of its ever having been imported or worked by the lapidaries of Western India. But the true Murrhine cups were probably made of fluor-spar (*Ency. Brit.*, x. 578). The writer of the article Murrhina, Murrea Vasa (Smith, *Dict. Greek and Roman Antiquities*, 3rd ed. ii. 181 f.) discusses the various substances from which they have been supposed to have been made, and regards the problem as unsolved. Also see Sir J. Frazer, *Pausanias*, iv. 255. On the modes of working the so-called Cambay stones, agate and carnelian, see Watt, *Commercial Products*, 561 f.

[2] Kalyān in Thānā District, 33 miles north-east of Bombay. Grant Duff (*Hist. of the Mahrattas*, Oxford, 1921, i. 110) states that it formerly belonged to Ahmadnagar and was ceded to Bījāpur under the treaty of 1636. The northern part extended from Bhiundī, the 'Bondī' of Tavernier, to Nagothana in Kolāba District. The other Kalyānā or Kalyāni is situated in the Kulbarga District, Nizām's Dominions. See Bilgrami & Willmott, *Hist. Sketch of the Nizām's Dominions*, ii. 616 ff.; Manucci, iv. 425; Bernier, 24, 28.

it to be partly demolished, and found in fact great riches, with which he supported his army, consisting of more than 30,000 men. It is impossible to disabuse these idolaters of their errors, because they will not listen to reason, and they entirely subordinate their own judgement to their ancient customs, the principal of which is to burn the bodies of the deceased.

CHAPTER VIII

Concerning the Idolaters' custom of burning the bodies of the deceased.

THE custom among the Gentiles of burning bodies after death is very ancient; they generally burn them on the banks of rivers, where they wash the bodies of the deceased to complete the cleansing of those sins from which they have not been purified during life. This superstition goes to such extremes that very often sick persons, when on the point of death, are carried to the margin of a river or tank, and their feet are placed in the water. According as nature fails the body is pushed forwards, and at last it is held by the chin only, so that at the moment when the spirit departs and leaves the body, both the one and the other can be purged of all defilement by plunging the body wholly into the water, after which it is burned in the same place, which is always close to some pagoda.[1] There are people who make it their business to collect wood, and there is a fixed rate of payment for their trouble.[2] When an idolater is dead, all those of his caste or tribe who are in the place assemble at the house of the deceased, and the body having been placed on a litter covered by some fine cloth, according to the station of the deceased and the property which he has left, they accompany it to the place where it is to be burnt, following the litter, which is carried on the shoulders of those appointed for that

[1] For the custom in Bengal see Ward, *The Hindoos*, 2nd ed., i. 192, and Bernier, 315.

[2] For the extortions of the Doms at Benares, who provide fuel for the funeral pyre, see Crooke, *Tribes and Castes, North-West Provinces and*
12 *Oudh*, ii. 329.

duty. They always proceed chanting some prayers to their god, and calling out Rām! Rām! and, while carrying the body, there is someone who sounds a small bell to give notice to the living to pray for the deceased. The body having arrived at the margin of the river or tank, it is plunged into the water, and afterwards burnt.[1] This is done in three different ways, as I shall describe in the following chapter. According to the wealth of the deceased, more or less sandal-wood or other scented wood is mingled with the ordinary wood which is collected for burning the corpse.

But the idolaters burn not only dead bodies; their cruel superstition goes further, for they also burn the bodies of the living. They make scruple about killing a serpent, and even a bug, yet they regard it as a highly meritorious action to cause a living woman to be burnt in the fire together with the body of her deceased husband.[2]

CHAPTER IX

How the women burn themselves with the bodies of their deceased husbands in India.

It is also an ancient custom among the idolaters of India that on a man dying his widow can never remarry; as soon, therefore, as he is dead she retires to weep for her husband, and some days afterwards her hair is shaved off, and she despoils herself of all the ornaments with which her person was adorned; she removes from her arms and legs the bracelets which her husband had given her, when espousing her, as a sign that she was to be submissive and bound to him, and she remains for the rest of her life without any consideration, and worse than a slave, in the place where previously she was mistress.[3] This miserable condition causes her to detest

[1] For the custom in Kāthiāwār see Mrs. S. Stevenson, *Rites of the Twice-born*, 149.

[2] See a curious case of self-inhumation of a water-carrier woman attendant with her mistress, mother of the Rāo (Mrs. M. Postans, *Cutch*, 72 ff.).

[3] In Gujarāt the widow on the day of her husband's death breaks her bracelets, and has her head shaved on the tenth day; but a young

life, and prefer to ascend a funeral pile to be consumed alive with the body of her deceased husband, rather than be regarded by all the world for the remainder of her days with opprobrium and infamy. Besides this the Brāhmans induce women to hope that by dying in this way, with their husbands, they will live again with them in some other world with more glory and more comfort than they have previously enjoyed. These are the two reasons which make these unhappy women resolve to burn themselves with the bodies of their husbands; to which it should be added that the priests encourage them with the hope that at the moment they are in the fire, before they yield up their souls, Rām will reveal wonderful things to them, and that after the soul has passed through several bodies it will attain to an exalted degree of glory for all eternity.

But it should be remarked that a woman cannot burn herself with the body of her husband without having received permission from the Governor of the place where she dwells, and those Governors who are Musalmāns, hold this dreadful custom of self-destruction in horror, and do not readily give permission.[1] On the other hand, it is only childless widows who can be reproached for not having loved their husbands if they have not had courage to burn themselves after their death, and to whom this want of courage will be for the remainder of their lives a cause of reproach. For widows who have children are not permitted under any circumstances to burn themselves with the bodies of their husbands; and so far from custom obliging them, it is ordained that they

Brāhman widow is allowed to wear her bracelets till she is about thirty years old, and then, when another death occurs in the family, her bracelets are broken, her head is shaved, and she wears the dark dress of a widow (*Bombay Gazetteer*, ix, part i, 50. Mrs. S. Stevenson, *Rites of the Twice-born*, 203).

[1] On Mughal efforts to repress Satī see Ovington, 344; Bernier, 306; Smith, *Akbar, the Great Mogul*, 226. At a later time Sleeman (*Rambles*, 18 ff.) was asked to allow a Satī, and failed to save the woman's life. Akbar prohibited the burning of a widow against her inclination (Smith, *Akbar, the Great Mogul*, 382). The custom was prohibited by the Sikh Gurus, and does not prevail among the Nāmbutirī Brāhmans of Malabar. (M. A. Macauliffe, *The Sikh Religion*, i. Introd. xxii; E. Thurston, *Castes and Tribes of S. India*, v. 189.)

shall live to watch over the education of their children. Those to whom the Governors peremptorily refuse to grant permission to burn themselves pass the remainder of their lives in severe penances and in doing charitable deeds. There are some who frequent the great highways either to boil water with vegetables, and give it as a drink to passers by, or to keep fire always ready to light the pipes of those who desire to smoke tobacco. There are others among them who make a vow to eat nothing but what they find undigested in the droppings of oxen, cows, and buffaloes,[1] and do still more absurd things.

The Governor, seeing that all the remonstrances with women, who are urged to burn themselves even by their relatives and by the Brāhmans, fail to turn them from the damnable resolution which they have taken to die in so cruel a fashion, when his secretary indicates by a sign that he has received a bribe, at length allows them to do what they wish, and in a rage tells all the idolaters who accompany them that they may 'go to the devil'.

Immediately on permission being obtained, all kinds of music are heard, and with the sound of drums, flutes, and other instruments, all go to the house of the deceased, and thence, as I have said, accompany the body to the margin of a river or tank, where it is to be burned.

All the relatives and friends of the widow who desires to die after her husband congratulate her beforehand on the good fortune which she is about to acquire in the other world, and on the glory which all the members of the caste derive from her noble resolution. She dresses herself as for her wedding-day, and is conducted in triumph to the place where she is to be burnt. A great noise is made with instruments of music and the voices of the women who follow, singing hymns to the glory of the unhappy one who is about to die. The Brāhmans accompanying her exhort her to show resolution and courage, and many Europeans believe that in order to remove the fear of that death which man naturally abhors, she is given some kind of drink that takes away her senses and removes all apprehension which the preparations for her

[1] See i. 226 above.

death might occasion.[1] It is for the interest of the Brāhmans that these unhappy women maintain the resolution they have taken to burn themselves, for all the bracelets which they wear, both on arms and legs, with their earrings and rings, belong of right to the Brāhmans, who search for them in the ashes after the women are burnt. According to the station and wealth of the women, the bracelets, earrings, and rings are either of gold or silver ; the poorest wear them of copper and tin ; but as for precious stones, they do not wear them at all when going to be burnt.[2]

I have seen women burnt in three different ways, according to the customs of different countries. In the Kingdom of Gujarāt, and as far as Agra and Delhi, this is how it takes place : On the margin of a river or tank, a kind of small hut, about 12 feet square, is built of reeds and all kinds of faggots, with which some pots of oil and other drugs are placed in order to make it burn quickly. The woman is seated in a half-reclining position in the middle of the hut, her head reposes on a kind of pillow of wood, and she rests her back against a post, to which she is tied by her waist by one of the Brāhmans, for fear lest she should escape on feeling the flame. In this position she holds the dead body of her husband on her knees, chewing betel all the time ; and after having been about half an hour in this condition, the Brāhman who has been by her side in the hut goes outside, and she calls out to the priests to apply the fire ; this the Brāhmans, and the relatives and friends of the woman who are present immediately do, throwing into the fire some pots of oil, so that the woman may suffer less by being quickly consumed. After the bodies have been reduced to ashes, the Brāhmans take what ever is found in the way of melted gold, silver, tin, or copper, derived from the bracelets, earrings, and rings which

[1] Preparations of bhang, or Indian hemp, used to be given for this purpose, but in many cases the excitement alone, in all probability, produced an insensibility to pain. In a case which occurred in Cutch, it was suspected that the woman had been dosed with opium, but when she was examined by two doctors, this was found not to be the case (Mrs. M. Postans, *Cutch*, 65).

[2] For some contemporary accounts see Bowrey, 36 ff., 86, 203 f ; Fryer, i. 95 f., ii. 18, 117.

the woman had on; this belongs to them by right, as I have said.

In the Kingdom of Bengal women are burnt in another manner. A woman in that country must be very poor if she does not come with the body of her husband to the bank of the Ganges to wash it after he is dead, and to bathe herself before being burnt. I have seen them come to the Ganges more than twenty days' journey, the bodies being by that time altogether putrid, and emitting an unbearable odour. There was one of them who came from the north, near the frontiers of the Kingdom of Bhutān, with the body of her husband which she had conveyed in a carriage, and travelled all the way on foot herself, without eating for fifteen or sixteen days, till she arrived at the Ganges, where after washing the body of her husband, which stank horribly, and bathing herself also, she had herself burnt with him with a determination which surprised those who saw it. I was there at the time. As throughout the course of the Ganges, and also in all Bengal, there is but little fuel,[1] these poor women send to beg for wood out of charity to burn themselves with the dead bodies of their husbands. A funeral pile is prepared for them, which is like a bed, with its pillow of small wood and reeds, in which pots of oil and other drugs are placed in order to consume the body quickly. The woman who intends to burn herself, preceded by drums, flutes, and hautboys, and adorned with her most beautiful jewels, comes dancing to the funeral pile, and ascending it she places herself, half-lying, half-seated. Then the body of her husband is laid across her, and all the relatives and friends bring her, one a letter, another a piece of cloth, this one flowers, that one pieces of silver or copper, asking her to give this from me to my mother, or to my brother, or to some relative or friend, whoever the dead person may be whom they have most loved while alive. When the woman sees that they bring her nothing more, she asks those present three times whether they have any more commissions for her, and if they do not reply she wraps all they have brought in a

[1] This remark is of interest as showing that the scarcity of fuel, which is now so much felt, had already been experienced in these regions.

taffeta,[1] which she places between her lap and the back of the body of her dead husband, calling upon the priests to apply fire to the funeral pile. This the Brāhmans and the relatives do simultaneously. There is, as I have remarked, but little wood in the Kingdom of Bengal; so as soon as these miserable women are dead and half burnt, their bodies are thrown into the Ganges with those of their husbands, where they are eaten by the crocodiles.

I should not forget here an evil custom which is practised among the idolaters of the same Kingdom of Bengal. When a woman is delivered, and the infant, as often happens, is unwilling to take its mother's breast it is carried outside the village and placed in a cloth, which is tied by the four corners to the branches of a tree, and is thus left from morning to evening. In this way the poor infant is exposed to the crows, which torment it, and some have been found whose eyes have been torn out of their heads, which is the reason why many idolaters are seen in Bengal who have but one eye, and others who have both injured or altogether gone. In the evening the infant is taken to try whether it is willing to suckle during the following night, and should it happen that it still refuses the breast, it is taken back on the following day to the same place; this is done for three days in succession, after which, if the infant is unwilling to take the breast, in the belief that it is a demon, they cast it into the Ganges, or some other river or tank which is nearer at hand. In places where there are many monkeys these poor children are not so exposed to the attacks of crows, for this reason, that as soon as a monkey discovers a nest of these birds he climbs the tree, and throws the nest on one side and the eggs on the other. On the other hand, there are among the English, Dutch, and Portuguese charitable persons who, moved to compassion for the misfortune of these infants, remove them when they are thus exposed and hung in a tree and take care to have them brought up as I have once seen

[1] Pers. *tāfta,* silken or linen cloth; *tāftan,* 'to shine, twist, spin'; originally applied to various kinds of silk cloth; at present various mixtures of silk, wool, cotton. or jute. (*New English Dict.* s.v.; Yule, *Hobson-Jobson,* 708.)

an example of at Hugly; this is done in the places near their factories.[1]

Let us see now what is the practice along the coast of Coromandel when women are going to be burnt with the bodies of their deceased husbands. A large hole of 9 or 10 feet deep, and 25 or 30 feet square, is dug, into which plenty of wood is thrown, with many drugs to make it burn quickly. When the hole is well heated, the body of the husband is placed on the edge, and then his wife comes dancing, and chewing betel, accompanied by all her relatives and friends, and with the sound of drums and cymbals. The woman then makes three turns round the hole, and at each time she embraces all her relatives and friends. When she completes the third turn the Brāhmans throw the body of the deceased into the fire, and the woman, with her back turned towards the hole, is pushed by the Brāhmans, and falls in backwards. Then all the relatives throw pots of oil and other drugs of that kind, as I have said is elsewhere done, so that the bodies may be the sooner consumed. In the greater part of the same Coromandel coast the woman does not burn herself with the body of her deceased husband, but allows herself to be interred, while alive, with him in a hole which the Brāhmans dig in the ground, about 1 foot deeper than the height of the man or woman. They generally select a sandy spot, and when they have placed the man and woman in the hole, each of their friends fills a basket of sand, and throws it on the bodies until the hole is full and heaped over, half a foot higher than the ground, after which they jump and dance upon it till they are certain that the woman is smothered.[2]

[1] The exposure of children is said to have been a Vedic practice, but it merely meant that the child, if a girl, was laid aside, while a boy was lifted up and acknowledged (Macdonell & Keith, *Vedic Index*, i. 395; ii. 114 f.). Various modes of infanticide are described by Chevers (*Manual of Medical Jurisprudence in India*, 750 ff.). In stating that in Bengal the excess of children blind of one eye is due to exposure, Tavernier exaggerated the case. Blindness in Bengal is largely due to climatic causes—glare and dust (*Census Report, Bengal*, 1901, i. 288; 1911, i. 419).

[2] Thévenot alludes to the custom of burying widows alive, but says that when they were covered with clay up to the neck, they were strangled by the Brāhmans (*Voyages*, 253). This probably gave rise to the tale of Sindbad the Seaman being buried with his dead wife (Burton,

When any of the idolaters of the Coromandel country are on the point of death, their friends do not act like those elsewhere, who carry them to die at the margin of a river or tank, so that their souls when leaving the body may be cleansed of their impurity. They simply carry them into the vicinity of the fattest cow which they are able to find.[1]

. . . .

If a cow happens to be sick the owner must lead it to the margin of a tank or river, for should it die in his house the Brāhmans inflict a fine upon him.[2]

CHAPTER X

Remarkable histories of several women who have been burnt after the death of their husbands.

AMONG several examples of this more than barbarous custom of the women of the idolaters of India of burning themselves with the corpses of their husbands, I will relate three remarkable cases, of two of which I was a witness.

A Thousand Nights and a Night, ed. 1893, iv. 381 ff.). Numerous other writers also refer to the custom. As is the case with Satī, this practice is now extinct, but were the restraint removed it is most probable that there would be reversion to both in some parts of India. For this form of Satī by burning in a pit see Fra Paolino da San Bartolomeo, *A Voyage to the East Indies*, trans. W. Johnston, 1800, p. 91 f.; Sleeman, *Rambles*, 19; Caesar Fredericke, in Hakluyt, *Principal Navigations*, Everyman's Library, iii. 214.

[1] The remainder of this passage has been omitted, as the ceremony described is too disgusting for reproduction. This refers to the common use of the Panchagavya, the five sacred products of the cow—milk, curds, butter, urine, dung (Dubois, *Hindu Manners*, 42 f., 152 ff.).

[2] These fines, as described by Ward, were very heavy, sufficient in some cases to cripple a man's resources for the remainder of his life. If one of the Tiyar caste in the Central Provinces kills a cow, he must live in the cowshed for 21 days, lying down when the cows lie down, standing up when they stand up; then he must make a pilgrimage, partake of the five products of a cow, and give a feast to the caste (Russell, *Tribes and Castes*, i. 415). Among the Tellis of Madras, if a cow dies with a rope round its neck, or on the spot where it is tethered, the family must get rid of the pollution by a pilgrimage, or by bathing in a sacred river (Thurston, *Castes and Tribes of Southern India*, vii. 16). See also Fra Paolino da San Bartolomeo, *A Voyage to the East Indies*, 299; F. Buchanan, in Martin, *Eastern India*, ii. 140.

The Rājā of Vellore,[1] of whom I have spoken in the first book of this account of India, having at the same time lost both this town and his life by the victory which the General of the King of Bījāpur gained over him, there was great mourning in all his Court. Eleven of the women of his household were keenly affected by his death, and all resolved to burn themselves when his body was burnt. The General of the Bījāpur army having heard of this resolve, thought that he would be able to dissuade these desperate women by flattering them, and promising them all kinds of good treatment. But seeing that this was of no effect, and that they were absolutely determined to be burnt with the body of the deceased, he directed that they should be kept shut up in a room. He who received this order, on going to execute it, was told by the infuriated women that it was in vain, that he might do his best, but that it was useless to keep them prisoners, and that if they were not allowed to do what they wished, they had resolved that in three hours there would not be one of them left alive. He jeered at this threat, and would not believe that it could be carried into effect. But the officer in charge of the women, on opening the door at the end of three hours, found the eleven all dead and stretched on the ground, without any apparent indications that they had hastened their deaths, either by steel, rope, or poison, nor could anyone see how they had been able to make away with themselves. On this occasion it was assuredly the case that the evil spirit had played his game. Let us pass to another history.

Two of the most powerful Rājās of India, who were brothers came to Agra in the year 1642 to pay their respects to Shāhjahān, who then reigned. As they had not behaved themselves properly on this occasion, in the opinion of the Grand Master of the Emperor's palace, he one day said to one of the two

[1] Velou in the original (see vol. i. 130). This refers to Rāma Rājā, of Vijayanagar, who was defeated at the battle of Talikota, 23rd January 1565, by a confederacy of the Kings of Bījāpur, Bīdar, Ahmadnagar, and Golkonda, and being captured, was beheaded by Husain Nizām Shāh of Ahmadnagar, with his own hands (Smith, *Oxford Hist. of India*, 296 f.). No contemporary account of the Satī, which certainly occurred, has been traced.

Rājās, who were together under the gallery of the palace, in the presence of the Emperor, that this was not the sort of demeanour that should be observed towards so great a monarch as the Emperor his master. As this Rājā regarded himself as a King and a great Prince, and had brought 15,000 or 16,000 horse in his suite with the other Rājā, his brother, he was offended by the boldness the Grand Master showed in reprimanding him in that fashion, and drawing his dagger slew him on the spot, in the presence of the Emperor, who witnessed the deed from an elevated position, where, as I have elsewhere said, he generally administers justice. The Grand Master fell at the feet of his brother, who was close to him, and the latter immediately set himself to avenge his death, but was anticipated by the brother of the Rājā, who stabbed him in the breast with his dagger and flung his dead body on that of the Grand Master. The Emperor, who beheld these two murders, one after the other, was frightened and withdrew into his harem; but forthwith all the Omrahs and other people who were present under the gallery, threw themselves on the two Rājās and cut them to pieces. The Emperor, indignant at such an action being committed in his palace and in his presence, ordered the bodies of the Rājās to be thrown into the river; but as soon as the troops they had left near Agra heard of the affront which was intended to the memory of their Princes, they threatened to enter the city and pillage it; this caused the Emperor, rather than expose the city to this danger, to order that the bodies should be handed over to them. This was done, and the Rājputs were appeased by this means. As they went to burn them they beheld thirteen women of the households of these two Rājās approaching, dancing and leaping, who forthwith encircled the funeral pile, holding one another by the hand, mounted it, and being immediately enveloped in the smoke, which suffocated them, they all fell together into the fire. The Brāhmans then threw upon them a quantity of wood, pots of oil, and other drugs, according to custom, in order that the bodies should be quickly consumed.[1]

[1] This refers to the famous tragedy of the assassination of Salābat Khān in the Palace at Agra, on 5th August 1644. See the narrative, with references, in Tod, *Annals of Rajasthan*, ed. 1920, ii. 976 ff.

I remember another strange occurrence which happened one day in my presence at Patna, a town of Bengal. I was with the Dutch at the house of the Governor of the town, a venerable noble, nearly eighty years old, who commanded 5,000 or 6,000 horse, when a young and very beautiful woman, scarcely more than twenty-two years of age, entered the reception room where we were seated. She, with a firm and resolute voice, required the Governor's permission to burn herself with the body of her deceased husband. The Governor, touched by the youth and beauty of the woman, sought to turn her from her resolution, but seeing that all that he could say was useless, and that she only became more obstinate, and asked him with a bold and courageous voice if he believed that she feared fire; he enquired if she knew any torment equal to fire, and if she had never happened to burn her hand. 'No, no,' this woman then replied to him with more courage than before; 'I do not fear fire in any way, and to make you see that it is so, you have only to order a well-lighted torch to be brought here.' The Governor, horrified at the language of the woman, did not wish to hear more, and dismissing her told her in a rage that she might go to the devil. Some young nobles who were by him asked him to allow them to test the woman and to order a torch to be brought, persuading him that she would not have the courage to burn herself with it. At first he was unwilling to consent, but they continued to urge him the more; so that at length, by his order, a torch was brought, which, in India, is nothing more than a cloth twisted and steeped in oil, and fixed on the end of a stick like a chafing dish; this, which we call a lamp (*fallot*), serves us at need in the crossways of towns. As soon as the woman saw the torch, which was well lighted, she ran in front of it, held her hand firmly in the flame without the least grimace, and pushed in her arm up to the elbow, till it was immediately scorched; this caused horror to all who witnessed the deed, and the Governor commanded the woman to be removed from his presence.

Since we are at Patna I shall relate yet another strange thing which happened there one day in my presence. A Brāhman from outside entered the town, summoned all his tribesmen and told them that they must give him 2,000 rupees and 27 cubits of cloth, which are, as I have said, the ells of this country. The principal among them told him that it was impossible, and that they were poor, but he persisted in his demand to have what he asked, and declared that he would remain there without drinking or eating till they had brought the cloth and the 2,000 rupees. With this resolution he climbed up a tree in the square, seated himself on a forked branch, and remained in this position without eating or drinking for several days. The report of this extravagance reached the ears of the Dutch, with whom I then was, and we gave money to keep men on the watch all night close to the tree, to see if it was true that this man was able to remain for so long a time without eating or drinking, which he did indeed for thirty days. Besides the people whom we had engaged for the purpose, there were more than 100 other witnesses whom his tribesmen had sent, who never moved day or night from the vicinity of the tree. At length, on the thirty-first day of such a surprising and extraordinary fast, the idolaters, fearing that the Brāhman would not be able to hold out longer against hunger, and having a scruple about allowing one of their priests to die for want of that which he asked, taxed themselves all round and took him the 27 ells of cloth and the 2,000 rupees.[1] As soon as the Brahman saw the money and cloth he descended from the tree, reproached all those of the tribe who were present at this spectacle with their want of charity to the poor, and distributed to the poorest the whole sum, reserving only 5 or 6 rupees for himself. He did the same with the cloth, which he cut up into many pieces, keeping for himself only what was sufficient to cover his waist, and when all this was done he disappeared, and in spite of inquiries no one knows what became of him. This

[1] This is what is known in India as sitting Dharnā—to enforce payment of a demand; it is now an offence under the Indian Penal Code. As to the possibility of a man remaining for so long a period without food, India furnishes numerous apparently well authenticated instances. Besides which we have Dr. Tanner's case in America, many in different countries of Europe, and that of McSwiney, Lord Mayor of Cork, who died in Brixton Prison, on 25th October 1920, after 73 days' hunger strike. (See p. 156 above.) On 'sitting Dharnā' see Yule, *Hobson-Jobson*, 315.

ought to show sufficiently that in these matters the work of the devil is manifested.

As there are many Chinese at Batavia, I shall give here an account of a custom which I have observed among these idolaters. When a Chinaman is at the point of death, all the relatives and friends crowd about him, and ask him, with tears, where he wishes to go, that if he wants anything he has only to say so and they will give it to him, be it gold, silver, or women.[1] When death occurs many ceremonies are performed at their funerals; these consist principally in displays of fireworks, in which the Chinese excel all the other nations of the world, for a man must be very poor if something is not expended on them at his death. Moreover, some silver is placed in a small box, which is buried near the deceased, and a quantity of food is placed near the grave in the belief that he will come to eat it. As some soldiers of the garrison are sent out of Batavia every evening to make the circuit of the town during the night, on one occasion they took it into their heads to go to the graves, and ate up that which had been left; this they continued to do for some nights in succession. When the Chinese were aware of this, in order to deter them from returning, on three or four occasions they poisoned the food which they placed on the graves of their dead; this caused a great disturbance in Batavia. The Chinese occupy a leading position in commerce, and are more cunning than the Dutch, but as they are not liked by the people of the town, the latter took the part of the soldiers, and accused the Chinese of having poisoned

[1] This is apparently a version of the custom of placing with the dead articles for their use in the next world. The exact custom in the text has not been traced. See J. J. M. de Groot, *Religious Systems of China*, i. 3 ff.; J. M. Gray, *China*, i. 278 ff. 'The Burials of the Chineses are perform'd with great Ceremony. When a sick Person is at the point of Death, all his Friends and Relations gather about him, and ask him frankly whither he is going, and why he will leave them? Questions very edifying and much to the purpose! They tell him he need only acquaint them what he wants, and assure him very obligingly he shall immediately have all he can ask' (*The Voyage of François Leguat*, Hakluyt Society, ii. 254 f.). Leguat, who speaks contemptuously of Tavernier, may have borrowed this passage from him.

some of them. But they defended themselves from this charge very cleverly, saying, that if greed had caused these soldiers to die from eating the food which had been left on the graves of their dead, they were not responsible, as it was not for the soldiers they had left it, and that till then among the great number whom they had interred not one of the dead persons had ever complained of such a thing; thus nothing more was said about it, and the soldiers dared not meddle with them any further.

CHAPTER XI

Concerning the most celebrated Pagodas of the Idolaters of India.

THE idolaters of India have, both in the towns and country parts, a great number of temples, large and small, called pagodas, where they go to pray to their gods and make offerings; but many of the poor people who dwell in the forests and mountains, far removed from villages, take a stone, and rudely trace a nose and eyes with yellow or red colour upon it, and all the family then worship it.[1]

The four most celebrated pagodas are, Jagannāth, Benares, Muttra, and Tirupati,[2] of each of which I shall give a separate description.

Jagannāth is the name of one of the mouths of the Ganges,[3] upon which the great pagoda is built, where the Great Brāhman, that is to say the High Priest of the idolaters, resides. The form of the choir or interior of this pagoda is as follows: it is similar, in proportion, to all the others, which are built upon the same model, in the form of a cross. The great idol on the altar of the choir[4] has two diamonds for his eyes and

[1] For stone worship in India see Hastings, *Ency. Religion and Ethics*, xi. 871 ff.

[2] Jagrenate, Banarous, Matura, and Tripeti in the original.

[3] The position of Jagannāth is on the sea coast of Orissa, at Purī, which is many miles from the nearest mouth of the Ganges. Bernier, Tavernier's contemporary, was better informed, as in a letter to M. Chapelain he states it was situated on the Gulf of Bengal (p. 304). For an account and plan of the temple see Hunter, *Orissa*, i. 128 and Bowrey, 12 f., who calls it Jno. Gernaet.

[4] Of late years no European has been allowed to enter Jagannāth.

a pendant from his neck which reaches to the waist, and the smallest of these diamonds weighs about 40 carats; he has bracelets on his arms, some being of pearls and some of rubies, and this magnificent idol is called Kesora.[1] The revenues of this great pagoda are sufficient to feed 15,000 or 20,000 pilgrims daily, and these numbers are often to be found there, the pagoda being the object of the highest devotion by the Indians, who visit it from all quarters. It should be remarked that jewellers, who come like others, are not now permitted to enter the pagoda, since one of them intending to steal it, who allowed himself to be shut up during the night, extracted a diamond from one of the eyes of the idol. As he was about to leave in the morning, when the pagoda was opened, this thief, they say, died at the door, and the idol performed this miracle as a punishment for sacrilege. What makes this grand building the principal pagoda in India, is, that it is situated on the Ganges, the idolaters believing that the waters of that river have a special virtue, which cleanses them from defilement when they bathe in it. The great wealth of this pagoda (for it supports upwards of 20,000 cows) depends upon the amount of the offerings made every day by the incredible multitude of people who arrive from all parts. But these alms are not altogether at the discretion of those who give them, as they are fixed by the High Priest, who before granting permission to the pilgrims to shave themselves, to bathe in the Ganges, and do the other things necessary

On the occasion of the late Lord Mayo's last journey, which was cut short by his murder in the Andaman Islands, he had it in contemplation to visit Purī on his return to Calcutta, and a rumour was then abroad that a special concession about entering the temple was to be made in his favour. The temple has been described by Hindus, and in especial detail by Dr. Rajendra Lāla Mitra, in his *Orissa*.

[1] Kesava Rāī, 'he with the flowing locks', or Krishna. The bones of Krishna, who had been killed by a hunter, were placed inside an image, which was never completed owing to the impatience of King Indra, who, however, obtained from Brahma a concession that the idol should become famous as Jagannāth. (Ward, *The Hindoos*, 2nd ed., ii. 163.) The story of the bones of Krishna is based on the veneration of relics in Buddhism, of which many survivals are found in the Vaishnava customs of Jagannāth (Hastings, *Ency. Religion and Ethics*, vii. 464).

in fulfilment of their vows, taxes each one according to his means, of which he is very exactly informed. Thus he receives enormous sums, from which he himself derives no profit, all being expended on the feeding of the poor and the support of the pagoda. The Grand Brāhman distributes each day to the pilgrims whatever food is required, consisting of butter, milk, rice, and flour; but to the poor, who are in want of utensils to cook their food with, it is given read cooked.[1] It is a surprising thing, and well worthy of notice, to observe how the food is distributed to the poor people who have no pots. In the morning the rice is cooked in earthen pots of different sizes, and when the hour has come when the poor pilgrims come for food, if, for example, there are five, the chief Brāhman orders another Brāhman to take a pot full of cooked rice, which he lets fall, and the pot is broken into five equal parts, of which each pilgrim takes one, and likewise in proportion, more or less, according to the number of people who present themselves to receive their shares. The Brāhmans never cook twice in the same earthen pot, but frequently use copper pots, and they have for plates certain leaves larger than our walnut leaves,[2] which are stitched together. They use, however, a kind of dish about a foot in diameter to melt butter, in which they dip the rice with their fingers when eating, and a small ladle for the melted butter, which is drunk as we drink a glass of Spanish wine after a repast.

I come now to a more detailed description of the idol on the altar of the pagoda of Jagannāth. It is covered from the neck to the base with a grand mantle which hangs on the altar, and this mantle is of gold or silver brocade according to the nature of the ceremonies. At first this idol had neither feet nor hands, and this is how this fact is explained. After one of their prophets was taken up into heaven, when they were all plunged in tears and lamentation at losing him, God sent to them from heaven an angel like the prophet, whom they treated with great honour and respect. But while

[1] This is a distorted version of the distribution of the consecrated food to the pilgrims. See Hastings, *op. cit.*, vii. 464 f.; Hunter, i. 146. The same custom prevails at other Vaishnava shrines (Mrs. S. Stevenson,
13 *Rites of the Twice-born*, 317).

[2] See ii. 60 above.

the angel was engaged in making the idol, impatience seized upon them, and they removed it to the pagoda, although, as yet, it was unprovided with feet and hands. But as it was deformed, they made hands for it out of the small pearls which we call 'pearls by the ounce'.[1] As for the feet, they cannot be seen, being concealed under the mantle. There is nothing left uncovered save the hands and face; the head and body are made of sandal wood.[2] Round the elevated dome in which the idol is seated, from the base up to the top, there are many niches containing other images, the majority of which represent hideous monsters made of stone of various colours. On each side of this great pagoda there are others, much smaller, where the pilgrims make their petty offerings, and those who, on account of sickness or in their business, have made a vow to some god, take there an image or semblance of the object in memory of the benefit which they believe they have received.[3] This idol is anointed every day with scented oils which make him quite black. He has on his right hand his sister who is called Sotora, who is also represented standing and clothed; and on his left his brother, also clothed, who is called Balbader.[4] In front of the great idol, somewhat to the left, his wife is to be seen, who is called Kemui,[5] she is of massive gold, and represented standing, the three others are made of sandal wood.

The other two pagodas are intended for the residence of the chief Brāhman, or High Priest, and the other priests who serve in the great pagoda. All these Brāhmans go about with bare heads, and the majority are shaved, having for sole garment a piece of cloth, a part of which is wrapped

[1] Seed pearls, aljofar of the Portuguese. (See p. 93.)

[2] The legend was invented to explain how a rude fetish block, an object of worship by some non-Aryan tribe, became adopted as a form of Vishnu (Hastings, *op. cit.*, vii. 464).

[3] A similar custom is followed in some Catholic countries of Europe; see vol. i, p. 210 above.

[4] The names are Subhadra and Balbhadra or Balarāma. The triple image is said to represent Buddha, his Law and Congregation (see Hastings, *op. cit.*, vii. 464).

[5] The word may represent Kāminī 'an amorous woman', applied to Rādhā, mistress of Krishna.

round the body, and the remainder worn like a scarf. Near the pagoda the tomb of one of their prophets, named Cabir,[1] to whom they do great honour, is to be seen. It should be remarked that all these idols are on a kind of altar surrounded by gratings, for no one is allowed to touch them, with the exception of certain Brāhmans appointed by the High Priest for that purpose.

I come to the pagoda of Benares, which, after that of Jagannāth, is the most famous in all India, and of equal sanctity, being built on the margin of the Ganges,[2] and in the town of which it bears the name. The most remarkable thing about it is that from the door of the pagoda to the river there is a descent by stone steps, where there are at intervals platforms and small, rather dark, chambers, some of which serve as dwellings for the Brāhmans, and others as kitchens where they prepare their food. For after the idolaters have bathed, and have gone to pray and make their offerings in the pagoda, they prepare their food without anyone but themselves touching it, through the fear they have lest anyone who approached it might be unclean. But above all things, they ardently desire to drink the water of the Ganges, because, as soon as they have drunk it, they believe, as I have said, that they are cleansed from all their sins. Every day large numbers of these Brāhmans are to be seen going to the clearest part of the river to fill round, small-mouthed, earthen pots, which hold about a bucketful, with this water. When they are full they are taken to the chief priest, who directs the mouth to be covered with a very fine cloth of fire-colour, in three or four folds, upon which he applies his seal. The Brāhmans carry this water at the end of a stick, flat like a lath, from which hang six small cords, and to each of them one of these pots is attached. They rest themselves by changing the shoulder frequently,

[1] Kabīr, a Saint and writer, flourished about the close of the fifteenth century. (Hastings, *op. cit.*, vii. 632 ff.) It is a corroboration of Tavernier's knowledge that a monastery, called after Kabīr, still exists at Purī (Hunter, *op. cit.*, i. 103).

[2] Here the mistake about Jagannāth, being on the Ganges (see p. 175, *n.*) is repeated, as it is also elsewhere in the following pages.

and they sometimes travel three or four hundred leagues of country with this load,[1] and then sell it, or make a present of it, but only to the richest persons, from whom they expect a liberal reward. Some of these idolaters, when they celebrate any festival—especially when their children are married—drink this water at a cost of 400 or 500 écus. It is drunk only at the end of the repast, as we drink hypocras or muscat in Europe, each guest receiving a cup, or two, according to the liberality of the host. The principal reason why thi water of the Ganges is so highly esteemed, is, that it neve becomes bad, and engenders no vermin; but I do not know whether we should believe what is said about this, taking into consideration the number of bodies which are constantly being thrown into the Ganges.[2]

Returning to the pagoda at Benares.[3] The building, like all the other pagodas, is in the figure of a cross, having its four arms equal. In the middle a lofty dome rises like a kind of tower with many sides terminating in a point, and at the end of each arm of the cross another tower rises, which can be ascended from outside. Before reaching the top there are many niches and several balconies, which project to intercept the fresh air; and all over the tower there are rudely executed figures in relief of various kinds of animals. Under this great dome, and exactly in the middle of the pagoda, there is an altar like a table, of 7 to 8 feet in length, and 5 to 6 wide,

[1] This is what is known as a banghy in India. Men who are accustomed to carrying weights in this way, when on occasion they have only a load for one end, make up an equipoise of a stone or clod of earth for the other. A similar carrying-stick is used in China. Formerly, if not still, troops of these water-carriers were to be seen on the Grand Trunk road, which affords a scene of much animation and interest. Photographs of men carrying water from the Ganges and Nerbudda will be found in Russell, *Tribes and Castes, Central Provinces*, i. 184, ii. 100.

[2] The reader will do well not to believe this story, but rather to conclude that much of the water when drunk is in a very unwholesome condition, and is the cause of disease. At the same time, it is believed that it becomes rapidly purified by oxidation.

[3] The mosque at the Panchgangā Ghāt, the minarets of which overlook the city, occupies the site, and is constructed out of materials of the great temple dedicated to Siva, known as Bisheshar (Visvesvara) and destroyed by orders of Aurangzeb in 1669 (Jadunath Sarkar, *Hist. of Aurangzīb*, iii. 321). Tavernier's account of the original temple is valuable.

with two steps in front, which serve as a footstool, and this footstool is covered with a beautiful tapestry, sometimes of silk and sometimes of gold and silk, according to the solemnity of the rite which is being celebrated. The altar is covered with gold or silver brocade, or some beautiful painted cloth. From outside the pagoda this altar faces you with the idols upon it; for the women and girls must salute it from the outside, as, save only those of a certain tribe, they are not allowed to enter the pagoda. Among the idols on the great altar one stands 5 or 6 feet in height; neither the arms, legs, nor trunk are seen, only the head and neck being visible; all the remainder of the body, down to the altar, is covered by a robe which increases in width below. Sometimes on its neck there is a rich chain of gold, rubies, pearls, or emeralds. This idol has been made in honour and after the likeness of Bainmadou,[1] formerly a great and holy personage among them, whose name they often have on their lips. On the right side of the altar there is also the figure of an animal, or rather of a chimera, seeing that it represents in part an elephant, in part a horse, and in part a mule. It is of massive gold, and is called Garou,[2] no person being allowed to approach it but the Brāhmans. It is said to be the resemblance of the animal which this holy personage rode upon when he was in the world, and that he made long journeys on it, going about to see if the people were doing their duty and not injuring anyone. At the entrance of the pagoda, between the principal door and the great altar, there is to the left a small altar, upon which an idol made of black marble is seated, with the legs crossed, and about two feet high. When I was there, near it, on the left, sat a small boy, son of the chief priest, and all the people who came there threw him pieces of taffeta, or brocade like handkerchiefs, with which he wiped the idol and then returned them to the owners.

[1] Benīmādho, Sanskrit *veni*, 'a triple braid', the impersonation of the junction of the three sacred rivers, Ganges, Jamnā and Sarasvatī, at Prayāg, or Allāhābād. Mādhava, 'honey-sweet', is a title of Vishnu or Krishna.

[2] Garuda, the mythical bird, vulture, half-man, half-bird, on which Vishnu rides, represented with the head, wings, talons, and beak of an eagle, and the body and limbs of a man.

Others threw him chains made of beads like small nuts, with a naturally sweet scent, which these idolaters wear on their necks and use to repeat their prayers over each bead. Others threw chains of coral or yellow amber, others fruits and flowers. Finally, with everything which is thrown to the chief Brāhmaṇ's child he wipes the idol and makes him kiss it, and afterwards, as I have just said, returns it to the people. This idol is called Morli Ram,[1] that is to say, the God Morli, brother of the idol on the great altar.

Under the principal entrance of the pagoda one of the chief Brāhmans is seated, and close to him is a large dish full of yellow pigment mixed with water. All the poor idolaters one after the other present themselves to him, and he anoints their foreheads with some of this colour, which is continued down between the eyes and on to the end of the nose, then on the arms and in front of the chest ; and it is by these marks that those who have bathed in the Ganges are distinguished.[2] Those who bathe only in their houses—for they are all obliged to bathe before eating, and even before cooking—those, I say, who have bathed only in well-water, or in that brought from the river, are not properly purified, and so they cannot be anointed with this colour. It may be remarked that the idolaters, according to their castes, are anointed with different colours ; and in the Empire of the Great Mogul, those who are anointed with yellow belong to the most important tribe, and are the least impure. For, when attending to the ordinary necessities of nature, the others content themselves with carrying a pot of water to wash themselves, while these always use a handful of sand, with which they first rub themselves, and then bathe. So they can say their bodies are clean, that no impurity remains, and that they may then take their food without fear.

Adjoining this great pagoda, on the side which faces the setting sun at midsummer, there is a house which serves as

[1] Muralīdhara, Krishna in the form of a flute-player, muralī, 'a flute or pipe'. See an engraving in W. J. Wilkins, *Hindu Mythology*, 186.

[2] The Tilak, or mark characteristic of the Vaishnava sect, is perpendicular ; that of the Saivas horizontal. See drawings in Russell, *op. cit.*, ii. 102 ; *Census Report, Bengal*, 1911, i. 254.

a college, which the Rājā Jai Singh,[1] the most powerful of the idolatrous princes in the Empire of the Great Mogul, has founded for the education of the youth of good families. I saw the children of the Prince, who were being educated there by several Brāhmans, who taught them to read and write in a language which is reserved to the priests of the idols,[2] and is very different from that spoken by the people. Entering the court of this college, being curious to see it, and throwing my eyes upwards, I perceived a double gallery which ran all round it, and in the lower the two Princes were seated, accompanied by many young nobles and numerous Brāhmans, who were making different figures, like those of mathematics, on the ground with chalk. As soon as I entered, the Princes sent to inquire who I was, and having learnt that I was a Frenchman they invited me to ascend, when they asked me many things about Europe, and especially about France. One of the Brāhmans had two globes, which the Dutch had given him, and I pointed out the position of France upon them. After some conversation of this kind they presented me with betel; and before I took leave I asked the Brāhmans at what hour I should be able to see the pagoda open. They told me to come on the following morning a little before sunrise, and I did not fail to be at the house by that time, where the Rājā had built a pagoda on the left of the entrance. In front of the door there is, as it were, a gallery sustained by pillars, where many people were already assembled—men, women, and children—awaiting the opening of the door. When the gallery and a part of the court are full of people, eight Brāhmans approach, four on each side of the door of the pagoda, each carrying a censer; and there are many other Brāhmans who make a great noise with drums and other instruments. The two oldest of the Brāhmans chant a canticle, and all the people, after they have intoned it, repeat it while singing and playing instruments, each one waving a peacock's tail, or other kind of fan, to drive away the flies; so that when the door of the pagoda is opened the

[1] At a later period than this, namely 1693, Jai Singh erected the famous observatory at Benares (Sherring, *Sacred City of the Hindus*, 131 ff.).

[2] Sanskrit.

idol may not be inconvenienced by them. All this fanning and music lasted a good half-hour, when the two principal Brāhmans began to sound two large bells three times, and, with a kind of small mallet, they then knocked at the door. At the same moment it was opened by six Brāhmans, who were inside the pagoda, and 7 or 8 paces from the door there was an altar with an idol upon it, which is called Ram-Kam, who is the sister of Morli Ram.[1] She has on her right a child in the form of Cupid, who is known as the god Lakshmī, and on her left arm she carries a small girl called the goddess Sītā. As soon as the door of the pagoda was opened, and after a large curtain had been drawn, and the people present had seen the idol, all threw themselves on the ground, placing their hands upon their heads and prostrating themselves three times; then rising they threw a quantity of bouquets and chains in form of chaplets, which the Brāhmans placed on the idol, and then returned to the people. An old Brāhman in front of the altar held in his hand a lamp with nine lighted wicks, upon which, from time to time, he threw a kind of incense when moving the lamp towards the idol. All these ceremonies lasted about an hour, after which the people retired, and the pagoda was closed. The people presented the idol with a quantity of rice, flour, butter, oil, and milk, of which the Brāhmans let nothing be lost. As this idol has the form of a woman, all the women invoke her, and regard her as their patron; this is the reason why the temple is always crowded with women and children.

The Rājā desiring to have this idol in the pagoda of his house and to remove it from the great pagoda, has expended in gifts to the Brāhmans and in alms to the poor more than 500,000 rupees, which make 750,000 livres[2] of our money.

On the other side of the street in which this college is

[1] The image of 'Ram-Kam' is that of Annapūrnā, 'she who fills with food', a beneficent goddess, represented as a fair woman, standing on a lotus, holding in one hand a rice bowl, and in the other the spoon with which the rice is stirred when it is being boiled (W. J. Wilkins, *Hindu Mythology*, 265 f.). Tavernier supposed that she was the sister of Muralidhara, Krishna represented as a flute-player. Lakshmī or Srī is the goddess of fortune, consort of Vishnu, and mother of Kāma, god of love, the Cupid of the text.

[2] £56,250.

situated, there is another pagoda called Richourdas,[1] from the name of the idol on the altar inside, and lower down on another small altar is the idol whom they call Goupaldas,[2] brother of this Richourdas. Only the faces of these idols, which are made of stone or wood, are exposed to view. They are black as jet, with the exception of the image of Morli Ram, which is in the great pagoda and is uncovered. As for the idol Ram-Kam, which is in the pagoda of the Rājā, it has two diamonds in the eyes which the Prince has placed there, together with a large necklace of pearls, and a canopy sustained by four silver pillars over its head.

At eight days' journey from Benares, due northwards, is a mountainous country [3] which at intervals has beautiful plains sometimes 2 to 3 leagues wide. They are very fertile, producing corn, rice, and vegetables, but what injures and ruins the people of this country is the abundance of elephants [4] which eat a considerable proportion of the vegetables and grain. If a caravan of travellers passes through this country where there are no caravansarāīs, as they are compelled to camp in the open fields, they have much trouble in defending themselves during the night from the elephants which often come to carry away the food. In order to prevent this the travellers light fires, fire musket-shots, and from time to time some of them cry with all their might, and make a great noise to frighten these animals.

In this country there is another pagoda, well-built and very ancient, and ornamented within and without with many figures, which are representations of girls and women only. Men never go there to worship, and on that account it is called the girls' pagoda. It has an altar in the middle like the other pagodas, and upon this altar there is an idol of massive gold about 4 feet high, which represents a girl, standing, whom they call Ram-Marion.[5] She has on her right an

[1] Ranchhordās, 'he who fled from the battle field', a form of Krishna.

[2] Gopāla, Krishna as a keeper of cows.

[3] Ajodhya, not in the hills, but in the plain of Oudh, on the river Gogra, about 105 miles north of Benares. It is the birthplace of the deified hero, Rāma, and the centre of his cultus (*Imperial Gazetteer*, v. 175 f.).

[4] See p. 205.

[5] Rāmnārāyan, the deified Rāma of Ajodhya. Nārāyana, usually

image of a child, standing, made of massive silver, and nearly 2 feet in height, and it is said that this girl living a holy life, the infant was taken to her by the Brāhmans to learn her creed and how to live well; but at the end of three or four years, during which the child had dwelt with the girl, it became so clever and accomplished that all the Rājās and Princes of the country wished for it, and, at last, one of them carried it off one night and it has not since been seen. This idol has on her left, at the base of the altar, another idol representing an old man, whom they say had been the servant of Rām-Marion and the child, and the Brāhmans pay great reverence to this idol. They come to it only once a year for worship, and it is necessary for them to arrive on a prescribed day, which is the first day of the moon in November, because the pagoda is only opened at full moon.[1] During the fifteen days which intervene all the pilgrims, both men and women, must fast at times, and bathe three times every day, without leaving a single hair on their bodies, all being easily removed by the use of a certain earth with which they rub themselves.[2]

CHAPTER XII

Continuation of the description of the principal Pagodas of the Idolaters of India.

After the pagodas of Jagannāth and Benares, the most considerable used to be that of Muttra,[3] about 18 coss from

interpreted to mean 'he that moves on the waters', really means 'Son of Nara, the Primal Male', in Hindu belief. Tavernier, writing from hearsay, represents the image as that of a goddess.

[1] The reference is perhaps to the Rāmlīlā, or miracle play describing the exploits of Rāma, held from the 8th day of the waning moon of the month Kuār, September–October, until the 15th of the waxing moon. But there is an important local bathing fair in honour of Rāma in October–November (*Imperial Gazetteer*, v., 176).

[2] The reference is to the use of lime and arsenic as depilatories.

[3] Matura in the original. The antiquities of Muttra, or, as it is properly called, Mathurā, have been very fully described by F. S. Growse, *Mathurā*, 3rd ed. Allāhābād, 1883. The temple on the platform described by Tavernier was that of Kesavadeva, Krishna with the long locks, which

Agra, on the road to Delhi. It is one of the most sumptuous buildings in all India, and was visited by the greatest concourse of pilgrims; but at present scarcely any are to be seen there, the idolaters having gradually lost the devotion which they had for this pagoda, since the river Jumnā, which used to pass close to it, has changed its course, and now flows half a league away.[1] For when pilgrims have bathed in the river it takes them too much time to return to the pagoda, and during that period they may encounter something which renders them impure and unclean. Although this pagoda, which is very large, is in a hollow, it is visible from more than 5 or 6 coss distance, the building being very elevated and magnificent. The stones which were used in its construction are of a red colour, and are obtained from a large quarry near Agra. They split like our slates, and some of them, which are 15 feet long and 9 or 10 feet wide, are not 6 fingers in thickness, that is to say, they are split by the quarrymen to the required size; beautiful columns are made of them also. The fortress of Agra, the walls of Jahānābād, the palace of the Emperor, the two mosques, and some houses of the great nobles are built of the same stone.[2]

Returning to the pagoda, it is seated on a great platform of octagonal shape faced with cut stone, around which there are two courses of animals, chiefly monkeys, carved in relief. One of the courses is only 2 feet from the ground floor, and the other 2 feet from the level of the platform. It is reached

was destroyed by Aurangzeb in 1669–70, and a mosque built on the site (Growse, 126 ff.; Jadunath Sarkar, *History of Aurangzib*, iii. 321).

[1] The main channel of the Jumnā can never in historic times have flowed near the temple. The traces of fluvial action are unmistakable, but they date from remote antiquity (Growse, 129).

[2] For an account of these sandstones, which are derived from the Vindhyan formation, reference may be made to the chapter on Building Stones in the *Economic Geology of India*. Tavernier's statements as to the fissile character and the large size of the pieces which can be obtained are quite accurate. One of the most remarkable, though not the most successful uses to which they have been put in modern times is in the manufacture of telegraph-wire posts. Latterly these have been replaced by metal posts. The best quarries are at Fatehpur Sīkrī, in Agra District, and Bansi Pahārpur in Bharatpur State (Watt, *Dict. Economic Products*, vi, part 3, 369 f.; *Imperial Gazetteer*, v. 78, viii. 82; *Āīn-i-Akbarī*, ii. 180 f.).

by two staircases of fifteen or sixteen steps each, the steps being only 2 feet long, so that two persons are unable to ascend side by side. One of these staircases leads to the great gate of the pagoda, and the other behind the choir. But the pagoda occupies scarcely half the platform, the other half serving as a grand area in front. Its form, like those of the other pagodas, is that of a cross, and in the middle there rises a lofty dome, with two others a little smaller at the sides. On the exterior of the building, from base to summit, there are numerous figures of animals such as rams, monkeys, and elephants, carved in stone, and all round are niches containing different monsters. From the foot of each of the three domes up to their summit, at intervals, there are windows from 5 to 6 feet high, and at each a kind of balcony where four persons can sit. Each balcony is covered by a small canopy, and some are sustained by four columns, others by eight, but then they are in pairs and in contact with one another. Around these domes there are also niches full of figures which represent demons, one with four arms, another four legs; some of them have the heads of men on the bodies of beasts, with horns and long tails which twine round their legs. There are, finally, numerous images of monkeys, and it is a terrible thing to have before the eyes so many ugly representations. The pagoda has but one door, which is very high, and on both sides there are many columns and images of men and monsters. The choir is enclosed by a screen of stone columns 5 to 6 inches in diameter, and no one may enter these except the principal Brāhmans, who have access by a small secret door which I could not see. When I visited this pagoda I asked some Brāhmans who were there if I might see the great Rām Rām, that is to say the great idol. They replied that if I gave them something they would go to ask leave of their Superior; this they did as soon as I had placed two rupees in their hands. I waited less than half an hour when the Brāhmans opened a door inside the middle of the screen, for on the outside there is none, the screen itself being closed. I saw across it, at about 15 or 16 feet from the door, as it were a square altar covered with a piece of old brocade of gold and silver, and on it the great idol which they call Rām Rām.[1] Only the head, which is of black marble, can be seen, and he has for eyes what appear to be two rubies. All the body from the neck to the feet is covered by a robe of red velvet with some embroidery, and the arms cannot be seen. There are two other idols beside him 2 feet in height or thereabouts ; they are arranged in the same manner, save that they have the faces white, and they are called Becchor.[2] I also saw in this pagoda a machine 15 to 16 feet square and about 12 to 15 feet high, covered with painted calico on which all kinds of demons are represented. This machine was supported on four small wheels, and I was told that it was the car on which their great god is placed at the solemn days when he goes to visit the other gods, and is taken to the river by the people on the occasion of their principal festival.[3]

The fourth pagoda is that of Tirupati,[4] in the province of Carnatic, towards the Coromandel coast and Cape Comorin. I went to see it when I was going from Masulipatam to Gandikota [5] to join the Nawāb Mīr Jumla. It is a large pagoda, surrounded by numerous small ones, and by many dwellings for the Brāhmans ; this makes it appear like a town. It has around it many tanks, and the superstition is so great that a passer-by dare not take water from them unless a Brāhman give it to him.

[1] Kesavadeva, Krishna.

[2] This word represents none of the many names of Krishna and his consorts unless the word is a corruption of Ranchhor (see p. 185 above).

[3] Growse (*op. cit.*, 261) gives a photograph of the great car used at the Seths' temple.

[4] Tripeti in the original ; more correctly it is Tirupati, commonly called Tripatty, in the District of North Arcot. In some respects it is regarded as the most sacred temple in Madras. The principal temple is at Tirumala, 6 miles distant. From all parts of India pilgrims flock there, bearing large offerings with them (*Imperial Gazetteer*, xxiii. 393 f.).

[5] Indecote in the original. In vol. i, p. 217, Tavernier gives his route between Madras and Gandikota when he saw this temple. There he speaks, however, of Courua or Kuruva-bandalu, which is a different place.

CHAPTER XIII

Concerning the pilgrimages of the Idolaters to their Pagodas.

ALL the idolaters who are subjects of the Great Mogul and other Princes on either side of the Ganges at least once in their lives make a pilgrimage to perform their devotions at one of the four pagodas which I have named, and most commonly to that of Jagannāth, it being the principal and most considerable of all. The Brāhmans and rich people make this pilgrimage more than once, some every four years, others every six or every eight years, when they place the idols of their pagodas in litters and accompany their Brāhmans in procession to the pagoda for which they have most reverence ; but it is most frequently, as I have said, to that of Jagannāth, and also to that of Benares, because both are on the Ganges, the water of which is held in special veneration by them.

These pilgrimages[1] are not made as in Europe, by one or two individual pilgrims, but the people of a town or several villages assemble and travel together in company. The poor who come from afar, sometimes 300 or 400 leagues, with all the savings which they have accumulated for that purpose during their lives, are unable to bear the expenses of the journey, and they are assisted by the rich, who expend very great sums in such alms. Each one travels according to his station and means, some in pallankeens or litters, others in carriages ; and the poor, some on foot and others on oxen, the mother carrying her child and the father the cooking utensils.

The god whom they carry in procession[2] from the place they are leaving, to visit and pay his respects to the great Rām Rām, reposes at full length in a rich pallankeen covered with gold brocade with silver fringes, with a mattress and cushion of the same material under his head, feet, and elbows, as we see in the effigies on our tombs. The Brāhmans distri-

[1] On pilgrimages in India see Sleeman, *Rambles*, 588 ff. ; Hastings, *Ency. Religion and Ethics*, x. 24 ff. Pilgrimages are not confined to the four temples described by Tavernier.

[2] See vol. i. 236.

bute among the most important persons in the troop fans with handles 7 or 8 feet long, and covered with plates of gold and silver, the fan being at the end in the form of a kiln-shovel of 2 to 3 feet in diameter, and covered with the same brocade as the pallankeens. It is surrounded with peacock feathers, and makes a great current of air; to it bells are sometimes attached to give a kind of music,[1] and there are generally five or six of these fans to drive away the flies from the face of the idol; those who carry them take turns from time to time, like those who carry the pallankeens, so that many may share in this honourable task. This custom should not appear more strange to us than that which I have seen practised in Saxony, and in many other parts of Germany, where, while a funeral oration for a man or a woman is delivered in the church, the body reposes at full length on a bier which is uncovered, and the people on both sides fan it constantly, when it is summer time, to drive away the flies attracted to the face of the deceased, who has then no more power of feeling than an idol.

In the year 1653, on the road from Golkonda to Surat in company with M. d'Ardilière, of whom I have elsewhere spoken, we met near Daulatābād more than 2,000 persons, including men, women, and children, who came from the direction of Tatta[2] with their idol, which they carried in a rich pallankeen, on their way to visit the great idol of the pagoda at Tirupati. The idol was laid on a mattress of red crimson velvet, and the covering and cushions were of the same stuff. The bamboo or stick which served to carry the pallankeen was covered with gold and silver brocade, and no one except the Brāhmans had permission to approach it. We saw this long procession pass, and we could not help

[1] And to scare evil spirits.

[2] M. Joret (*l.c.* p. 131) is probably mistaken in assuming that this occasion of meeting pilgrims is identical with one described in vol. i. 236, which took place in the year 1652 at Emelipata, i.e. Vemulakota, a stage between Gandikota and Golkonda. He adds as a further mistake of Tavernier's that M. d'Ardilière had died before 1653. (See Preface.) As we know that Tavernier went back to Golkonda in 1653, and was in Surat in 1654, he may very possibly have met the pilgrims exactly as he says, when on his return towards the end of 1653.

feeling much compassion for the blindness of these poor people.

[Here are the figures of the most famous idols, which I had the curiosity to have drawn on the spot.[1]]

CHAPTER XIV

Concerning various customs of the Idolaters of India.

THE Brāhmans possess much knowledge of astrology, and know how to predict eclipses of the sun and moon for the people.[2] On the 2nd of July 1666 at one o'clock p.m. an eclipse of the sun was visible at Patna, a town of the Kingdom of Bengal.[3] It was a wonderful sight to watch the multitude of people, men, women, and children, who came from all quarters to bathe in the Ganges. But they must begin this bathing three days before they see the eclipse, during which time they remain day and night on the banks of the river preparing all kinds of rice, milk, and sweetmeats to throw to the fishes and crocodiles. Immediately when the Brāhmans give the word, and they know it is the fortunate hour, whichever kind of eclipse it may be, of the sun or moon, the idolaters break all the earthen vessels used in their households, and

[1] These figures are not given in any of the editions which are accessible. Probably they were never reproduced.

[2] 'The Brachmanes of this Kingdome [Bengal] are great Students of the Magick art, and make their Sorceries more apparent than they of any Other Kingdome in Asia' (Bowrey, 205). Similar accounts will be found in Roe, i. 192; Terry, 236 f.; Fryer, ii. 102; Bernier, 161, 244 f. For modern accounts see A. K. L. Anantha Krishna Iyer, *Cochin Tribes and Castes*, ii. 217 ff.; Russell, *Tribes and Castes, Central Provinces*, iii. 255 ff.; Thurston, *Castes and Tribes, Southern India*, i. 10; Dubois, *Hindu Manners*, 379 ff.

[3] Bernier (p. 300) gives a lively account of eclipse observances at Delhi in 1666. On modern ceremonies see Crooke, *Popular Religion and Folklore of N. India*, i. 21; *Bombay Gazetteer*, ix, part i, 395; Mrs. S. Stevenson, *Rites of the Twice-born*, 351 f. Compare Fryer, i. 275, ii. 306 f. The 'fortunate hour', mentioned by Tavernier, is the Sā'at or Mahūrat. The earthen vessels are broken because they are believed to be defiled by the presence of the demon Rāhu, who causes the eclipse by swallowing the sun or moon.

leave not one piece whole—this causes a terrible noise in a town.

Every Brāhman has his book of magic, in which there are a number of circles and semicircles, of squares and triangles, and many other kinds of figures.[1] They draw divers figures on the ground, and when they perceive that the fortunate hour has arrived they all cry aloud to the people to throw food into the Ganges. Then a terrible noise is made with drums, bells, and large disks made of a metal similar to that of our cymbals, which they strike one against the other; and as soon as the food is thrown into the river all the people should enter and continue rubbing themselves, and bathing until the eclipse is over. As this eclipse appeared at a time when the Ganges is usually very low, after the end of the rains, which last from the month of July to the end of October, for more than 3 leagues above and below the town, and as many as the river extends in width, nothing was to be seen but heads in the water. As for the Brāhmans, they remain on land to receive the richest pilgrims and those who give them most, dry their bodies, and give them fresh clothes to cover their waists. Then they make them sit in chairs, at a place where the richest of the idolaters have brought abundance of Indian corn, rice, and all kinds of vegetables, with milk, butter, sugar, flour, and wood. Before each chair the Brāhman makes a very clean place about 5 or 6 feet square, after which he takes cattle droppings steeped in a great dish of yellow pigment, to rub over all the place, through fear lest some ant might come there and be burnt.[2] If possible their ceremonies are conducted without burning any wood, and for cooking their food they generally use cattle droppings. When they are obliged to use wood they take care that it has no maggots or other insects inside it, as I have elsewhere remarked, because of their belief in the transmigration of souls into different bodies, lest the soul of a relative or friend may be burnt with this small animal. In the place which they have carefully cleaned,
14 they trace many kinds of figures, such as triangles and half

[1] Bernier (p. 244) explains how this book is used.

[2] The true object is to preserve the purity of the enclosures.

triangles, ovals and half ovals, made with powdered chalk. On each figure they place a little cow-dung, with two or three small branches of wood, which they rub well for fear any insect should be present ; and they place on one of the branches wheat, on another rice, on the others vegetables, and all the kinds of food they have. Then they throw on each heap a quantity of butter, and set fire to them, when according to the appearance of the flames they predict whether there will be in that year an abundant harvest of corn, rice, and other products.[1]

At the March full moon there is a solemn festival for the idol in the form of a serpent, of which I have spoken in the first Book of this account of India.[2] This festival lasts nine days, and while it lasts both men and beasts remain idle ; the majority of the latter are ornamented with circles of vermilion around the eyes, with which the horns are also painted, and when any animal is specially loved leaves of tinsel are added. Every morning the idol is worshipped, and the girls dance round it for an hour to the sound of flutes and drums, after which all eat together and enjoy themselves till the evening, when they worship the idol again and dance round it a second time.

Contrary to the usual custom of the idolaters who consume no kind of drink, during this festival they drink palm wine, and, in villages far removed from the great routes, a spirit is made from this wine, because Musalmān governors do not

[1] For the Homa or fire-sacrifice see Monier-Williams, *Brahmanism and Hinduism*, 4th ed. 366 ff. ; Mrs. S. Stevenson, *Rites of the Twice-born*, 225 ff. Omens are taken from the direction in which the smoke rises. This is also done in Northern India in the case of the Holi, or spring fire-festival. See for the rules Crooke, *Rural and Agricultural Glossary, North-West Provinces and Oudh*, 125.

[2] Snake worship. See vol. i. 35. The chief snake festival is the Nāgpanchamī, held on 5th Srāvan (July–August), in the rainy season, when snakes are most dangerous (B. A. Gupte, *Hindu Holidays and Ceremonials*, 2nd ed. 176 ff.). The feast mentioned in the text has not been exactly identified : but in Madras the Nagarapanchamī is held in the beginning of February, to propitiate the cobra (Dubois, 571). Mr. A. L. K. Anantha Krishna Iyer writes that snakes are venerated in Madura and other places in South India in connexion with the worship of Subrahmanya or Kārttikeya, god of war, in the month of Phālgun, February–March.

allow them to distil it, or to sell wine brought from Persia or elsewhere. The spirit is made in this way—In large earthen vessels, glazed inside, which are called martabans,[1] and of different sizes, holding as much as 300 Paris pints of palm wine, they place 50 or 60 pounds of black sugar—unrefined, and looking like yellow wax—with about 20 pounds of a thick black bark of a kind of thorn,[2] very like that which our tanners use in Europe to tan their leather. This bark serves to make the palm wine ferment in four or five days like our new wine, so that the sweetness changes into sourness like that of our wild pears. The whole is then distilled, and, according to the flavour which is desired, they throw into a kettleful either a small bag of cloves, or three or four handfuls of aniseed or mace, large cauldrons serving for the distillation. This spirit can be made of whatever strength is desired. One day, as I had a fancy to distil some for myself, I filled ten of those bottles which come from England, the glass of which is of the thickness of a white crown (écu blanc); they hold each about 4 pints, Paris measure, and are used for wines which it is desired to keep. But during the night the spirit effervesced in the bottles and I found them all cracked in the morning by the strength of the liquor.

When I was at Agra in the year 1642 a somewhat strange thing happened. An idolater called Voldas,[3] who was the Dutch broker, and about seventy years old, received news that the Chief Priest of the pagoda of Mathura was dead. Immediately he went to see the Chief of the Dutch factory to ask him to examine his accounts and close them, because, as he said, their Chief Priest being dead he also wished to die, to serve that holy man in the other world. As soon as

[1] Martavane in the original. This name was given to large vessels of glazed pottery, which were made in Martaban, and thence largely exported. A number of examples of its use will be found in Yule, *Hobson-Jobson*; Dames, *Book of Duarte Barbosa* ed. 1921, vol. ii. 158.

[2] This does not appear to be the common Cutch or Catechu (Acacia catechu); but the gum of *acacia leucophloea*, which is used in distillation (Watt, *Commercial Products*, 15, 759). For methods of distillation see *ibid.*, 1043 ff.

[3] His name may have been Vitthaldās, called after Vitthal or Vithobā, the form of Vishnu worshipped at Pandharpur in Sholāpur District (*Bombay Gazetteer*, xx. 420).

his accounts had been examined he entered his carriage accompanied by some relatives who followed him, and as he had neither eaten nor drunk since he had received the news, he died on the road, refusing to take any food.

The idolaters of India observe this custom, that when any one yawns they crack their fingers, while crying out many times Ginarami,[1] that is to say, remember Narami, who passes among the idolaters as a great saint. This cracking of the fingers is done, it is said, to prevent any evil spirit entering into the body of the yawner.

When I was at Surat in the year 1653 one of the soldiers called Rājputs, who had upon his horse two or three pieces of cloth, was brought before the Governor to be made pay duty on them. The Rājput in a firm tone of voice asked the Governor boldly, if a soldier who had served the Emperor all his life ought to pay duty on two or three miserable pieces of calico which were not worth more than 4 or 5 rupees, and were intended to clothe his wife and children. The Governor, stung by this protest, called him Bethico, that is to say, son of a strumpet,[2] adding that even if he were a Prince he would make him pay the Emperor's due. The soldier, exasperated by this abuse, made as though to take out the money to pay what was demanded, and advancing towards the Governor gave him seven or eight stabs with his dagger in the stomach, from which he died, and the soldier was at once hacked to pieces by the attendants.

Although these idolaters are in the depths of blindness as to a knowledge of the true God, that does not prevent them from leading in many respects, according to nature, moral lives.[3] When married they are rarely unfaithful to

[1] Jai Nārāyan! a name of Vishnu, with the exclamatory prefix Jai! signifying 'victory to'. The custom referred to is well known, its object being to prevent evil spirits taking advantage of the involuntarily open mouth in order to obtain an entrance into the body of the yawner, or that his soul may not escape. See Crooke, *Popular Religion and Folk-lore of N. India*, i. 240; P. Saintyves [M. Nourry], *l'Éternuement et le Baillement dans la Magie, l'Ethnographie, et le Folk-lore Médical*, Paris, 1921.

[2] This is not an exact translation of the term, but may be allowed to pass as such here (Yule, *Hobson-Jobson*, 56). [See Introd.]

[3] Many early travellers give a favourable account of Hindu morals,

their wives, adultery is very rare among them, and one never hears unnatural crime spoken of.[1] They marry their children at the age of seven or eight years, through fear lest they should abandon themselves to this crime. And, in a few words, these are the ceremonies which are observed at their marriages. On the eve of the nuptials the bridegroom, accompanied by all his relatives, goes to the house of the bride with a pair of large bracelets two fingers in thickness, but hollow inside, and in two pieces, with a hinge in the middle to open them by. According to the wealth of the bridegroom these bracelets are more or less costly, being of gold, silver, brass, or tin,[2] those of the poorest being of lead only. When the bridegroom arrives, he places one of these bracelets on each leg of his bride, to indicate that he holds her thenceforward enchained, and that she can never leave him. On the morrow the feast is prepared in the house of the bridegroom, where all the relatives on either side are present, and at 3 p.m. the bride is brought.[3] Several Brāhmans are present, and their Chief makes the head of the bridegroom touch that of the bride, and pronounces several words while he sprinkles water on their heads and bodies. Then on plates or on large leaves of the fig tree[4] many kinds of food and pieces of stuff and calico are brought. The Brāhman asks the bridegroom if what God gives to him he will share with his wife, and if he will strive to support her by his labour. When he has said 'yes,' all the guests seat themselves at the feast which has been prepared for them, and each one eats apart. According to the wealth of the bridegroom and the credit he enjoys with great persons, the nuptials

as Friar Jordanus, *Wonders of the East*, 22; Marco Polo, ii. 303. Max Müller has made a large collection of similar evidence (*India, What can it teach us?* ed. 1905, p. 34 ff.). Both sides of the question are discussed in *Bombay Gazetteer*, ix, part i, 78.

[1] This testimony as regards homosexual practices is very different from that given by some other writers of the same period as Tavernier, who himself describes cases (vol. i, pp. 44, 100). See Fryer, i. 245; Linschoten, i. 100; Dubois, 311; Grose, 219; Chevers, *Handbook of Medical Jurisprudence*, 705 ff.; Russell, *Tribes and Castes, Central Provinces*, iii. 209 ff.

[2] Leton and estain in the original.

[3] For the rites among Brāhmans see Mrs. S. Stevenson, *Rites of the Twice-born*, 46 ff.

[4] The plantain (vol. i. 197, and vol. ii. 3).

are celebrated with pomp and great expenditure. He is seated on an elephant and his bride in a carriage, all who accompany them bearing torches in their hands. He borrows, moreover, for this ceremony from the Governor of the place and from other great nobles among his friends as many elephants as he can, together with show horses, and they march about thus for a part of the night with fireworks, which are exploded in the streets and open spaces. But the chief outlay is on Ganges water,[1] for those who are sometimes 300 or 400 leagues distant from the river; as this water is considered sacred, and drunk from religious motives, it has to be brought from a great distance by the Brāhmans in earthen vessels glazed inside, which the Grand Brāhman of Jagannāth has himself filled with the cleanest water in the river,[2] and has marked with his own seal. This water is not given except at the end of the repast, as I have said before; for each of the guests three or four cupfuls are poured out, and the more of it the bridegroom gives them to drink the more generous and magnificent he is esteemed. As this water comes from so far, and the Chief Brāhman charges a tax on each pot, which is round and holds about as much as one of our buckets, there is sometimes 2,000 or 3,000 rupees worth of it consumed at a wedding.[3]

On the 8th of April, when I was in Bengal at a town called Mālda,[4] the idolaters made a great feast which is peculiar to the inhabitants of that place. They all leave the town and attach hooks of iron to the branches of trees, to which many of these poor people hook themselves, some by the sides and others by the middle of the back. These hooks enter their bodies, and they remain suspended, some for an hour and others for two, till the weight of the body drags the flesh, when they are compelled to retire.[5] It is a surprising

[1] See vol. ii. 180. [2] See vol. ii. 179.

[3] Ganges water is used as a means of purification, more usually at funeral than at marriage rites.

[4] Malde in the original. See vol. i. 110. Mālda is a well-known town at the junction of the Kālindrī and Mahānadī rivers in the district of the same name in Bengal. Formerly it was a port and centre of manufactures, but is not now important. (*Imperial Gazetteer*, xvii. 82.)

[5] This is the so-called Charakh pūjā or swinging festival, now forbidden

thing not to see a drop of blood come from this cut flesh, and not to see a sign of it even on the hook, and in two days they are entirely cured by the drugs which the Brāhmans give them. There are others at this festival who make beds for themselves with points of iron and lie upon them; these points enter deep into the flesh, and while both are doing these penances their relatives and friends bring them presents, such as betel, money, or pieces of calico. When the penance is finished the penitent takes all these presents and distributes them to the poor, not wishing to profit by them himself.[1] I asked some of these people why they gave this feast and underwent this penance, and they said it was in memory of the first man, whom they called Adam like us.[2]

I shall relate also an example of a strange kind of penance which I saw when sailing up the Ganges on the 12th of May 1666. A clean place on the margin of the river had been prepared, in which one of these poor idolaters was condemned to place himself on the ground many times during the day, supported only on his hands and feet, and to kiss the ground three times before rising, without daring to touch it with the rest of his body. When he rose it was necessary for him to do so on the left foot, with the right foot in the air, and every morning during a whole month, before drinking or eating, he was obliged to place himself in this position fifty times in succession, and kiss the ground one hundred and fifty times. I was told that the Brāhmans had inflicted this penance on him for having allowed a cow to die in his house, not having taken it to the margin of the water according to custom, in order that it might be bathed while dying.[3]

in British India. On one occasion, in the Rājmahāl hills, a deputation of Santāls waited on Ball to ask for his intercession with the Government to permit its revival, on the ground that their neglected deities, out of revenge, caused injury to their families and flocks. See a full account of the rite by J. H. Powell, *Folk-Lore*, xxv. 147 ff., with photographs. It is not peculiar to the Mālda District. On swinging as a magical rite see Frazer, *The Golden Bough*, The Dying God, 277 ff.

[1] For the penance of lying on a spiked bed see Crooke, *Popular Religion and Folk-lore*, i. 92; *Id.*, *The People of Northern India*, 128; Greaves, *Kashi*, 54, with photographs.

[2] Tod (*Annals of Rajasthan*, iii. 1754) heard a Rājput call Siva-Mahādeva Bābā, or Father, Adam.

[3] See vol. ii. 169.

Here is yet another rather curious custom. When an idolater loses a coin or a sum of gold, be it by mistake or that he has been robbed, he is bound to take as much as he has lost to the Chief Brāhman, and if he does not do so and it gets known he is driven with ignominy out of his caste, through policy, to make people careful.[1]

Beyond the Ganges, northwards, towards the mountains of Nagarkot,[2] there are two or three Rājās who, like their people, believe neither in God nor devil. Their Brāhmans have a certain book which contains their creed, and which is only filled with rubbish for which the author, who is called Baudou, gives no reason.[3] These Princes are vassals of the Great Mogul and pay tribute to him.

Finally, as a last remark and to finish this chapter, I may say that the Malabaris in general carefully preserve the nails of their left hands, and allow their hair to grow like that of a woman. Their nails, which are sometimes half a finger long, serve them as combs, indeed they have no others, and it is with this left hand also that they perform all impure duties, never touching their faces nor that which they eat save only with the right hand.[4] I now come to some remarks

[1] Dr. L. D. Barnett and Mr. S. K. Chatterjī have kindly inquired into this custom, of which they have found no corroboration. It seems to be based on a misunderstanding.

[2] Naugrocot in the original. Nagarkot is to a certain extent synonymous with Kāngrā, the capital of which is situated on the Rāvi Bāngangā Torrent. The name in many early travels indicates the mountainous region of the N.W. Himalayas. See *Āīn-i-Akbarī*, ii. 312 f.

[3] This is rather an unceremonious way of discussing the tenets of Buddhism. The Buddhists form a comparatively small part of the population of Kāngrā at present. For Buddhism in the Panjāb hills see Rose, *Glossary, Tribes and Castes Panjāb and N. W. Frontier Province*, 166 ff.; *Census Report, Panjāb*, 1911, i. 192.

[4] The Nāyars of Malabar let their nails grow, according to Linschoten, (i. 282) to show that they are 'gentlemen' and do not engage in manual labour. As is well known, the Chinese do so likewise, for the same reason. Alberuni (*India*, i. 180) erroneously notes it as a general custom. The Nambūtiri Brāhmans of Malabar grow their nails more than a foot long, 'which serve several useful purposes' (Thurston, *Castes and Tribes of Southern India*, v. 169). Compare the Chinese customs (J. F. Davis, *The Chinese*, i. 267 f.; S. W. Williams, *The Middle Kingdom*, 4th ed., ii. 38).

which I have made in my journeys regarding kingdoms which lie to the north-east of the territories of the Great Mogul, as those of Bhutān, Tippera, Assam, and Siam, of which I believe that we Europeans have not much knowledge; and I would also speak of the Kingdom of Tonquin,[1] if I did not know that two different authors have filled two volumes with it.

CHAPTER XV

Concerning the Kingdom of Bhutān, whence comes musk, good rhubarb, and some furs.

THE Kingdom of Bhutān is of very wide extent, but we have not been able to acquire an exact knowledge of it as yet.[2] This is what I have ascertained during several journeys in India, from people of the country who come from there to trade; but I was better informed regarding it on the last occasion than I had been previously, as I was at Patna, the largest town in Bengal and the most famous for trade—at the time that the merchants of Bhutān arrive to sell their musk. During the two months I spent there I bought to the extent of 26,000 rupees worth of musk, an once (Fr.) in the capsule costing me 4 livres and 4 sols of our money, and out of the capsule at the rate of 8 francs,[3] and were it not for the custom duties which have to be paid in India, as well as in Europe, there would be a great profit to be made on it. The best kind of rhubarb[4] also comes from the Kingdom of Bhutān; the same country produces also the seed which yields worm powder,[5] and other kinds of drugs, and from

[1] In his third volume Tavernier gives an account of Tonquin, or Tunquin as he calls it. In the opinion of some critics it is very inaccurate. See S. Baron, *A Description of the Kingdom of Tonqueen*, in J. Pinkerton, *A General Collection of Voyages and Travels*, ix. 656 ff., who criticizes some of Tavernier's statements.

[2] For a full account of Bhutān see *Imperial Gazetteer*, viii. 154. The name is derived from Sanskrit Bhotānta, 'the end of Bhot or Bod', Tibet (L. A. Waddell, *Buddhism of Tibet*, 44).

[3] See vol. ii. 115 for another account of this purchase, and a comparison showing the discrepancy. Here for francs we should probably read livres.

[4] See p. 203 *post*.

[5] This is probably a species of *Artemisia*—*A. maritima* (Watt,

thence also beautiful furs are brought. But as for rhubarb, you risk much in its carriage, by whatever road you take it; for if you go by the north towards Kābul the damp spoils it, and if you take the southern direction, as the way is long, the rains which may supervene are still more to be feared, so that there is no kind of merchandise which is more likely to be spoilt, and requires more care than it does.

As for musk, during the hot season the merchant does not make any profit by it, because it becomes dry and loses weight. Upon this article 25 per cent. duty has generally to be paid at Gorakhpur,[1] the frontier town of the territories of the Great Mogul in the direction of the Kingdom of Bhutān,[2] although they extend 5 or 6 leagues farther. When Indian merchants arrive in that town they call on the customs officer, and tell him that they are going to the Kingdom of Bhutān, one to buy musk, another rhubarb, and they make declarations of the sums which they intend to expend, these the customs officer enters in his register with the names of the merchants. Then the merchants, instead of 25 per cent., which they ought to pay, agree for 7 or 8 per cent., and take a certificate from the customs officer or the Kāzī,[3] so that on their return they may not be asked for any more. If it should happen that they are unable to obtain a fair composition from the customs officer, they take a different road, which is both very long and very difficult, as the mountains are nearly always covered with snow, and in the level country

Commercial Products, 93. It is the *Flores cinæ*, or *Semen cinæ*, or *Santonica* of the pharmacopœias. Most of it which reaches Europe comes through Russia, but the drug now to be found in Indian bazars is similar, consisting of the small unopened flower heads. It is found in great abundance on the steppes of the Kirghiz, in the northern part of Turkestan. (See *Pharmacographia*, by Hanbury and Flückiger. London, 1874.)

[1] Gorrochepour in the original. Gorakhpur is the chief town of the District of the same name in the United Provinces of Agra and Oudh. It adjoins Nepāl on the north, through which territory the merchants travelled to Bhutān.

[2] This geographical indication is not correct, as Northern Bengal lies nearer to Bhutān; but it is evident from other references that Tavernier's knowledge of the extent and position of Bhutān was vague.

[3] For the Kāzī, a State minister in the Himalayan Kingdoms, see Yule, *Hobson-Jobson*, 475.

there are vast deserts to be crossed. They have to go up to the 60th degree of latitude, and then they turn towards the west to Kābul,[1] which is at the 40th, and it is in that town that the caravan divides, one portion going to Balkh,[2] and the other to Great Tartary. It is where those who come from Bhutān barter their goods for horses, mules, and camels, for there is little money in these countries. Then these Tartars carry their goods into Persia, to Ardabīl,[3] and Tabrīz ; this it is which makes Europeans believe that rhubarb and the seeds (*semencine*)[4] come from Tartary. It is quite true that rhubarb comes from thence, but it is not nearly so good as that which comes from the Kingdom of Bhutān, as it is much more tainted, rhubarb being subject to decay at the heart. The Tartars carry away from Persia silken stuffs of small value which are made at Tabrīz and Ardabīl, and some English and Dutch cloths which the Armenians bring from Constantinople and Smyrna, whither they are brought from Europe. Those merchants who come from Bhutān and Kābul go to Kandahār and on to Ispahān, and they generally take back coral beads, yellow amber, and lapis wrought into beads when they can obtain them. The other merchants, returning from the regions about Multān, Lahore, and Agra, take calicoes, indigo, and an abundance of carnelian and

[1] That they travelled so far north as the 60th degree is most improbable. That there was a northern route is well known, however. The true latitude of Kābul (Caboul) is only 34° 21′.

[2] Balch in the original. Balkh is an ancient city of Turkestan, south of the Oxus. (See vol. i. 75 *n.*)

[3] Ardeüil in the original. Ardabīl is near the Caspian, in the rugged northern province of Persia called Azarbaijān, wherein Tabrīz is also included.

[4] See *ante*, p. 201. Commercial rhubarb, known as Chinese and East Indian, is said to be obtained from Rheum officinale and R. palmatum, which grow in South-east Tibet and North-West China (Watt, *Commercial Products*, 912 f.) Nishapur, in North Persia, is also famous for its rhubarb. Sir P. Sykes (*Hist. of Persia*, ii. 20) quotes a verse by Ya'qūb :

'Its stones are turquoises, its bushes rhubarb,
And its dust edible clay. How could I leave such a land ?'

Barbosa names rhubarb as one of the products of Malabar, but his editor, Dames, suggests that it came from China via Malacca (i. 93, f., ii. 230).

crystal beads. Finally, those who return by Gorakhpur, and have an understanding with the customs officer, take from Patna and Dacca coral, yellow amber, tortoise-shell bracelets, and others of sea shells,[1] with numerous round and square pieces of the size of our 15-sol coins, which are also of the same tortoise-shell and sea shells. When I was at Patna four Armenians, who had previously made a journey to the Kingdom of Bhutān, came from Dantzic, where they had had made numerous images of yellow amber, which represented all kinds of animals and monsters; these they were taking to the King of Bhutān to place in his pagodas, he being, like his people, exceedingly idolatrous. Wherever the Armenians see that money is to be made they have no scruple about supplying materials for the purposes of idolatry,[2] and they told me that if they had been able to get an idol made which the King had ordered from them they would have been enriched. It was a head in the form of a monster, which had six horns, four ears, and four arms, with six fingers on each hand, the whole to be of yellow amber,[3] but the Armenians could not find sufficiently large pieces for the purpose. I was inclined to believe that they lacked money, for it did not appear that they had much of it; it is, however, an infamous trade to furnish the instruments of idolatry to these poor people.[4]

Coming now to the road which must be followed from

[1] For the Chank or Conch fishery and industry see J. Hornell, *The Sacred Chank of India*, Madras, 1914: Watt, *op. cit.*, 989.

[2] Ball notes that 'Bohemia, it is said, at present sends idols made of cast glass to India, which undersell the marble images of Agra.'

[3] Huge pieces of amber were employed in the manufacture of the boxes made in the shape of geese included in the King of Burma's treasure, which is in the South Kensington Museum. It has been stated that the largest piece of amber ever known was recently discovered near the Nobis Gate at Altona. It weighed 850 grammes. Dr. Meyer of Dresden (*Nature*, 29th November 1888), commenting on this, says that besides smaller pieces, elsewhere, there are specimens in the Berlin Mineralogical Museum weighing 6·5 and 9·5 kilogrammes; they were obtained on the sea-coast of North Germany.

[4] For an example of a form of trade equally disgraceful see A. Hamilton, *New Account of the East Indies*, in Pinkertom, *Voyages and Travels*, viii. 439.

Patna to the Kingdom of Bhutān, upon which the caravan spends three months.[1] It leaves Patna generally at the end of December and arrives on the eighth day at Gorakhpur, which, as I have said, is the last town in this direction in the territories of the Great Mogul, where the merchants obtain their supplies for a portion of the journey. From Gorakhpur to the foot of the high mountains there are still eight or nine days' marching, during which the caravan suffers much, because the whole country is full of forests, where there are numerous wild elephants,[2] and the merchants instead of sleeping at night must remain on the watch, making large fires and firing their muskets to frighten these animals. As the elephant moves without noise, he takes the people by surprise, and is close to the caravan before they are aware of it. He does not intend to do injury to man, for he contents himself with carrying off whatever food he can seize, a sack of rice or flour, or a pot of butter, of which there is always a large supply. One can go from Patna to the foot of these mountains in Indian carriages or pallankeens, but oxen, camels, or the horses of the country are generally used. These horses are by nature so small that when a man is upon them his feet nearly touch the ground, but they are otherwise strong, and go at an amble, doing up to 20 leagues at a stretch, and eating and drinking but little. There are some of them which cost as much as 200 écus,[3] and when you enter the mountains you can only use that means of carriage, it being necessary to leave all the others behind, which become useless on account of the numerous and very narrow passes. The horses even, though strong and small, often have difficulty in getting through, and it is for this reason, as I shall presently

[1] Three months is a long time for the journey to have lasted between Patna and any portion of Bhutān territory, as now known. The Bhutān of Tavernier seems to have included Lhassa.

[2] The Tarāi. It was in a part of this region that the Prince of Wales, afterwards King Edward VII, took part in the elephant captures arranged for him by Sir Jang Bahādur.

[3] £45, a very high price indeed for a country pony in Ball's day. These hill ponies, known as Gūnth, or Tāngan, stand usually about 13 hands high, are short-bodied, clean-limbed, deep in the chest, and extremely active and sure-footed (Yule, *Hobson-Jobson*, 387, 898).

say, that one has recourse to other expedients for traversing these lofty mountains.

At 5 or 6 leagues beyond Gorakhpur you enter the territories of the Rājā of Nepāl,[1] which extend to the frontiers of the Kingdom of Bhutān. This Prince is a vassal of the Great Mogul, and sends him an elephant every year as tribute.[2] He resides in the town of Nepāl, of which he bears the name, and there is very little trade or money in his country, as it consists of forests and mountains.

The caravan having arrived at the foot of the high mountains, known to-day by the name of Nagarkot,[3] which cannot be crossed in less than nine or ten days, as they are very high and narrow, with great precipices,—many people come from different places, the majority being women and girls, who strike a bargain with the people of the caravan, to carry the men, goods, and provisions to the other side of the mountains. This is the method by which they carry them. The women have a strap on the shoulders to which a large cushion hanging on the back is attached; upon it the man seat himself.[4] It takes three women, who change in turns, to carry a man; and as for the baggage and provisions, they are loaded on goats which carry up to 150 livres weight each. Those who desire to take horses into these mountains are often obliged, in the narrow and difficult passes, to haul them up with ropes; and it is, as I have said, on account of this difficulty that but little use is made of horses in this

[1] See p. 202 *n.* It is Nupal in the original.

[2] The finest elephant Ball ever saw he met on its way down the Grand Trunk Road to Calcutta from Nepāl. It was a gift from Sir Jang Bahādur to Lord Mayo. If the Mughals claimed suzerainty over Nepāl, it was of a very shadowy kind. The capital of Nepāl is Kathmāndū. The finest elephant Sir S. W. Baker ever saw belonged to the Rājā of Nandgaon in the Central Provinces. A perfect elephant should be 9 feet 6 inches high at the shoulder: Baker gives the other points. (*Wild Beasts and their Ways*, 44.)

[3] See p. 200, *n.* This takes us to the Panjāb hills, a long way from the Gorakhpur route.

[4] In some parts of the Himalayas women still offer themselves for carrying travellers on their backs. But in Kāngrā the practice seems to have ceased, though the women are so strong that one of them is said to have carried a grand piano up the hill.

country. They are fed only in the morning and evening. In the morning a pound of flour, half a pound of black sugar and half a pound of butter, are mixed together with water for the horse. In the evening it must be contented with a few horn peas,[1] crushed and steeped in water for half an hour; this is all their food during the space of twenty-four hours. The women who carry the men receive only 2 rupees each, for the ten days of the journey, and as much is paid for every quintal [2] that the goats or sheep carry, and for every led horse.

After passing these mountains, for carriage to Bhutān, oxen, camels, and horses, and even pallankeens [3] are procurable for those who wish to travel more at their ease. The country is good, and produces corn, rice, vegetables, and wine in abundance. All the people, both men and women, are clad during the summer in coarse cotton or hempen cloth, and during the winter in a thick cloth like felt. The headdress for both sexes is a cap made very like those English caps which they call bouquin-kans,[4] and it has pigs' teeth around it for ornament, with round and square pieces of tortoise-shell of the size of one of our 15-sol coins; the richest add to them beads of coral or yellow amber, of which the women also make necklaces. The men, like the women, wear bracelets only on the left arms, and from the wrist to the elbow. Those worn by the women are very narrow, but those of the men are two fingers wide. They wear a silken cord on the neck, to which a bead of coral [5] or yellow amber is suspended, or a pig's tooth, which hangs down to the waist; and on their

[1] 'd'un peu de poids cornus,' i. e. gram, cicer arietinum.

[2] Quintal, Arabic qintār, 100 lb.

[3] Probably a modified form of pallankeen, or dooly, suitable for hill travelling.

[4] We have not found a full explanation of the term. Bouquin means an old book-cover. The caps of felt worn in these regions are somewhat similar to what used to be called 'pork pie' hats a few years ago in England. C. A. Sherring (*Western Tibet and the British Borderland,* 1906) does not mention the use of pigs' teeth as ornaments, but they are worn in Assam (p. 223 below).

[5] Tibetan women wear silver disks on the sides and back of their heads, 'and all were loaded with coral and sham or real turquoise' (W. Gill, *The River of Golden Sand,* 201).

left side they have bands from which more of these same beads of coral, amber, or pigs' teeth hang in strings. Although they are great idolaters they eat all kinds of meat, except that of the cow, which they worship as the mother and nurse of all men, and they are very fond of spirits. They also observe some of the Chinese ceremonies; for, after having fed their friends, when the repast is finished they burn yellow amber, although they do not worship fire like the Chinese. I have elsewhere given the reason why the Chinese burn amber at the conclusion of their feasts;[1] this causes this article to have a good sale in China. In Patna, even, pieces of yellow amber which are not worked, of the size of a good nut, clear and of good colour, are bought by these Bhutān merchants at 35 and 40 rupees the ser, and the ser, both for amber, as also for ambergris, musk, coral, rhubarb, and other drugs, is equal to 9 onces (Fr.) of our weight. Saltpetre, corn, rice, sugar, and other articles of food, are also sold by sers in Bengal; but this ser is 72 of our livres at 16 onces to the livre, and 40 sers make a maund, which would amount to 2,880 livres weight of Paris.[2] When I left that country the maund of rice was selling for 2 rupees.

To return to the yellow amber, for a piece of a ser or 9 onces (Fr.) weight, according to its colour and beauty, from 250 to 300 rupees is paid, and the other pieces cost the same in proportion to their size and beauty.[3] Coral in the rough or worked into beads is saleable with sufficient profit, but the rough is much preferred, for this reason, that it can be cut according to their own fashion; and most frequently women and girls are employed at this work. They also make beads of crystal and agate, and the men bracelets of tortoise-shell and sea shells, as also those small pieces of the same shell, both round and square, of which I have spoken above.[4] All

[1] See vol. ii. 108.

[2] This is an extraordinary jumble of figures. A ser of 72 livres, 40 of which went to the maund, making a maund of 2,880 livres, is surely due to a copyist's mistake. It is possible that a Bengal maund of 40 sers may have been equal to 72 livres, or more than double the Surat maund of 40 smaller sers = 34 livres (see vol. i. 334), but the statement as it stands is clearly wrong.

[3] See vol. ii. 108.

[4] See vol. ii. 204.

the people of the north, men, women, girls, and boys, suspend them from their hair and ears. There are in Patna and Dacca more than 2,000 persons who occupy themselves with these trades, all that is produced by them being exported to the Kingdoms of Bhutān, Assam, Siam, and other countries to the north and east of the territories of the Great Mogul.[1]

As for the semencine,[2] or worm powder, it cannot be harvested like other grains. It is a herb which grows in the fields, and must be allowed to die, and the evil is that when it approaches maturity the wind causes a great part to fall among the herbage, where it is lost, and it is this which makes it so dear. As it cannot be touched by the hand, because it would thereby be quickly spoilt, and even when taking a sample, it is collected in a porringer ; when they want to gather what remains in the ear, the following is the method adopted. The people who collect it have two baskets with handles, and when walking in the fields they wave one of these baskets from right to left, and the other from left to right, as though they cut the herb, of which nevertheless they only touch the upper part—that is to say, the ear, and all the grain thus falls into the baskets. Semencine also grows in the Province of Kermān,[3] but it is not so good as that of Bhutān, and there is not more of it than is required in the country itself. This grain not only serves to relieve children from worms, but the Persians and all the people who live towards the north, and even the English and Dutch, use it like aniseed to flavour comfits.

As for rhubarb, it is known to be a root which is cut in pieces, ten or twelve of them being strung together and then dried.

If the people of Bhutān had as much skill as the Muscovites in slaying the marten, an abundance of rich furs might be obtained, since there are numbers of these animals. As soon as it shows its head outside its hole the Muscovites, who are

[1] For the Sānkhārīs, or shell-workers of Dacca and other parts of Eastern Bengal see J. Wise, *Notes on the Races, Castes, and Trades of Eastern Bengal*, 364 ff. ; T. N. Mukharji, *Art-Manufactures of India*, 135, 281.

[2] See p. 201, *n.* 5.

[3] In South-East Persia.

on the watch, shoot it without fail, generally in the nose or the eyes, for if it is shot in the body the skin will be worth nothing on account of the blood which flows from the wound, and causes the hair moistened by it to fall out.

The King of Bhutān always employs 7,000 or 8,000 men as his guard. These people are armed with bows and arrows, and the majority also carry axes and shields, the former having a point on one side like a war mace. It is long since the Bhutānese first acquired the use of the musket, iron cannon, and gunpowder,[1] which is of long grain, and is very strong. I have been assured that on their guns figures and letters are visible which are more than 500 years old.[2] They cannot be taken out of the kingdom without the express permission of the Governor, and no one dare carry away a musket unless his nearest relatives go bail that it will be faithfully returned. Except for this difficulty I would have brought one away with me. By the characters on the gun, as those who were able to read assured me, it had been made 180 years. It was very thick, the mouth shaped like a tulip, and the interior polished like a mirror. On two-thirds of the gun there were bands in relief, and some gilt and silvered flowers between two of them, and the ball which it carried was an once (Fr.) in weight. The merchant of Bhutān being so particular about the return of the musket, no matter what offer I made, I could never persuade him to sell it to me, and

[1] In his paper on *Early Asiatic Fire Weapons* General Maclagan says, 'While there appears to be no good evidence in support of the idea that Asia had a knowledge of gunpowder and used firearms before Europe, there are plain indications that the knowledge of the most improved weapons of war, both before and since the introduction of gunpowder, and the skill to make and use them, came from Europe to India and other Asiatic countries': *Journ. Asiatic Society of Bengal*, vol. xlv, p. 64. He concludes, too, that there is no good evidence to support the belief that the Arabs were the first to use powder. He considers the European nations were the first to discover its most important form and application: p. 70 (*Ency. Brit.*, xii. 723 f.; *Cambridge Hist. of India*, i. 271). Were space available, much interesting information might be given here of the huge size of the guns which were used in India. One at Bījāpur was 4 feet 8 inches diameter at the muzzle, and had a calibre of 2 feet 4 inches. It was cast at Ahmadnagar in 1549. (*Asiatic Journ.*, 1827, p. 65; *Bombay Gazetteer*, xxiii. 638 ff.)

[2] This carries back to the year A. D. 1150 or thereabouts. See p. 217.

he even refused to give me a sample of his powder. But I have brought to France two guns of nearly the same kind, one of which was made in the island of Ceylon, and the other in Bengal.[1]

There are always fifty elephants about the house of the King of Bhutān for his guard, and twenty or twenty-five camels, which carry on the saddle a small piece of artillery, with a ball of about half a pound in weight. A man is seated on the crupper of the camel, as I have elsewhere described, and he manipulates this piece as he pleases, high or low, to the right or to the left, it being fixed on a fork attached to the saddle.[2]

There is no king in the world who is more feared and more respected by his subjects than the King of Bhutān, and he is even worshipped by them. When on the seat of justice or when he gives an audience, all those who present themselves before him raise their joined hands to their foreheads, and at some distance from the throne, prostrate themselves to the ground without daring to raise the head. In this humble posture they make their supplications to the King, and when they withdraw they walk backwards till they are out of his presence. The Brāhmans make these poor people believe that the King is a god upon earth, and principally those who come from the north.[3] . . . [Passage not translated.]

The people of Bhutān are robust men and of fine stature, but have somewhat flat faces and noses. I am informed that the women are taller and more vigorous than the men, but that they are more subject than them to goitre, from

[1] This is the bell-mouthed blunderbuss, not uncommon, sometimes called Sherbachha, 'tiger-cub' (Hon. W. Egerton, *Illustrated Handbook of Indian Arms*, 142.)

[2] Known as Zambūrak, 'little wasp', Shuturnāl, 'camel-gun', Shāhīn, 'falcon' (Irvine, *Army of the Indian Moghuls*, 135 f.; Bernier, 217).

[3] It seems probable that this so-called King of Bhutān, who was described to Tavernier, was really the Grand Lama of Tibet, and this is the more likely from the statement as to his sanctity in the passage which is not reproduced, being unsuitable for publication. The armaments and elephants mentioned above seem, however, to be scarcely compatible with the surroundings of the Grand Lama. On this use of stercus humanum see Manucci, ii. 440, iv. 438; Dubois, 594.

P 2

which few of them escape. They know nothing of war, and have no one to fear but the Great Mogul. But his territory, which lies to the south of them, is, as I have said, a country of high mountains and narrow passes; on the north there is nothing but forests and almost perpetual snow, and both on the east and west there are vast deserts where one finds nothing but bitter water; and whatever inhabited country there is belongs to Rājās who have not much power.

There is apparently a silver mine in the Kingdom of Bhutān,[1] for the King coins pieces of the value of rupees. These pieces are not round but octagonal, and there are characters on them which are neither Indian nor Chinese. Nevertheless, the merchants of Bhutān, who told me at Patna of all these things, could not inform me where the mine was, and as for gold the little they have of it is brought to them by the merchants who come from the east.

This is all that I have been able to learn concerning the Kingdom of Bhutān, beyond which the ambassadors passed whom the Duke of Moscovie sent to China in the year 1659. They passed through the length of Great Tartary to the north of Bhutān, and arrived at the court of the King of China with considerable presents. They were some of the most distinguished nobles of Moscovie, and were at first very well received. But when it became necessary for them to salute the King—the custom being to prostrate oneself three times on the ground—they would not consent to do so, saying that they would salute according to their own method, and in the manner that they saluted their own Emperor, who was as great and as powerful as he of China. As they remained firm in this resolution they had no audience,

[1] This is extremely probable; but it is inconsistent with our author's own statement on p. 128 that there are no silver mines in Asia except in Japan. Ainslie (*Materia Medica*, vol. i. 563) gives a number of references to authorities on the subject. Silver mines in the Patkāi country, between Assam and Upper Burma, have been recently described by Colonel Woodthorpe. (See *Pro. Geogl. Soc.*, January 1887.) A number of mines where argentiferous ores occur in India will be found enumerated in the chapter on silver in the *Economic Geology of India*. On Tibetan gold mines see N. Elias & E. D. Ross, *Hist. of the Moghuls of Central Asia*, 409, 411 f.

and returned with their presents without having seen the King.[1] It would have answered better if the Grand Duke had chosen for this embassy some persons of lower rank than these three nobles, who would have shown themselves less scrupulous about formalities, which are often the cause of envoys being unable to accomplish great designs. If these Moscovite ambassadors had consented to conform to the customs of China—which they might have done without compromising the honour of their master—we should have, without doubt, at this time, a road opened by land from Moscovie to China, through the north of Great Tartary, and a greater knowledge of the Kingdom of Bhutān, which is in its vicinity, and of some others of which we scarce know the names; this would have been a great advantage for all Europe.[2]

As I have just spoken of the Moscovites, I remember that in my journeys, and particularly on the road from Tabrīz to Ispahān, where you generally meet Moscovite merchants, several of them have assured me that in the year 1654, in one of the towns of Moscovie, a woman aged eighty-two gave birth to a male child, which was taken to the Grand Duke, who wished to see it, and had it brought up at his own court.[3]

[1] Envoys to the Emperor of China about the year 713, who refused to kotow, were tried and pronounced worthy of death, but were subsequently pardoned. See Yule, *Marco Polo*. i. 349; *Cathay and the Way Thither*, i. lxxxi. The Russian embassy to China arrived in 1656 (*Ency. Brit.*, vi. 198).

[2] This passage is of considerable interest when regarded in connexion with the subsequent extension of Russia's influence in this direction, and our own hitherto futile attempts to establish a regular trade route through Tibet, which however, have been advanced by the war in 1903–4.

[3] Mr. A. Keith, F.R.C.S. LL.D. Conservator of the Museum of the Royal College of Surgeons, in a letter dated 12th January 1921, writes: 'Two years ago a correspondence was carried on in the *British Medical Journal* to ascertain the latest age at which a woman was known to have borne a child. It was found that there was no authenticated case of any one over 50 bearing a child, and that such cases were very rare.'

CHAPTER XVI

Concerning the Kingdom of Tippera.

SOME persons up to this hour believe that the Kingdom of Pegu bounds China, and I myself shared this error until three merchants of the Kingdom of Tippera corrected me. They passed as Brāhmans in the hope that they might be treated with special respect, but they were in truth only merchants who came to Patna and Dacca, where I saw them, to buy coral, yellow amber, tortoise-shell, and sea-shell bracelets, and other toys which, as I have said in the preceding chapter, are made in these two towns of Bengal. I saw one of them at Dacca, and met the two others at Patna, and invited them to dine with me. They were people who spoke but little, either because it was their nature, or the usual custom of their country; one of them knew the Indian language. When they bought anything they made their calculations with small stones resembling agates, and of the size of the finger nail, upon which there were figures. They each had scales made like steelyards.[1] The arms were not of iron, but of a kind of wood as hard as bresil,[2] and the ring which held the weights, when put in the arm to mark the livres, was a strong loop of silk. By this means they weighed from a dram up to ten of our livres. If all the inhabitants of the Kingdom of Tippera resemble these two merchants whom I met at Patna, one might conclude that this nation loves drinking very much; and I experienced a pleasure in giving them sometimes spirits, sometimes Spanish wine, and other kinds, such as those of Shīrāz, Rheims, and Mantua, never having been without a supply in all my journeys, except during the last, in the deserts of Arabia, which I was unable to traverse in less than sixty-five days, for the reasons I have elsewhere stated. I should have been able to learn

[1] See H. Ling Roth, 'Oriental Steelyards and Bismars', *Journal, Royal Anthropological Institute*, xlii, 1912, p. 200 ff.

[2] The Brazil wood of commerce is at present derived from Cæsalpinia Brasiliensis, a native of Pernambuco. (*Ency. Brit.*, iv. 463.) The Indian Sappan wood is Cæsalpinia Sappan: Watt, *Economic Products*, 194 ff. (See Yule, *Hobson-Jobson*, 113.)

many things from these Tippera merchants in reference to the nature and extent of their country if they had known how to give me as good as account of it as they did of my good wine when I proposed a health. For my interpreter had scarce finished paying them a compliment, on my behalf, before the wine was drunk, when they gazed at one another, smacked their lips, and strook their hands two or three times on their stomachs with a sigh.[1] These three merchants had come by way of the Kingdom of Arakan, which lies to the south and west [2] of that of Tippera, partly bounded by Pegu in the direction of the winter sunset, and they told me that they spent about fifteen days in traversing their country, from which one cannot very well estimate its extent, because the stages are unequal, being sometimes longer and sometimes shorter, according as water is to be found.

For the conveyance of goods they use, as in India, oxen and horses, which are similar to those I have described above, small in size, but otherwise excellent. As for the King and the great nobles, they travel in pallankeens,[3] and have elephants trained for war. The inhabitants of Tippera are not less troubled by goître than those of Bhutān. I was told that it attacked some of the women on the breasts. Of the three men from Tippera whom I saw in Bengal, the one who was at Dacca had two goîtres, each of the size of the fist; they are caused by the bad water, as in many other countries of Asia and Europe.[4]

Nothing is produced in Tippera which is of use to foreigners. There is, however, a gold mine, which yields gold of very low standard; and silk, which is very coarse.[5] It is from

[1] 'Drunkenness among them [the Tipperas] does not take an amorous or a pugnacious direction; it generally expends itself in vehement dancing, until such time as the head becomes giddy, and the dancer lies down to sleep off what he has drunk' (T. H. Lewin, *Wild Races of South-Eastern India*, 201).

[2] East.

[3] The King, without reason, claims descent from the Rājput Lunar Race (*Imperial Gazetteer*, xiii. 118).

[4] For early explanations of the origin of goître see Mundy, i. 117. It seems to be due to telluric or malarial causes, combined with drinking water impregnated with salts of lime and magnesia (*Ency. Brit.*, xii. 192). It is prevalent in the Sub-Himalayas and the adjoining districts.

[5] Tippera, as now understood, does not produce gold—the gold brought from thence may have been originally obtained elsewhere

these two articles that the King's revenue is derived. He levies no taxes from his subjects, save that those below the rank, corresponding to that of the nobility of Europe, have to work for him for six days every year either in the gold mine or at the silk. He sends both the gold and silk to be sold in China, and receives silver in return, with which he coins money of the value of 10 sols.[1] He also coins small gold money like the aspres [2] of Turkey, and has two kinds of them, of one of which it takes four to make an écu, and of the other a dozen. This is all I have been able to ascertain concerning a country which has been unknown to us up to the present, but about which we shall hereafter have more information, as also of others which the accounts of travellers have made known to us, all not having been discovered in a day.[3]

CHAPTER XVII

Concerning the Kingdom of Assam.

It was never properly known what the Kingdom of Assam was till after that great Captain Mīr Jumla, to whom I have often referred in the history of the Moguls, had secured the Empire for Aurangzeb by the death of all his brothers and the imprisonment of his son. He concluded, that when the war was finished, he would be no longer esteemed at Court

(see vol. ii, p. 157 *n.*). In Assam, it is said that it was once the custom for the Rājās to require their subjects to wash for gold for a certain number of days every year. Regular gold washers were taxed. For gold in Upper Burma see Scott & Hardiman, *Gazetteer*, Part i, vol. ii. 304 f.

[1] These coins were therefore worth 9*d.*

[2] The Turkish asper (ἄσπρος, 'white': see *New English Dict.* s.v. asper) was both a small coin, and a money of account. Its value varied with that of the piastre. It therefore represented about a halfpenny in value, if there were 80 to 100 in a piastre. The coins here mentioned by Tavernier were worth 1*s.* 1½*d.* and 4½*d.* respectively.

[3] For the people of Tippera see 'On the Manners, Religion, and Laws of the Cucis, or Mountaineers of Tipra' by J. Rawlins (*Asiatic Researches*, ii, 1799, pp. 187 ff.); and more recent accounts by Sir E. Gait (*Bengal Census Report*, 1901, vol. i. 186 f., 438), Sir H. Risley (*Tribes and Castes of Bengal*, ii. 323 ff.); T. H. Lewin (*Wild Races of South-Eastern India*, 190 ff.).

as highly as he had been when Commander-in-Chief of the armies of Aurangzeb, and all powerful in the Kingdom where he had a great number of supporters. In order, therefore, to retain for himself the command of the troops, he resolved to undertake the conquest of the Kingdom of Assam, where he knew he would not meet with much resistance, the country having had no war for 500 or 600 years, and the people being without experience in arms.[1] It is believed that this people in ancient times, first discovered gunpowder and guns, which passed from Assam to Pegu, and from Pegu to China; this is the reason why the discovery is generally ascribed to the Chinese. Mīr Jumla brought back from this war numerous iron guns, and the gunpowder made in that country is excellent. Its grain is not long as in the Kingdom of Bhutān, but is round and small like ours, and is much more effective than the other powder.

Accordingly Mīr Jumla left Dacca with a powerful army for the conquest of the Kingdom of Assam.[2] At 5 leagues from Dacca one of the rivers which comes from the Lake of Chiamay,[3] which like other rivers of India takes different names according to the places it passes, joins an arm of the Ganges, and at the place where these two rivers meet there are forts on each side, both armed with good pieces of bronze cannon, which shoot at a level with the water. This is where Mīr Jumla embarked,[4] his army ascending the river to the

[1] Bernier (p. 171) says that Mīr Jumla was sent to Assam because 'Aurangzeb justly apprehended that an ambitious soldier could not long remain in a state of repose, and that, if disengaged from foreign war, he would seek occasion to excite internal commotions.' Ostensibly he was appointed Viceroy of Bengal to punish the lawless Zamīndārs of Assam and Arakan (Jadunath Sarkar, *History of Aurangzīb*, iii. 178).

[2] On 1st November 1661. An account of Assam at the time of its conquest by Mīr Jumla in 1663, based on the '*Ālamgīr-nāma* of Muhammad Kāzim-ibn-Muhammad Amīn Munshī, by Kavirāj Syāmal Dās, translated by Bābū Rāma Prasāda, has been published in the *Indian Antiquary* for July 1887, pp. 222-6. The authorities for the campaign are Elliot & Dowson, *Hist. of India*, vii. 144; *Asiatic Researches*, ii. 172 ff.; Jadunath Sarkar, iii. 166 ff.

[3] Lake Chiamay was a myth believed in by early travellers. (Yule, *Hobson-Jobson* 190; Scott & Hardiman, *Gazetteer of Upper Burma*, Part ii, vol. ii, 659 f.)

[4] Gorāghāt on the west bank of the Karatoyā river in the district

29th or 30th degree, where the frontier of Assam is situated, and thence he led it by land through a country abounding with all the necessaries of life, and with but little means of defence, especially as the people were taken by surprise. As they are all idolaters, the army, which consisted wholly of Musalmāns, did not spare their pagodas, but destroyed them wherever they met with them, burning and sacking all, up to the 35th degree.[1] Mīr Jumla then heard that the King of Assam was in the field with a larger force than had been expected; that he had many guns, and an abundance of fireworks, somewhat like our grenades, which are fixed at the end of a stick as long as a short pike, as I have elsewhere described, and carry more than 500 paces.[2] When Mīr Jumla received this intelligence he did not consider it prudent to advance farther, but the principal cause of his return was that the cold season had commenced, and to effect the conquest of that country it would have been necessary to go as far as the 45th degree of latitude; this would have involved the loss of his army. For the Indians are so susceptible to cold, and fear it so much, that it is impossible to make them pass the 30th, or at the most the 35th degree, except at the risk of their lives, and of all the servants whom I took from India to Persia, it was a great feat for them to come as far as Kasvīn,[3] and I never succeeded in taking any of them to Tabrīz. As soon as they saw the mountains of Medea covered with snow I had to allow them to return home.

As Mīr Jumla was unable to go farther north, he resolved to turn to the south-west, and laid siege to a town called Azoo,[4] which he took in a short time, and found great riches

of Dinājpur, an ancient city now marked by ruins, according to Muhammad Ḳāzim, was the starting point of Mīr Jumla on the 21st November 1662. This was after he had conquered Kuch Bihār. The route is fully given by Jadunath Sarkar, and cannot be reconciled with the text (Jadunath Sarkar, iii. 181 ff.).

[1] The Mughal forces can scarcely have gone beyond Garhgāon, which they reached on 17th March 1662 or about the 28th degree of latitude, at the farthest.

[2] Rockets (see vol. i, p. 311).

[3] Casbin in the original.

[4] Azoo or Koch Hājo, a kingdom on the left bank of the Brahmaputra river, extending up to Kāmrūp. The town of Hājo was on the frontier of Assam. A full account of it will be found in the *Pādishāh-*

there. Many are of opinion that his original design was merely to take this town and pillage it, and afterwards return, as he in fact did.[1] It is in this town of Azoo that the tombs of the Kings of Assam and of all the members of the royal family are situated. Although the Assamese are idolaters, they do not burn the bodies of the dead, but bury them. They believe that after death they go to another world, where those who have lived well in this world lack nothing, and enjoy all kinds of pleasure; but, on the contrary, those who have lived badly, and have taken the property of others, suffer much, principally hunger and thirst, and accordingly it is prudent to bury something with them to serve them at need. Thus it was that Mīr Jumla found such a quantity of riches at Azoo,[2] since for many centuries every King has built for himself in the great pagoda a sort of chapel where he was to be buried, and during their lifetime, each of them sent, to be placed in the grave where he was to be buried, a quantity of gold and silver, carpets and other articles. When the body of a dead king is buried, all his most precious possessions are also placed in the grave, such as the household

nāma. (See Blochmann in *Journ. Asiat. Soc. Bengal*, vol. xli. p. 53.) Here Tavernier copies Bernier (p. 172), but it is difficult to follow his story. The Mughals seem to have been in possession of Hājo since 1612 (Jadunath Sarkar, iii. 169).

[1] Muhammad Kāzim says that Mīr Jumla, finding his army tired of the difficulties with which they were surrounded, 'came to terms with the Assamis (on the 17th January 1663), who, besides surrendering two districts, which were added to the crown lands, gave 20,000 tolās of gold, 128,000 rupees in hard cash, 120 elephants, and the King's daughter to the conqueror. He then returned to Bengal via Lakhughar and Kajli, and reached Khizarpur on the 8th April A. D. 1663, where he paid the debt of nature after suffering for a time from consumption' (*l.c.*, p. 223). For the terms of peace and a review of the results of the campaign, which, except for the blockade of the Mughals, was successful, see Jadunath Sarkar, iii. 201 ff.; Bernier, 172 f. It was at Garhgāon, not Hājo, that the booty was taken.

[2] Muhammad Kāzim says 90,000 rupees worth of gold and silver was obtained by Mīr Jumla's soldiers from these graves (*l.c.* 225). 'The tumuli constructed over the graves of the Asam (Ahom) sovereigns are very extensive, and when opened the remains of the dead have been found in coffins of massive timber, with gold and silver ornaments, and outside the coffin various utensils, arms, and implements of agriculture.' (E. T. Dalton, *Descriptive Ethnology of Bengal*, 9.)

idol of gold or silver which he worshipped during life, and all things which it is believed will be required by him in the other world. But it is most strange, and savours much of barbarism, that as soon as the King is dead, some of his most beloved wives and the principal officers of his house kill themselves by means of a poisoned decoction, in order to be interred with him, so that they may serve him in the other world. Besides which an elephant, twelve camels,[1] six horses, and numerous sporting dogs are buried with him, it being believed that all these animals will come to life again, after they are dead, and serve the King.

This Kingdom of Assam is one of the best countries in Asia, for it produces all that is necessary to the life of man, and there is no need to go for anything to the neighbouring States. There are mines of gold, silver, steel, lead, and iron,[2] and much silk, but it is coarse. There is a kind of silk which is produced on trees, and is made by an animal like our silkworm, but it is rounder and remains for a whole year on the trees.[3] The stuffs which are made of this silk are very brilliant, but soon fray and do not last long. These silks

[1] Muhammad Kāzim gives a similar account, but does not mention camels. Elsewhere he states camels were unknown in Assam (*l. c.*, p. 224). The climate of Assam does not suit camels. (*Imperial Gazetteer*, vi. 36.) The practice, if it once prevailed, of burying animals with the dead, has now practically disappeared from India, though among some of the tribes in the Vindhyan hills the habit of placing in the grave tools or implements used by men or women still survives as in the case of the Majhwārs of the United Provinces (Crooke, *Tribes and Castes of the North-Western Provinces*, iii. 433). And in Bengal, when a Khambu dies, a pig is brained with the pestle used for husking corn, its tail and ears being cut off and placed under the dead man's armpits before he is buried (*Census Report, Bengal*, 1911, i. 512).

[2] Muhammad Kāzim says, 'Gold and silver are got from the sand of the rivers draining the Gol (i. e. northern circle). About 12,000 Assamis according to some people, 20,000 as others state, are generally engaged in washing these noble metals, and have to pay one tola of gold per head per annum to the Chief' (*l. c.*, 224). See *Economic Geology of India*, p. 231, for details as to the gold of Assam. See also *ante*, p. 128, where it is stated incorrectly that there are no silver mines in India. Iron is still worked to a small extent; alluvial gold is no longer washed; there is some silver and platinum (*Imperial Gazetteer*, vi. 71 f.).

[3] The production of silk is now important (*ibid.*, vi. 73). For Upper Burma see Scott & Hardiman, *Gazetteer*, Part i, vol. ii, 372 f.

are produced, and the gold and silver mines are situated in the southern part of the country. The country also produces an abundance of shellac, of which there are two kinds.[1] That formed on trees is of a red colour, with it they dye their calicoes and other stuffs, and when they have extracted the red colour they use the lac to lacquer cabinets and other objects of that kind, and to make Spanish wax.[2] A large quantity of it is exported to China and Japan, to be used in the manufacture of cabinets ; it is the best lac in the whole of Asia for these purposes. As for the gold, no one is permitted to remove it out of the Kingdom, and it is not coined into money but is kept in large and small ingots, which the people make use of in local trade, and do not export it ; but as for silver, the King coins it into money of the size and weight of rupees, and of an octagonal shape, and they may be taken outside the Kingdom. Although the country abounds, as I have said, with all things necessary to life, among all articles of food the flesh of the dog[3] is especially esteemed ; it is the favourite dish at feasts, and every month, in each town in the Kingdom, the people hold markets where they sell only dogs, which are brought thither from all directions. There are also quantities of vines and good grapes, but no wine, the grapes being merely dried for distilling spirits. Finally, as regards salt, there is none in the Kingdom but what is manufactured, which is done in two ways.[4] The first is to collect vegetable matter which

[1] The manufacture of shellac is declining (Watt, *Economic Products*, 1059).

[2] See p. 18 for an account of shellac and lac dye. For shellac in Upper Burma see Scott & Hardiman, *Gazetteer*, Part i, vol. ii. 393 ff. 'In his [King of Pegu] country there is found much lacca' (Varthema, 222).

[3] Muhammad Kāzim says the Nanaks (Nāgas) eat the flesh of dogs, cats, serpents, &c. (*l.c.*, p. 224). The Nāgas still eat dog's flesh (Dalton, *Descriptive Ethnology of Bengal*, 43 ; T. C. Hodson, *Naga Tribes of Manipur*, 59 f. ; J. H. Hutton, *The Angami Nāgas*, 81) ; and so do the Akhas in Upper Burma (Scott & Hardiman, *Gazetteer*, Part i, vol. i. 589).

[4] The chief sources of supply of salt in Assam were formerly the brine springs at Borhāt and Sadiyā in Lakhimpur. The vessels used in the manufacture for boiling the brine were simply sections of bamboos, which were pared so thin that the percolating moisture prevented their

is found in stagnant water, such as ducks and frogs eat. This is dried and burnt, and the ashes derived from it being boiled and strained as is described below, serve as salt. The other method, which is that most commonly followed, is to take some of those large leaves of the kind of fig tree which we call Adam's fig,[1] they are dried in the same manner and burnt, and the ashes from them consist of a kind of salt which is so pungent that it is impossible to eat it unless it is softened, this being done in the following way. The ashes are put into water, where they are stirred about for ten or twelve hours, then this water is strained three times through a cloth and boiled. As it boils the sediment thickens, and when the water is all evaporated, the salt, which is white and fairly good, is found at the bottom of the pot.

From the ashes of fig leaves in this country the lye is made to boil silk, which becomes as white as snow, and if the people of Assam had more figs than they have, they would make all their silks white, because white silk is much more valuable than the other, but they have not sufficient to bleach half the silks which are produced in the country.

Kemmerouf[2] is the name of the town where the King of Assam resides, twenty-five or thirty days' journey from the former capital of the Kingdom and it bore the same name. The King takes no tribute from his people, but all the mines of gold, silver, lead, steel, and iron belong to him, and to avoid oppressing his subjects, he employs only the slaves

burning. Imported salt is now largely used in Assam. (See *Economic Geology of India*, p. 491.) The manufacture of salt is now confined to some hill tribes (Watt, *Dict. Economic Products*, vi, part 2, 400).

[1] This manufacture of salt from the leaves of the plantain is mentioned by Muhammad Kāzim, *l. c.*, p. 224. (See *ante*, p. 3.) The pungency is probably due to the presence of potash salts. The ashes of the leaves are, as Tavernier says, still used for dyeing in Bengal (Watt, *op. cit.*, v. 296).

[2] Kāmrūp, now known as the name of a District in Assam of which Gauhātī is the chief town. It is certain that Mīr Jumla was defeated by the Ahāms here, and this was the seat of the Ahām Viceroy, but the King of Assam's capital was at Nāzira or Garhgāon (Kargānv) in the Sibsāgar District. (See Jadunath Sarkar, iii. 183 ff.; *Imperial Gazetteer*, xix. i f.) The palace is described in Robinson's *Descriptive Account of Assam*. According to Muhammad Kāzim, who also describes it, its circuit was 1 kos and 14 chains (= 840 yards).

whom he buys from his neighbours for working the mines.[1] Thus all the peasants of Assam are at their ease, and there is scarcely anyone who has not a separate house in his land, a well surrounded by trees, and the majority even keep elephants for their wives. These idolaters, unlike those of India, who have but one wife, have four, and when a man marries one, in order that there may be no dispute among them, he says to her, 'I take you to serve me in my household for this purpose', and to another, 'I destine you for another', and thus each of the women knows what she has to do in the house. The men and women are of fine build, and of very good blood; but the people dwelling on the southern frontier are somewhat olive coloured, and are not subject to goître like those of the north. The latter are not of so fine stature, and the majority of their women have somewhat flat noses. The people of the southern part go about naked, having only a piece of calico with which they cover that which modesty requires them to conceal, with a cap like English caps, around which they hang an abundance of pigs' teeth.[2] They have their ears pierced so that one might easily pass the thumb through the holes, some carry ornaments of gold in them and others of silver.[3] The men wear their hair down to their shoulders, and the women let it grow as long as it can. In the Kingdom of Assam, as well as that of Bhutān, there is a large trade in tortoise-shell bracelets, and sea shells as large as an egg, which are sawn into small circles, but the rich wear bracelets of coral and yellow amber.

[1] This may have been true of the silver mines, but as above stated, subjects had to wash for gold.

[2] Muhammad Kāzim says, 'A head-piece of gunny (*gonī*), a cloth round the loins, and a sheet over the shoulders, form all the articles of their dress' (*l.c.*, p. 225). Dalton, *op. cit.*, plate xiii, gives a photograph of an Abor chief whose head is decorated with tusks of the wild boar.

[3] On the practice, common among Hindu women, of distending the ears with heavy rings see P. della Valle, i. 195; Pyrard de Laval, i. 343, 419; Barbosa, ed. Dames, i. 114; Linschoten, i. 77. In the Central Provinces 'to have the hole torn open is one of the worst social mishaps which can happen to a woman. She is immediately put out of caste for a long period, and only readmitted after severe penalties, equivalent to those inflicted for getting vermin in a wound' (Russell, *Tribes and Castes*, iv. 529).

When a man dies all his relatives and friends should come to the burial, and when they place the body in the ground they take off all the bracelets on their arms and legs and bury them with the deceased.

CHAPTER XVIII

Concerning the Kingdom of Siam.[1]

THE greater part of the Kingdom of Siam is situated between the Gulf of the same name and the Gulf of Bengal, adjoining Pegu on the north and the peninsula of Malacca on the south. The shortest road and the best which Europeans can take to reach this Kingdom is to go from Ispahān to Hormuz, from Hormuz to Surat, from Surat to Golkonda, and from Golkonda to Masulipatam, where they should embark for Denouserin,[2] which is one of the ports of the Kingdom of Siam. From Denouserin to the capital town, which bears the name of the Kingdom, there are about thirty-five days' journey; one part is traversed by ascending a river, and the remainder in a cart or upon elephants. The road both by land and water is uncomfortable, because on the land portion one must always be on guard against lions[3] and tigers; and by water, as the river makes rapids in many places, it is difficult to make the boats ascend, but this is accomplished by the aid of machinery. It is the route which I recommended, on the return from one of my voyages to India, to three bishops whom I met on the road. The first was the Bishop of Beryte,[4] whom I met at Ispahān; the second the Bishop of Megalopolis,[5] when crossing the Euphrates;

[1] One of the most important early accounts of Siam is that of Simon de la Loubère, *Du Royaume de Siam*, Amsterdam, 1691, of which an English translation, by A. P. Gem, R. S. S., was published in London, 1693, under the title of *A New Historical Relation of the Kingdom of Siam*. The references in the notes are to the latter work.

[2] Tenasserim, which, however, was included in the Kingdom of Pegu, though at times conquered and held by Siam (Yule, *Hobson-Jobson*, 914).

[3] There are no lions in Siam.

[4] Beyrout, in Syria.

[5] Metellopolis of Finlayson, *Mission to Siam*, 257: perhaps Megalopolis in Arcadia.

the third the Bishop of Heliopolis,[1] who arrived at Alexandretta as I was leaving it for Europe. The whole of Siam abounds with rice and fruits, the principal of which are called mangues, durions, and mangoustans.[2] The forests are full of deer, elephants, tigers, rhinoceros, and monkeys, and everywhere is to be seen an abundance of bamboos, which are large and very tall canes, hollow throughout, and as hard as iron.

At the ends of these canes nests, of the size of a man's head, are suspended; they are made by ants from a fat earth which they carry up. There is but a small hole at the base of these nests, by which the ants enter, and in these nests each ant, like honey bees, has his separate chamber. They build their nests on the canes, because if they made them on the ground, during the rainy season, which lasts four or five months, they would be exterminated, all the country being then inundated. One must take precautions after night-fall against snakes. There are some snakes which are 22 feet long and have two heads,[3] but the head at the extremity which answers to the tail, and where the snake ends, does not open the mouth and has no movement. There is also in Siam a very venomous animal which is not more than a foot long. Its tail is forked and has two points, and its form is somewhat like what we picture the salamander.[4]

The rivers of this Kingdom are very beautiful, and the

[1] Heliopolis or Bambyke, near Carchemish on the Euphrates. Le Blanc identified Hieropolis with Aleppo (*Voyages*, Paris Edition, 1648, p. 8).

[2] Mangoes, durians, and mangosteens.

[3] This fable of two-headed snakes is common in India; sometimes it is said of the Dhamin snake—Ptyas mucosus. The statement that the head, at the tail end, has no movement, and that the mouth does not open, is a charmingly ingenuous admission. See Mundy, 308 f., with an illustration; *Bombay Gazetteer*, x. 48. Like the case of the Birds of Paradise, referred to on p. 13, the description illustrates the persistence of myths.

[4] This poisonous, forked-tailed reptile was certainly mythical. A species of Eublepharis? is called bishkhaprā by the natives of India, and though unprovided with fangs is believed to be very poisonous. (Yule, *Hobson-Jobson*, 95 f.) A. Hamilton describes a dangerous animal, shaped like a lizard, and called Jackoa (Pinkerton, *Voyages*, viii. 453).

one at Siam is of nearly uniform size throughout.[1] The water in it is very wholesome, but it is full of crocodiles of enormous size, which often devour men who are not on their guard.[2] The rivers are in flood during the time that the sun traverses the northern signs; this contributes much to the fertility of the land where the waters spread themselves, and where, by a wonderful provision of nature, the ear of rice ascends to the surface as the waters rise.[3]

Siam,[4] the capital town of the Kingdom, and the ordinary residence of the King, is surrounded by walls, and is more than 3 of our leagues in circuit. It is on an island, the river surrounding it on all sides; canals might easily be made through all the streets if the King were willing to expend on that work a part of the vast amount of gold which he lavishes on the idol temples.

The Siamese have thirty-three letters in their alphabet;[5] they write as we do, from left to right, or contrary to the people of Japan, China, Cochin-China, and Tonquin, who write from the right hand to the left, and from the top of the page to the bottom.

All the common people of this Kingdom are in slavery either to the King or to the nobles.[6] The women cut their hair like the men, and their garments are not very copious. Among the civilities which the Siamese observe towards

[1] The principal rivers of Siam are the Menam, Mekong, Meklong, Petriü, Tachin, and the Chantibun (Crawfurd, *Dictionary*, 380).

[2] The Siamese take their revenge by eating crocodiles' eggs.

[3] The period of floods is during the south-west monsoon, from June to November, and the plain fertilized by them has an area of 6,750 geographical square miles.

[4] Bangkok, on both banks of the Menam river, 24 miles from the sea, is the present capital of Siam. The old capital, called Siam or Yuthia, or Ayuthia, from Sanskrit Ayodhya, is 54 miles farther to the north; it was destroyed by the Burmese in 1768, and Bangkok was founded in 1769 (Crawfurd, *Dictionary*, 384 f.; Yule, *op. cit.*, 56 f., 465 f.).

[5] The Siamese alphabet contains 32 vowels and 44 consonants—in all, 76 distinct characters (*Ency. Brit.*, xxv. 9). The language consists of two dialects—the court and the vulgar. The sacred language is distinct, being Pali or Prakrit (Crawfurd, *Dictionary*, 387).

[6] For an interesting account of slavery or serfdom in Siam at the present day, see E. Young, *The Kingdom of the Yellow Robe*, 125 ff.; de la Loubère, 77 f.

one another, one of the principal is never to pass anyone to whom respect is due, without previously asking permission; this is done by elevating both hands. The richest have many wives, as is the case in the Kingdom of Assam.[1]

The money of the country is of silver and nearly of the shape of a musket bullet.[2] The lowest denomination consists of small shells, which are brought from the Manillas. There are good tin mines in Siam.[3]

The King of Siam is one of the wealthiest monarchs in the East, and he calls himself in his edicts King of heaven and earth, although he is a tributary to the Kings of China. He shows himself but rarely to his subjects, and gives audience only to the principal persons of his court, strangers having no admission to his palace. He confides the government to his ministers, who very often make ill use of the authority with which they are invested. He shows himself in public only twice in the year; this he does with much splendour. The first time is when he goes in state to a pagoda in the town,[4] the tower of which is gilt throughout, both inside and outside. It contains three idols, from 6 to 7 feet high, and made of massive gold; by means of liberal alms to the poor, and presents to the priests of these false gods, he believes that he makes himself pleasing to them. He goes there accompanied by all his court, and displays all his richest possessions. Among other indications of magnificence there

[1] Young, 99 ff.

[2] The coins here referred to are probably those which our author figures in his chapter on coins (p. 22 of the original Paris ed. of 1676). Ball suggests that this peculiar form imitates the curious-shaped cocò-de-mer, or double coco-nut of the Seychelles islands, for which fabulous prices were given in the Malayan countries and India. (See Yule, *Hobson-Jobson*, 229 for an account of this coco-nut.) Gold and silver bullet coins are still current (Young, 140). See an illustration of these coins in de la Loubère, 72. Porcelain coins are still current (Carl Bock, *Temples and Elephants*, 142).

[3] Tin is obtained in four of the provinces, which extend from Lat. 8° to Lat. 13°; and also in the tributary Malay States (*Ency. Brit.*, xxv. 5).

[4] This pagoda, or the one next referred to, is probably the one still standing, though much ruined, near Yuthia; it is 400 feet high, and has a gigantic gilt bronze statue of Buddha. It is said to have been built in the year 1387 A. D. (Crawfurd, *Dictionary*, 387).

are 200 elephants in Siam, one of them being white; and it is so highly esteemed by the King that he glories in calling himself 'the King of the white elephant'.[1] .These elephants live for several centuries, as I have elsewhere remarked.[2]

The second time that the King goes forth in public is for the purpose of visiting another pagoda, 5 or 6 leagues from the town up the river. No one can enter this pagoda save the King and his priests. As for the people, as soon as they see the door of it each one must fall with his face to the ground. On this occasion the King appears on the river with 200 richly gilt and decorated galleys of an enormous length, each having 400 rowers.[3] As this second sortie of the King happens in the month of November, when the river begins to fall, the priests make the people believe that it is the King alone who is able to arrest the course of the waters by the prayers and offerings which he makes in this pagoda; and these poor people persuade themselves that the King goes to cut the waters with his sword, to dismiss them and order them to retire into the sea.[4]

The King goes, moreover, but on this occasion without any state, to a pagoda which is in the island where the Dutch have their factory. There is, at the entrance, an idol seated after the manner of our tailors, having one hand on one of

[1] In the year 1821–2 the envoys from the Governor-General of India found five white elephants in the possession of the King. Finlayson gives an interesting account of them (*Mission to Siam*, p. 154). See Sir J. Bowring, *Siam*, i. 220 f. 'In Siam the representation of the white elephant is everywhere conspicuous. The national flag is a white elephant on a scarlet ground. The mercantile flag is a white elephant on a blue ground. On every temple and official building in the land there is a representation in stone, plaster, or colour, of this wonderful creature' (E. Young, *The Kingdom of the Yellow Robe*, 389); Hastings, *Ency. Religion and Ethics*, xi. 483. Dames, *Book of Duarte Barbosa*, ed. 1921, ii. 154 f.

[2] See vol. i, p. 223.

[3] Drawings and descriptions of these fine royal barges, called Balon (see Yule-Burnell, *Hobson-Jobson*, 53), are given by de la Loubère, p. 40, and see Turpin, *Hist. of Siam*, in Pinkerton, *Collection of Voyages*, ix. 581; Young, 349; and compare the royal boats in the Burmese Court (Scott & Hardiman, *Gazetteer Upper Burma*, part i, vol. ii. 157 ff.).

[4] A good instance of mimetic magic.

his knees and the other at his side. It is more than 60 feet high, and around this large idol there are more than 300 others of different sizes, which represent all kinds of attitudes of men and women.[1] All these idols are gilt, and there is a prodigious quantity of these pagodas in all the country. This results from the fact that every rich Siamese builds one to perpetuate his memory. These pagodas have towers and bells, and the walls inside are painted and gilt, but the windows are so narrow that they give but little light. The altars are laden with costly idols, among which there are generally three of different sizes close to one another.[2] The two pagodas to which, as I have said, the King goes in state, are surrounded by many beautiful pyramids, all well gilt; and that in the island where the Dutch have their house has a cloister connected with it, the facade of which is very fine. In the middle there is, as it were, a great chapel all gilded within, where a lamp and three wax candles are kept alight in front of the altar, which is covered with idols, some being of fine gold and the others of gilt copper. The pagoda in the middle of the town, and one of the two which the King visits once in the year, as I have related, contains nearly 4,000 idols, and it has around it, like that 6 leagues from Siam, a number of pyramids, the beauty of which causes one to wonder at the industry of this nation.

When the King appears all the doors and windows of the houses have to be closed, and all the people prostrate themselves on the ground without daring to raise their eyes towards him. As no one should be in a place more elevated than the King when he is passing through the streets, all those who are in their houses must descend. When his hair is cut one of his wives is employed on that duty, as he does not allow

[1] It is possible that this is a mistake, as some images of Buddha have an effeminate appearance. For images in pagodas at Bangkok, see Young, *op. cit.*, 272 ff.; Hastings, *Ency. Religion and Ethics*, xi. 482.

[2] Vast accumulations of figures of Buddha characterize these temples, even those which are deserted. The well-known seated and recumbent figures of Buddha, made of marble or lacquered wood, which are brought to Europe, have generally been obtained from deserted pagodas in Burma or Siam.

a barber to place a hand upon him.[1] This prince is passionately attached to certain elephants, which he supports as the favourites and ornaments of his kingdom. When they are sick the greatest nobles of the court show the utmost care for them in order to please their sovereign; and when they die, as much magnificence is displayed for them as at the funerals of the nobles of the Kingdom.[2] These funerals of the nobles are conducted in the following manner:—A kind of mausoleum is adorned with reeds covered on both sides with paper of many colours. As all kinds of scented wood are sold by weight, as much as the body weighs is placed in the middle of the mausoleum, and after the priests have finished pronouncing some benedictions they burn the whole to ashes. Those of the rich are preserved in urns of gold or silver, but as for those of the poor they are cast to the winds.[3] As for criminals who have finished their lives with a disgraceful death, the Siamese do not burn their bodies, but bury them.[4]

The King authorizes public women, but they have to live in their own separate quarter, under a chief who protects them from insult. When one of them dies her body is not burnt as is that of a respectable woman, but is thrown into a place where it becomes the food of dogs and crows.

It is estimated that there are in this Kingdom more than 200,000 priests called Bonzes,[5] who are held in great veneration

[1] On respect paid to the heads of royal personages, see Young, *op. cit.*, 131. It is a well-known characteristic of these sacred kings that their heads are regarded as sacrosanct. Hence no one is allowed to appear above the level of the King's head, and this must not be touched except under careful precaution (Sir J. G. Frazer, *The Golden Bough*, 3rd ed.; *Taboo and the Perils of the Soul*, 252 ff.).

[2] Turpin (Pinkerton, ix. 590) describes the cremation of a favourite parrot of the King.

[3] See the account by de la Loubère, 123 f.; Young, *Kingdom of the Yellow Robe*, 239 ff.

[4] According to Turpin (Pinkerton, ix. 590) the honour of cremation is denied to executed criminals, women dying in childbed, and all who have perished by a violent death. Young (*op. cit.*, 245) describes a poor man's funeral, while the corpses of paupers and criminals are exposed to be devoured by vultures at one of the Bangkok temples, see Hastings, *Ency. Religion and Ethics*, xi. 487.

[5] This is the ordinary term to denote the priests of Buddha in Siam. Its origin is obscure (Yule, *Hobson-Jobson*, 105).

both by the court and by the people. The King himself regards some of them with such awe as to humiliate himself in their presence. The extraordinary respect which everyone shows them has sometimes inspired in them so much pride, that they have ventured to attempt to occupy the throne, But when the King discovers anything of the kind he takes their lives, as was the case some time ago in a rebellion, the author of which was a Bonze, whom the King executed.

These Bonzes are clad in yellow, and wear on their loins a small red cloth as a waistband. They make an outward show of great modesty, and they never appear to manifest the smallest degree of passion. At four o'clock in the morning they rise at the sound of bells to say their prayers, and they do the same towards evening. There are certain days of the year when they withdraw from the conversation of men to live in retreat.[1] Some live on charity, and others have well-endowed dwellings. As long as they wear the garb of Bonzes they cannot possess wives, and they must relinquish it if they desire to marry. They are for the most part very ignorant, and know not what they believe. It appears, however, that like the idolaters of India they believe in the transmigration of the soul into many bodies. They are forbidden to take the lives of animals; nevertheless, they make no scruple about eating animals which others have slain, or which have died naturally.[2] The god whom they worship

[1] This is the retreat practised by monks in the rainy season (vassavāsa, vassa, Sanskrit vārsika) when the country is swamped, and the roads are impassable (H. Kern, *Manual of Indian Buddhism*, 80).

[2] Ball quotes a story, which may be a libel, of Burmese chasing fowls till they died of exhaustion, by which kind of 'killing no murder' they believed they had not done wrong, though they ate the fowls. The Burmese are always glad to dispose of any animal a sportsman may shoot, and will even eat snakes if he kills them. The King of Burma (Ava), it is said, used to keep sheep, one of which would conveniently die whenever meat was required at the palace. (See H. Gouger, *The Prisoner in Burmah*, 1860, p. 52.) Buddha did not forbid the use of meat, and he is said to have died after a meal on wild boar's flesh which, as a Rājput, he was permitted to eat; but Rhys Davids (*Buddhism*, 80) thinks that it means mushrooms. A saying of his is quoted: 'Those who take life are in fault, but not the persons who eat the flesh: my priests have permission to eat whatever food it is customary to eat in any place or country' (Hardy, *Manual of Buddhism*, 327). Modern

is a phantom, of whom they speak blindly, and they are so obstinate in maintaining their gross errors that it is difficult to confute them. They say that the God of the Christians and theirs are brothers, but that theirs is the elder. If any-one asks them where their god is they reply that he has disappeared, and that they know not where he is.

The standing army of the kingdom consists mainly of infantry, which is fairly good. The soldiers are inured to fatigue, and have for their sole garment a piece of calico to cover their waists. All the remainder of the body—the chest, back, arms, and thighs—is uncovered, and the skin, which is all tattooed,[1] as when one applies cupping-glasses, represents many kinds of flowers and animals. After the skin is cut and the blood has flowed from it, these figures of flowers and animals are rubbed in with whatever colours they wish; and seeing these soldiers from a distance you would say that they were clad with some flowered silken stuff or painted calico, for the colours once applied never fade. They have for arms bow and arrow, musket and pike, and an azagaye,[2] which is a stick of 5 or 6 feet long, tipped with iron at the end, which can be hurled with skill against an enemy.

In the year 1665 there was in the town of Siam a Neapolitan Jesuit called Father Thomas.[3] He fortified the town and the King's palace, which is on the margin of the river, and he had previously erected good bastions on both sides. On account of this the King allowed him to dwell in the town, where he had a small church with a house where M. Lambert, Bishop of Beyrout, went to lodge on arriving in Siam. But these two did not long remain on good terms, and the Bishop found it advisable to have a separate chapel.

The port where vessels arrive from Cochin-China and other

Burmese occasionally, but not often, eat meat (Sir J. G. Scott, *Burma*, 1906, p. 90).

[1] As is well known, tattooing is a fine art in Siam (de la Loubère, 276): and in Burma, Sir J. G. Scott, *op. cit.*, 77 f.

[2] Assegai (vol. ii, 127).

[3] De la Loubère (p. 91) tells how a few years before his time the King employed a priest of the Mission of St. Lazarus at Paris, named Brother René Charbonneau, to make a wooden fort on the Pegu frontier.

places is only half a league from the town, and as there are always some Christian sailors there, the Bishop built a small house and a chapel there in order to perform mass.[1]

CHAPTER XIX

Concerning the Kingdom of Macassar and the Dutch Embassy to China

THE Kingdom of Macassar, otherwise called the Island of Celebes,[2] commences at the 5th degree of south latitude. The heat is excessive during the day, but the nights are fairly temperate, and the land is beautiful and very fertile; but the people of this island do not know how to build well. The capital town bears the same name as the kingdom, and is situated close to the sea. The port is free; and the vessels which carry thither a quantity of merchandise from the neighbouring islands do not pay any custom dues. The inhabitants poison their weapons, and the most dangerous poison which they use is made of the juice of certain trees which grow in the island of Borneo; they temper it according to the effect, whether slow or quick, which they wish the poison to produce.[3] It is said that the King alone knows the secret of weakening its effect, and he boasts of having some of it so quick that there is no remedy in the world capable

[1] On the whole, this must be allowed to be an excellent account of Siam. Very probably Tavernier obtained his information from the bishops and Jesuit priests. The reader is referred to Crawfurd's *Dictionary of the Indian Islands* for a valuable epitome of information on this subject, and to other authorities referred to on p. 224 above. Full bibliographies will be found in *Ency. Brit.*, 11th ed., xxv. 8 f.; Hastings, *Ency. Religion and Ethics*, xi. 488. Finlayson's *Account of the Mission to Siam*, p. 379, London, 1826, contains an interesting account referring to a period when Siam had scarcely been affected by European nations. On Siam as it now is, there are numerous authorities.

[2] The Island of Celebes extends from Lat. 1° 45′ north to 5° 45′ south (*Ency. Brit.*, v. 596 ff.). For Macassar, *ibid.*, xvii. 193.

[3] The reference is perhaps to the upas poison, for which see Yule, *Hobson-Jobson*, 952 ff.; *Journal Royal Anthropological Institute*, xxxii. 239 ff.; Skeat & Blagden, *Pagan Races of the Malay Peninsula*, i. 263, ii. 315.

of neutralizing it. One of my brothers,[1] whom I had taken to India, and who died there, one day witnessed a remarkable proof of the quickness with which this poison takes effect. An Englishman in a rage killed one of the subjects of the King of Macassar, and the Prince forgave him, but all the Franks, English as well as Dutch and Portuguese, who were in Macassar, feared that if this murder was left unpunished the islanders would take their revenge by attacking some of them, and besought the King to execute the Englishman, and they urged him so strongly that at length he consented. My brother was much beloved by the King, who invited him to take part in all his amusements, and especially at drinking parties. When the Englishman was condemned to death, the King told my brother that he would not allow the victim to languish long, and at the same time to prove the extraordinary power of his poison, he would wound the criminal himself with one of his arrows. These are small poisoned arrows which are fired with a sumpitan,[2] and the King, in order to show his skill, asked my brother in what part of the body he wished him to strike the criminal. My brother, who was anxious to see if what the King had told him of the rapid effect of his poison were true, asked him to strike him on the great toe of the right foot; this the King did exactly and with wonderful skill. Two surgeons, one English and the other Dutch, were ready to cut the toe well below the wound, but they were unable to accomplish it before the poison, more rapid, had reached the heart, and the Englishman died at the same moment. All the kings and princes of the East similarly cherish with care the strongest poisons, and the King of Achīn one day made a present of fifteen or twenty of these poisoned arrows to M. Croke,[3]

[1] This was his brother Daniel. (See Introduction, vol. i, p. x.)

[2] The word is sarbatane in the original; it means a blow-tube, or rather the object blown through. Owing to the virulence of the poison on the darts it is a terrible instrument of offence. Though frequently mentioned by writers, there is no stronger testimony of its power than that given by our author. As an alleged antidote stercus humanum, diluted with water, is mentioned by Friar Odoric (see Yule, *Cathay*, 91; *Hobson-Jobson*, 795, 868).

[3] Later on Tavernier calls him M. Croc (vol. ii, 249).

Envoy-General of Batavia, who was subsequently Chief of the factory at Surat. He had not thought of trying them for some years after they came into his possession, and one day when I was with him we shot many squirrels which fell dead immediately on being struck.

The King of Macassar is a Musalmān, and he allows none of his subjects to become Christians. The Jesuit fathers in the year 1656 found means to build a fairly good church at Macassar, but in the following year the King ordered it to be thrown down, as also that of the Dominican fathers, who said mass for the Portuguese traders in the kingdom. The parochial church, which was conducted by some secular priests, remained standing until the Dutch attacked Macassar with a powerful fleet, and by force of arms they compelled the King to drive all the Portuguese out of his territories.[1] The bad conduct of the Prince was partly the cause of this war, to which the Dutch were also driven by the resentment they felt in consequence of the Portuguese Jesuits having opposed their embassy to China. Besides which they had committed serious outrages against the Dutch at Macassar, having even flung on the ground the hat of one of the envoys who had come to conclude a treaty with the King. Thus the Dutch, unable to avoid resenting this affront, resolved to unite their forces with the Bugis,[2] who were in rebellion against their King, and to avenge, at whatever cost, so gross an insult. On the other hand, as I have said, the Dutch had been much ill-used by the Portuguese Jesuits, who by their intrigues prevented the Deputy whom the former sent to the Emperor of China from accomplishing what he desired, and it happened in this way:

Towards the end of the year 1658 the General of Batavia and his Council sent one of the chiefs of the Dutch Company to the Emperor of China. On his arrival at the Court with splendid presents, he sought to obtain access to the Mandarins, who are the great nobles of the kingdom, so that by their

[1] In 1660 (Crawfurd, *Dict.*, 91).

[2] Bouquins in the original. The Bugis are so called by the Malays, their proper name is Wugi. They are the dominant race in Celebes (Crawfurd, *Dict.*, 74; *Ency. Brit.*, iv, 759 f.).

credit he might obtain permission to trade in China. But the Jesuits, who knew the language and were acquainted with the nobles of the Court, in consequence of the long sojourn they had made in the country, in order to prevent the Dutch Company from gaining a footing, to the prejudice of the Portuguese nation, represented many things to the Emperor's Council to the disadvantage of the Dutch. They told them that in Ceylon they had broken the promise they had given to the King of that island to make over to him the places which they jointly captured from the Portuguese; that they were not people of good faith; and that they had likewise fooled the King of Achīn after the capture of Malacca, and many other Princes in the Molucca islands; that after having taken, by terms of capitulation, the country of some of them together with their persons, promising to maintain them all their lives according to their dignity, they had not treated them with any further consideration once they got them into their power, but had transported them as slaves to the Island of Maurice[1] to cut ebony wood. All these things and many others of the same kind having been represented to the Emperor's Council, the Dutch deputy was immediately dismissed, and left China without having accomplished anything. He learnt from a letter which a spy wrote to him after his departure, the bad turn which the Portuguese Jesuits had played him, and on his return to Batavia he reported it to the General and his Council, who were much annoyed, and resolved to take ample vengeance. According to the accounts which the Deputy handed in, the cost of the voyage amounted to 50,000 écus;[2] and the Council reflected how they could recover double that amount from the Portuguese. They were aware of the trade which the Jesuit fathers conducted annually in the island of Macao and the Kingdom of Macassar, and that they fitted out on their own account as many as six or seven vessels laden with all kinds of Indian as well as Chinese goods. The Dutch calculated the time when these vessels should arrive at Macassar, and on the 7th of June 1660 there appeared at that port two of the Company's vessels, which came in advance to facilitate the withdrawal

[1] Mauritius.

[2] £11,250.

of the Dutch who were on land. The Dutch fleet was composed of more than thirty sail, and anchored at the island of Tanakeke,[1] at 7 leagues from Butagne.[2]

The King felt compelled to defend himself against these enemies whose power he feared, and with the vessels of Macao, which were in the roads, attempted for some time to resist the Dutch attack. The combat was obstinate on both sides, the Dutch divided their fleet, and while thirteen vessels devoted themselves to the Portuguese, the remainder incessantly battered the fortress, which was carried without much resistance. It is said that on this day the Dutch fired more than 7,000 cannon shots, and that the King was so much terrified that he ordered the Portuguese not to fire any more, so as not to irritate the enemy further. The Prince Patinsaloa died during this engagement, and this was a great loss to the King of Macassar, who had become formidable to his neighbours by the diplomacy of this minister, upon whom he entirely relied. As the vessels of Macao found themselves surprised and unprepared for defence, it was not difficult for the Dutch fleet to destroy the Portuguese; they burnt three of their vessels, sent two to the bottom, and took from them a quantity of costly goods; thus it was that the Dutch reimbursed themselves profitably for the cost of the deputation to China.

On the 13th of June the King of Macassar, named Sumbaco, through fear of seeing himself reduced to the last extremity, ordered a white flag to be hoisted on another fortress, whence, surrounded by his wives, he watched the fight. During the truce which they granted him, he sent one of the highest of the nobles of his court to the General of the Dutch fleet to ask for peace, which was granted to him only on condition that he would send an ambassador to Batavia, that he would expel the Portuguese from the island, and that his subjects should no longer trade with them.

As the articles of the treaty were to be ratified at Batavia

[1] Tanahkeke, or the 'Island of Sorcerers', in S. Lat. 5° 30′ towards the extreme end of the south-western peninsula of Celebes (Crawfurd, *Dict.*, 426).

[2] Bontaing, Bonthein, Bonti (*ibid.*, 57) on S. coast of Celebes.

by the General and his Council, the King of Macassar equipped his galleys and sent there eleven of the grandest nobles of his court with a following of 700 men, and the chief of this embassy was the brother of the late Prince Patinsaloa. They were instructed to present to the General of Batavia 200 loaves (*pains*) [1] of gold to redeem the royal fortress, and had orders to submit to all the conditions which the Dutch proposed to them, provided that they did not affect the law of Muhammad. The General received this embassy, which was a great honour for him, and profiting by the opportunity, and the good fortune of his arms, he himself prepared the terms of the capitulation, which were signed by the ambassadors of Macassar and were strictly observed. For immediately all the Portuguese left the country, some passing to the Kingdoms of Siam and Cambodia,[2] and the remainder withdrawing to Macao and Goa. Macao, which was some years ago regarded as one of the most famous and richest towns of the East, was the principal object of the Dutch embassy to China, and as it was the best port which the Portuguese then had in these regions, the design of the Dutch was to ruin it completely. To-day this town, which is at the 22° of north latitude, in a small peninsula of the Province of Canton,[3] which is a part of China, has lost much of its former renown.

The Jesuit fathers and the Portuguese merchants were not recompensed by it for the disgrace which they had experienced at Macassar, and they sustained still another blow close to Goa. The Chief of the Dutch factory at Vengurla, which is only 8 leagues from that town, heard of the ill-success of Dutch affairs in China, and thought of a means to avenge it. On his part he was not ignorant of the fact that the Jesuit fathers of Goa and other places in India did a large trade in rough diamonds which they sent to Europe, whither they carried them when returning to Portugal. And in order to conceal this trade they used to send one or two of their number

[1] 'Loaves' of gold. (See Appendix, vol. i. 331. 200 = £9,000.)

[2] Camboye in the original.

[3] Xanton in the original. Macao is near the mouth of the Canton river and belongs to the Portuguese. The local, not the foreign, trade of Macao is still very considerable, but largely in the nature of smuggling (*Ency. Brit.*, xvii. 191).

in the garb of Fakīrs or Indian pilgrims; this was easy for them to do, because there are among them fathers born in the country, who know the Indian language perfectly. The garb of Fakīrs consists of the skin of a tiger, worn on the back, and one of a goat which covers the waist and hangs down to the knees. For cap they have the skin of a lamb or a kid, the four feet of which hang on the forehead, and neck, while their ears are pierced, and in them are inserted large rings of crystal. Their legs are naked, and they have large wooden sandals on the feet, and carry a bundle of peacocks' feathers to fan themselves with, and drive away the flies. One day as I was dining in company with MM. L'Escot and Raisin,[1] at the house of the Augustin fathers who reside at the Court of the King of Golkonda, one of these Jesuit fathers who had come from Goa entered the chamber clothed in the manner I have described. He told us that he was going to St. Thomé on the business of the Viceroy of Goa; upon which I remarked that to travel through India it was not necessary to disguise himself, and that other religious persons, to whatever order they belonged, did not disguise themselves in that manner.

The chief of the Vengurla factory then seized his opportunity to revenge himself on the Jesuit fathers, and having learnt that two of them were going to the mines to buy 400,000 pardos [2] worth of diamonds, he gave orders to two men who purchased some for him, that as soon as the fathers had completed their purchase they should give notice of it to the master of the customs at Bicholim.[3] Bicholim is a large town on the frontier, which separates the territories of the King of Bījāpur from those of the Portuguese, and there is no other road but by this place, because one cannot elsewhere pass the river which forms the island of Salsette where the town of Goa is built. The Jesuit fathers, believing that the officer of customs knew nothing of the purchase which they had made, embarked in the boat to cross the water, and they

[1] Manucci (ii. 344) tells how M. Raisin presented an emerald to Shāhjahān; for L'Escot, see p. 356 below.

[2] This, with the pardao at 2*s*., would represent a sum of £40,000.

[3] Bicholi in the original, Bicholly in vol. i, p. 146, is now known as Bicholim, and the District bearing the name is included judicially in Bardez in the 'old conquests' (Fonseca, *Goa*, 1).

had no sooner done so, than they were searched, and all the diamonds found on them were confiscated.

I return to the King of Macassar, whom the reverend Jesuit fathers strove to convert, and would possibly have accomplished their design, were it not for a condition which he imposed upon them, which they neglected to fulfil. For at the same time that the Jesuits laboured to attract him to Christianity, the Musalmāns on their part made equal efforts to induce him to embrace their Law; and the Prince, who wished to relinquish idolatry, not knowing which side he should take, told the Musalmāns to summon two or three of their most learned Mullās from Mecca, and the Jesuits to send him an equal number of their ablest men, that he might hear them and instruct himself thoroughly in the two religions; both promised to do so. But the Musalmāns made more haste than the Christians, and eight months afterwards, when they brought two learned Mullās from Mecca, the King, as the Jesuits sent no one, embraced the Law of Muhammad.[1] It is true that three years afterwards two Portuguese Jesuits arrived at Macassar, but it was too late, as the King was then no longer inclined to become a Christian.

The King of Macassar having been made a Musalmān, the Prince, his brother, was so annoyed that he was unable to restrain himself from giving signs of his feeling by a deed which resulted in his disgrace. As he knew that the Musalmāns had a horror of pork, which is one of the common articles of food of the idolaters of Macassar, as soon as the mosque which the King built was finished, he entered it one night, caused ten or twelve pigs to be slaughtered in his presence, and the blood to be sprinkled in all directions, both the walls and the niche[2] where the Mullā places himself to offer up prayers being soiled with it. The King, by the Law of the

[1] This, according to Crawfurd (*Dictionary*, 91), took place in the year 1603; but the people generally did not follow his example till 1616, or a century after the Portuguese had been in occupation of Malacca and the Moluccas.

[2] The Mihrāb, which marks the direction of Mecca. See a drawing of the fine Mihrāb in the Jāmi' or Çathedral Mosque at Fatehpur-Sīkrī (Smith. *Hist. of Fine Art in India and Ceylon*, 429).

religion which he had embraced, was obliged to demolish the mosque and build a new one; the Prince, his brother, withdrew with some other idolatrous nobles, and has never again appeared at Court since that time.

This is all that I have been able to collect of the most singular facts regarding the Kingdoms of the East included in the territories of the Great Mogul and the Empire of China, of which I also have good memoirs; but as I know that several persons have written fully regarding them, I think the reader would prefer that I should give him the result of my own travels and that I should amuse him only with accounts of what I have witnessed with my own eyes.

CHAPTER XX

The Author pursues his journey in the East and embarks at Vengurla for Batavia; the danger which he runs on the sea, and his arrival in the Island of Ceylon.

I LEFT Vengurla, a large town of the Kingdom of Bījāpur, 8 leagues from Goa, on the 14th of April 1648, and embarked on a Dutch vessel which had just brought silks from Persia and was going to Batavia. It had orders to stop at Bakanor [1] *en route*, in order to take in rice, and we arrived there on the 18th of the same month. I landed with the captain, who went to see the King to ask his permission to take the rice; this he gave willingly. It was necessary for us to ascend by the river nearly 3 leagues, and we found the King close to the water, where there were only ten or twelve huts made of palm leaves. He sat in his own hut on a Persian carpet spread beneath him, and there were five or six women, some of whom fanned him with fans made of peacocks' tails, while the others gave him betel and filled his pipe with tobacco. The most important persons of the country were in the other huts, and we counted about 200 men, the majority armed

[1] Bārkūr, an old port on an estuary on the west coast of India, Lat. 13° 28½′. According to the *Imperial Gazetteer* (vii. 22) it was 'the capital of the Jain Kings of Tulava . . . and subsequently a stronghold of the Vijayanagar Rājās. It is often mentioned by the older travellers' (see Yule, *Hobson-Jobson*, 45).

with bows and arrows. They also had with them two elephants. It appeared as if they had some retreat elsewhere, and that they had come to this place merely to enjoy the coolness afforded by the trees and streams. When we left the King and re-embarked on our boat, he sent us, as a present, a dozen fowls and five or six pots of palm wine. We slept the same evening, after a march of a league, in a hamlet where there were but three or four houses, but we had taken with us ample provisions from our vessel. In the morning when we were ready to leave we saw on the river one of our pilots with three or four young men, who came up to us and brought breakfast. When they were landed and we had begun to eat they asked for some tārī[1] or palm wine, and the owner of the hut where we had slept offered to bring us some, which was very good, but he told us that it was strong, and that it might send fumes to the head. Our sailors jeered at that because they drank it often, and sometimes to excess without being inconvenienced. But when you drink it as soon as it is drawn from the tree, and do not allow it to ferment, it is harmless, but if you take too much you feel it ferment in the stomach. The peasant brought us a pot of his palm wine, and each of us drank of it as he felt inclined, one three glasses, another four or five, but I was contented with only one, which contained nearly half a pint. But to tell the truth, we all suffered such severe headaches from it that for two days we were unable to cure ourselves. We asked the natives of the country why this wine had thus troubled us, and they said that it was due to the fact that pepper was planted around the palms, and that it was this which gave so much strength to the wine. We were still somewhat giddy from it when we returned on board, where a governor of the country immediately met us, settled the price of the rice, and asked how much was required. It had to be brought from some distance; this troubled us much, because the wind began to change, and the captain was unwilling to leave, as he had not laden all the cargo he required.

During the night, between the 28th and 29th, the wind began to change, and the pilots told the captain, who had

[1] See vol. i. 128.

never before sailed along the coasts of India, that he ought to hoist the anchor and set sail, although we had not received our full cargo ; but the captain would not consent, replying that we wanted water. The wind having been strong throughout the night, on the following day it calmed a little, and the loading up of the rice was continued. On the day after we strongly urged the captain to leave, and as he saw that we all murmured he sent two boats to get water. But they had scarcely reached the mouth of the river when the wind became so furious that the sailors hastened to return without water ; this they accomplished with much trouble and danger of being lost. When they came on board the two boats were tied astern of the vessel, according to custom, and fourteen men were put in the larger one to watch her and prevent the waves dashing her against the vessel. We wished then to start hoisting the anchor, but the wind became still stronger and more adverse ; of thirty or forty men who were about the winch more than twelve were injured by the bars, the violence of the wind driving them backwards. The captain, wishing also to assist in the work of easing the cable, had his hand badly crushed. At length the sea became so rough that instead of hoisting the anchor it became necessary to put others out, as the wind was driving us on shore. Every one then began to examine his conscience, and prayed thrice in a space of two hours. By midnight we had lost all our anchors, to the number of seven, so that as we had no more and knew not what to do, our pilots called out that every one should try to save himself as soon as the vessel touched the land, and being exhausted they lay down on their beds. A long time before, the captain had gone to rest on account of the great pain in his hand, which was in a dreadful condition. As the moon was shining, I leant against the bulwarks of the vessel watching how the billows urged it towards the shore. While I was in this position the vessel touched land, and everyone believed that she would go to pieces. At this moment two sailors told me that I need fear nothing, and that they would take precautions to ensure our safety, but if God permitted us by His grace to reach the land I must reward them for their trouble. I exhorted them to do their best to save us, and told them there would be 500 écus ready for them as soon as we reached the land. They were two Hamburghers, who had seen me previously at Bandar-'Abbās and Surat, and they well knew that I had all my goods on my person, and needed no camels or mules to carry them. As soon as I promised them this sum they took a spar of wood as thick as a man's thigh and 8 or 10 feet long, and attached to it thick ropes in five or six places, to each of which they allowed a length of only 3 or 4 feet. As they worked at it I kept my eyes constantly fixed in the direction of the land, and I observed that the vessel did not go straight as it had done previously. I feared that it was only the darkness which made me think so, for the moon began to set. I hastened at once to the compass to assure myself, and I saw as a matter of fact that the wind had altogether changed and came from the land. Immediately I cried out to the sailors that the wind had become favourable, and at the same moment the boatswain, who directs the vessel, made a great noise and called all the sailors. He also hailed the fourteen men who were in the large boat, supposing that they were there still; but no one replied, and we saw at daybreak that the cable had parted, and we were never able to ascertain what had become of them. As for the captain, he was unable to rise on account of a severe attack of fever which the pain in his hand had caused. At first everyone took courage, although they were in difficulty how they should steer the vessel, the top of the rudder being broken. To remedy this evil the pilot set a small sail, which was set first on one side and then on the other as he directed, and a rope was tied to the rudder to make it work, for it was only the socket above which was broken, and consequently they could not fix the tiller which comes on board for the steersman. At length the wind blew from the north-east, and the darker the night became, on account of the setting of the moon, the more the wind freshened, and each one gave thanks to God. We were nevertheless not beyond all danger, because it was necessary to pass three great rocks which projected above the water, but the night was so dark we were unable to see them. When ships come to this port where we had taken the rice, they do not generally pass inside these rocks; but our captain, as he had but little time to spare for loading, brought his vessel as close as possible to the mouth of the river for the convenience of those who carried the rice, who were in consequence able to make more frequent trips. At length by God's grace we were, at daybreak, some 3 or 4 leagues from the land. Then we held a consultation in order to settle what direction we should take, because we had no anchors left. Some advised that we should return to Goa to winter [1] there, others that we should go to Pointe de Galle, the first town which the Dutch took from the Portuguese in the Island of Ceylon, for we were about equidistant from both, and the wind was equally favourable for both places. My opinion was that we should not sail for Goa, but for Pointe de Galle; because it was to be feared that at Goa the sailors, who are much addicted to drink, would say or commit some folly which would give an occasion to the Inquisition for arresting them, joined to which there are in that town many facilities for dissipation, so that when time came to put to sea again, the captain would not find, it may be, a single man on board. But in going to Point de Galle there would be no danger, we would meet friends, and we should be able to change to another vessel in order to continue the voyage; this in fact happened. However, we were always in terror lest some tempest might come and throw us on land, as not a single anchor was left to moor the vessel.

Among our sailors there was, by chance, one who had served for many years in this vessel, who assured us that there was a very heavy anchor at the bottom of the hold, but that it had only one arm. Although we desired to get it, we foresaw great difficulty on account of the quantity of goods in the vessel. Nevertheless it was resolved to move the whole cargo, and four or five very skilful carpenters, who had worked at the house at Gombroon for the Company, and were returning to Batavia, said that if they could only get up the anchor they would fix it so as to work as well as if it had two arms. This they did, and in two days both

[1] That is, to remain during the monsoon (Yule, *Hobson-Jobson*, 970 f.).

the anchor and the rudder were in a condition to serve us. To incite the men to work it cost three or four cases of Shīrāz wine, which was distributed to all those who assisted in removing the goods and getting out the anchor.

Eight days afterwards we found that we were off Pointe de Galle, and we took in some of our sails in order to gain the port, one of the worst in all India, on account of the rocks, which are at a level with the water in many places.[1] For this reason as soon as a vessel is sighted at sea the Governor-General sends two pilots to direct and bring her into port. But as both weather and sea were sufficiently favourable, the captain and pilots, who had never been there before, not realizing that we had passed the reefs, which they thought were nearer land, and seeing that no pilot came to bring the vessel into port, put out to sea again ; this caused much surprise to the Governor and the pilots, who did not come out because they saw that we had passed the danger. The wind then beginning to change, drove us 9 or 10 leagues out to sea, and consequently we were two or three days beating about before we could regain the port. If the wind had driven us a little farther to sea we should have been obliged to go to winter at Masulipatam, in the Gulf of Bengal. At length the pilots of Pointe de Galle came out for us, and we entered the port and landed on the 12th of May. I immediately went to visit the Governor Madsuere,[2] who is at present General at Batavia, and he did me the honour to invite me to dine with him during my sojourn there.

I did not find anything remarkable in this town, and scarcely anything remains but the ruins, and mines, and the marks which the cannons made when the Dutch besieged it and drove away the Portuguese.[3] The Company gave land and sites for building to those who wished to dwell there, and had already erected two good bastions, which command the port. If it had accomplished the design which it then formed, it would have made this town a fine place.

[1] 'In addition to being incommodious and small, [it] is obstructed by coral rocks, reefs of which have been upreared to the surface, and render the entrance critical to strange ships' (Tennent, *Ceylon*, i. 52)

[2] In the edition of 1713 he is called Masudere. [Joan Maatsuiker, Governor 1646–50].

[3] In 1640. See Tennent ii. 42 ff.

The Dutch, before they had captured all the settlements which the Portuguese had in the Island of Ceylon, whence they have been entirely driven, persuaded themselves that the trade of the island would yield them enormous sums if they were sole masters of it. This might have happened if they had kept to the agreement they had made with the King of Kandy, who is the King of the country, when they began to make war with the Portuguese. But they broke faith with him, and that gave them a very bad character in these parts.

The treaty with the King of Kandy provided that this King was always to be in charge of the passes, with 18,000 or 20,000 men, to prevent the reinforcements which might come from Colombo, Negombe,[1] Manār, and many other places which the Portuguese held along the coast. And the Dutch were to bring in their large vessels sufficient troops to besiege Pointe de Galle both by sea and land. They agreed, also, with the King of Achīn that he should hold the coast with a sufficient number of small armed frigates, of which he always maintained several.

When the Dutch captured the town, they began to repair some breaches, on which the King of Kandy sent to know when he might come there to receive possession. For it had been agreed in the event of the Dutch taking the town that they would give it back to the King, who by way of recompense was to provide them with a certain quantity of cinnamon every year, and, in case of necessity, to aid them as far as he was able. The Dutch replied that they were willing to hand over the town to him provided he paid them the costs of the war, which they said amounted to many millions; but if he had possessed three kingdoms like his own he could not have paid half the sum. In truth money is scarce in that country, and I do not believe that the King has ever seen a sum equal to 50,000 écus[2] at one time. His whole trade consisted in cinnamon and elephants; but since the Portuguese have been in India he has derived no profit from either. As for the elephants, that is a small matter, for only five or six are captured in a year; but at the same time those

[1] Negombo. [2] £11,250.

of Ceylon are more highly esteemed than the elephants of other countries, because they are more courageous in war; and there is not a King in India who does not desire to have one. I may here state a fact which some may find it difficult to believe, but it is nevertheless quite true; it is that when any king or noble possesses one of these Ceylon elephants, and others are brought into its presence from the places where the merchants obtain them, such as Achīn, Siam, Arakan, Pegu, the Kingdom of Bhutān, the Kingdom of Assam, the territories of Cochin and the coast of Melinde,[1] as soon as these latter elephants see one of Ceylon, by a natural instinct they pay it reverence by placing the ends of their trunks on the ground, and then raising them.[2] It is true that the elephants which the great nobles keep, when brought before them to be examined whether they are in good condition, make a sort of salute thrice with their trunk. This I have often seen; but they are trained to it, and their masters teach them to do it when young.

The King of Achīn, with whom the Dutch failed to keep their promise, had other means for revenging himself than by the aid of the King of Kandy, because the Dutch were not allowed to ship the pepper which comes from his territories; for a long time he refused them permission, and even

[1] This reference to Malinda would seem to imply that the African elephant was domesticated in Tavernier's time (see vol. i. 221): but this is doubtful.

[2] Sir Emerson Tennent, alluding to the common belief that Tavernier had made a statement to this effect, adds that 'a reference to the original shows that Tavernier's observations are not only fanciful in themselves but are restricted to the supposed excellence of the Ceylon animal in war'. This statement is simply incomprehensible, since Tavernier's original passage, which is here translated, is quoted in full in a footnote on the same page (*Ceylon*, ii. 380). Fryer (i. 73) also says that the Ceylon elephants exact homage from all others, which prostrate themselves submissively before them. In reference to the fact that the elephants of Sumatra have points of affinity with the Ceylon variety, it has been suggested that the original stock of the Sumatra elephants was introduced in a domesticated condition from Ceylon. It is on record that some elephants sent as a present to the Sultān of Sulu (or Soolo) by the East India Company, as he was unable to maintain them, were let loose on Cape Unsang in Borneo. (Hornaday, *Two Years in the Jungle*, 220.)

declared war upon them; and without this pepper their trade could not prosper.

This is the kind of pepper which we call 'small', and all Orientals prefer it, because without skinning or crushing they place it whole on their plates of rice, as I have elsewhere said.[1] At length the Dutch were compelled to agree with the King of Achīn, and ambassadors were sent by both sides for this purpose. The envoy who arrived on behalf of the King at Batavia, was treated with much magnificence. When he was about to depart the General and all his Council entertained him splendidly, and the ladies sat at table; this greatly surprised this Musalmān ambassador, who was not accustomed to see women drink and eat with men. But that which astonished him still more was that at the end of the repast, after drinking many healths, they drank that of the Queen of Achīn, who ruled the state during the minority of the King, her son.[2] And in order to honour him still more, the General desired Madame la Générale to kiss the ambassador. The King and Queen of Achīn did not receive the ambassador sent to them from Batavia with less honour. He was M. Croc, who for fifteen years suffered from a languishing sickness; and it was believed that someone had administered to him some kind of slow poison. On the occasion of his third audience with the King, who knew that he had lived for so long a time in languor and without appetite, he asked him if he had ever kept any girl of the country, and how he had left her, if by mutual agreement or whether he had sent her away by force. He admitted that he had left one in order to get married in his own country, and that since that time he had always been languishing and indisposed, upon which the King said to three of his physicians, who were by his side, that having heard the cause of the ambassador's sickness he would give them fifteen days to cure him, and that if they did not

[1] See vol. ii. 11.

[2] 'There were Kings of Achin from 1521 till 1641, when the tyrant King died, and a Queen apparently assumed office, first as regent, and afterwards as absolute monarch. Her reign was not extraordinarily long, only 28 years, but the idea that female rule in Achin had prevailed for many years soon became common belief' (Temple's note, Bowrey, 295 f.; Fryer, i. 121; de la Loubère, 82).

accomplish it in that time he would have them all executed. The physicians replied that they would answer to him for the cure of the ambassador, provided he consented to take the remedies which they would give him, and M. Croc resolved to consent. They gave him in the morning a decoction, and in the evening a small pill, and at the end of nine days a great fit of vomiting seized him. It was thought he would die of the strange efforts which he made ; and at length he vomited a bundle of hair as large as a small nut, after which he was at once cured. The King afterwards took him to a rhinoceros hunt, and invited him to give the mortal shot to the animal. As soon as it was killed they cut off the horn, which the King also presented to the ambassador ; [1] and at the conclusion of the hunt there was a great feast. At the end of it the King drank to the health of the General of Batavia and his wife, and ordered one of his own wives to kiss the ambassador. On his departure he presented him with a pebble of the size of a goose's egg, in which large veins of gold were to be seen like the tendons in a man's hand, and it is thus that gold is found in this country.

M. Croc, when at Surat as chief of the factory, broke the pebble in two, and gave half to M. Constant, who, under him, held the highest authority there. When he was returning to Holland, I offered him 150 pistoles for it in order to present it to the late Monseigneur le Duc d'Orléans, but he would not consent to part with it.

CHAPTER XXI

Departure of the Author from the Island of Ceylon, and his arrival at Batavia.

On the 25th of July [2] [1648] we left Pointe de Galle on a different vessel from that by which we had arrived, because when it was examined, it was found that it could not make

[1] The horn of the rhinoceros was, and is still in South Africa and Hindostān, valued as an antidote to poison. See the authorities quoted in Fryer, ii. 298.

[2] The July of the original and the June of the edition of 1713 appear to be both wrong, as the month must have been May.

the journey without danger. Accordingly, all the goods were discharged from it and transhipped to that in which we embarked for Batavia.

On the 2nd of June [1] we crossed the line, and on the 6th reached the island called Nazacos.[2] On the 17th we sighted the coast of Sumatra, on the 18th the island of Ingagne,[3] and on the 19th the island of Fortune. On the 20th we saw several other small islands, and the coast of Java, and among these islands there are three which are called Prince's Islands.[4] On the 21st we saw the island of Bantam, and on the 22nd we anchored in the roads at Batavia. On the following day I landed, and went to salute General Vanderlin and M. Caron,[5] the Director-General, who was the second officer in the council.

On the 25th, two days after my arrival, the General sent one of his guards to invite me to dinner, where there were assembled M. Caron, two other councillors, the Avocat Fiscal, the Major, and their wives. Whilst we were at table they conversed about the news from foreign countries, and principally of the court of the King of Persia, and after dinner some began to play backgammon, while waiting till it became cool enough to take exercise outside the town by the river's bank, where there are very fine bathing places. The General went to his office, where he asked me to accompany him. After some conversation on indifferent matters he asked me for what purpose I had come to Batavia. I told him I had principally come to see so renowned a place; and as I had an opportunity of doing service to the Company at the request of the Chief of the factory at Vengurla, I had been

[1] In the 1713 edition this is given, probably incorrectly, as July. June appears to be correct.

[2] Not identified, but it may be remarked that *nusa* is Javanese for a small island, and like *pulo* is used as a prefix to the true name. (Crawfurd, *Dictionary*, 303.)

[3] Ball suggests that it may be Indragiri, a Malay State on the coast of Sumatra: but there is an island named Engano, about 200 miles SSE. of Nassau Island (A. Hamilton, in Pinkerton, viii. 449).

[4] There is a Prince Island in Sunda Strait, between Java and Sumatra.

[5] M. Caron, a renegade Dutchman, founded the first French factory in India, at Surat, in 1668. (*Imperial Gazetteer*, ii. 463, xii. 104.)

led to undertake the voyage, as he might see for himself by the letter which he had received from there. I told him, at the same time, as the Commander of Vengurla had requested me, of the discovery which had been made by a caravel of Portugal, which a storm had driven into a bay situated 30 leagues from the Cape of Good Hope, as I have related at length in the description of the town of Goa.[1] The Commander thought that the General would be able to send a small vessel there from Batavia, and that by conveying the news I would do a service to the Company; and it was also with this in view that he offered me a passage in the vessel which was in the roads at Vengurla. After I had finished my account of the matter the General thanked me somewhat coldly, as if my news was of small importance, although I have since learnt that he sent to seek for the bay, but the vessel was unable to find it. After about half an hour's interview I left him in his office, when three councillors entered at the same moment, and as I left he said that if I would wait for a little we might go together to promenade outside the town. I then joined Madame la Générale, and the other ladies who were keeping her company, and an hour afterwards two trumpets began to sound. The General and Madame, with four of the wives of the councillors, entered a carriage with six horses, and the councillors rode on horseback. I was allotted a horse with Persian saddle and bridle, the furniture of which was very beautiful. There are always forty or fifty saddle-horses in the stables of the General, for there is not a vessel that does not bring him some, either from Arabia or Persia or other places. A squadron of cavalry marched in front of the General's carriage, each dragoon having a collar of buffalo skin and long scarlet hose with silver lace, a hat with a bundle of plumes, a great scarf with a fringe of silver, the sword-guard and spurs of massive silver, and all the horses had very beautiful trappings. Three bodyguards marched at each door carrying halberds, and well clad. Each had a doublet of yellow satin, and the upper part of the hose of scarlet covered with silver lace, and below with yellow silk,

[1] See vol. i. 173, for accounts of this discovery. The details given there are somewhat different

and very fine linen. Behind the carriage there marched a company of infantry, besides another which went an hour or two in advance to clear the way. When the councillors go abroad, as well as when they are at home, they have each two musketeers for their guard, and when they wish for horses the General's equerry sends them what they require. They have also their small boats to row about on the sea, the river, or on the canals, where each of them has his garden. Our promenade was not long, because when we left the fort two vessels were seen approaching, but no one was able to say what they were. As the General and councillors were impatient to hear the news, they returned to the fort sooner than they had intended; and as soon as we arrived I took leave of the General, the councillors, and the ladies, and withdrew to my lodging.

For three or four days I received numerous visits, which caused me no small expenditure, because custom requires that when any visitor comes you offer him wine. One hundred écus are soon spent; for a pint of wine, of about Paris measure, holds only four glasses. Spanish wine when cheap costs an écu at Batavia, Rhine and French wine cost two, and one must pay 40 sols for a pint of beer, whether English or of Broncevimont.[1]

The people of Batavia are greatly delighted when vessels come from Holland, for they bring all kinds of drinks, which the publicans buy from the Company, and every private person also may buy them. But whether they find more pleasure in drinking at public-houses than in their own houses, or that it is more convenient to them, when they wish to amuse themselves in company, they generally make all their rejoicings in these places. It is a time of great festival when these new drinks arrive, and you meet women and girls in the streets who wager you for a pint or two of wine or beer. Whether one loses or gains, it is a point of honour never to allow the women to pay, and others come also, whose healths you have to drink. This often empties the purses of young people.

[1] These prices in English money were, for Spanish wine, 4*s.* 6*d.*; for Rhine and French wine, 9*s.*; and for a pint of beer, 3*s.* Mr. E. Heawood, Librarian of the Royal Geographical Society, has kindly traced the word 'Broncevimont'. It is Tavernier's way of writing Brunswick Mum, or beer

CHAPTER XXII[1]

Concerning an affair which was raised unseasonably for the Author in the Council at Batavia.

THERE are two Councils in Batavia, the Council of the Fort, at which the General[2] presides, where the affairs of the Company are discussed; and the Council that sits in the Town Hall, and deals with the police and the minor disputes which arise among the citizens. M. Faure, a member of the Town Council, was one of those who came to visit me on my arrival, and during nine or ten days he, with one of his friends, was with me four times. Both of them spoke frequently of M. Constant, who had been Commander at Gombroon, and was for many years the second officer of the factory at Surat, where he had amassed much wealth. He had often trusted me with a part of it, and we had always been good friends. One day, as I was about to leave Surat on my way to the diamond mine, he asked me to purchase diamonds on his account to the extent of 16,000[3] rupees' worth, giving me a letter of credit for that sum on Golkonda, where it was paid me, and I invested it as he desired. I expected on my return to find him at Surat; but during my journey he had received orders to start at once for Batavia, and as soon as he got there he married the widow of General Vandime and went with her to Holland. I was much surprised on my return to Surat to find that he had left without giving orders to any of his friends, Dutch or English, to receive what I had for him, and send it to him by one of the vessels which go to England. I remained at Surat about two months,

[1] This chapter is omitted in the English Translation by John Phillips, but an abstract of its contents is included in ch. xxi.

[2] [Governor-General].

[3] £1,800. (See Index for further references to this traffic carried on by Tavernier on behalf of the Dutch officials.) At a latter period we find English officials engaging in the same trade. (See Colonel Yule's account of the Pitt diamond in Hedges' *Diary*, Hakluyt Society, iii. 91, 161 f.) Thomas Pitt, was Governor of Madras from 1698 to 1709. Another Pitt, Governor from 1730-35, George Morton or Moreton Pitt, appears to have been notable, also, for his private trade in diamonds. (*Kistna Manual*, 106 n.; Wheeler, *Madras in the Olden Time*, 505.)

and as I wished to travel, in order not to risk what M. Constant had entrusted to me I placed the whole in the hands of Sr. Francis Breton,[1] the second officer in the English factory at Surat, who, at M. Constant's request, afterwards forwarded it to him in Holland. I had previously asked the Dutch Commander, named Arnebar, to be good enough to take charge of this parcel, as he was a friend of M. Constant; but he excused himself, telling me that if the General or Council at Batavia came to know that he had such goods in his hands they would treat him as a receiver who had not declared them, in other words, he would be deposed from his office and all his property confiscated.

One day, then, while I was at Batavia, M. Faure, whom I have just mentioned, came to see me with three others, bringing a large bottle of Rheims wine and another of English beer. For my part I had contributed a collation, and as we began to drink they asked me if I had not heard the news of M. Constant which had come by land while I was at Surat; to which I replied that I had not received any intelligence, either by sea or land, since he had left Batavia. They expressed surprise at this reply, and told me that they were much astonished, that having been such great friends, and having done such considerable trade together which still lasted, he had not made me acquainted with his movements. I saw from the first that they were come with no other design than to inquire whether I had with me the parcel of diamonds which I had bought at the mine for M. Constant, or whether I had left it with some Dutchman to send to him. I thought it advisable to remove this doubt from their minds, for unless I did so they would be unable to drink the wine they had brought, with comfort. Without keeping them longer in suspense, therefore, I told them that I was astonished that they had not spoken to me of this matter on the first occasion when they had done me the honour to visit me, and I perceived clearly that they wished to know if the last time I had been at the diamond mine M. Constant had not given me a commission to buy for him; that they need not have brought

[1] Francis Breton, President of Surat 1644–9. See the epitaph on his tomb (Rawlinson, *British Beginnings in Western India*, 136). [Cf. p. 62].

wine for that purpose to make me drink, because I differed from most men, who speak much and say more than they know when they have drunk, but, as for myself, it is then I talk least; nevertheless, since I desired to satisfy them, so that they might not have any regret for their good wine, I would tell them the truth frankly. It is true, then, I told them, that M. Constant not only gave me a commission to buy him a parcel of diamonds, but he also gave me money to pay for them, and I purchased them for 16,000 rupees. I had no sooner finished speaking than M. Faure, turning to the three others, 'Gentlemen,' said he, 'you will bear me witness that M. Tavernier has 16,000 rupees' worth of diamonds for M. Constant, which he left me an order to receive when he departed for Holland.' I replied without disturbing myself, that if he wished for them he would have to run after them, but that I did not believe he would overtake them; that it was more than six months since I had dispatched them by land, and that I was much surprised at his having taken this commission, and wondered how M. Constant and he could have known that I would go to Batavia. I saw that it annoyed him to find that he had not got what he expected, and as they did not wish to drink any more they all four departed.

On the following day, early in the morning, an officer of the Company handed me a summons to appear at 11 o'clock before the Town Council, where the Avocat Fiscal was present to take up the case on behalf of the Company. I did not fail to be present at the Town Hall at the hour named, when, immediately, these gentlemen called me in, and with great compliments asked me if it was true that M. Constant had asked me to make an investment in diamonds to the amount of 16,000 rupees, and also where they were. I said that as regards the purchase of the diamonds it was true that I made it, but that I knew not where they were, because more than six months had elapsed since I forwarded them to him from Surat by land. Upon that the gentlemen of the law delivered sentence that it was not for M. Faure to interfere in the matter, but it was the duty of the Avocat Fiscal to follow it up; that at that time M. Constant was in the Company's

service, and that, without having defrauded it, he could not out of his wages have amassed so large a sum. At this mention of his having defrauded the Company I was unable to prevent myself from laughing ; this astonished them, and the President of the Council asked me why I laughed. I told him that it was seeing his astonishment at the fact that M. Constant had defrauded the Company of 16,000 rupees, and that if he had only carried off so much, it would have been a small matter, adding that there was scarcely a servant of the Company who had held M. Constant's offices, and had enjoyed the opportunity of trading, as he had, without fear of the Fiscal, who had not made at least 100,000 écus.[1] Two or three members of the Council, then present, were uneasy at hearing me talk in this way, as these remarks particularly affected them For to say the truth, the Commanders and their subordinates in the factories know well how to appropriate large sums for their own benefit, to the great detriment of the Company ; and as they cannot do so without having an understanding with the broker, he does the same on his own account, those below him also taking what they can. I made an estimate once of all the money of which the Company is defrauded on the trade in each factory, and I ascertained that as they annually defraud it in all the factories taken together to the extent of 1,500,000 or 1,600,000 livres,[2] they have abundant opportunity for consoling themselves. For to speak but of Persia alone, I have known Commanders who, both by the sale of spices and on the purchase of silks, have laid apart for themselves in one year more than 100,000 piastres.[3] They practice marvellous artifices which it is difficult for the Company, especially the directors and shareholders of the Company, who are in Holland, to discover. For, as regards the Commanders in India, the scandal must become notorious before the General of Batavia and his council have recourse to law, and most frequently the commanders shut the mouth of the Avocat Fiscal, by a present amounting to more than the third part which would be his share if all were confiscated, another third belongs to the
18 Company, and the other to the Hospital. Thus all passes

[1] £22,500. [2] £112,500 to £120,000. [3] £22,500.

in silence, for every one of these Commanders has his patron at Batavia, to whom he sends valuable presents yearly, besides which there is not one of these gentlemen of the Council who has not done the same himself. Moreover, if anyone who is cognizant of a wrong done by a Commander to the Company reports it to the General, he is certain never to be appointed to any factory, and sooner or later an opportunity is found for removing him from the office he holds, and he is sent as a soldier to some island to end his life miserably.

As for the trade which these Commanders do on their own account, there is no one who knows more about it than the poor sailors, who are sometimes very badly treated by the Commanders themselves, or the officers of the vessels who when they go on shore report to the chief of the factory that so and so has so many bales of goods on his private account. Most frequently the chief of the factory, who knows his part, sends to advise the person to whom the goods belong to have them removed, and to arrange to have them carried on shore by night. In order to give him time to discharge all, the informer is so well supplied with drink that he is drunk for a day or two, and when all has been removed the Commander goes to the vessel to make an examination, well assured that he will find nothing. Then the poor sailor or soldier, for the falsehood which they force him to believe he has told, is severely punished, his wages are confiscated, and in most cases he is sent for three or four years to work on the galley dispatched for a cargo of stones. There are, then, some of these Commanders who have defrauded the Company, and have returned to Holland with great booty, 400,000 or 500,000 livres [1] worth of diamonds, pearls, ambergris, and other goods which occupy but small space. For if all is not well concealed, and if the Company is able to discover it, it is lost, and their wages are confiscated. But they have wonderful ways for escaping, even when they have bulky goods, like calicoes and other things which occupy much space, for all cannot go to the places where diamonds are to be purchased, and moreover they more frequently experience

[1] £30,000 to £37,500.

loss than gain by carrying them, while on coarse goods there is always much profit to be made.

As the captain and other officers of the vessel try to do private trade as well as the Commanders, knowing that it will be difficult to take their goods out of the vessels without being discovered, they sometimes discharge them on the coast of Norway, making believe that it is bad weather which has driven them thither. Moreover, when the Dutch are at war with the English, they send vessels of war to meet those coming from India, and into these vessels those who wish to defraud the Company tranship their bales of goods, before arriving at Holland. They also employ, for the same purpose, the fleet of herring fishers when they meet them. In short, there is no kind of artifice of which they do not make use. But when the Company entertains a suspicion that anyone has cheated them, they order the Commanders to undress and put on other clothes, and more than once diamonds have been found in those which were taken off. In conclusion, it has been remarked that the majority of those who have defrauded the Company and have returned to Holland with great wealth have not left their heirs any the richer; all this wealth being, as it were, evaporated in a few years. This proves that wealth ill-acquired does not profit.

Returning to the affair which had been stirred up against me at Batavia. On the order which the members of the Council had given, that the Avocat Fiscal should take the cause in hand on the Company's behalf, three days afterwards he sent me many pages of paper containing written charges, so that I might reply to each. The first demanded that I should declare to what extent M. Constant and I had traded together since we had known one another. The others were mere nonsense, for instance the demand for a reply from me, who was in no wise responsible to the Company, and had only come to Batavia to render it a service; so I had no need to trouble myself about the Fiscal's order. There was a special query that the General and his Council wished to know what M. Constant had done at Bandar 'Abbās, where he had been sent as Commander; that they were aware of the fact that we were together day and night, and that consequently I must be well acquainted with his affairs. They were right in this, but I was not bound to render an account to them. This inquiry lasted fully four or five weeks, during which an officer came to summon me several times to accompany him to the Town Hall to give a reply. I gavé always the same answer, that I knew nothing of M. Constant's affairs, and that when he did anything he did not ask my advice. As they saw they could get nothing from me by politeness, they began to threaten me with arrest. I replied boldly that I did not fear them, and that if they arrested me I had the honour to serve a Prince, the late Monseigneur le Duc d'Orléans, who would get me safely out of their hands, and would resent the affront they had done me. At the same time I left their presence without saying another word, and they also said nothing to me. Fifteen days passed without reference to this affair, and during this time I went to take exercise and even to dine with some of these gentlemen. One day the Avocat Fiscal, who had read much and liked to hear about foreign countries, asked me to supper; when we had left the table he took me apart and told me that he had to summon me on the following day, having received an order from the General, who wished to know, absolutely, what I had seen M. Constant do at Gombroon. 'If it is to say what I have seen,' I replied, 'I shall do so willingly, but I desire to speak in the presence of the judges.' Next morning the officer did not fail to summon me. I followed him forthwith, and when I entered the chamber, the President asked me at first if I would tell them something of what I had seen of M. Constant. I said, 'I would satisfy him, and that I desired to give the account at full length,' with which reply the President and Council told me they were quite content. As they had ordered silence for me, and I saw they awaited with impatience what I had to say to them, I spoke in the following terms :—

'The day M. Constant disembarked at Gombroon the Khān or Governor of the town and country made much of him, and kept him to supper, together with those who had accompanied him. The repast was magnificent, and the dishes were much better prepared than usual; I have been at many feasts of Khāns or Governors of Provinces in Persia, where they know of nothing but ragouts, not even understanding how to roast a fowl properly. But at this repast all was well arranged, and it looked as if a Frank cook had a hand in it. All the baladines of Gombroon were present, to dance in their own manner according to custom, and there was much gaiety. The following day M. Constant entertained several Franks at dinner, and at the close of the repast the Khān sent one of his officers to present his compliments to Commander Constant, and to tell him that he would sup with him ; this he received very well, as he appreciated the honour the Khān wished to do him. Compliments being finished, the Commander took a large glass and drank to the health of the Khān, and all those who were at table did likewise. As soon as the officer had left, the Commander asked some of those who were dining with him, how a governor should be treated when he did the honour to a commander of coming to see him at home ; one told him that the first care he should have would be that as soon as night had come numbers of lamps should be lighted, both outside and in the house. In that country these are little saucers full of oil attached to the walls of the house, and about a foot from each other.[1] But the Commander desiring to do more honour than that to the Khān and to the Company, instead of these lamps ordered white wax candles to be used, so that both within and without the house there was light everywhere. The Khān expressed himself highly pleased with this liberal expenditure, which was done specially to enhance his honour ; and all the merchants, both Christians and Musalmāns, were also surprised. It is true', said I to the members of the Council,' that you know that this wax does not cost so much to the Company as it does to private persons, because all the Dutch vessels which come from Mocha carry much of it, as it is very cheap there.'

'The baladines were present in large numbers at this repast, to amuse the company with their dances and graceful attitudes, for there was money to be earned, as they know that the Commanders pay them well, and that it is not the case with

[1] The Chirāgh, used in the same way in India.

them as with the Khān, who generally considers he has paid liberally when he gives them supper.

'Next day those who were in charge of these baladines (for each troupe had an old woman as guardian and directress, whom the baladines call their mother[1]) came to pay their respects to M. Constant, who showed himself so liberal toward them that no one asked for anything from the guests—this is very contrary to their usual custom. Some of those who had slept there, and had passed all the night in making these women dance, were much surprised, on leaving in the morning, at not being compelled to put their hands in their pockets, and took occasion to extol the generosity of the Commander who had so liberally paid for all. Throughout the night the signals which were on the terrace of the lodge were fired, and at each health a dozen were fired to warn the vessels to make a salute.

'Two hours before sunrise the Khān rose from where he had seated himself on his arrival, and where they had drunk and eaten, and his officers bore him away, observing that the wine began to heat him. As soon as he had left, a part of the company returned to eat and drink and the others to see the baladines dance, and the debauch lasted till ten o'clock in the morning. Everyone, when leaving, remarked to another, "It must be admitted that this new Commander is honourable, and does all things with a good grace."

'When M. Constant,' I continued to these gentlemen of the Council, 'arrived at Gombroon, and had to go to the dwelling of the Khān, the finest horses in the Company's stable were brought to him. That for the Commander had rich brocaded trappings, but as the bridle was only of silver he appeared to be surprised, and asked why there was not a golden bridle on his horse, considering that he was not inferior to the other Commanders who had preceded him at Gombroon. They told him that, by order of the Company, the Commander Vanderlin had sent the two golden bridles from Gombroon to Batavia, the gold of one weighing 600, and of the other 450 ducats, and that it had been ordered

[1] Known in Indian Musalmān cities as Sāqan, feminine of Sāqī, 'a cup-bearer', or Nā'ika, 'conductor'.

that, for the future, no Commander should use one of gold on his horse, but must content himself with one of silver. As I saw that this annoyed M. Constant, I told him privately that it would be easy for him to have a golden bridle on his horse without the Company being able to reproach him. That he had only to send to the Khān the present which he had to make him on behalf of the Company on a little more liberal scale than the other Commanders, his predecessors, had done, and he should see that he would soon have a golden bridle. M. Constant believed me, and made a very handsome present to the Khān.

'These presents consist generally of all kinds of spices, porcelain, Japanese cabinets, Dutch cloths, and other things of that kind. But the best part of the present was a ring of diamonds for which he had paid me 1,500 écus [1]; and 1,000 gold ducats of which the King caused a golden bridle to be made, which he sent as a present to the Commander; it weighed but 643 ducats of gold, and the balance remained in the Khān's purse. It is the custom in Persia, when a stranger makes a present to a great person, that he gives another in return, but certainly when one makes one to a King he never receives in return nearly the value of that which he has given.[2] The Khān was altogether amazed at so magnificent a present, and although, according to custom, he should have sent his gift, which is usually a valuable horse, and sometimes two, on the following day, he waited for five or six days, because it required that time to make the bridle. As soon as it was finished the Khān sent two fine horses to the Commander, one with the bridle of gold, and the other with a bridle of silver, the saddles of the Turkish pattern with brocade of gold and silver. Out of politeness it was necessary that the Commander when mounting his horse, should have the golden bridle put on; and thus the Company was not able to say anything.'

This was the account I gave to the Council of Batavia of what I had seen at Gombroon in reference to M. Constant, and it should be remarked, before going further, that all

[1] £337 : 10*s*.

[2] See under Peshkush in Yule, *Hobson-Jobson*, 701.

the presents which the kings and great nobles make to the commanders and the other principal officers of the Company ought to be handed over, when they go to Batavia, to the charge of the General of the Council as property belonging to the Company, but they are sometimes allowed to retain them.[1]

When I spoke in this way to these gentlemen of the Council of Batavia, and told them ingenuously what M. Constant had done during the first days after his arrival at Gombroon, they wished to know what happened afterwards, and they told me that they had already been sufficiently informed of what I had just told them, but wished that I should let them know what trade M. Constant had done. It was then I began to speak to them in a different way, and told them I was not dependent on them and was not their spy; that if they wished to know so much they should have ascertained it when he was at Batavia, or they might write to him in Holland, and would thus be able to satisfy themselves. The President, who saw that I mocked them, rose from his place to talk with some of the councillors, and then told me that they would give me four days to reflect on my reply to the Council, both in reference to the trade which I had done with M. Constant, and that which I knew he had done with other persons. Upon this I retired, without replying, and went to dine with one of the councillors without speaking further of the matter.

The four days having expired, I waited for them to send for me, but they delayed eight days longer, after which they sent an officer to tell me that the President would expect me at the Council at 11 o'clock. When I entered the chamber, the Avocat Fiscal delivered a long discourse, referring to my refusal to reply to the questions which had been given me in writing, and as for himself he required that I should be placed in gesselin, i. e. under arrest, until I had replied. I replied to that 'that I was not the least astonished at what he said, and that I believed the gentlemen of the Council would think more than once before they carried it into execu-

[1] As presents in India are sent to the Government's Toshakhāna, 'wardrobe' or 'store'.

tion; that if he wished me to reply to what he asked, it was necessary to convey it to me in a language which I understood, and not in Dutch.' He replied to this 'that he had often heard me speak Dutch,' to which I answered 'that in truth I did know something of the language, but not enough to enable me to read and understand chicanery.' As I perceived that he was offended by the use of the word 'chicanery' I said to him again in a firmer tone than before, 'that I was not in receipt of wages from the Company, and that I had not been appointed to observe the conduct and actions of M. Constant.' The Council at length ordered the Fiscal to give me his questions in French; this he did, and fixed the period for replying at eight days. I laughed at all these questions, being well assured that I was able to put an end to the proceedings whenever I pleased. I deferred replying for another eight days beyond the eight which they had given me; but seeing that the Council began to be annoyed, I thought that it was time to put an end to the affair.

As soon as the Fiscal had given me his questions in French, I communicated them to M. Potre, the ablest counsel in Batavia, who told me that, not being employed by the Company, I was not obliged to reply to any of these articles; nevertheless, being desirous of putting an end to the affair, I went to the President's house shortly after sunrise, and he came to receive me in his sleeping garment, 'preferring', he said, 'to come to me in that condition rather than make me wait while he dressed.' The reply which I made to this compliment was 'that since he wished me absolutely to tell him all that I knew of M. Constant, I would conceal nothing that had come to my knowledge, even were it to the disadvantage of the General himself and many members of the Council, and of you yourself who urge me to speak,' I added, after he had made his guard withdraw, and he and I remained alone. I told him, then, that 'when leaving Surat to go to the diamond mine, M. Constant entrusted me with 44 000 [1] rupees, asking me to expend it on diamonds, and especially on large stones, that my services would be well rewarded, and that as this sum belonged to the General

[1] £4,950.

he would be glad to have an opportunity of obliging him. Moreover, that the General himself had purchased from M. Constant, when he visited Batavia, all the parcels I had sold him while he was the second officer at the factory of Surat. They were all stones which I had cut, their value being more than 40,000 écus.[1] As for the pearls which M. Constant had bought for the General during the time he was at Hormuz, I did not exactly know the value, but I so far knew that they included two pear-shaped pearls which cost 170 tomāns.[2] That I had also received somewhat considerable sums to invest for M. Carles Renel, M. Cam, and some others, and that he himself could not have forgotten that when M. Constant left Batavia to become Commander in Persia, he entrusted to him 36,000 rupees,[3] asking him to give it to some of his friends to invest it in a parcel of diamonds. That the said M. Constant expected to find me at Surat to place this sum in my hands, but as I had left for Hormuz some days before on an English vessel, he thought to find me there, and place the sum in my hands, supposing that during the same season I should return to India, and to the diamond mine. And in order to make you see,' I further said to the President, 'how M. Constant was devoted to your interest, he purchased with the greater part of your money goods of Sironj and Burhānpur, and as soon as he arrived at Gombroon he was offered 30 per cent. profit on them. It is true', I added, 'that to calculate it at the rate which the other merchants have to pay it would only amount to 5 per cent., but he made all pass as if on the account of the Company, which neither pays the freight of the vessel nor the customs at Gombroon, these two items amounting, in the case of the merchants, to 25 per cent.; that when the vessel which had carried him returned to Batavia, although the goods were not sold, he did not forget to write to you that he had refused 30 per cent. profit in the hope of receiving more; that, however, three vessels arrived at Gombroon laden with the same kinds of goods, so that he had difficulty in getting for them what they had cost in India; this compelled him to

[1] £9,000. [2] £586 : 10*s*., the tomān being equal to £3 : 9*s*.
[3] £4,050.

give those which he had bought for you at the current price; that, nevertheless, M. Constant had been so generous that he never asked anything from you, but that he had told me in private that he had lost more than 15 per cent. by the transaction.'

Having given all this detail to the President, he appeared to be very much alarmed, and besought me to make no noise about it, in which he did wisely, for I could have named others, all the devices [1] of the chiefs of the Company having come to my knowledge, and the principal part of the large sums which they had invested in diamonds having passed through my hands. Observing then that the President did not wish to hear more, I took leave of him and went to tell my counsel all that had passed. His dwelling being near that of the President, I observed that the latter went to the fort, apparently to see the General. Between 11 o'clock and noon I was about to go to the Town Hall to know what the Avocat Fiscal would say to me, because I knew that the President had gone there when leaving the fort, and that they had conversed together. But I met him half-way, and approaching me with a laughing face he asked me where I was going. I replied that I was going to the Town Hall to reply to some of his questions. 'I beg you,' he replied quickly, 'let us leave that affair to go and have dinner together. I was presented yesterday with two cases, one of French wine and the other of Rhine wine, we shall see which is the best. All I ask from you is a word written with your own hand, that you have nothing belonging to M. Constant.' This I gave very willingly, and in this way the whole case came to an end.

[1] 'Adresses', 'dexterities', or worse. Not 'addresses', as Ball rendered the term.

CHAPTER XXIII

The Author goes to see the King of Bantam,[1] *and describes several adventures in connexion therewith.*

HAVING freed myself of an affair which had been raised so inconveniently for me, I forthwith formed a resolution to visit the King of Bantam, having often heard that he was very fond of men of our nation ; this I can confirm on account of the good treatment which I received from him. As soon as one passes beyond the Kingdoms which yield obedience to the Great Mogul, the language which is called Malay is, among Orientals, what the Latin language is in Europe.[2] On the voyage I made to India in the year 1638 I took with me one of my brothers [3] who was my junior, and had a special talent for foreign languages. He required but five or six months in order to learn one, and he spoke eight of them perfectly well. Moreover he was well made in person and was considered brave, of which he gave many proofs. One day he fought a duel at Batavia with an infantry captain, over whom he obtained considerable advantage, and General Vandime, who liked men of spirit, and the principals of the Council, who had much esteem for him, permitted the matter to pass in silence, and as a mark of the affection with which they regarded him they gave him permission to equip a vessel on his own private account and to trade in such goods as he pleased, with the exception of spices. Accordingly my brother bought a vessel of fourteen guns, with which he made many voyages. The first was to Siam, where he made

[1] In the native language, Bantan. It forms the western end of Java and has an area of 2,568 geographical square miles. It is a mountainous country of volcanic formation. An English station was established there as early as 1603, but the Dutch ultimately proved the superior in this region. It is now a Dutch Province, having been taken possession of in 1643. (Crawfurd, *Dictionary*, 38.) *Ency. Brit.*, iii. 355 f. [But see Introd.]. The King of Bantam appears in English literature (Jonson, *The Alchemist*, ii. 1 ; Congreve, *Love for Love* ; Aphra Behn, *The Court of the King of Bantam*).

[2] This is still the case, Malay being the lingua franca in these regions.

[3] This was his brother Daniel (see Introduction, pp. xii and xvi).

a sufficiently large profit, but he lost 5,000 or 6,000 écus of it to the King, who invited him to gamble with him and five of the principal nobles of his court, as he was much pleased at meeting a European who spoke the Malay language so well. It cannot be doubted that the profits are great in this kind of trade, since those who advance the money to traders, on loan, obtain for it cent. per cent. But it is also true that they risk much, because if the vessel is lost the money is lost to them also, and this is called 'the great speculation'. He also made some voyages to the King of Macassar, but they did not yield so much profit as those to the Kingdoms of Siam, Tonquin, and Cochinchina.

Having, then, resolved to go to Bantam, and not knowing the Malayan language, I took with me my brother who was then at Batavia. It was necessary for me to have the permission of the General, according to custom, and he refused because he was not on good terms with the King of Bantam. But two hours afterwards M. Caron, who was at that time Director-General, sent to me to say that I might leave on my voyage for Bantam in all safety, as soon as I wished. Accordingly I set out with my brother in a small barque which we hired to carry us to Bantam, where, on arrival, our first visit was to the English President, who gave us a grand reception, and desired that we should not take other quarters but stay with him. He had still about fifty pots of Mantua wine with which he desired to regale us. This wine is not exported in glass bottles, in which it goes bad, but in earthen pots, in which it always keeps good.

On the following morning my brother went to the King's palace, where he was well known and welcome, in order to ascertain when His Majesty would be able to receive us. But as soon as the King knew that he was there, he would not allow him to return to fetch me, but ordered a messenger to be sent to seek me, and tell me that if I had any rare jewels I should please him by bringing them.

When the King's people came to conduct me to the palace, and I did not see my brother with them, I was on the point of refusing to follow them, and I recalled the manner in which the King of Achīn had treated M. Renaud, who had left Nantes with his brother on the vessels which M. de Montmorency sent to India. I shall record the history of it in a few words, and this short digression will possibly not be displeasing to the reader. A French Company of Commerce established for India sent there four vessels, three large and one small one of eight guns, on board which among others were the two brothers Renaud, who entered the service of the Company. Their journey was the shortest and the most fortunate of any ever heard of, as they arrived off Bantam in less than four months. The King received them with great joy, and in eight or ten days' time he gave them as much pepper as they asked for, and at a very fair price, more than 20 per cent. cheaper than the Dutch do. But as our Frenchmen had not come for pepper only, but wished also to obtain information about the trade in cloves, nutmegs, and mace, they sent the smaller vessel with the greater part of their money to Macassar, where the King's stores are generally full, as I have elsewhere said, because the Dutch, with all their skill, are unable to prevent the people of this island trading with the other islands where the spices grow;[1] this annoys them much, since they desire to compel the trade of all other nations to pass through their hands.

Our Frenchmen having obtained their cargo of pepper so quickly at Bantam, had not patience to await the return of the small vessel which they had sent to Macassar, and, to amuse themselves, decided to go to Batavia, which is not more than 14 leagues distant from Bantam. When the wind is favourable one can go there in a single tide, and they reached the roads at 8 o'clock in the morning. As soon as they had cast anchor the General of the French fleet sent to pay his compliments to the General of Batavia, who did not fail to reply to this civility by asking the General to come on shore that he might entertain him. He sent at the same time to those who remained in the vessel a quantity of refreshments, and especially Spanish and Rhine wine, with instructions to those who carried it to make them drink well and to intoxicate them. This order was so well obeyed that it was easy for the Dutch afterwards to set fire to the

[1] Vol. ii. 13.

vessels according to the orders which they had received, and as, from the saloon of the fort where the General of Batavia receives strangers, all the roads are visible, one of the Indian Councillors who was at the table, seeing the flames, cried out that he believed the French vessels were on fire. The General of Batavia appeared to be much astonished, and the French General, who rightly concluded how it had come about, looked unmoved at the company: 'But that', said he, 'need not prevent us from continuing to drink—those who have lighted the fire shall pay for it.' But he did not remember then that time was worth money, and the Dutch did not pay for a quarter of the damage. The French vessels were all burnt and the crews were saved on the frigates which were dispatched for them in haste. The General of Batavia made the men liberal offers, which they refused, and they returned to Bantam to await their small vessel. When it arrived they could think of no better plan than to sell their goods and the vessel itself to the English, and the money was divided among all according to the rank of each. The English offered them a passage to Europe, but the General and some of the principal officers alone accepted it. The greater part of the French remained in India and took service with the Portuguese, with whom there was some advantage to be gained at that time.

The Dutch did not ill-treat the French alone, after this fashion, as they did a still more serious injury to the English. The English were the first to realize that the voyage to Japan from Surat, Masulipatam, and other places, was too dangerous to attempt in one stretch, without having some place to rest at when the winds were contrary. They found it desirable to build a fort in the island of Formosa;[1] and this has prevented the loss of many vessels, in addition to the great profit which it brought them. The Dutch, jealous that the English had seized so good a position as that, the only

[1] According to W. Milburn (*Oriental Commerce*, 1813, ii. 547) the Dutch had formerly a considerable fort at Tai-wan on the east coast of Formosa, from which they were expelled by the Chinese. 'The English also made some unsuccessful attempts to form an establishment here.'

place in all the island where vessels could lie in safety, as they were unable to take it by force, decided to accomplish their design by treachery. They sent two of their vessels, on board which they put their best soldiers, who feigned to have been very badly injured by a storm, making their vessels appear dismasted and broken in many directions, and all the soldiers pretending sickness. The English, touched by this misery, which was only a sham, invited the chief officers to come on shore to refresh themselves ; this invitation they immediately accepted, ordering as many of their people as possible to leave the vessel, under pretext that they were ill, and could be treated better on shore than on board. While the principal officers were at table with the English, who had civilly invited them to dinner, to accomplish their object, they took with them more attendants than politeness permitted, and, to make more come on shore they ordered them to bring from the vessels, from time to time, many kinds of wine, and those who brought it had the word to remain there, of which the English, who were not on their defence, took no notice. The Dutch, seeing that they had drunk well, and that it was time to execute their design, started a quarrel with the English chief ; and drawing their arms which they had concealed, threw themselves upon the English garrison, whom they murdered without meeting with much resistance. It was thus they made themselves masters of the fort, which they possessed till they were driven from it by the Chinese. I could tell of many other treacheries by the Dutch,[1] but it is time to return to that which followed the burning of the French vessels in the Batavia roads.

The two brothers Renaud, of whom I have above spoken, received at Bantam a small amount of money from the distribution which was made of the proceeds of the sale of the small vessel, and of the goods which it had brought from Macassar, found means to go to Goa, and knew so well how to gain the good opinion of the Portuguese, that they were permitted to trade in all places where the Portuguese were

[1] Tavernier subsequently resolved to do so, and in his third volume we have his accumulated charges against the Dutch, under the title, *Conduite des Hollandois en Asie.*

in authority. In five or six years they had each earned to the value of 10,000 écus.[1] The elder dealt in cottons and other coarse goods, and the younger in precious stones. The Portuguese had been accustomed to send three or four vessels to Achīn every year to obtain pepper, elephants,[2] and gold, and they took there all kinds of white and coloured calicoes, especially blue and black. They also sent jewels to the King, because he loved and highly valued them. The two brothers Renaud decided to go there, each for his own particular trade, the elder one carrying cottons, and the younger jewels, amongst which he had four rings of the value of about 18,000 écus. On their arrival at Achīn, they went with the other Portuguese to the King's palace, which is 2 leagues from the sea, and showed the King and the nobles who were with him whatever they had brought. As for the jewels, as soon as the King had cast his eyes on the four rings he desired to have them, but refused to pay more than 15,000 écus for them, but the younger Renaud asked 18,000 écus. Not having been able to agree, he took them away, which much displeased the King, who sent for him on the following day. Renaud, who had returned to the vessel, was a long time in doubt whether he should go to the King again or not; but the officers of the vessel advising him to go, he at length resolved to do so, and the King took the four rings for the 18,000 écus, which he paid him forthwith. But after Renaud left the presence of the King no one ever knew what became of him; apparently he was secretly murdered in the palace.

This adventure came to my memory when I saw that the King of Bantam sent to ask for me, and that my brother was not with those who came to summon me. Nevertheless, I resolved to go, and took with me 12,000 or 13,000 rupees' worth of jewels, the largest part consisting of rings with diamonds arranged in roses, some of seven stones, others of nine, and others of eleven, with some bracelets of diamonds

[1] £2,250.

[2] This statement as to the importation of Sumatran elephants is of interest, but requires confirmation. See vol. ii. 248 for suggested origin
19 of the elephants in Sumatra.

and rubies. I found the King with three of his captains and my brother seated in the Oriental fashion, and they had before them five large plates of rice of different colours. For their drink they had Spanish wine and brandy, with many kinds of sherbets. After I saluted the King, and presented to him a diamond ring, another of blue sapphires, and a small bracelet of diamonds, rubies, and blue sapphires, he invited me to be seated, and told the attendants to give me a cup of brandy to excite my appetite. This cup held about half a septier of Paris,[1] but I refused to take it from the officer who presented it to me; this astonished the King. My brother then asked him to excuse me, saying that I never drank brandy; but that I could drink a little Spanish wine, upon which the King ordered some to be given me.

Whether the repast had already lasted a long time, or that the King was impatient to see what I had brought, he did not delay about finishing, and seated himself in a kind of arm-chair, the woodwork of which was gilt with gold and moulded like the frames of our pictures. His feet and legs were uncovered, and beneath him there was a small Persian carpet of gold and silk. His garment was a piece of calico, a part of which covered the body from the waist to the knees, the remainder bound on his back and about his neck like a scarf. He wore as a head-band, a kind of three-cornered handkerchief; and his hair, which was very long, was twisted and tied together on the top of his head. In place of slippers he had placed by the side of his chair sandals with leather straps to go over his feet, like those attached to a spur, which were embroidered with gold and small pearls. Two of his officers stood behind him with large fans, the handles of which were 5 or 6 feet long, and at the ends there were bundles of peacocks' plumes, as large as the bottom of one of our barrels. On his right side there was an old black woman, who held in her hands a small mortar and a pestle of gold, in which she crushed the betel leaves, with which she mixed areca [2] nuts and dissolved seed pearls. When she saw that

[1] Equal to one-fourth of an English pint. It is apparently the one-seventh of a litre, whence the name.

[2] Araque in the original: the nuts of Areca catechu (Watt, *Commercial Products*, 83 ff.).

the whole was well pounded she placed her hand on the King's back, who at once opened his mouth, and she put the betel in with her fingers as women do who give pap to their infants,[1] because the King had no teeth; for he had eaten so much betel, and smoked so much tobacco, that his teeth had fallen out.

The palace of the King of Bantam did not need a very skilful architect. It is a square building surrounded by small lacquered pillars of different colours, 2 feet in height, against which one leans when seated. There are at the four corners large pillars planted in the earth at 40 feet distance from each other, and the floor is covered by a mat woven of the bark of a kind of tree, as if it were a piece of cloth, and neither fleas nor bugs will approach it. The roof is of coco-nut fronds. Close by, under another roof, sustained also by four large pillars, there were sixteen elephants, the most courageous of those which the King keeps—for he has a large number of them—which are destined for war and do not fear fireworks. For his guard he has about 2,000 men, who were seated in squads under the shade of some trees. They are good soldiers both on sea and land, strict Musalmāns who do not fear death. His harem, where his women dwell, must be a small affair, for when he had seen what I had brought he summoned two old black women, to whom he gave some of the jewels to show them to his wives. The two old women entered by a miserable door, and the place was enclosed only by a kind of palisade, with earth mixed with cow-dung between the posts. I observed that nothing which he sent by these women was brought back, this made me conclude that I should stick to the price. Thus I sold him profitably what he took from me, and I was paid at once. After having drunk a cup of sherbet—while my brother drank spirits with the King—we took leave of him, and he made us promise that, on the following day towards evening, we should return to see him, because he wished to show me a dagger which he was having made after the Turkish fashion,

[1] Ball saw the famous hairy woman of Mandalay being supplied with betel by her Burmese attendant in much the same way; being blind, the packet had to be prepared for her and placed in her mouth.

but he did not possess sufficient diamonds to cover the handle, and he desired that I should procure enough to finish it. We then returned with our money to the English House, and our friends were much astonished that the King had spent 20,000 rupees, as they believed it was the most part of his treasure.[1]

Next day my brother and I went to see the King again at the hour which he had fixed, and we found him seated in the same place as on the preceding day. A Mullā read and interpreted to him something from the Korān, which was in Arabic. When the reading was finished the King and the Mullā rose to pray, after which the King sent for the dagger, the handle and sheath of which were of gold. The upper part of the handle was already covered with diamonds, and in the plaque at the end there was a large one cut into facettes, which, as far as I could judge, was worth at least 15,000 or 16,000 écus.[1] The King told me that he had received it as a present from the Queen of Borneo, and that he had sent it to be cut at Goa, but he valued it much higher than what I considered it to be worth. All the handle and the sheath were covered with bezels [1] applied without order, which proved to me that he did not understand design. The King had no other stones, neither diamonds nor rubies, nor anything to place in these bezels, and he wished to induce me to obtain for him some that would fit. I made him understand that this would be impossible, and that he ought not to limit himself to these bezels; that when he had acquired the quantity of stones which were required to cover the dagger, other bezels of the shapes of the stones should be made, and that in Europe when we begin a work of this kind we first arrange all the available stones on wax; this I exemplified to him at the same time, but that was beyond his understanding, and he told me that he did not care to destroy a design which he had himself taken the trouble to arrange, and to have made for his own use. In spite of

[1] As the value of the jewels is stated on page 273 to have been only 12,000 to 13,000 rupees, the transaction was a profitable one for Tavernier.

[2] £3,375 to £3,600.

[3] Bezels (chatons in the original), mountings for individual stones.

any reasons which I could give for the purpose of escaping from a commission which I was not able to execute, the King wished positively that I should take the dagger with me to Batavia. I represented to him then that as I was a stranger he risked much, and that I might go off with the dagger without returning it, but he said to me smiling that he feared nothing on that account, and that he well knew that Frenchmen were incapable of so disgraceful an action. At length, unable to excuse myself further, I took charge of the dagger, and having taken leave of the King, my brother and I went to bid farewell to the English President, and to thank him for the civilities we had received from him.

CHAPTER XXIV

The Author returns to Batavia, and some days afterwards goes again to visit the King of Bantam, giving an account, in connexion therewith, of the dangerous extravagances of some Fakīrs, or pilgrims, on their return from Mecca.

MY brother and I, after supper this evening with the English President, went on board a barque between 11 o'clock and midnight, for the land-wind that we required generally blows at night, and on the following day between 10 and 11 o'clock in the morning we arrived at Batavia.[1] I remained there twenty days, merely to make the King of Bantam believe that I had not misrepresented the matter, and that during that time I had been looking for what it was impossible to find. As I had nothing to do, these twenty days appeared very long to me; for at Batavia there is scarcely any other amusement but gambling, and all the gain goes in drink; this did not suit me. During the day, on account of the great heat, one cannot even think of taking exercise, which can only be done towards the cool of the evening, and it is moreover necessary to make it very short, because as soon as the sun sets they close the gates, unless the General or Madame or some of the Councillors of India are outside the

[1] See *Voyage of François Leguat*, Hakluyt Society, i. 220 ff.

town in their gardens. During these twenty days M. Cant, one of the Councillors of India, died, and was buried with great honour. A company of infantry attended and bore a large standard, upon which were the arms of the deceased, although when he first came to India he held the lowest office in the vessel. A stick, to the end of which spurs were attached, was borne behind, though, to say the truth, I do not believe he had ever mounted a horse save to go for exercise outside the town. One of the captains carried his sword, another his helmet, and his body was borne by eight military officers. The son-in-law of the deceased followed with the General; after whom walked the gentlemen of the Council; a number of people followed from the fort and town. The four corners of the pall with which the bier was covered were carried by four captains, and all these honours were rendered to him in consideration of the good services which the Company had received from him—as the General and members of the Council proclaimed; but the people used very different language and complained bitterly of the great injustice he had done, both to sailors and soldiers.

Having passed these twenty days at Batavia, I resolved to carry back the dagger to the King of Bantam, without having looked for the diamonds or other stones, for if I had remained years I should not have found any suitable for these bezels. My brother accompanied me again, and I took with me some jewels which the King had not yet seen. On our arrival at Bantam we intended to go first to visit the English President, but, before we had done so, one of the King's officers came to us, and told us that he had been instructed that we should be lodged in one of the King's houses in the town. These houses are made of bamboos, which are, as I have elsewhere said, hollow canes, and though they are as hard as iron, nevertheless split like our osiers, and it is of them that the Indians make nearly everything. We had not spent more than half an hour in this house when the King sent us some pateches,[1] which are very sweet water-melons, and red as scarlet inside. There were also mangoes,

[1] More properly pateca, a water-melon, *Citrullus vulgaris* (Schrader). The name is from the Arabic al-bittīkh. (Yule, *Hobson-Jobson*, 684 f.)

of which I have elsewhere spoken, and another large fruit called pompone,[1] which is also red inside, the flesh being soft like a sponge, and very good. The servant who brought these fruits told us that as soon as we had taken our food we were to go to see the King; this we did, and we found him again in the same place with the old betel pounder, who from time to time made him open his mouth and gave him some with her fingers in the way I have described. There were five or six captains seated round the room, who were looking at some fireworks which the Chinese had brought, such as grenades, fusees, and other things of that kind to run on the water; for the Chinese surpass all the nations of the world in this respect.[2] As soon as I saw the King in a condition to speak to me I presented to him his dagger in the same state as he had given it to me, and told him that Batavia was not a place where one could obtain precious stones, and when I did find some they wanted double their value for them; that this commission could not be fulfilled except by someone who went to Goa, and that I could have accomplished it when at Goa, or at Golkonda, or, better still, at the diamond mine, where parcels of stones of all shapes and sizes are procurable and might be cut with but little loss to suit the bezels. Upon this the old woman took the dagger, carried it into the harem, and the King never spoke to me about it again. Afterwards I showed him the jewels I had brought, and I sold a parcel of them as advantageously as on the first journey. As the sun was setting, which is the time when the Musalmāns say their prayers, the King told us to return on the following day, and said he would arrange for payment being made to us. On arriving at our lodging we found one of the servants of the English President, who came to invite us to have supper with him, and taste some new liquors which had arrived from England on the Company's account. For during the twenty days we spent at Batavia two vessels had arrived, laden with French and Spanish wine,

[1] More properly pommelo, *Citrus decumana* (L.), the shaddock of the West Indies. (*Ibid.*, 721 f.)

[2] On Chinese fireworks see J. D. Ball, *Things Chinese*, 3rd ed., p. 238 ff.

and especially a large quantity of beer. We remained till midnight with the President, who showed much joy at seeing us again.

Next day at 10 o'clock a.m., when going to the palace, with my brother and a Dutch surgeon, who was prescribing for one of the King's wives, we passed along a road with the river on one side and on the other a large garden enclosed by a palisade, and there were intervals between each pair of posts. Behind the palisade a rascal of a Bantamese was concealed who had returned from Mecca and was running a muck,[1] which means in their language, that when someone of the lower class of Musalmāns, who has returned from Mecca, takes it into his head to seize his crease [2] which is a kind of dagger with generally half of the blade poisoned, he runs through the streets and kills all whom he meets who are not of the Musalmān faith, until he is himself killed. These fanatics think they do a service to God and to Muhammad by killing the enemies of his Law, and thus they will be saved. After they are killed the Musalmān mob inter them as though they were saints, and everyone contributes to build them splendid tombs. Often some great mendicant dresses as a Dervish and builds a hut close to the tomb, which he is careful to keep tidy and adorn with flowers. According as donations are given he adds some ornament, because the more beautiful the grave is, so much the more worship and sanctity does it acquire, and by so much the more do the donations increase. I remember in the year 1642 a vessel of the Great Mogul arrived at Suwālī,[3] which is the port of Surat, from Mecca,

[1] À Moqua in the original. The French edition of 1713 has it 'joüoit à Mocca'. This is what is more commonly known as running a muck. See Yule, *Hobson-Jobson*, 18 ff. for etymology and examples of the use of the term.

[2] Cric in the original. The term crease or cris, signifying a dagger, is adopted in the Malay from the Javanese kris or kiris. Ball had seen an ingenious explanation for the waved form of these blades; it is that it is a survival of the outlines of the knives and spears made of obsidian by flaking, and indeed the resemblance is somewhat striking. See Romilly, *West Pacific and New Guinea*; Yule, *Hobson-Jobson*, 274 ff. gives examples of the use of the term. On the magical significance of these marks see W. W. Skeat, *Malay Magic*, 525 ff.

[3] Souali in the original (vol. i. 5).

where there were a number of these Fakīrs or Dervishes. For every year the Great Mogul sends two large vessels there to carry pilgrims, who thus get a free passage. When these vessels are ready to depart the Fakīrs come from all parts of India to embark. The vessels are laden with good articles of trade, which are disposed of at Mecca, and all the profit made is given in charity to the poor pilgrims. The principal only is retained, and it serves for another year, and this principal is, at the least, 600,000 rupees.[1] It is considered a small matter when 30 or 40 per cent. only is made on these goods, for some yield cent. per cent. Besides this all the principal persons of the Great Mogul's harem, and other private persons, send considerable donations to Mecca. I have mentioned at the end of my account of the seraglio of the Grand Seigneur the rich and magnificent present which the Great Mogul sent to Mecca in the year 1644, over and above the ordinary presents which he makes annually.[2]

One of these Fakīrs returned from Mecca in the year 1642, and on landing at Suwālī he forthwith showed signs of diabolical fury. He had no sooner said his prayers than he took his dagger and attacked some Dutch sailors, who were on shore discharging goods from four vessels in the port. Before they saw him and were able to put themselves on their defence, this fanatical Fakīr wounded seventeen, of whom thirteen died. The khanjar[3] which he had was a kind of dagger, the upper part of the blade of which was three fingers wide, and as it is a very dangerous weapon I give a figure of it here. At length the Dutch soldier who was on guard at the entrance to the tent where the Commander and the merchants were seated, shot this madman through the body, and he fell dead. Forthwith all the other Fakīrs in the place, and even the Musalmāns, carried off the body and buried it, and at the end of fifteen days a handsome tomb had been built over it. It is broken each year by the English and Dutch sailors when

[1] £67,500.

[2] On the embassies from the Grand Sharīf of Mecca to Aurangzeb and the gifts sent by the latter see Manucci, ii. 114 f.: Bernier, 133.

[3] Canjare in the original (see vol. i. 82, 246). It is not necessary to reproduce the figure here.

their vessels are in port, because they are then strong; but as soon as they depart the Musalmāns have it rebuilt and place many standards about it. Some also say their prayers there.

To return to the Fakīr of Bantam—This rascal was concealed, as I have said, behind the palisades, and as my brother and I and the Dutch surgeon went along, all three, side by side, and came opposite him, he thrust out his spear, thinking to transfix one of us in the body. By God's grace he was too quick, and the point passed in front of all three. The Dutchman being on my left on the river side, and slightly in advance of my brother and me, the point of the spear cut his high hose and immediately he and I caught hold of the handle, the Fakīr pulling with all his might to recover his spear. My brother, who was on my right on the palisade side, being young and strong, leaped over it, and gave him three sword cuts in the body of which he died on the spot. Immediately a number of Chinese and other idolaters who were close by kissed my brother's hands and thanked him for having slain this fanatic. Thence we went to see the King, who had already heard of what my brother had done, and showed his approval by making him a present of a waistband. For the Kings and Governors, although they are Musalmāns, are well pleased when someone slays these ruffians, knowing well that they are desperadoes of whom it is well to be rid.

The King paid me for what he had purchased on the preceding day; but he was unwilling that my brother should return with me, because he was going to make a great rejoicing, and wished him to be present. It was on the occasion of the launch of four large vessels which he had had built. Never had any King of Bantam built such large ships, and for five or six days there was to be nothing but feasts, dances, and fireworks. Thus I took leave of the King, who presented me with a beautiful embroidered waistband, and we went to sup and sleep at the Dutch surgeon's house.

Next day I went to bid farewell to the English President, who kept me for dinner. While waiting for it to be served, he showed me two strings of diamonds which had come to him from England, and two services of silver, the whole being worth, perhaps, 25,000 écus. He wanted to sell me all, but I bought only one of the strings of diamonds for 2,600 reales, for the stones on the other string were too foul; and as for the vessels of silver, if money had still been coined at Batavia I would certainly have been able to buy them. They coined there formerly, but all their coins contained more than ten per cent. of alloy. This was done on account of the Chinese, who prefer silver to gold, as I have elsewhere remarked,[1] because they have no silver mines in their own country,[2] and they used to carry into China as much of the silver money which was coined at Batavia as they could. These were reales, half reales, and quarter reales, which have no other mark than that of the Company, as is to be seen in the figure which I give here.[3] On one side was a vessel, and on the other a V, an O, and a C, interlaced, these three letters signifying in Dutch 'Vor Oost Indien Compagnie', i. e. for the Company of the East Indies.

This lasted for some years; but in the end all the nations of the East, who had trade with the Dutch, began to be tired of it, especially the people whose sovereigns did not coin silver money; for in fact there are very few who coin after one passes beyond the Empire of the Great Mogul, and it is still bar silver only which comes from Japan. As for gold, there are many Kings who coin it, as the King of Pegu, the King of Achīn, and the King of Macassar; and besides their golden money, they have also copper and tin money. The Chinese—who are careful in all things—in selling their goods calculate according to the standard of the silver; for when they have come home, they reduce all that they received in foreign countries to their own standard, and keep it in ingots.

The principal part of the profit derived from these reales which were coined at Batavia, used to go into the purses of the General, the Councillors, and the Master of the Mint. The

[1] See vol. ii. 122.

[2] There are silver mines in China, in the island of Hainan and elsewhere (*Ency. Brit.*, vi. 178; S. W. Williams, *The Middle Kingdom*, i. 244).

[3] This figure is not reproduced here.

States-General having had notice of it, considered it very singular that the gentlemen of the Company had assumed authority to coin money without permission, and forbade the Company to continue to do so. They condemned them likewise to a large fine, and ordered a careful search to be made for all these reales, in order to give an equal number of good ones to those who had received the bad ones. On this voyage to Batavia, when in the island of Ceylon, I sold some jewels to a lady of Pointe de Galle, who paid me with these reales. When I was leaving, an officer of the Company came on board to ask if I had not received some of these reales, and added that if I had he would give me good ones, piece for piece, without my losing anything; this he did forthwith.

CHAPTER XXV

Concerning the Dutch War with the Emperor of Java.[1]

BEFORE leaving the English President, with whom I dined the day I left Bantam, he discussed with me the reasons why the General of Batavia and his Council had refused me a passage to Surat or the coast of Bengal, where they often send vessels. The President, to compensate me for this refusal, kindly offered me a passage to England; for the season was then past for returning to India. Attracted by his offer, I accepted it without ceremony; and he told me he would be much gratified at having my company, because he himself intended to go home, as the period of his service had expired. But the vessels, English or Dutch, could not leave for Europe for more than three months; and I thought I should do best to pass that time at Batavia, where I might be able to buy something to make my money yield a profit during the voyage. Accordingly, I took leave of the President till the time when the vessels should sail; and he presented me with a large cask of English beer to take with me to Batavia, where he said I should find scarcely any, because the General had made it contraband, knowing that it had come to the English Company. 'But if he does us only this

[1] *La Iave* in the original.

injury,' continued the President, 'the Company will not trouble itself, and will not be the poorer because its beer remains unsold.' It is not really the case that if this prohibition of the Dutch General and his Council had continued it would not have been injurious to the English, for they make a considerable profit on beer, and it yields them a large sum of money annually. I have said above that it is the principal delight of the people of Batavia to see new drinks arrive, especially English beer, and that which they call mom,[1] which comes from Brunswick. It is thought that they contribute to health; and the majority fear that they will not survive till the year's end if they do not receive these supplies. Accordingly all the people murmured loudly against the General and his Council; and even the publicans risked buying beer from the English, the General shutting his eyes, and the wives of the Councillors being very glad to drink it.

As soon as I landed at Batavia one of the guards ran to the entry office to give notice that I had arrived with a cask of beer; however, I landed it from the barque and placed it near the guard. The chief of the office came to me and said that he could not give permission for the cask to be carried to my lodging; that I must be aware of the order of Council; and that it would be best to reship it on the barque, and send it back to Bantam. Seeing that there was no favour to be hoped for, and as there are close to the guard-house cannons, in position, for the defence of the port, and an abundance of cannon balls, I took one of these balls and with it stove in one end of the cask. That done, I cried out to the soldiers and passers-by: 'Children, come and empty this cask, and drink the health of the King of France, my sovereign lord, and that of the Prince of Orange', after which I mentioned the General and the members of the Council. As no one refused to drink, the cask was already half emptied when an officer on the part of the General came to tell me that I might carry my cask of beer to my lodging. Immediately I replaced the end of the cask and had it carried

[1] Mum, German Mumme, Brunswick beer, largely imported into England in the 17th and 18th centuries (*New English Dict.* s. v.)

away, after which I filled a canteen of six bottles, and sent them as a present to the General, knowing well that it would be the first he had to drink that year, and with the rest I regaled my friends.

I had designed, as I have said, to spend at Batavia the three months which remained till the departure of the vessels for Christendom, but the life led in that place being one of idleness is tiresome, and as I had no other amusement than gambling and drinking, I resolved to employ a part of the time in going to see the King of Japara,[1] who is otherwise called the Emperor of Java. He was formerly King of all the island, before the King of Bantam, who was only governor of a province, rebelled against him, the Dutch being maintained in this country by the division of these two powers. For whenever the King of Japara wished to besiege Batavia, the King of Bantam immediately aided the Dutch and when they have been attacked by the King of Bantam, which has happened many times, the King of Japara has come to their aid. In the same way, when these two Kings make war upon one another, the Dutch assist whichever of them is the weaker.

The King of Japara resides in a town of that name, about 30 leagues distance from Batavia, and accessible only by sea along the coast, though nearly 8 leagues inland. From the town you pass down a fine river to the sea, where there is a good port and finer houses than those in the town. The King would prefer to make his ordinary residence at the port, but thinks he would not be safe there.

On the eve of the day I had intended to start, I went to take leave of one of the Councillors of India, and mentioning to him that I was going to the King of Japara, he was much astonished, because the King and the Dutch were then mortal enemies. He explained the matter to me in this way. The

[1] Japar in the original. Japara is the name of a province of Java, comprehending Juwana, situated in the country of the proper Javanese. Its area is 672 square miles, and the population amounts to 671 per square mile, it being the most thickly inhabited region of Java. (Crawfurd, *Dictionary*, 165; Milburn, *Oriental Commerce*, ii. 364; *Ency. Brit.*, xv. 290.)

deceased King, he said, father of the King who reigns at present, ever since the Dutch Company had built the fort at Batavia in his territories, had never been willing to make peace with it : although during the war the King had taken some Dutchmen prisoners, and the Dutch, on their side, had taken twenty times as many of his subjects, offering to give in exchange ten of his for one of theirs, yet he would not give up one, either on that condition, or for money, and on his deathbed he advised his son, who succeeded him, never to give liberty to one of them. This obstinacy troubled the General and all the people of Batavia very much, and obliged them to think of some means to bring him to reason. It is the custom that as soon as a Musalmān King dies, his successor sends some of the principal nobles of his court to Mecca with presents to make the priests pray for the soul of the deceased, and also to give thanks to God and to Muhammad because the new King has come to the throne without any obstruction, and to pray that he may always be victorious over his enemies. The new King and his Council were in much difficulty how they should make this voyage for two reasons, one because the King had only small vessels, and to undertake so long a journey on such vessels was risking much, besides which the native pilots and sailors are able to sail only along the coasts, sighting from point to point, because they do not understand how to take observations. The other difficulty was that the King of Japara could not ignore the fact that the Dutch were always cruising about his harbours to capture his subjects if they went outside. In order, then, to secure that those who went on the pilgrimage should be in safety, he bethought him that it would be best to come to an understanding with the English, believing that the Dutch would not dare to do anything to the pilgrims if they were on board English vessels. With this object, an envoy was dispatched to Bantam to the English President and his Council, who promised to give the King one of the largest and best appointed vessels which the Company sent to India. They stipulated as a recompense that on the trade which the English might do in the future in the Kingdom of the King of Japara, they should not have to pay more than half the custom dues which they had hitherto paid, and that this privilege should be perpetual. This treaty being made, the English equipped a very fine vessel and placed a larger crew and more guns on her than usual. The King of Japara's Envoy and two English merchants embarked on the vessel to ratify the treaty with the King, who at once signed it, being very well satisfied at seeing so fine a vessel, and he concluded that the voyage both ways would be accomplished in safety. Nine of the principal persons of his court, and the majority of his relatives, with eighty or a hundred servants, and some other private persons, delighted to find so good an opportunity of accomplishing their pilgrimage, embarked with much joy on this large vessel. All this was not done without the Dutch being aware of it, as, like the English, they had their spies everywhere. As it was necessary to pass Bantam in order to get out of the Straits, this being the only route, the General of Batavia, who had notice of the time of departure, kept three large war-vessels ready, of which M. Chevres,[1] a Councillor of India, and the Major were placed in command. They met the English vessel off Bantam, and as it was about to enter the Straits sent a cannon-shot as a signal to her to bring to; this the English were unwilling to do, seeing which the Dutch commenced to fire from all three vessels. The English, who well knew that if this continued they would be sent to the bottom, lowered sails and prepared to yield; but all the Javanese nobles, and those who accompanied them, cried out to the English that they were traitors, and that the agreement which had been made was intended to sell them and deliver them over to the mercy of the Dutch. The Javanese at length seeing that no hope of safety was left, and that the Dutch began to board the vessel, seized their creases, or poisoned daggers, and began to run a muck [2] among the English, of whom they killed a large number before the latter had time to place themselves on their defence. It is possible that not one would have escaped if the Dutch had not speedily come on board, when some of the Javanese nobles, twenty or thirty

[1] Cheveres in ed. of 1678.

[2] À Mocca in the original. The French edition of 1713 has it 'to cry *Mocca*' (cf. p. 280 *n.* above).

of their servants, and the passengers refused to accept quarter. The combat was bloody, and seven or eight Dutchmen were killed. When the English vessel was taken to Batavia, the General treated the crew with much civility, and sent them back with their vessel, and afterwards gave notice to the King of Japara that if he consented to make an exchange of the Dutch prisoners, he would give him all satisfaction. But the King would not listen to it, and replied that if the General had taken three times as many of his subjects he would not give up the Dutch prisoners whom he had in his power. Thus the poor Dutch remained in slavery, and the Javanese died of poverty at Batavia, although, through policy, they were sometimes stealthily assisted, so that the King of Japara coming to know of it, through his spies, it might cause him to treat the Dutch prisoners less harshly.

The Javanese are very good soldiers. While Batavia was besieged by the King of Bantam in the year 1659, a Dutch soldier was in ambuscade in a march, and a Javanese advanced to see what the enemy were doing, not thinking any of them were so close. The Dutchman thrust a pike into him, and the Javanese feeling himself wounded, instead of withdrawing the pike, pushed it into his body up to the hilt, where the Dutchman held it, so as to be able to get near him, and give him two stabs with his dagger in the stomach, of which the Dutchman died.

CHAPTER XXVI

The Author renders the last duties to his brother, who died at Batavia, and has fresh difficulties with the General and his Council.

FINDING myself without hope of being able to visit the King of Japara, I resolved to embark in a small vessel which belonged to one of the citizens of Batavia, and traded along the whole length of the western coast of Sumatra. Here the principal part of the trade of this island, which consists of very poor gold and pepper, is carried on. What induced me to go was the opportunity it afforded of disposing of some diamond rings made according to the fashion of the country. For although these people have for their sole garment only two or three ells of calico, nevertheless, they always like to have some diamond rings or earrings, and they pay well for them. When I was at the port, ready to embark, a small barque arrived from Bantam with my brother, who was very ill with a bloody flux, which arose from the debauches he had indulged in with the King of Bantam. The sight of his condition caused me to give up my voyage and to do what I could for his cure, but all my care and all the remedies which could be applied availed nothing, and at the end of thirty days God took him from this world. For his funeral I was obliged to follow the somewhat strange customs, which the Dutch have invented to cause expenditure of money by the heirs of a deceased [1] person. The first is the fee to those who go to pray at the burial, for the more prayers are said the more honourable is the interment. If only one be engaged he pays him but 2 écus, but if two he must pay 4 écus to each ; if three, each ought to receive 6 ; and if twelve, the payment goes on increasing in the same ratio. As I wished that the thing should be done in an honourable manner, and in ignorance of this pleasant custom, I engaged six of these persons, and when it came to paying them I was astonished to find that each one demanded 12 écus, and that I had to pay 72 for this single item. As for the pall which is placed on the bier, it must be hired at the hospital, and it is a right which the poor enjoy who derive profit therefrom. The commonest is of cloth, and the three others of velvet, one without fringe, another with fringe, and a third with fringe and large tassels at the four corners. This causes an expenditure of from 5 to 30 écus, and I paid 20 for the one which was placed on my brother's bier. A cask of Spanish wine, which was drunk at the interment, cost me 200 piastres.[2] I gave 26 for three hams and some ox tongues, and 22 for

The foregoing lines of this chapter are in the English translation by John Phillips, compressed into the following quaintly expressed sentence :—'While I stay'd at Batavia my brother dy'd ; and it was pretty to consider what the Dutch made me pay for his funeral.'

[2] £45.

some pastry. It is also the custom to send on the following day some money to entertain those who have carried the body to the burial ground, and as there were eight of them I paid them 20 écus. It cost 16 for the grave site—100 écus being asked for interment in the church. Thus the whole funeral cost me 1,223 livres [1] of French money, and after I had paid this sum I resolved, for my own part, not to die in a country where it cost so much to be interred. I praised God that notwithstanding the troubles I had experienced in Batavia, and of which I have as yet told only a part, and the small dissipations which one cannot altogether avoid in this country, I have taken such good care of myself that I have never been inconvenienced by the least headache, or by a bloody flux, which is the ailment that carries away many people. That which in my opinion has contributed most to my health is, that I do not think I have ever grieved on account of any misfortune which has happened to me. I have sometimes made great profits, and I have sometimes experienced severe losses; but when in unpleasant circumstances I have never been more than half an hour in deciding what course I should adopt, without thinking more of the past, having always in my mind the thought of Job, that God gives and takes away as it pleases Him, and that one should render thanks for all that happens, whether it be good or evil.

Seeing that the two voyages which I had proposed to myself to make, one to Japara and the other to the coast of Sumatra, in order to dispose of some jewels which remained in my hands, had been prevented, I at length resolved to sell the jewels at Batavia with the least possible loss, and then try to invest the money in something which would yield me a profit in Holland. My jewels having been sold, three or four of my friends told me that as I had ready money I could not invest it better than by buying rekenings from the Company's servants. These rekenings [2] are their accounts of the balance the Company owes them, which are paid when

[1] £91 : 14*s*. 6*d*.

[2] Requenings (for rekenings) in the original, meaning statements of account or pay certificates. (*New English Dict. s. v.* reckonings.)

they return to Holland. But as there are many of them who, after their term of service is completed, remain at Batavia and become citizens there, or in other places where the Company has settlements, as Malacca, the island of Ceylon, the coast of Coromandel, and other places, each has his account closed with the balance that the Company owes him. In order to obtain this money, since they are domiciled there, and do not think of ever returning to Europe, they sell these statements of account to those who have money and are returning home, and the Company pays them in Holland. Those who buy these vouchers get them as cheaply as they can—thus, for 100 piastres they generally give but 60 or 70, or at the most 80, and they are allowed by the notary to sign a declaration that the seller is content, and had received his payment. Whenever these poor people sold their vouchers in this way to reasonable persons, it was a convenience to them; but most frequently they sold them to hotel keepers and publicans, from whom they did not obtain more than 40 or 50 per cent. at the most. When the latter had thus purchased up to 2,000 or 3,000 écus, they placed the 'statements' in the hands of a notary to resell them to the commanders who were returning to Holland, and who generally gave for them 85 or 90 per cent., contenting themselves with being thus able to conceal what they had taken from the Company, while they were chiefs of the factories.

The Company freely borrows money from those who are willing to lend it, and gives them 25 per cent. interest, but the commanders and other officers take care not to lend the full amount which they have amassed, because they may be asked by what means they have gained so much money, and be obliged to render an account; for some of them, as I have said, on their return to Holland take with them from 400,000 up to 500,000 livres.[1] I dealt then with one of these notaries of Batavia who had about 11,000 guilders'[2] worth

[1] £30,000 to £37,500. (Vol. i. 327).

[2] Guldes in the original. The florin or guilder of Batavia is given by Kelly as being of the intrinsic value of 1*s*. 7·77*d*., and the Dutch coin of the same denomination at 1*s*. 8·49*d*. The currency value was about 1*s*. 8*d*. and 1*s*. 9*d*. respectively in round numbers. Perhaps the true

of these 'statements' at 82 per cent., and on the following day, the transfer was completed, and I paid for them. As I was taking these papers to my lodgings I met the Avocat Fiscal, who asked me what papers my servant carried. I told him they were 'statements' which I had just purchased at a certain price, to which he replied that it was rather dear, and that he knew of some amounting to 6,000 guilders, at a cheaper rate; these I obtained with his assistance at 79 per cent. I sought to buy more, but more were not to be found, for a ship's captain who was returning had bought for himself alone to the amount of upwards of 100,000 guilders; many other persons had also done the same, and the whole amounted in value to more than 400,000 livres.

Five or six days afterwards, while I was still seeking for something in which to invest the remainder of my money, I met the Avocat Fiscal, who asked me if I had bought many of those rekenings. I told him that I had not found any more, and that I had only the two parcels he knew of, amounting to about 17,500 guilders; upon which he told me with many compliments that he was much distressed for those who had bought them, because the General and his Council had ordered him to make them give back all these rekenings, as it had been decided that it was not just that a poor man should lose so much of his wages. I told him that I would willingly give them back into the hands of the parties from whom I had purchased them, provided that I was repaid my money at the same time, and that I would get them over from Bantam, where I had sent them with my baggage, as I intended to return in a few days in order to go to England with the English President, who had civilly offered me a passage. At 6 p.m. one of the General's halberdiers came to tell me that the General wished to speak to me. I immediately went to him and he asked me forthwith why I had not given these rekenings to the Avocat Fiscal when he asked for them in the names of himself and his Council. I replied to him coldly that I was unable to give him that which I had not got, and that they were in Bantam. 'You intend

exchange value of the latter was about 1*s*. 9½*d*. At 1*s*. 9*d*. the 11,000 guilders represented a sum of £9,625.

then,' he said, 'to go to Europe?' 'Yes,' I replied, 'and the President of the English has done me the honour to give me a passage and the use of his table.' I added that it was very true that the long journey which I was about to make to Surat, and thence to the diamond mine, where my usual trade was, would cause me much loss, and that if he had so willed it he might have enabled me to save all this time and avoid the dangers inseparable from these long journeys, by allowing me to embark, as I had asked, on one of the vessels which sailed for Bengal, Surat, or Hormuz; that it would have caused no injury to the Company, and that I believed such courtesy the General and his Council should not have refused me, since I had come to Batavia only in their service. When I had finished speaking all the members of the Council looked at one another, and the General whispering to M. Caron, told me that as I was resolved to go by sea, their vessels were as good as those of the English, and that I should enjoy equally good treatment, and he offered me a passage by one of them. This offer, which I did not expect, amazed me a little, and I did not at first know whether I ought to accept it or not. But at length I accepted, fearing that by refusing it they might detain me for another year without being able to sail in any direction, a friend having told me in confidence that the design of the General and his Council was to so arrange, that, either from Batavia or from Europe, I should not return to India again, and that by this means they hoped to prevent the Commanders or chiefs of the factories, which they have both in India and Persia, from making further use of me to invest for them in diamonds the money of which the Company was defrauded.[1] It was this which led me to accept the passage, for which I thanked the General and his Council. Subsequently the General told me to select the particular vessel I preferred to go by, and that when I informed him he would order a cabin to be prepared for my own special convenience, but if I would take his advice I should go on the Vice-Admiral,[2] because of the good company

[1] The object of the Dutch was in short to deport Tavernier, whom they regarded as a dangerous interloper.

[2] The second ship of the fleet. (Fryer, i. 71.)

which would be on board, and that I should find old friends whom I had known in Persia and in the territories of the Great Mogul. I tendered him my thanks for having placed me in such good company; but after he had made this obliging offer he added that it was absolutely necessary that I should place all the rekenings which I had bought in the hands of the Avocat Fiscal, and that until I did so I should not be permitted to leave Batavia. He received no further reply from me than that I had already given, that the rekenings were at Bantam, and that I should have them sent for, provided he returned my money, on which he told me that for the amount I had disbursed, when I was about to leave, he would give me an order from himself and the Council to be paid in Holland by the Company. Some days passed without the matter being further discussed, save that once or twice I met the Fiscal, who asked me whether I had not yet obtained the rekenings from Bantam. My last reply was that I had written about them to the English President, who had my box in his house, and that I had asked him to send them to me; but that he had replied that I must go for them in person, or at the least send a man with an order in my own hand, and without that he could not send back my box. The truth was that it would have been difficult for him to send them, for the whole were with me, and I wished to see whether the time would not come when I should be asked no more about them. However, all those who had purchased these rekenings, merchants as well as captains and other persons who were returning this year, were put in prison, and the Council took from them, by force, all their papers, dismissed them from their offices, and they were sent to Holland as common soldiers.

Four or five days before the fleet left, the Avocat Fiscal came to tell me that he had the General's command to arrest me if I still refused to place in his hands the rekenings which he had already so often demanded. When I replied I had nothing to give him, he said, 'Be so good then as to follow me'; this I did willingly. He conducted me to a beautiful place on one of the bastions, called 'Sapphire,' where there is a pleasant house devoted to the amusement of the officers, where the majority of the respectable people of the town came to visit me, and sent me presents of the best wines. On the following day two Councillors came to see me, and told me that they knew not what objection I had to place in their hands that which they asked for, especially as they, with good grace, offered me an order for payment on the Company in Holland. I replied that it was not with a sufficiently good grace, and that when I saw the order I should make it my business to get back the rekenings. Two or three days more passed, during which the vessels commenced to set sail. This caused these gentlemen, both those of the Council of India and those of the town to the number of eight or ten, to come to see me. The Major, a very respectable man, was in their company, and he promised me that as soon as I had got the papers and handed them to the members of the Council to calculate the amount, he would so arrange it that the General would give me the order to be paid in Holland on my arrival there. Seeing that the vessels were about to leave and that I could not do otherwise, I told them that they must allow me to go to Bantam; this they were unwilling to agree to, preferring to send someone on my behalf to bring them. Having given my word, they told me that I might go out on parole, and that they were much distressed at what had happened. I replied that they had reason to be distressed, because I had the honour to belong to a great Prince, who was the late M. le Duc d'Orléans, who did me the honour to love me, and he would be able to fully resent the injustice which they had done me, and complain of it to the States. At length, forced by their unjust pressure, and by the necessity of leaving with the fleet, of which I did not wish to lose the opportunity, I gave them my rekenings, and from day to day I went to see if they had counted them, so as to give me the order they had promised. For the Vice-Admiral on which I was to embark remained more than fifteen days after the other vessels, because it was desired to send news by it to Holland, of what had been accomplished by a fleet which the General had sent to take possession of the Philippines by capturing them from the Spanish. On the voyage they met with bad weather so that three or four were lost; and they were obliged to return without accomplishing anything.

It is the custom, when the vessels are about returning to Holland, that the General entertains all the principal officers of the fleet with the Council and the most important personages of the town, and he did me the honour to invite me also. The repast commenced at 2 p.m., and at four tables there were fully sixty persons of both sexes. I was seated between the Major and the Secretary of the Grand Council; they were both men of worth, whose conversation was agreeable. We had been seven or eight hours at table, and they had already asked the General if it pleased him that the comedy should commence, which the youth of the town were to enact; whereupon I reminded the Major that he had promised me that as soon as I had delivered my papers to the Council they would give me an order to be paid on my arrival in Holland. I told him that the Secretary, to whom I had spoken in the morning, had given me reason to hope that I should have it before dinner; but the Secretary then said in my ear that I need not expect it, and when he said this he rose from the table to go to the comedy. I then asked our Vice-Admiral and three or four merchants who were returning to Holland to bear in mind what I should say to the General and his reply to me, and serve me as witnesses before the Directors of the Company when we arrived in Holland. In the *entre actes* of the comedy everyone took a glass and drank healths, and the General, glass in hand, addressed our Vice-Admiral, 'I drink your health,' said he, 'and that of M. Tavernier, whom may God vouchsafe to bless and protect on sea during this journey, as he has done in all the others which he has made by land.' I replied that I thanked him, and that I sincerely hoped that God would bless our journey, but that I should not make it without displeasure and without resentment for their failure to keep their promise—neither he nor his Council having kept the promise which they had made me to give an order on my handing them my rekenings, which amounted to 17,500 guilders; that now, when they had the papers which they asked for, they mocked me; but that I assured them I would publish their proceedings throughout the world. The General replied to this that I need not trouble myself, and that I might be cheerful during the voyage, as the order which he had promised me would be in Holland as soon as myself, and that I should have no cause to complain of them. Though but ill satisfied with the General, I took leave of him, and did not await the remainder of the comedy, being anxious, amongst other things, to prepare for my departure.

CHAPTER XXVII

The Author embarks on a Dutch Vessel in order to return to Europe.

Next day, at a very early hour, I took a small Chinese boat to go on board, where, on my arrival, I found one of the General's bodyguards, who came to convey to me once more his good wishes for my voyage, and to tell me that Madame la Générale begged me to accept a cask of Rhine wine, and some pots of fruits preserved in vinegar, which she sent me. There were cucumbers, mangoes, citrons, and eggs in their shells, which prevents them from becoming salt. I had taken no provisions with me, because some days before our departure the captain of the vessel told me that if I brought any they would not be received on board, as it was forbidden by the General. It is the custom that the General gives 200 écus to each captain of a vessel to furnish himself with all kinds of stores, and as I embarked by his advice on the Vice-Admiral, he caused double the sum to be given to the captain on my account, in order to have the honour to cause no expenditure to a stranger to whom he had offered a passage. Madame la Générale, when sending this present, bethought herself, possibly, of that which I had done some days previously for her daughter. Some friends seeing that I had easy access to the principal ladies of Batavia, begged me to intercede for a young man, a native of Paris, who in consequence of dissipation had come out to India as a soldier, and was in danger of the surgeons cutting off his leg, where he had an ulcer. To accomplish it I made a present to the

General's daughter, in order that she might ask the Major and the Avocat Fiscal not to appear to see this young man when he was leaving.

We were still three days in the roads before setting sail. On the first day the principal merchant of the fort, who kept a record of all the goods which had been embarked, both for Holland and other places, came to the vessel according to custom to examine the bill of lading, and have it read over by the captain of the vessel and the merchants who came with him, whom he made sign it. This bill of lading was placed in the box where they shut up all the account books and records of all that had passed in the factories of India, both concerning trade and as regards civil and criminal justice, and the covering over all the goods was then sealed.

On the second day the Major with the Avocat Fiscal and the chief surgeon also came, according to custom, to examine all those who were in the vessel returning to Holland—the Major to see whether there were any soldiers who were going without leave, for everyone must have his passport with him; the Avocat Fiscal to ascertain if any of the writers were concealed who wished to escape before their term was finished. The Chief Surgeon of the fort comes to see that all the sick persons who are being sent home have ailments which are incurable in the country, because some soldiers may obtain leave from the Major by the influence of friends, as he did, whom as I have said, I carried off; for the surgeon is obliged by oath not to allow anyone to go unless he considers that he cannot be cured but by going to Europe. The Major is bound to give the roll of all the soldiers, both of those who are well and those who are ill, to the Avocat Fiscal, who makes them come on the vessel one after the other; and it is then that the sick men are examined by the surgeon. It was perhaps not impossible that he whom I took might have been healed of his illness in the country; but by the favour of the Fiscal he was not called with the others, and escaped in that way.

On the third day the principal persons of the town and many ladies came to bid adieu to their friends who were leaving, and brought with them wine and food to entertain them, music accompanying the good cheer, and at 6 p.m. all of them returned home.

On the following day at daybreak we set sail, and were clear of the Straits sooner than we expected, because generally the wind is contrary, and besides we were leaving twenty-four days after all the others, the season for going to sea being nearly over. As soon as we had left the Straits we saw Prince's Island.[1] From thence our direction was to make for the Cocos Islands,[2] and when in the latitude of these islands we spent two or three days scouring the sea, expecting to sight them, but we were unable to do so, and this caused us to direct our course straight for the Cape of Good Hope.

On the forty-fifth day after our departure from Batavia—for I do not wish to weary the reader with a journal of our voyage—our Vice-Admiral neglected to order the ship's lantern to be lighted, in the belief that the whole fleet had already arrived at the Cape of Good Hope. It happened that a vessel of the same fleet called the 'Maestricht' also omitted to light its lantern the same night, and as it was very dark and the sea was high, it came into collision with our vessel; this threw everyone on both vessels into great consternation. All began to pray to God, believing that one or other of the vessels would be lost. Ours, which was called 'Les Provinces', was considered to be the largest and the best of the vessels which sailed to India; this was apparent from this collision, when it received so severe a shock. Everyone realizing the danger we were in, laboured to disengage

[1] Prince's Island is at the western end of the Straits of Sunda (p. 251 above).

[2] There are several groups of islands called Cocos: first, there is one in the Bay of Bengal between the Andamans and the mainland; second, a group of four coral-girt islands, in Lat. 3° N., near Hog (or Sinalu) Island on the W. coast of Sumatra; and third, the Cocos or Keeling Islands, from 700 to 800 miles SW. of Sumatra, in Lat. 12° 10′ S. and Long. 97° E. It was probably the last which Tavernier refers to. They produce coco-nuts in abundance, and have for many years been in the possession of an English family, several of whose members and a few Malays reside there. A recent account of this group will be found in A. D. Forbes, *A Naturalist's Wanderings*, and *Ency. Brit.*, xv. 112.

the other vessel from ours, and good fortune willed that the yards of the 'Maestricht', which were entangled in our rigging, broke away, and in order to help matters we cut some of them with an axe. Thus, with great trouble, the 'Maestricht' was disengaged, drifted all along the length of our vessel, and when she was passing the prow she broke off the beak-head.[1]

On the fifty-fifth day of our voyage we came in view of the Cape of Good Hope, and we remained outside five or six days, because the waves were so high that we did not venture to enter the roads to cast anchor. This was not because there was much wind, but because the south wind had blown so long that it had raised a sea on the coast. When the sea calmed down, we cast anchor, and this is what I have been able to observe there.

Of all the races of men I have seen in my travels I have found none so hideous nor so brutal as the Comouks,[2] whom I have mentioned in my account of Persia, and as the inhabitants of the Cape of Good Hope, whom they call Cafres or Hottentots. When the latter speak they make the tongue click (*peter*) in the mouth, and although their voice is scarcely articulate they easily understand one another. They have for their sole garments the skins of wild beasts which they kill in the forests, and when it becomes cold in the winter in this place, which is in 35° and some minutes of latitude, they turn the fur inside, and when it is warm they turn it outside. But it is only the better-to-do among them who are thus clothed, the others having only some miserable scrap of cloth to cover their nakedness. Both men and

[1] 'A small platform at the forepart of the upper deck; the part of a ship in front of the forecastle, fastened to the stem, and supported by the main knee.' (*New English Dictionary. s.v.*)

[2] Comouks in the original, and Comouchs in the *Persian Travels*, Book III, chap. xi, where Tavernier describes them as robbers living at the foot of the mountains of Comanie (i. e. the region between the Caucasus and the north-western shores of the Caspian Sea, bounded on the north by the Terek river). He distinguishes them from another people, the Kalmouchs (Kalmucks), who, he says, inhabit the coast of the Caspian between Moscovie and Great Tartary. For the Kumuk tribe see Keane, *Man Past and Present*, ed. 1920, p. 312

women are of spare habit and small stature, and as soon as a male is born his mother partially castrates him, and gives him sea-water to drink, and tobacco to eat. They perform this partial castration because it makes them swifter in running, so they say. It is true that there are some of them who can capture roebucks by running them down. I have had the curiosity to examine many of these Cafres, and I found they had all been castrated on the right side.[1] They have no knowledge of gold, silver, or any kind of money, and have not, so to speak, any religion.[2]

On our arrival in this place after we had cast anchor, four women came on board bringing with them four young ostriches, which were cooked for some of our sick men. Subsequently they brought many turtles and ostrich eggs, and another kind of eggs as large as the eggs of a goose. The birds which lay these eggs are a kind of goose, and have so much fat that it is impossible to eat them, as they taste rather of fish than of flesh.[3] These women, observing that our cook threw into a wooden bucket the entrails of two fowls and a goose which were for our supper, took them, squeezed them from one end to the other in order to express the contents, of which only half was ejected, and ate them in that condition,[4] being

[1] The object of this mutilation is to prevent the birth of twins (Hastings, *Ency. Religion and Ethics*, v. 580.)

[2] For an account of the religion of the Hottentots see Dr. E. Sidney Hartland's article, *ibid.*, vi. 820 ff., and that on Bantu and South Africa, *ibid.*, ii. 350 ff.

[3] These birds were penguins. (See vol. i, p. 174, *n.*, and ii, p. 307.) They are mentioned by Castanheda as occurring at St. Blaze, 60 leagues to the east of the Cape of Good Hope :—'On the rock also there are great numbers of birds as large as ducks, which do not fly, having no feathers in their wings, and which bray like so many asses.' *Note.*—Lichfield calls them stares, as large as ducks. Osorius says that the natives called them solitario, and that they were as big as geese. (Kerr's *Voyages and Travels*, ii. 309, 393.) Sir T. Roe says, 'They are a strange fowle, or rather a miscelanius creator of beast, bird, and fish, but most of bird, confuting that difinition of man to be *Animall bipes implunæ*, which is nearer to a discription of this Creature.' (*Journal*, ed. Foster, i. 12 : Mundy, ii. 327 f.)

[4] 'They eate the skinns of beasts or fowls, only sindgeing the haire and feathers a little, halfe scortched. Also the intralls, small guts and garbage, excrement and all, only quarter boiled or warmed in the fire' (Mundy, ii. 322).

much pleased also because our captain gave each of them two cups of spirits to drink. Neither men nor women have the slightest shame about exposing their nudity, and they live almost like beasts.

When they see vessels arriving they drive cattle to the shore and bring what they have to barter for tobacco, spirits, and beads of crystal and agate, which are cheap at Surat, and for some hardware. When they are not content with what is offered them they immediately take to flight, and at the sound of a whistle all their animals follow them, and you see no more of them. Some persons on one occasion, saw them fly, and fired musket-shots in order to slay the cattle, but for some years past, these Cafres have not brought their beasts, and there has been much trouble in inducing them to return. It is a great convenience for the vessels which touch there to obtain supplies, and the Dutch have had good reason for building a fort there. There is now a fine village inhabited by people of all nationalities who live with the Dutch, and all kinds of grains which are imported, both from Europe and Asia, on being sown, grow much better than in the places whence they have been brought. It is a very good country, as I have said, at the 35th degree and some minutes of latitude, and it is neither the air nor the heat which makes these Cafres so black as they are. Desiring to know the explanation of it, and why they smell so strongly, I inquired from a young girl who was taken as soon as her mother had brought her forth, and was nursed and reared in the fort, being as white as one of our European women. She told me that the reason that the Cafres are so black, is that they rub themselves with an ointment which they make of different simples known to them, and that if they do not rub themselves often, and as soon as they are born, they become dropsical like other blacks of Africa, and like the Abyssinians, and the inhabitants of Saba, who have one leg twice the size of the other;[1] few of these people live more than forty years. It is true that these Cafres, brutal as they are, have nevertheless a special knowledge

[1] The disease known as elephantiasis. On the use of grease by Cafres see J. G. Wood, *Natural History of Man*, i. 36 f.

of simples, and know how to apply them to the maladies for which they are specifics ; this the Dutch have very often proved.[1] Whether the Cafres are bitten by a venomous animal, or that an ulcer or other disease appears, by means of these simples, which they know how to select, they accomplish the cure in a short time. Of nineteen sick men who were in our vessel, fifteen were placed in the hands of the Cafres, their maladies consisting of ulcers in the legs or wounds received in war, and in less than fifteen days all were perfectly cured. Each sick man had two of these Cafres to attend upon him, and as soon as they saw what the condition of the wound or ulcer was, they sought for the drugs, crushed them between two pebbles and applied them to the sore. As for the four others, they were not given into their hands, being so infected with venereal disease that they could not be cured at Batavia. All four died between the Cape and the Island of Saint Helena.

In the year 1661 there returned from Batavia on a vessel named the 'West Frisland', a young Breton gentleman, who squandered all his money in Holland, and then entered the Company's service. When he arrived at Batavia a multitude of mosquitoes bit him on his leg during the night, and an ulcer appeared on which all the surgeons of Batavia had expended their skill and remedies ; if the General had not given him permission to go home it would have been necessary to amputate his leg. When the ship arrived at the Cape, the captain sent the Breton on shore to give him some ease, these Cafres began to examine him, and said that if they were allowed to treat him they would cure him in a short time. The captain placed him in their hands, and in less than fifteen days his leg was rendered as sound as the other which had never had anything the matter with it.

As soon as a vessel has anchored at the Cape, the commander gives some of the soldiers and sailors permission to go on shore to refresh themselves. Those who during the voyage have been most indisposed go first, each in his turn, to the town, where they are fed for 7 or 8 sols a-day, and enjoy good cheer.

[1] Tavernier's statement is repeated by F. Leguat (*Voyage*, ii. 294.)

It is the custom of the Dutch to send parties from time to time to explore the country, and those who go furthest are best rewarded. A number of soldiers went in a party with a sergeant who commanded them, and advanced far into the country, where they made a large fire at midnight, both to protect themselves from lions and for warmth, and lay round it to rest. When they were asleep, a lion seized one of the soldiers by the arm, and immediately the sergeant fired a shot and slew the animal. When it was dead its jaws had to be forced open, with great effort, in order to release the soldier's arm, which was pierced from side to side. It is apparent from this story that it is an error to suppose that lions do not approach a fire.[1] The Cafres healed the soldier's arm in twelve days. There are in the fort several skins of lions and tigers.[2] Among others there is the skin of a horse which the Cafres killed. It is white barred with black stripes pricked out like a leopard, and without a tail.[3] At a distance of two or three leagues from the fort the Dutch found a dead lion with four porcupine's quills in its body, which had penetrated the flesh three-fourths of their length. It was accordingly concluded that the porcupine had killed the lion. The skin is still kept with the spines sticking in the foot.[4]

At one league's distance from the fort there is a fine village which grows from day to day. When the vessels of the Dutch Company arrive, if any soldier or sailor wishes to remain there he is welcomed. He takes as much land as he can manage,[5] and, as I have above said, all kinds of vegetables

[1] Ball notes that some African travellers have been of opinion that a fire attracts lions, and that a substantial fence is requisite for the protection of a camp.

[2] By tigers here we must understand leopards, as tigers do not occur in Africa any more than lions do in the eastern and southern parts of India, where Tavernier has so often referred to their presence in previous pages.

[3] Zebra; it should have had a tail. On the zebra sent from Abyssinia to Aurangzeb, see Bernier, 135, 143.

[4] Numerous cases are recorded of tigers having died in India from this cause, and some have been found, when shot, to have porcupine quills sticking in them.

[5] Here we have an early reference to the first Dutch Boer settlement
21 at the Cape. In 1671 the first purchase of land from the Hottentots,

and pulse, and even grapes grow readily, and rice also is cultivated. These people have young ostriches, beef, and sea and fresh water fish in abundance. When they wish to catch the young ostriches, as soon as the birds are seven or eight days old they go to the nests, drive a stake into the ground and tie the young birds by one of their feet in the nest, so that they cannot escape, leaving them to be fed by their parents till they are of good size, when they are taken to be sold or eaten.

When the Dutch began to inhabit the Cape of Good Hope, they took, as I have said, the daughter of one of these Cafres as soon as she was born. She is white and beautiful, save that she has a slightly depressed nose, and she serves as interpreter to the Dutch. She had a child by a Frenchman, but the Company would not allow him to marry her. On the contrary, they confiscated 800 livres of his wages; this was somewhat hard on him.

In this country there are many lions and tigers, and the Dutch have discovered a contrivance which answers well for killing them. They fasten a gun to a stake driven into the ground, and fix some meat at the end of the gun, which is bound to a cord attached to the trigger. When the animal comes to take this meat the cord draws the trigger, and the balls lodge in its mouth or body. The Cafres eat a root which resembles our root of cherüy,[1] which they roast, and it serves them as bread. Sometimes they make it into flour, and it tastes like chestnuts. As for flesh, they eat it raw, and fish also in the same condition; and as for the entrails of animals,

beyond the fort built by Riebeck, marked the beginning of the colony (*Ency. Brit.*, v. 237), see Ovington, 499, and Du Bois, p. 151.

[1] Dr. E. Sidney Hartland has kindly searched many authorities on South Africa in order to identify this root. F. Leguat (*Voyage*, Hakluyt Society ed., ii. 287) says of the Hottentots: 'They set great store by a Root that resembles our skirrets [a perennial umbelliferous plant, Sium sisarum, *New English Dict. s.v.*]. They roast it, and oftentimes make it into Past, which is their Bread, and somewhat like our Chestnut.' It is apparently a kind of ground-nut, which Junod (*Life of a South African Tribe*, ii. 12) says 'is extensively cultivated, being of every-day use in the Thonga culinary art, which it provides with the fatty principles. . . . Its taste is delicious, either prepared as a sauce to season mealie flour, or roasted'. [In mod. Fr. chervi or -is = skirret.]

as I have already said,[1] they merely squeeze them to exclude the digested matter and then eat them. Most of the women bind these entrails, when dried, round their legs, especially those of wild beasts which their husbands slay in the woods, and they wear them as ornaments. They also eat turtles after they have roasted them for a short time, so that the shells can be removed. They are very skilful in hurling the assegai, a kind of dart, and those who have not got one, use a stick an inch thick, of a very hard wood, and of the same length as the dart. They make a point on it and hurl it to a considerable distance with their hands. They take these sticks with them to the margin of the sea, and as soon as a fish comes to the surface they do not fail to transfix it.

As for those birds which are like our ducks, their eggs contain no yolk; there are a great number in the country, and in a bay which is eighteen miles from the Cape they are killed with blows of a stick.[2]

. . . .

During the time while M. Vandime was General, the Dutch captured a young Cafre boy at the Cape and sent him to Batavia. The General took great pains to have him instructed in languages, so that in seven or eight years he learned Dutch and Portuguese in perfection. He then wished to return to his country, and the General not desiring to constrain him to remain, equipped him with linen and clothes, thinking that when he arrived at the Cape he would live like the Dutchmen, and would aid them in obtaining supplies for their vessels whenever they arrived. But he was no sooner at the Cape than he threw his garments into the sea and fled with the other blacks, eating raw flesh as before, and since then he has remained with them without having any intercourse with the Dutch.[3]

[1] See above p. 302. [2] See i. 174, ii. 302.

[3] Some curious examples of this kind of speedy relapse into savagery, after a long course of education from infancy, have occurred among the inhabitants of the Andaman islands. A good case of a similar reversion to savagery is that of Billy Button, told by Charles Darwin (*Voyage of a Naturalist*, chap. x). Miss Gordon Cumming gives instances of the same kind in Fiji (*At Home in Fiji*). The question forms the subject of a story by Grant Allen, 'The Reverend John Creedy' (*Strange Stories*, 1892).

When these Cafres go to hunt in the forest they collect in large numbers, and cry or shout, so that the beasts are frightened by them, and it is then easy to slaughter large numbers of them. I have even been told that these cries frighten the lion.

CHAPTER XXVIII

The Dutch fleet arrives at St. Helena, and the Author gives a description of that Island.

When we had stayed twenty-two days at the Cape of Good Hope, and found that the wind was very favourable to us, our Vice-Admiral ordered the anchor to be hoisted, and we directed our course for the Island of St. Helena.[1] As soon as the sails were set and prayers had been said, all the sailors and soldiers declared they would go to rest and sleep till they got to St. Helena. For a steady wind always prevails and bears you, generally in sixteen or eighteen days, to the anchorage at that island. During the whole course the sails were not touched, because the wind was always astern, and the only trouble the sailors had was that fourteen days after our departure two of them were sent to the main-mast top to watch, in order to sight the island ; for as soon as it is sighted the pilots should take good care to be ready to cast anchor on the side facing northwards, and it is necessary to approach the land in order to cast it, otherwise no bottom can be found. If these precautions are not taken, and if the anchors do not find bottom, the currents in the air and ocean carry the vessel quickly past the anchorage and there is then no hope of returning, because the wind is always contrary and never changes.

As soon as two of our anchors were cast into the sea the soldiers and sailors were summoned, and the crew made the vessel as tight as they could. They also fixed stages outside to scrape the hull and grease it ; this was accomplished in two days. Then all on board were divided into two watches, and the Vice-Admiral addressed them from the quarter-deck

[1] Compare Ovington, 89 ff. ; *Voyage of F. Leguat*, ii. 298 ff.

as follows: 'Gentlemen, we shall remain here twenty-two days, arrange which of you desire to go first on shore to refresh yourselves and hunt, and let all return here on the eleventh day so that the others may also go in turn.' Each of the men who went on shore was given a pair of shoes, and they carried large cauldrons, and supplies of rice, biscuit, spirits, and salt. On reaching land they ascended the mountain, but three or four remained below to collect sorrel, which grows to two or three feet in height and is very good. When they had collected a load of it they went to find the others, who were in pursuit of wild pigs, which abound in the island. When they had killed some they cooked the flesh with the rice and sorrel, which make a fairly good kind of soup, and purges insensibly without one's knowing it. While on shore they did nothing but sing, drink, and eat, and they had to send some of the pigs to the vessel every day. For each pig an écu and a pair of shoes were given them, because the mountain was high and steep, and this chase gave the men much trouble. I have elsewhere spoken of the Persian greyhounds which are taken to St. Helena for hunting wild pigs, and after having been used they are thrown into the sea, and not carried farther for the reason I have pointed out in the same place.

While those who are on land occupy themselves with this sport, those who remain in the vessel spend their time in fishing; for there is a great abundance of fish around the island, especially mackerel.[1] Each sailor and soldier is given a measure of salt, with which they salt the fish, and then hang them to dry in the wind. They feed themselves upon this dried fish after leaving the island, and generally have sufficient for thirty or forty days, and each receives only a little oil and rice cooked in water; this saves the Company a quantity of food.

All the pigs, sheep, geese, ducks, and hens which were on board were sent on shore, and as soon as these animals had eaten the sorrel, which purges them as well as it does men, in a few days they became so fat that when we approached

[1] Of sixty-five species of sea-fish caught off the island, including mackerel, seventeen are peculiar to St. Helena (*Ency. Brit.*, xxiv. 7).

Holland it was almost impossible to eat them, especially the geese and ducks, on account of the fat.

There are two places off the coast of St. Helena where one can anchor. The best of them is where we were, because the bottom is very good for anchorage, and the drinking water which comes from the top of the mountain is the best on the island. In this part of the island there is no level ground, for the mountain rises from the very shore. There is only a small flat place close to the sea, where formerly there was a chapel where a Portuguese priest of the sect of St. Francis lived for fourteen years; but at present this chapel is half ruined. While this priest lived there he made presents to the vessels which touched there, furnishing them with fish, which he caught and dried, and they gave him in exchange rice, biscuit, and Spanish wine. After he had dwelt there for the time I have said, and had lived a very austere life, he fell ill, and by good fortune it happened that a Portuguese vessel arrived just then. Everything was done to relieve him, but he died five days after the vessel had anchored, and was interred by people of his own nationality.

The anchorage is not so good at the other roads, but on shore there is a beautiful plain where all that is sown arrives at maturity. The orders of the Dutch Company are at present, that, if a vessel takes cabbages, salad, or other vegetables, seeds must be sown for the benefit of those who may come afterwards. There are many lemon and some orange trees, which the Portuguese planted. For this nationality has this to its credit, that wherever it goes it seeks to do something for the benefit of those who afterwards visit the place. The Dutch do the reverse and seek to destroy everything, so that those who come afterwards shall find nothing. It is true that it is not the superior officers who act in this way, but the common sailors and soldiers, who say to one another, 'We shall not return any more', and in order to get fruit from a tree more quickly, they cut it down instead of plucking the fruit.

A serious disturbance was on the point of breaking out. In the fleet although our vessel left Batavia the last of all, since she was a good sailer, she was the second to arrive at

St. Helena. One day the Vice-Admiral, the captain, and other officers of the vessel determined to go in the skiff towards this plain, to obtain some vegetables and lemons. When we arrived there—for I was with the party—we were much surprised to find nothing on the trees, and only some remains of cabbages and radishes on the ground. We did not doubt that the crew of the vessel called the *Encuse,* which had arrived some days before us, had done all this damage, and our Vice-Admiral resolved to go on board to inquire into the matter. When we got there we found quantities of lemons and vegetables in the cabins of the captain and pilot, and all the sailors presented lemons, with which they were well provided, to our men. The captain of the vessel offered a present of some to the Vice-Admiral, which he refused to accept, saying that it was treason to all the fleet, and that all these delicacies must be collected and put together in one place until all the vessels had arrived. so that each poor invalid might have some of them. The sailors and soldiers who had filled their chests with them were very unwilling to consent; but the Vice-Admiral, exerting his authority, said that if they did not bring all the lemons which were still remaining, he would hang a number of the men, when the Admiral and the remainder of the fleet, which consisted of eleven vessels, arrived. The captain, fearing his threat, put so much pressure on his crew that the whole were brought into his cabin and safely shut up until the fleet had arrived, so that each vessel had its share of this small refreshment.

When all the fleet had anchored in the roads of St. Helena, there was nothing but feasting and rejoicing, sometimes on one vessel and sometimes on another; and the English fleet, which consisted of nine vessels, arrived soon afterwards.[1] There arrived, moreover, two Portuguese vessels laden with slaves of both sexes, which came from the Guinea coast, on their way to the mines of Peru. Some Dutchmen in our fleet who had dwelt at Castel de Mine, knew the language of these poor people. They went on board, to see them, and also some Dutch sailors who were in the Portuguese service;

[1] For a summary of the voyages of the early English adventurers see *Imperial Gazetteer,* ii. 453 f.

and on the following night about 250 of these poor blacks threw themselves into the sea. It was believed that the Dutch, who knew their language, had told them that they would be miserably treated when they reached the mines, and this had driven them to despair. It is true that it is a very hard and miserable slavery; for frequently, after having worked for some days, some of the softer strata collapse and suddenly bury 400 or 500 of these poor people. As soon as they are put to mining their faces, eyes, and skin entirely change colour; this is caused by the vapours in the excavations, and slaves are kept alive in these places only by the quantity of spirits which are supplied to both the men and women.

Some of these people are no longer slaves, their masters having given them liberty, but they do not cease to work in the mines and earn large wages. But as they leave the mines on Saturday evening to return on Monday morning, during the interval they drink so much spirit, which is very dear, that they spend all they earn during the week, and thus they are always in a miserable condition of poverty.

While the two fleets were in the roads at St. Helena the English and the Dutch entertained each other in turns, and there was continual festivity. The day our Vice-Admiral entertained our Admiral and some of the chiefs of the English fleet, it was not on board our vessel, for as soon as he told me of his intention, I advised him to give his feast on land; this he did with greater credit and more freedom than the others had done. I offered him for the purpose my tent, and the carpet and cushions which I had still with me, and had used in my journeys by land; and I further promised to open, on his account, my cask of Rhine wine, which Madame la Générale had presented me with, and even to contribute to the collation half a dozen bottles of Mantua wine, and a similar quantity of that of Shīrāz. He was delighted with the offer I made him, and immediately we went on shore to pitch the tent; this gave us some trouble, because we could not find any level spot even of the size of the tent; but our sailors made one near the river, whence, while eating, we might contemplate the high mountains and the pointed rocks, where we saw the male and female goats leaping from one side to the other.

On the following day, between 9 and 10 a.m., he had the pleasure of seeing all the guests in their boats, some with trumpets and drums, others with violins and other musical instruments; this could not have been if the Vice-Admiral had given his entertainment in the vessel, where all these different classes of people could not have come. As the feast, then, was on land, the majority of the ladies, both English and Dutch, who were in the fleet also came, without being invited; and so instead of one table three were required, and those who expected to eat in the tent, under shade, were obliged to yield their places out of politeness to the ladies. During the repast there was a great noise of trumpets and other musical instruments, and at each health all the guns of the vessels fired a discharge. The first health which was drunk was that of the King of England, after which followed those of the States General, of the Prince of Orange, and of the Companies, and then came the healths of the chief officers of the fleet and of some private persons. At the close of the repast, when we were ready to return on board, a disaster happened which somewhat marred the enjoyment of the company. The Admiral's trumpeter, having drunk a little more than he ought to have done, mounted on a high rock in order to blow his trumpet, and from time to time he rolled down large stones. Although ordered to stop, because it was seen that some injury might happen, he did not cease, however, finding some amusement in it; and at length he let go a very large one, which, jumping from rock to rock, went through the tent, where it broke a case of wine and killed a small boy born at Batavia of Dutch parentage. He was being sent to Holland to learn the language properly, and to be taught to read and write. For these children, though born of parents who have come from Holland, never learn Dutch properly while they remain at Batavia, being brought up among servants and slaves, who use the Portuguese language more than Dutch. These children also learn from them a thousand wickednesses, and at the age of nine years they know more lechery than do youths of twenty years in Europe.[1] After burying the child the company returned on board sooner than they would otherwise have done, and they were distressed that a day which had been so joyful had so sad an ending.

On the next two days we had numerous visits, and there was not a lady who did not come to our vessel; I believe it was less on our own account than to ascertain if we had still any Rhine wine, which they had found to be excellent at our Vice-Admiral's feast.

After our vessel had been twenty days at anchor—for the others which arrived later had less time to refresh themselves—the Admiral fired three cannon, and hoisted a large flag on the poop of his vessel, as a signal to all the captains and pilots to come on board; when they arrived, they held council to settle what route should be taken for Holland. The majority maintained that they should go to the west rather than to the south, because the season for navigation was much advanced, and by sailing towards the West Indies we should find the proper winds for Holland. But it happened otherwise; for as soon as we had passed the line we found the winds contrary to what our pilots had expected; this was the reason why we were afterwards obliged to go to the 64th degree in the latitude of Iceland, and return to Holland from the north.

CHAPTER XXIX

The Dutch fleet leaves the Island of St. Helena, and the Author arrives safely with it in Holland.

On the day after the council had been held, the Admiral ordered the three signal shots for parting, to be fired, and at ten o'clock p.m. all the fleet set sail. The English still remained there and we did not know why, unless it was to try to catch one of their sailors, who was ill-treated by his pilot, one day went on shore with him to get water, and slew him with two stabs of his dagger, after which he escaped into the mountain. If he remained there he must have

[1] There is, it is to be feared, some applicability in these remarks to the case of children reared in India at the present time.

passed a bad time, as there is no house in the island. Three days after our departure from St. Helena the crew commenced to pray every morning and evening, but I remarked that they had not done so during the twenty-two days we spent in the roads; this I thought strange, as if one should not pray to God when out of danger as well as while in danger.

On the eleventh day after our departure we crossed the line with a favourable wind. I know that many have written that the heat is insupportable under the line, and that the water and some of the provisions become decomposed, but we experienced nothing of the kind; elsewhere in the voyage we felt much greater heat. I am quite ready to admit that if a calm had caught us under the line, instead of the propitious wind which we experienced, we should have felt the heat more than we did.

After some days' sailing we spent three in passing a bank where the sea is full of a plant, the leaf of which resembles the leaves of the olive.[1] This plant has fruits like large white gooseberries, but they contain nothing inside. At length, after many more days' sailing, we sighted the coasts of Iceland, and afterwards the Island of Ferelle,[2] where the Dutch fleet already awaited us, constantly firing cannon shots to intimate its position to us. As soon as the two fleets sighted one another, each vessel fired all its guns, and took up position by its patron, that of the Admiral by the Admiral, that of the Vice-Admiral by the Vice-Admiral, and so of all the others. We numbered eleven vessels, there came also eleven other vessels to meet us, and after each had recognized its mate, the first thing that was done was to send on board the vessels from India a quantity of supplies, such as casks of beer, smoked meat, butter, cheese, good white biscuit, and for every vessel one cask each of Rhine, French, and Spanish wines. As soon as the supplies were on board our vessel, the soldiers and sailors took three or four of the casks of beer, which they placed on end close to the mainmast, broke them open with a cannon-ball, and they were then

[1] This was the sargossa weed, Fucus natans, or sargassum bucciferum which is found in the Pacific. The so-called fruits are the floats.

[2] Faroe Islands.

free to whoever wished to drink. It was the same with the food, for both drink and food were at the discretion of the crew during the remainder of the voyage. Next day each pilot resigned his charge, giving over the direction to the pilots brought by the convoy. There were three of them for each vessel, and for that purpose pilots of from sixty to eighty years of age, who knew these seas perfectly, and how the sand-banks had changed during the current year, were selected.

Next day the Admiral of the convoy fired three cannon shots, and hoisted his flag on the poop, to give notice to all the officers of both fleets to assemble in council. All the reports and processes which have been made against those who have misbehaved during the voyage are taken to it, and the whole being examined, according as the council adjudicates the accused are brought from each vessel on the following day, and judgement is pronounced. Formerly they took them to Holland, but when it was so, they found friends who obtained their pardon, and they all got off. But at present all are afraid, as there is no longer chance of pardon. This is the reason why the soldiers and sailors are not guilty of insolence and mutiny during the voyage as they were formerly. There were two men of our fleet hanged for having stabbed officers; many were sentenced to the stocks and whipping before the mainmast, and the wages of others were confiscated.

We passed through a fleet of herring fishers, and they did not fail to bring casksful to each vessel. The captains presented them with rice, pepper, and other spices.

As soon as we had sighted the coasts of Holland, all the soldiers of our fleet who had been with those who went to besiege the Manillas, from joy at beholding their country again, fixed a quantity of large and small wax tapers about the poop and bow of the vessel, where the wind, when they were lit, could not extinguish them. The same was done in five or six of the vessels; this gave out such an extraordinary light that the whole fleet was alarmed. On our vessel alone, there were more than 1,700 of these wax tapers, both large and small. The sailors had kept them since they were at the Manillas, from whence they had brought a large quantity, as also from Pointe de Galle in the Island of Ceylon. For when on shore they pillaged and burnt some convents which were in the country, and as wax is cheap in India, and is easily bleached, every religious house always has a large supply of wax tapers for the festivals, when numbers are lighted before the grand altar and in all the chapels. Thus the least of the Dutch sailors had thirty or forty of these tapers for his share, and some of them had some as thick as a man's thigh.

The command was, according to custom, that our vessel, as Vice-Admiral, should go to Zealand. We were on the coast seven whole days without being able to enter Flushing,[1] on account of the sand which frequently changes its position. As soon as we had cast anchor, more than fifty small boats came about our vessel, but kept a short distance off, being forbidden to come alongside. Each then began to call out and ask the names of persons in order to carry the news of their arrival to their relatives and friends.

On the day following that on which we anchored off Flushing, two of the members of the Company came on board to welcome us all, and to tell us to close our chests and place our marks thereon. They were then carried into a hall of the India House, and the day was fixed upon which each should return to claim what belonged to him. It is the custom that before the chests are given up they are opened to be examined, through fear lest they should contain anything contraband.

These two gentlemen summoned the crew on deck between the poop and the mainmast, and taking the captain, whom they placed at their side in front of all, 'Gentlemen,' they said to all on board, 'on behalf of the Directors we order you to tell us whether the captain has ill-treated you during this voyage.' The crew, who wanted to be on shore, where the majority saw father or mother, brothers or sisters, or friends awaiting them, began to cry out that the captain was a good man, that he knew how to act for the interests of the Company and his own also; but that if, when leaving Batavia, God had delivered them from him, they would have

[1] Flessingue in the original.

been much more happy during the voyage. At once, without another word, they all jumped into the boats and went on shore, where they received many kisses and embraces, and immediately all hastened to the public-house. Most of the soldiers and sailors first go there after their debarkation, and generally they do not leave it save to claim their baggage or receive their pay, or to join a party. Some of these soldiers and sailors returning from India have been known to expend, in two months' continual debauch, nearly 1,000 écus, which they had had much trouble in earning in fifteen or twenty years' service to the Company. I have known a sailor at Middelburg, who in a debauch broke glass to the value of 250 livres, when drinking the health of his friends. But the publicans do not receive all the money of these people, as the women of pleasure get their share of it too.

The two Directors of the Company, who came on board as soon as the anchor was cast, to give permission to the crew to go on shore, and appoint persons for the protection of the vessel, did me the honour to salute me at once, and I received many expressions of kindness from them. They ordered a collation to be served at the same time, and, drinking to my health, asked me if I had anything to complain of with regard to any of the officers of the vessel. I replied that on the contrary I had every reason to praise them, that they had all treated me with great civility, and that I gave thanks to the Vice-Admiral, to the captain, and to all the merchants of the vessel for the good friendship they had shown me during the voyage. For it should be stated that besides the Vice-Admiral we had a captain under him. The Directors told me that they were much pleased that I was satisfied with the treatment I had received, telling me that if I had any chests I had only to place my mark on them, and that they would take care to have them carried to the Company's House at Middelburg, where I might come to claim them in four days. It required fully this time for them to discharge a part of what was in the vessel, which could not reach Middelburg with a full cargo. I thanked them for their goodwill, and, having placed my mark on my chests, left the vessel and went by land to Middelburg.

It was the year that the Chamber General was held there, for it is held for four years in succession at Amsterdam, and two years at Middelburg. The reason is, that Amsterdam owns half the Company; Middelburg a quarter; and Rotterdam, Delft, Horne, and Encuse each a sixteenth; and the Company is not bound to hold the Chamber in either of these four last, which only make up one-fourth, and have the right only to have a vessel each year between the four, one year at Rotterdam, one year at Delft, and similarly the others. For the same reason Amsterdam has eight Directors, Middelburg four and the other four towns each its own one; this makes the number sixteen, though they always speak of seventeen Directors, because the President has two votes.

On the fourth day of my arrival at Middelburg I went to the India House, where I found two of the Directors, who were already engaged in delivering the chests to those to whom they belonged, and as soon as they saw me they told me to claim mine; this I did, at the same time handing them the keys of my boxes, so that they might see for themselves whether I carried anything which was contraband. Of these two gentlemen one was from Zealand, and the other from Horne, and the latter took the keys to open my boxes. But the Zealand Director, more civil than he of North Holland, told him I was free, that I was not subject to the Company, and that it had afforded me a free passage. My keys were at once returned to me, and one of the people of the store was ordered to summon some sledges, which are used in Holland instead of waggons, to convey my chests. I may say in passing, that it is not only on this occasion that I have remarked that the more one approaches the north the less civility and honesty we meet among the inhabitants, and that manners follow the harshness and roughness of the climate.

The same evening the Directors did me the honour to send one of their officers to invite me to dine with them on the following day. Many persons interested in the Company were at the repast, and I believe that they were there less for the good cheer than to hear me talk, thinking that I might know many things in regard to the private trade which the representatives of the Company carry on in India. They were not mistaken; and I may say that no one could be better informed than I was of the methods of these agents, who have the management of the factories in Persia and India, to enrich themselves. For they never return to Holland empty-handed, and when they take but 100,000 or 150,000 florins they count it a poor thing. I have known many of them who have amassed up to 600,000 and 700,000 florins; as, for instance, among others the Sieur Nicolas Obrechit,[1] who was chief of the Dutch factories both at Ispahān and Hormuz and other places in Persia, during the years from 1635 to 1640. His friends and those who had done business with him estimated that he carried away more than 15,000 tomāns, which are equal to about 690,000 livres,[2] without estimating what he had expended on the gout with which he was afflicted, and the other ailments which more often arise from relationships with the courtesans of Persia, than from the trouble expended in packing silk, weighing it, examining its quality, and seeing whether it has any bad skeins mixed with the good. The Sieur Obrechit was well able to spend freely, for his profits were large, but such as are rarely permitted or approved of by honest people. All the spices, sugar, and other goods of the Company are sold wholesale, generally at Hormuz or Gombroon, and amount in value, annually, to 15 or 16 tonnes of gold, each tonne being equal to 100,000 guilders, which are equivalent in our money to 120,000 livres, and the 16 tonnes of gold to 1,920,000 livres. The Sieur Obrechit did not sell all these goods without receiving annually for himself, 80,000 or 100,000 guilders,[3] which the Persian merchants presented to him, underhand, through the broker, so that he might allow the goods to be sold at a low price. But he was not the inventor of this fine means of enriching himself, others practised it before him,

[1] The correct name of this official, as Sir W. Foster points out, was Nicolaas Overschie, President der Commissarissen van Huwelykze- en Kleine Zaken in 1741 at Batavia, after which year he disappears.

[2] Equal to £51,750.

[3] Taking the Dutch guilder or florin at 1*s*. 9½*d*. (vol. i, p. 328) the value of the tonne would be about £9,000. Perhaps the guilder ought to be a fraction more, but it is important to have here independent testimony that the livre as understood by Tavernier was about 1*s*. 6*d*.—the proportion being 5 guilders = 6 livres, or 9*s*.

and since his time others have employed it, especially the Sieurs Constant and Van-Wück.

Moreover, there is also the profit that these gentry make on silk. It is true that for some years past the Company has not esteemed Persian silk so highly as it did formerly, because it has not so great a sale in Japan as it would have had if the trade had continued as it was in the years 1636 and 1637.[1] All the chiefs of the factory who succeeded Obrechit could not have made as much as he did; for in the two above-named years silk was dear in Japan, because the people of China and Tonquin were then at war with the Dutch, and the latter prevented them from trading with Japan; so the Chinese and Tonquinese could not obtain silk except through the hands of the Dutch. Whatever it may cost they must have it to clothe themselves with, as they use no other materials for their garments. It was in these two years, 1636 and 1637, that the Sieur Obrechit filled his purse; for instead of 500 or 600 bales of silk, which is the most they receive from the King of Persia, the General of Batavia and his Council wrote to him that at any cost he must send them 2,000 loads. I have alluded, in the first volume of my history, to the agreement made between the King of Persia and the Dutch Company; and I have also made mention, in connexion with this subject, of the small success of the negotiation of the Ambassadors of Holstein, of which the secretary of that embassy has without doubt not boasted in the account which he has given to the public. Therefore, for fear of wearying the reader, I shall not repeat it here, and I shall only ask him to remember that the arrival of these Ambassadors, which caused apprehension and jealousy among the Dutch, caused the latter to raise the price of silk so much that they removed all desire in other nations to outbid them.

Thus Obrechit, having then received an order from Batavia
for 2,000 loads of silk, irrespective of cost, and this quantity
being all that Persia could supply, as he was shrewd and
22 loved profit beyond all things, succeeded so well in intriguing

[1] For an account of the Persian silk trade see Curzon, *Persia*, i. 366 ff.

with the Armenians and other merchants in Persia that he obtained the 2,000 loads of silk which had been ordered. It is true that beyond the 500 or 600 loads which the Dutch receive from the King, according to the agreement made between his Majesty and the Company, Obrechit was obliged to pay at a high rate for the others; and he bought them from the Armenians, who sold them to him at the same rate as those they had sold to Aleppo and Smyrna. During these two years there was not a single load of silk for which he did not place 4 tomāns in his purse, and he said some loads cost him 60 tomāns. It was represented to him that it would be better not to send so large a quantity of silk, as it was so dear, and that the merchants of the country, both Christians and Musalmāns, were laughing at him; but he only replied that he must obey the Company's order. One day when I was alone with him we were talking together about my travels, and he told me how astonished he was, after my experience of the greater part of the trade of Asia, that I underwent so much trouble in my long journeys; that I should do much better by serving the Company, and that if I wished he would send me to the diamond mines on its account; but I believe it would have been on his own. When I had thanked him for his goodwill, and told him I had no such intention, he replied that I did not know what I was refusing, that I would derive great profit, and that in his factory, with a scratch of the pen, or by changing a figure, he obtained what he wished. I replied to him that on three or four occasions my horoscope had been cast, and on all occasions it had been agreed that I should live to a good age; and so, if I was able to acquire wealth, I desired to acquire it honestly and by my labour, as God had ordained for me, in order to be able to possess it with greater security and comfort to my soul for the remainder of my days, and that my heirs might enjoy it peaceably. If we were not to act in this way, replied he, we should be miserable; for the wages the Company gives us would not suffice to clothe us. On my return from one of my voyages I went to see him at a village bearing his name, situated one league from the Hague. I saw him ill in bed, and suffering from several diseases, and I believe that he often then recalled to mind what I had said to him at Ispahān.

I must now return to the Directors and the members of the Company with whom I dined at Middelburg. Most of them desired that I should inform them of the manner in which the agents of the Company behaved in Persia and India, and the others asked me to speak of my travels. I preferred to satisfy the latter, and avoided all referenec to trade. It is true that if I had not had some suspicion of the deception which they played me subsequently, I would possibly have told them many things from which they might have derived benefit. For in the space of the forty years during which I have often visited Persia and India, most persons in the service of the Company have told me all the tricks they made use of in order to acquire money. In return for this confidence, when they were about to return home, I endeavoured to furnish them with a good parcel of diamonds, which occupy but little space. If then I had declared to these gentlemen what I knew of this matter, they would have gained much in studying the record I should have given, and by discovering the knavery of their servants, and by doing rightly by me, their conscience would not be charged as it is, concerning the 17,500 florins which General Vanderlin and his Council seized from me at Batavia.

What astonishes me most is, as I have elsewhere remarked, that when the General and his Council took from me the value of these 17,500 florins, they made a hundred promises that I should be paid immediately I set foot in Holland, but this was not done in spite of all the steps I could take for recovering the amount. For when leaving the feast that was given at Batavia on the departure of the fleet, I took four witnesses of the fact, namely, our Vice-Admiral and three merchants, to whom, when taking leave of the General and Council, I said aloud in their presence that they would be my witnesses if God permitted us to arrive in Holland or Zealand, and would remember that the General and his Council did not give me on my departure what they had promised, namely, an order which I could show to the Directors of the Company, by which they would see that 17,500 florins were due and payable to me on my arrival. The General's reply was to take a glass of wine and wish me a pleasant journey, assuring me that the order would arrive in Holland before me. The Directors, to justify their refusal to pay me, told me that the General and his Council had written nothing to them concerning the matter, and that when they received an advice of it they would at once pay it. I was at length obliged to bring an action against them which lasted two years, before I was able to find, either at Amsterdam or the Hague, a notary who would serve a summons, every one fearing them, as they were both judges and parties to the suit. During these two years I often entered their assembly, where they always gave me some hope, but in reality they were laughing at me. I have hardly ever been deceived when looking a man in the face, as I know almost exactly what is in his mind. I remarked that many of these men had the appearance of loving their own interests and caring little for those of others, and among others there was a young man who represented Encuse, who gazed earnestly at me. After looking at me for some time he asked why I had been to Batavia, where strangers have no business. I replied that all these gentlemen were sufficiently acquainted with it, and that as he was the only one who did not know, his beard was too young to oblige me to explain to him. As their procedure annoyed me, and I was enraged at seeing myself treated so unjustly, I added in speaking to this young man that he would do better at Encuse selling his butter and cheese than where he was. The President interrupted me gently, and told me that I must offend no one, to which I replied that I had seen too much to render an account of my doings in this manner, and that what I did at Goa and Batavia was at the request of the Chief of the factory at Vengurla, and solely for the purpose of rendering a service to the Company. This discourse being finished, the President asked me to go outside for a short time, which I did. Afterwards, when I returned, he told me that he still knew nothing about the matter, and that all these gentlemen believed that I would not remain there, but would still make another journey to Asia, and as I praised the good treatment I had received on their vessels on my return voyage, they again offered me a passage, and promised to give orders that I should be treated even still better than before; that as soon as I arrived at Batavia I should be paid; that they would send an order to that effect to the General and his Council, and that I might embark on the first vessel which left for Surat or Hormuz. I thanked these gentlemen for all their fine offers, and told them that I preferred to make three journeys by land rather than one voyage by sea. In conclusion, at the end of five years the Directors wrote to my brother—for I had then returned to India—that if he was willing to take 10,000 livres in satisfaction of my claim, he might come to receive them. This my brother did, and he gave them a receipt in full. I leave the reader to judge of the equity and conscience of these gentry. For either they owed me 17,500 florins or they did not. If they did not, why pay me 10,000 livres? And if they did owe me, why not pay me fully? I am not the only person to whom they have done injustice of this kind. I know many other more serious cases, the recital of which would not be to their advantage.[1]

Such was my return from India in the year 1649, the only time I returned by sea, having made, as I have said, all my Asiatic journeys by land, both when going and returning, counting as nothing the short passage in the Mediterranean; and my first journey was wholly by land, from Paris by Germany and Hungary to Constantinople, where I also went on the return from my last journey in the year 1669. From Constantinople I went to Smyrna, where I embarked for Leghorn, and from Leghorn I travelled by land to Genoa, from Genoa to Turin, and from Turin to Paris, where I took the King that beautiful parcel of diamonds of which I have spoken in the discourse on precious stones.[2] His Majesty had the goodness to give me a very favourable reception,

[1] As to the merits of this case, without the other side of the question before us, we cannot venture to decide. But, on the whole, Tavernier got off much easier than did the Dutch subjects, who also bought rekenings at the same time, for they not only had to give them up but were imprisoned and sent to Holland as common soldiers (vol. ii. 295).

[2] See vol. ii. 100.

which was a glorious conclusion to my long journeys, in which I have always had for my primary object to spare nothing in order to make known to the great monarchs of Asia, that there is one grander than them all, in Europe, and that our King infinitely surpasses them both in power and glory.

My first thoughts on finding myself in Paris, on the return from my sixth journey, were to return thanks to God for having preserved me, during the space of forty years, among so many perils which I had run, by sea and land, in regions so far distant.

THE KING'S LICENCE

LOUIS, by the grace of God, King of France and of Navarre, to our beloved and liege Councillors, the Members of our Courts of Parliament, Masters of the Requests ordinary of our House, Bailiffs, Seneschals, or their Lieutenants, and to all others whom it may concern, greeting: our well beloved Jean-Baptiste Tavernier, Esq., Baron of Aubonne, having informed us that he has written a book which has for title, 'Six Voyages made in Turkey, Persia, and India, during the space of forty years, and by all the routes that can be taken,' which he desires to print and sell, if it pleases us to grant our letters, necessary to him who humbly seeks them: for these reasons we have permitted and shall permit the Petitioner to have the said Book printed in such volume, margin, or type, as he may be advised, and to sell and dispose of it throughout our Kingdom and the territories subject to us, during the space of fifteen years, to date from the day on which the said impression may be completed; during which time we expressly inhibit all Booksellers and Printers from printing, selling, or disposing of the said Book, and also reprinting it, except with the consent of the Petitioner or of those who hold the right to do so from him, on pain, to those acting otherwise, of a penalty of three thousand livres fine, one-third to us, one-third to the Hotel Dieu of our City of Paris, and the remaining third to the said Petitioner; also of confiscation of the counterfeit copies, and of all expenditure, damages, and interest; on condition of placing two copies of the said Book in our Public Library, one in that of our Chamber in the Palace of the Louvre, and one in that of our beloved and loyal Chevalier and Chancellor of France, the Sieur Daligre, before offering it for sale, on pain of nullifying these presents, which will be registered in the proper place; and in placing at the beginning and end of them a statement acknowledging that they are bound by the terms agreed upon, and of their willingness to allow the Petitioner to enjoy them quietly and peaceably.

We command in the first place our Usher or Sergeant, on this requisition, to undertake for the execution of these presents all necessary deeds and actions without further permission, notwithstanding 'Clameur de Haro', 'Charte Normande', and all else to the contrary. For such is our pleasure. Given at Versailles the 7th day of October, in the year of Grace one thousand six hundred and seventy-five, and of our reign the thirty-third. By the King in Council.

(Signed) DESVIEUX.

Registered on the Book of the Society of Booksellers and Printers of Paris, the 14th November 1675, according to the resolution of Parliament of the 8th April 1653, and that of the King's Privy Council of the 27th February 1665.

(Signed) THIERRY, Syndic.

And the said Jean-Baptiste Tavernier, Esq., Baron of Aubonne, has ceded and transferred his rights to Gervais Clouzier and Claude Barbin, Merchant Booksellers, in accordance with the agreement made between them.

Printed for the first time the 1st of October 1676.

APPENDICES

[By Dr. V. Ball]

APPENDIX I

1. The Great Mogul's Diamond, and the true history of the Koh-i-Nūr.
2. Summary history of the Koh-i-Nūr.
3. The Grand Duke of Tuscany's Diamond, otherwise known as the Austrian Yellow, or the Florentine; and some further notes on the absolute weights of the carat and rati as they were used by Tavernier.
4. On the Weights of the Diamonds, other precious stones and Pearls, mentioned by Tavernier.

APPENDIX II

List of all the Diamond Mines in India of which there are authentic records; and extracts from an Early Account of the Diamond Mines of Southern India.

APPENDIX III

The Diamond Mines of Bengal.

APPENDIX IV

The Diamond Mines of Borneo.

APPENDIX V

1. The Ruby Mines of Burma.
2. The Sapphire Washings of Ceylon.

APPENDIX VI

A Review in the Philosophical Transactions of Chappuzeau's work entitled 'Histoire des Joyaux' published in 1665 or 1666.

APPENDIX I

1. *The Great Mogul's Diamond and the true History of the Koh-i-Nūr.*

Although the writers on this subject are very numerous, still it is believed that almost everyone of them who has contributed to its elucidation has been consulted in the preparation of this account; and it is certain that many, whose writings have also been consulted, are chiefly noteworthy for the amount of confusion which they have unfortunately introduced into it. The principal authorities are enumerated in the note below.[1] It would only prove puzzling to the reader and cloud the main issue were any considerable space devoted to refuting the errors and correcting the misquotations regarding it, which are so common in works on precious stones. It seems to be a better course to endeavour to secure close attention to the facts of the case supported

[1] It will be convenient to classify the principal authorities according to the theories which they have respectively adopted, as follows:

First, those who maintain the identity of the Koh-i-Nūr with Bābur's Diamond:

Erskine, *Life of Bābur*, 1918, ii, pp. 191–2; Rev. C. W. King, *Natural History of Precious Stones*, Bohn's ed., 1870, p. 70; E. W. Streeter, *The Great Diamonds of the World*, p. 116.

Second, those who maintain the identity of the Koh-i-Nūr with the Great Mogul's Diamond, and who either treat Bābur's Diamond as distinct or make no special reference to it:

James Forbes, *Oriental Memoirs*, 1834, vol. ii, p. 175; Major-General Sleeman, *Rambles and Recollections*, 1918, pp. 288 ff.; James Tennant, *Lecture on Gems and Precious Stones*, 1852, p. 84; V. Ball, *Journ. As. Soc. of Bengal*, 1880, vol. l, pt. ii, p. 31, and *Economic Geology of India*, 1881, p. 19.

Third, those who maintain the identity of the Koh-i-Nūr with both Bābur's and the Great Mogul's Diamonds:

Official Descriptive Catalogue of the Great Exhibition of 1851, pt. iii, p. 695; Kluge, *Handbuch der Edelsteinkunde*, Leipzig, 1860, p. 240; Professor N. S. Maskelyne, Roy. Inst. of Great Britain, March 1860, and *Edin. Rev.*, 1866, pp. 247–8; Gen. Cunningham, *Arch. Reports*, vol. ii, p. 390; Professor Nicol, *Encyclopædia Britannica*, 9th ed., Art., 'Diamond'; Dr. H. A. Miers, quoting Ball and N. S. Maskelyne, *Nature*, 1891, p. 44; p. 555, in *Ency. Brit.*, 11th ed.

It would not be difficult to add to the above a score of names of writers who have supported one or other of these theories.

by well-verified references, so that the reader may be in a position to pronounce for himself a verdict on definite evidence alone, and accept or reject the conclusions which are here suggested.

In order, so to speak, to clear the way for the discussion, it will be necessary, as a preliminary, to give short accounts of all the large diamonds with which authors have sought to identify the Koh-i-Nūr.

Firstly, there is the diamond of Sultān Bābur, which his son Humāyūn received in the year A.D. 1526 from the family of Rājā Bikramajit, when he took possession of Agra. It had already then a recorded history, having been acquired from the Rājā of Mālwā by Alā-ud-dīn in the year 1304.[1] Regarding its traditional history, which extends 5,000 years farther back, nothing need be said here; though it has afforded sundry imaginative writers a subject for highly characteristic paragraphs. We have no record of its having been at any time a cut stone.

According to Sultān Bābur the diamond was equal in value to one day's food of all the people in the world. Its estimated weight was about 8 mishkāls, and as he gives a value of 40 ratis to the mishkāl—it weighed, in other words, about 320 ratis. Ferishta [2] states that Bābur accepted the diamond in lieu of any other ransom, for the private property of individuals, and that it weighed 8 mishkāls or 224 ratis. Hence 1 mishkāl = 28 ratis, from which we may deduce that the ratis Ferishta referred to were to those of Bābur, of which 40 went to the mishkāl, as 28 : 40; and this, on the supposition that the smaller rati was equal to 1·842 troy gr., gives a value of 2·63 troy gr. for the larger, which closely approximates to the value of the pearl rati of Tavernier. If on the other hand we deduce the smaller from the larger (at 2·66 gr. for the pearl rati) we obtain for it a value of 1·86. So far as I am aware, this explanation of Ferishta's figures [3] has not been published before. The value of the mishkāl in Bābur's time, as being a more tangible weight than the variable rati, has been investigated by Prof. Maskelyne,[4] and he concludes that it was equal to about 74 gr. troy, and that if taken at 73·69 gr. troy, and multiplied by 8, it would yield a weight exactly corresponding to that of the Koh-i-nūr when brought to England, namely 186·06 carats. Accepting the second estimate for the value of the mishkāl, that of

[1] See Erskine's *Memoirs of Sultan Bābur*, 1918, ii, p. 191; *History of India*, i. 438.

[2] *History of the Rise of the Mahomedan Power in India*, &c., trans. by J. Briggs, London, 1829, Calcutta, 1909, ii. 46.

[3] See also Dow, *History of Hindostan*, 1812, ii. 105.

[4] *Lecture at the Royal Institution*, March 1860.

Bābur's rati would be 1·842 gr. troy, and the value of his diamond in carats might be expressed by the following equation.

$$\frac{320 \times 1{\cdot}842}{3{\cdot}168 \text{ (troy gr. in a carat)}} = 186{\cdot}06 \text{ carats.}$$

In such a calculation it is well to bear in mind that a very slight variation in the rati, as a unit, would, when multiplied, produce a considerable difference in the result. Thus, if 1·86 were put instead of 1·842, the resultant would be enhanced above the desired figure, namely the weight of the Koh-i-Nūr.

Here I must leave Bābur's diamond for the present, without expressing any more decided opinion as to the absolute accuracy of the data which make its weight appear to be actually identical with that of the Koh-i-Nūr, being, however, as will be seen in the sequel, quite content not to dispute their general correctness, though my deduction therefrom does not accord with Professor Maskelyne's.

In the year 1563 Garcia da Orta, in his famous work on the Simples and Drugs of India,[1] mentioned four large diamonds, one of which he was told had been seen at Bisnaguer, i. e. Vijayanagar, and was the size of a small hen's egg. The others weighed respectively—

120 mangelins	= 200 ratis	= 150 carats.[2]
140 ,,	= $233\frac{1}{3}$,,	= 175 ,,
250 ,,	= $416\frac{2}{3}$,,	= $312\frac{1}{2}$,,

None of these three last can be identified with the Great Mogul's diamond, because, even supposing it had been already discovered at so early a date as 1563, it must then, as will be seen hereafter, have been uncut, and had a weight of $787\frac{1}{2}$ carats, or more than double the weight of the largest of them; but it might have been the one spoken of as being of the size of a small hen's egg, as that was probably its form in its early condition when acquired by Mīr Jumla. As to whether any of the stones mentioned by Garcia could have been the same as Bābur's diamond, it is quite useless to speculate; but, as none of them are said to have belonged to the Mogul, it seems to be most improbable.

In the year 1609, De Boot, in his work on gems, &c., referred to all these diamonds mentioned by Garcia, but when doing so, was guilty of three serious blunders, which were, however, detected by his editor, Adrian Toll; they have misled many

[1] *Colloquios dos simples e drogas e cousas medicinaes da India*, p. 159: *Colloquies on the Simples and Drugs of India*, trans. Sir C. Markham, London, 1913, p. 347.

[2] He says the mangelin = 5 gr., the carat 4 gr., and the rati 3 gr. (of wheat). Sir C. Markham gives the weights as 140, 120, 250 carats.

subsequent authors, who have apparently overlooked the editorial comments, including Professor Maskelyne (*Nature*, x. 91). The first was in giving Monardes instead of Garcia as his authority; the second in treating the mangelin as though it were the equivalent of the carat; and thirdly, in making, on the supposed authority of Monardes, a statement to the effect that the largest known diamond weighed 187½ carats.[1]

The explanation of De Boot's confusion between the names of Monardes and Garcia is that Écluze (Clusius) published a work in 1574, in which he incorporated in the same volume the writings of these two authors; and, as pointed out by Adrian Toll, Monardes does not even allude to diamonds, his work being on the drugs of the West Indies.[2]

The question remains—Where did De Boot obtain the figure 187½, which approximates to the weight of the Koh-i-Nūr, when brought to England, and the weight of Bābur's diamond as estimated above? It has been seized upon by Professor Maskelyne, who quotes it from King, as a link in the chain connecting the two just mentioned diamonds. It is a worthless link, however. It originated in a further manifestation of De Boot's carelessness.[3] What he really quoted from may have been a passage in Monardes's work, as he says, or in that of Garcia this time, as he had already disposed of the diamond mentioned by him; but a commentary or note on the latter's statement about Indian diamonds, by the editor Écluze, and, as will be seen, the note itself, which is of sufficient importance to be given in the original Latin, refers to the largest diamond ever seen in Belgium![4] its weight being 47½ carats, or 190 gr. There can be no doubt that the statement by De Boot regarding a diamond weighing 187½ carats was, as pointed out by Adrian Toll and De Laet, utterly spurious. It was therefore quite unworthy of the notice it has received from the above-named authors, and is of no value whatever for the purposes of this history.

No attention has hitherto been given by writers to a large diamond which, as pointed out in a footnote,[5] was obtained

[1] *Gemmarum et Lapidum Historia*, 3d ed., by De Laet, 1647, p. 29.

[2] It was first printed at Seville in 1565.

[3] Rosnel, in *Le Mercure Indien*, Paris, 1667, evidently quoting from De Boot, makes the same mistake.

[4] Majorem vero Adamantem in Belgio conspectum haud puto, quam Philippus II. Hispaniarum Rex ducturus Elizabetham, Henr. II. Gall. Regis filiam majorem natu emit, de Carolo Affetato Antwerpia, Anno 1559, Octogies Millenis Cronatis; pendebat autem Car. xlvii, cum semine (=47½), id est grana 190.—*De Gemmis et Lapidibus*, Lib. II.. J. de Laet, *Lug. Bat.*, 1647, p. 9

[5] See vol. ii. 42.

by a Portuguese who worked the mine at Wajra Karūr in Bellary about the beginning of the seventeenth century. It weighed, apparently, 434·7 carats. Nothing of its subsequent history is known; but it cannot have been the one presented by Mīr Jumla to Shāhjahān. It may, however, have been the Pitt diamond, which, when offered to Pitt in 1701, weighed 426 carats; but if so, it remained uncut for nearly a century, and the generally accepted story of the Pitt diamond is that it was obtained at the mine at Partial.

We may now pass to a brief summary of the facts contained in Tavernier's several independent references to the Great Mogul's diamond—

First, in order of sequence, after describing the Mogul's jewels, he mentions (vol. i. 315) its weight as being 319½ ratis, or 280 carats, the rati being ⅞th of a carat. When first presented to Shāhjahān by Mīr Jumla it weighed, he says, 900 ratis or 787½ carats, and had several flaws, but when he saw it it was round, rose cut, very steep at one side, with a notch on the basal margin, and an internal flaw; its water was beautiful.[1]

Secondly, when describing (vol. ii. 58) the mine of Kollūr (Gāni or Coulour) he says that there was found in it the great diamond which weighed 900 carats (?) before cutting, and was presented to Aurangzeb (?) by Mīr Jumla. This account, as already pointed out, contains several mistakes. Tavernier adds that the mine had been opened 100 years previously.

Thirdly (vol. ii. 75), he states that the Great Mogul's diamond was of perfect water and good form, and weighed $279\frac{9}{16}$ carats. Its value he estimated as amounting to 11,723,278 livres, 14 sols, 3 liards, or £879,245 18*s.* 1½*d.* If it had weighed 279 carats only it would have been worth 11,676,150 livres, and consequently the value of the $\frac{9}{16}$th of a carat, owing to the geometrical method of calculation, amounted to 47,128 livres, 14 sols, 3 liards, or £3,534 13*s.* 1½*d.*

Fourthly (vol. ii. 97), he states that he was permitted to weigh the diamond, and ascertained its weight to be 319½ ratis, or $279\frac{9}{16}$ carats, and adds, 'when in the rough it weighed, as I have elsewhere said, 907 ratis, or 793⅝ carats'. Its form was as of an egg cut in two.

Tavernier's figure of the diamond (see Plate II) has been referred to by Mr. King as being carefully drawn. It is true that very neat representations of it have appeared in works on mineralogy and precious stones, and glass models have been made on the same lines, but the original figure can only

[1] The *Ma'āsir-ul-umarā* ii. 535, gives the weight of this diamond as 216 surkh, or 9 tānk, and values it at Rs. 216,000, or £21,600. Manucci says that it weighed 360 carats (Manucci, i. 237).

be correctly described as a very rude unprojected diagram, in which the facets are bounded by three transverse series of parallel lines which intersect one another irregularly.

The only other early mention of this diamond is by Bernier, who calls it 'matchless', and states that it was presented to Shāhjahān by Mīr Jumla when he advised him to dispatch an army for the conquest of Golkonda.[1]

Let us now endeavour to reduce these statements to a common denomination. First, it must be stated that Tavernier and Bernier, both of whom refer expressly to the famous topaz belonging to Aurangzeb, are not likely to have been mistaken as to the nature of the stone examined; that it was a diamond may be safely accepted, in spite of any suggestions which have been made by authors to the contrary.

With regard to Tavernier's second statement, it is clearly wrong in two particulars, both of which may be attributed to the errors of a copyist, who wrote Aurangzeb for Shāhjahān, and 900 carats in mistake for 900 ratis. This statement, therefore, being put aside from consideration, we have then left for comparison the following:

Original weight 900 ratis = $787\frac{1}{2}$ carats; after cutting, $319\frac{1}{2}$ ratis = 280 carats.

Original weight 907 ratis = $793\frac{5}{8}$ carats; after cutting, $319\frac{1}{2}$ ratis = $279\frac{9}{16}$ carats.

Calculated according to Tavernier's own statement that the rati was equal to $\frac{7}{8}$ of the carat, the equivalents would more correctly be stated as follows:

$$\left.\begin{array}{l} 900 \text{ ratis} = 788\frac{1}{2} \text{ carats}^{2} \\ 907 \quad ,, \quad = 793\frac{5}{8} \quad ,, \end{array}\right\} 319\frac{1}{2} \text{ ratis} = 279\frac{9}{16} \text{ carats.}$$

We have then, at first sight, the remarkable apparent coincidence in weights between this diamond, when cut, of $319\frac{1}{2}$ ratis, and Bābur's of about 8 mishkāls (i. e. about 320 ratis); but the ratis were of very different values, the former being equal to 2·66[3] troy gr., and the latter to about 1·842 (or 1·86 ?) gr. The respective weights, in carats, as already shown, are $186\frac{9}{16}$ and $279\frac{9}{16}$, the difference in weights of the two stones being therefore, apparently, $93\frac{1}{2}$ carats. But in anticipation of the discussion to be found on page 346 as to the reasons which have led to the conclusion that

[1] *Travels in the Mogul Empire*, 1918, p. 22.

[2] The discrepancy between these two accounts of the original weight of the stone, which Tavernier probably obtained from native reports, one being 900 ratis and the other 907 ratis, does not in the least affect the question here discussed, as it is only the weight of the stone after cutting that we have to do with.

[3] On page 347 Ball explains his reasons for modifying the first conclusion, stated in vol. i, Appendix, as to the value of the pearl rati.

Tavernier used the light Florentine carat, it should be stated here that the weight of the Mogul's diamond, in English carats, was 4 per cent. less than Tavernier's figures, in terms of Florentine carats; hence its weight, in order to be compared with other diamonds given in terms of English carats, should be $268\frac{18}{50}$, from which, if we subtract $186\frac{1}{16}$, the difference would be $82\frac{1}{3}$ carats, nearly. The similarity between the weight of Bābur's diamond at 320 ratis, and the Mogul's at $319\frac{1}{2}$ ratis, is delusive, as in ratis of the same denomination the former figure should be given at about 224 ratis, which is Ferishta's equivalent for 8 mishkāls. So that the real difference amounted to $319\frac{1}{2} - 224 = 95\frac{1}{2}$ ratis, or, expressed in carats, at $\frac{7}{8}$ths of a carat = 1 rati, $83\frac{1}{2}$ carats. This is sufficiently close to the $82\frac{1}{3}$ carats, independently deduced, to justify the conclusion that the weight of Bābur's diamond was about 83 carats less than that of the Mogul's, when cut.

There is, I believe, no direct record of the size and weights of the diamonds carried away from Delhi by Nādir Shāh, but before dealing with that portion of the history, it will be convenient to refer here to an interesting statement by Forbes[1] which has been overlooked by most writers on the subject. He states that a Persian nobleman, who possessed a diamond weighing 117 carats, which was subsequently lost at sea, informed him when at Cambay in the year 1781, long before it had been taken to Kābul, that there had been two diamonds in the Royal Treasury at Ispahān, one of which, called Koo-i-toor (Koh-i-Nūr ?), 'The Hill of Lustre', weighed 264 carats, and its value was estimated at £500,000. The other, called Dorriainoor (Daryā-i-Nūr), 'The Ocean of Lustre,' was of a flat surface. Both formed a portion of the treasure, amounting in value to from 70 to 80 millions sterling, which Nādir Shāh carried away from Delhi in 1739.

Forbes suggests that the first was the Mogul's diamond, described by Tavernier, remarking that the difference between the weights 264 and $279\frac{9}{16}$ carats may easily be allowed between the accounts given by a Persian and a European traveller. (If, as above suggested, the weight of the latter was $268\frac{9}{60}$ English carats, the approximation is still closer.) The Daryā-i-Nūr, as we shall presently see, still belongs to Persia; it weights 186 carats, and there is no known fact which in the slightest degree affects the possibility of its being identical with Bābur's diamond.

Several writers, among them Professor Schrauf of Vienna,[2] have suggested that the Mogul's diamond is to be identified
23 with the similarly shaped Orloff, now belonging to Russia.

[1] *Oriental Memoirs*, 2nd ed., ii. 175.

[2] *Handbuch der Edelsteinkunde*, Vienna, 1869, p. 103.

Apart from the discrepancy in the weights and in the size, as shown by Tavernier's drawing, which was intended to represent the natural size of the former, it is tolerably certain that the Orloff was obtained from the temple of Srīrangam on an island in the Cauvery river, in Mysore. It was therefore a possession of the Hindus, and it is most improbable that it ever belonged to the Moguls.

Reference has been made by some authors to the long historical chain which, they say, connects Bābur's diamond with the Koh-i-Nūr. As to the length of the supposed chain, it would extend over a period of 500 years at the least ; but as to the links composing it, there is this to be said—they are all utterly unsound. In making so emphatic a statement I feel the necessity of being very sure of the grounds of my argument, especially as it is opposed to the views of many authorities, who, however, do not agree with one another as to details.

In deference to the opinions of Erskine, Professor Maskelyne, and General Cunningham, it may no doubt with perfect safety be admitted that the weight of Bābur's diamond in 1526 was, as stated above, about 8 mishkāls or 320 ratis, and that these were equivalent to about 186 or 187 modern English carats. But it must be at once plainly stated that there is no direct evidence that any diamond of that weight was in the possession of the Mogul emperors at any subsequent period, up to the time of Nādir Shāh's invasion. We know nothing as to the weight of the Koh-i-Nūr, as such, till about the time it was brought to England, namely, the year 1850 ; and then, although its weight was 186$\frac{1}{6}$ carats, the trustworthy evidence, as to its condition at that time, as will be seen, is to the effect that it was not identical with Bābur's diamond.

In order to put this clearly it is necessary to summarize what has already been stated about other diamonds. Those mentioned by Garcia da Orta were not apparently in the possession of the Mogul, and their weights do not correspond to those of either the Mogul's or Bābur's diamonds. The diamond of 187$\frac{1}{2}$ carats referred to by De Boot has been shown to be mythical. Again, Tavernier did not see any stone of the weight above attributed to Bābur's diamond in the possession of the Great Mogul, Aurangzeb, nor can we suppose that he heard of any such diamond being in the possession of Shāhjahān, who was then confined in prison, where he retained a number of jewels in his own possession.[1] If either he or Bernier had heard of such a stone he would surely have mentioned it. It is possible, that Bābur's diamond may have been in Shāhjahān's possession when

[1] See vol. i. 295.

Tavernier saw Aurangzeb's jewels, and that the latter obtained possession of it when Shāhjahān died, and so ultimately it passed to Persia with other jewels taken by Nādir Shāh.[1]

Tavernier's statements, in so far as they relate to this history, are—I. That the Great Mogul's diamond was found in the mine at Kollūr, when, we cannot say, though Murray, Streeter, and other writers have ventured to assign precise dates. II. It was acquired by Mīr Jumla, and presented by him to Shāhjahān about the year 1656. III. It originally weighed 900 ratis or 787½ carats; but having been placed in the hands of Hortensio Borgio, it was so much reduced by grinding, distinctly not by cleavage, that, when seen by Tavernier in 1665, he personally ascertained that it only weighed 319½ ratis or $279\frac{9}{16}$ carats. IV. The figure given by Tavernier, though very rudely drawn, is of a stone which must have weighed more than $279\frac{9}{16}$ carats (Florentine), and it corresponds fairly with his description. V. This description mentions a steepness on one side and certain flaws, &c.

In order to identify the Mogul's diamond with Bābur's, certain authorities, notably Professor Maskelyne, have suggested that Tavernier's description did not really apply to the diamond presented by Mīr Jumla to Shāhjahān; that the stone he describes had therefore not been found at Kollūr; that he was mistaken as to the particular kind of ratis which he mentions, and that consequently his equivalent in carats—calculated on the supposition that they were pearl ratis—was incorrect; finally, Professor Maskelyne maintains that Tavernier's drawing of the stone differs from his description of it, and was wholly incorrect and exaggerated in size.

Thus, in order to establish this supposed link of the chain, we are invited to whittle down Tavernier's account until it amounts to a bare statement that he saw a large diamond, about which all that he records as to its weight and history is incorrect.

If I were not prepared to maintain that a jeweller of Tavernier's large experience could not possibly have made the mistakes which have thus been suggested, I should feel that I had rendered a very ill service in editing these volumes. It is incredible that having actually handled and weighed the stone, at his leisure, he could have made so great a mistake as to believe that it weighed $279\frac{9}{16}$, or in round numbers 280 carats (Florentine), while it was really one of only 186 carats (English).

The custom, which has been followed by many writers, of adopting or rejecting Tavernier's statements according

[1] See vol. i. 275.

as they agree or disagree with their independently conceived hypotheses, is one against which we are bound to protest. It is a kind of treatment which no author should receive. If supposed to be guilty of so many blunders and inaccuracies of statement, the proper course would be to leave all that such a writer states severely alone.

Judging from Tavernier's drawing and description, the stone had been ground by Hortensio Borgio to a fairly symmetrical shape as a round rose, one side being, however, steeper than the other, which feature, though indicated to some extent in the original drawing, is not generally faithfully reproduced in the copies in various works on diamonds, and some of the glass models which have been made are not only defective in this respect, but are altogether too small. This is mentioned here because these models are sometimes referred to as though they afforded authentic evidence of the true form of the stone.

We have now arrived at a stage when we can agree with those authorities who have maintained that Bābur's diamond and the Mogul's were distinct; but with most, if not all of them, we must part company, as they maintain that the Mogul's diamond no longer exists, and that it was upon Bābur's diamond that Nādir Shāh conferred the title Koh-i-Nūr in the year 1739. But the Mogul's diamond has a stronger and more immediate claim to be regarded as *the* diamond, so denominated, which was taken from Muhammad Shāh, Aurangzeb's feeble descendant. The name was an eminently suitable one to apply to the Mogul's stone as it was when seen by Tavernier, though not equally applicable to it in its subsequent mutilated condition, in which it has been so confidently identified by some writers with Bābur's diamond.

The stone which now bears the title Koh-i-Nūr was taken by Nādir to Persia, and from thence we have rumours of its having been cleaved into several pieces, when or by whom is doubtful. Acceptance of these stories has been rendered difficult by some authors having attempted to assign names and weights to these pieces, the sum of the latter being greater than the total weight of the Mogul's stone, as it was when seen by Tavernier. Thus the Orloff, the Great Mogul itself, and the Koh-i-Nūr have been spoken of as having formed parts of the same stone.[1] This hypothesis is in opposition to everything connected with the histories of these stones which can be relied on; but as regards the possibility of the Koh-i-Nūr alone having been carved out of the Great Mogul's diamond, it is not argument—but is simply begging the whole question—to assert that the Koh-i-Nūr existed 120 years before Borgio handled the Mogul's diamond. This

[1] Quenstedt, *Klar und Wahr*, Tübingen, p. 79.

Mr. Streeter has done,[1] and in his accounts of these diamonds he several times repeats that 'all are agreed' that Bābur's diamond and the Koh-i-Nūr are identical, and the Mogul's distinct, which are precisely the points at issue. Indeed, he might be reminded that in his own previously published work [2] he states that 'any doubt as to the Mogul and Koh-i-Nūr being identical is but rarely entertained'; this, I venture to believe, was the sounder opinion than the one more recently advocated by him.

At the meeting of the British Association in 1851 [3] Dr. Beke referred to a diamond found among the jewels of Razā Kuli Khān at the conquest of Khorāsān by 'Abbās Mīrzā in 1832. It weighed 130 carats, and showed marks of cutting on the flat or largest face. It was presented to the Shāh, and the jewellers of Teherān asked £16,000 for recutting it. Dr. Beke suggests that it was a part of the Koh-i-Nūr, meaning thereby the Mogul's diamond. This could not have been the case, because, as we have seen, the Mogul's diamond, if identical with the Koh-i-Nūr, had only a margin of about $82\frac{1}{3}$ carats to lose, while if the latter be identical with Bābur's diamond it could have lost nothing. At the subsequent meeting of the Association [4] Professor Tennant improved on this by suggesting that the Russian diamond, i. e. the Orloff, formed a part of the same. Other suggestions about the Orloff have already been dealt with above.

A host of other writers have taken up this story, and lastly, Professor Nicol in his article on the diamond in the *Encyclopædia Britannica* has unfortunately suggested that these three stones formed portions of the Mogul's stone seen by Tavernier, which amounts to saying that these three, weighing respectively $194\frac{3}{4}$, $186\frac{1}{16}$ and 130 carats,[5] or in all $510\frac{13}{16}$ carats, were portions of one which weighed only between 279 and 280 (Florentine) carats. His statement that 'the three united would have nearly the form and size given by Tavernier' is simply incomprehensible.

If, however, we merely suppose that the Mogul's stone, while in the hands of one or other of its necessitous owners, after it was taken to Persia by Nādir, had pieces removed from it by cleavage, which altogether (there were at least three of them) amounted to the difference between its weight and that of the Koh-i-Nūr as it was when brought from India, namely, $279\frac{9}{16}$ Florentine carats $= 268\frac{19}{50}$ English carats $- 186\frac{1}{16} = 82\frac{1}{3}$ carats, we at once arrive at a simple explana-

[1] *Great Diamonds of the World*, 119. [2] *Precious Stones*, p. 126.
[3] See *Athenæum*, July 5, 1851. [4] *Ibid.*, September 25, 1852.
[5] Professor Nicol gives the weights at $194\frac{3}{4}$, $186\frac{1}{16}$, and 132, the sum being $512\frac{13}{16}$. Compare the article by Dr. H. A. Miers, *Ency. Brit.*, 11th ed., viii. 163.

tion of the cause of the difference in weight between the stones, and are, moreover, thus enabled to show that Tavernier's account requires no whittling down, though the stone itself, after he saw it, appears to have been subjected to that process.

This would be but an hypothesis based on the rumours above referred to, were it not so strongly corroborated by the appearance presented by the Koh-i-Nūr itself when taken by the British from the Treasury at Lahore. Mr. Tennant [1] describes it as exhibiting, when brought to England, two large cleavage planes, *one of which had not even been polished, and had been distinctly produced by fracture.*

No one can examine the authentic sketches and models of the Koh-i-Nūr without feeling a strong presumption that it must have been mutilated, after cutting, and that it cannot have been left in such an incomplete condition by the jeweller who cut and polished it. In addition to its possessing defects similar to some of those described by Tavernier as having been in the Mogul's diamond, Mr. Tennant records that the Koh-i-Nūr had a flaw near the summit which, being on a line of cleavage parallel to the upper surface, may very possibly have been produced when the upper portion was removed—the weight of which, together with that of two portions removed from the sides, and the loss occasioned by the re-grinding of four facets on the upper surface, may very easily have represented the difference in the weights of the two stones, namely $82\frac{1}{3}$ carats.

This too, in a measure, explains the discrepancies between Tavernier's description, which, as Professor Maskelyne [2] admits, very fairly characterizes the Koh-i-Nūr (i.e. certain flaws and defects in it, which happened to be in the portion preserved), and the figure, which, as it represents the whole stone, does not, at first sight, seem to resemble the Koh-i-Nūr. The accompanying illustration (Plate VI) and descriptive notes prove not only the possibility of the Koh-i-Nūr having been thus carved out of the Mogul's diamond, but the represent graphically the extreme probability of the truth of that suggestion.

Tavernier's account of the Mogul's diamond has, I think, been fully proved in the preceding pages to be quite inapplicable to Bābur's diamond, while all his facts and the balance of probability favour the view that in the Koh-i-Nūr we are justified in recognizing the mutilated Mogul's diamond. Thus, while this theory, which has been built up on the basis of Tavernier's statements, is consistent with the literal acceptance of all of them, and with the physical condition of the

[1] *Lecture on Gems and Precious Stones*, London 1852, p. 83.
[2] *Proceedings of the Royal Institution of Great Britain*, March 1860.

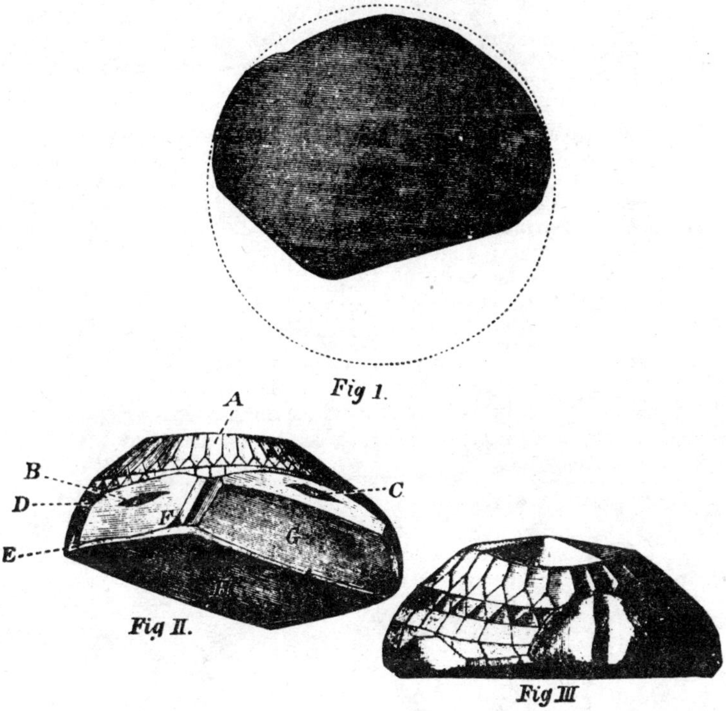

Figures of the Koh-i-Nūr

Koh-i-Nūr when it came to Europe, of none of the other theories can the same be said; but, on the contrary, to suit their respective exigencies, they require the total rejection of one or more of the carefully recorded observations on the condition of the Mogul's stone when placed in the hands of this experienced jeweller for examination.[1]

The necessary conclusion is that it is not the Mogul's diamond which, through failure of being historically traced, as some authors assert, has disappeared, but it is Bābur's diamond of the history of which we are really left in doubt. The fixing of the weight of Bābur's diamond at a figure identical, or nearly so, with that of the Koh-i-Nūr when brought to England, though used as a link in the chain, has, as I think I have shown, effectively disposed of its claim to be identified with the Mogul's diamond in the first place, and secondly with the Koh-i-Nūr.

It has already been intimated that the Daryā-i-Nūr, a flat stone which weighs 186 carats, and is now in the Shāh's treasury,[2] may very possibly be Bābur's diamond, with regard to which I can only say that I have in vain sought for any well authenticated fact which in the slightest degree controverts or even throws doubt upon that suggestion.

2. *Summary History of the Koh-i-Nūr.*

This diamond, as related by Tavernier, was obtained in the mine of Kollūr on the Kistnā (see vol. ii, 58). The precise date of its discovery is mere matter of conjecture; but about the year 1656 or 1657 it was presented, while still uncut, to Shāhjahān by Mīr Jumla, who had previously farmed the mines at Kollūr and elsewhere. The stone then weighed 900 ratis or $787\frac{1}{2}$ carats (these, if Florentine carats, were equal to about 756 English carats).

In the year 1665 this diamond was seen by Tavernier in Aurangzeb's treasury, and it then weighed, as ascertained by himself, only $319\frac{1}{2}$ ratis, or $279\frac{9}{16}$ carats (which, if Florentine carats, equalled $268\frac{19}{80}$ English carats). It had been reduced to this size by the wasteful grinding treatment to which it had been subjected by a Venetian named Hortensio Borgio.

In the year 1739 it was taken from Aurangzeb's feeble descendant, Muhammad Shāh, by Nādir Shāh, when he

[1] Among other difficulties introduced into the subject are such as follow from misquotation. Thus Kluge says that Tavernier himself described the stone as weighing $319\frac{1}{2}$ ratis = 186 carats! For this unfortunate and mischievous error there can be no excuse, as he goes on to say quite correctly that the earlier weight was $793\frac{5}{8}$ carats. *Handbuch der Edelsteinkunde*, Leipzig, 1860, p. 341.

[2] See Benjamin, *Persia*, p. 71.

sacked Delhi and carried away to Persia, it is said, £70,000,000 or £80,000,000 worth of treasure.[1] On first beholding it he is reported to have conferred upon it the title Koh-i-Nūr or Mountain of Light, a most suitable name for the stone described by Tavernier.

On the murder of Nādir Shāh at Kelāt, in 1747, it passed with the throne to his grandson Shāh Rukh, who resided at Meshed, where he was made a prisoner and cruelly tortured by Aghā Muhammad (Mīr Alam Khān), who in vain sought to obtain the Koh-i-Nūr from him.[2] In the year 1751 Shāh Rukh gave it, as a reward for his assistance, to Ahmad Shāh, the founder of the Durrānī dynasty at Kābul, and by him it was bequeathed to his son Taimūr, who went to reside at Kābul. From him, in 1793, it passed by descent to his eldest son Shāh Zamān, who, when deposed by his brother Muhammad, and deprived of his eyes, still contrived to keep possession of the diamond in his prison, and two years afterwards it passed into the hands of his third brother Sultān Shujā'. According to Elphinstone,[3] it was found secreted, together with some other jewels, in the walls of the cell which Shāh Zamān had occupied. After Shujā''s accession to the throne of Kābul, on the dethronement and imprisonment of Muhammad, he was visited at Peshāwar by Elphinstone in 1809, who describes how he saw the diamond in a bracelet worn by Shujā', and he refers to it in a foot-note as the diamond figured by Tavernier. Shujā' was subsequently dethroned by his eldest brother Muhammad, who had escaped from the prison where he had been confined.

In 1812 the families of Zamān and Shujā' went to Lahore, and Ranjīt Singh, the ruler of the Punjab, promised the wife of the latter that he would release her husband and confer upon him the kingdom of Kashmīr, for which service he expected to receive the Koh-i-Nūr.[4]

When Shāh Shujā' reached Lahore, soon afterwards, he was detained there by Ranjīt, who wished to secure both his person and the diamond; but the Shāh for a time evaded compliance with his demand for the stone, and refused offers of moderate sums of money for it. At length 'the Mahārājā visited the Shāh in person, mutual friendship was declared, an

[1] According to the *Imperial Gazetteer* 1st ed. (vi. 314) only £30,000,000. In the edition of 1907 (ii. 409) the words used are 'a huge ransom': Smith (*Oxford Hist. of India*, 459) 'incalculable riches': Keene (*Fall of the Moghul Empire*, 25) says the plunder 'has been estimated at eighty millions sterling'.

[2] Sir J. Malcolm, *Hist. of Persia*, 2nd ed. ii. 195 f.

[3] *Account of the Kingdom of Caubul*, ed. 1907, ii. 325 *n*.

[4] Cunningham, *History of the Sikhs*, Oxford, 1918, p. 153.

exchange of turbans took place, the diamond was surrendered, and the Shāh received the assignment of a jāgīr in the Punjab for his maintenance, and a promise of aid in recovering Kābul'.[1] This was in 1813: the Shāh then escaped from Lahore to Rājāurī, in the hills, and from thence to Ludhiāna, after suffering great privations.[2] Here he and his brother Shāh Zamān were well received by the Honourable East India Company, and a liberal pension was assigned by the Government for their maintenance. The above statements, except where other authorities are quoted, are taken from General Sleeman's [3] account, which was founded on a narrative by Shāh Zamān, the blind old king himself, who communicated it to General Smith, he being at the time in command of the troops at Ludhiāna.

In the year 1839 Shāh Shujā', under Lord Auckland's Government, was set up on the throne of Kābul by a British force, which two years later was annihilated during its retreat.

The testimony of all the writers up to this period, and, it is said, the opinions of the jewellers of Delhi and Kābul also, concur in the view that the diamond which Ranjīt thus acquired was the Mogul's, i.e. the one described by Tavernier. It seems probable that the mutilation and diminution in weight by about 83 carats, to which, as we have shown, it was subjected (see p. 342), took place while it was in the possession of Shāh Rukh, Shāh Zamān, or Shāh Shujā', whose necessities may have caused one of them to have pieces removed to furnish him with money.

Ranjīt during his lifetime often wore the diamond on state occasions, and it is referred to by many English visitors to Lahore, who saw it during this period.[4] It is said to have then been dull and deficient in lustre.

In 1839 Ranjīt died, and on his deathbed expressed a wish that the diamond, then valued at one million sterling, should be sent to Jagannāth,[5] but this intention was not carried out,[6] and the stone was placed in the jewel chamber till the infant Rājā Dhalīp Singh was acknowledged as Ranjīt's successor.

[1] Cunningham, *History of the Sikhs*, Oxford, 1918, p. 153. The Shāh's own account (*Autobiography*, chap. xxv) of Ranjīt's methods to get possession of the diamond is more favourable to the latter than Captain Murray's. (See his *Rangeet Singh*, 96.)

[2] Dr. W. L. M'Gregor, *History of the Sikhs*, London, 1847, i. 170.

[3] *Rambles and Recollections of an Indian Official*, 288 ff.

[4] Dr. M'Gregor, *History of the Sikhs*, London, 1847, i. 216; Baron C. von Hügel, *Travels in Kashmir and the Panjab*, 1845, p. 303.

[5] Lieut.-Colonel Steinbach, *The Punjab*, London, 1846, p. 16.

[6] Miss Eden, *Up the Country*, ii. 130, says that the Mahārāja ultimately consented to its not being sent.

When the Punjab was annexed, in the year 1849, the diamond was formally handed to the new Board of Government at one of its earliest meetings—and it was then personally entrusted by his colleagues to the care of John Lawrence, afterwards Lord Lawrence, who, on receiving it, placed the small tin box containing it in his waistcoat pocket, and then forgot all about it till he was called upon to produce it six weeks later, in order that it might be sent to Her Majesty the Queen.

Recalling the circumstances when thus reminded of them, he hurried home and, asked his bearer whether he had got the box which had been in his pocket some time previously. Careful about trifles, like most Indian servants, the bearer had preserved it, though he thought it only contained a useless piece of glass. This strange vicissitude in the history of the stone is related by Bosworth Smith in his life of Lord Lawrence.[1] He adds that he had been told on good authority that it had passed through other dangers, on the way home, before it was safe in the possession of the Queen.

In 1851 the Koh-i-Nūr was exhibited in the first great Exhibition, and in 1852 the recutting of the stone was entrusted by Her Majesty to Messrs. Garrards, who employed Voorsanger, a diamond cutter from M. Coster's atelier at Amsterdam. The actual cutting lasted thirty-eight days, and by it the weight was reduced to $106\frac{1}{16}$ carats. The cost of the cutting amounted to £8,000.

3. *On the Grand Duke of Tuscany's Diamond, otherwise known as the Austrian Yellow or the Florentine; and on the absolute weights of the carat and rati as known to Tavernier.*

When writing of the carat (see vol. i, Appendix, p. 332), and when making the several references to the Grand Duke of Tuscany's diamond, I had not seen Dr. Schrauf's original paper [2] on the weighment of the stone, and, having obtained my information of it indirectly, I was misled as to its precise purport, which does not prove that the absolute weight of the stone is less than Tavernier gave it, but demonstrates that the difference in weight is only apparent. The absolute weight is 27·454 grm. which converted into carats, gives

Florentine (= 197·2 milligrams)	. .	$139\frac{1}{5}$ carats.
Paris (= 205·5 ,,)	. .	$133\frac{3}{5}$,,
Vienna (= 206·13 ,,)	. .	$133\frac{1}{5}$,,

In English carats (= 205·4 milligrams) the weight would

[1] *Life of Lord Lawrence*, i. 327.

[2] *Sitz. der K. Akad. der Wissen.*, Wien, Math.-Nat. Classe, Bd. liv., Abth. i. 479, 1866.

be 133⅗ carats nearly. The conclusions to be drawn, therefore, are, that, in the first place, the stone has not had any additional facets cut upon it, and that it is, in fact, in the same condition as when Tavernier gave its weight at 139½ carats; the difference between that weight and the 139⅕ Florentine carats is so small, amounting to only $\frac{3}{10}$ths of a carat, that it may be fairly attributed to difference in the accuracy of the methods of weighment employed by Tavernier and Schrauf respectively.

Hence we may fairly conclude that in this instance, at least, the carat used by Tavernier was the 'Florentine'; and that being so, it is hardly conceivable that, when mentioning Indian stones on the very same pages as those where he describes the Grand Duke of Tuscany's diamond, he had other carats in view. Consequently, with greater confidence than I could venture to assume when the Appendix of vol. i. was written, I now suggest the hypothesis that Tavernier's carats were the light Florentine carats, which are exactly 4 per cent. lighter than modern English carats. Thus the English carat of ·2054 grm. less 4 per cent. (·0082) = ·1972 grm. which is the precise value of the Florentine carat.

The conclusion thus arrived at as to the carat of Tavernier having been the light Florentine, involves a reduction in the value of the rati, which has been calculated in the earlier part of his work on the supposition that it was equal to ⅞ths of the modern French and English carat. It must therefore be reduced by 4 per cent. likewise, so that instead of 2·77 troy gr., it must stand at 2·66 troy gr. This value, it should be added, is identical with that derived from Tavernier's own statement, that 6 melscals or 181⅛ ratis = 1 French ounce (i. e. 482·312 gr. troy), since 482·312 ÷ 181⅛ = 2·66. I am accordingly compelled to accept this value finally as being that of Tavernier's pearl rati; and I must ask readers to accept this conclusion, which was given as an alternative to 2·77, in the Appendix to vol. i,[1] instead of the latter, which was adopted in the text.

In the following table the weights in carats of the principal stones mentioned by Tavernier are enumerated, and in the last column these weights, reduced by 4 per cent., show the equivalent values in English carats.

4. *On the weights of some of the Diamonds, other Precious Stones, and Pearls, mentioned and figured by Tavernier.*

Assuming that our argument is well founded as to the carats mentioned in the text having been Florentine carats,

[1] See vol. i. 332 ff.

it is necessary in order to reduce them to English carats, to subtract 4 per cent. from them, as in the following table :

DIAMONDS.

	Tavernier's Carats (Florentine).	English Carats.
1*a*. Great Mogul's (uncut) . .	787½	756
1*b*. Great Mogul's (cut) . . .	$279\frac{9}{16}$	$268\frac{19}{50}$
2. Golconda	$242\frac{1}{16}$	$232\frac{19}{50}$
3*a*. Ahmadabad (uncut) . .	157¼	$150\frac{24}{25}$
3*b*. Ahmadabad (cut) . . .	94½	$90\frac{18}{25}$
4. Grand Duke of Tuscany's (139½)	139⅕	$133\frac{16}{25}$
5. Blue	$112\frac{3}{16}$	$107\frac{7}{10}$
6. Bazu	104	$99\frac{21}{25}$
7. Mascarenha	67½	64⅘
8. Kollúr	63⅜	$60\frac{21}{25}$

RUBIES.

1. King of Persia's (192 ratis ?) .	168	$161\frac{7}{25}$
2. Banian	50¾	$48\frac{18}{25}$
3. Bijapur (Visapour) . . .	17½	16⅘

TOPAS.

1. Aurangzeb's . .	157¾ should be 158½	$152\frac{4}{25}$

PEARL.

1. American, sold to Shāista Khān[1]	55	52⅘

APPENDIX II

List of all the Diamond Mines in India of which there are authentic Records, arranged in Districts.

SINCE this list was first published[2] it has been repeatedly checked, and it contains several additions. Although in various works on precious stones, &c., names are given as being those of diamond mines in India which are not to be found here, they are for the most part either synonyms of names that are, or are spurious. Want of space prevents such synonyms being dealt with, which is to be regretted, as the confusion in the nomenclature cannot be easily described without recourse to details. Names of villages, towns, rivers,

[1] Several other pearls of about this size and smaller were in the Mogul's Treasury. See vol. i. 316.

[2] See *Economic Geology of India*, chap. i. The Madras lists were founded originally on Dr. King's in *Mem. Geol. Surv. India*, vol. iii. but have been considerably amplified.

provinces, &c., are misplaced and jumbled together in almost inextricable confusion. One author gives Pegu as a diamond mine in Southern India; in the Mount Catti of another we trace a reference to the Ghāts of Southern India; and in the Malacca of many authors we must recognize, not as they do, either a place supposed to be in Southern India or the true Malacca, but Borneo, which used to be so called by the Portuguese in the fifteenth century. (See Appendix IX.) For some time I was unable to identify a certain Mr. Cullinger, who was quoted by one writer in connexion with diamonds. Will it be believed that this gentleman ultimately proved on investigation to be the fort of Kālanjar?

MADRAS

Kadapa (or Cuddapah) District

Chennūr on the Penner River: Lat. 14° 34′; Long. 78° 51′ 30″.

Condapetta (or Kanuparti), opposite Chennūr.

Gandikota ?, mentioned by some authors: Lat. 14° 49′; Long. 78° 20′ 30″.

Goorapur ?, close to Chennūr. Not identified: [? *Goulapalli*, *v.* i, 226].

Goulagoonta (close to Jammalamadugu): Lat. 14° 51′; Long. 78° 26′. [? *Gogeron*, *v.* i, 227.]

(Jammalamadugu, close to Goulagoonta which see.)

(Kanuparti, or Condapetta which see.)

Lamdur ? Not identified, mentioned by Heyne.

Ovalumpally (or Woblapully): Lat. 14° 34′; Long. 78° 51′ 35″.

Pinchetgapadu ? Not identified, mentioned by Heyne.

(Woblapully, or Ovalumpally which see.)

Bellary District [1]

Gunjeegoonta, 2 miles south of Wajra Karūr.

Gutidrug ?: Lat. 15° 7′; Long. 77° 42′. (Foote-King, *Annual Report Geol. Survey of India,* 1889.)

Hotoor ?, 6 miles WSW. of Wajrā Karūr.

Wajrā Karūr, Lat. 15° 2′; Long. 77° 27′.

Karnūl (or Kurnool) District

Banganapalle: Lat. 15° 18′; Long. 78° 16′; 37 miles SE. of Karnūl (see A.S. No. 76). Mines.

Bannur, close to Gudipaud; in Nandikotkūr Tāluk.

Baswapur: Lat. 15° 25′; Long. 78° 43′ 30″; in Nallamalai Hills; mines and alluvial washings.

Byanpalle: Lat. 15° 32′; Long. 78° 14′ 15″; 24 miles SSE. of Karnūl.

[1] A locality called Nizam in Bellary is mentioned by M. Chaper. See *Engineering,* 1884, 29th February.

Coomroly (close to Gooramankonda, which see); Nandiāl Tāluk.

Deomurru: Lat. 15° 49′ 30″; Long. 78° 11′. Left bank of Tungabhadra.

Devanur: Lat. 15° 44′; Long. 78° 19′. Diamonds found in banks of Kundur river; in Nandikotkūr Tāluk.

Dhone: Lat. 15° 23′ 30″; Long. 77° 56′.

(Gazerpalle close to Baswapur, which see.)

Gooramankonda: Lat. 15° 32′; Long, 78° 14′ 15″; 24 miles SSE. of Karnūl. Rock workings.

Gudipaud, 2 miles W. of Devanur; in Nandikotkūr Tāluk.

Hassanapur in Doopaud. Not identified.

Jorapur. A diamond of 44 carats found in débris of irrigation works, near Karnūl.

Kannamadakalu: Lat. 15° 42′; Long. 78° 14′ 30″. Alluvial.

Lanjapoleur: Lat. 15° 45′ 30″; Long. 78° 4′; 7 miles SSW. of Karnūl; Rammalakota Tāluk.

Muddavaram: Lat. 78° 9′ 30″; Long. 78° 30′. 9 miles ESE. of Rammalakota; Nandiāl Tāluk.

Munimadagu: Lat. 15° 15′; Long. 78° 2′ 10″; in Pattikonda Tāluk, 16 miles W. by S. of Banaganapalle (formerly included in Bellary District).

Muravakonda: Lat. 16° 1′; Long. 78° 9′; on the Kistnā. Diamonds found below the ford, according to Ferishta and Newbold.

Oruvakal (or Woraykal of A.S.): Lat. 15° 41′; Long. 78° 14′; 14 miles SE. of Karnul; Nandiāl Tāluk.

Panchalingala, left bank of Tungabhadra; Rammalakota Tāluk.

Pendekallu, 5 miles SE. of Rammalakota; Rammalakota Tāluk.

Polúr ?: Lat. 15° 31′ 30″; Long. 78° 19′; 4 miles NW. of Nandiāl; in Nandiāl Tāluk.

Pyapali; Palikonda Tāluk.

Rammalakota: Lat. 15° 34′; Long. 78° 3′ 15″; 18 miles W. by S. of Karnūl. Rock and alluvial.

Saitankota, right bank of Tungabhadra, ENE. of Karnūl.

Tandrapad: Lat. 15° 51′; Long. 78° 71′; left bank of Tungabhadra, opposite Karnūl. Alluvial.

Timmapuram: Lat. 15° 32′ 30″; Long. 78° 6′ 30″; 6 miles ESE. of Rammalakota. Rock workings.

Yembye: Lat. 15° 32′; Long. 78° 14′ 15″; 24 miles ESE. of Karnūl.

Kistnā and Godāvarī Districts

Ātkur: Lat. 16° 38′; Long. 80° 23′ 30″.

Barthenypadu: Lat. 16° 38′; Long. 80° 23′ 30″.

Bhadrachalum (doubtful; a diamond said by Newbold to have been found there), on the Godāvarī.

Damarapad: Lat. 16° 35′ 3″; Long. 79° 30′.
Golapalle (or Golapilly): Lat. 16° 43′ 30″; Long. 80° 57′.
[1] Kodavatakullu: Lat. 16° 40′; Long. 80° 23′ 30″ (A.S. 75).
Kollūr (the Gāni or Coulour of Tavernier): Lat. 16° 42′ 30″; Long. 80° 5′; right bank of Kistnā.
Madagalu? (in Palnād Tāluk), 8 miles from the Kistnā.
Malawaram: Lat. 16° 35′ 3″; Long. 79° 30′.
Moonaloor (or Moogaloor): Lat. 16° 38′; Long. 80° 23′ 20″.
Muléle (or Mullavilly): Lat. 16° 41′; Long. 80° 56′.
[1] Oostapully (or Ustapalle): Lat. 16° 40′; Long. 80° 23′ 30″.
[1] Partiāl: Lat. 16° 39′; Long. 80° 27′ (A.S. 75).
(Ustapalle, or Oostapully which see.)

CENTRAL PROVINCES

Sambalpur District

Sambalpur, town on the Mahānadī River, and some of the tributaries above the town. (The country of the Sabarai of Ptolemy.)

Chāndā District

Wairāgarh (the Bairagarh of the Āīn-i-Akbarī): Lat. 20° 26′; Long. 80° 10′ (A.S. 73). Probably the Kosala of the Chinese pilgrims. (V. A. Smith, *Early Hist. of India*, 3rd ed., 285.)

WESTERN BENGAL

Lohārdagā District

Sānkh River, a tributary of the Brāhminī.

Sema, on the Koel (the Soumelpour on the Gouel of Tavernier): Lat. 23° 35′; Long. 84° 21′. This was probably the Sambalaka, in the country of the Mandalai, of Ptolemy.

BUNDELKHAND

Pannā

Baghin, Bargari, Brijpur, Etwa, Kamariya, Majgoha, Myra, Pannā, Sakeriya, Saya-Lachmanpur, Udesna, and many others around Pannā town. It is not known when these mines were first discovered. So far as I can ascertain, Tieffenthaler was the earliest European visitor to them who has left any record of them; he appears to have been at Pannā in 1765. He says the diamonds found there could not compare either in hardness or fire with those of Orissa (Soumelpour ?) or of Raoulcound (i. e. Rammalakota). There is no record of any exceptionally large diamonds having been

[1] The three villages, so marked, were reserved by the Nizām on account of their diamond mines when the Kondupelle Circar was ceded to the East India Company in 1766.

found at Pannā. Though it is believed by some that the mines are of very great antiquity, the history of them is defective. However, the *Āīn-i-Akbarī*, by Abū'-l Fazl (1590),[1] refers to small diamonds having been found at 8 coss distance from the fort of Kālanjar. It seems probable that these mines were worked in Tavernier's time, though he was not aware of the fact.

NORTH-WEST PROVINCES

SIMLA? This is a very doubtful locality, but there are several diamonds in the Calcutta Museum which were said to have been found in a stream near Simla.

NOTE ON THE GOLKONDA AND BĪJĀPUR DIAMOND MINES

There is a very important early description of the diamond mines of these regions, which is of special interest, as it gives a clue to the original source of many names of diamond sites which are to be found in the modern literature of the subject. It was published in the *Philosophical Transactions*, vol. xii. 1677, p. 907, having been presented to the Royal Society by the Earl Marshal of England, who was then Henry Howard, afterwards Duke of Norfolk. His term of office as Earl Marshal lasted from 1672–83. I am inclined to think it may have been written by Mr. Cholmley, who is described by Sir Streynsham Master[2] as having been engaged for several years before 1679 in making the annual purchases of diamonds for the Company, especially at the mines of Gollapalle (or Golapilly) and Malavalle (Mulēli or Mullavilly).

The diamond mines of the Kistnā District belonged to the Kings of Golkonda, Kutb-Shāhī dynasty, from the downfall of the Bāhmanī Kings of the Deccan (*c*, 1500) until their defeat and extinction in 1686. The mines in the Karnūl District also belonged to them after the Rājās of Vijayanagar were driven to the south in 1564. (See *Kistna Manual*, p. 244.)

It is curious to note that while Tavernier only mentions three localities in these regions by name, namely, Rammalakota (his Raolconda), Kōllūr (his Coulour), and Gandikota, together with another unnamed locality (which was Gazerpalle, see p. 371), this paper, published only a year after Tavernier's first edition appeared, enumerates 23 mines in the Kingdom of Golkonda, and 15 in the Kingdom of Bījāpur—in all 38.

As will be seen some of these names correspond with names in the preceding list, others seem to be identical with names of villages in the region, about which there is no independent evidence of their having been diamond producing. The remaining names I have failed to identify. As I hope on

[1] Ed. Jarrett, ii. 159.

[2] *Kistna Manual*, p. 147. Nathaniel Chumley, who lived many years at Golkonda: *Eng. Factories, 1661–1684*, p. 274 *n*.

some future occasion to republish this paper of the Earl Marshal's *in extenso*, with annotations, I shall at present limit myself to a brief enumeration of the localities, their proper modern names being given in brackets.

The Golkonda Mines are—1. Quolure; this is Tavernier's Coulour or Gani [Kollūr]. This is said to have been the first mine worked in Golkonda, but was then, 1677, almost exhausted. 2. Codawillicul [Kodavatakullu]. 3. Malabar [Malawaram]. 4. Buttephalem [Barthenypadu, near Partiāl]. 5. Ramiah [?]. 6. Gurem [?]. 7. Muttampellee [near Karūr ?]. These five (? six) were under the same government as that of Melwillee [Malavalle or Mulēli], see below. 8. Currure [Wajrā- or Vajrā-Karūr, in the Guty Tāluk of the Bellary District]. This identification is confirmed by the statement that it, the most famous and most ancient of all the mines, was taken some years previously, with the Carnatic, by Mīr Jumla from the Hindu Rājās. It is said that diamonds up to 'a seize (? ser) weight, which was equal to about 9 ounces troy, or 81½ pagodas, had been found there; the mine was privately worked by the King, and the stones produced from it were large and well spread', &c. I have elsewhere quoted, see vol. ii, p. 42, the account of this mine having been worked by a Portuguese gentleman. 9. Ganjeeconta [Gunjeegonta]. 10. Lattawar[1] [Lattwārā]. These two last are respectively 1 and 10 miles SW. of Wajrā-Karūr. 11. Jonagerre [?]. 12. Pirai [?]. 13. Dugulle [?]. 14. Purwillee [?]. These four last I cannot identify. 15. Anuntapellee [Anantapur ? is 20 miles from Wajrā-Karūr. Dr. King (*Mem. Geol. Surv. India*, vol. viii, p. 101) alludes to a diamond being found there]. 16. Girregeta [Goulagoonta]. 17. Maarmood [?]. 18. Wazzergerre [Wajirābād ?]. 19. Munnemurg [Munimadagu in Karnūl]. The two last are said to have been the deepest mines; they were carried to depths of 40 to 50 fathoms. Some interesting details are given as to the process of mining. 20. Langumboot [?]; process of mining as in the preceding. 21. Whootoor [Hotoor ?] near Karūr. 22. Muddemurg [Madagula ? in centre of Palnād Tāluk, Kistnā District. This identification is founded on the statement that the locality was about 9 miles from the Kistnā river]. 23. Melwillee, or new mine [Malavalle or Mulēli], worked first from 1670–71, then closed, but reopened in 1673 by the King's licence, owing to the Kollūr mine becoming exhausted.

In Bījāpur there were 15 mines, of which only those yielding the smallest stones were allowed by the King to be worked,

[1] This, as also some of the other localities, are given by Dutens and Castellani as being in Asia!—a rather wide geographical expression; they have long been objects of search to me, till traced by means of this paper.

partly to prevent large stones becoming too common, and partly to avoid exciting Aurangzeb's cupidity. The mines were—1. Ramulconeta [Rammalakota, i. e. Tavernier's Raolconda]; diamonds of a mangelin weight were seldom found there, generally they were much smaller. Broken diamonds, called shemboes, were found there. 2. Banugunnapellee [Banaganapalle, 37 miles SE. of Karnūl]. 3. Pendekull [Pendekallu]. 4. Moodawaram [? Muddāvaram, 7 miles ESE. of Rammalakota]. 5. Cumerwille [Coomroly of A.S. close to Gooramankonda]. 6. Paulkull [?]. 7. Workull [? Oruvakal]. 8. Lungeepoleur [Langapolūr, 5 miles S. of Karnūl]. 9. Pootloor [Polūr]. 10. Punchelingull [Panchalingala, left bank of Tungabhadra]. 11. Shingarrampent [?]. 12. Tondarpaar [Tandrapād, left bank of Tungabhadra]. 13. Gundepelle [?]. 14. Donee [Dhone]. 15. Gazerpellee [this is close to Baswapur].

I would venture to commend the identification of those mines which are unplaced in the above list to someone with local knowledge.[1]

We are told in the Earl Marshal's paper that in Golkonda the miners and merchants were much oppressed, and in a miserable state of poverty, from having to submit to tyrannical squeezing and heavy duties on provisions, tobacco, and betel. With extraordinary inconsistency, although the King of Golkonda, 'Abdulla Kutb Shāh, and the King of Bījāpur, 'Ādil Shāh, had agreements with the miners that all diamonds above a certain weight were to be reserved for them, still they would not only pay highly for large stones conveyed to their capitals secretly by the merchants, but would bestow dresses of honour upon those who brought such stones to them for sale.[2]

APPENDIX III

The Diamond Mines of Bengal.

ALTHOUGH it is possible that many persons in India may be surprised at the statement that there were formerly diamond mines of considerable importance and value in the region of Bengal, which is about to be described; and although it is probably the case that many who have resided for long periods in the very District itself have never heard of the

[1] There is a mountain in the kingdom of Bījāpur 'where they dig out diamonds, which mountain is a league distant from the city, and is surrounded by a wall, and is kept by a strong guard' (Varthema, 118).

[2] Major Leonard Munn has published an interesting paper on 'Ancient Mines and Megaliths in Hyderabad', *Memoirs and Proceedings of the Manchester Literary and Philosophical Society*, vol. lxiv (1921), part ii, No. 5.

A MAP SHEWING THE POSITION OF THE DIAMOND RIVERS OF BENGAL

I *Soumelpour on the Gouel i.e. Semah on the Koel in the Palamow Subdivision.*

II *An intermediate locality on the Sunk river in Burwa, Palkot & Jushpur*

III *Position of the washings on the Mahanadi near Sambalpur in the Central Provinces.*

Diamond rivers

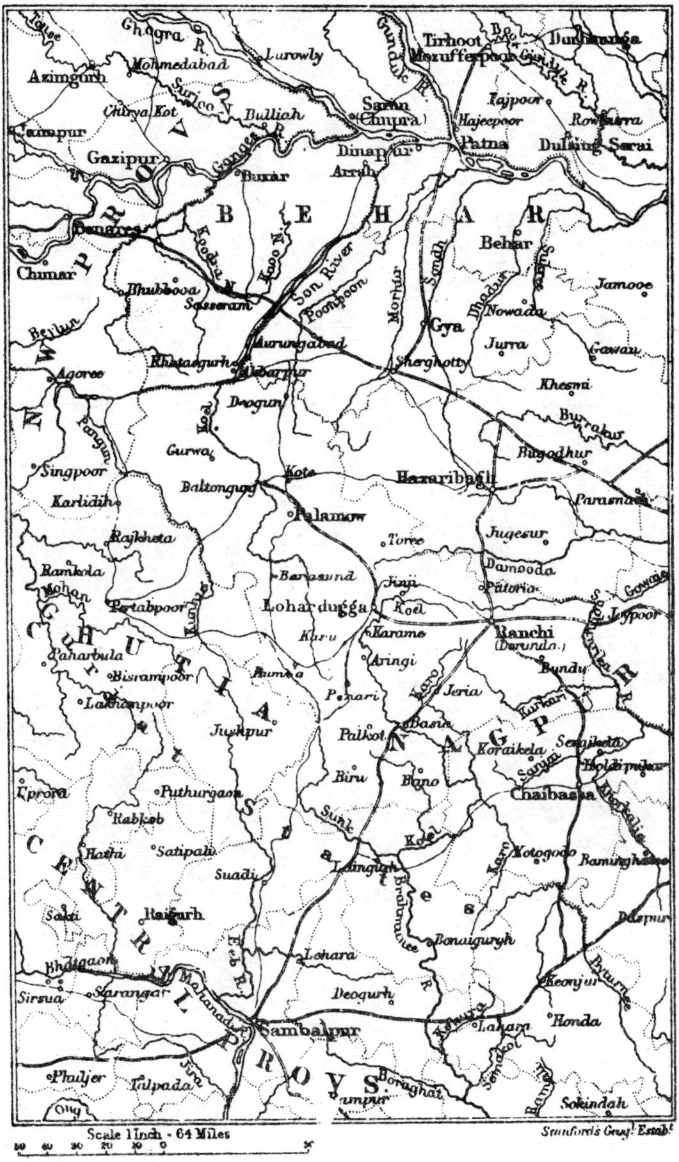

fact, all local traces of the industry being now extinct still the cumulative evidence which can be brought forward is such that I do not anticipate that any serious objections can be urged to the natural conclusions derivable from that evidence.

Gibbon, in the *Decline and Fall of the Roman Empire*, for some reason which he does not give, arrived at the conclusion that it was the mines described by Tavernier at Soumelpour[1] on the Gouel (i. e. Sema or Semulpur on the Koel, in the Sub-Division of Palāmau), rather than any of the localities in Southern India, which supplied Rome with diamonds.

Ptolemy mentions Sambalaka[2] as a city in the country of the Mandalai which produced the finest diamonds in the world. Now, although it is possible that he may have referred to Sambalpur on the Mahanādī, where diamonds are known to occur, I prefer to identify it with Tavernier's Soumelpour, as above, because it was situated in the country generally recognized as that of the Mandali or Mundas, while Sambalpur is beyond its limits.

Further, it may be conveniently remarked here that Ptolemy's Adamas river, although he clearly indicates its origin in Chota Nāgpur (Kokkonage or Kokra), has by some authors been identified with the Mahānadī, while others have with greater probability identified it with one or other of the rivers rising in Chota Nāgpur, namely, the Dāmudā, Subanrikhā or Brāhmanī, with its tributaries the Sānkh and Southern Koel, to which we shall presently again refer. The Mahānadī is probably Ptolemy's Manada,[3] rising in the country of the Sabarae or Savaras, where diamonds were also obtained.

Our next reference to this locality is a very definite and explicit one; it is separated by a long period of time from Ptolemy. In Professor Blochmann's translation[4] of the Tuzuk-i-Jahāngīrī, we find that 'On the 3d Isfandiármuz of the 10th year of my reign (A.D. 1616) it was reported to me (Jahāngīr) that Ibrāhīm Khān (governor of Bihār) had overrun Kokrah and taken possession of its diamond washings.

[1] By a misprint given as Jumelpur, in Bengal, *Decline and Fall*, ii. 281, *note*.

[2] See *Indian Antiquary*, vol. xiii, 1884, p. 364, where it is identified with Sambalpur. J. W. McCrindle (*Ancient India as described by Ptolemy*, 133) writes: 'Sambalaka is Sambhal, a town in Rohilkhand. Sambalaka or Sambhala is the name of several countries in India, but there is only one town of the name that is met with in the Eastern parts. It is a very ancient town and on the same parallel as Delhi.' (See *Imperial Gazetteer*, xx. 18 f.)

[3] So McCrindle, *op. cit.*, 71.

[4] *Journ. As. Soc. Bengal*, xl. 113: *Āīn-i-Akbarī*, 480 n.

This District belongs to Sūbah Bihār, and the river which flows through it yields the diamonds.' Then follow accounts of the mines and Ibrāhīm Khān's operations, all of which will be found quoted in the *Economic Geology of India*, p. 25. The account goes on to say, 'The District is now subject to me. All diamonds found in the river are forwarded to court. Only a few days ago a diamond arrived which had a value of Rs.50,000, and I hope many more will be added to my store of jewels.' Among those received from Ibrāhīm Khān was one which was coloured like a sapphire, it weighed several ratis, and the lapidaries valued it at Rs.3,000, though they would have given 20,000 had it been white and stood the test. Professor Blochmann gives a quotation from a MS. history of the Mahārājas of Chota Nāgpur, in which a method of testing diamonds for flaws is described as consisting in fixing them on the horns of fighting rams.

General Dalton recorded that the family of the Rājā of Chota Nāgpur possessed a diamond from these mines valued at Rs.40,000.[1] A large picture, representing the attack on the Palāmau fort in 1660 by Dāūd Khān, contains a figure of the Zamīndār-i-kān-i-almās or Lord of the Diamond Mine. General Dalton was, I believe, rather inclined to think these mines somewhat mythical, while Professor Blochmann[2] identified the river with the Sānkh. As I had conversations with both of them on the subject, I am satisfied that neither of them knew of Tavernier's references to this region, nor did I know of them then, and it was not till some time after I became aware of them that I was able to show that his Soumelpour was quite a different locality from Sambalpur on the Mahānadī, with which most writers had identified it.

In addition to Tavernier's own direct account of this locality, there is another somewhat earlier in date, but which there is reason to believe was derived from information obtained from him. Reference will be found in Appendix VI to a work by Chappuzeau. In it there appears to be reference to the locality in Bengal which produced diamonds under the name Nage (i. e. Kokkonage or Chota Nāgpur). In the year 1657 L'Escot of Orleans (see p. 239) went there to purchase a diamond of 42 carats, but he failed to get it.

Although Tavernier's locality was on the Gouel River—i. e. the Koel, which runs northwards to join the Son, and so reaches the Ganges—the Sānkh and another Koel also take their rise close by, and running southwards they form the Brāhmanī, which joins the delta of the Mahānadī, near the coast of the Bay of Bengal. The Ebe River, a tributary

[1] *Ethnology of Bengal*, 163 n.
[2] *Journ. As. Soc, Bengal*, xliii, pt. i. 240.

of the Mahānadī also, rises in the same neighbourhood, and it is locally called the Hīra or diamond river, and its bed is said to have yielded diamonds. Hence it is a natural deduction that the source of the diamonds found in the beds of these rivers, which pursue such different courses, is common to all, and that the diamond-bearing rocks will be found there. Unfortunately before leaving India I had no opportunity of putting this theory to the test, and I am not aware that the area has been as yet fully explored.[1]

The accompanying map will convey a clear idea of the relative positions of the three localities, which have hitherto been much confused in the accounts by different authors. In the south there is Sambalpur, on the Mahānadī, of which I have elsewhere [2] published detailed accounts of the geology, and of the records of the yield of diamonds there in former times; farther north is the locality on the Sānkh river, which, as stated above, is one of the tributaries of the Brāhmanī; and lastly, on the other side of the watershed, is the site of the locality, Sema on the Koel, a tributary of the Son, which I identify with the Soumelpour of Tavernier.

As Sambalpur is in the Central Provinces, and is therefore beyond the region of the present discussion, not being included in Bengal, we may now pass to the mention of the other two localities, as they are referred to by various authorities since Tavernier's time.

Sumelpur (Mine de diamans), near a tributary of the Solon (i. e. Sone, called in its upper portion Rivière d'Andi, see *ante*, vol. i, p. 45), is represented on the Carte de l'Indoustan by M. Bellin, which was published in 1752 in the *Histoire générale des Voyages*.

Tieffenthaler,[3] somewhere about the year 1766, wrote of Sommelpour as a place producing an abundance of diamonds of good quality in the river Gouel, 30 *milles* S.E. from Rohtās. He did not visit it himself, and perhaps he quoted from Tavernier.

Pennant,[4] in the year 1798, mentions that a diamond mine was then being worked on the Sānkh river, but he does not name his authority. He also states that Soumelpour on the Gouel was the most noted and most ancient locality for

[1] In connexion with the diamonds of Bihār, it may be noted that in 1585 the King of Chota Nāgpur was reduced to the status of a feudatory, and in the reign of Jahāngīr, up to which time the Musulmān governors had been satisfied with a tribute of two or three diamonds, Ibrāhīm Khān Fath Jang, governor of Bihār, defeated the Rājā and carried off his family diamonds (Sarat Chandra Roy, *The Mundas*, 151).

[2] *Economic Geology of India*, p. 30.

[3] Bernoulli, *Descr. de l'Inde*, Berlin, 1791, i. 433.

[4] *View of Hindoostan*, ii. 140.

diamonds.[1] Here he evidently quotes from Tavernier, as also did Buffon,[2] who calls the locality Soonelpour on the Gouil, which Buchanan Hamilton in 1838 [3] refers to as being probably identical with a diamond mine which he had heard of on the southern Koel. Karl Ritter in 1836 detected the incompatibility of Tavernier's statements as to the position of his Soumelpour with that of Sambalpur on the Mahānadī; but his correction did not serve to mitigate the confusion which is to be found even in the most recent authors upon the subject. I may add that I was pointed out on the map a locality on the Sānkh by a resident in Chota Nāgpur, where local tradition asserts that diamonds used to be found.

Having referred above to Sambalpur in the Central Provinces it may be of interest to add that this Indian Province includes another locality which, though of importance in early times, was so forgotten even a century ago, that Rennell, and after him Karl Ritter, altogether failed to identify it. It was mentioned as being in the country conquered by Ahmad Shāh Walī Bahmanī, both by Garcia de Orta and Ferishta. In the *Āīn-i-Akbarī* the locality is spoken of as at Bairagarh, which is now identified with Wairāgarh in the Chānda District, about 80 miles from Nāgpur. It was probably the Kosala of the Chinese pilgrims and perhaps the Kosa of Ptolemy.[4]

It is just possible that a locality mentioned by Nicolò Conti in the fifteenth century as a diamond mine called Albenigaras may have also been Wairāgarh. He mentions that the diamonds were obtained then by means of pieces of meat, which were flung on to the mountain, where the diamonds could not be collected owing to the number of serpents. The pieces of meat with diamonds sticking to them were then carried to their nests by birds of prey, from whence they were recovered by the diamond seekers.[5] This, with variations, is the story told by Marco Polo, and in the travels of Sindbad the Sailor. Elsewhere I have described the probable origin of this myth. It appears to be founded on the very common practice in India, on the opening of a mine, to offer up cattle to propitiate the evil spirits who are supposed to guard treasures—these being represented by the serpents in the myth. At such sacrifices in India, birds of prey invari-

[1] *View of Hindoostan,* ii. 113.

[2] *Hist. Nat., Minéraux,* Paris, 1786, iv. 280.

[3] Montgomery Martin, *Eastern India,* i. 535.

[4] McCrindle (*op. cit.,* p. 158 f.) fixes Kosa in the neighbourhood of Baital, north of the sources of the Tāptī and Varadā, a tributary of the Tungabhadrā (*op. cit.,* 179).

[5] R. H. Major, *Travels of Nicolò Conti, India in the Fifteenth Century* Hakluyt Society, part ii, 29 f.

ably assemble to pick up what they can, and in that fact we probably have the remainder of the foundation of the story.

It is probable, also, that the story by Pliny and other early writers, of the diamond being softened by the blood of a he-goat, had its origin in such sacrifices.

As to whether these or other diamond mines in India could be profitably worked again I cannot now discuss here; but I may say that I do not believe that they can be truly described as being exhausted.

APPENDIX IV

The Diamond Mines of Borneo.

In the Colloquies of Garcia da Orta, in the Travels of Linschoten, in the works of De Boot [1] and De Laet,[2] and in many treatises on precious stones, up to some of those most recently published, we find, as has already been stated in the note on p. 67, that Malacca is mentioned as a locality where diamonds occur. This was for a long time a sore puzzle to me, especially as among modern writers on Malacca, with the exception of Miss Bird,[3] none claimed that Malacca was known to be a diamond producing country, while some local inquiries which I made through the late Mr. W. Wynne, of the Straits Civil Service, confirmed an opinion, founded on the character of the geological structure, that probably none had ever been found there.

The solution of the difficulty is afforded by the fact that the name Malacca was applied by the early Portuguese writers to Borneo, and that the Taniapura which they mention was Tanjongpura in Borneo.

I am indebted to Mr. D. F. A. Hervey for the information that Tanjong pūra (the Tandjong Poera of the Dutch) is situated about 30 miles up the river Pawān in the northern part of the Mātan District, adjoining Sukadana. The name, he states, is a hybrid, Tanjong being the Malay for a point (of land), and pūra a Malayan version of the Sanskrit pûr, a town.

Such is the true explanation, and not that Malacca was

[1] *De Lapidi. et Gemm.*, 3rd ed., by De Laet, Lug. Bat. 1647, p. 121 When enumerating the localities where the diamond is obtained, he says, 'Alia est rupes ad fretum Tanian in Malacca que etiam profert adamantes qui de rupe veteri vocantur'. De Boot's original work was published in 1609.

[2] *De Gemm. et Lapidi.*, Lug. Bat. 1647, p. 2, 'Juxta fretum Taniapurae haud longe ab Emporio celeberrimo Malacca aliā earumdem gemmarum fodina est unde vulgo Malacenses appellantur'.

[3] *The Golden Chersonese*, 261.

a place situated in the Eastern Ghāts! as stated by Castellani; nor that the idea originated in some jumble about malachite, as has I think been suggested by one writer.

As it was with Pliny, so it has been with a host of other compilers; we find in the literature of precious stones the same places or the same objects called by different names, and treated as though they were distinct. It has been shown on p. 56 that Gāni was a prefix signifying 'mine of' to the name Kollūr, a diamond locality on the Kistnā, though it is commonly treated as though it were a name itself; and when we find Malacca mentioned side by side with Borneo, as a diamond-producing region, we should not suspect that its appearance in the lists is simply due to a survival of an old name for Borneo. It is perhaps needless to add, therefore, that it should be expunged from all future lists.

The following facts with regard to the occurrence of the diamond in Borneo are chiefly extracted from Crawfurd's *Dictionary* and a paper by Dr. Posewitz.[1] The original matrix of the diamonds of Borneo is, as yet, unknown; but, as they are found in alluvial deposits, in the beds of certain rivers, and in older alluvial or diluvial deposits together with gold and platinum, it may be concluded with some probability that all come from the same sources. The platinum is not known to have been met with in the original matrix, but gold has been found *in situ* in Palaeozoic rocks.

The most famous and apparently the earliest known diamond mines were situated in West Borneo, in the Districts of Landak and Sangau, while some diamonds are reported to have been obtained in Sarawak. Dr. Posewitz does not refer to their occurrence at Tanjongpura, on the Pawān river, nor in Sukadana, where earlier writers state they were found.

In Southern Borneo the most abundant mines and washings are in the neighbourhood of the Tanahlaut hills, which form the boundary between Southern and Eastern Borneo, near Martapura and Tjempaka. The produce of these localities is best known in connexion with the name Banjarmasin, a territory and seaport now held by the Dutch. It should be added that there are some minor localities in the region between Banjarmasin and Sukadana. In Eastern Borneo the territory of Kusan, to the east of the Tanahlaut range, also includes some mines. In British North Borneo there are believed to be some diamond-bearing localities, but as

[1] *Das Diamantvorkommen in Borneo, Mitth. a. d. Jahrb. d. K. Geol. Anst.*, Bd. vii, Budapesth, 1885. 'Borneo is amazingly rich in minerals, gold, silver, coal, iron, and even diamonds being won from it, mostly by the industrious Chinese, while in other parts there are rich oil-wells, for which a rich future has been predicted' ('Natural Wealth in British North Borneo,' *The Times*, 24 May, 1921).

yet they have not been proved to be of any very great promise.

In connexion with the subject of Borneo diamonds, mention is frequently made of a supposed diamond in the possession of the Rājā of Mātan. Its great size, 367 carats, and its reputed value, £269,378, as estimated by Crawfurd, have for many years caused it to be an object of Dutch cupidity, and many stories are told of the efforts made by them to induce the Rājā to part with it. It is stated that early in the century the Rājā was offered 150,000 dollars, two large war brigs fully equipped, besides other war material, in exchange for the diamond ; but from superstitious or other reasons he refused to part with this emblem of royalty, and it has never been cut. Hugh Low states that the real diamond was not shown to visitors, but that a rock crystal was kept for the purpose. Dr. Posewitz, however, records that in 1868 the so-called diamond was itself definitely proved to be merely a piece of rock crystal, thus proving the accuracy of von Gaffron's previous assertion that it could be scratched by corundum, and had a specific gravity of only 2·63 (namely, that of quartz).

Although diamonds weighing up to 70 and even 80 carats have been found in Borneo, for many years past stones of even 4 or 5 carats have been but rarely met with.

APPENDIX V

The Ruby Mines of Upper Burma and the Sapphire Washings of Ceylon.

Position.—The principal ruby mines of Burma are situated in three valleys, which are known by the names of their chief villages respectively, namely Mogok (or Mogout), Kathé, and Kyatpyen.[1] The elevated tract including these valleys is situated at a distance of about 90 miles NNW. from Mandalay, and is at elevations of from 4,000 to 5,500 feet above the sea. The mountains surrounding the Mogok valley culminate in the peaks of Chenedoung, 7,362 feet, and Toungee, 7,775 feet. The ruby tract, as now defined by the most recent scientific examination, occupies an area of 66 square miles, but mining is at present limited to an area of about 45 square miles. The region is described as being very beautiful, and presenting a thriving appearance ; but the climate is somewhat malarious, and Europeans, although the country

[1] For a full account of the Ruby Mines District see Sir J. G. Scott, J. P. Hardiman, *Gazetteer of Upper Burma and the Shan States*, Rangoon, 1901, part i, vol. ii, 213 ff. ; part ii, vol. iii, 3 ff. ; *Imperial Gazetteer*, xxi. 326 ff.

is so elevated, are subject to attacks of fever on first arrival there.

A totally distinct ruby tract is situated in the marble hills at Sagyin, which is only 16 miles from Mandalay. So far as is known, it is comparatively of little importance, the rubies and other gems which are found there being of inferior qualities. Other localities about 15 miles to the north and north-east of Sagyin are reported to produce rubies, but nothing certain is known about them.

History.—The ruby mines of Burma were first made known by European writers towards the end of the fifteenth century. In the sixteenth century there are more definite references by Portuguese travellers, but they are not of much practical importance. Tavernier,[1] as we have seen, gives an account of the mines and their produce from hearsay; from which it would appear that the reputation they then bore was not very high, or he would probably have made an effort to visit them. The yield, he says, did not exceed 100,000 *écus* (say £22,500) per annum, and he found it profitable to carry rubies from Europe to Asia for sale.

The principal authorities of the present century, previous to the conquest of Upper Burma, are Mr. Crawfurd[2]; the Père Giuseppe d'Amato,[3] who visited the mines about the year 1833; Dr. Oldham,[4] who visited Ava and collected information about the mines in the year 1855, when with Sir Arthur Phayre's mission; Mr. Bredmeyer, who was in the service of the King and visited the mines in the year 1868; and Mr. Spears and Capt. Strover, of the British Burma Commission, both of whom have placed on record their observations. From these authorities we learn that the rubies which were found were generally small, not averaging more than a quarter of a rati, and that the large stones were generally smuggled away, but few of them reaching the King. It was supposed that the Chinese and Tartar merchants who visited Mogok and Kyatpyen conveyed most of them out of Burma. The large rubies were generally flawed, and Mr. Spears states that he never saw one exceeding half a rupee in weight, i.e. about 22 carats.

The King's revenue derivable from the monopoly was variously estimated by these authorities at from £12,500 to £15,000. The more recent information now available confirms these estimates. The figures stated on official authority are 90,000 to 100,000 rupees, the highest sum being 150,000 rupees paid in one year. Besides which, however, was the reserva-

[1] Vol. ii. pp. 77 f. below.

[2] 'Mission to Ava,' *Edin. New Phil. Journ.*, 1827, p. 366.

[3] *Journ. As. Soc. Bengal*, vol. ii, p. 75.

[4] Yule's *Mission to Ava*, p. 347.

tion of stones above a certain size ; but it seems to be generally admitted that few large stones were found, and of these a proportion, in spite of severe punishments for concealment, never reached the King ; there is no basis then for an estimate of the total revenue which he received from the mines.

If one may judge from the appearance of the rubies forming part of the treasure taken at Mandalay, and which are now exhibited at the South Kensington Museum, valuable stones were rare, as, except a few of the smaller ones, none seem to be perfect.

As is well known, recent accounts by experts have represented the prospects of the mines in a much more favourable light, and the true value will probably be ere long ascertained by the energetic operations of a company conducted on scientific principles.

The different kinds of precious stones found in the mines.—Although the rubies have given their name to the mines, several other varieties of corundum are also found, such as sapphires, oriental emeralds, oriental amethyst, oriental topaz, and white sapphires ; and besides these there are to be found spinels of various colours, hyacinth (or zircon), iolite (or dichroite, a stone resembling sapphire), and lastly the semi-precious rubellite, which is a variety of the mineral called tourmaline, of which some exceptionally fine examples have been brought from Ava, one of which has long held an honoured position in the mineral collection of the British Museum.

According to Mr. Spears, the proportion of sapphires to rubies was as 1 to 100, but the former are often of large size and fine quality.

Pegu has been mentioned by some early writers[1] as producing diamonds, but there are no real grounds for supposing that either the diamond or true emerald occur in any part of Burma.

Mode of occurrence and source of the gems.—Although it has for some time been known that the rubies of Sagyin were derived from crystalline limestones or marble, the source of the gems in the principal region at Mogok, Kyatpyen, and Kathé was not actually ascertained till recently, when these localities were visited by Mr. Barrington Brown. It was known that they were for the most part actually obtained in derivative gravels, and it had been inferred that the so-called clefts and lodes, of a report which appeared before his examination, were really fissures in limestones, where the stones had accumulated as the result of the solution of limestone, and by gravitation into these recesses.

[1] See *Description of the Diamond Mines of India, Phil. Trans.*, vol. xii, 1677, p. 907.

Mr. Brown has shown that the geological formation consists of recent deposits of hill wash and alluvium and old crystalline limestones, schists, pegmatite, and other metamorphic rocks. In order to explain the relationship which exists between these formations and the rubies, it will be convenient to describe the various systems of mining, by which the mode of occurrence will be made apparent. The mines, as worked by the natives, may be divided into four classes, as follows :

I. Twinlones, or pits sunk in the alluvium of the valleys.
II. Mewdwins, or open cuttings in the hill-wash over which water is led.
III. Loodwins, or workings in caves and fissures.
IV. Quarries in a bed of coarse calcspar in the limestone, which appears to be the true original matrix of the gems.

The Twinlones are square pits which are sunk in the alluvium of the valleys down to the gem-bearing gravels, which occur at varying depths. These pits have to be timbered to support the sides and, as far as possible, exclude water, which, however, finds access, and the first operation, every day, is to bale out the water which has accumulated during the night. The gravel is hoisted out in baskets by means of balance poles similar to those which are used in India for raising water from wells. The gravel is then washed in shallow baskets made of closely-woven bamboo, and the rubies, as they are picked out, are placed in a bamboo tube full of water and are sorted at the close of the day's work. The larger pits are generally cleared out in about ten days and the smaller in half that time ; when working in one is finished, the timber is removed and another pit is started.

Mewdwins.—These are open cuttings on the slopes of the hills to which water is conducted, often from a considerable distance, and discharged with as great a head as possible on the ruby clay and sand, which is shovelled under it by the miners. The lighter portions are carried down by the stream, the boulders removed by hand, and the residue placed in the sluice and washed, where it is caught by riffles, from whence it is removed and washed in baskets as in the preceding process. The circumstances appear to be such as would suit a more scientific application of hydraulic methods than are known to the natives.

Loodwins.—These are natural caves and fissures in the limestone rock, in the floors and crevices of which the rubies have accumulated in consequence of the solution by water of the limestone matrix. In the ordinary sense of the term these are not mines, i. e. the miners do not excavate the rock, but merely scramble through the natural passages and tunnels to the spots where the loam containing the rubies is found—this they either carry to the surface in baskets or it is hoisted up by means of balance poles—and it is then washed at the surface at the nearest watercourse.

From such caves the finest rubies ever found have been obtained, and from one in the Pingu Hill, near Kyatpyen, Mr. Brown states that, after the detritus had been passed, of every basketful of the ruby clay which was raised half consisted of rubies.

A certain royal mine of this character is said to have produced a ruby as large as a walnut, and in another the rubies were found in association with the bones of some extinct animal of very large size.[1]

This description opens up a somewhat wide vista of speculation, and one can hardly resist the temptation of prophesying as to the wonderful discoveries which *may* be made when adits and shafts are driven to afford access to these natural caves and fissures in the mass of the marble hills. In such safe receptacles it is not unreasonable to suppose that stones which have suffered but little from attrition and fracture may be found, and that there the greatest prizes will be obtained.

Quarries.—To the north of Mogok village, at a distance of about three-quarters of a mile, a bed of calcspar in the limestone, which is 20 feet wide, produces rubies, but in order to obtain them the use of powder has to be employed as well as the hammer, and when chipped out the gems are generally more or less fractured; but good stones have been obtained. Whether any method can be devised of avoiding the injury resulting from the use of explosives is at present doubtful. It is not easy to suggest how a firm rock, such as this calcspar, could be mined without recourse being had to violent methods of some kind.

The rose-pink rubellite (a variety of tourmaline) is obtained on the margin of the Meobychoung river, 15 miles S. of Mogok and 3 miles from Mamlong. The mines in the alluvium are worked by a rude hydraulic system, and the produce is sent to China, large pieces obtaining a good price.

Under the arrangements which have been made with the New Burma Ruby Mine Company, the rights and interests of the miners have apparently been very fully safeguarded, but whether the miners on their part will refrain from smuggling and comply with the regulations, and disclose their more valuable finds and submit them to taxation, remains to be seen. The total production of rubies in 1887, when the

[1] The fossil remains of Mastodons and other large mammalia, allied to those found in the Siwālik hills of India, have long been known to occur in Burma.

country was disturbed, amounted to only 42,486 rupees' worth, but in the first two months of 1888 21,883 rupees' worth had been obtained. Stones of from 5 to 20 carats weight were sold during this period, and the highest price obtained for one was 500 rupees.

The mode of occurrence of the rubies in calcspar is, I believe, somewhat unusual, though spinel is known to be found in calcareous rocks. It is generally the case that the corundum minerals are found in mica schists; such is stated to be the case in Zanskar in the Himalayas, and also in Ceylon; with reference to the latter it may be of interest, in addition to the remarks on p. 102, to add here some particulars as to the sapphire washings of that island.

THE SAPPHIRES OF CEYLON.—Under British rule the monopoly in precious stones, which existed under the Kandyan sovereigns, was early abolished as a source of revenue, and no licence is now required by jewel hunters. Great numbers of people are attracted annually to the washings, to the great detriment of agriculture and the demoralization of the villagers, who are brought into contact with dissolute adventurers. Sir Emerson Tennent, from whom the above facts are quoted, estimated the annual total value of the precious stones which were found as not exceeding £10,000 *per annum*.[1]

According to the *Handbook for Ceylon*, recently published in connexion with the Colonial and Indian Exhibition, the search is conducted in a rude fashion, and, despite the advice and reports by experts, there has been no improvement in the method. It is stated in the same work that, though some returns are attempted by the Government, it is impossible to estimate the annual yield at present, and the mines have never, I believe, been successfully worked by Europeans.

APPENDIX VI

A Review or Abstract in the 'Philosophical Transactions' of Chapuzeau's (sic) work, entitled 'Histoire des Joyaux,' published in 1665; and Note on the English edition of the same work.

THE following is a contemporary abstract published in the *Philosophical Transactions*[2] of a book which seems to be of extraordinary rarity—there being no copy of it, I believe, in any of the great libraries in Great Britain, nor even in the Bibliothèque Nationale—it is therefore of sufficient interest

[1] Tennent, *Ceylon*, i. 37.

[2] Vol. ii, 1667, pp. 429-36.

to justify its republication in its original quaint form. But it has in connexion with Tavernier a special interest, because from the glimpse of the contents of the book which it affords, we can see that Chapuzeau (or rather Chappuzeau), by whatever means he acquired them, was in possession of many of the facts recorded in Tavernier's *Travels* at least ten years before the *Travels* were published, and while Tavernier was absent on his last journey. None of the biographies of Chappuzeau mention this work; and although I have not failed to make inquires I have been unable as yet to find any explanation of the mystery.

In Emanuel's bibliography of works on precious stones,[1] the book is mentioned with its full title, and the place and date of publication are given as Geneva 1665.

An Account
Of a small Book in French, entituled
HISTOIRE DES JOYAUX
ET
*Des Principales Richesses de l'*Orient *et de l'*Occident,
par le Sr. Chapuzeau.

This History treats of Diamonds, Rubies, Emeralds, Pearls, Coral, Bezoar, Yellow Amber, Ambergris, Indigo, &c.

Of *Diamonds*, the Author shews:

I. The *Places* whence they are taken; of which he finds but five in all the *East-Indies*, whereof *two* are *Rivers*, vid. *Saccadan* in Borneo and *Nage* in the Kingdom of *Bengala*;[2] at the bottom of both which, *he saith*, the Diamonds are found among the sand, after the waters, that fall as great Torrents from the Mountains, are run off; and the three others are Mines, in the Kingdoms of *Decan*, *Cuncan*, and *Golconda*. In this Relation he observes, that the Diamonds which are found at the bottom of those Rivers, have the best *Water*; but those in Mines have often *Flaws* (which he imputes to the violent knockings of the Rock) and *Blebs*, ascribed to the condition of the Earth or Sand they are found in, *vid.* when that is not pure, but fattish or black. He takes also notice, that Diamonds are the heaviest of precious Stones, as Gold is of Mettals.

II. The *Manner*, how they are found and separated; which is the same in substance with that described in *Num.* 18, p. 328.[3]

[1] *Diamonds and Precious Stones*, second ed., London, 1867, p. 246.

[2] See *ante*, pp. 41 *et seq.* of vol. ii, and Appendix III, p. 356.

[3] This is a reference to another Review, on the *Voyage de l'Évêque de Beryte.* &c.; it is in *Phil. Trans.*, vol. i, pp. 327–8.

III. The *Price* of them, according to the proportion of their weight; for which he gives this Rule. Take, saith he, a Diamond of 10 *Carats*: this number is to be squared (which makes 100). Then, if the Stone be clean, each Carat, according to its perfection, may be worth 40 to 60 Crowns: if it have no good water, or have a Bleb or Flaw, the Carat will not be worth but from 10 to 30 Crowns. So multiplying the said 100 by the number, which each Carat of such or such a Stone may be worth, the product is the price of the Stone.

For *Rubies*, he discourses also of the *Places* where *they* are found, and of their *Price*.[1] The Places are, the Kingdom of *Pegu*, and the Isle of Ceylon; whence very few are suffered to be carried away. The Price is, that a good *Rubi* of the weight of 1 *Rati* (which is $\frac{7}{8}$ of a Carat) is esteemed at 20 old *Pagodes* in India, each *Pagode* being about ten shillings *English*.

(A Rubi) of	2	*Ratis*	is valued at	100	*Pagodes*.
,,	3	,,	,,	250	,,
,,	4	,,	,,	500	,,
,,	5	,,	,,	900	,,
,,	6	,,	,,	1,500	,,
,,	7	,,	,,	2,300	,,
,,	12	,,	,,	12,000	,,

Concerning *Turquois*, they are found in *Persia*, in the Province *Chamaquay*, north of *Ispahan*, in two Mines, called the *Old* and the *New* Rock. These of the *New*, are of an ill, whitish Blew; but those of the *Old* are not suffered to be digged out, but by the King of *Persia* himself.[2]

Emeraulds are affirmed by him, never to be found in the *East-Indies* but in *Perou*,[3] whence they were carried by that trading people to the *Moluccas*, even before *America* was discovered by the Europeans; and so they come from the Orient; of much less value than they were formerly, by reason of their commonness. The Author notes, that Emeraulds grow in stones, just as Chrystals, forming a Vein, in which they are by little and little refined and thickened: and that some of them are seen, half white and half green: others, all white: and others all green and perfect.

To Pearls he assigns in the *Orient* four places where they are fished: The Isle of *Baharem*, in the *Persian Gulf*: the Coast of *Arabia Felix*, near the Town of *Catif*, over against *Baharem*: the Isle of Ceylon about Manar: the Isle of Japan. The best at *Ceylon*, but small: the biggest at *Japan*, but uneven. In the *West-Indies* they are fished in the *North-Sea*,

[1] See *ante*, p. 78 of vol. ii.
[2] See *ante*, p. 81 of vol. ii.
[3] See *ante*, p. 82 of vol. ii.

in the Isles of *Marguerite*, *Cubagua*, *St. Marthe*: and at *Comana*, *Comanagote*, near the Continent: and in the *South-Sea*, near *Panama*: which *American* sort, though they are much inferiour to the *Oriental*, in Lustre, yet they far excel them in bigness, amounting sometimes (saith this *Author*) to 42 *Carats*.[1]

In this Relation 'tis mentioned, that sometimes 5 or 6 *Pearls* are found in one Oyster: That *Pearl-fishers* are fed with dry and roasted meat, to give them better breathing: That Pearl-bearing Oysters are not good to eat, being flat and hard of digestion, &c.

As to the *Price* of good *Pearls*, well fashioned, he marketh it, as follows:

Such a Pearl of

Grain 1	*Crowns* 1	*Carats* $4\frac{1}{4}$	*Crowns* 289
,, 2	,, 4	,, $4\frac{1}{2}$	,, 324
,, 3	,, 9	,, $4\frac{3}{4}$	,, 361
Carats 1	,, 16	,, 5	,, 400
,, $1\frac{1}{4}$	,, 25	,, $5\frac{1}{4}$	,, 441
,, $1\frac{1}{2}$	,, 36	,, $5\frac{1}{2}$	,, 484
,, $1\frac{3}{4}$	,, 49	,, $5\frac{3}{4}$	,, 529
,, 2	,, 64	,, 6	,, 576
,, $2\frac{1}{4}$	,, 81	,, $6\frac{1}{4}$	,, 625
,, $2\frac{1}{2}$	,, 100	,, $3\frac{1}{2}$	,, 675
,, $2\frac{3}{4}$	,, 121	,, $6\frac{3}{4}$	,, 729
,, 3	,, 144	,, 7	,, 784
,, $3\frac{1}{4}$	,, 160	,, $7\frac{1}{4}$	,, 841
,, $3\frac{1}{2}$	,, 196	,, $7\frac{1}{2}$	,, 900
,, $3\frac{3}{4}$	,, 225	,, $7\frac{3}{4}$	,, 960
,, 4	,, 256	,, 8	,, 1,024

Of Corals, he taketh notice *where* they are fished, and *in what manner*.[2] The *Places, he saith*, to be *Eight*: *Three* upon the Coasts of *Corsica* and *Sardinia*, *vid.* at *Argueil* (where is the best) *Baza*, and near the *Isle of St. Peter*: one upon the Coast of *Sicily*, near *Drepanum*: *Two* upon the coast of *Africa*, near the *Bastion of France*, and at *Tabarca*: *One* more, upon the Coast of *Catalonia*, at the *Cape of Quiers*: And the last, about *Majorca*. Observing, that red Coral is not found, but in the *Mediterranean* alone, where 'tis fished from the beginning of *April* till the end of *July*, employing commonly about 200 Boats. The *manner* of fishing them, is with two big beams of wood, laid crosswise, with a good piece of Lead on the middle, to make it sink, casting about it coarse Hemp, carelessly twisted, and tying this Wood to

[1] See *ante*, pp. 88–9 of vol. ii. [Seemingly '42' here should be 55.]

25 [2] See *ante*, pp. 104 ff. of vol. ii.

two Ropes, whereof one hangs at the Sterne, the other at the fore-part of the Boat: and so letting this contrivance fall into the Current, along the Rocks, where the Hemp being turned about, and engaged in the Coral, there need sometimes many Boats to draw away the Instrument.

Bezoar, he saith, is not only found in *Golconda*, in the Province of *Renquery*, in the Maw of Goats, whereof some are at times furnisht with a dozen a piece: but also at *Macassar*, in the Isle of *Celebes*, in the body of Apes: bigger than those found in *Golconda*. He mentions, that the people in those parts, to find whether a Goat hath any of those *Bezoar-stones* in its body, do beat his belly with their hands and rub it, till all the stones in the Animal come together, and tell them as you do stones in a bag, &c.[1]

The English Edition of the 'Histoire des Joyaux'.

Since the foregoing pages were printed I have had the good fortune to obtain a copy of a small volume entitled *The History of Jewels, and of the Principal Riches of the East and West, Taken from the Relation of Divers of the most Famous Travellers of our Age; Attended with Fair Discoveries conducing to the Knowledge of the Universe and Trade.*[2] Although not stated to be a translation, the identity of its contents with those of Chappuzeau's *Histoire des Joyaux*, as shown by the above abstract, admits of no doubt that it is the same work in an English dress.

Neither Chappuzeau nor Tavernier are mentioned in it; but the internal evidence conclusively proves that it must have been largely founded on Tavernier's original memoirs. If it be the case that Chappuzeau appropriated these without acknowledgment, it would also appear that the English editor pirated Chappuzeau's book.

A general resemblance of facts alone would not prove Tavernier to have been the original author, but the *History* casually refers to certain dates in connexion with places where we know Tavernier to have been in the same years. Thus on p. 26 reference is made to Mīr Jumla and his occupation at Gandikot in the year 1652, i. e. when Tavernier visited him (see vol. i, p. 227). On p. 23 the depreciated condition of the diamond mines at Kollūr in the year 1660 is referred to, and Tavernier alludes (see *ante*, p. 59) to a falling off in the number of miners since his first visit, and we have otherwise seen that he had visited the mines in 1660 (see vol. i, Introduction, p. xix. On p. 123 the facts stated in reference

[1] For account of Bezoar, see *ante*, pp. 115 ff. of vol. ii.

[2] London, printed by T. N, for Hobart Kemp, &c., 1671, small 8vo, pp. 128.

to bezoar are substantially the same as Tavernier's own personal record (see p. 116 f. *ante*). Tavernier's personal stories about Bohemian rubies (see p. 80 *ante*) and a living worm in dead coral (see p. 106 *ante*) are both in the *History*, pp. 60 and 106.

Short as it is, the *History* contains some facts not given in the *Travels*, but they, for the most part, do not refer to India.

Of facts given in the *History* which are omitted accidentally or are misprinted in the *Travels*, some, as will be seen, confirm corrections and additions already made in the footnotes on preceding pages. On p. 24 of the *History* we find the name of the diamond mine which Tavernier omitted to mention (*ante*, pp. 41 *n.* and 61); it was Gazerpoli (i. e. Gazerpalle or Baswapur, see p. 349 *ante*), two days' journey from Raolconda (i. e. Ramulkota). It is said to have been discovered in 1448, which is not recorded in the *Travels*. On p. 54 Ava is correctly given instead of Siren, where a mistake occurs in the *Travels* (see p. 77 *n.*). On p. 20 there is the same mistake as occurs once in the *Travels* (see p. 57) in reference to the weight of the Mogul's diamond—it being given as 900 carats instead of 900 *ratis*.

The *History* also contains some important facts about the Bengal diamond mines; these have been already noticed (see p. 356).

The value of the rupee is stated in the *History* to be 28 pence, but I venture to think that 27 pence, which has been adopted in the footnotes and in Appendix I, vol. i, is a closer approximation to the value.

The principal discrepancy to be found between the *History* and the *Travels* is in the tables of values of rubies; they are quite discordant.

The concluding paragraph of the *History*—read in the light of this identification of Tavernier as the original author of the work—is of interest. The writer says: 'This is all I have at present collected of what is remarkable in the modern and faithful Relations of our Travellers upon the subject of Jewels, and other rich productions of which I have given a short Account as a platform for a greater work.'

[Owing to administrative changes of recent years, certain tālūks are no longer in the Districts stated above. *E.g.* Palnād tāluk is now in the Guntūr District, and Gutī in that of Anantapur: *v. Imp. Gazetteer of India*, Index, vol. xxv., *svv.*]

INDEX AND GLOSSARY

Words and names in Tavernier's French text are given in italics. D.=Dutch; Fr., French, t., town, and r., river. A few of Ball's identifications of places are retained, though eliminated from the text of his translation by the late Dr. Crooke.

THE END